Cracking the ACT®

2010 Edition

Geoff Martz, Kim Magloire, and
Theodore Silver

Updated by Melissa Hendrix and
the Staff of The Princeton Review

PrincetonReview.com

Random House, Inc. New York

The Independent Education Consultants Association recognizes The Princeton Review as a valuable resource for high school and college students applying to college and graduate school.

The Princeton Review, Inc.
2315 Broadway
New York, NY 10024
E-mail: editorialsupport@review.com

ISBN 978-0-375-42962-0
ISSN 1030-5507

Editor: Heather Brady
Production Coordinator: Kim Howie
Production Editor: Jennifer Graham

Printed in the United States of America.

10 9 8 7 6 5 4 3 2 1

2010 Edition

Editorial
Rob Franek, VP Test Prep Books, Publisher
Seamus Mullarkey, Editorial Director
Laura Braswell, Senior Editor
Rebecca Lessem, Senior Editor
Heather Brady, Editor
Selena Coppock, Editor

Production Services
Scott Harris, Executive Director, Production Services
Kim Howie, Senior Graphic Designer

Production Editorial
Meave Shelton, Production Editor
Jennifer Graham, Production Editor

Random House Publishing Team
Tom Russell, Publisher
Nicole Benhabib, Publishing Manager
Ellen L. Reed, Production Manager
Alison Stoltzfus, Associate Managing Editor
Elham Shabahat, Publishing Assistant

Acknowledgments

A test-preparation course is much more than clever techniques and powerful computer score reports; the reason our results are so great is that our teachers really care. Eleven years ago, a small group of Princeton Review instructors enthusiastically created a program to prepare students for the previous version of the ACT. We would like to thank John Cauman, Judy Moreland, Bill Lindsley, and Jim Reynolds for their commitment to the original ACT project.

The completion of this book would not have been possible without the help and dedication of several individuals. We would like to thank Melissa Hendrix and Liz Rutzel, in particular, for their work on this edition. Thanks also to those who have updated previous editions.

Special thanks to Adam Robinson, who conceived of and perfected the Joe Bloggs approach to standardized tests and many other successful techniques used by The Princeton Review.

Contents

Foreword

In 2008, a record number of high school students took the ACT. This is a good trend. The ACT is a better test than the SAT, and since every four-year college and university now accepts either, there's no reason to take that other test.

More students are prepping for the ACT as well, and scores are up for the third time in the last five years. I'm glad you've chosen this book to prepare and hope you are too. We've always tried—in our tutoring, online courses, classroom programs, and books—to be effective and efficient. We know the key to raising your ACT score does not lie in memorizing dozens of math theorems, the periodic table of elements, and the complete rules of English grammar. The information needed to do well on the ACT is surprisingly limited, and we'll concentrate on a small number of crucial concepts.

If you feel that standardized test scores don't reflect your high school grades, you might suspect that there's more to mastering this test than just honing math, verbal, and science skills. At its root, this test is trying to measure your reasoning. The test writers do this by leading you to wrong answers (called, fittingly, distracters). Some of our techniques address distracters; I think you'll find them fun and useful on every standardized test you take.

Despite the strength of our approach, a book can't mold itself around your strengths and weaknesses. We've set up an array of online tools that you can access at **PrincetonReview.com** once you register the serial number at the back of your book. We'll be adding new tools and lessons throughout the year, so check back from time to time.

Good luck on the ACT! And if you need more help, or just want to find the right college or the best way to pay for it, please stop by **PrincetonReview.com** or call us at 800-2Review.

John Katzman
Chairman and Founder

...So Much More Online!

More Lessons...

- Step-by-step guide to solving difficult problems
- Tutorials that put our strategies into action
- Interactive, click-through learning for English, Math, Reading, and Science
- Overview of the question types you will find on the ACT

More Practice...

- Reading Drill with passages, questions, and hints
- English Drill on Grammar, Sentence Structure, and Punctuation
- Full-length practice test

More Scores...

- Automatic scoring for online test
- Instant scoring and analysis for your book tests
- Optional essay scoring with our LiveGrader℠ service
- Performance analysis to tell you which topics you need to review

More Good Stuff...

- Sign up for e-mail tips and tricks
- Chat with other ACT students

...then College!

- Detailed profiles for hundreds of colleges help you find the school that is right for you
- Information about financial aid and scholarships
- Dozens of Top 10 ranking lists including Quality of Professors, Worst Campus Food, Most Beautiful Campus, Party Schools, Diverse Student Population, and tons more

princetonreview.com/cracking

Look For These Icons Throughout The Book

 Go Online

 More Great Books

Getting The Most Out Of Your Princeton Review Materials

princetonreview.com/cracking

1 Register

Go to PrincetonReview.com/cracking. You'll see a Welcome page where you should register your book using the serial number. What's a serial number, you ask? Flip to the back of your book and you'll see a bunch of letters and numbers printed on the inside back cover. Type this into the window, dashes included. Next you will see a Sign Up/Sign In page where you will type in your e-mail address (username) and choose a password. Now you're good to go!

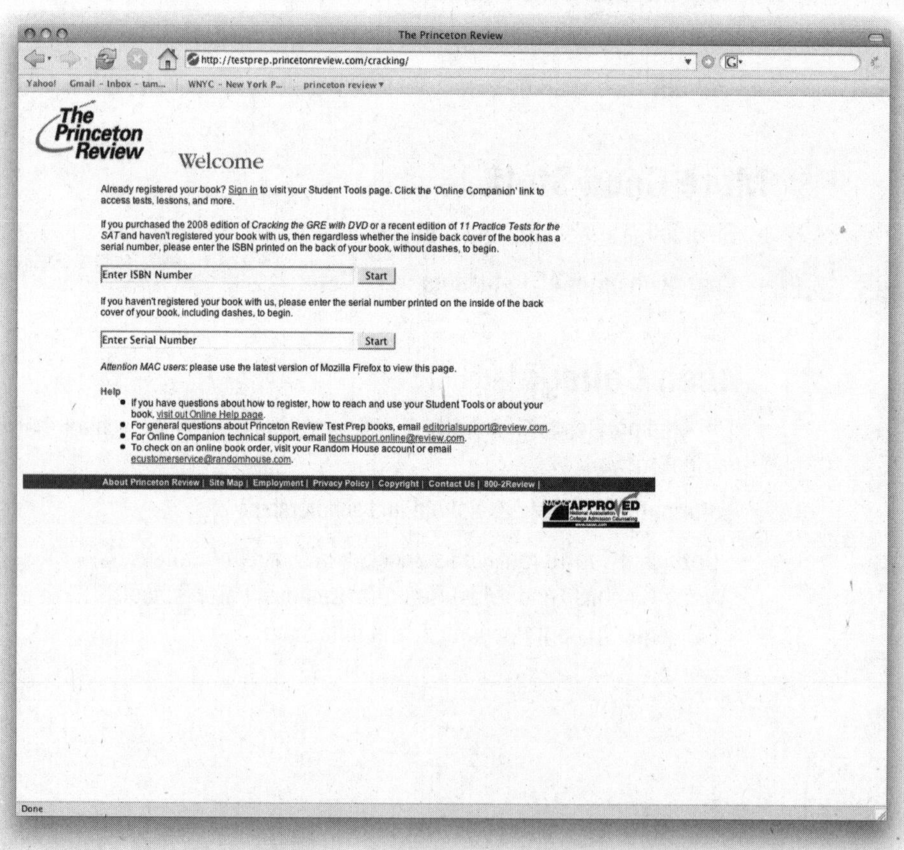

2 Check Out Your Student Tools

Once you are logged in and registered, click on "Your Student Tools." From there, you can access practice tests, online course demos, class information (for current students), important dates and more. Check out the "Advice Library" and "What's New" for additional information. But first, look under "Your Course Tools" and click on the name of your book. Be sure to enable pop-ups! The window that will pop-up when you click on your book is called the dashboard and it will lead you to tons of helpful online components.

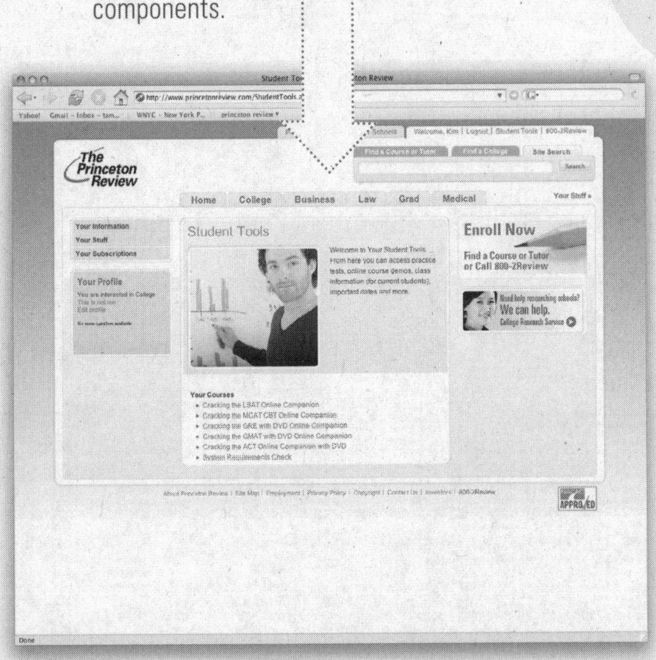

3 Make Use of the Dashboard

The dashboard has 5 buttons displayed vertically. Click on each of these buttons to explore your options. There's a lot of fantastic online content, including drills, problem-solving strategies worked out in examples, a full practice test with automatic grading, discussion area, and more.

Find the college that is right for you with our ranking lists. See which school has the best cafeteria food, the best dorms, the most red-tape and lines, the worst library, the best parties, and many more categories. Sign up for email tips about the ACT and check out the vocabulary "Word du Jour" for a new word each day. Our website is your resource for tons of practice exercises and college information.

Part I
Orientation

Chapter 1
Introduction to the ACT

So, you have to take the ACT? What will you need to do first? This chapter presents an overview of the ACT as a whole and discusses registration requirements, when to take the test, how to have your scores reported to colleges (or how not to), and the ways in which colleges use your scores.

THE ACT

The Princeton Review has a reputation for test bashing that is richly deserved. In general, we don't have many nice things to say about the tests we tackle or the organizations that write them. So it's a pleasure to take on what we feel is (by comparison) a fair and good-hearted test, written by intelligent people.

The ACT measures what it says it does—academic achievement. It doesn't pretend to measure your analytic ability or your intelligence. The people at ACT admit that you can increase your score by preparing for the test. They even put out their own coaching book.

So if we ever seem to be poking fun at the test or the people who write it, we want you to remember that it does not lessen our underlying affection and respect for the exam and its authors.

If there is any flaw in the ACT, it is that, in its attempt to be fair, it has become a little, well, predictable. Of course, when we say that the ACT is a completely predictable test, we mean it in the nicest possible way. We *like* predictable tests, and so should you.

The ACT Is a ~~Standardized~~ *Predictable* Test

From now on, whenever you see the word *standardized*, think *predictable* instead. The ACT tests the same information the same way, year after year. For example, there are always 14 plane geometry questions on the ACT, not 13, not 15, exactly 14. There are exactly 10 questions on punctuation. You can count on it. Even the way the test asks the questions is predictable, based on the need for a standardized product.

The review in this book is based on the very specific knowledge you need to do well on this test. The test-taking strategies we have developed are designed to take advantage of the ACT's predictability.

Do I Need to Prepare if I Have Good Grades?

Let's take the hypothetical case of Sid. Sid is valedictorian of his class, editor of the school paper, and the only teenager ever to win the Nobel Prize. To support his widowed mother, he sold more seeds from the back of comic books than any other person in recorded history. He speaks eight languages in addition to being able to communicate with dolphins and wolves. He has recommendations from Colin Powell *and* Bill Gates. So if Sid had a bad day when he took the ACT (the plane bringing him back from his Medal of Freedom award presentation was late), we are pretty sure that he is going to be just fine anyway. But Sid wants to ensure that when his colleges look at his ACT score, they see the same high-caliber student they see when they look at the rest of his application, so he carefully reviews the types of questions asked and learns some useful test-taking strategies.

I Have Lousy Grades in School. Is There Any Hope?

Let's take the case of Tom. Tom didn't do particularly well in high school. In fact, he has been on academic probation since kindergarten. He has caused four of his teachers to give up teaching as a profession, and he prides himself on his perfect homework record: He's never done any, not ever. But if Tom aces his ACT, a college might decide that he is actually a misunderstood genius and give him a full scholarship. Tom decides to learn as much as he can about the ACT.

Most of us, of course, fall between these two extremes. So is it important to prepare for the ACT?

If you were to look in the information bulletin of any of the colleges in which you are interested, we can pretty much guarantee that somewhere you would find the following paragraph:

> Many factors go into the acceptance of a student by a college. Test scores are *only one* of these factors. Grades in high school, extracurricular activities, essays, and recommendations are also important and may in some cases outweigh test scores.
>
> (2008 University of Anywhere Bulletin)

Truer words were never spoken. In our opinion, just about *every* other element in your application "package" is more important than your test scores. The Princeton Review (among other organizations) has been telling colleges for years that scores on the ACT or the SAT are pretty incomplete measures of a student's overall academic abilities. Some colleges have stopped looking at test scores entirely, and others are downplaying their importance.

Size Matters
Large schools process more applications, so they rely heavily on standardized test scores. Small schools have the time to read the rest of your application.

So Why Should You Spend Any Time Preparing for the ACT?

Out of all the elements in your application "package," your ACT score is the easiest to *change*. The grades you've received up to now are written in stone. You aren't going to become captain of the football team or editor of the school paper overnight. Your essays will be only as good as you can write them, and recommendations are only as good as your teachers' memories of you.

On the contrary, in a few weeks you can substantially change your score on the ACT (and the way colleges look at your applications). The test does not pretend to measure analytic ability or intelligence. It measures your knowledge of specific skills such as grammar, algebra, and reading comprehension. Mostly, it measures how good you are at taking this test.

When It Comes to the ACT, *Nothing* Is Written in Stone

It doesn't matter how well you've done in school up to now. Good grades are not a guarantee that you will do well on the ACT. It doesn't matter if you've always been bad at taking standardized tests. Colleges aren't going to see any of your scores from earlier standardized tests. It doesn't matter if you hate math in general or English in general or science in general. The ACT doesn't measure math in general. It measures the math that is on the ACT.

By reviewing the very specific knowledge that the people who write the ACT think is important and by learning good test-taking strategies, you should be able to increase your ACT score significantly. This is not just our opinion. Even the people who write the test agree.

What Is the ACT?

The ACT is a multiple-choice standardized exam that is supposed to measure your knowledge of some of the subjects taught in high school. The ACT takes about three and a half hours and has one break. It is divided into four tests, which are always given in the same order. (ACT calls them tests, but we may also use the term "sections" in this book to avoid confusion.)

1. English Test (45 minutes—75 questions)

Power Booking
If you were getting ready to take a history test, you'd study history. If you were preparing for a basketball game, you'd practice basketball. So if you're preparing for the ACT, study the ACT!

In this section, you will see 5 essays on the left side of the page. Some words or phrases will be underlined. On the right side of the page, you will be asked whether the underlined portion is correct as written or whether one of the three alternatives listed would be better. This is a test of grammar, punctuation, sentence structure, and rhetorical skills. Throughout each essay, commonly known as a "passage," there will also be questions about overall organization and style or perhaps about how the writing could be revised or strengthened.

2. Math Test (60 minutes—60 questions)

These are the regular, multiple-choice math questions you've been doing all your life. The easier questions, which test basic math proficiency, *tend* to come first, but the folks at the ACT try to mix in easy, medium, and difficult problems throughout the Math Test. A good third of the test covers pre-algebra and elementary algebra. Slightly less than a third covers intermediate algebra and coordinate geometry (graphing). Regular geometry accounts for less than a quarter of the questions, and there are four questions that cover trigonometry.

3. Reading Test (35 minutes—40 questions)

In this test, there will be 4 reading passages of about 750 words each—the average length of a *People* magazine article but maybe not as interesting. There is always one prose fiction passage, one social science passage, one humanities passage, and one natural science passage, and they are always in that order. After reading each passage, you have to answer 10 questions.

4. Science Reasoning Test (35 minutes—40 questions)

No specific scientific knowledge is necessary for the Science Reasoning Test. You won't need to know the chemical makeup of hydrochloric acid or any formulas. Instead, you will be asked to understand six sets of scientific information presented in graphs, charts, tables, and research summaries, and you will have to make sense of one disagreement between two or three scientists. (Occasionally, there are more than three scientists).

There may be one additional section on the ACT. During this section, you will pay for the privilege of being a guinea pig while the test writers at ACT try out some experimental questions on you. This section typically comes at the end of the test and is usually very easy to recognize, as it is much shorter than a regular section—just 10 to 15 minutes long. In other words, it's not a big deal. This section usually shows up on the June exam, and it won't count toward your score.

More great titles by The Princeton Review
Word Smart

5. Optional Writing Test (30 minutes)

The ACT contains an "optional" writing test featuring a single essay. We recommend you take the "ACT Plus Writing," version of the test because some schools require it. While on test day you may think you don't need it, you might later decide to apply to a school that requires a writing score. The last thing you want is to be forced into taking the whole ACT all over again... this time *with* the writing test. The essay consists of a prompt "relevant" to high school students on which you will be asked to write an essay stating your position on the prompt. Two people will then grade your essay on a scale of 1 to 6 for a total score of 2 to 12. In this book, we will teach you how to write the best possible essay for the ACT.

Where Does the ACT Come From?

The ACT is written by a company that used to call itself American College Testing but now just calls itself ACT. The company's main offices are in Iowa City, Iowa. The people at ACT have been writing a version of this test since 1959. Even if you aren't looking forward to taking the ACT this year, you would probably prefer it to the version they used to give. In the old days, the test included detailed questions about topics like the Constitution of the United States, electrostatic forces, and planets in the solar system.

The people at ACT also write a number of other tests, including a test for professional golfers and a test for dieticians. They provide a broad range of services to educational agencies and business institutions.

How Is the ACT Scored?

Scores for each of the four tests are reported on a scale of 1 to 36 (36 being the highest score possible). The four scores are averaged to yield your composite score, which is the score colleges and universities primarily use to determine admission. Next to each score is a percentile ranking. Percentile ranking refers to how you performed on the test relative to other people who took it at the same time. For instance, a percentile ranking of 87 indicates that you scored higher than 87 percent of the people who took the test and 13 percent scored higher than you.

Closed Loop
The ACT tests how well you take the ACT.

Some of the scores have subcategories. English is broken down into Usage/Mechanics and Rhetorical Skills. The subcategories may be of some marginal use to colleges; they are much more useful to you if you decide to take the test again, because they pinpoint your strengths and weaknesses. In these subcategories, scores are reported on a scale of 1 to 18 (18 being the highest score possible). They are also reported as percentiles.

If you decide to take the ACT Plus Writing Test, you will receive standard ACT scores plus two additional scores. One will be a scaled score from 1 to 36, which combines your performance on the Writing test and the English Test. The other will be a subscore, ranging from 2 to 12, which reflects how you did on your essay. Neither score contributes to your composite score. The Writing Test costs an additional $15, which you will be charged when you sign up for the ACT. The ACT with the Essay section is more expensive than the ACT without the Essay section. Check **www.act.org** for current costs.

Three to seven weeks after you take the ACT, you and the colleges you have selected, if any, will receive your ACT scores in the mail. If you want, you can pay to see your scores a bit earlier (about 10 to 14 days after your test date).

Who Actually Receives the Scores?

More great titles by The Princeton Review
College Essays that Made a Difference

You might think that your scores will be mailed directly to your home, but this is not always the case. If you take the June administration of the test, scores are mailed to colleges and to you. For all other administrations, scores are sent to colleges and to your high school counselor, not directly to you, unless your high school has given ACT permission to send them to you. You then get the scores from the counselor. We've checked with ACT, and the people we talked to there said that if you choose not to provide a High School Code, your scores simply won't be sent to your high school. So, if you want your scores sent to your home (and not your high school), leave the High School Code blank. All colleges you list will get copies of your score regardless of whether you leave the High School Code blank.

There is one potential downside to not reporting your scores to your high school: If you're likely to receive a state-awarded scholarship on the basis of your ACT score, such a score is usually reported to the state's scholarship-awarding entity through—you guessed it—the high school. If you anticipate receiving such a score and are counting on such a scholarship (taking at least one test as a reality check is a good idea), go ahead and provide your High School Code. As the owners of your transcript, you and your parents can go to your high school and have a score removed from it later if you feel the score doesn't reflect your abilities. In any event, because ACT allows score choice (sending scores from just one testing date to colleges), the test scores on your high school transcript ultimately don't matter that much.

When Should You Take the ACT?

The test is given four times each year in New York and five times each year in most of the rest of the country, usually at 8:00 A.M. on a Saturday morning. In some states, there are six administrations each year (they include a September test date as well). Most students take the ACT in the spring of their junior year or in the fall of senior year. Check out **www.act.org** to determine which administrations are best for you. A good case can be made for taking it at the earlier date. For one thing, you'll have a better idea of where you stand. If your score is about what you want, you can spend the summer visiting colleges or getting started on your applications. If your score is lower than you want, you can use the summer to prepare to take the test again in the fall.

The cost of the ACT changes from time to time and depends on whether you decide to take the Writing Test. In 2009, the test without the writing portion is $31 and $46 with it. You can obtain a registration packet for the ACT at your high school guidance office, online at **www.actstudent.org/forms/stud_req.html**, or by writing or calling ACT at the address and phone number below.

ACT Registration
P.O. Box 414
Iowa City, IA 52243
319-337-1270

You can also register directly online via ACT's website at **www.actstudent.org**. But before you decide on a test date, there are other things that you should know.

Special Considerations

The ACT offers accommodations to students with special needs, learning or otherwise. You cannot, however, get accommodations without prior arrangement with ACT. A detailed description of the types of special accommodations available and of ACT's documentation requirements is available at **www.act.org/aap/disab**.

Some ACT Test Dates Are Better Than Others

On certain dates, the ACT offers what it calls "Test Information Release." If you take the ACT on one of these dates, you can, for $17.00 (as of 2009), receive a copy of the test that you took and a photocopy of your actual answer sheet. We strongly advise that you take the test on one of these dates. It is not unheard of for ACT to make a mistake when scoring. You certainly won't find out about this unless you can see the test you took and your own answers. For example, it is possible to fill in an oval on the answer sheet darkly enough for the human eye to see, but not darkly enough for the machine that scores the test to read. In this case, if you point it out to them and pay another small, additional fee, the people at ACT will hand-score your test and change your grade if they indeed made a mistake.

Flying Standby

You don't have to register in advance for the ACT. It is possible to register on the spot on the day of the test for an additional fee, but you *must* bring a completed registration booklet. Also, be sure to arrive extra early if you're testing on standby, because just like on airplanes, there are a limited number of seats, and it's first-come, first-served.

What If I've Already Taken the ACT Once Before?

The nice folks at ACT allow you to decide which of your ACT scores they report to colleges. If you want to have full control over this, it is a good idea *not* to take advantage of the four free score reports ACT offers to send to colleges directly after the test. Why send colleges scores you might not want them to see? While it costs a few extra dollars to get ACT to send scores to schools later, it is well worth being able to send the colleges your best results.

How to Prepare for the ACT

The Princeton Review materials and test-taking techniques contained in this book should give you all the information you need to improve your score on the ACT.

Other popular coaching books contain several complete practice ACT exams. We strongly advise you *not* to waste your time taking these tests. In some cases, the questions in these books are not modeled on real ACT questions. Some of them cover material that is not even on the real ACT. Others give the impression that the ACT is much easier or more difficult than it really is. Taking the practice tests offered in these books could actually hurt your score.

One reason these coaching books do not use real ACT questions is that the folks at ACT won't let them. They have refused to let anyone (including us) license actual questions from old tests. You may have chosen our book because it contains two practice ACT exams. Rest assured that these tests are *modeled very closely after actual ACT exams,* with the proper balance of questions reflective of what the ACT actually tests.

Cynics might suggest that no one else can license ACT exams because ACT sells its own review book called *The Real ACT Prep Guide.* Although *The Real ACT* doesn't contain a very full review section and offers only limited test-taking strategies (after all, no one wants to rob his or her own house), we think ACT's book is well worth the price just for the three real tests it contains. We recommend that you either buy the book or ask your high school to send away to ACT for actual ACT Tests. You can also buy real ACT Tests on **www.act.org**. You should get a copy of *Preparing for the ACT Assessment* from your counselor. It's free, and it contains a complete, real ACT. The same test can be downloaded for free from ACT's website.

While we advise you to obtain these practice tests to further your preparation for the ACT, it is important that you use them properly. Many students like to think that they can prepare by simply taking test after test until they get the scores they want. Unfortunately, this doesn't work all that well. Why? Well, in many instances, repetitive test taking only reinforces some of the bad test-taking habits that we address in this book. You should use practice tests for the following three key purposes:

- to build up familiarity with the exam
- to learn how to avoid the types of mistakes you are currently making
- to master our techniques and strategies so you can save time and earn more points

More great titles by The Princeton Review
1,296 ACT Practice Questions
ACT or SAT? Choosing the Right Exam for you

The ACT vs. the SAT

You may have to take the ACT anyway, but most of the schools in which you're interested also accept the SAT. We think the SAT is nowhere near as fair a test as the ACT. Whereas the ACT says it measures "achievement" (which we believe *can* be measured), the SAT says it measures "ability" (which we don't think can be measured at all; and if it can, the SAT sure isn't doing it).

What Exactly Are the Differences?

The SAT tends to be less time-pressured than the ACT. However, many of the questions on the SAT are trickier than those on the ACT. The SAT Verbal sections have a stronger emphasis on vocabulary than do the ACT English and Reading Tests. The SAT Math section Tests primarily algebra and plane geometry and includes no trigonometry at all.

Both tests include an Essay section, although ACT has made this new essay optional because some colleges require it while others do not. ACT doesn't want to force students to take (and pay for) a test they don't need. The implication then is that many students can ignore the new Writing Test altogether depending on what the schools to which they are applying require.

To find out if the schools in which you are interested require the ACT essay, visit the ACT writing test page at **www.actstudent.org/writing** or contact the schools directly.

While we are obviously not tremendously fond of the SAT, you should know that some students end up scoring substantially higher on the SAT than they do on the ACT and vice versa. It may be to your advantage to take a practice test for each one and see which is more likely to get you a better score.

More great titles by The Princeton Review
Best 371 Colleges, Complete Book of Colleges

Check out the Best Fit College Search at
PrincetonReview.com

What Is The Princeton Review?

The Princeton Review is the world's leading test-preparation and educational services company. We run courses at hundreds of locations worldwide and offer web-based instruction at **PrincetonReview.com**. Our test-taking techniques and review strategies are unique and powerful. We developed them after studying all the real ACTs on which we could get our hands and analyzing them with the most sophisticated software available. For more information about our programs and services, feel free to call us at **800-2Review.**

A Final Thought Before You Begin

The ACT does not measure intelligence, nor does it predict your ultimate success or failure as a human being. No matter how high or how low you score on this test initially, and no matter how much you may increase your score through preparation, you should *never* consider the score you receive on this or any other test a final judgment of your abilities.

Chapter 2
Triage

The ACT is a time-limited test. You can develop strategies to help you use the time you are given to your advantage. One simple strategy is to prioritize the questions rather than answer them in the order in which they appear. In this chapter, you'll learn how to use a two-pass, or triage, system for approaching the ACT efficiently and effectively.

How Questions Are Organized

Wouldn't it be great if all the questions on the ACT were arranged in order of difficulty? Then you could do the easiest questions first and move on from there. That way you wouldn't waste a lot of time trying to answer difficult questions before you had answered all the easy questions, which count for the same number of points anyway.

Unfortunately, the ACT is not organized that way.

According to the ACT writers we interviewed, the English section of the test is not in any order of difficulty. In the Math Test, according to ACT literature, "most people find the first questions on the test easier...than the ones that come later," but these are only very rough guidelines. Many Princeton Review students find that some questions toward the end of the test are easier than many of the questions in the beginning.

Oh. But What If...

Equality
Remember that easy questions are worth just as much as difficult questions, so do the easy ones first!

But what if the Science Reasoning and Reading *passages* were arranged in order of difficulty? Some of the other test-preparation books maintain that they are. According to one ACT writer, this is true, "...only in an average sense. We believe in the philosophy that if students are running out of time, the questions they don't get to should be ones they would have difficulty with anyway. But students will find plenty of exceptions." So by its own admission, ACT does not use a definite order of difficulty in the Science Reasoning or Reading Tests.

Oh. But...

But nothing! On the ACT, if you want to do the easy questions first, you're going to have to find them for yourself. We have a good way to think about this. We call it "triage."

TRIAGE

Triage is the medical term that describes the technique used by emergency-room doctors when they have several emergencies at the same time. To save the most lives, doctors separate patients into three groups: those who will die regardless of intervention, those who require immediate medical attention, and those who can afford to wait a little while. The routine patients are left until last.

In ACT triage, you adapt this strategy somewhat. See that really tough algebra problem sitting over there? Forget it; it's a goner. How about that problem on frequency and amplitude? That would take far too long, and even if you got it right, it would still only be worth one point. Now this problem involving basic arithmetic—this is something different altogether. It's an easy question, so you should do it right away.

See that tough, horrible-looking passage about European authoritarianism during the nineteenth century? Let's see if it's still breathing after we finish the one about Ronald Reagan's election in 1980.

Just One More Minute...

If you find yourself stuck on a question, waiting for divine inspiration, it's time to move on to another, easier problem. Save your time and live to fight another day (or question, that is). The temptation to get stubborn and stay with a particular problem can be very strong, especially when you've already invested some time on it. Nonetheless, you need to move on. Why stick with a question that's giving you problems when there are easier questions to be answered?

For more help check out our academic tutoring offers at PrincetonReview.com

"Oh, Yeah!"

We've all had the experience of riding home in the car and suddenly slapping our hand to our forehead as we finally realized exactly how to do question number five. By using triage, you can sometimes have this sudden revelation *before* the test is over, when you can still do something about it. So how does triage work exactly?

Now, Later, Never

Do you want to do the problem *now*? That is the question you should constantly be asking yourself during the exam. If you finish reading a problem and immediately know how to solve it, then of course you should do it right away.

But what if you finish reading a problem and you aren't really certain how to begin? If you think you might be able to figure it out on your second pass, circle the question number and move on. This might seem hard to do at first, but it is one of the central tenets of good test taking, and it gets easier with practice. You aren't necessarily skipping the problem forever. You're just putting it at the back of the line.

However, if the problem is a goner and you're sure you'll never figure it out, fill in your guess answer and forget it. There are other problems out there waiting for you; don't worry about the ones you just *can't* do.

Two Passes

First Pass, Second Pass

On the first pass, do the questions you know how to do and guess on the questions that you have no idea how to do. On the second pass, answer all the questions that are doable but likely to take you more time.

We want you to do each section in two passes. During the first pass, the object is to nail every single question you can answer. By answering all the questions of which you're sure, you will never have to hear the words, "Okay, pencils down," and know that there were several more questions you could have done if only there had been more time. You will have already done them.

What Happens if I Think I Know How to Do It, but then I Realize I Was Wrong?

Nobody's right all the time. As soon as you realize you're stuck, you should put a big circle around the question and move on. This is the time when people tend to get stubborn. They think, "But I've already spent so much time on this question. It would be a waste to skip it now."

You Haven't Wasted the Time; You've Invested It

When you come back to this question on the second pass, you won't be starting from scratch. You'll already have read the question once. You may have made some notes in the margin. Perhaps reading it again will make you realize an important point you missed the first time. If not, throw it to the back of the line and count your blessings: You could still be back there working on question number five!

The Second Pass

After you've finished everything you can do on the first pass and bubbled in your Letter of the Day on all questions that you're sure you can't do, come back to the questions you circled for a second pass. Again, think ACT triage. Most of the "patients" in your emergency room have now been handled. Look over the remaining problems and ask yourself the same question: Which one do I want to do *now*? Obviously, none of them struck you as easy the first time or you would have answered on the first pass. On the contrary, among the remaining problems, some are probably more likely bets than others.

Sometimes when you read a question again, you suddenly realize what the point of the question really is. This will save you from having that "Oh, yeah!" revelation on the car ride home. But other times when you re-read a question, you suddenly realize that you will hate this question for the rest of your life and you never, ever want to see it again. Fine. Throw it to the back of the list and keep looking. These are "never" questions: Do them only if you have time to spare.

Sometimes you reject a question initially because you think it will take too much time. Well, now you have time. You've already locked in all the sure points, so maybe this is the question to do now.

Time to Spare

Let's face it—the ACT is designed to be difficult to finish in the time given. Most students are not going to finish early. But what if you do? Do you lay your head down and catch a few z's? No way! Go back to the problems that you skipped the first time through or that you wondered if you'd done right. There's always something to check!

Scoring More Points with ACT Triage

Deciding whether you will do a question *now*, *later*, or *never* is a crucial part of improving your results on the ACT. The whole point of ACT triage is to help you invest your time more profitably. By utilizing the two-pass approach and the concept of triage, you will, unlike most test takers, spend the majority of your time working on questions that seem easy or at least doable. As a result, you will score more points.

I've Done All the Questions I Know How to Do and All the Questions I Think I Know How to Do. Now What?

You guess. Guessing on the ACT is so important that we've given it its own chapter.

Chapter 3
Guessing and POE

There is no penalty for guessing on the ACT, so it is to your advantage to fill in an answer for every question. In this chapter, you'll learn how to take advantage of the multiple-choice nature of the ACT and get more points by understanding and using the Process of Elimination.

NO PENALTY FOR GUESSING

Imagine for a moment that you are a game show contestant. It's the final, big deal of the day. The host asks you, "Do you want curtain number one, curtain number two, or curtain number three?" As you carefully weigh your options, the members of the audience are screaming out their suggestions, but you can bet there is one suggestion no one in the audience is going to shout at you.

"Skip the question!"

Be Test Smart
Many students with good grades get below-average scores because they refuse to guess.

It wouldn't make sense. You have a one-in-three shot of winning, and there is no penalty for guessing wrong. (Okay, you might have to cart home a lifetime supply of toilet paper.)

On the ACT, you don't even have to worry about the toilet paper because there is no guessing penalty at all.

You Must Fill in an Answer for Every Single Question on the ACT

There are 215 questions on the ACT. If you went into the test room, filled out your name, and then went to sleep for the entire test, your composite score would be just about what you might expect: 0.

If, however, you went into the test room, filled out your name, went to sleep for most of the time, then woke up and picked answer choice (B) or (G) 215 times, your composite score would be a 12!

We would not recommend random guessing as an overall strategy (unless all you need is a 12, and that's only the first percentile), but you can see that it is in your interest to guess on every question you either can't answer or don't get to in time.

Ah, but there's guessing, and then there's *guessing.*

How to Score Higher on the ACT

Multiple Choice
The ACT is a multiple-choice test. This means you don't have to come up with an answer; you just have to identify the correct one from among the four or five choices provided.

Try the following question:

1. What is the French word for "eggplant"?

What? You don't know? Well then, you'd better guess at random. (By the way, there are no questions about vegetables, French or otherwise, on the ACT. We're just using this question to make a point.)

If you really don't know the answer to a question, of course, you should always guess. But before you choose an answer at random, take a look at the problem the way you would see it on the ACT.

1. What is the French word for "eggplant?"

   A. のみもの
   B. すきやき
   C. Aubergine
   D. デザート

Suddenly the question looks a lot easier, doesn't it? You may not have known the correct answer to this question, but you certainly knew three answers that were incorrect.

POE

The Process of Elimination (POE for short) enables you to make your guesses really count. Incorrect answer choices are often easier to spot than correct ones. Sometimes they are logically absurd; sometimes they are the opposite of the correct answer. If you find a wrong answer, eliminate it. While you will rarely be able to eliminate all of the incorrect answer choices, it is often possible to eliminate one or two, and each time you can eliminate an answer choice, your odds of guessing correctly get better.

A Moral Dilemma
What if someone approached you moments before the ACT began and offered to give you the answers to the test? You'd be SHOCKED, right? But what if we told you that the person making the offer was the proctor running the test? The fact is that every student who takes the test gets to see all the answers ahead of time; they're printed in the test booklet, right underneath each question.

Try another question.

1. What is the capital of Malawi?

   A. New York
   B. Lilongwe
   C. Paris
   D. Kinshasa

This time you could probably eliminate only two of the answer choices. However, that meant you were down to a fifty-fifty guess—much better than random guessing.

The Process of Elimination is a tremendously powerful tool. We refer to it in every single chapter of this book, and explain how to use it on a variety of specific types of questions.

Letter of the Day

Which makes more sense—guessing the same letter every time or switching around? If you think you're better off switching around, think again. As counterintuitive as it may seem, you will pick up more points consistently if you always guess the same letter. Sure, you won't get all of your random guesses correct, but you'll get some points. On the contrary, if you vary your guess answer, you might get some correct, but you might miss all of them just as easily.

It doesn't matter what letter you pick as your Letter of the Day. Contrary to popular opinion, you won't get more questions right if you guess (C) rather than any other choice. Go crazy, guess (A) or (F) on the next ACT you take. Just be consistent.

Chapter 4
Taking the ACT

Preparing yourself both mentally and physically to take the ACT is important. This chapter helps you learn exactly what you're in for, so you can plan ahead and be as comfortable as possible on test day. We not only talk about what to do but also what *not* to do.

PREPARING FOR THE ACT

The best way to prepare for any test is to find out exactly what is going to be on it. This book provides you with just that information. In the following chapters, you will find a comprehensive review of all the question types on the ACT, complete information on all the subjects covered by the ACT, and some powerful test-taking strategies developed specifically for the ACT.

To take full advantage of the review and techniques, you should practice on the tests in this book as well as on real ACT questions. We've already told you how to obtain copies of real ACT exams. Taking full practice exams allows you to chart your progress (with accurate scores for each test), gives you confidence in our techniques, and develops your stamina.

The Night Before the Test

Unless you are the kind of person who remains calm only by staying up all night to do last-minute studying, we recommend that you take the evening off. Go see a movie or read a good book (besides this one), and make sure you get to bed at a normal hour. No final, frantically memorized math formula or grammatical rule is going to make or break your score. A positive mental attitude comes from treating yourself decently. If you've prepared over the last several weeks or months, then you're ready.

If you haven't really prepared, there will be other opportunities to take the test, so get some rest and do the best you can. Remember, colleges will see only the score you choose to let them see. No *single* ACT is going to be crucial. We don't think night-before-the-test cramming is very effective. For example, we would not recommend that you try going through this book in one night.

On the Day of the Test

It's important that you eat a real breakfast, even if you normally don't. We find that about two-thirds of the way through the test, people who didn't eat something beforehand suddenly lose their will to live. Equally important, bring a snack to the test center. You will get a break during which food is allowed. Some people spend the break out in the hallways comparing answers and getting upset when their answers don't match. Ignore the people around you and eat your snack. Why assume they know any more than you do?

Don't Leave Home Without 'Em

Here are some items you'll want to have on test day.

- admissions ticket
- photo ID or letter of identification
- plenty of sharpened No. 2 pencils
- a watch
- an acceptable calculator with new batteries

Warming Up

While you're having breakfast, do a couple of questions from an ACT on which you've already worked to get your mind going. You don't want to use the first test on the real exam to warm up. And please don't try a hard question you've never done before. If you miss it, your confidence will be diminished, and that's not something you want on the day of the test.

At the test center, you'll be asked to show some form of picture ID or provide a note from your school—on school stationery—describing what you look like. The time or time remaining is often *not* announced during the test sections, so you should also bring a reliable watch—not the beeping kind—and, of course, several No. 2 pencils, an eraser, and a calculator. Check **www.actstudent.org/faq** to see if your calculator model is permitted. If you haven't changed the batteries recently (or ever), you should do that before the test or bring a back-up calculator.

When you get into the actual room in which you'll be taking the exam, make sure you're comfortable. Is there enough light? Is your desk sturdy? Don't be afraid to speak up; after all, you're going to be spending three and a half hours at that desk. And it's not a bad idea to go to the bathroom *before* you get to the room. It's a long haul to that first break.

ZEN AND THE ART OF TEST TAKING

Once the exam begins, tune out the rest of the world. That girl with the annoying cough in the next row? You don't hear her. That guy who is fidgeting in the seat ahead of you? You don't see him. It's just you and the exam. Everything else should be a blur.

As soon as one test ends, erase it completely from your mind. It no longer exists. The only test that counts is the one you are taking right now. Even if you are upset about a particular test, erase it from your mind. If you are busy thinking about the last test, you cannot focus on the one on which you are currently working, and that's a surefire way to make costly mistakes. Most people aren't very good at assessing how they performed on a given section of the exam, especially while they're still taking it, so don't waste your time and energy trying.

Some Things to Remember

- Make sure you know where the test center is located and where you need to go once you are at the test center.
- Show up early; you can't show up right when the test is scheduled to begin and expect to get in.
- Lay out your pencils, calculator, watch, admission ticket, and photo identification the night before the test. The last thing you want to be doing on the morning of the test is running around looking for a calculator. Also, it's important to have your own watch because there's no requirement that the room you're in have a working clock.
- Bring a snack and a bottle of water just in case you get hungry. There's nothing worse than testing on an empty stomach.

Keep Your Answers to Yourself

Please don't let anyone cheat off you. Test companies have developed sophisticated anti-cheating measures that go way beyond having a proctor walk around the room. We know of one test company that gets seating charts of each testing room. Its computers scan the score sheets of people sitting in the immediate vicinity for correlations of wrong answer choices. Innocent and guilty are invited to take the exam over again, and their scores from the first exam are invalidated.

Beware of Misbubbling Your Answer Sheet

Probably the most painful kind of mistake you can make on the ACT is to bubble in (A) with your pencil when you really mean (B), or to have your answers be one question number off (perhaps because you skipped one question on the test but forgot to skip it on the answer sheet). Aargh! The proctor isn't allowed to let you change your answers after a section is over, so it is critical that you either catch yourself before a test section ends or—even better—that you don't make a mistake in the first place.

Write Now
Feel free to write all over your test booklet. Don't do computations in your head. Put them in the booklet; you paid for it. Go nuts!

We suggest to our students that they write down their answers in their test booklets. This way, whenever you finish a page of questions in the test booklet, you can transfer all your answers from that page in a group. We find that this method minimizes the possibility of misbubbling and it also saves time. Of course, as you get near the end of a test, you should go back to bubbling question by question.

If you get back your ACT scores and they seem completely out of line, you can ask the ACT examiners to look over your answer sheet for what are called "gridding errors." If you want to, you can even be there while they look. If it is clear that there has been an error, ACT will change your score. An example of a gridding error would be a test in which, if you moved all the responses over by one, they would suddenly all be correct.

Should I Ever Cancel My Scores?

We recommend against canceling your scores, even if you feel you've done poorly. If you have registered as we recommended and not sent the scores to any colleges and possibly not to your high school, then the score you receive won't go anywhere unless you send it on later. There is no need to panic and cancel your score without knowing what it is if no one will ever see it. You never know—perhaps you did better than you think. Furthermore, if you've taken the ACT two or more times (something we heartily recommend), you can choose which score you want colleges to see when you request reports from ACT.

If you do decide to cancel your scores, ACT allows you to do it only at the test center itself. However, you can stop scores from reaching colleges if you call ACT by 12:00 P.M., Central Time on the *Thursday* following the test. The number to call is 319-337-1270.

Part II
How to Crack the ACT English Test

Chapter 5
Introduction to the ACT English Test

The English test does not test how well you write. It tests how well you know and can apply the rules of standard written English. The ACT is a standardized test, so it always tests the same basic concepts. If you don't know what the question is testing, you can look at the answers for clues. In this chapter, you'll learn how you can find these clues and use them along with test strategy to get a higher English score.

What's Good Writing?

Deciding what constitutes good writing is difficult. So much depends on the context, on what the writer is trying to accomplish, and on who is doing the deciding.

Call Us Ignorant, but We Prefer "Four Score and Seven"

For more great titles by The Princeton Review:
Grammar Smart, Illustrated Word Smart

These days, there are computer programs that are supposed to fix our writing. Mike Royko, the national columnist, once decided to try out one of these computer programs on Abraham Lincoln's Gettysburg Address, with predictably humorous results. "Four score and seven years ago" became "eighty-seven years ago" and it went downhill from there, turning a moving document of history into trite, conventional, standard written English.

What the English Test Tests

The English test measures how well you understand "the conventions of standard written English." There are 5 passages to read. Portions of each passage will be underlined, and you must decide whether these portions are correct as written or whether one of the other answer choices is better.

On Your Mark...
You have 45 minutes for 75 questions.

Some questions are designed to measure your knowledge of punctuation, grammar, and sentence structure. Other questions are designed to see if you know how to revise and strengthen a passage, how to change particular words for style or clarity, or how to "explain or support a point of view [more] clearly and effectively." There are a total of 75 questions to answer in 45 minutes.

What Your Score Means

Good writing is, to some extent, a matter of opinion. No matter how well or how poorly you do on the English test, you should not feel that your ACT English score truly represents your ability to write. A good score does not make you the next Jane Austen; a bad score does not make you the next Bart Simpson.

We don't mean to imply that ACT is doing a bad job. It's tough to measure English skills, and we think the test writers have constructed a fair test. In the end, however, what the ACT English test measures is how well you take the ACT English test.

Remember, This Is a Standardized Test

Every time the ACT is given, it tests the same things in the same way. You don't need to be a strong writer to do well on this test. You *do* need to know what types of errors crop up again and again and how to fix them. By going into the exam armed with this knowledge, you can more easily identify both the intentional errors and the correct answers for these questions.

We are going to review all punctuation, grammar, sentence structure, and rhetorical skills that are tested on this exam.

What Do the Passages Look Like?

Here is part of a sample passage.

[1]

When studying a foreign language, its[1] helpful to have a grasp with[2] other foreign languages, if only[3] because one has already learned what things are most important to know how to say first.

1. A. NO CHANGE
   B. its'
   C. it's
   D. it, is

2. F. NO CHANGE
   G. of
   H. to
   J. OMIT the underlined portion

3. A. NO CHANGE
   B. languages. Only
   C. languages, only if
   D. language: only if

[2]

[1] I am proud to tell you that I can ask, "Where is the bathroom?" in four different languages. [2] We both, however, admire the accomplishments of my clumsy friend, Al. [3] He can says[4] he is sorry in fourteen different languages. [5]

4. F. NO CHANGE
   G. say
   H. said
   J. says that

5. Suppose the author wants to add the following sentence to Paragraph 2:

   My friend Alice can ask for directions in five different languages.

   The best place to insert this sentence would be:

   A. before Sentence 1.
   B. before Sentence 2.
   C. before Sentence 3.
   D. after Sentence 3.

Question 6 asks about the preceding passage as a whole.

6. Suppose the author had chosen to write a short essay on the value of studying Japanese. Would this essay successfully fulfill the writer's goal?

F. No, because the writer is speaking about the general experience of learning a language.
G. No, because the writer fails to mention which languages are the easiest to learn.
H. Yes, because the writer explains how to learn additional languages.
J. Yes, because the writer offers such facts as how to say "Where is the bathroom?"

Most of the questions refer to individual words or phrases in the passage; these words are underlined and numbered. A few of the questions (such as question 5) ask you about the organization of a paragraph. You can tell what paragraphs they ask about by looking for the question number in a box at the end of a paragraph. (See the number 5 in a box at the end of the passage?) You will also see a few questions (such as question 6) that ask you about the passage as a whole. By the way, the answers are 1. (C), 2. (G), 3. (A), 4. (G), 5. (B), and 6. (F).

TRIAGE

In Chapter 1, we introduced you to the concept of triage and told you that it would be useful on every test on this exam. In the English test, the ACT writers have concocted their own brand of triage so that the specific questions (on subjects such as punctuation, grammar, and sentence structure) tend to come earlier in each passage. Usually there will be one or two questions about style or rhetoric at the end of each passage, dealing with the passage as a whole.

First Pass, Second Pass
On your first pass, answer all the questions that you know you can answer quickly and confidently. On your second pass, answer the questions that require more thought or that you skipped the first time through. Use POE to help you get rid of wrong answers.

Some rhetorical questions are sprinkled throughout the passages, and just because a question is at the beginning of a passage or only deals with a small mistake in grammar doesn't mean that you will necessarily spot the correct answer right away. If you are not sure what point of grammar, punctuation, or sentence structure is being tested, you should probably use POE (Process of Elimination) and move on: If you can eliminate any of the answer choices because you are sure they are wrong, you should cross out those choices and guess from what is left. You get the most out of your ability when you really attack the answer choices.

In our students' experience, the format of this test—passages side by side with the questions—tends to make them want to guess too quickly. The impulse to pick the first answer that sounds good is sometimes very strong. After all, this *is* English, which for many of us is our first language.

The problem is, of course, that it is *not* the English we speak every day.

ACT Island

The Laws of ACT Island
Don't just rely on what sounds incorrect: Look for specific errors.

Imagine that a bunch of ACT writers were shipwrecked on a desert island about 20 years ago. Not having much to do, they continued to write tests, which they slipped into empty bottles and cast into the sea. The tests regularly wash up on the coast of Iowa (yes, we know that Iowa is landlocked), where the national headquarters of ACT is located. The company is grateful and uses the tests regularly.

The only problem is that, after 20 years, the test writers' English is feeling a little old-fashioned and stilted. Still, the company feels a lot of loyalty to these shipwrecked grammarians and wouldn't dream of changing their tests.

If you make a lot of mistakes in this test, it is probably because you are relying on your ear, which is used to hearing a less formal English than is tested on the ACT. Moreover, English is a funny language—lots of things that sound all right are grammatically incorrect, while other things that sound incorrect are perfectly fine. A much better way to approach this test is to look for the specific errors that appear on the test all the time. By looking for these errors, you can take the guesswork out of your approach to the ACT English test.

For more great titles by The Princeton Review:
Reading Smart, Word Smart

Looking for Clues

One of the best ways to look for errors is to search the answer choices for clues. The underlined portions are very short—usually only a few words—so it's easy to see how each choice is different from the others. These differences offer a strong indication of what is on the minds of the ACT writers.

Look at the following example:

27. A. NO CHANGE
B. one goes
C. you go
D. he goes

Clearly, this question is about pronouns. Even if you do not spot something wrong with the underlined portion of the passage as you read it, the answer choices are telling you to check to see which of these pronouns agrees with the noun referred to in the passage. (Don't worry if you are rusty on pronouns; we'll cover them in detail later in this section.)

In the sections that follow, we show you the key elements for which to look in the passages and in the answer choices.

What If There Is More Than One Thing Wrong?

There is often more than one error in the underlined portion of a sentence. The best way to approach these questions, however, is not to try to see everything at once. Find *one* error. Eliminate the answer choices that contain the same error, then compare the remaining answer choices. Regardless of the number of errors you find in the question, keep your focus on the *differences* in the answer choices.

POE

You've probably already noticed that sometimes, even though you're not sure what the right answer is, you're *certain* that some of the answers are WRONG. Whenever you know an answer is wrong, cross it out. That's called POE (Process of Elimination), and it's a powerful tool for raising your score on the ACT.

When you come across an English question you're not sure how to answer, don't immediately circle it for later consideration and move on. First, take a look at the answers and see if there are any obvious mistakes in them. If there are, use POE. Cross out the wrong answers and guess from what's left. You should still circle the question and come back to it later if you have the time, but this way, you're getting the most out of the passage right as you're doing it. By crossing out the wrong answers and guessing now, you're preventing yourself from accidentally picking an answer you *know* is wrong when you use your Letter of the Day.

What's Wrong?
About 25 percent of the time...absolutely *nothing.*

No Change

Many of the questions in this test have NO CHANGE as the first of the answer choices. Just because this is a test is no reason to assume that there is always something wrong. NO CHANGE turns out to be the correct answer a little less than a quarter of the time it is offered. So don't be afraid to select it.

OMIT the Underlined Portion

A few of the questions in this test will have "OMIT the underlined portion" as the last of the four answer choices. When this choice is offered, it has a high probability of being correct—better than half the time on some recent tests. Unfortunately, a couple of recent tests we've seen had OMIT as the correct choice *less* than half the time, so you can't just choose it every time you see it.

It is worth noting that when you see OMIT, you should examine it very carefully.

What If Time Is Running Out?

Remember that as good as the techniques in the next chapters are, this is still a timed test. What should you do if you are running out of time? First, fill in every question with your guess answer. That way, if the proctor calls time, you at least have something filled in. Then go to the questions you haven't done and see which look like they would be the fastest to do. Usually, these are the questions with the shortest answer choices, not the longer rhetorical skills questions. Do as many of these as you can, changing the answers that you've already bubbled in as you go.

A Warning

To forestall the objections of the expert grammarians out there, let us say at the outset that this discussion is not designed to be an exhaustive discourse on English grammar and usage. You are reading this chapter to do well on the English test of the ACT. Thus, if we seem to oversimplify a point or ignore an arcane exception to a rule, it's because we feel no further detail is warranted. A rule is unlikely to be tested if it is obscure or controversial.

Before We Begin, Some Terminology

The ACT is not going to ask you to identify parts of speech or diagram a sentence, but it will be helpful for the following discussion if you know some basic definitions. Here's a simple sentence.

Tom broke the vase.

This sentence is made up of two nouns, a verb, and an article.

- A **noun** is a word used to name a person, a place, a thing, or an idea.
- A **verb** is a word that expresses action.
- An **article** is a word that modifies or limits a noun.

In the sentence above, *Tom* and *vase* are both nouns. *The* is an article. *Broke* is a verb. *Tom* is the **subject** of the sentence because it is the person, place, or thing that is "doing" the action (the passive voice is an exception and will be discussed later). *Vase* is the **object** of the sentence because it receives the action of the verb (again, the passive voice is an exception).

Here's a more complex version of the same sentence.

Tom accidentally broke the big vase of flowers.

We've added an adverb, an adjective, and a prepositional phrase to the original sentence.

- An **adverb** is a word that modifies a verb, an adjective, or another adverb.
- An **adjective** is a word that modifies a noun.
- A **preposition** is a word that notes the relation of a noun to an action or a thing.
- A **phrase** is a group of words that acts as a single part of speech. A phrase is missing either a subject, a verb, or both.
- A **prepositional phrase** is a group of words beginning with a preposition.

In the sentence above, *accidentally* is an adverb modifying the verb *broke. Big* is an adjective modifying the noun *vase. Of* is a preposition because it shows a relationship between *vase* and *flowers. Of flowers* is a prepositional phrase that acts like an adjective by modifying *vase.*

Here's an even more complex version of the same sentence.

As he ran across the room, Tom accidentally broke the big vase of flowers.

Now we've added to the original sentence a secondary clause containing a pronoun.

- A **pronoun** is a word that takes the place of a noun.
- A **clause** is a group of words that contains a subject and a verb.

Tom accidentally broke the big vase of flowers is considered the **independent clause** in this sentence because it contains the main idea of the sentence and could stand by itself. *As he ran across the room* is also a **clause** (it contains a subject and a verb), but because it is not a complete thought, it is called a **dependent clause**. In this clause, *he* is a pronoun taking the place of *Tom*.

Summary

- Do the questions in order, leaving only tougher rhetorical questions for the end. If you're having trouble with a particular question, leave it and come back. Often a later question will help you with an earlier one.
- Search the answer choices for clues. Focus on the differences between the answer choices, and use that information to determine the error(s) being tested.
- Look for one error at a time. It is a good idea to start by narrowing down the choices on the basis of errors in sentence structure and grammar, and then use punctuation to make your selection between the remaining choices. For instance, if the choices offer you a list of items or actions, first check for parallel construction and then look for correct use of serial commas.
- Don't forget that NO CHANGE is correct a little less than a quarter of the time. If you can't find anything wrong with the underlined portion, it may be correct as written.

Chapter 6
Sentence Structure and Punctuation

The ACT English test contains a number of questions that test sentence-structure issues and punctuation errors. This chapter takes a look at the primary errors in sentence structure: sentence fragments, comma splices and run-ons, misplaced modifiers, and non-parallel construction. It also covers the basics of how and when to use certain punctuation marks. Often, sentence-structure and punctuation questions can be spotted by looking at the variations in the answer choices.

THE BASICS OF SENTENCE STRUCTURE

Good sentence structure is about putting together words, phrases, and clauses—the essential building blocks of sentences—in logical ways. Before we talk about the *errors* of sentence structure, let's spend a moment talking about correct structure. Here is that example again.

As he ran across the room, Tom broke the vase.

This sentence consists of two clauses. Each clause has a subject and a verb. The second clause ("Tom broke the vase") is considered the main clause and is independent because it can stand alone. The first clause ("As he ran across the room,") is called dependent because it cannot stand alone.

You can easily change a dependent clause into an independent clause and vice versa. Often, all it takes is a single word.

He ran across the room.

By removing "as" from the dependent clause, we suddenly have a sentence that can stand on its own. By adding an "as" to the second clause, we can instantly change it into a dependent clause.

As Tom broke the vase,...

If we stuck these two new clauses together now, the meaning of the sentence would be very different. Could we have kept the meaning more or less the same and still made the first clause independent? Sure. Try this:

Tom ran across the room, breaking the vase.

Now the first half of the sentence contains the main independent clause. We had to change "he" to "Tom" so that the reader would know about whom the sentence was talking. We also had to change the second half of the sentence from a clause into a modifying phrase. **While a clause has a subject and a verb, a phrase is missing at least one of these.**

PUTTING THE PIECES TOGETHER

Proficient writers use a mixture of dependent clauses, independent clauses, phrases, and varied punctuation to add variety to their writing and to create emphasis. By combining these building blocks in different ways, writers create a rhythm and show readers which thoughts are most important.

Here are the most often used structures.

- Independent clause (period) new independent clause (period)
  Jane lit the campfire. Frank set up the tent.

- Independent clause (comma plus conjunction) independent clause (period)
  Jane lit the campfire, and Frank set up the tent.

- Independent clause (semicolon) independent clause (period)
  Jane lit the campfire; Frank set up the tent.

- Independent clause (comma) dependent clause (period)
  Jane lit the campfire, while Frank set up the tent.

- Dependent clause (comma) independent clause (period)
  As Jane lit the campfire, Frank set up the tent.

All of these examples are correct. A writer might choose one over another to emphasize one thought over another. For example, in the last sentence, the writer is choosing to make "setting up the tent" the focus. Perhaps in the next sentence the tent is going to collapse with Frank inside it.

THE GLUE

Punctuation serves as the glue that holds the pieces of our sentences together. It's important to use the correct punctuation; otherwise, the pieces of a sentence won't form a coherent sentence.

There are several types of punctuation that are used in different ways. Some types, such as the period, are only used in one way (to end a sentence). Other types, such as the apostrophe, can be used in many situations (denoting contractions or possession, for example). If that sounds confusing, don't worry—we'll go through each type and explain how it works and affects sentence structure.

As you saw previously, there are many different ways to combine clauses and phrases. Now let's see how punctuation works in these scenarios.

Two Independent Clauses

Mary wondered why there was a bird in the classroom and she decided to ask the teacher what the bird was doing indoors.

When two independent clauses appear in the same sentence, they are usually joined by a conjunction (a word like *and, or, but, for, nor,* or *yet*). Thus, the two independent clauses above are: "Mary wondered why there was a bird in the classroom" and "she decided to ask the teacher what the bird was doing indoors." A comma belongs before the conjunction that joins the two independent clauses.

> *Mary wondered why there was a bird in the classroom, and she decided to ask the teacher what the bird was doing indoors.*

Alternatively, you could separate the two clauses with a period or a semicolon. To do that, you would also need to remove the conjunction *and.*

> *Mary wondered why there was a bird in the classroom. She decided to ask the teacher what the bird was doing indoors.*

Or:

> *Mary wondered why there was a bird in the classroom; she decided to ask the teacher what the bird was doing indoors.*

The first example using a period separates the two clauses completely. A semicolon, the other hand, indicates that the two clauses are related. However, the ACT doesn't tend to differentiate between the two.

You can also use a colon to connect two independent clauses if the second is an expansion or explanation of the first clause. Let's look at an example.

> *I didn't know what to do: I could either go camping or stay home and study for the ACT.*

An Independent Clause and a Dependent Clause

Commas are also used to separate independent clauses from dependent clauses. You'll remember that a dependent clause is one that cannot stand on its own as a sentence. Identify the dependent clause in the sentence below.

> *Before Mary could reach the teacher she saw the woman offer the bird part of the bagel.*

Check for Commas
Look out for
- words and phrases in a series
- introductory phrases and words
- mid-sentence phrases that are not essential to the sentence

The first clause, "Before Mary could reach the teacher," cannot stand by itself and therefore is a dependent clause. "She saw the woman offer the bird part of the bagel" can stand by itself, so it is an independent clause. Here, the two must be separated by a comma.

> *Before Mary could reach the teacher, she saw the woman offer the bird part of the bagel.*

An Independent Clause and a Modifying Phrase

Commas are also used to separate independent clauses from modifying phrases of more than just a couple of words. A modifying phrase modifies or describes something else, usually a noun. Identify the modifying phrase in the sentence below.

Hungry and excited the bird snapped up the bagel.

"Hungry and excited" is a modifying phrase (it modifies the noun "bird"). "The bird snapped up the bagel" is an independent clause. The two must be separated by a comma.

Hungry and excited, the bird snapped up the bagel.

Additional Information Within an Independent Clause

You might decide to include some extra information or details in your independent clause. You can set that information apart from the rest of the sentence by using commas or dashes. You can also use a colon to add a list of related details.

Josh, who needed to stock up for the party, went to the store to buy the necessary supplies: soda, chips, balloons, and weasels.

Commas

Commas can change restrictive clauses or phrases to being nonrestrictive. What does that mean?

A "restrictive" clause or phrase is essential to the meaning of a sentence, and it should not be separated from the rest of the sentence by commas.

People who snore are advised to sleep on their sides.

"Who snore" is essential to the meaning of this sentence. The sentence is not saying that *all* people should sleep on their sides, just the ones who snore.

A "nonrestrictive" clause or phrase is not essential to the meaning of a sentence. It merely adds a parenthetical thought, and therefore, it needs to be separated from the rest of the sentence by commas.

My father, who snores loudly, always sleeps in his long johns.

Identify the nonrestrictive clause in the sentence below.

Mary who by now was very confused stopped in front of the woman.

The nonrestrictive clause is "who by now was very confused." This clause modifies the noun that precedes it—in this case, "Mary"—but is not essential to the meaning of the sentence. "Mary stopped in front of the woman" does not need the clause in order to make sense as a sentence. To set off the clause from the rest of the sentence, you need to surround it with a *pair* of commas.

> *Mary, who by now was very confused, stopped in front of the woman.*

Identify the restrictive clause in the sentence below.

> *"Only a person who is a little peculiar would feed a bagel to a bird!" thought Mary.*

"Who is a little peculiar" is a restrictive clause because it adds essential information to the sentence. Thus, it does *not* require separation by commas.

How Do You Spot Restrictive/Nonrestrictive Comma Errors?

As always, the answer choices provide you with a very small menu of options from which to choose. If you see differences in punctuation among the choices, check to see whether the underlined portion of the sentence is part of a restrictive or nonrestrictive phrase or clause.

Dashes

Dashes Often Travel in Pairs
Dashes (like parentheses) are used to set off a phrase that is not essential to the meaning of the sentence.

Dashes (—) separate a word or group of words from the rest of the sentence. Dashes are used either to indicate an abrupt break in thought or to introduce an explanation or afterthought.

In the example below, which group of words should be separated from the rest of the sentence?

> *I tried to express my gratitude not that any words could be adequate but she just nodded and walked away.*

The clause "not that any words could be adequate" must be isolated from the rest of the sentence.

> *I tried to express my gratitude—not that any words could be adequate—but she just nodded and walked away.*

When the group of words that needs isolating is in the middle of a sentence, dashes function as a pair of less formal parentheses. However, when the phrase that needs isolating is at the end of the sentence instead, only one dash is required.

> *Just outside the door to the cabin we heard the howling of wolves—a sound that made our hair stand on end.*

How Do You Spot Dash Errors?

If the underlined portion *or any of the answer choices* contains a dash, compare the dash to the punctuation marks available in the other answer choices. Also check the non-underlined portion of the passage for dashes that might be linking up with this one to isolate a clause or phrase. Ask yourself whether the sentence contains a sudden break in thought, an explanation, or an afterthought.

Remember that if the group of words that needs isolating is in the middle of the sentence, there should be a *pair* of dashes. If the group of words is at the end of the sentence, there should be only one.

Colons

Colons are usually used after a complete statement to introduce a list of related details. The list can have many items or just one. In the following sentence, try to decide where the statement ends and the details begin.

Check for Colons
Look out for
- an underlined phrase that contains a list

> *Maria just purchased all the camping supplies for our trip, a backpack, a sleeping bag, and a pair of hiking boots.*

"Maria just purchased all the camping supplies for our trip" is the complete statement in the sentence above. "A backpack, a sleeping bag, and a pair of hiking boots" are the related details. A colon belongs between the two.

> *Maria just purchased all the camping supplies for our trip: a backpack, a sleeping bag, and a pair of hiking boots.*

How Do You Spot Colon Errors?

If the underlined phrase *or any of the answer choices* contains a colon, you should ask yourself the following question:

Is a list of some kind introduced by an independent clause?

If so, a colon preceding the list or statement is correct. If not, a colon is probably incorrect.

One of ACT's favorite tricks is to write a sentence that utilizes a colon to introduce a list but to do so incorrectly because it follows an incomplete thought. Look out for colons that follow the verb including or the phrase *such as*.

> *Maria just purchased all the camping supplies for our trip, including: a backpack, a sleeping bag, and a pair of hiking boots.*

In this example, the colon is used improperly. By adding the word "including," the part of the sentence preceding the colon is no longer an independent clause, and therefore, the sentence, as written, is incorrect.

To make a sentence more complex, you can always add more clauses and phrases (with the appropriate punctuation, of course), but those are the basic building blocks. Now that we know how to put these pieces together, let's look at some of the ways the ACT tests sentence structure errors.

AVOID THESE COMMON ERRORS IN SENTENCE STRUCTURE

There are four main types of errors in sentence structure.

1. sentence fragments
2. run-ons and comma splices
3. misplaced modifiers
4. non-parallel construction

All of these errors are the result of incorrect placement of the building blocks that make up sentences. Sentence structure on the ACT is closely tied to punctuation. The two are related because sentence structure errors can often be fixed by using the appropriate punctuation. In fact, you will find that by using punctuation clues from the answer choices, you will often be able to zero in on sentence structure errors in the passages.

Error #1: Sentence Fragments

Fragments
The ACT always contains. A few sentence fragments. Like these.

A complete sentence must have a subject and a verb, and it must be able to stand alone. In other words, it must be or contain an independent clause. Remember the very first example in this chapter?

Tom broke the vase.

Check for Sentence Fragments
Look out for
- a dependent clause by itself
- punctuation changes in the answer choices

This is an independent clause. We can change it into a dependent clause by adding just one word.

When Tom broke the vase,...

Even though it still has a subject and a verb, this clause can no longer stand alone. It is now waiting for an independent clause to finish the sentence.

When Tom broke the vase, Sid ran to tell their aunt Sally.

You can turn any independent clause into a dependent clause by *adding* one of the words in the box below to the beginning of the clause.

when, where, why, how, if, as, because,

although, while, despite, that, who, what

(You may see these words referred to in *The Real ACT* or in grammar books as subordinating conjunctions, relative pronouns, or prepositions, but these terms are not important.)

By the same token, you can turn most dependent clauses into independent clauses by *taking away* these words.

The First Type of Sentence Fragment

There are two kinds of sentence fragments. The first is just a dependent clause waiting for a second half that isn't there. Here's an example.

The bride and groom drove away in their car. As the children ran behind, shouting and laughing.
(underlined: "As the" — 1)

1. A. NO CHANGE
   B. While the
   C. During which the
   D. The

Here's How to Crack It

The second "sentence" in the example isn't a sentence at all; it is a dependent clause Answer choices (B) and (C) repeat the error. The only answer that makes the clause independent is (D).

Could we have combined the second "sentence" with the first to make a correct sentence? Yes, but in this case, ACT doesn't give us that option: The period at the end of the first sentence isn't underlined, so we can't change it.

The Second Type of Sentence Fragment

In the second type of sentence fragment question, the ACT writers ask you to *incorporate* the sentence fragment into the complete sentence coming immediately before or after the fragment through the use of different punctuation marks. In the example that follows, notice that the underlining extends from the end of one sentence through the beginning of the next sentence, so it includes the punctuation as well.

Although it will always be associated with Shakespeare's famous literary character. The castle at Elsinore was never home to Hamlet.
(underlined: "character. The" — 2)

2. F. NO CHANGE
G. character, the
H. character; the
J. character. A

Here's How to Crack It

The underlined portion of this passage includes pieces of two sentences and the punctuation in between. We have to check both "sentences" to make sure they are complete. Let's check the first "sentence" first. Can it stand on its own? No. It's a dependent clause. Aha! This is the error. Could we have removed the "Although" at the beginning to create an independent clause? Sure, but that isn't an option in this case because "Although" isn't underlined.

This time, the only way to fix the passage is to combine the dependent clause with the independent clause to form one big sentence. As we mentioned earlier in the chapter, you need a comma between a dependent and an independent clause. The only answer choice that contains a comma is (G). This must be the correct answer.

How Do You Spot Sentence Fragments?

You will often be able to spot this type of error as you read the passage itself, now that you know to look for a dependent clause all by itself. If you don't see the error as you read the passage the first time, however, don't despair. There are three terrific clues waiting for you—the three remaining answer choices after NO CHANGE.

The Answer Choices Contain Valuable Clues

If you're having trouble deciding whether a passage has a sentence-construction error, it helps to look at the answer choices. They often contain great clues as to what is going on in the minds of the test writers. In the last question, for example, it may have helped to look at the differences in *punctuation* among the answer choices. Some of the choices break the two clauses into two sentences. Others combine them. This should make you ask, "Why would ACT give me this choice? Maybe this question is about sentence construction. Would it be better to combine the two clauses? Hmm. Let me check for sentence fragments."

Sometimes, of course, there will be no need to change the sentence at all. Remember, the answer NO CHANGE is correct slightly less than a quarter of the time. However, the flip side of this is that NO CHANGE is wrong slightly more than three-quarters of the time.

Error #2: Comma Splices and Run-Ons

In a comma splice, two independent clauses are jammed together into one sentence, with only a comma to try to hold them together.

Aunt Sally ran into the room, Tom was already gone.

There are several ways to fix this sentence. The easiest way would be to break it up into two sentences.

Aunt Sally ran into the room. Tom was already gone.

If there is a clear reason that one clause might be connected to the other (for example, if Tom has just broken Aunt Sally's vase), you can also fix it by putting a **conjunction** (such as "and" or "but") between the two thoughts.

Aunt Sally ran into the room, but Tom was already gone.

You can also break up the two thoughts with a semicolon instead of a period.

Aunt Sally arrived home several hours later; Tom was already gone.

Conjunctions

Conjunctions plus commas can be used to link two independent clauses.

Mary wondered why there was a bird in the classroom, and she decided to ask the teacher what the bird was doing indoors.

You will also see conjunctions linking dependent clauses to independent clauses, as in this example.

Susie was sick because she ate seven hamburgers.

The first part of the sentence does give a complete thought, but the "because" in the second part means that clause cannot stand on its own. The "because" is a conjunction, however, and links the dependent clause to the independent clause.

A **run-on** sentence is the same thing as a comma splice but without the comma.

Aunt Sally swept up the shards of glass she was furious.

Again, the easiest way to solve the problem is to break up the sentence into two new sentences.

Aunt Sally swept up the shards of glass. She was furious.

A run-on sentence is often much longer than our example, running on and on, you might actually run out of breath if you read it out loud and then wonder whether perhaps it would have been better to split it up into more than one sentence. That last sentence, of course, was a run-on as well.

Check for Comma Splice

Look out for

- punctuation changes in the answer choices

Here's How They Look on the ACT

Here's how a comma splice or run-on might look on the ACT.

There is not much difference between the decision to enter politics and the decision to jump into a pit full of <u>rattlesnakes, in fact,</u> [3] you might find a friendlier environment in the snake pit

3. A. NO CHANGE
   B. rattlesnakes. In fact,
   C. rattlesnakes in fact
   D. rattlesnakes, in fact

Here's How to Crack It

Check the punctuation. As soon as you see that one or more of the answer choices gives you the option of breaking up the sentence into two pieces, you should immediately consider that there might be a comma splice or a run-on problem. Are the two clauses surrounding the punctuation both independent? Yes! This is probably a comma splice error. Now the question is how to fix it. Only one of the answer choices breaks the long sentence into two smaller ones. Answer choice (B) is probably correct. Remember, however, that there are other ways to fix a comma splice; to be certain, try out the other answer choices in the sentence. Perhaps one of them will use a conjunction to bridge the two clauses. Is that the case here? No. Therefore, the correct answer is (B).

The college's plans for expansion included a new science building and a new <u>dormitory if</u> [4] the funding drive is successful, there will be enough money for both.

4. F. NO CHANGE
   G. dormitory, if
   H. dormitory; if,
   J. dormitory. If

Here's How to Crack It

If you could start from scratch, there would be many different ways of expressing the thoughts in this passage. However, as always, you must find the way that the ACT writers decided to use.

Again, the answer choices provide immediate clues. In some, the sentence is broken up into two smaller sentences. Check to see if there are independent clauses on either side of the punctuation. Bingo: This is a run-on sentence. Which choices can we eliminate? (F) and (G) bite the dust. Both (H) and (J) successfully break up the two clauses. (Remember, a semicolon will often do the trick if the subjects of the two clauses are related.)

Is there anything else wrong with either of them? Come to think of it, the comma at the end of (H) is unnecessary. The correct answer is (J).

Error #3: Misplaced Modifiers

A modifying phrase needs to be near what it is modifying. If it gets too far away, it can get misplaced.

> *Sweeping up the shards of glass, the missing key to the jewelry box was found by Aunt Sally.*

As written, this sentence gives the impression that the *missing key* was sweeping up the shards of glass. When a sentence begins with a **modifying phrase** (a group of words without a subject), the noun being modified must follow the phrase. *Who* was sweeping up the shards of glass? Aunt Sally, of course. The correct version of this sentence would be:

> *Sweeping up the shards of glass, Aunt Sally found the missing key to her jewelry box.*

A more subtle version of the same type of error:

> *Ecstatic and happy, Aunt Sally's key opened the jewelry box for the first time in weeks.*

At first glance, it looks like the modifying phrase "ecstatic and happy" is modifying Aunt Sally. However, what is the real subject of this sentence, as written? The key. "Aunt Sally's" is actually modifying the key. A correct version of this sentence would be:

> *Ecstatic and happy, Aunt Sally used her key to open the jewelry box for the first time in weeks.*

Check for Misplaced Modifiers

Look out for

- modifying phrases followed by commas. Do the nouns being modified appear right after the modifiers?

Here's How They Look on the ACT

Here's how a misplaced modifier might look on the ACT.

Walking to the pawnshop, Bob's watch dropped into the sewer.

5. A. NO CHANGE
   B. Bob's watch dropped in the sewer
   C. Bob dropped his watch into the sewer
   D. Bob's dropped watch into the sewer

Here's How to Crack It

Bob's watch may have dropped into the sewer, but it certainly isn't walking to the pawnshop. We've got to get Bob closer to the comma so it's clear that the modifying phrase in the first half of the sentence refers to him. Only (C) does that.

How Do You Spot Misplaced Modifiers?

That's easy! If the underlined portion of the sentence is part of a modifying phrase, check to make sure it modifies the correct noun. If the underlined portion of the sentence includes the noun that is supposed to be modified, check to make sure it is the correct noun.

Check for Construction Shifts

Look out for

- shifting phrases in the answer choices

Construction Shifts

A related type of error is what the ACT writers call a construction shift. These resemble misplaced modifiers in that the modifier is in the wrong place, but construction shifts require no words to be changed. Instead, the modifying word or phrase simply has to be moved over slightly.

Stepping to avoid the large puddle,

I carefully tripped and fell.
6

6. F. NO CHANGE
G. (Place after *Stepping*)
H. (Place after *and*)
J. (Place after *fell*)

Here's How to Crack It

These questions require just a little common sense. "Carefully" is an adverb. It must modify a verb. The only question for us is, which verb? Only a stunt man trips or falls "carefully." This effectively disposes of answer choices (F), (H), and (J). If we put "carefully" after "stepping," does the sentence make sense? Yes, so the answer is (G).

Need more Grammar help?
Check out *Grammar Smart*

How Do You Spot Construction Shifts?

That's easy. The answer choices in construction shifts are either presented as shown above, or as follows:

Stepping to avoid the large puddle, I
7
carefully tripped and fell.
7

7. A. NO CHANGE
B. Stepping carefully over the puddle, I tripped and fell.
C. Stepping over the puddle, I tripped and carefully fell.
D. Stepping over the puddle, I tripped and fell carefully.

Here's How to Crack it

In either case, it is easy to see that the only difference in each of the answer choices is the position of the word "carefully." This should alert you to consider the position of the modifier. Once again, you must keep your focus on the differences among the answers.

Error #4: Non-Parallel Construction

There are two major types of parallel construction errors tested on the ACT. They both involve some kind of list. You might see a list of verbs.

> *When Tom finally came home, Aunt Sally <u>kissed</u> him, <u>hugged</u> him, and <u>gives</u> him his favorite dessert after dinner.*

The sentence above has an error because all of the items on the list must be in the same tense. The first two verbs in the example above ("kissed" and "hugged") are in the past tense, but the third verb ("gives") is in the present tense. It is not "parallel" with the other two. The correct sentence should read

> *When Tom finally came home, Aunt Sally <u>kissed</u> him, <u>hugged</u> him, and <u>gave</u> him his favorite dessert after dinner.*

Check for Non-Parallel Construction
Look out for

- a series of nouns or verbs

You also might see a list of nouns.

> *Three explanations for Sid's locking himself in his room were <u>a desire</u> to do his homework, <u>a sense</u> that he needed to hone his college essays, and <u>disliking</u> his brother Tom, who always got away with murder.*

The sentence above is wrong because while "a desire" and "a sense" are both nouns, "disliking" is a gerund, or a verb functioning as a noun. Is there a more noun-like way to say the same thing? If you said "a dislike of," you are absolutely right. Now the sentence is parallel. Here's the corrected version.

> *Three explanations for Sid's locking himself in his room were <u>a desire</u> to do his homework, <u>a sense</u> that he needed to hone his college essays, and <u>a dislike of</u> his brother Tom, who always got away with murder.*

The lists do not have to have *three* nouns or *three* verbs. Sometimes there are only two.

> *<u>To see</u> the beauty of a sunset in Venice is <u>experiencing</u> perfection.*

This is wrong because if the first half of the sentence begins with the infinitive "to see," the second half of the sentence must also begin with an infinitive.

> *<u>To see</u> the beauty of a sunset in Venice is <u>to experience</u> perfection.*

The Serial Comma

Commas are used to separate items in a series. Let's look at an example.

> *When Mary walked into the classroom, she saw a school teacher, a doctor, a woman eating a bagel and a bird.*

A comma should be placed after each item in a series. Thus, we need a comma after the phrase "a woman eating a bagel." As this sentence stands, you might get the impression that the woman was eating the bird as well.

In some writing, it is acceptable to omit the comma before the "and" in a series of three or more items. However, the ACT test writers prefer a more formal version of English (no surprise there), so use a comma to separate every item in a series, including the last one.

Reminder
Don't forget that some of the punctuation questions will be correct *as is.* Many punctuation questions on the ACT concern commas.

How Do You Spot Parallel-Construction Problems?

That's easy. First, as you read the passage, be on the lookout for a series of actions or nouns. Now that you know what to look for, you may spot an error even without having to go to the answer choices. Second, look for changes in verb tense or the way in which nouns are set up among the answer choices.

"Just the Punctuation, Ma'am"

The ACT also likes to test one kind of punctuation all by itself: the apostrophe. These errors aren't related to sentence structure, but they are fairly common.

Apostrophes

An apostrophe is used either to indicate possession or to mark missing letters in a word.

When it is used to indicate possession, it appears either right before or right after the *s* at the end of the possessive noun.

Peter's new car is extremely expensive.
Women's issues will be important in the next election.
The girls' room will be renovated this summer.

The apostrophe tells us that the car belongs to Peter. If the noun in possession is singular—as in the case of Peter—the apostrophe falls before the "s." If the noun in possession is singular and ends in "s"—such as "boss"—add an apostrophe and an "s" *if* the possessive form would be pronounced as would the plural form (in this case, "boss's" is pronounced "bosses"). The ACT does not test the few exceptions to this rule.

If it is plural and it doesn't end in "s"—as in the case of women—the apostrophe falls before the "s." If it is plural and it ends in "s"—as in the case of "girls"—the apostrophe falls after the "s." Note: Don't worry too much about the plural nouns. ACT seems more interested in your ability to form singular possessives correctly.

The ACT folks also seem very interested in whether you know when an apostrophe is *unnecessary*; some apostrophe questions require you to *drop* an apostrophe. Remember, for the apostrophe to be correct when forming a possessive, the noun containing it must be followed by another noun or an adjective and a noun.

Peter's new car
Women's issues
Girls' room

The apostrophe is also used to indicate missing letters in a word.

I'm sorry. I couldn't make it to your party.

In the sentences above, the apostrophe takes the place of "a" (*I'm* instead of *I am*) and the place of "o" (*couldn't* instead of *could not*). Words that use apostrophes in this way are called **contractions**. Common contractions include *don't, isn't, won't,* and *can't.*

Its/It's/Its'

The most common apostrophe error you'll see tested on the ACT is misuse of *it's* and *its,* which have their own special rules.

The word "it's"—with an apostrophe—is used only when you want to say "it is" or "it has."

It's important. (It is important.)
It's been nice talking to you. (It has been nice talking to you.)

Pronouns Most Frequently Misused
The ACT test writers will sometimes try to confuse you by presenting both a possessive pronoun and the same pronoun in a contraction as answer choices. Do you know the difference between these words: *whose, who's, its, it's*?

The word "its"—without an apostrophe—is (in this case only) the possessive form of the word "it."

The baby bear could not find its mother.

We realize this is a little confusing because you usually use an apostrophe to form the possessive. The ACT writers realize this is confusing, too; that's why this error is on the test. Possessive pronouns (such as *his, her, your, our*) NEVER take apostrophes.

The word *its'* isn't a word at all. That doesn't stop ACT from throwing it on the test to try to trip you up. Most ACT English tests have at least one made-up word on them somewhere.

How Do You Spot Apostrophe Errors?

If a word in the underlined portion *or any of the answer choices* contains an apostrophe, you should ask yourself whether the apostrophe is meant to form a contraction or to make a noun possessive and which you need for the sentence. When the word(s) *it's* or *it is* is in the underlined portion *or any of the answer choices,* use the special rules we just discussed.

What About !(")*?

It seems that the ACT test writers just aren't that interested in whether you know how to use exclamation points, parentheses, asterisks, and question marks correctly. They mention in their guide that the ACT tests some of these points, but not one of the ACTs in *The Real ACT Prep Guide* contains any such questions.

Quotation marks sometimes surround words in the underlined portion and the answer choices, but when they do appear, they show up in every answer choice (you aren't given the option of removing them) and seem intended to distract you from some other error.

As a result, we think you're safe spending your time worrying about other kinds of punctuation. The most common punctuation errors on the ACT deal with commas, semicolons, colons, dashes, and apostrophes. Learn how to use these correctly, and you should be covered.

PUTTING IT ALL TOGETHER

How Do You Spot Punctuation Errors?

That's easy. Look for changes in punctuation among the answer choices. These changes tell you what the ACT writers are up to.

Look at the following example:

A. NO CHANGE
B. cities environmental problems
C. city's environmental problems
D. citys' environmental problems

Clearly, this question is about proper use of the apostrophe. Read the entire sentence and use the rules you've learned in this chapter to pick the best answer.

For more practice, go online!
If you haven't registered yet, go to PrincetonReview.com/cracking

One Last Note

There are some forms of punctuation that can be used interchangeably. As we stated above, a semicolon can sometimes take the place of a period. Dashes can sometimes be used instead of parentheses. Sometimes a colon can be replaced by a dash. We haven't discussed these possibilities at length because on the ACT, you will never be asked to make a decision between two correct alternatives.

If two kinds of punctuation can both be considered correct, only one will appear among the answer choices. After all, questions can't have two right answers, can they?

Sentence Structure and Punctuation Drill

In the drill below, you will find only questions that focus on sentence construction. Before you start, take a few moments to go back over the review material and techniques. If you don't spot an error as you read, remember that the answer choices may help to suggest an error for which you should look. Answers in Part VII.

When you see the gingerbread houses of Roskilde with their neatly thatched roofs, the gardens filled with flowers, blooms, [1] and the happy smiles on the fresh-faced inhabitants, it is difficult to believe that this town was once the home of a more warlike people—the Vikings. Roskilde's main museum is devoted to those early inhabitants, the Vikings [2] once wandered throughout Europe, and by some reports, may have travel [3] all the way to North America as well. The museum sits on a site at the edge of Roskilde fiord. Where [4] the Viking ships were once launched on voyages of conquest and plunder. Until 20 years ago used only by the fishermen who still ply their trade in the fiord, tourists now arrive in buses at the craggy shoreline [5] to watch local artisans build the Viking ships in the traditional manner. [6]

High above the fiord is Roskilde Cathedral, built by the famous Viking King Harold Blue-toothe in the 1200s the king [7] is said to have converted to Christianity when a visiting priest was able to cure his toothache.

1. A. NO CHANGE
B. flowers and blooms,
C. flowers; blooms
D. flowers, blooms

2. F. NO CHANGE
G. inhabitants the Vikings
H. inhabitants. The Vikings
J. inhabitants, the Vikings,

3. A. NO CHANGE
B. travels
C. traveled
D. had traveled

4. F. NO CHANGE
G. fiord. Where,
H. fiord, where
J. fiord; where

5. A. NO CHANGE
B. the craggy shoreline must now be shared with tourists who arrive in buses
C. tourists now arrive at the craggy shoreline in buses
D. the craggy shoreline must now share itself with tourists who arrive in buses

6. F. NO CHANGE
G. (Place after artisans)
H. (Place after build)
J. (Place after watch)

7. A. NO CHANGE
B. in the 1200s. The king
C. in the 1200s, the king
D. in the 1200s, the king,

In one corner of the cathedral is a column on which the heights of some other famous historical figures who visited the cathedral are recorded. The tallest (more than seven feet tall, if the markings are to be believed) was Peter the Great; the shortest was a king of <u>Siam; who</u> one hopes was only a boy at the time.
8

8. F. NO CHANGE
G. Siam. Who
H. Siam, whom
J. Siam, who

My most memorable vacation as a child was a trip I took to the Grand Canyon with my grandfather. I was only eleven at <u>the time; and</u> I'd never been outside the city of Boston. My <u>grandfather, a true adventurer,</u> decided that it was time for me to discover the great West. My romantic picture of the <u>West complete with cowboys and Indians</u> was a little out of date, but the incredible scenery took my breath away.
9 10 11

9. A. NO CHANGE
B. at the time and
C. at the time, and
D. at the time. And

10. F. NO CHANGE
G. grandfather, a true, adventurer,
H. grandfather: a true adventurer
J. grandfather, a true adventurer

11. A. NO CHANGE
B. West—complete with cowboys and Indians—
C. West—complete with cowboys and Indians
D. West; complete with cowboys and Indians,

<u>On our first day we</u> decided that the best way to explore the vast beauty of the canyon would be to take a mule-packed trip down one of the trails. As I rode along <u>on my mules back,</u> I noticed that each rock stratum displayed a distinctive <u>hue; gray</u> and violet in some places, dark brown and green in others. The rock layers of the Grand Canyon are mostly made of <u>limestone, freshwater shale and sandstone.</u> The Grand Canyon was truly magnificent. As I looked up from the floor of the canyon, <u>it's imposing</u> peaks made me realize how small I really was.
12 13 14 15 16

12. F. NO CHANGE
G. On our first day we,
H. On our first day, we
J. On, our first day, we

13. A. NO CHANGE
B. on my mules' back
C. on our mules' back
D. on my mule's back

14. F. NO CHANGE
G. hue. Gray
H. hue, gray
J. hue: gray

15. A. NO CHANGE
B. limestone, freshwater, shale, and sandstone.
C. limestone, freshwater shale, and sandstone.
D. limestone freshwater shale and sandstone.

16. F. NO CHANGE
G. its imposing
H. its' imposing
J. its, imposing

Summary

- ACT writers like to test your knowledge of whether sentences are put together and punctuated correctly.
- Watch for sentence fragments, run-ons and comma splices, serial commas, restrictive/nonrestrictive clause separation errors, misplaced modifiers, and non-parallel construction.
- ACT test writers also like to test semicolon usage. Semicolons should be used to connect two related yet independent clauses.
- You might also see colons being used in sentences. A colon typically introduces a list that follows an independent clause.
- Dashes can be used to separate a word or group of words from the rest of a sentence, but a dash cannot be combined with a comma. Dashes typically come in pairs unless the isolated group of words is at the end of the sentence.
- Watch for apostrophes. They can either indicate possessives or contractions.
- *It's* can be used only to replace *it is* or *it has*. *Its* is the possessive form of the word *it*. *Its'* is not a word.
- If you are not sure what the question is asking you to do, check the answer choices. The differences among the answer choices can provide clues to what the ACT is testing.

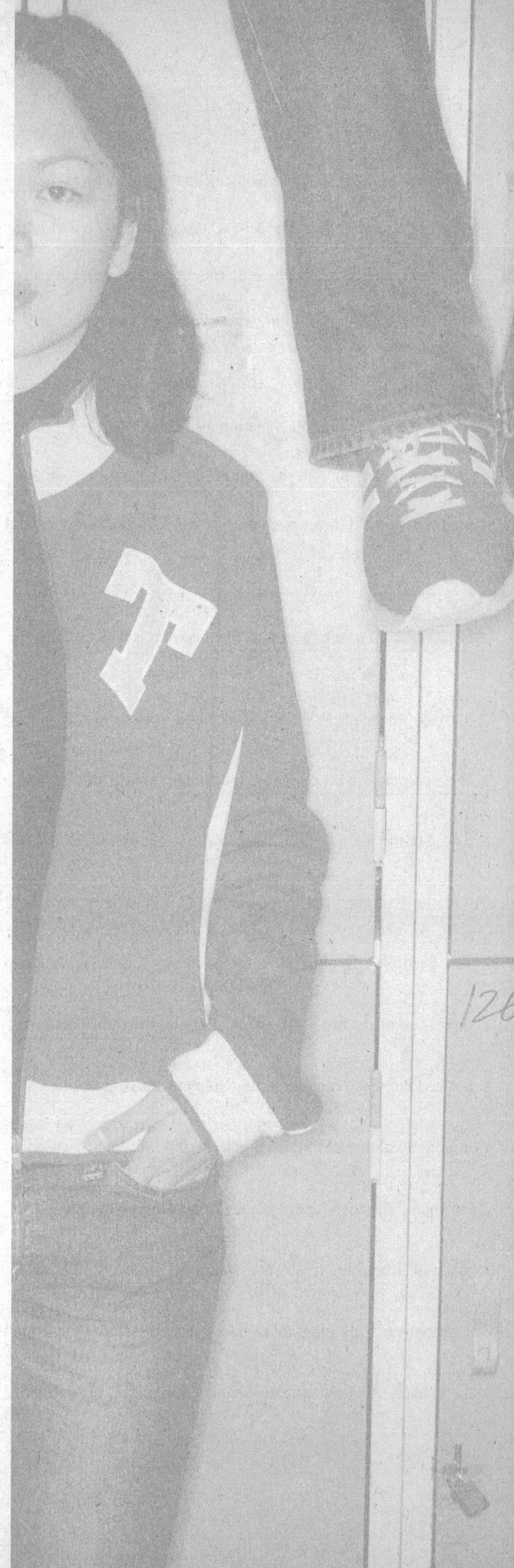

Chapter 7
Grammar and Usage

The ACT heavily tests grammar and usage. The test writers focus on pronoun and verb questions, with particular emphasis on agreement issues. The ACT test writers like to include lots of extra language to hide these errors and lure students into picking the wrong answer. In addition to the pronoun and verb questions, there are many questions that involve adjectives, adverbs, and idioms. This chapter will help you learn the rules you need to crack these questions on the English test.

PRONOUNS

Pronouns—words such as *he, she, it,* and *they*—are used to replace nouns. The ACT writers like to see if you understand the rules of pronouns. There will probably be several pronoun questions on the test you take.

The First Pronoun Rule: Agreement

Be Familiar with the Rules of Pronouns
Agreement—
singular/plural
Case—
subject/object

A pronoun must always agree with the noun to which it refers. Sound straightforward? Try to spot the error in the sentence below.

> *Any young boy who watched the first moon landing probably spent the next few years wishing that they could become an astronaut.*

In spoken English, people make pronoun agreement errors all the time. In written English, you have to be precise. As you look at the sentence above, try to decide which noun is being referred to by the word "they." If you decided that "they" was referring to "boy," you were absolutely correct. However, because "boy" is singular, the pronoun referring to "boy" has to be singular as well. "He" correctly refers back to "boy."

> *Any young boy who watched the first moon landing probably spent the next few years wishing that he could become an astronaut.*

The charts below contain some commonly used singular and plural pronouns.

Singular Pronouns		
Subject	**Object**	**Possessive**
I	me	my, mine
you	you	you, yours
he	him	his

Singular Pronouns		
she	her	hers
it	it	its

Plural Pronouns		
Subject	**Object**	**Possessive**
we	us	our, ours
you	you	you, yours
they	them	their, theirs

Here's another example.

> *Neither of the two young girls with whom I watched the first moon landing expressed their feelings out loud, but I knew that all three of us wanted to be astronauts.*

Neither and *either* are considered singular. Therefore, in this sentence, it is incorrect to use the possessive pronoun "their." We should use "her" instead.

> *Neither of the two young girls with whom I watched the first moon landing expressed her feelings out loud, but I knew that all three of us wanted to be astronauts.*

That's an Error?

Remember ACT Island? It takes the writers of the ACT a while to catch up to the way we use English. For example, your English teacher at school may think it's okay to use "they" to replace a singular noun, although technically it is not. We get so used to using language incorrectly that when the ACT comes along and tests the formal rules of pronoun usage, the right answers sound wrong even though they are grammatically correct. This is one place where you really can't use your ear. You need to learn the pronoun rules.

The following indefinite pronouns are all singular.

anybody	each	somebody
anyone	everybody	someone
either	everyone	nobody

Let's look at an example in ACT format:

Although the American bald eagle has been on the endangered species list for years, they have been [1] sighted in wildlife preserves much more frequently during the past two years.

1. A. NO CHANGE
   B. they are
   C. it can be
   D. it has been

Here's How to Crack It

As you read the sentence, look to see if there is a pronoun in the underlined portion. If you find one, check to make sure the pronoun agrees with the noun to which it refers. What does "they" refer to here? Obviously, it must refer to "the American bald eagle." Although the sentence is clearly talking about the American bald eagle in its *general* sense, we need to use a singular pronoun to agree with the singular noun. Thus, we can eliminate (A) and (B). Choices (C) and (D) both contain the correct pronoun, "it." How do we decide which one to pick? Note the difference between (C) and (D). Choice (C) uses the present tense, while (D) uses a type of past tense. According to the sentence, when were these birds sighted? "In the past two years." Which answer do you want to pick? If you said choice (D), you were absolutely correct.

Even if you missed the pronoun as you read the sentence, you almost certainly would have noticed that the *answer choices* offered you two different pronouns. The answer choices are always great clues to what might have been going on in the ACT writers' minds. Don't forget to use your answer choices as clues if you can't find the error on your own.

The Second Pronoun Rule: Case

Check for Pronouns
Look out for

- **pronouns in the answer choices.** Should the pronoun be singular or plural? Is the pronoun being used as a subject or an object?

If a pronoun is the subject of a sentence, it must be expressed as a subject. Subject pronouns include *I, we, you, he, she, it, they,* and *who.* If a pronoun is the object of a sentence, or the object of a preposition, it must be expressed as an object. Object pronouns include *me, us, you, him, her, it, them,* and *whom.*

Which choice best fits the sentence below?

> *(She/her) bought a souvenir NASA sweatshirt.*

Because the person who buys the shirt is the subject of the sentence, the correct pronoun is "she."

> *Jane bought a souvenir NASA sweatshirt for (he/him).*

Because the person who receives the shirt is the object of the preposition "for," the correct pronoun is "him."

ACT's favorite pronoun case errors involve the use of *who* and *whom,* both of which are called relative pronouns. Let's look at a correct example first.

> *The TV announcer, who was quite an expert, told us many interesting facts about the lunar mission.*

The group of words "who was quite an expert" is functioning here as an adjective describing the TV announcer. Is this group of words a phrase or a clause? You may remember that a phrase often does not contain a subject, but a clause must contain both a subject and a verb. In this group of words, the relative pronoun "who" functions as a subject, which means that this group of words is a clause. You should always use "who" when the relative pronoun is functioning as the subject of a clause or as the subject of the entire sentence. The phrase "… whom was quite an expert" would be wrong here.

Now try an incorrect example.

> *Before the moon landing, the TV announcer gave some additional background on the astronauts, about who we were all quite interested.*

If you spot *who* following a preposition (in this case, "who" follows the word "about") on the ACT, it will almost certainly turn out to be incorrect. A pronoun following a preposition is supposed to be the object of that preposition. The sentence should read

> *Before the moon landing, the TV announcer gave some additional background on the astronauts, about whom we were all quite interested.*

Let's try an example in ACT format.

The students, <u>who had been studying the space program,</u> were thrilled to [2] witness the lunar landing.

2. F. NO CHANGE
   G. about whom had been studying the space program,
   H. whom had been studying the space program,
   J. who had been studying the space program

Here's How to Crack It

The group of words "who had been studying the space program" functions as an adjective clause describing the students. Is "who" the subject of this adjective clause? Yes, it is, so we are down to (F) (NO CHANGE) and (J), both of which contain the correct form of the pronoun—"who." How do the two remaining choices differ? Answer choice (F) contains a comma after "program" while choice (J) does not. Is the comma necessary? We look back at the passage and see that a comma precedes the clause, which is a nonrestrictive clause. "The students were thrilled to witness the lunar landing" would be perfectly acceptable in this example. Nonrestrictive clauses require commas on either side of them, so (F), NO CHANGE, is correct.

Professors Get High Marks

1. Wellesley College
2. Harvey Mudd College
3. Middlebury College
4. Sarah Lawrence College
5. Simon's Rock College of Bard
6. Ripon College
7. St. John's College (NM)
8. Wabash College
9. Reed College
10. Sweet Briar College

Source: *Best 366 Colleges*, 2008 Edition

How Do You Spot Pronoun Errors?

Look for pronouns! Whenever you see a pronoun in the underlined portion of the sentence or in the answer choices, you must first determine which noun the pronoun is replacing. If the pronoun is replacing a singular noun, it must be singular; if it is replacing a plural noun, it must be plural.

> Reminder
> Don't forget that many indefinite pronouns are singular. These are words such as *each*, *either*, *somebody*, *anyone*, *everyone*, and *neither*. The language sounds awkward, but it's still correct.

If the pronoun is being used as a subject, it must be in its subject form. If the pronoun is being used as an object, it must be in its object form.

If *who* or *whom* appears in the underlined portion of the passage or in the answer choices, you must determine whether the pronoun is the subject or the object of the clause in which it appears. If it is the subject, *who* is correct. If it is the object, *whom* is correct. Generally, if the relative pronoun follows a preposition, the correct form will be "whom."

SUBJECT-VERB AGREEMENT

The verb of a sentence must always agree with its subject. If a sentence contains a singular subject, the verb that goes with it must also be singular. If a sentence contains a plural subject, then the verb that goes with it must also be plural.

> **Check for Subject-Verb Agreement**
> Look out for
> - **a verb in the underlined portion of the sentence.** Do the answer choices contain different forms of the verb?

Let's look at an example.

> *The best moment during a broadcast filled with many great moments were when the astronaut stepped out of the lunar lander and bounced on the moon.*

The subject of this sentence is "moment," which is singular. See if you can find the main verb of the sentence. If you said "were," you were absolutely correct. But because the subject is singular, the verb should also be singular. The correct form of the verb is "was."

> *The best moment during a broadcast filled with many great moments was when the astronaut stepped out of the lunar lander and bounced on the moon.*

Now, if the original sentence had been written like this

> *The best moment were when the astronaut stepped out of the lunar lander and bounced on the moon.*

the error would have been a *lot* easier to spot.

ACT writers like to stick many modifying phrases and clauses between the subject and the verb in the hope that you will forget what the subject was by the time you get to the verb. The best way to check subject-verb agreement is to cross out all the words between the subject and the verb so that you can see if the subject and verb really agree.

PRONOUN-VERB AGREEMENT

Sometimes, the subject of a sentence turns out to be a pronoun; don't let that throw you. The verb must still agree with the subject, even if the subject is just a pronoun. Let's look at an example.

> *Each of these moments have played in my mind again and again as I try to recapture the excitement of that momentous day in June.*

The subject of this sentence is "each," which you'll recall is singular (along with *either, neither, anyone, everybody,* and *everyone*). The verb is "have played," which is plural. The subject (in this case a pronoun) and the verb don't agree. How do you fix the sentence?

> *Each of these moments has played in my mind again and again as I try to recapture the excitement of that momentous day in June.*

Sounds awkward, doesn't it? It's correct, though. This is a great example of an instance in which knowing and applying the rules leads you to the correct answer while using your ear may not.

Check for Verb Agreement

Look out for

- **a verb in the underlined portion of the sentence.** Does it agree with the subject? Is the verb's tense consistent with the other verbs in the sentence?

How Do You Spot Subject-Verb Agreement Errors?

That's easy. Isolate the subject and the verb of the sentence. To see the relationship between the subject and the verb, try drawing a line through any words, phrases, or clauses in between them. As always, remember that the answer choices themselves can provide valuable clues. If the underlined portion of a sentence contains a verb, you should check to see whether the answer choices contain different forms of that verb. If they do, you have a potential subject-verb agreement error.

More Great Titles From The Princeton Review

Grammar Smart

VERB TENSE

Verb tense tells us when the action of the sentence is taking place—in the past, in the present, or in the future. Let's review the different verb tenses.

The **present tense** indicates an action that is happening right now.

He runs the 440 in 50 seconds.

The simple **past tense** indicates an action that took place entirely in the past.

He ran the 440 in 50 seconds last week.

The **future tense** indicates an action that will take place at some point down the road.

He will run the race next Saturday.

The **present perfect tense** indicates an action that started in the past but that may continue into the present.

He has run the 440 in under 50 seconds in the last four races.

The **past perfect tense** indicates an action that happened in the past and that preceded another action also in the past.

He had run 100 yards of the race when he twisted his ankle.

The **future perfect tense** indicates that an action will be completed by a definite time in the future.

He will have finished the race by next Sunday.

How Does the ACT Test Verb Tense?

The ACT writers don't care whether you know the names of the verb tenses or sometimes even whether you know in which tense a particular passage should be written.

What the ACT writers want to see is whether you can spot *inconsistencies* in verb tense (they are testing a form of agreement here). If a verb in a non-underlined portion of the sentence is in one tense, the verb in the underlined portion tends to be in the same tense. What's wrong with the following sentence?

Sam is walking down the street when he found a large suitcase.

The verbs "is walking" and "found" are in two different tenses. "Is walking" is in the present tense and "found" is in the past tense. One or the other has to change.

The new sentence can read either.

Sam is walking down the street when he finds a large suitcase.

or

Sam was walking down the street when he found a large suitcase.

On the ACT, you generally will not be asked to make a decision as to which tense (in this case, past or present) would be most appropriate for the sentence. Only one of the verbs will be underlined, and it will be up to you to look at the other verb in the sentence or the verbs in surrounding sentences to decide how to change the underlined verb.

Look at underlined verbs in the "–ing" form very carefully. This is especially true when the sentence uses the verbs "having" and "being," which are almost always used improperly.

How Do You Spot Verb Tense Agreement Errors?

That's easy. If you see a verb in the underlined portion of the sentence or in any of the answer choices, you should immediately anticipate that the error could be one of two types: subject-verb agreement (about which we've already spoken) or tense.

You should begin by asking yourself whether the verb agrees with its subject. If that is not the problem, then ask yourself whether the verb's tense is consistent with the tense of other verbs in the sentence or in surrounding sentences. If there is an inconsistency, then you've probably spotted the error.

Be careful, though, because sometimes a verb-tense change within a sentence is correct. For instance

Once he has finished reading, he will set the table.

This sentence actually requires a change from present to future tense.

One More ACT Verb Error

Sometimes, ACT will put together two perfectly fine past tense verbs to create a past tense construction that does not work. For example

Mike has ate all the cookies in the cookie jar.

In this sentence, either "ate" or "has eaten" would be correct, but "has ate" is incorrect.

ADJECTIVES AND ADVERBS

Adjectives modify nouns. Adverbs modify everything else—verbs, adjectives, and other adverbs. The ACT sometimes tests to see whether you know the difference between adjectives and adverbs. You may remember from grade school a method that often helps to decide if a word is an adjective—simply put the word you aren't sure about into the following sentence: "He (or she or it) is very ______." If the word fits the blank, then the word is an adjective. Let's try it out.

He is very <u>intelligent</u>.

He is very <u>intelligently</u>.

Adjectives and Adverbs
Adjectives and adverbs can usually be distinguished from each other by the "He is very—" test (if the word fits, it's probably an adjective) or by their form (most adverbs end in "–ly").

Intelligent fits the blank in the first sentence, so *intelligent* must be an adjective. *Intelligently* does not fit the blank in the second sentence. In fact, *intelligently* is an adverb. You can often recognize an adverb by the "–ly" at the end of the word.

She thinks intelligently.

A comparative adjective is often used when a sentence is comparing two things.

Juanita is taller than Jane.

("Taller" is a comparative adjective.)

In general, if an adjective has only one syllable, you can make it comparative by adding an "–er" to the end of the word. If an adjective has more than one syllable, you can usually make it comparative by adding a "more" or a "less" in front of the adjective.

Sid is more careful than Tom.

Tom is less careful than Sid.

A comparative adverb is often used when a sentence is comparing two actions.

Juanita dances more gracefully than Jane.

("More gracefully" is a comparative adverb.)

To make most adverbs comparative, you also need to add a "more" or "less" in front of the adverb.

Sid behaves more politely than Tom does.

Tom behaves less politely than Sid does.

When more than two things are being compared, a sentence needs a superlative adjective.

Of the many men in the room, John is the strongest.

("Strongest" is a superlative adjective.)

To make a comparison among three or more people or things, add "–est" to the adjective. When more than two actions are being compared, a sentence often needs a superlative adverb.

Compared with the other boys in the school, Sid behaves the most politely.

("Most politely" is a superlative adverb.)

IDIOMATIC EXPRESSIONS

Why do we say, "I am in love *with* you," instead of, "I am in love *for* you?" The answer is,

"Well, just because!"

Each idiomatic expression is a law unto itself. There are no general rules to go by. Of course, it would be difficult to memorize every single idiom in the English language, at least on short notice. Fortunately, it turns out that you already know most of the idioms that come up on the ACT. Here's an example.

My sculpture is based after Rodin's Thinker.

Do you base something "after?" No; the correct expression is

My sculpture is based on Rodin's Thinker.

Idioms
Idioms are expressions that require the use of a specific preposition. Fortunately, you'll be familiar with many of the idioms on the test. The best way to spot them is to look for prepositions in the answer choices.

How Do You Spot Idiomatic Errors?

You already know most of the idiomatic expressions likely to appear on the ACT. The only problem will be spotting the error in the first place. As always, the answer choices provide excellent clues. Let's see how that last example would have looked on the ACT.

My sculpture is based after Rodin's *Thinker.* (3)

3. A. NO CHANGE
   B. is based over
   C. is based on
   D. based on

Here's How to Crack It

Even if you didn't spot the error as you read the sentence, when you went to the answer choices, you would have noticed that the question seemed to be mostly concerned with the preposition that followed the word "based."

The best way to check out a potential idiom error is to try making up your own sentence using the idiomatic expression.

My term paper is based after the discoveries of Edison.

Does that sound correct? No! We need to say "is based on…" Answer choice (D), while it uses the correct idiomatic expression, creates a sentence fragment. Thus, the best answer is choice (C).

Grammar Drill

In the drill below, you will find questions focusing only on grammar. Before you start, take a few moments to go back over the review material and techniques. If you don't see an error as you read, examine the answer choices for clues as to the errors for which you should look.

Have you ever had a day when you realized in retrospect that it would have been better <u>if one had</u> [1] stayed in bed? Yesterday was one of those days. I woke up at 10:30 to find that my alarm clock <u>has failed</u> [2] to go off. I was already an hour and a half late for work. I jumped into my clothes and ran to my car, only to discover that I had left the lights <u>on the previously evening</u> [3] and the car wouldn't start. Each of the first three taxis I saw <u>were</u> [4] too far away to hail. The taxi driver <u>who finally picked</u> [5] me up didn't have change for a ten dollar bill. When I finally arrived at the office, my boss was not only furious that I was late, <u>and she</u> [6] was also mad that I had forgotten to bring the report I had been preparing at home. Of all the bad days I have experienced in my life, this <u>was the worse.</u> [7]

1. A. NO CHANGE
   B. if you had
   C. if you has
   D. had one

2. F. NO CHANGE
   G. have failed
   H. had failed
   J. having failed

3. A. NO CHANGE
   B. on the evening previously
   C. on the evening previous
   D. on the previous evening

4. F. NO CHANGE
   G. was
   H. are
   J. is

5. A. NO CHANGE
   B. whom finally picked me up
   C. whom picked me up finally
   D. who finally picks me up

6. F. NO CHANGE
   G. and her
   H. but her
   J. but she

7. A. NO CHANGE
   B. was the more worse
   C. was the worst
   D. was the worser

Summary

- Many ACT questions include pronoun errors, subject-verb agreement errors, and other grammatical mistakes.
- If a verb is underlined, check for subject-verb agreement, verb tense errors, and verb parallelism.
- If a pronoun is underlined, check for noun-pronoun agreement, pronoun-verb agreement, and pronoun case (subject or object).
- ACT test writers like to mix up adjectives and adverbs. Be careful that you are using the correct type of modifier for what is being modified.
- Idioms are expressions that require the use of a specific preposition. If you know the correct idiom, great. If not, just guess.
- If you are not sure what the question is asking you to do, check the answer choices. The differences among the answer choices can provide clues to what the ACT is testing.

Chapter 8
Rhetorical Skills

In the ACT English test, 35 of the 75 questions are designed to test what the ACT test writers call rhetorical skills. These questions include strategy, transition, organization, and style questions. You may be asked to reorder sentences or paragraphs, to reword something, or to evaluate whether the writer of a passage has satisfied a particular assignment. Rhetorical skills questions vary more widely than grammar and usage questions, and we'll talk about the best strategies to get you through them.

Questions that test your rhetorical skills are not necessarily harder than the types we've been discussing up to now; they're just different. Rather than asking you about specific points of grammar, rhetorical skills questions get into the realm of style and editing. A few will concern the passage as a whole; save these for last. For the most part, the test writers have placed those at the end of the passage anyway.

The Real ACT Prep Guide suggests two strategies for rhetorical skills questions with which, frankly, we disagree.

No Points for Reading!
You get points only for answering questions.

First, *The Real ACT* (we're going to stick with the abbreviated name from now on) suggests that you read or skim the entire passage quickly for content and then start answering the questions. We think this is a waste of time. You don't get any points for *reading* these passages. The proctor is not going to walk around the room saying, "Ah, excellent reading form there. Five points." You get points for *answering questions* correctly. Because most of the questions (including many of the rhetorical skills questions) can be answered just by looking at the particular sentence that contains the underlined portion related to that question, you may as well wade in there and start racking up points.

Second, *The Real ACT* suggests that it might be a good idea to answer the general rhetoric questions first. *The Real ACT* points out that if a general question asks you to rearrange the order of paragraphs, your new order will make it easier for you to answer other questions. Unfortunately, we think it's equally distracting to try to read a passage for content when every other sentence has something grammatically wrong with it.

The ACT writers break down rhetorical skills into three subcategories: strategy, organization, and style.

STRATEGY QUESTIONS

Among the strategy questions, many concern **transitions** of ideas. Transition questions pop up throughout the passage, not just at the end. They are probably the easiest of the rhetorical skills questions.

A transition is sometimes needed at the *beginning* of a clause, sentence, or paragraph, as the writer attempts to move smoothly from one thought to another. Writers use what are called sentence connectors to get from one thought to the next. There are only three main types of sentence connectors in the world: *but*, *also*, and *therefore*. Try filling in each of the blanks below with one of these three words.

> Fred and Sue were looking forward to going to dinner at a Chinese restaurant with their friends, ____ their friends wanted to go to an Italian restaurant.
>
> When European children hear the word *Chicago*, the first thing they think of is gangsters; ____ it must be a disappointment to them when they get off the plane and see that no one is wearing spats or carrying a tommy gun.
>
> The campers were very tired. ____ they were very hungry.

There's a food fight brewing in the first sentence. To indicate that the friends are in disagreement with Fred and Sue, we need a word implying *contradiction*. That word is *but*.

In the second sentence, we want to imply a *cause-and-effect* relationship. The first part of the sentence is meant to cause the second half. The word that suggests this relationship is *therefore*.

The third example connects two sentences. Surely the two are related but much less directly than in either of the first two examples. Our transition word needs to stress that the second idea is an addition to the first. The word to use here is *also*.

Of course, there are many different ways of saying *but*, *therefore*, and *also*. Here's a partial list.

The Big Three Transitions
but, also, therefore

but (contradiction)—*however, quite the contrary, despite, rather, notwithstanding, contrarily, on the other hand, on the contrary, although, yet, nevertheless*

therefore (cause and effect)—*hence, and so, thus, consequently, for example, because of, finally, in conclusion*

also (in addition)—*in addition, for example, furthermore, another, and, first, second, moreover, by the same token, besides, so too, similarly*

Each of these words has a slightly different shade of meaning. We don't mean to imply that all the "but" words, for example, are interchangeable. However, the answer choices in a transition question generally won't give you a choice among four different kinds of *but*s. Often, your choice will be between a *but* and three *also*s, or a *therefore* and three *but*s.

How Do You Spot Transition Questions?

The underlined portion in a transition question is almost always at the *beginning* of a new clause, sentence, or paragraph.

The answer choices themselves will help you to spot transition questions. They are invariably made up of different sentence connectors from the list we just gave you. You have to decide which sentence connector is appropriate.

Now go back to the passage. Think *but*, *therefore*, or *also*. Which type of sentence connector would be most appropriate to express the transition from one thought to the other? Look at the answer choices again to see which version of the sentence connector you want is available to you this time. Here's an example.

Funds provided by the Stafford program are not considered scholarships; so too, they are part of the extended student loan system.

1. A. NO CHANGE
   B. in addition,
   C. rather,
   D. moreover

Here's How to Crack It

There are two clues that might immediately point you in the right direction on this question: The underlined portion is at the *beginning* of a new clause; it also contains one of the sentence connectors we just listed. If you still aren't sure what type of question this is, look at the other answer choices. What do you see? More sentence connectors. This is a transition question.

Check for Transitions
Look out for
- underlining at the *beginning* of sentences

As the passage stands, what type of transition is being used? "So too" is an *also.* Is this what we need? No. The next clause is not an *additional* thought but rather a contrary thought. If we eliminate any answer choices that contain *alsos*, (A), (B), and (D) all bite the dust. The answer must be (C).

Note that in this case, it might have been harder to decide among the answer choices if one of them had been a *therefore*. Fortunately, that was not an option.

The Other Strategy Questions

Other strategy questions involve *improving* the passage rather than fixing errors. Many of these questions require you to choose a correct answer based on the purpose of a sentence or the effect of the passage on the reader.

Let's see some examples.

Many dog owners turn to animal trainers when they find they can no longer control their pets. Most experts find that a poorly trained dog has received plenty of affection but not enough discipline or exercise. [2]

2. Which of the following sentences provides new, specific guidelines about the proper training of a dog?
   - **F.** Behavior that was cute in a twenty-pound puppy is alarming in a one hundred-pound adult dog.
   - **G.** Would-be dog owners should consider their own lifestyles and the temperament of a specific breed before adopting the animal.
   - **H.** Dogs should be walked at least three times a day and should never be given a treat without first obeying a command.
   - **J.** Small children should never be left unsupervised with a dog.

Here's How to Crack It

Pay careful attention to the question itself when confronted with strategy questions. Not only do we have an actual question, as opposed to just answer choices, but the text in the question also provides a valuable clue. According to the question, one of these choices *provides new, specific guidance about the proper training of a dog.* We don't even need to go back into the passage. Find an answer choice that fulfills the purpose. Answer choices (F), (G), and (J) all may be true, but they do not offer any specific information about training a dog. Only (H) does that, and it is our correct answer.

ORGANIZATION QUESTIONS

There are three kinds of organization questions.

- The first asks you to check the placement of an underlined word or a phrase in a sentence and possibly relocate it, according to what the underlined word or phrase should logically modify.
- The second asks you to reorder sentences within a paragraph.
- The third asks you to reorder paragraphs within the passage as a whole.

Let's talk about sentences within a paragraph first. Here's an example.

---

[1] Particularly in his later paintings, van Gogh creates thick swirls of paint that perhaps mirror the emotional storm raging within. [2] DuFevre piles the paint onto the canvas in thick swatches that rise off the canvas by a good half inch at times. [3] Perhaps the most telling similarity between van Gogh and DuFevre, the little-known modern surrealist, lies in their use of brushstrokes. [4] It is almost as if he is challenging van Gogh to a contest to determine who was more emotionally disturbed.

3. Which of the following ordering of sentences will make the paragraph most logical?

A. NO CHANGE
B. 1, 3, 2, 4
C. 1, 4, 3, 2
D. 3, 1, 2, 4

Here's How to Crack It

Although you might not think so at first, organization questions are actually easier when they ask you to reorder all of the sentences in the paragraph, as they do in this example. The trick is to figure out which of the sentences should come *first.*

Look at the answer choices to see which sentences you have to consider as contenders for the first slot. In this case, the options are Sentence 1 and Sentence 3. You don't have to consider the other sentences yet. You should look for any obvious transition words, especially those that suggest either the introduction of the paragraph or its conclusion. This should eliminate several of the answer choices and make your job much easier.

In this case, the word "perhaps" is used to set up our story, which talks about the similarities between van Gogh and DuFevre.

The third sentence suggests a similarity between two painters that is explained and amplified in the other sentences. Which of the answer choices has Sentence 3 in the lead-off position? Only one. The answer must be (D). In this case, you are done!

If you can't decide which of the choices comes first, another trick is to pair sentences that you can connect in some way. For example, in the paragraph on the previous page, you may have looked at Sentence 4 and noticed that the pronoun "he" could refer only to DuFevre. This implies that Sentence 4 comes right after Sentence 2. This would eliminate (A) and (C). This technique is also useful for ordering the remaining sentences.

Check for Organization
Look out for

- words like *ordering, organize,* and *summary*

Ordering Whole Paragraphs

When the ACT writers ask you to reorganize the paragraphs in a passage, they always position the question at the end of the passage after all the other specific questions. That's exactly where this question belongs. Don't spend large amounts of time re-reading the entire passage. If you are struck by something strange in the ordering of paragraphs during the first read, go back and look at that place; otherwise, do some quick elimination and guess.

Again, you don't need to be sure of the position of *all* the paragraphs to do some quick elimination. Look for either the first paragraph or a pair of paragraphs that you are pretty sure go together, and use POE.

Here's a small-scale example. Let's assume that you've worked a passage and summarized each of the paragraphs in your head. Here are the summaries.

Summary of Paragraph 1 Most people believe eating healthy, nutritious food is good for you.

Summary of Paragraph 2 Carrying the heavy boxes home, I pulled a muscle.

Summary of Paragraph 3 I recently went to the health food store and bought big boxes of wheat germ, carrot juice, and tofu.

Summary of Paragraph 4 But you can take this health kick too far, as I discovered.

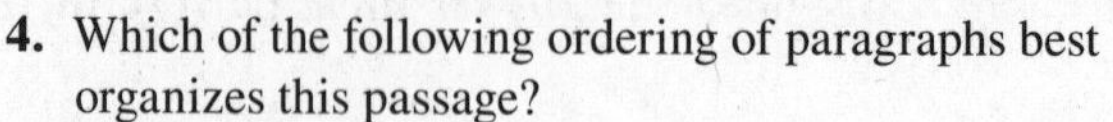

4. Which of the following ordering of paragraphs best organizes this passage?

F. NO CHANGE
G. 1, 4, 3, 2
H. 4, 2, 1, 3
J. 2, 3, 4, 1

To check out our ACT Academic Tutoring options take a look at our website, PrincetonReview.com.

Here's How to Crack It

There are several ways to approach this question. You could look for the first paragraph of the passage. (In this case, we have a choice of four paragraphs, so this won't be as easy as the last question.) You could try to establish some relationship between any two of the paragraphs. You could try to spot the last paragraph of the passage.

Let's begin by trying to establish some relationship between any two paragraphs. In this passage, is there any observable cause and effect going on? Yes. Lifting the boxes caused a pulled muscle in the narrator. He couldn't pull the muscle until after he bought the boxes, which means Paragraph 2 must come after Paragraph 3. This option exists in only one of the answer choices. It begins to look as if (G) must be correct.

To check, we can look to see what (G) offers us as the beginning and end paragraphs. However, bear in mind that you don't want to spend too much time on any one question. Reading an entire passage again with a new beginning is a laborious task. Bubble in (G) on your answer sheet and move on.

STYLE QUESTIONS

The largest number of style errors stems from **redundancy.** Put simply, redundancy means saying the same thing twice.

How Do You Spot Redundancy?

Some redundancy errors are easier to see than others. Here are a couple of easy examples.

Cheap and inexpensive gifts can be found in the shopping district.

Weak and without strength, the old car could not make it up the hill.

In both of the examples above, two adjectives are saying exactly the same thing. Because there is really no need for both, the best way to correct the sentences would be to remove one of the superfluous adjectives.

> *Inexpensive gifts can be found in the shopping district. The weak, old car could not make it up the hill.*

Slightly more difficult

> *After birth, the newborn babies are weighed by a nurse. In the year 1992…*

These examples would be perfectly acceptable in normal speech. However, newborn babies have obviously just been born, and 1992 is already a year. To fix these sentences, simply remove one of the superfluous items.

> *After birth, the babies are weighed by a nurse. In 1992…*

Check for Redundancy
Look out for
- **redundancy**
  Oh, and check for sentences that say the same thing twice too.

A comprehensive list of all the possible redundancies would be too long to do you any good. All you have to do in questions like these is spot the redundancy, and that's easy enough. Look for repetition in the underlined portion of the sentence or among the answer choices. When you see it, expunge it ruthlessly.

The Vietnam veterans were recently memorialized by a memorial sculpture in Washington.

5. A. NO CHANGE
   B. memorialized by a
   C. memorialized with a new memoria
   D. memorialized in a recent

Here's How to Crack It

This is an obvious case of redundancy. We need to find an answer choice that does not repeat itself. Choice (D) seems possible until we realize that "recently memorialized in a recent sculpture" merely makes the same error with another word, "recently." The only possible answer is (B).

The Other Style Questions

A small number of style questions relate to the overall tone of the passage and to the suitability of individual words. Some deal with issues of irrelevancy, wordiness, or slang. Remember, ACT prefers formal English. There are relatively few of these questions, and because many of the answer choices are extreme or clearly do not conform to ACT's formal style, you can use POE with relative ease.

Rhetorical Skills Drill

[1]

The golden age of television means many things to many people, <u>and to</u> [1] the small band of actors, writers, and directors who would rise to <u>prominence</u> [2] in the late 50s and early 60s, without a doubt it meant the "live" television shows such as *Playhouse 90*, where many of them <u>initially worked for the first time.</u> [3]

1. A. NO CHANGE
   B. thus to
   C. but to
   D. In addition to

2. F. NO CHANGE
   G. prominent famousness
   H. famous prominence
   J. famousness

3. A. NO CHANGE
   B. initially for the first time worked.
   C. for the first time worked initially.
   D. worked for the first time.

[2]

[1] Each week, a new "teleplay" was created from scratch—written, cast, rehearsed, and performed. [2] *Playhouse 90* was truly a remarkable training ground for the young talents. [3] Such future luminaries as Paddy Chayefsky, Marlon Brando, and Patricia Neal worked long hours honing <u>to a knife edge</u> [4] their craft. [4] In some cases, when there were problems with the censors, it would have to be created twice. [5]

4. F. NO CHANGE
   G. to an edge
   H. edges
   J. OMIT the underlined portion.

5. Which of the following sequences would best organize the sentences in Paragraph 2?
   A. NO CHANGE
   B. 1, 2, 4, 3
   C. 2, 1, 4, 3
   D. 2, 3, 1, 4

[3]

<u>Despite</u> [6] the frantic pace, accidents happened frequently. David Niven once revealed that, during an early show, he inadvertently locked his costume in his dressing room two minutes before air time. As the announcer read the opening credits, the sound of axes splintering the door to Niven's dressing room could be heard in the background. [7]

6. F. NO CHANGE
   G. Due to
   H. In spite of
   J. Thus

7. If the writer wished to make the tone of Paragraph 3 more lighthearted, she could change the word "accidents" to
   A. NO CHANGE
   B. casualties
   C. mishaps
   D. grave errors

Question 9 asks about the preceding passage as a whole.

8. Which of the following would best summarize the passage as a whole?

F. The golden age of television meant many things to many different people.

G. Early television shows such as *Playhouse 90* provided the training ground where talented new entertainers could learn their craft.

H. The golden age of television had many amusing moments.

J. The rise of Paddy Chayefsky, Marlon Brando, and Patricia Neal helped to make *Playhouse 90* a success.

9. Which of the following sequences of paragraphs would make the structure of the passage as a whole the most logical?

A. NO CHANGE

B. 3, 2, 1

C. 3, 1, 2

D. 2, 3, 1

Summary

- Do the questions in order. However, if you're having trouble with a particular question, or if it seems to be taking too much time, circle the question number, leave it, and come back on your second pass. Often a later question will help you with an earlier one.
- Search the answer choices for clues. Focus on the differences between the answer choices, and use that information to determine the error(s) being tested.
- Look for one error at a time. Eliminate all answers that do not correct the first error you spotted. Compare the remaining answers and choose the most concise answer choice free of any additional errors.
- Don't forget that NO CHANGE is correct a little less than a quarter of the time. If you can't find anything wrong with the underlined portion, it may be correct as written.
- Remember to look very carefully at any question with OMIT as an answer. If you can OMIT and the passage/sentence is still correct, then do so.

Part III
How to Crack the ACT Mathematics Test

Chapter 9
Introduction to the ACT Mathematics Test

The second section of the ACT will always be the Math test. To perform your best, you'll need to become familiar with the structure and strategy of the ACT Math test. In this chapter, we discuss the types of questions you can expect to see and how you can use organizational strategy, estimation, and elimination skills to improve your Math score.

WHAT TO EXPECT ON THE MATH TEST

You will have 60 minutes to answer 60 multiple-choice questions based on "...topics covered in typical high school classes." For those of you who aren't sure if you went to a typical high school, these questions break down into rather precise areas of knowledge.

There are usually

33 Algebra questions

- 14 pre-algebra questions based on math terminology (integers, prime numbers, etc.), basic number theory (rules of zero, order of operations etc.), and manipulation of fractions and decimals
- 10 elementary algebra questions based on inequalities, linear equations, ratios, percents, and averages
- 9 intermediate algebra questions based on exponents, roots, simultaneous equations, and quadratic equations

23 Geometry questions

- 14 plane geometry questions based on angles, lengths, triangles, quadrilaterals, circles, perimeter, area, and volume
- 9 coordinate geometry questions based on slope, distance, midpoint, parallel and perpendicular lines, points of intersection, and graphing

4 Trigonometry questions

- 4 questions based on basic sine, cosine, and tangent functions, trig identities, and graphing

What Not to Expect on the Math Test

Because the ACT test writers care more about your math skills than do the SAT test writers, the ACT does not provide any formulas at the beginning of the Math test. Before you panic, take a second look at the chart on the previous page. Because the ACT is so specific about the types of questions it expects you to answer, preparing to tackle ACT Math takes a few simple steps.

CAN I USE MY CALCULATOR?

You sure can, and you should. Although the folks who write the ACT state that none of the math questions requires a calculator, the fact is the math on the test has become steadily more complex since calculators were first allowed. The test writers clearly expect you to have a calculator.

Furthermore, there are plenty of questions on the test that will go much more quickly and smoothly if you know how to use your calculator properly. As we go through the math in this book, we'll be pointing out which questions are particularly calculator-friendly and telling you just what to do with your calculator to succeed. The key, of course, is that you need to know how to use your calculator before the test begins. So when we tell you to make sure you can do a certain type of operation on your calculator, be sure to check right away.

Throughout the rest of the Math chapters, we discuss ways to solve calculator-friendly questions in an accurate and manageable way. Because TI-89 and TI-92 calculators are not allowed on the ACT, we will show you how to solve problems on the TI-83. If you don't plan to use a TI-83 on the test, we recommend that you make sure your calculator is acceptable for use on the test and that it can do the following:

- handle positive, negative, and fractional exponents
- use parentheses
- graph simple functions
- convert fractions to decimals and vice versa
- change a linear equation into $y = mx + b$ form

THE PRINCETON REVIEW APPROACH

Because the test is so predictable, the best way to prepare for ACT Math is with

1. a thorough review of the very specific information and question types that come up repeatedly
2. an understanding of The Princeton Review's test-taking strategies and techniques

In each chapter of the Math test, you'll find a mixture of review and technique, with a sprinkling of ACT-like problems. At the end of each chapter, there is a summary of the chapter and a drill designed to pinpoint your math test-taking strengths and weaknesses. In addition to working through the problems in this book, we strongly suggest you practice our techniques on some real ACT practice tests. Let's begin with some general strategies.

Easy, Medium, Difficult

You get 60 minutes for 60 questions. This seems fairly straightforward, but don't let the symmetry of these two numbers fool you; some problems will take much less than a minute, and others could take forever if you let them.

The first few questions are designed to be easier than the rest of the test, then the questions get a bit tougher for the remainder of the test—at least, this is ACT's intention. However, what the people at ACT think is easy may not strike you the same way. Similarly, you may find some of the problems in the middle or end of the test to be a piece of cake.

In fact, if you took a room full of high school students and asked them to vote on which type of ACT math question they would prefer to do, you would almost certainly get different answers: While one student may prefer algebra questions, another student would choose geometry questions instead. Is one of the students more justified in his or her selection? Absolutely not. On the ACT, establishing an order of difficulty for the questions is a *personal* process. Only you can determine which questions are most worth your time investment. Again, we can use triage to help plan our math strategy.

MATH TRIAGE

In Chapter 2, we introduced the concept of triage. Let's apply this concept to ACT Math. Here's a problem.

1. Cynthia, Peter, Nancy, and Kevin are all carpenters. Last week, each built the following number of chairs:

Cynthia–36 Peter–45 Nancy–74 Kevin–13

What was the average number of chairs each carpenter built last week?

A. 39
B. 42
C. 55
D. 59
E. 63

Now, Later, Never

When the average test taker begins the ACT Math test, what do you think the person's first instinct is? If you said, "Work questions 1 through 60 as quickly as possible until time runs out," you're 100 percent correct. After all, isn't that what we do on our high school math tests?

The problem with taking such an approach on the ACT is that you are probably robbing yourself of points. Instead of starting with question 1 and finishing with question 60 (if you even make it that far), use the triage approach to actively seek out questions that fit your Personal Order of Difficulty. If question 5 is about a topic with which you're not comfortable, mark it for review and see what else lies ahead. The next page may have several questions that are more worthy of your immediate attention. Attempting easier questions on your "first pass" will guarantee that your time investment actually yields points. As you consistently identify and attempt questions that fit your first pass criteria, your confidence will increase as well; you'll be surprised by how much easier the second pass questions will seem once you've established a successful pattern. Don't get caught up in the psychology of the test. Use your practice time to study ACT's question types and categorize them according to your Personal Order of Difficulty.

First Pass
Do the problems you're *sure* you know how to do.

Second Pass
Do the problems you *think* you know how to do. For seemingly impossible questions, pick a Letter of the Day and move on.

I'm Almost Done...

The temptation to get stubborn and stay with a particular problem can be very strong. But if it takes you four minutes to solve question 5, then it might mean that you don't have the time to do several problems later on that you may have found easier. As we mentioned in Chapter 2, you might have the "oh, yeah!" revelation on this problem before you finish the test.

That Was an Easy One

Of course, to solve the problem about the four carpenters, you were probably not going to have to depend on a revelation. Did you want to do it right away? Sure. It's a moderately easy average problem.

An Easy Problem
has one or two steps.

Here's How to Crack It

To find the average of a group of numbers, add the numbers together and divide by the number of terms.

$$\frac{\text{sum of everything}}{\text{number of things}} = \text{average}$$

In this case, the thing we don't know is the average, but we do know everything else, so let's put the numbers into our formula.

$$\frac{36+45+74+13}{4} = \text{average}$$

(By the way, we cover average problems more fully in Chapter 11. The answer to this question is (B).)

You distinguish an easy problem from a tough one in part by deciding whether it can be done in one or two steps or whether it will require three or more steps.

Here's a Medium ACT Problem

A Medium Problem
has two or three steps.

22. Four carpenters built an average of 42 chairs each last week. If Cynthia built 36 chairs, Nancy built 74 chairs, and Kevin built 13 chairs, how many chairs did Peter build?

F. 24
G. 37
H. 45
J. 53
K. 67

This is still an average problem, but it is less straightforward and requires an extra step to get the final answer.

Here's How to Crack It

Let's put the information we have into the same formula we used before.

$$\frac{36+74+13+\text{Peter}}{4} = 42$$

More great titles by The Princeton Review
Math Smart

You might want to substitute the variable x for Peter. Medium and difficult average problems often give you the number of terms and the average. What they don't give you—and the important thing to figure out—is the sum of the numbers to be averaged.

If we multiply both sides by 4, we get the sum of all four numbers.

$$36 + 74 + 13 + \text{Peter} = 168$$

To find out Peter's number of chairs, we just have to add the other numbers and subtract from 168. 168 – 123 = 45. The answer is (H).

Here's a Hard ACT Problem

A Difficult Problem has more than three steps.

41. Four carpenters each built an average of 42 chairs last week. If no chairs were left uncompleted, and if Peter, who built 50 chairs, built the greatest number of chairs, what is the **least** number of chairs one of the carpenters could have built, if no carpenter built a fractional number of chairs?

A. 18
B. 19
C. 20
D. 39.33
E. 51

The concept behind this question is really no more difficult than either of the first two problems. It is still about averages. But now there are several more steps involved, including a small leap of faith. You can tell it's more difficult than the first two questions partly because of the language it uses: "If no chairs were left uncompleted" is closing a potential loophole. Easy problems are usually too simple to have loopholes. "What is the **least**" implies the need for reflection.

Here's How to Crack It

Let's put what we know into the same formula we have used twice already.

$$\frac{50 + x + y + z}{4} = 42$$

The only individual about whom we know something specific is Peter. We've represented the other three carpenters as x, y, and z. Because the sum of all four carpenters' chairs adds up to 168, we now have

$$50 + x + y + z = 168$$

By itself, an equation with three variables can't be solved, so unless we can glean a little more information from the problem, we're stuck, and it's time to put a circle around the problem and move on.

Let's assume you skipped the problem temporarily, and you have now come back to it after completing all the problems you thought were easier.

The problem asks for the *least* number of chairs one carpenter could have built. To figure this out, let's have the other two carpenters build the *most* number of chairs they could build. According to the problem, Peter constructed 50, and no one else built as many as he did. So let's say two of the other carpenters constructed 49 each—the largest possible amount they could build and still have built fewer than Peter. By making carpenters x and y construct as many chairs as possible, we can find out the *minimum* number of chairs carpenter z would have to make.

Now the problem looks like this:

$$50 + 49 + 49 + z = 168$$

If we add 50 + 49 + 49 and subtract it from 168, then $z = 20$, and the correct answer is (C).

USE PROCESS OF ELIMINATION (POE)

Even if you weren't sure how to do that last problem, you may have been able to eliminate two answer choices right away using the major technique we introduced in Chapter 3: POE. Remember, ACT doesn't take away any points for wrong answers, so it is in your interest to guess on every question you can't solve using other methods. But your guesses will be much more valuable if you can eliminate some of the answer choices first. The problem said Peter built the greatest number of chairs—50 of them. Therefore, could any of the other carpenters have built *more* than that? No, so (E) doesn't make sense. And because no carpenter built a fractional number of chairs, (D) doesn't make sense, either.

At this point, you're down to three answer choices. But before you guess, you can try a few more tactics. What if you decide to try (A)? If (A) is the correct answer choice, then one carpenter (the one who made the least number of chairs) produced 18 chairs. So what do you do now? Well, that would leave 100 chairs for the other two carpenters, which either means that both of them made 50 chairs or one made more than 50. However, that can't be true because Peter, who made the most chairs, made only 50. So (A) is eliminated. If you try (B), you'll find that the same holds true, and thus, only (C) remains.

BALLPARK

You can frequently get rid of several answer choices in an ACT math problem without doing any complicated math. Narrow down the choices by estimating your answer. We call this ballparking. Let's look at an example:

Cross Out the Crazy Answers

What's the average of 100 and 200?

~~A. 500~~
B. 150
~~C. a billion~~

---

3. There are 600 school children in the Lakeville district. If 54 of them are high school seniors, what is the percentage of high school seniors in the Lakeville district?

A. .9%
B. 2.32%
C. 9%
D. 11%
E. 90%

Here's How to Crack It

This is not an advanced problem. ACT wants us to write a simple equation, and we will review just how to do that in the arithmetic chapter. But before we do any heavy math, let's see if we can get rid of some answer choices by ballparking.

The question asks us to find a percentage of 600. Just to get a rough fix on where we are, what is 10 percent of 600? If you said 60, you are right. To find 10 percent of anything, you simply move the decimal point over one place to the left. If 60 is 10 percent, then 54 must be slightly less than 10 percent. Which answer choices don't make sense? Choices (D) and (E) don't work because we need something less than 10 percent. On the contrary, we need something only *slightly* less than 10 percent. Could the answer be (A) or (B)? No. On this problem, it is just as easy to eliminate wrong answers as it is to solve for the right answer. The answer is (C).

Of course, your calculator is certainly handy for narrowing down the answer choices on questions like this. If you were to enter 54/600 and press [ENTER], you would know exactly which numbers should appear in the answer choices. After you eliminate the answers that don't match, it's just a matter of taking your result and multiplying by 100 to determine the percentage. We will discuss accurate calculator methods in detail later in this chapter, but the process is as simple as typing (54/600) * 100 and hitting [ENTER].

On most ACT problems, you will be able to eliminate only one or two answer choices by ballparking, but it's still vital that you always think about what a reasonable answer might be for a particular problem *before* you solve it mathematically. This is because the ACT has some trap answers waiting for you.

Pop Quiz

Q: What percent of the ACT Math tests trigonometry?

AVOID PARTIAL ANSWERS

Sometimes students think they have completed a problem before the problem is actually done. The test writers at ACT like to include trap answer choices for these students. Here's an example.

---

4. A bus line charges $5 each way to ferry a passenger between the hotel and an archaeological dig. On a given day, the bus line has a capacity to carry 255 passengers from the hotel to the dig and back. If the bus line runs at 90% of capacity, how much money did the bus line take in that day?

F. $1,147.50
G. $1,275
H. $2,295
J. $2,550
K. $2,625

Here's How to Crack It

The first step in this problem is to determine how much money the line would make if it ran at total capacity. If there were 255 passengers, each of whom paid $10 (remember, the bus company charges $5 each way), that would be $2,550.

If you were in a hurry, you might decide at this point that you were already done and go straight to the answer choices. And there is (J), beckoning seductively. Unfortunately, of course, (J) is not the right answer. The bus line is running at only 90 percent of capacity. To get the real answer, we have to find 90 percent of $2,550.

You also may have missed, or put aside temporarily, the information that each passenger has to pay coming *and* going, in which case you may have multiplied 255 by 5 to get $1,275, and then found 90 percent of that, $1,147.50, which just happens to be (F).

Both (F) and (J) were partial answers. Students who picked one of these answers did not make a mistake in their math, nor did they misunderstand the overall concept of the problem; they simply stopped before they were finished. All you had to do to $1,147.50 to get the right answer was double it so that you included both trips. All you had to do to $2,550 to get the right answer was to take 90 percent of it. The answer is (H).

Are Partial Answers Fair?

You may decide that it is not very sporting of ACT to try to trip up students with partial answer choices. However, if this had been a short-answer test, students might well have made exactly the same mistake on their own. Besides, if partial answers represent the downside of multiple-choice testing, there is a tremendous upside as well: Let's see how taking bite-size pieces can help us on long word problems.

Taking Bite-Size Pieces

As you have probably noticed by now, difficulty on many ACT questions is directly related to the number of steps required to determine the correct answer. To avoid partial answers on multistep problems, break down lengthy questions into manageable steps. You can chew on one bite-size piece at a time. Let's walk through an example.

Pop Quiz

A: 4 questions out of 60 is equal to roughly 6.67%.

8. Each member in a club had to choose an activity for a day of volunteer work. $\frac{1}{3}$ of the members chose to pick up trash. $\frac{1}{4}$ of the remaining members chose to paint fences. $\frac{5}{6}$ of the members still without tasks chose to clean school buses. The rest of the members chose to plant trees. If the club has 36 members, how many of the members chose to plant trees?

F. 3
G. 6
H. 9
J. 12
K. 15

How to Avoid Partial Answers

You can prevent yourself from picking partial answers by doing the following three things:

1. Slow down. It isn't going to help to do a problem so quickly that you miss important information and get the question wrong.
2. Once you've read the question, underline what it's really asking. Now go back and do the question piece by piece. If you find yourself reading the whole question over again, STOP! You're not going to do the whole problem all at once, and if you did, you'd probably make a mistake. So just take it one step at a time.
3. When you finish the problem, re-read what you underlined to make sure you've answered the question that was asked by the ACT test writer.

Here's How to Crack It

Although your gut reaction may be to jam everything into your calculator and circle whatever pops up on the screen, think about how neatly the information is divided. If you were to translate each part of the question into math language and write each step in your test booklet, wouldn't you be less likely to make a mistake? Try this.

1. Because the question is dealing with fractions, we'll need to start with the number of members in the club. Write "36 members" down in your scratch work area.

2. Now, let's work the question in steps. The first thing we read is "$\frac{1}{3}$ of the members chose to pick up trash." We'll just need to take $\frac{1}{3}$ of 36, so write the equation down before completing it or entering it into your calculator. After you find out that 12 people picked up trash, be sure to label the information so you don't forget what the number is.

3. The next thing we read is "$\frac{1}{4}$ of the remaining members chose to paint fences." Be careful here—we want to take $\frac{1}{4}$ of the *remaining* members, not of the original 36. If 12 people are already picking up trash, we know there are 24 people remaining. Write down the proper equation to express this: $\frac{1}{4} \times 24 = 6$ people. Again, be sure to note that 6 is the number of people painting fences.

4. What's next? We see a line saying, "$\frac{5}{6}$ of the members still without tasks chose to clean school buses." In the last step, we were down to 24 members; if 6 are painting fences, how many are left over? 18. The answer is 18. Use this to write your next equation: $\frac{5}{6} \times 18 = 15$ people. We now know that 15 people are cleaning school buses.

Pop Quiz

Q: Is 0 positive or negative?

5. Almost there…the next line says, "All of the remaining members chose to plant trees." We don't need to do much math here. If 15 out of 18 people ended up cleaning school buses, then we know there are only 3 people left. Those 3 are planting trees.
6. Finally, we arrive at what the question is asking. Now that all the math involved is nicely mapped out and labeled, we should have no problem finding the answer. The question asks, "How many of the members chose to plant trees?" If we refer to our scratch work, we see that 3 people planted trees. We can safely pick answer choice (F) and move on. Your scratch work for this problem should look something like this.

36 members

$\frac{1}{3} \times 12 = 12$ *(trash)*

24 remaining

$\frac{1}{4} \times 24 = 6$ *(fences)*

18 remaining

$\frac{5}{6} \times 18 = 15$ *(buses)*

3 remaining (trees)

By taking a more manageable approach, you can guarantee that you won't pick any of the distracter answers. To illustrate the point, take a look at the steps above and compare them with the answer choices. Notice anything? (J) was the number of people picking up trash. Similarly, (G) was the number of people painting fences, and (K) was the number of people cleaning school buses. As you can see, being too quick on the draw can get you into trouble on multistep word problems. If you take bite-size pieces of word problems, you'll be able to move many of them into your first-pass question group.

RED HERRINGS

Of the 60 problems in the Math section, several will contain extra information that is not, strictly speaking, necessary to solve the problems. The test writers want to see if you can distinguish important information from filler. Because there are so few of these questions, it isn't necessary to examine each new piece of information with a magnifying glass to see if it might be a red herring. In almost every problem on the ACT, you will need *all* the information given to solve it. However, if you're staring at a particular number that doesn't seem to have anything to do with the solution of the question you're doing, it might be a red herring. Here's an example.

Pop Quiz

A: 0 is neither positive nor negative, but it is an even number.

---

5. Susan's take-home pay is $300 per week, of which she spends $80 on food and $150 on rent. What fraction of her take-home pay does she spend on food?

A. $\frac{2}{75}$

B. $\frac{4}{15}$

C. $\frac{1}{2}$

D. $\frac{23}{30}$

E. $\frac{29}{30}$

Here's How to Crack It

The last line tells us what we need to do. A fraction is a part over a whole. In this case, the whole is $300. The part is the amount of money spent on food.

$$\frac{\$80}{\$300} \text{ which reduces to } \frac{4}{15}$$

Where does the $150 fit in? It doesn't. The question isn't asking about rent. The test writers just threw that in to confuse you. Note that if you got confused and found the fraction of the take-home salary that was paid in rent, $150/$300, you would pick (C). The correct answer is (B).

Summary

- On the ACT Math test, you have 60 minutes to attempt 60 questions. The questions fall into the following categories:
    - 33 Algebra questions (14 pre-algebra, 10 elementary algebra, 9 intermediate algebra)
    - 23 Geometry questions (14 plane geometry, 9 coordinate geometry)
    - 4 Trigonometry questions
- Use triage and your Personal Order of Difficulty to establish a two-pass system.
    - On the first pass, actively search for questions that require only a few steps and/or deal with topics you find manageable.
    - Save any multistep, unfamiliar, or difficult questions for your second pass. As time runs out, or if a question seems exceedingly difficult, pick a Letter of the Day and invest your time in something more worthwhile.
- You can use POE to cancel out wrong answer choices. Sometimes it is easier to get rid of wrong answers than to find the correct answer.
    - Incorrect answers are sometimes partial answers—answers you arrive at on the way to the final solution if you quit before you are really done.
    - Incorrect answers sometimes don't really make sense if you look at them in the cold light of day. Frequently, you can eliminate answer choices because they are nowhere near what common sense says the answer would have to be.
    - Incorrect answers are sometimes based on red herrings—pieces of information that are not really necessary to solve the problem.
- Take bite-size pieces of questions with multiple steps. Use the space in your test booklet to translate each sentence into its math equivalent, and be sure to label your information to avoid confusion.
- Be sure you put an answer down for every question—even the ones you don't have time to do. There's no penalty for wrong answers.

Chapter 10
Basics

To successfully tackle the questions you'll encounter on the ACT Math test, you must have a strong command of mathematical nuts and bolts. In this chapter, we'll discuss math terminology, properties of numbers, basic operations, and processes involving exponents and roots.

Look at the following problem:

1. How many even prime numbers are there between 0 and 100 ?

   A. 0
   B. 1
   C. 2
   D. 3
   E. 4

If you know what the terms *even* and *prime* mean, this problem is a snap. Without a knowledge of these terms, the problem is impossible. Let's begin our math review by going over all the basic math terms and operations covered on the ACT. By the way, the answer to the question is (B).

BASIC TERMS

Pop Quiz

Q: Is 0 even or odd?

Q: Is 0 a prime number?

Real Numbers

Real numbers are all the numbers you think of when you think of numbers: 5, $\frac{1}{4}$, 7.9, 100, –43, $\sqrt{2}$, etc. They include everything *except* imaginary numbers, which appear only occasionally on the ACT. An example of an imaginary number is i, which is the square root of –1.

Rational Numbers

Any number that can be written as a whole number, a fraction (an integer over another integer), or as a repeating decimal is a rational number. This means that 5, $\frac{1}{5}$, and $.33\overline{3}$ are rational numbers. In fact, most of the numbers you'll see on the ACT are rational numbers.

Irrational Numbers

An irrational number cannot be written as an integer over another integer. π is irrational. Like other irrational numbers, it goes on forever. While you may think of π as 3.14, it can be written out to as many decimal places as you feel like writing down—3.141592, etc.—and as many places as you take it, you will never find a repeating pattern.

Other irrational numbers? Any square root of a number that does not have a perfect square root. For example, $\sqrt{3}$ or $\sqrt{2}$. By contrast, $\sqrt{4}$, which simplifies to 2, is a rational number.

Integers

Integers include everything *except* what we normally think of as fractions or decimals: 2, 134, –56, 0, and 7 are all integers. $\frac{1}{2}$, 6.7, and $\frac{-31}{2}$ are not.

Positive and Negative

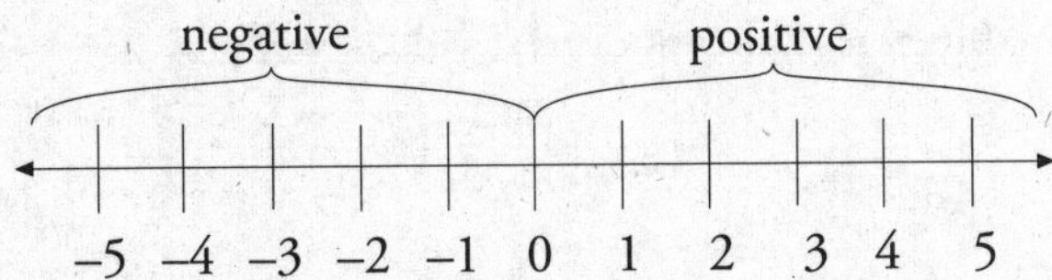

Positive numbers are to the right of the 0 on the number line above. Negative numbers are to the left of zero on the number line above. Zero itself is neither negative nor positive.

Note that positive numbers get bigger as they move away from 0. Negative numbers get smaller. For example, –3 is smaller than –1.

There are three rules regarding the multiplication of positive and negative numbers. They are

positive × positive = positive

positive × negative = negative

negative × negative = positive

When you add a positive number and a negative number, you're subtracting the number with the negative sign in front of it from the positive number.

$$5 + (-3) = 2$$

Pop Quiz

A: 0 is even.

A: Nope, 0 doesn't count as a prime number.

When you add two negative numbers, you're adding the two numbers as if they were positive and then putting a negative sign in front of the sum. In the process, you are going farther away from zero.

$$-3 + -4 = -7$$

When entering negative numbers into your calculator, use the negative key (–) rather than the subtraction key. This will ensure that you don't end up with the incorrect answer by entering too many or too few operands.

Even and Odd Numbers

Even numbers are integers that can be divided evenly by 2 (leaving no remainder.)

–4, –2, 0, 2, 4, 6, etc.

Odd numbers are integers that cannot be divided evenly by 2.

–5, –3, –1, 1, 3, 5, etc.

Note that 0 is even. There are several rules regarding multiplication and addition of even and odd numbers. They are

even × even = even

odd × odd = odd

even × odd = even

even + even = even

odd + odd = even

even + odd = odd

Pop Quiz

Q: What's the only even prime?

Digits

There are ten digits: 0, 1, 2, 3, 4, 5, 6, 7, 8, 9.

The number 364 has three digits—3, 6, and 4. In this number, the 4 is called the **ones** digit, or **units** digit. The 6 is called the **tens** digit. The 3 is called the **hundreds** digit.

The number 4.56 has three digits—4, 5, and 6. The 4 is called the ones digit or units digit. The 5 is called the **tenths** digit, and the 6 is called the **hundredths** digit.

Prime Numbers

A prime number can be divided evenly by two and only two distinct factors—1 and itself. Thus, 2, 3, 5, 7, 11, and 13 are all prime numbers. The number 2 is the only even prime number. Neither 0 nor 1 is a prime number. There are no negative prime numbers.

For more help, check out our ACT Academic Tutoring options at our website, PrincetonReview.com.

Absolute Value

The absolute value of a number is the distance between that number and 0 on the number line. The absolute value of 6 is expressed as $|6|$.

$$|6| = 6$$

$$|-6| = 6$$

Variables and Coefficients

In the expression $3x + 4y$, x and y are called **variables** because we don't know what they are. 3 and 4 are called **coefficients** because you multiply the variables by them.

BASIC OPERATIONS

Divisibility Rules

If a number can be divided evenly by another number, it is said to be divisible by that number. A good way to save time dividing is to know the rules of divisibility for some common numbers. The rules are as follows:

1. A number is divisible by 2 if its units digit can be divided evenly by 2 (in other words, if it is even). 46 is divisible by 2. So is 3,574.
2. A number is divisible by 3 if the sum of its digits can be divided evenly by 3. We can quickly determine that 216 is divisible by 3 because the sum of the digits (2 + 1 + 6) is divisible by 3.
3. A number is divisible by 4 if the number formed by its last two digits (tens digit and units digit) is also divisible by 4. Thus, 316 is divisible by 4 because 16 is divisible by 4. 728 is also divisible by 4 because 28 is divisible by 4.

Pop Quiz

A: 2. (It's also the smallest prime number. That's right: 1 is *not* prime.)

4. A number is divisible by 5 if its last digit (units place) is either 0 or 5. For example, 60, 85, and 15 are all divisible by 5.
5. A number is divisible by 6 if it is also divisible by the factors of 6, which are 2 and 3. For example, 228 is divisible by 6 because it is even (divisible by 2) and the sum of its digits is divisible by 3.
6. A number is divisible by 8 if the number formed by its last three digits (hundreds, tens, and unit digits) is also divisible by 8. Thus, 9,128 is divisible by 8 because 128 is divisible by 8.
7. A number is divisible by 9 if the sum of its digits can be divided evenly by 9. For example, 873 is divisible by 9 because the sum of the digits (8 + 7 + 3) is divisible by 9.

The Four Horsemen

Make sure you can identify terms that invoke the four basic operations.

- **Sum** is the result of addition.
  The sum of 3 and 4 is 7.
- **Product** is the result of multiplication.
  The product of 5 and 2 is 10.
- **Difference** is the result of subtraction.
  The difference between 7 and 3 is 4.
- **Quotient** is the result of division.
  If you divide 14 by 7, the quotient is 2.

Pop Quiz

Q: If a number is divisible by 2 and by 3, it's also divisible by...

Factors and Multiples

A number is a **factor** of another number if it can be divided evenly *into* that number. Is 3 a factor of 15? Yes, because 3 can be divided evenly into 15. The complete list of factors of 15 is 1, 3, 5, and 15.

A number is a **multiple** of another number if it can be divided evenly *by* that number. For example, multiples of 15 include 15, 30, 45, and 60.

All integers have a limited number of factors and an infinite number of multiples. You can remember this with the following mnemonic: Factors, Few; Multiples, Many.

What is the only factor of 15 that is also a multiple of 15? 15.

STANDARD SYMBOLS

Symbol	Meaning
=	is equal to
≠	is not equal to
<	is less than
>	is greater than
≤	is less than or equal to
≥	is greater than or equal to

EXPONENTS

An exponent is a short way of writing the value of a number multiplied several times by itself. $4 \times 4 \times 4 \times 4 \times 4$ can also be written as 4^5. This is expressed aloud as "4 to the fifth power." The lower and larger number (4) is called the **base**, and the upper number (5) is called the **exponent**. There are several rules to remember about exponents.

Multiplying Numbers with the Same Base

When you multiply numbers that have the same base, you simply add the exponents.

$$6^2 \times 6^3 = 6^{(2+3)} = 6^5 \qquad \left(y^2\right)\left(y^3\right) = y^{(2+3)} = y^5$$

Pop Quiz

A: 6

Dividing Numbers with the Same Base

When you divide numbers that have the same base, you simply subtract the bottom exponent from the top exponent.

$$\frac{4^7}{4^2} = 4^5 \quad \frac{x^7}{x^2} = x^5 \quad \frac{y^3}{y^5} = \frac{1}{y^2} = y^{-2}$$

Negative Powers

In that last example, we also wrote the result as y^{-2}. A negative power is simply the reciprocal of a positive power. (The reciprocal of 3 is $\frac{1}{3}$.)

$$3^{-1} = \frac{1}{3} \quad 3^{-2} = \frac{1}{9} \quad 3^{-3} = \frac{1}{27}$$

Fractional Powers

When a number is raised to a fractional power, the **numerator** (the number above the line in a fraction) functions like a real exponent, while the **denominator** (the number below the line in a fraction) tells you what power radical to make the number. (Radicals will be defined on page 114.)

$$9^{\frac{1}{2}} = \sqrt{9} = 3 \quad 8^{\frac{2}{3}} = \sqrt[3]{8^2}$$

Raising a Power to a Power

When you raise a power to a power, you simply multiply the exponents.

$$(4^2)^6 = 4^{(2 \cdot 6)} = 4^{12} \qquad (y^3)^2 = y^{(3 \cdot 2)} = y^6$$

Pop Quiz

Q: What number is both a factor and multiple of 21?

The Zero Power

Anything to the zero power is 1.

$$4^0 = 1 \qquad x^0 = 1$$

The First Power

Anything to the power of 1 is itself.

$$5^1 = 5 \quad y^1 = y$$

Distributing Exponents When several numbers are inside parentheses, the exponent outside the parentheses must be distributed to all of the numbers within.

$$(4y)^2 = 4^2y^2 = 16y^2$$

But Watch Out For...

Exponents are shorthand for multiplication, so the rules apply only when you multiply or divide the same base.

Does $x^2 + x^3 = x^5$? NO!

Does $x^4 - x^2 = x^2$? NO!

Does $\dfrac{x^2 + y^3 + z^4}{x^2 + y^3} = z^4$ NO!

You would expect that raising a number to a power would increase that number, and usually it does, but there are exceptions.

- If you raise a positive fraction of less than 1 to a power, it gets smaller.

$$\left(\frac{1}{2}\right)^2 = \frac{1^2}{2^2} = \frac{1}{4}$$

- If you raise a negative number to an odd power, the number gets smaller (unless it is between 0 and –1).

$$(-3)^3 = (-3)(-3)(-3) = -27$$

(Remember, –27 is smaller than –3.)

- If you raise a negative number to an even power, the number becomes positive.

$$(-3)^2 = (-3)(-3) = 9$$

Pop Quiz

A: 21

RADICALS

The **square root** of a positive number x is the number that, when squared, equals x. For example, the square root of 16 equals 4 because $4 \times 4 = 16$. On the ACT, you will not have to worry about negative square roots; for ACT purposes, the square root of 16 is just 4.

The symbol for a positive square root is $\sqrt{\ }$. The symbol $\sqrt{\ }$ is also called a **radical**.

$$\sqrt{16} = 4$$
$$\sqrt{9} = 3$$

The **cube root** of a positive number x is the number that, when cubed, equals x. For example, the cube root of 8 equals 2 because $2 \times 2 \times 2$ equals 8.

$$\sqrt[3]{8} = 2$$
$$\sqrt[3]{27} = 3$$

Roots Are Positive on the ACT
When you're asked for the square root of any number, supply the positive root only. Although 5^2 and $(-5)^2$ both equal 25, 5 is the only square root of 25.

Be sure that you know how to use your calculator to find more than just square roots and simple exponents like 4^2. The ACT is going to have fractional exponents, negative exponents, and all sorts of weird roots, and you'll need to be able to solve them quickly and accurately. Can you do the two examples above on your calculator? What about questions 4 and 5 in the drill at the end of this chapter? If you can't, be sure to learn how.

Rules to Remember About Radicals

- $\sqrt{x} + \sqrt{x} = 2\sqrt{x}$

For example, $2\sqrt{5} + 20\sqrt{5} = 22\sqrt{5}$

- $\sqrt{x} \cdot \sqrt{y} = \sqrt{xy}$

For example, $\left(\sqrt{12}\right)\left(\sqrt{3}\right) = \sqrt{36}$, or 6.

$$3\sqrt{5} \cdot 6\sqrt{2} = 18\sqrt{10}$$

- $\sqrt{\frac{x}{y}} = \frac{\sqrt{x}}{\sqrt{y}}$

  For example, $\sqrt{\frac{3}{16}} = \frac{\sqrt{3}}{\sqrt{16}} = \frac{\sqrt{3}}{4}$

- To simplify a radical, try factoring. Look for a perfect square to factor out.

  $\sqrt{32} = \sqrt{16}\sqrt{2} = 4\sqrt{2}$

  $2\sqrt{5} + 4\sqrt{125} = 2\sqrt{5} + 4\left(\sqrt{25}\right)\left(\sqrt{5}\right) =$

  $2\sqrt{5} + (4)(5)\left(\sqrt{5}\right) = 22\sqrt{5}$

- The square root of a positive fraction less than 1 is actually larger than the original fraction.

  For example, $\sqrt{\frac{1}{4}} = \frac{1}{2}$

- Always try to have a ballpark idea of how large the number you are dealing with actually is. $\sqrt{63}$ is a bit less than $\sqrt{64}$ or 8. $\sqrt[3]{9}$ is a bit more than $\sqrt[3]{8}$ or 2. Some good approximations to memorize and helpful hints to remember them are as follows:

  $\sqrt{2} \approx 1.4$ (Valentine's Day is 2/14.)

  $\sqrt{3} \approx 1.7$ (St. Patrick's Day is 3/17.)

- Your calculator can make working with radicals even easier. Choose [2nd], then [x^2] for square roots.
- For cube roots, hit [MATH] and choose $\left[4:\sqrt[3]{(}\right]$.
- For all roots, always remember to close the parentheses after you enter your number.

Basics Drill

1. Which of the following expresses the prime factorization of 54 ?

   A. 9×6
   B. $3 \times 3 \times 6$
   C. $3 \times 3 \times 2$
   D. $3 \times 3 \times 3 \times 2$
   E. 5.4×10

2. $\dfrac{(-5)(4)|-6|}{-3} =$

   F. –120
   G. –40
   H. 40
   J. 60
   K. 120

3. The number 1,134 is divisible by all of the following except

   A. 3
   B. 6
   C. 9
   D. 12
   E. 14

4. $(-2)^3 + (3)^{-2} + \dfrac{8}{9} =$

   F. –7
   G. $-1\dfrac{7}{9}$
   H. $\dfrac{8}{9}$
   J. $1\dfrac{7}{9}$
   K. 12

5. $27^{\frac{2}{3}}$

   A. –9
   B. –4
   C. 9
   D. 18
   E. 81^3

6. For all $x \neq 0$, $y \neq 0$, $\dfrac{(xy)^3 z^0}{x^3 y^4} =$

   F. $\dfrac{1}{y}$
   G. $\dfrac{z}{y}$
   H. z
   J. xy
   K. xyz

7. When is $\dfrac{11-a}{2}$ an integer?

   A. Only when a is negative
   B. Only when a is positive
   C. Only when a is odd
   D. Only when a equals 0
   E. Only when a is even

8. How many even integers are there between –4 and 4 ?

   F. 1
   G. 3
   H. 4
   J. 5
   K. 7

9. If the four-digit number 47W6 is divisible by 6 (W represents the tens digit), which of the following could be the value of W ?

   A. 2
   B. 3
   C. 4
   D. 6
   E. 8

10. If $9^x = \dfrac{1}{3}$, then $x =$

    F. –3
    G. –2
    H. –1
    J. $-\dfrac{1}{2}$
    K. $-\dfrac{1}{3}$

Summary

- Make sure you are familiar with math terminology. Many partial answers rely on the misinterpretation of key terms; don't be a victim.
- Knowing the rules of divisibility can be very useful on the ACT. In case you forget the rules, you can also test divisibility by entering the numbers into your calculator. If you get an integer result, the number is divisible by its factor.
- For any given number, the factors and multiples are *always* distinct, with one exception—the number itself. The number 10, for instance, is both a factor and a multiple of itself.
- Know the rules for multiplying and dividing exponents, raising a power to a power, and expressing fractional and negative exponents.
- On the ACT, square roots must be positive. However, exponents have both positive and negative roots.

Chapter 11 Arithmetic

Most of the arithmetic operations you'll come across on the ACT will seem like ancient history. While some questions will deal with only your ability to follow the correct order of operations, others will ask you to apply the same rules to a problem involving exponents and fractions. What do all these questions have in common? Getting them correct hinges on your command of basic arithmetic topics. In this chapter, we show you how to identify and attack questions that deal with the types of numbers and operations we commonly see in arithmetic questions.

Pay close attention to questions that deal only with arithmetic and do them first. Remember the concept of triage? These are exactly the type of questions that are points ready for the taking, so make sure you work them out carefully and get them right.

Here are the specific arithmetic (and related) topics tested on the ACT.

1. Order of operations
2. Fractions
3. Decimals
4. Ratios
5. Percentages
6. Averages
7. Charts and graphs
8. Combinations

First, let's discuss the fundamentals of each topic before we show you how ACT constructs questions based on those fundamentals.

Calculators

Students are permitted (but not required) to use calculators on the ACT. You should definitely bring a calculator to the test. Remember: We'll point out the calculator-friendly questions and tell you what you need to be able to do with your calculator on the ACT. Be sure to confirm that you can do each of the operations we mention. If it's been awhile since you used your calculator to figure out material tested on the ACT, put it through its paces again.

ORDER OF OPERATIONS

For problems that involve several different operations, you must perform the operations in a particular order. Here's an easy way to remember the order of operations.

Please Excuse My Dear Aunt Sally

First, you do operations enclosed in Parentheses; then you take care of Exponents; then you Multiply, Divide, Add, and Subtract, working from left to right. Most calculators follow the correct order of operations, but you have to be sure to enter the equations into your calculator correctly. Now's the time to test your calculator's ability to handle order of operations (and your ability to push tiny buttons properly).

Try this one.

$$((-5)+4)^2\left(\frac{8}{2}\right)+4-8=$$

Now try this one.

$$(-8)+\left(\frac{8}{2}\right)(4-5)^2+4=$$

If your calculator follows order of operations, then you should have gotten the same answer both times: 0.

The Associative Law: When adding a string of numbers, you can add them in any order you like. The same thing is true when multiplying a string of numbers.

$5 + 6 + 7$ is the same as $7 + 6 + 5$

$2 \times 3 \times 4$ is the same as $3 \times 4 \times 2$

The Distributive Law: Some combinations of addition and multiplication can be written in two different formats, which often proves extremely useful in finding ACT answers. The distributive law states that

$$a(b + c) = ab + ac$$

and that

$$a(b - c) = ab - ac$$

What Comes First?
Perform all operations within parentheses first. The distributive law is something of an exception; it gives you two ways to get the same result.

If a problem gives you information in factored format, which is $a(b + c)$, you should distribute it immediately. If the information is given in distributed form, which is $ab + ac$, you should factor it. An ACT problem might look like this.

---

1. For all $x \neq -2$, $\frac{2x+4}{x+2} = ?$

   A. $x+2$
   B. x
   C. 2
   D. $x+4$
   E. 4

For more great titles by The Princeton Review
Math Smart II

Here's How to Crack It

Let's use the distributive property on the numerator of this fraction and rewrite it in factored form.

$$\frac{2(x+2)}{(x+2)}$$

$\frac{(x+2)}{(x+2)}$ equals just 1. Therefore, we can cancel out both terms and the answer must be (C).

FRACTIONS

Calculators and Fractions

Your calculator is an excellent tool to perform many of the basic operations concerning fractions. Many of the common calculator errors, however, involve fractions. We have found that the best way to avoid these errors is to know how to perform basic operations on fractions by hand. Even if you use a TI-83/84 on the ACT, the next few pages will provide you with an understanding of what fractions are and how they work.

Fractions can be thought of in two ways. A fraction is just another way of expressing division. The expression $\frac{1}{2}$ means 1 divided by 2. $\frac{x}{y}$ is nothing more than x divided by y. A fraction is made up of a numerator and a denominator. The numerator is on top; the denominator is on the bottom. Just think, *denominator* starts with "d," just like *downstairs.*

$$\frac{1}{2} \quad \frac{\text{numerator}}{\text{denominator}}$$

The other way to think of a fraction is as a part over a whole.

$$\frac{1}{2} \quad \frac{\text{part}}{\text{whole}}$$

In the fraction $\frac{1}{2}$, we have one part out of a total of two parts.

In the fraction $\frac{3}{7}$, we have three parts out of a total of seven parts.

Reducing Fractions

To reduce a fraction, see if the numerator and the denominator have a common factor. It may save time to find the largest factor they share, but getting this information isn't crucial. Whatever factor they share can now be canceled. Let's take the fraction $\frac{6}{8}$. Is there a common factor? Yes: 2.

$$\frac{6}{8} = \frac{\cancel{2} \times 3}{\cancel{2} \times 4} = \frac{3}{4}$$

Get used to reducing all fractions (if they can be reduced) before you do any work with them. It saves a lot of time and prevents errors that crop up when you try to work with large numbers. Use your calculator's [FRAC] function under the MATH menu to reduce as well.

Fraction Reduction
In any fraction involving large numbers, try to reduce the fractions before you do anything else.

Comparing Fractions

Sometimes a problem will involve deciding which of two fractions is larger. If your calculator can convert fractions to decimals at the touch of a button, that's the way to compare them. If not, keep reading, and we'll explain how to do it by hand.

Which is larger, $\frac{2}{5}$ or $\frac{4}{5}$? Think of these as parts of a whole. Which is bigger, two parts out of five or four parts out of five? $\frac{4}{5}$ is clearly larger. In this case, it was easy to tell because they both had the same whole, or the same denominator.

Try this one. Which is larger, $\frac{2}{3}$ or $\frac{3}{7}$? To decide, we need to find a common whole, or denominator. You change the denominator of a fraction by multiplying it by another number. To keep the entire fraction the same, however, you must multiply the numerator by the same number.

Let's change the denominator of $\frac{2}{3}$ into 21.

$$\frac{2\times7}{3\times7}=\frac{14}{21}$$

$\frac{14}{21}$ still has the same value as $\frac{2}{3}$ (it would reduce to $\frac{2}{3}$) because we multiplied the fraction by $\frac{7}{7}$, or one.

Let's change the denominator of $\frac{3}{7}$ into 21 as well.

$$\frac{3\times3}{7\times3}=\frac{9}{21}$$

$\frac{9}{21}$ still has the same value as $\frac{3}{7}$ (it would reduce to $\frac{3}{7}$) because we multiplied the fraction by $\frac{3}{3}$, or one.

Now we can compare the two fractions. Which is larger, $\frac{14}{21}$ or $\frac{9}{21}$? Clearly, $\frac{14}{21}$ (or $\frac{2}{3}$) is bigger than $\frac{9}{21}$ (or $\frac{3}{7}$). Why did we decide on 21 as our common denominator? The easiest way to get a common denominator is to multiply the denominators of the two fractions you wish to compare: $7 \times 3 = 21$.

Let's do it again. Which is largest?

$$\frac{2}{3} \text{ or } \frac{4}{7} \text{ or } \frac{3}{5}?$$

To compare these fractions directly, you need a common denominator, but finding a common denominator that works for all three fractions would be complicated and time-consuming. It makes more sense to compare these fractions two at a time. Let's start with $\frac{2}{3}$ and $\frac{4}{7}$. An easy common denominator is 21.

$$\frac{2}{3} \qquad \frac{4}{7}$$

$$\frac{2\times7}{3\times7}=\frac{14}{21} \qquad \frac{4}{7}\times\frac{3}{3}=\frac{12}{21}$$

Because $\frac{2}{3}$ is larger, let's compare it with $\frac{3}{5}$. This time, the easiest common denominator is 15.

$$\frac{2}{3} \qquad \frac{3}{5}$$

$$\frac{2}{3}\times\frac{5}{5}=\frac{10}{15} \qquad \frac{3}{5}\times\frac{3}{3}=\frac{9}{15}$$

So $\frac{2}{3}$ is larger than $\frac{3}{5}$, which means it's also the biggest of the three.

Using the Bowtie

A more streamlined way to do this is to use the **Bowtie**. Let's compare the last two fractions again. We get the common denominator by multiplying the two denominators together.

$$\frac{2}{3 \rightarrow} \frac{3}{5} = \frac{}{15}$$

Easiest Common Denominator

Your teachers wanted you to calculate the Least Common Denominator (LCD) of a fraction. They even made you "show your work." The ACT doesn't care. This gives you the luxury of finding the Easiest Common Denominator by using the Bowtie.

We get the new numerators by multiplying as shown below.

$$\overset{(10)}{} \quad \overset{(9)}{}$$
$$\frac{2}{3 \rightarrow} \times \frac{3}{5} = \frac{}{15}$$

So $\frac{2}{3}$ is larger.

Adding and Subtracting Fractions

Now that we've reviewed finding a common denominator, adding and subtracting fractions is simple. Let's use the Bowtie to add $\frac{2}{5}$ and $\frac{1}{4}$.

$$(8) \quad (5)$$
$$\frac{2}{5 \rightarrow} \times \frac{1}{4 \rightarrow} = \frac{8+5}{20} = \frac{13}{20}$$

Let's use the Bowtie to subtract $\frac{2}{3}$ from $\frac{5}{6}$.

$$(15) \quad (12)$$
$$\frac{5}{6 \rightarrow} \times \frac{2}{3 \rightarrow} = \frac{15-12}{18} = \frac{3}{18} \text{ or } \frac{1}{6}$$

Multiplying Fractions

To multiply fractions, line them up and multiply straight across.

Half Empty or Half Full?
On the ACT, always think about what's left over. If a pizza is three-quarters eaten, there's still one-quarter left.

$$\frac{5}{6} \times \frac{4}{5} = \frac{20}{30} = \frac{2}{3}$$

Was there anything we could have canceled or reduced *before* we multiplied? Yes. We could cancel the 5 on top and the 5 on the bottom. What's left is $\frac{4}{6}$, which reduces to $\frac{2}{3}$.

Sometimes students whose math skills are a bit rusty think they can cancel or reduce in the same fashion *across an equal sign.*

$$\frac{\cancel{5}x}{6} = \frac{4}{\cancel{5}} \quad \text{NO!}$$

You *cannot* cancel the 5s or reduce the $\frac{4}{6}$ in this case. When there is an equal sign, you have to cross-multiply, which yields $25x = 24$, so x in this case would equal $\frac{24}{25}$.

Dividing Fractions

To divide one fraction by another, just invert the second fraction and multiply.

Fractional Calculators
Many calculators can add, subtract, multiply, and divide fractions and return the answer as a fraction. If yours can, it will save you lots of time on the ACT.

$$\frac{2}{3} \div \frac{3}{4} \text{ is the same thing as } \frac{2}{3} \times \frac{4}{3} = \frac{8}{9}$$

You may see this same operation written like this.

$$\frac{\frac{2}{3}}{\frac{3}{4}}$$

Again, just invert and multiply. Try the next example.

$$\frac{6}{\frac{2}{3}}$$

Think of 6 as $\frac{6}{1}$ and do the same thing.

$$\frac{6}{1}\times\frac{3}{2}=\frac{18}{2}=9$$

Converting to Fractions

An integer can always be expressed as a fraction by making the integer the numerator and 1 the denominator. $8=\frac{8}{1}$.

Sometimes the ACT gives you numbers that are mixtures of integers and fractions (e.g., $3\frac{1}{2}$). It is often easier to work with these numbers by converting them completely into fractions. Because the fraction is being expressed in halves, let's convert the integer into halves as well. $3=\frac{6}{2}$. Now just add the $\frac{1}{2}$ to the $\frac{6}{2}$. $3\frac{1}{2}=\frac{7}{2}$.

Now How Does the ACT Test Fractions?

An ACT fraction problem combines several of the elements we've just discussed. Here's a typical problem.

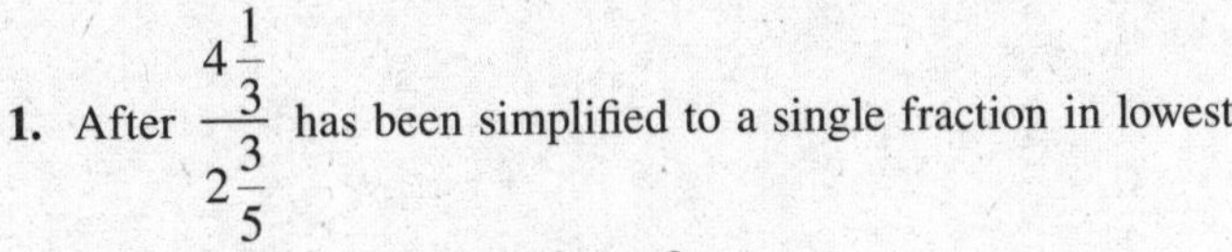

1. After $\dfrac{4\frac{1}{3}}{2\frac{3}{5}}$ has been simplified to a single fraction in lowest terms, what is the denominator?

A. 2
B. 3
C. 5
D. 9
E. 13

Here's How to Crack It

First, let's convert the mixture of integers and fractions into fractions. $4\frac{1}{3} = \frac{13}{3}$, $2\frac{3}{5} = \frac{13}{5}$. Remember, to divide fractions, simply flip and multiply $\frac{13}{3} \times \frac{5}{13}$. The 13s cancel, leaving $\frac{5}{3}$. The answer is (B).

More complicated fraction problems might test your ability to recognize that every fraction implies another fraction—what's left over. If a glass is $\frac{3}{5}$ full, what part of the glass is empty? $\frac{2}{5}$.

2. On Friday, Jane does one-third of her homework. On Saturday, she does one-sixth of the remainder. What fraction of her homework is still left to be done?

F. $\frac{4}{9}$

G. $\frac{1}{2}$

H. $\frac{5}{9}$

J. $\frac{5}{6}$

K. $\frac{7}{12}$

Here's How to Crack It

Jane did $\frac{1}{3}$ on Friday. How much is still left to be done? That's right: $\frac{2}{3}$. On Saturday she did $\frac{1}{6}$ *of the remainder.* In math, the word "of" always means multiply, so let's set it up.

Friday	**Saturday**
$\frac{1}{3} \times 1$	$\frac{1}{6} \times \frac{2}{3} = \frac{2}{18}$
$\frac{1}{3}$ done	$\frac{2}{18}$ or $\frac{1}{9}$ done (on Saturday)

If we find a common denominator, we can add up what she's done. Then we get

$$\frac{3}{9} + \frac{1}{9} = \frac{4}{9}$$

Altogether, she has done $\frac{4}{9}$ of the assignment. If you thought you were done at this point, you may have picked (F), but the question doesn't ask how much was done but rather how much remained *undone.* How much is left? $\frac{5}{9}$. The answer is (H).

POE Pointers

In that last problem, (F) was a *partial* answer designed to catch people who thought they were done before they really were. Choice (G), on the contrary, was designed to catch people who slightly misunderstood the question. If you missed the words "of the remainder" as you read the question, you probably added $\frac{1}{6}$ to $\frac{1}{3}$ and got $\frac{1}{2}$.

DECIMALS

Most simple decimal problems are easier to figure out on a calculator than on paper. However, unless you understand the theory behind them, it is easy to make a mistake.

A fraction can be written as a decimal and vice versa. Take the fraction $\frac{3}{5}$. Remember what we said before: A fraction is just another form of division.

$$\frac{3}{5} = 3 \div 5 = .6 \qquad 5\overline{)3.0}^{\,.6}$$

You can also express any decimal as a fraction.

$$.4 = \frac{4}{10} = \frac{2}{5} \qquad .03 = \frac{3}{100}$$

The test writers frequently ask questions using decimals but want answers as fractions, or vice versa, so the ability to go back and forth between the two is essential to succeeding on the test. If your calculator can do this for you, be sure you know how to use that function.

Adding and Subtracting Decimals

To add or subtract decimals, just line up the decimal points and proceed as if it were regular addition or subtraction. To add 9.25, 3.2, and 8.567

Stay in Line
When adding or subtracting decimals, keep all decimal points lined up.

$$\begin{array}{r} 9.250 \\ 3.200 \\ +\ 8.567 \\ \hline 21.017 \end{array}$$

It helps to add zeros to fill out the decimal places of the numbers with fewer digits. 3.2 is the same as 3.200.

Multiplying Decimals

To multiply decimals, simply ignore the decimal points and multiply your numbers. When you've finished, count all the digits to the right of the decimal points in the original numbers you multiplied. Now place the decimal point in your answer so that there are the same number of digits to the right of it.

Here's an example.

$$\begin{array}{r} 2.32 \\ \times .03 \\ \hline .0696 \end{array}$$

$3 \times 232 = 696$. There are a total of four digits to the right of the decimal point in the original numbers. Therefore, we now place the decimal so that there are four digits to the right in the answer.

Dividing Decimals

Place Value
Compare decimals place-by-place, going from left to right.

The best way to divide one decimal by another is to convert the number you are dividing *by* (in mathematical terminology, the **divisor**) into a whole number. You do this simply by moving the decimal point as many places as necessary.

This works as long as you also remember to move the decimal point in the number that you are dividing (in mathematical terminology, the **dividend**) the same number of spaces.

To divide 12 by .6, set it up the way you would an ordinary division problem.

$$.6\overline{)\,12.}$$

To convert .6 into a whole number, move the decimal point over one place to the right. Now you must move the decimal point in 12 one place as well. The operation looks like this:

$$6\overline{)120} \quad \begin{array}{r} 20 \\ 6\overline{)120} \end{array}$$

SCIENTIFIC NOTATION

The purpose of scientific notation is to express very large numbers or very small numbers without endless strings of zeros.

$$3.24 \times 10^2$$

All you have to do to simplify this expression is move the decimal point over to the right by the same number as the power of ten—in this case, two places. If the power of ten is negative, you move the decimal point to the left instead.

$$3.24 \times 10^3 = 3{,}240$$

$$3.24 \times 10^2 = 324$$

$$3.24 \times 10^{-1} = .324$$

$$3.24 \times 10^{-2} = .0324$$

An ACT scientific notation problem might look like this.

---

1. $(9 \times 10^{-3}) - (2 \times 10^{-2}) = ?$

A. –0.007
B. –0.07
C. –0.011
D. –0.11
E. 0.11

Here's How to Crack It

$$9 \times 10^{-3} = .009$$

$$2 \times 10^{-2} = .02$$

$$\begin{array}{r} .009 \\ -.02 \\ \hline -.011 \end{array}$$

The answer is (C).

RATIOS

Ratio vs. Fraction
Keep in mind that a ratio compares part of something with another *part.* A fraction compares part of something with the whole thing.

There are relatively few ratio problems on the ACT. The important thing to remember is the difference between a ratio and a fraction. While a fraction is a $\frac{\text{part}}{\text{whole}}$, a ratio is a $\frac{\text{part}}{\text{part}}$.

Take the ratio of $\frac{4 \text{ cats}}{3 \text{ dogs}}$. What is the whole of this ratio? If you said the total number of animals, or 7, you are absolutely correct. So what fractional part of the animals is dogs? Let's change the ratio $\left(\frac{\text{part}}{\text{part}}\right)$ into a fraction $\left(\frac{\text{part}}{\text{whole}}\right)$. The part made up of dogs is 3. The whole is 7. Thus, the fractional part of the animals that is dogs is $\frac{3}{7}$.

Ratio problems don't often need to be converted to fractions, but knowing what a ratio is is important.

---

1. If the ratio of $2x$ to $5y$ is $\frac{1}{20}$, what is the ratio of x to y ?

A. $\frac{1}{40}$

B. $\frac{1}{20}$

C. $\frac{1}{10}$

D. $\frac{1}{8}$

E. $\frac{1}{4}$

Here's How to Crack It

$$\frac{2x}{5y} = \frac{1}{20}$$

To isolate $\frac{x}{y}$ on the left side of this equation, what do we have to do to it? Let's multiply both sides by $\frac{5}{2}$.

$$\frac{5}{2}\times\frac{2x}{5y}=\frac{1}{20}\times\frac{5}{2}$$

$$\frac{x}{y}=\frac{5}{40}$$

$\frac{5}{40}$ reduces to $\frac{1}{8}$. The answer is (D).

PERCENTAGES

A percentage is a fraction in which the denominator equals 100. In literal terms, the word *percent* means "divided by 100," so any time you see a percentage in an ACT question, you can punch it into your calculator quite easily. If a question asks for 40 percent of something, for instance, you can express the percentage as a fraction: $\frac{40}{100}$. Any time you are looking for a percent, you can use your calculator to find the decimal equivalent and multiply the result by 100. If four out of five dentists recommend a particular brand of toothpaste, you can quickly determine the percent of doctors who recommend it by typing $\frac{4}{5}\times 100$ and hitting the ſ key. The resulting "80" just needs a percent sign tacked onto it. To properly translate all percent questions, it is helpful to have a decoding table for the various terms you'll come across.

English	Math Equivalent
percent	/100
of	multiplication (×)
what	variable (y, z)
is, are, were	=
what percent	$\frac{y}{100}$

Using the above table, let's say you had a word problem in which you had to translate the following sentence into math terms: "What percent of 7 is 14?" Word for word, substitute the math terms above in the appropriate places. You should end up with

$$\frac{y}{100} \times 7 = 14$$

Now, solve for y to arrive at 200. Tack on your percent sign and call it a day.

Percentage Shortcuts

In the last problem, we could have saved a little time if we had realized that $\frac{1}{5}$ = 20 percent. Therefore, $\frac{4}{5}$ would be 4 × 20 percent or 80 percent. Below are some fractions and decimals whose percent equivalents you should know.

Another fast way to do percents is to move the decimal place. To find 10 percent of any number, move the decimal point of that number over one place to the left.

10% of 500 = 50

10% of 50 = 5

10% of 5 = .5

To find 1 percent of a number, move the decimal point of that number over two places to the left.

1% of 500 = 5

1% of 50 = .5

1% of 5 = .05

You can use a combination of these last two techniques to find even very complicated percentages by breaking them down into easy-to-find chunks.

- 20% of 500: 10% of 500 = 50, so 20% is twice 50, or 100.
- 30% of 70: 10% of 70 = 7, so 30% is three times 7, or 21.
- 32% of 400: 10% of 400 = 40, so 30% is three times 40, or 120.
- 1% of 400 = 4, so 2% is two times 4, or 8.

Therefore, 32 percent of 400 = 120 + 8 = 128

You may also have to convert a decimal into a percentage. This is similar to converting a fraction to a percentage, which we just reviewed. Remember the dentists? We turned four out of five dentists into a fraction, but we could have turned it into a decimal as well. If you divide four by five, you get .8. To turn that into a percentage, take it to two decimal places and then put it over 100 (removing the decimal point).

$$.8 = .80 = \frac{80}{100}$$

That's the same as 80 percent, which is the same answer we got before (good thing).

Here's what an ACT percentage problem might look like.

The Big Four: Fraction/Percent Equivalents You Should Know

$$\frac{1}{5} = .2 = 20\%$$

$$\frac{1}{4} = .25 = 25\%$$

$$\frac{1}{3} = .\overline{33} = 33\frac{1}{3}\%$$

$$\frac{1}{2} = .5 = 50\%$$

---

1. At a restaurant, diners enjoy an "early bird" discount of 10% off their bill. If a diner orders a meal regularly priced at $18 and leaves a tip of 15% of the discounted meal, how much does he pay in total?

A. $13.50
B. $16.20
C. $18.63
D. $18.90
E. $20.70

Here's How to Crack It

A combination of bite-size pieces, percent translation, and calculator work will make this problem easy to tackle. When we take fractions or percentages of something, we need to start with the original number. The first thing we'll have to do is figure out how much the discounted meal costs. Write out the steps.

$$\text{Discount taken: } \left(\frac{10}{100}\right) \times 18 = \$1.80$$

$$\text{Discounted meal price: } \$18 - \$1.80 = \$16.20$$

$$\text{Tip paid for meal: } \left(\frac{15}{100}\right) \times 16.20 = \$2.43$$

$$\text{Total meal price: } \$16.20 + \$2.43 = \$18.63$$

Circle (C). Take your time and make it painless.

POE Pointers

Even before you began this problem, you could have eliminated one answer choice through POE. Did you spot it? Answer choice A was way too small. The diner is getting a discount of only 10 percent off the $18 and he must still pay the tip, which will add a bit more money. Could the answer be as low as $13.50? Nope. Cross off answer choice A.

Even if you didn't notice that answer choice A was too small, once you figured out that 10 percent of $18 was $16.20, you could have eliminated choices A and B because there was still the tip to pay, so the total had to be larger than $16.20.

AVERAGES

There are only three parts to any average question. Fortunately for you, the ACT must give you two of these parts, which are all you need to find the third. The average pie is an easy way to keep track of the information you get from questions dealing with averages. If you have the total, you can always divide by either the average or the number of things in the set (whichever you are given) to find the missing piece of the pie. Similarly, if you have the number of things and the average, you can multiple the two together to arrive at the total (the sum of all the items in the set).

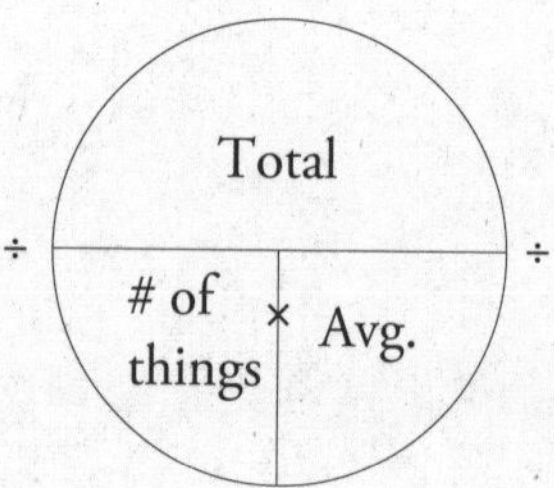

For example, if you want to find the average of 9, 12, and 6 using the average pie, you know you have 3 items with a total of 27. Dividing the total, 27, by the number of things, 3, will yield the average, 9. Your pie looks like this:

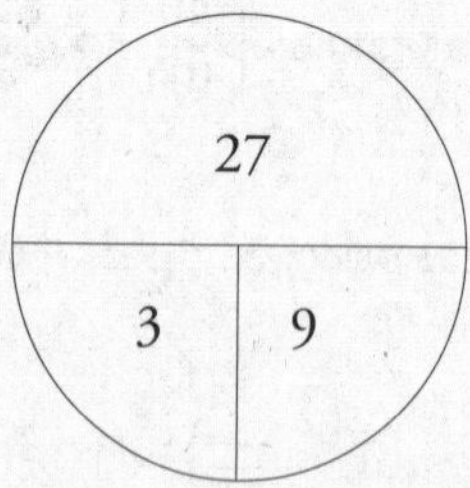

Although you probably could have done that without the average pie, more difficult average questions involve multiple calculations and lend themselves particularly well to using the pie. Let's take a look at one:

3. Over 9 games, a baseball team had an average of 8 runs per game. If the average number of runs for the first 7 games was 6 runs per game, and the same number of runs was scored in each of the last 2 games, how many runs did the team score during the last game?

A. 5
B. 15
C. 26
D. 30
E. 46

Here's How to Crack It

Let's use bite-size pieces to put the information from the first line of this problem into our trusty average pie.

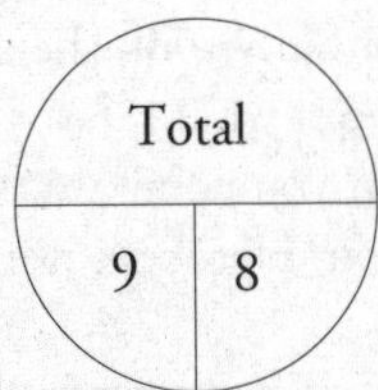

What is the sum of everything for these 9 games? 9×8, or 72.

Now let's put the information from the second line into the average equation.

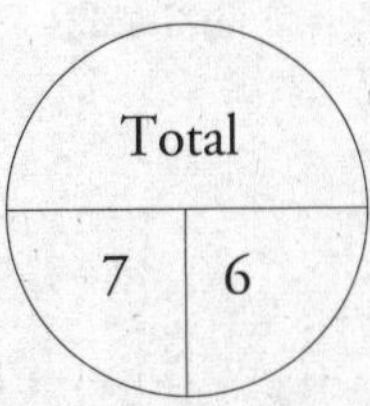

What is the sum of everything for these 7 games? 7×6, or 42.

If all 9 games added up to 72, and 7 of these games added up to 42, then the remaining 2 games added up to $72 - 42$, or 30. In case you are feeling smug about getting this far, the ACT writers made 30 the answer for (D).

But of course, if you read the last line, you know that they only want the runs they scored in the last game. Because the same number of runs was scored in each of the last two games, the answer is $\frac{30}{2}$ or 15, (B).

The Weighted Average

ACT writers have a particular fondness for "weighted average" problems. First, let's look at a regular unweighted average question.

> **Playing the Averages**
>
> **Arithmetic mean**—just a fancy way of saying "average."
>
> **Median**—the one in the middle, like the median strip on the highway.
>
> **Mode**—you're looking for the element that appears most. Get it? MOde, MOst.

If Sally received a grade of 90 on a test last week and a grade of 100 on a test this week, what is her average for the two tests?

Piece of cake, right? The answer is 95. You added the scores and divided by 2. Now let's turn the same question into a weighted average question.

If Sally's average for the entire year last year was 90, and her average for the entire year this year was 100, is her average for the two years combined equal to 95?

The answer is "not necessarily." If Sally took the same number of courses in both years, then yes, her average is 95. But what if last year she took 6 courses while this year she took only 2 courses? Can you compare the two years equally? ACT likes to test your answer to this question. Here's an example.

---

1. The starting team of a baseball club has 9 members who have an average of 12 home runs apiece for the season. The second-string team for the baseball club has 7 members who have an average of 8 home runs apiece for the season. What is the average number of home runs for the starting team and the second-string team combined?

A. 7.5
B. 8
C. 10
D. 10.25
E. 14.2

Here's How to Crack It

The ACT test writers want to see whether you spot this as a weighted average problem. If you thought the first-string team was exactly equivalent to the second-string team, then you merely had to take the average of the two averages, 12 and 8, to get 10. In weighted average problems, the ACT test writers always include the average of the two averages among the answer choices, and it is always wrong. 10 is (C). Cross off (C).

The two teams are not equivalent because there are different numbers of players on each team. To get the true average, we'll have to find the total number of home runs and divide by the total number of players. How do we do this? By going to the trusty average formula as usual. The first line of the problem says that the 9 members on the first team have an average of 12 runs apiece.

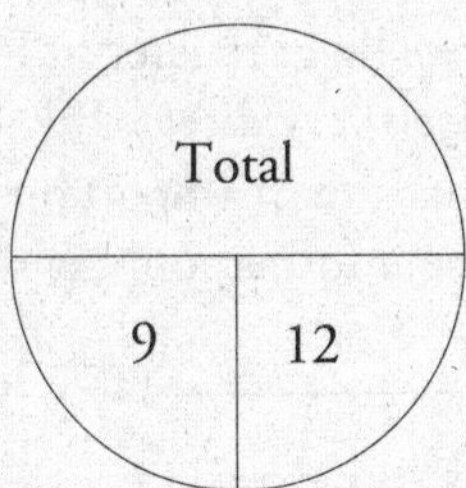

So the sum of everything is 9 × 12, or 108.

The second sentence says that the 7 members of the second team have an average of 8 runs each.

The Missing Number
The ACT loves to leave out totals on average problems. You aren't done until you've found it.

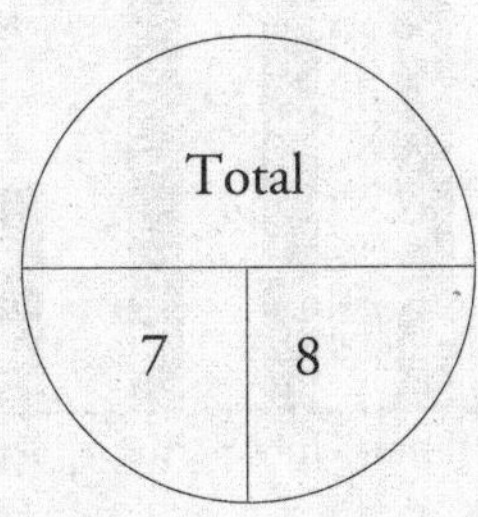

So the total is 7 × 8, or 56.

Now we can find the true average. Add all the runs scored by the first team to all the runs scored by the second team: 108 + 56 = 164. This is the true total. We divide it by the total number of players (9 + 7 = 16).

The answer is 10.25, or (D).

POE Pointers

Although we could eliminate (C) in that last problem because it represented the "unweighted" average, there were several other answers we might have eliminated through POE. If the average of the first team was 12 and the average of the second team was 8, it stood to reason that the correct answer would be somewhere between those two numbers. Could the answer really have been higher than 12? Answer choice (E) bites the dust. Could the answer really have been equal to or lower than 8? Answer choices (A) and (B) also fall by the wayside.

CHARTS AND GRAPHS

Since calculators were added to the arsenal you're allowed to bring with you when you take the ACT, more and more of the test has been composed of questions on which calculators are of little or no use, such as questions based on charts and graphs. On this type of question, your math skills aren't really being tested at all; what ACT is interested in is your ability to read a simple graph (not unlike on the Science Reasoning test, which we'll get to later in Part V). All of the questions we have seen in this format have been very direct. If you can read a simple graph, you can always get them right. What's most important on questions like these is paying attention to the labels on the information. Let's take a look at a graph.

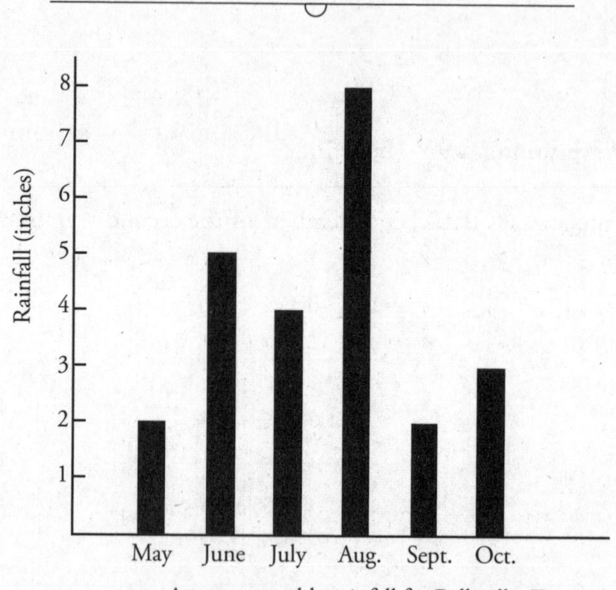

Average monthly rainfall for Belleville, IL.

3. Between which two months was the change in total rainfall the greatest?

A. May and June
B. June and July
C. July and August
D. August and September
E. September and October

Here's How to Crack It

The ACT test writers want to see if you can decipher the information presented in the graph. Before you read the question then, you need to take a look at the graph. What is measured here? It says on the bottom: Average monthly rainfall in Belleville, IL. You should look at the values along the left side and bottom of the graph as well. When you do, you'll see that the rain is measured in inches (left-hand side), and the measurements were made each month (bottom).

Now for the question. To determine which two months had the greatest change, we need to compare the change between each pair of months, discarding the smaller ones until we have only one left. The difference from May to June is about 3, and that's larger than June to July and September to October, so (B) and (E) are out. July to August is larger still, though, so (A) is out, leaving only (C) and (D). It should be pretty apparent that the August to September change is larger than the July to August change, though, so the correct answer must be (D).

Although most questions involving graphs on the Math test are this simple, you may see slightly more complicated variations. Here's another question based on the same bar graph.

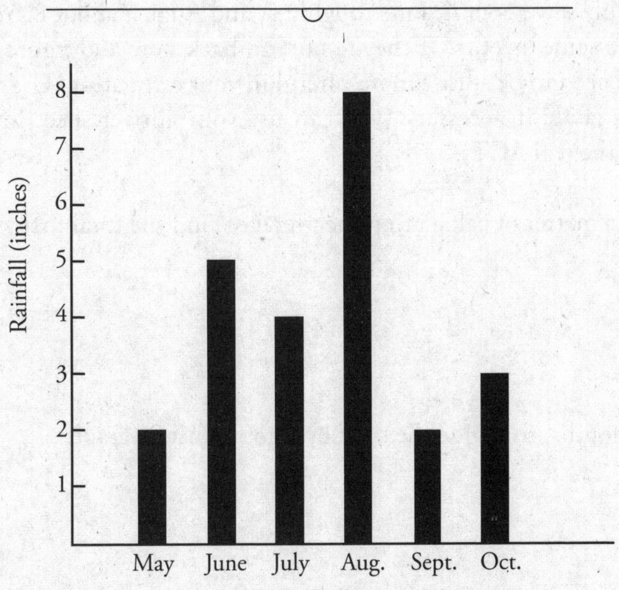

Average monthly rainfall for Belleville, IL.

24. Based on the information presented in the graph above, what is the approximate average monthly rainfall in Belleville, IL, for the period given?

F. 2
G. 3
H. 4
J. 5
K. 8

Here's How to Crack It

As with the last question, the first thing you want to do is examine the graph and figure out what information is being given to you and how it is being presented. Because you already did that for this graph, we'll skip that step on this one.

This question combines graph reading with average calculation, so the next thing you'll have to do is estimate the rainfall for each month. Because the question uses the word *approximate*, you don't have to worry too much about making super-exact measurements of the heights of the bar graphs. Eyeballing it and rounding to the closest value given on the left-hand side will be good enough to get you the right answer. Do that now before you read the next sentence.

To us, it looks like about 2 inches fell in May and September, and around 3 fell in October. July saw about 4, June roughly 5, and August about 8. Your estimates should be the same as ours. If they're not, go back now and figure out why not. You probably need to be a little more careful in your estimating. Use another piece of paper as a guide if necessary (you can use your answer sheet in this manner when taking the real ACT).

Now it's just a matter of calculating the average. Find the total first.

$$2 + 2 + 3 + 4 + 5 + 8 = 24$$

There are 6 months, so divide the total by 6 to find the average.

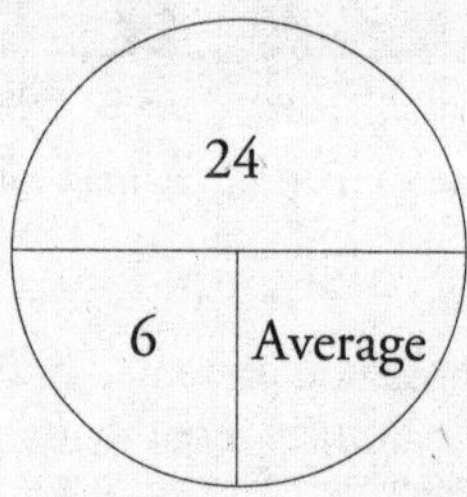

So the answer is 4, or (H).

COMBINATIONS

Combination problems ask you how many different ways a number of things could be chosen or combined. The rule for combination problems on the ACT is straightforward.

> The number of combinations is the **product** of the number of things of each type from which you have to choose.

Here's an example.

---

4. At the school cafeteria, students can choose from 3 different salads, 5 different main dishes, and 2 different desserts. If Isabel chooses one salad, one main dish, and one dessert for lunch, how many different lunches could she choose?

F. 10
G. 15
H. 25
J. 30
K. 50

Here's How to Crack It

Isabel is going to choose her lunch by choosing one of each of the items. The numbers of items she has to choose from for each type of dish are 3, 5, and 2. The number of possible combinations she could choose from is always the product of the number of things of each type she can choose from, so there are $3 \times 5 \times 2 = 30$ possible lunch combinations. Therefore, the answer is (J).

On a more difficult problem, you may run into a combination with more restricted elements. Just be sure to read the problem carefully before attempting it; if the question makes your head spin, pick your Letter of the Day and return to it later.

College Lingo

Direct Loan Program: With this federal educational loan program, funds are lent directly by the U.S. government through the school's financial aid office, with no need of a private lender or bank.
Source: *Best 366 Colleges*, 2008 Edition

55. At the school cafeteria, 2 boys and 4 girls are forming a lunch line. If the boys must stand in the first and last places in line, how many different lines can be formed?

A. 2
B. 6
C. 48
D. 360
E. 720

Here's How to Crack It

Let's think about the restricted spots first. If only boys can stand in the first spot, how many people in the question can be first in line? Because there are only 2 boys available, there are only two options for spot #1. Now, what about the last spot in line? Again, if only boys can stand there, and if one of the boys is going to have to stand in the first spot, there is only 1 boy left to fill the position. The spots in the middle must go to the girls. Because the question does not set any additional limits on the girls, we can assume they can be placed in any of the 4 remaining spots. Thus, any of the 4 girls can stand in spot #2, leaving 3 girls to stand in spot #3, 2 girls to stand in spot #4, and the last girl to stand in spot #5. Now all we need to do is multiply all the possibilities together. If you drew a picture of the line and wrote in the above arrangements, it should look like this.

$$\frac{2}{B} \times \frac{4}{G} \times \frac{3}{G} \times \frac{2}{G} \times \frac{1}{G} \times \frac{1}{B}$$

When you multiply everything, you'll get 48, which is answer choice (C).

Arithmetic Drill

1. The ratio of boys to girls at the Milwood School is 4 to 5. If there are a total of 27 children at the school, how many boys attend the Milwood School?

   A. 4
   B. 9
   C. 12
   D. 14
   E. 17

2. Linda computed the average of her six biology test scores by mistakenly adding the totals of five scores and dividing by five, giving her an average score of 88. When Linda realized her error, she recalculated and included the sixth test score of 82. What is the average of Linda's six biology tests?

   F. 82
   G. 85
   H. 86
   J. 87
   K. 88

3. In the process of milling grain, 3% of the original is lost because of spillage, and another 5% of the original is lost because of mildew. If the mill starts out with 490 tons of grain, how much (in tons) remains to be sold after milling?

   A. 425
   B. 426
   C. 420.5
   D. 440
   E. 450.8

4. $5\frac{1}{3} - 6\frac{1}{4} = ?$

   F. $\frac{-11}{12}$
   G. $\frac{-1}{2}$
   H. $\frac{-2}{7}$
   J. $\frac{1}{2}$
   K. $\frac{9}{12}$

5. $1{,}245 \div .05 = ?$

   A. 200
   B. 2,490
   C. 2,500
   D. 24,900
   E. 25,000

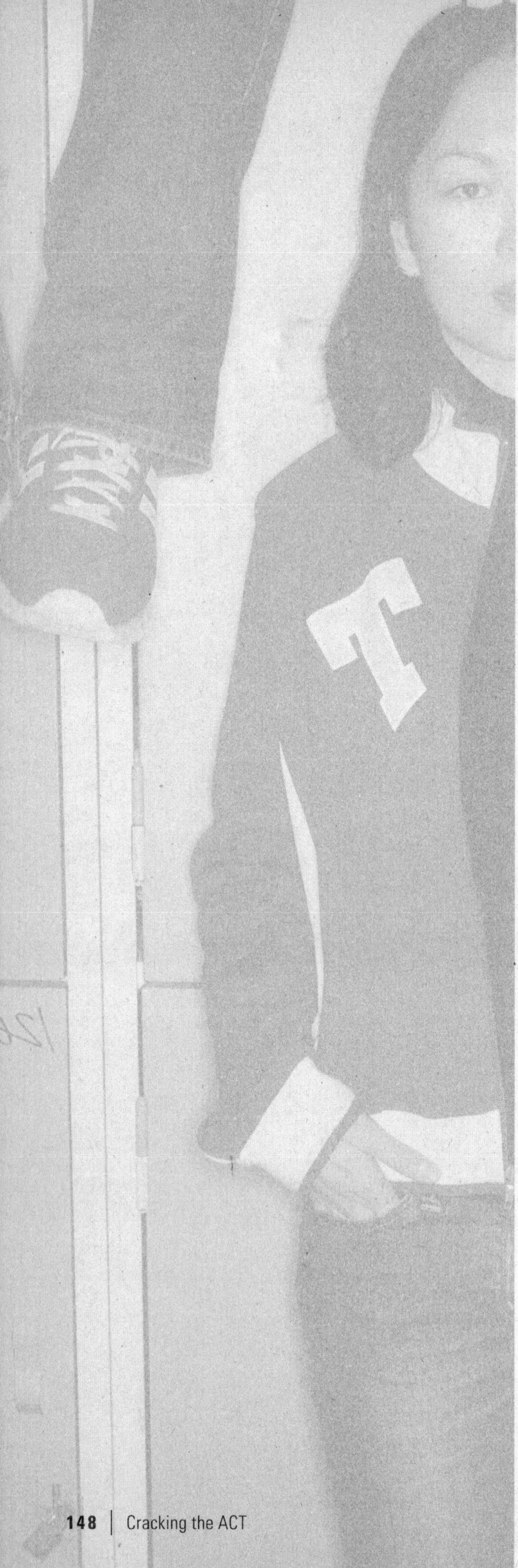

Summary

- The eight main topics of arithmetic are
    - order of operations
    - fractions
    - decimals
    - percentages
    - ratios
    - averages
    - charts and graphs
    - combinations

- Your calculator can be an extremely powerful tool on the ACT. Having command of 9 or 10 simple operations on the calculator will raise your score and lower your blood pressure significantly.

- Arithmetic operations must be performed in a particular order. Here's an easy way to remember the order of operations: Please Excuse My Dear Aunt Sally. First, you do operations enclosed in parentheses; then you take care of exponents; then you multiply, divide, add, and subtract.

- When you add or multiply a group of numbers, you can put them in any order that suits you. This is called the associative law.

- The distributive law states that $a(b + c) = ab + ac$ and that $a(b - c) = ab - ac$. On the ACT, if you see a problem in one form, you will make the problem much easier by immediately putting it in the other form.

- A fraction can be thought of as a $\frac{\text{part}}{\text{whole}}$.

- You must know how to reduce, multiply, divide, compare, add, and subtract fractions. The Bowtie is a great method for doing the last three items mentioned, but your calculator is even better—if you know how to use it.

- Every fraction implies another fraction—what is left over. If a glass is $\frac{3}{5}$ empty, it is $\frac{2}{5}$ full.
- A decimal is just another way to express a fraction.
- You must know how to add, subtract, multiply, and divide decimals as well as be familiar with scientific notation.
- A ratio is different in one respect from a fraction: A ratio is a $\frac{\text{part}}{\text{part}}$. If the ratio of cats to dogs is $\frac{3}{4}$, the whole is 7.
- A percentage is just a fraction in which the denominator is equal to 100. Most percentage problems can be set up to look like this: $\frac{\text{part}}{\text{whole}} = \frac{x}{100}$.
- On word problems dealing with percentages, you can use the percent translation table to create a calculator-friendly equation.
- In average questions, you should immediately think

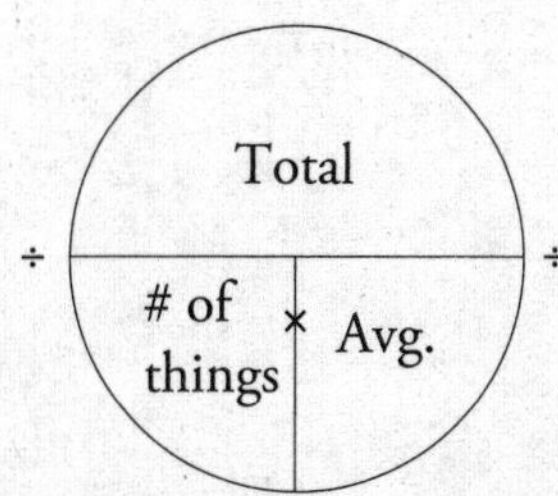

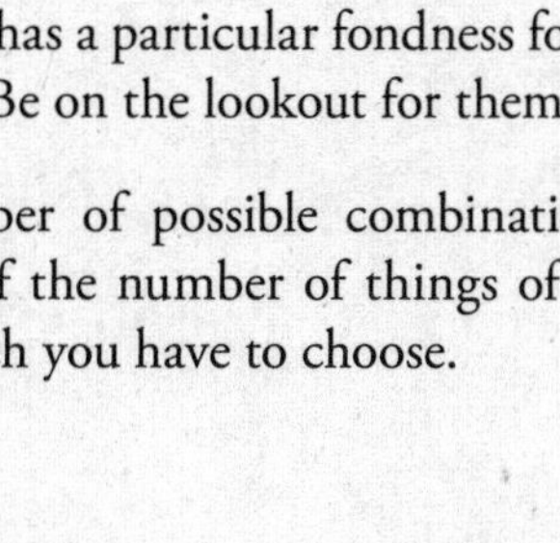

- The ACT has a particular fondness for weighted averages. Be on the lookout for them.
- The number of possible combinations is the product of the number of things of each type from which you have to choose.

Chapter 12
Algebra

Algebra is all about solving for an unknown quantity. In this chapter, we'll take a look at the different ways you will see algebra on the ACT and give you some strategies to tackle it. You'll get plenty of practice with these techniques while you brush up on topics such as factoring, quadratic equations, simultaneous equations, inequalities, and logarithms.

Algebra is all about solving for an unknown quantity. The unknown is usually represented by a variable such as x or y. There are two general kinds of algebra questions on the ACT. The first kind asks you to solve for a particular x. The second kind asks you to solve for a more cosmic x (don't worry, we'll explain). Let's begin with the particular.

WHEN *X* HAS A PARTICULAR VALUE: THE BASIC EQUATION

Here is a simple example of a basic equation.

The Golden Rule of Algebra
Whatever you do to one side of an equation, you have to do to the other side.

$$3x + 7 = 28$$

There is only one number in the world that will satisfy this equation. To find it, we need to isolate x on one side of the equation and get all of the numbers on the other side. To get rid of the 7 that is being added on the left side, we must do the opposite of addition and subtract 7 from the left side. However, to avoid changing the entire equation, we also have to subtract 7 from the right side. Whatever is done to one side must also be done to the other.

$$\begin{array}{r} 3x+7=28 \\ -7\ \ -7 \\ \hline 3x=21 \end{array}$$

Calculator Tip
Although many calculators can solve equations involving only one variable, it's usually faster to do the simple ones by hand.

To get rid of the 3 that is being multiplied on the left side, we must do the opposite of multiplication and divide the left side by 3. If we are dividing the left side by 3, we must also divide the right side by 3.

$$\frac{3x}{3} = \frac{21}{3} = 7$$

$$x = 7$$

But in this last problem, we left out one very important thing: ACT questions always have multiple-choice answers. Let's look at this question the way it would have appeared on the actual test.

1. If $3x + 7 = 28$, what is x ?

A. 4
B. 5
C. 6
D. 7
E. 8

You might say, "Well, what's the difference? It's the same problem." But in fact, it's not the same problem at all.

Most Particular *X* Problems Can Also Be Solved *Backward*

Algebra is a wonderful discipline, and we do want you to be able to solve problems like the one above algebraically, particularly when they are easy. However, there is another way to do most particular x problems—a way that can, in some cases, save you huge amounts of time and trouble. It's called "Working Backward."

If we asked you to *guess* the value of x in this question, it might take you a long, long time. After all, there's only going to be one number in the whole world that satisfies this equation, and there is a limitless supply of numbers from which to choose. Or is there?

In fact, on the ACT there are always just five—the five possible answer choices—and one of them has to be the correct answer. Let's try doing the problem backward. To do this, you take the answer choices one at a time and put them into the equation to see which one makes the equation work. With which choice should we begin?

The one in the middle. Numeric answers are always presented in order on this test, from least to greatest. There are three steps to **Working Backward.**

1. Start with the middle answer—(C) or (H).
2. If it's too big, go to the next smaller choice.
3. If it's too small, go to the next larger choice.

Here's the problem again.

1. If $3x + 7 = 28$, what is x ?

A. 4
B. 5
C. 6
D. 7
E. 8

Here's How to Crack It

Let's start with (C): 3(6) + 7 equals only 25. Could this be the right answer? No, it's supposed to equal 28. Do we need a smaller or a larger x? Because we need a larger number, we can immediately knock out (A) and (B). Let's try (D). 3 times (7) + 7 = 28. Bingo! We have our answer.

Note that if (D) had still been too small, the only possible answer would have been (E), and you would not have had to check it. Remember, if you've eliminated 4 wrong answers, what's left *must* be right. One of the great things about Working Backward is that you will usually have to do only two actual calculations. You start with (C). If (C) is correct, you're done. If (C) is too big, then you're down to (A) and (B). Now you try (B). If (B) is correct, you're done. If it isn't, you're still done. The answer must be the only remaining choice: (A).

Now we know that many of you are thinking, "This technique is a waste of time. It would have been way easier to just solve for x." You know what? You're right. On this example, solving for x would have been easier, but if you don't learn how to do the Working Backward technique on easy questions, you won't be able to do it effectively on more complex questions (and believe us, the questions get *much* more complex). So do yourself a favor and use Working Backward on these easy questions so that you have a good feel for it when it's time to do the tough ones.

Let's Do It Again

Here's another problem.

2. If \$600 was deposited in a bank account for one year and earned interest of \$42, what was the interest rate?

F. 6.26%
G. 7.00%
H. 8.00%
J. 9.00%
K. 9.50%

Which Way?
Sometimes, it's hard to tell which way to work backward after eliminating (C). Should you go higher or lower? Don't fret; just pick a direction and try. Find a choice with an easy-to-manipulate number. It may turn out to be wrong, but it won't take long to find out. It may also tell you whether to go higher or lower.

Here's How to Crack It

Of course, we could write an equation. On the contrary, one of these answer choices is correct, and all we have to do is find out which one it is. Why not work backward?

We'll start, as always, in the middle, this time with (H). If the interest rate is 8 percent, then 8 percent of 600 should equal 42. Use percent translation (and your calculator) to check the equation: Does $\frac{8}{100} \times 600 = 42$? Nope—it equals 48, which means our percentage is too large. Eliminate (H), (J), and (K), and try (G).

Does $\frac{7}{100} \times 600 = 42$? It does, so we circle (G) and continue on to the next problem.

How Do You Know When to Work Backward?

You can *always* work backward when you see numbers in the answer choices and when the question asked in the last line of the problem is relatively straightforward. For example, if there are numbers in the answer choices and the question asks, "What is x?" you can work backward.

However, if the question asks instead, "What is the difference between x and y?" then you probably don't want to work backward. In this case, the answers won't give us a value to try for either x or y.

The Reverse Question

Sometimes the ACT test writers will make your job even easier by giving you the value for the variable within the question itself.

1. What is the value of $3x^2 + 5x - 7$ when $x = -1$?

A. –15
B. –9
C. –1
D. 5
E. 15

Here's How to Crack It

There is still only one number in the world that will satisfy this question, and in this case, you know what x is supposed to be. This time the ACT test writers ask you to find the value of the entire polynomial. (A **polynomial** is a type of equation.) These problems are about as easy as this test gets.

Note that it would be pointless to work backward on this problem, because the answer choices don't give you possible values for x but rather for the entire polynomial. Simply plug –1 into the polynomial and solve.

$$3(-1)^2 + 5(-1) - 7 =$$
$$3 - 5 - 7 = -9$$

Choice (B) is the correct answer.

Now There's a Choice

When you are asked to find a particular value for x, you have a choice: You can solve for x or you can work backward. There are times when one technique is more suitable than the other, but as we cover different algebra topics in this chapter—factoring, quadratics, inequalities—we will keep returning to the concept of Working Backward. You will find it extremely useful, particularly on the more difficult questions that you might not want to take the time to solve the old-fashioned way. That's why we now want you to practice Working Backward on the easier questions.

WHEN *X* HAS NO PARTICULAR VALUE: THE COSMIC EQUATION

Now let's look at the following problem:

1. What is 5 more than the product of 4 and a certain number x ?

A. $4x - 5$
B. $4x$
C. $-x$
D. $5x - 4$
E. $4x + 5$

In this problem, there is *no* one value for x. The variable x could be 5 or 105 or –317. In fact, the ACT test writers are asking you to create an expression that will answer this question no matter what the "certain number" is.

In other words, this is a cosmic problem. The correct answer choice will be correct *for any value of x*. There are two methods for approaching cosmic problems.

Translation Revisited

On the ACT, many word problems require you to translate English terms into their math equivalents. In Chapter 11, we discussed using translation to tackle word problems dealing with percentages; on many of the algebraic problems you're tasked with, you'll want to use the same method. We've expanded the percent translation table to include some of the common phrases you'll find in algebra questions.

ACT English →	ACT Math
is (any form of the verb "be") is the same as	=
of *product* *times*	× (multiplication)
what *a certain number*	*x, y, z* (your favorite variable)
percent	100 (Alternatively, we could use "over 100.")
30 percent	$\frac{30}{100}$
what percent	$\frac{x}{100}$
more than	+ (addition)
less than	– (subtraction)

Let's translate the problem word for word.

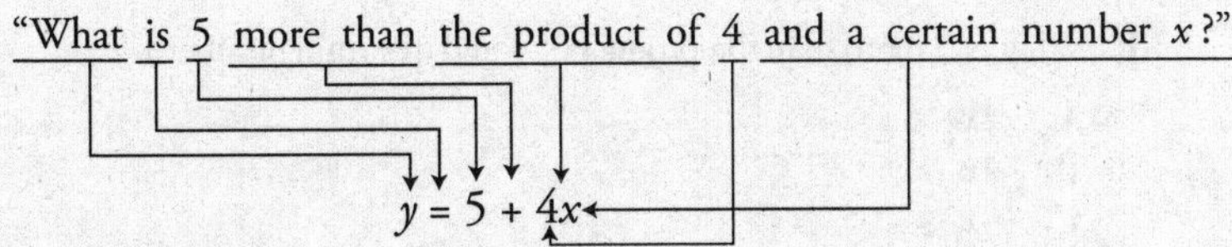

Does this look like any of the answer choices? Yes—(E).

While translation is a fine way to solve this problem, we want you to try thinking about cosmic problems in a slightly different way. If a problem is truly cosmic—if the correct answer is correct for *every* value of "a certain number"—then it should be correct for *any* value you can think of, right?

A Few More Translations/Math Terms

English	Math
more than	+ (addition)
the sum of	+ (addition)
increased by	+ (addition)
is added to	+ (addition)

The Other Method Is Plugging In

Why don't we pick our own value? Let's make $x = 7$. (Why? Why not? We could just as easily have chosen 5 or 12 or whatever you like. Try it and see.) The advantage of using a specific number is that our minds do not think naturally in terms of variables. We don't go into a store and ask for an x-pack of soda. We have a specific number in mind. There are three steps involved in **Plugging In**.

1. Pick numbers for the variables in the problem (and write them down).
2. Using your numbers, find an answer to the problem.
3. Plug your numbers into the answer choices to see which choice equals the answer you found in step 2.

Here's the problem again.

1. What is 5 more than the product of 4 and a certain number x ?

A. $4x - 5$
B. $4x$
C. $-x$
D. $5x - 4$
E. $4x + 5$

Here's How to Crack It

Let's make $x = 7$. In the space over the x in the problem above, write down "7." Now, let's figure it out. Reread the question with "7" for the x. The product of 4 and 7 is 28. 5 more than 28 is 33. So, if $x = 7$, then the answer to the question is 33. We're done. All we have to do now is check to see which of the answer choices equals 33.

- Let's start with (A). Because $x = 7$, $4(7) - 5 = 23$. Not the answer.
- Let's look at (E). Because $x = 7$, $4(7) + 5 = 33$. The answer is (E).

You might be thinking, "Wait a minute. It was easier to solve this problem algebraically. Why should I plug in?" There are a couple of reasons.

- This was an easy problem. Plugging In makes even difficult problems easy, so you should learn how to do it by practicing on the easy ones, just as we advised with the Working Backward technique for particular *x* problems.
- The ACT test writers try to anticipate how you might mess up this problem using algebra. If you make one of these common mistakes, your answer will be among the answer choices; you will pick it and get it wrong.

Get Real
There's nothing abstract about the ACT. So if a problem says Tina is x years old, why not plug in your own age? That's real enough. You don't have to change your name to Tina.

How Do You Spot a Cosmic Problem?

Any problem with variables in the answer choices is a cosmic problem. You may not choose to plug in on every one of these, but you *could* plug in on *all* of them. However, there are also some cosmic problems that do *not* have variables in the answer choices. For example,

16. A number q has a remainder of 5 when divided by 6. What is the remainder when $3q$ is divided by 6 ?

F. 0
G. 1
H. 3
J. 4
K. 15

Here's How to Crack It

In this case, the unknown is very explicitly stated, so we can go ahead and think of a number that fits the bill. First and foremost, we must choose a number that satisfies the restrictions imposed by the question. When we divide q by 6, we must have 5 left over. Could we make $q = 12$? Definitely not, because it would divide evenly and leave 0 as the remainder. We could, however, make q equal to 17; if we divided $\frac{17}{6}$, we would be able to divide evenly only twice (giving us 12). What's the remainder? $17 - 12$ would leave us with 5, so we know our numbers work.

Let's move to the second step in the problem: What would the remainder be if $3q$ were divided by 6? In our scenario, $3q$ would equal 51. How many times can we divide 6 into 51? Only 8 times, because $6 \times 8 = 48$. How much is left over before we get to 51? Only 3. Thus, our answer is (H).

So Now There's Another Choice

When x has *no* particular value, you also have a choice: You can translate or you can plug in. There are times when one technique is more suitable than the other. As we cover the different algebra topics in this chapter, we will keep returning to the concept of Plugging In.

FACTORING

Many ACT problems involve factoring of one kind or another. Here is the most basic kind of factoring problem.

$$x^2 + 7x + 12 = ?$$

Some Numbers Are Better than Others

In that last problem, only certain numbers could be plugged in for q—numbers that agreed with the conditions set forth in the problem.

In most cosmic problems, you can pick any number you like. However, there are some numbers that work better than others. In general, you might want to stick to small numbers just because they're easier to work with. If a problem is about days and weeks, 7 might be a particularly good number. If the problem is about percents, 100 is probably a good number.

Some numbers to avoid are 0, 1, and numbers that are already being used in the problem. Why? If you plug in one of these numbers, you may find that more than one answer choice appears to be correct.

If your calculator can solve quadratics, now's the time to make sure you know how to put it through its paces.

To factor this expression by hand, put it into the following format, and start by looking for the factors of the first and last terms. Note that the factors for the last term have to meet two conditions: Their product is the last term and their sum is the coefficient of the second term.

$$x^2 + 7x + 12 =$$
$$(\quad)(\quad) =$$
$$(x \quad)(x \quad) =$$
$$(x \quad 3)(x \quad 4) =$$
$$(x + 3)(x + 4) =$$

To ensure that you've factored correctly, you can also use the FOIL (First, Outer, Inner, Last) method to check your math. Let's try it on the above polynomial.

1. First—multiply the first two terms in each polynomial: $(x)(x)$. The result should equal the first term of your quadratic expression: x^2.
2. Outer/Inner—multiply the outer terms from each polynomial: $(x)(4)$. Do the same with the inner terms: $(3)(x)$. Add the two terms to arrive at the middle term of your quadratic expression: $3x + 4x = 7x$.
3. Last—multiply the last terms in each polynomial: $(3)(4)$. This should be equal to the last term in your quadratic expression: 12.
4. When you add your First, Outer, Inner, and Last terms together, you get back to where you started.

$$x^2 + 7x + 12$$

The ACT test writers might use that last expression to make a problem like this.

---

1. If $\dfrac{x^2+7x+12}{(x+4)} = 5$, for $x \neq -4$ then $x = ?$

A. 1
B. 2
C. 3
D. 5
E. 6

Here's How to Crack It

This is a specific x question. If we factor the top expression as we did a moment ago, we get.

$$\frac{(x+3)(x+4)}{(x+4)} = 5$$

Now we can cancel the $(x + 4)$s, with the result that $x + 3 = 5$. To get rid of the 3, we subtract it from both sides. Now $x = 2$, and the answer is (B).

POE Pointers

1. Note that, like all specific x problems, this could also have been solved by Working Backward.
2. If there isn't an obvious clue, try thinking of factors of the last term (2 and 6; 3 and 4) and then checking if their sum matches the coefficient of the middle term.
3. If you were having trouble factoring $x^2 + 7x + 12$, it may have helped to wonder why—of all the numbers in the world—ACT picked $(x + 4)$ as the denominator of its problem. It was almost bound to be one of the factors of the polynomial in the numerator. Always look for clues in the question itself or in the answer choices when dealing with factoring questions.

---

1. If $\dfrac{x^2 + 7x + 12}{(x + 4)} = 5$, then $x = ?$

A. 1
B. 2
C. 3
D. 5
E. 6

Here's How to Crack It

The question asks, "What is x?" Let's start with 3—(C).

$$\frac{(3)^2 + 7(3) + 12}{(3 + 4)}$$

$$= \frac{9 + 21 + 12}{7}$$

$$= \frac{42}{7}$$

$$= 6$$

Because the answer was supposed to be 5, we know that we need a smaller x. Eliminate answer choices (C), (D), and (E). Let's try 2.

$$\frac{(2)^2+7(2)+12}{(2+4)}$$
$$=\frac{4+14+12}{6}$$
$$=5$$

Again, the answer is (B).

The same kind of equation could have been used in a cosmic problem.

1. For all $x \neq -3$, which of the following is equivalent to the expression $\frac{x^2-x-12}{x+3}$?

A. $x-4$
B. $x-2$
C. $x+2$
D. $x+4$
E. $x+6$

Here's How to Crack It

Again, we could solve this by factoring.

$$x^2-x-12=$$
$$(\quad)(\quad)$$
$$(x\quad)(x\quad)$$
$$(x\ \ 4)(x\ \ 3)$$
$$(x-4)(x+3)$$

Therefore, we can write the problem as $\frac{(x-4)(x+3)}{(x+3)}$.

The $(x+3)$s cancel and we get $(x-4)$, or (A).

POE Pointers

1. As in the preceding problem, if you were having trouble factoring v $x^2 - x - 12$, it may have helped to wonder why—of all the numbers in the world—ACT picked $(x + 3)$ as the denominator of its problem. It was almost bound to be one of the factors of the polynomial in the numerator.
2. Because this was a cosmic problem (variables in the answer choices), we also could have done this problem by Plugging In.

Here's how. Let's choose a value for *x*. How about 3?

$$\frac{(3)^2 - (3) - 12}{(3+3)}$$

$$= \frac{9 - 3 - 12}{6}$$

$$= \frac{-6}{6}$$

$$= -1$$

Now all we have to do is plug 3 (our value for *x*) into the answer choices to see which one gets us the answer –1. Let's try (F), *x* – 4. Bingo.

$$3 - 4 = -1$$

Factoring: Advanced Principles

More advanced factoring problems set a factorable expression equal to zero. This is called a **quadratic equation.**

$$x^2 + 7x + 6 =$$
$$(\quad)(\quad) =$$
$$(x \quad)(x \quad) =$$
$$(x \quad 6)(x \quad 1) =$$
$$(x + 6)(x + 1) =$$

Quadratic equations often have two values that solve the equation. In this example, *x* could be either –6 or –1. These two solutions are sometimes called the **roots** or **zeros** of the equation. Let's try an ACT-type quadratic equation.

1. What is the positive value of x in the equation $2x^2 - 4x - 6 = 0$?

A. -1
B. 2
C. 3
D. 4
E. 6

Here's How to Crack It

Before we can factor the expression the way we did in the previous problems, we need to reduce it. Look to see if all of the terms have any factor in common. Yes, each of the terms can be divided by 2.

$$\frac{2x^2}{2} - \frac{4x}{2} - \frac{6}{2} = \frac{0}{2}$$

Let's rewrite the equation.

$$2\left(x^2 - 2x - 3\right) = 0$$

Now we can factor. The expression becomes.

$$2(x+1)(x-3) = 0$$

x could equal -1 or 3. Unfortunately, both our values are among the answer choices. Which one is correct? If we reread the question, we realize that we were asked to find the *positive* value of x. Therefore, the answer is 3, (C).

POE Pointers

1. Because the problem asked us for a *positive* value, we should have crossed out (A) even before we factored the expression. If we had done this, we would not have been tempted by it when we finished factoring and discovered it was one of the solutions to the problem.
2. This was a particular *x* problem. That's right; you could have worked backward. Start with (C) and put it back into the equation. Does $2(3)^2 - 4(3) - 6 = 0$? It sure does. The answer must be (C).

A warning: When you work backward with a quadratic problem, remember that there may be two solutions. The problem will usually find a way to ask you for only one of them, but sometimes the ACT test writers will ask you for the *sum* or the *product* of the two solutions. Remember what we said before: If a question asks, "What is *x*?" you can work backward; if a question asks, "What is *x* + *y*?" then you probably can't.

The ACT's Three Favorite Quadratics

The test writers are really fond of three quadratic equations in particular. The first is called the difference of perfect squares (although the name isn't important).

$$x^2 - y^2 = (x + y)(x - y)$$

For some reason, they use this one all the time. You should just memorize it. The idea is that whenever you see this expression in the form on the left, you should immediately put it into the form on the right. If you see it in the form on the right, you should immediately put it into the form on the left. That's all there is to it. Here's an example.

The ACT's Favorite Factors

Train yourself to recognize these quadratic expressions instantly in both factored and unfactored form:

$x^2 - y^2 = (x + y)(x - y)$

$x^2 + 2xy + y^2 = (x + y)^2$

$x^2 - 2xy + y^2 = (x - y)^2$

Learn them, love them. Better yet, if your calculator can factor quadratics, use these to make sure you know how to use that function.

1. If for all $x \neq -3$, $\dfrac{x^2 - 9}{x + 3} = 12$, then x = ?

A. 10
B. 15
C. 17
D. 19
E. 20

Here's How to Crack It

Do you recognize the form of the numerator? Great, so let's factor it.

$$\frac{(x+3)(x-3)}{(x+3)}=12$$

Now we can cancel the $(x + 3)$ terms and are left with $(x - 3)$. The answer is 15, or (B).

POE Pointers

Could you have worked backward to solve this problem? Yes, although it wouldn't have been much fun squaring those large numbers. In this case, it was definitely faster to solve by factoring if you recognized the difference of perfect squares.

The two other quadratic equations ACT test writers are fond of are these.

$$x^2+2xy+y^2=(x+y)^2$$

$$x^2-2xy+y^2=(x-y)^2$$

As with the difference of perfect squares, the important thing is to recognize the two forms that each of these equations takes. Whichever form is used in the problem, the solution lies in immediately putting it into its *other* form. Memorize both forms and look for them on the test.

SIMULTANEOUS EQUATIONS

If you see one equation with two variables, can you solve for either variable? For example, if $x + y = 4$, do we know exactly what x and y equal? No. If x is 2, then y is 2, but if x is 3, then y is 1. You can *never* solve one equation with two variables. However, if there are *two* equations, each of which contains the same two variables, then you can solve it using a process known as simultaneous equations. An easy problem might look like the problem on the following page.

If $4x + 2y = 5$ and $6x - 2y = 15$, then what is x?

To solve, set one equation above the other and add or subtract one equation to or from the other so that one of the variables disappears.

$$\begin{array}{r} 4x+2y=5 \\ +6x-2y=15 \\ \hline 10x \quad\;\; =20 \end{array}$$

$$x = 2$$

In more difficult simultaneous equations, you'll find that neither of the variables will disappear when you try to add or subtract the two equations. In such cases, you must multiply both sides of one of the equations by some number to get the coefficient in front of the variable you want to disappear to be the same in both equations.

This sounds more complicated than it really is. A difficult problem might look like this:

2 Variables—2 Equations
You can't solve one equation with two variables. But if you have two different equations with the same two variables, you're in business.

1. What is the value of y in the system of equations below?

$3x+4y=5 \qquad 6x+2y=2$

A. $\frac{4}{3}$

B. $\frac{8}{3}$

C. 6

D. 7

E. 9

Here's How to Crack It

Line up the two equations.

$$3x+4y=5$$

$$6x+2y=2$$

Because we want to end up with a value for y, we need to make x disappear. To do this, let's multiply the entire top equation by 2.

$$6x + 8y = 10$$
$$6x + 2y = 2$$

When we subtract one equation from the other, all the x's will disappear.

$$\begin{array}{r} 6x + 8y = 10 \\ -6x + 2y = 2 \\ \hline 6y = 8 \end{array}$$

$y = \frac{8}{6}$ or $\frac{4}{3}$, and the answer is (A).

INEQUALITIES

There is one difference between an inequality and an equality. You solve both in exactly the same way, except that when you multiply or divide both sides of an inequality by a negative number, the direction of the inequality sign flips. Here's an example.

Warning!
When you multiply or divide an inequality by a negative number, you must reverse the inequality sign.

$$\begin{array}{ll} 3x + 7 > 28 & -3x + 7 > 28 \\ -7 \quad -7 & -7 \quad -7 \\ 3x > 21 & -3x > 21 \\ \frac{3x}{3} > \frac{21}{3} & \frac{-3x}{-3} < \frac{21}{-3} \\ x > 7 & x < -7 \end{array}$$

Because most inequalities on the ACT involve graphing, we will be discussing them in more detail in the Graphing and Coordinate Geometry chapter.

LOGARITHMS

$\log_x y = z$ means $x^z = y$

Logarithm questions are not too common on the ACT (at most, one per test), but they *do* come up, and they're not too tough once you understand how they work. Logarithms are just another form of notation for exponents, and you know how to deal with exponents, right?

Take a look at the formula above. Let's work it from right to left, because the stuff on the right is that with which people are most familiar.

As you know, $5^2 = 25$. Well, as a logarithm, you'd write that as $\log_5 25 = 2$. Compare that with the formula on the previous page and you'll see how to go from one to the other. Now if ACT were to give you $\log_5 25 = x$ and ask what x was, you'd know that it's 2 because you have to raise 5 to the 2nd power to get 25.

Try this one.

41. If $\log_x 32 = 5$, what is the value of x ?

A. 1
B. 2
C. 5
D. 6.4
E. 27

Here's How to Crack It

Use the formula in the box above to rewrite this in simple exponential form and you'll be on the way to the answer.

According to your formula, $\log_x 32 = 5$ is the same as $x^5 = 32$.

So you can plug in the answers and see which one works here.

Let's start in the middle with (C). If $x = 5$, then we've got $5^5 = 32$, but that's not right because $5^5 = 3{,}125$, not 32. (C) is clearly way too big, so we can eliminate it, as well as (D) and (E), and move on to something smaller.

So let's try (B). If $x = 2$, we have $2^5 = 32$. Yep, that's right, so we're done. The answer is (B).

Algebra Drill

1. If $x = -3$, then $\frac{(x+3)(x-3)}{9} = ?$

A. 0
B. 1
C. 3
D. 5
E. 6

2. What is the largest value of x that solves the equation $x^2 - 4x + 3 = 0$?

F. 1
G. 2
H. 3
J. 4
K. 5

3. If $x + 2y = 8$ and $\frac{x}{2} - y = 10$, then $x = ?$

A. −7
B. 0
C. 10
D. 14
E. 28

4. For all $x \neq -9$, $\frac{x^2 + 6x - 27}{(x+9)} = ?$

F. $x + 9$
G. $x - 3$
H. $x + 3$
J. $2x - 4$
K. $2x + 3$

5. If 2 less than 3 times a certain number is the same as 4 more than the product of 5 and 3, what is the number?

A. 7
B. 10
C. 11
D. 14
E. 15

6. A certain number of books are to be given away at a promotion. If $\frac{2}{5}$ of the books are distributed in the morning and $\frac{1}{3}$ of the remaining books are distributed in the afternoon, what fraction of the books remains to be distributed the next day?

F. $\frac{1}{5}$
G. $\frac{2}{5}$
H. $\frac{1}{3}$
J. $\frac{5}{7}$
K. $\frac{8}{9}$

Summary

- There are two main types of algebra questions on the ACT: particular value questions, which ask you to solve for a particular x, and no particular value questions, otherwise known as cosmic problems.
- On particular value questions, you can use algebra or you can work backward from the answer choices. Working Backward is frequently easier. When you work backward, begin with the middle answer choice to see whether you need a larger number or a smaller number. You can always work backward if you see specific numbers in the answer choices and the question in the last line is relatively straightforward.
- On cosmic problems, you can use algebra or you can plug in. Plugging In is frequently easier. You can always plug in if you see variables in the answer choices or if the problem itself does not depend on specific numbers.
- You must know how to factor quadratic equations. ACT's favorites are $x^2 + 2xy + y^2 = (x + y)^2$, $x^2 - 2xy + y^2 = (x - y)^2$, and $x^2 - y^2 = (x + y)(x - y)$. Remember that many quadratic problems can be solved by Working Backward, Plugging In, or using FOIL.
- In solving simultaneous equations, add or subtract one equation to or from another so that one of the two variables disappears. You can also Work Backward if you're having trouble solving the equation.
- When you solve an inequality, remember that if you multiply or divide by a negative number, the sign flips.

Chapter 13 Geometry

The ACT test writers tell us there will be 23 geometry questions on the Math test. Fortunately, the types of geometry questions you'll see won't deal with proofs, theorems, or complex three-dimensional figures. Instead, you'll need to focus on a small cross-section of very commonly tested formulas and concepts. This chapter primarily deals with plane geometry, which appears in 14 questions on the ACT Math test.

Even if geometry was your least favorite subject in school, you should count on getting most of the ACT geometry questions correct after you've finished reading this chapter. They are trickier than they are difficult, as long as you know your rules.

PRELIMINARY TIPS ON CRACKING ACT GEOMETRY

Before we begin our review, however, ask yourself the following important questions:

All a Matter of Degree
Degrees in a circle: 360
Degrees in a line: 180
Degrees in a perpendicular angle: 90
Degrees in a triangle: 180
Degrees in quadrilateral: 360

To Scale or Not to Scale?

That is the question. In the instructions to the Math portion of the ACT, the test writers say that the diagrams are "NOT necessarily drawn to scale." On the contrary, in the ACT's own *The Real ACT,* one of the suggested strategies is to use the diagrams to estimate the correct answer. The book says that "some of the figures are reasonably accurate."

We didn't think measuring the diagrams would be a very successful strategy if some of them were accurate and some of them weren't. So we carefully measured the diagrams on every geometry problem of every ACT test we could get our hands on. The results? EVERY diagram was drawn EXACTLY to scale. When we asked an ACT spokesperson about this, he said that ACT diagrams were never intended to be misleading, but that there might be rare instances in which it was impossible to draw a problem to scale. Because we couldn't find a single one of these problems, you should consider it a very rare possibility indeed.

POE and Crazy Answers

In the previous chapters, you've seen how POE can be used to prevent picking careless or partial answers when you know how to do a problem. You've also seen how POE can narrow down the range of reasonable answers when you *don't* know how to do a problem and just need to guess.

In geometry, because the problems are *always* drawn to scale, it will be possible to get very close approximations of the correct answers *before you even do the problems.*

How Big Is Angle *NLM*?

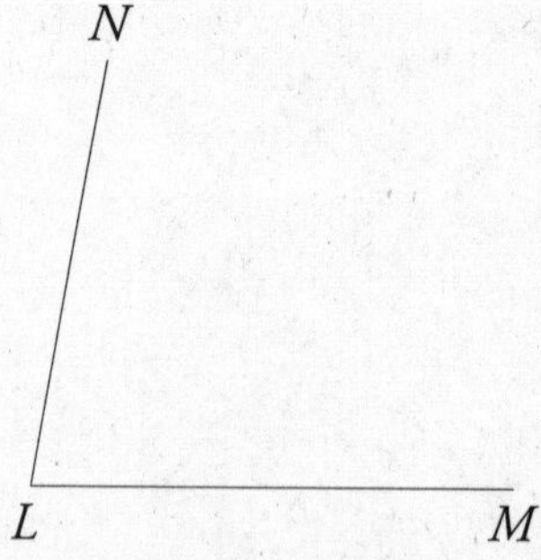

Obviously, you don't know exactly how big this angle is, but it would be easy to compare it with an angle whose measure you *do* know exactly. Let's compare it with a 90-degree angle.

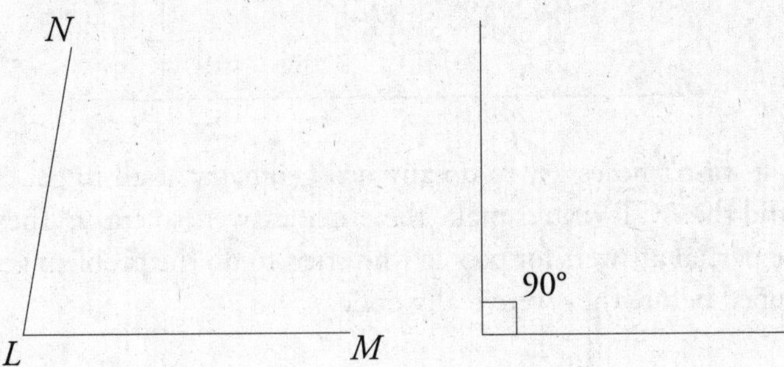

Angle *NLM* is clearly a bit less than 90°. Now look at the following problem, which asks about the same angle *NLM*.

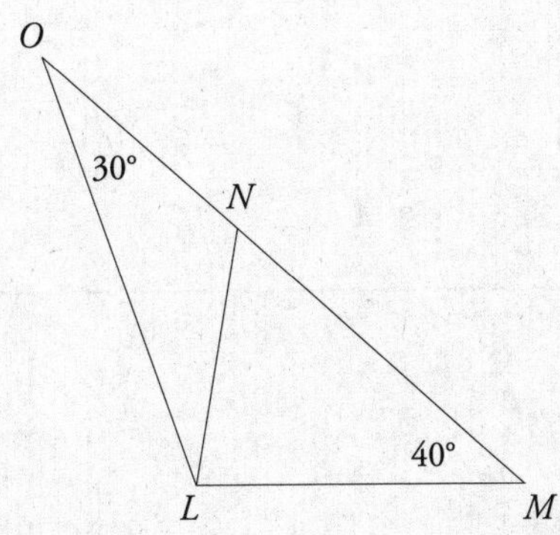

1. In the figure above, *O*, *N*, and *M* are collinear. If the lengths of $\overline{ON}$ and $\overline{NL}$ are the same, and the measure of angle *LON* is 30° and angle *LMN* is 40°, what is the measure of angle *NLM* ?

A. 40
B. 80
C. 90
D. 120
E. 150

Here's How to Crack It

This is a relatively easy problem, and we will show you its geometric solution later in the chapter (as well as explaining terms like "collinear" and which angle is meant by angle *LON*).

For now, however, let's focus on eliminating answer choices that don't make sense. We've already decided that $\angle NLM$ is a little less than 90°, which means we can eliminate (C), (D), and (E). How much less than 90°? 40° is less than half of 90°. Could angle *NLM* be that small? Of course not. The answer to this question must be (B).

In this case, it wasn't necessary to do any real geometry at all to get the question right. Why did the ACT writers make the other answers so crazy? They wanted to include some partial answers for people who tried to do the problem geometrically but who stopped before they were really done.

For example, students who used the information that segments $\overline{ON}$ and $\overline{NL}$ were the same may have realized that triangle *ONL* is isosceles (has two equal sides) and that $\angle ONL$ is equal to 120°. This was a possible first step to getting the correct answer geometrically. However, if they felt carried away with their own brilliance at getting this far and looked straight to the answers, the folks at ACT wanted 120° to be one of the possible answer choices.

Let's Do It Again

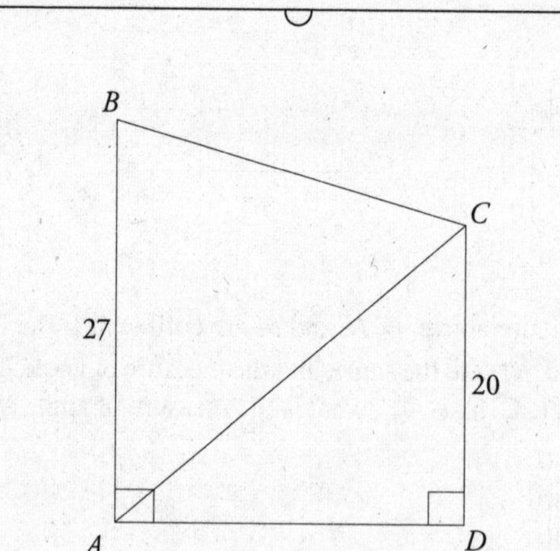

2. In the figure above, if $\overline{AB} = 27$, $\overline{CD} = 20$, and the area of triangle $ADC = 240$, what is the area of polygon $ABCD$?

   F. 420
   G. 480
   H. 540
   J. 564
   K. 1,128

Here's How to Crack It

Again, we will solve this problem using geometry a little later in the chapter. For now, let's concentrate on eliminating crazy answers. This polygon is not a conventional figure, but if we had to choose one figure that the polygon resembled, we might pick a rectangle. Try drawing a line at a right angle from the line segment $\overline{AB}$ so that it touches point C, thus creating a rectangle. It should look like this:

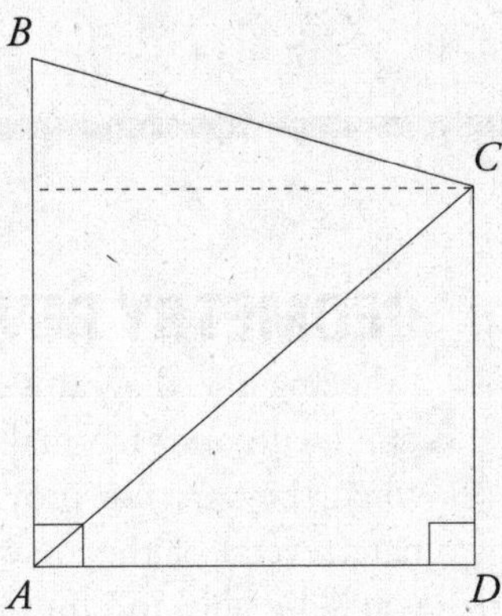

The area of polygon *ABCD* is equal to the area of the rectangle you've just formed, plus a little bit at the top. The problem tells you that the area of triangle *ADC* is 240. What is the area of the rectangle you just created? If you said 480, you are exactly right, whether you knew the geometric rules that applied or whether you just measured it with your eyes.

So the area of the rectangle is 480. Roughly speaking, then, what should the area of the polygon be? A little more. Let's look at the answer choices. (F) and (G) are either less than or equal to 480; get rid of them. Choices (H) and (J) both seem possible; they are both a little more than 480; let's hold on to them. Answer choice (K) seems pretty crazy. We want more than 480, but 1,128 is ridiculous.

Thus, on this problem, which was of medium difficulty, we were able to eliminate three of the five answer choices without doing any real geometry. Now what should you do? If you know how to do the problem, you do it. If you don't or if you are running out of time, you guess and move on.

Important Approximations

In some cases, you may want to estimate problems that contain answer choices with radicals or π. Here are some useful approximations.

$$\sqrt{2} \approx 1.4$$
$$\sqrt{3} \approx 1.7$$
$$\pi \approx 3+$$

What Should I Do if There Is No Diagram?
Draw one! It's always easier to understand a problem when you can see it in front of you. If possible, draw your figure to scale so that you can estimate the answer as well.

GEOMETRY REVIEW

By using the diagrams ACT has so thoughtfully provided, and by making your own diagrams when they are not provided, you can often eliminate several of the answer choices. In some cases, you'll be able to eliminate every choice but one. Of course, you will also need to know the actual geometry concepts that ACT is testing. We've divided our review into the following four topics:

1. Angles and lines
2. Triangles
3. Four-sided figures
4. Circles

ANGLES AND LINES

Here is a line.

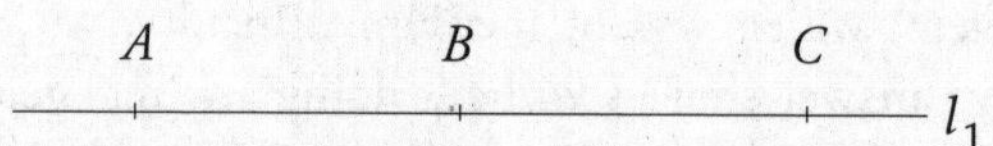

A line extends forever in either direction. This line, called l_1, has three points on it: *A*, *B*, and *C*. These three points are said to be **collinear** because they are all on the same line. The piece of the line in between points *A* and *B* is called a line **segment**. ACT will refer to it as segment *AB* or simply $\overline{AB}$. *A* and *B* are the **endpoints** of segment *AB*.

A line forms an angle of 180°. If that line is cut by another line, it divides that 180° into two pieces that together add up to 180°.

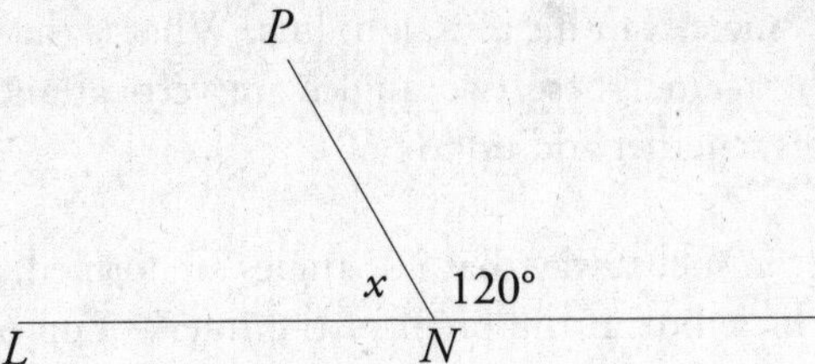

In the above diagram, what is the value of x? If you said 60°, you are correct. To find $\angle x$, just subtract 120° from 180°.

An angle can also be described by points on the lines that intersect to form the angle and the point of intersection itself, with the middle letter corresponding to the point of intersection. For example, in the previous diagram, $\angle x$ could also be described as $\angle LNP$. On the ACT, instead of writing out "angle LNP," they'll use math shorthand and put $\angle LNP$ instead. So "angle x" becomes $\angle x$.

If there are 180° above a line, there are also 180° below the line, for a total of 360°.

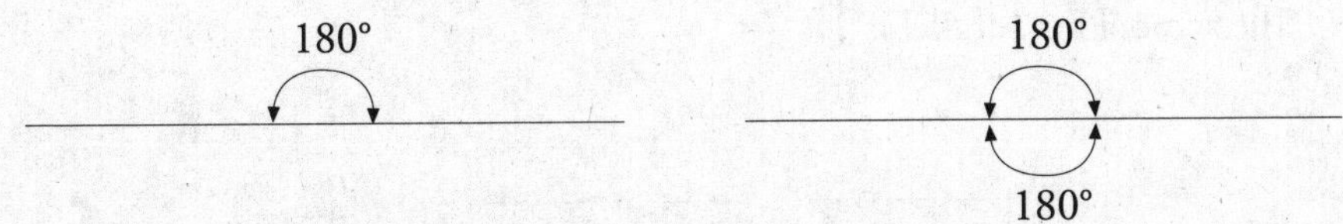

When two lines intersect, they form four angles, represented below by letters A, B, C, and D. $\angle A$ and $\angle B$ together form a straight line, so they add up to 180°.

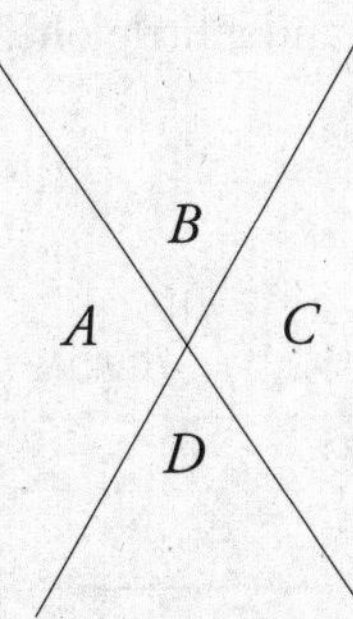

Angles that add up to 180° are called **supplementary** angles. $\angle A$ and $\angle C$ are opposite from each other and always equal each other, as do $\angle B$ and $\angle D$. Angles like these are called **vertical** angles.

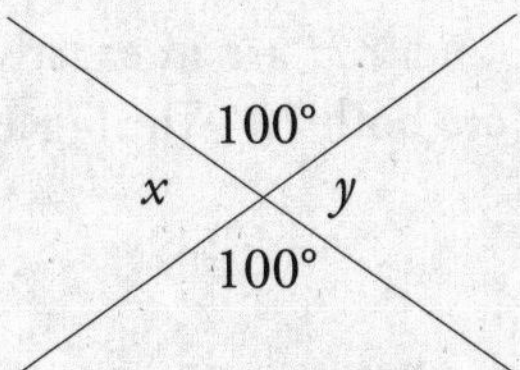

In the previous figure, what is the value of $\angle x$? If you said 80°, you're right. Together with the 100° angle, x forms a straight line. What is the value of $\angle y$? If you said 80°, you're right again. These two angles are vertical and must equal each other. The four angles together add up to 360°.

When two lines meet in such a way that 90° angles are formed, the lines are called **perpendicular.** The little box at the point of the intersection of the two lines below indicates that they are perpendicular. It stands to reason that all four of these angles have a value of 90°.

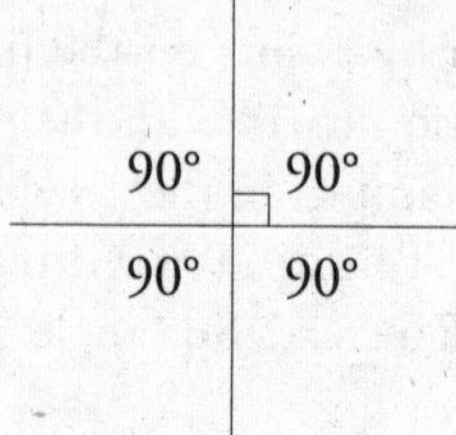

When two lines in the same plane are drawn so that they could extend into infinity without ever meeting, they are called **parallel.** In the figure below, l_1 is parallel to l_2. The symbol for parallel is $||$.

When two parallel lines are cut by a third line, eight angles are formed, but in fact, there are really only two—a big one and a little one. Look at the diagram below.

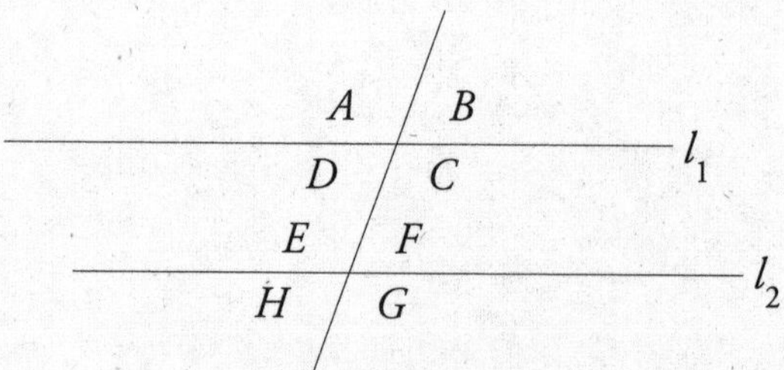

If $\angle A = 110°$, then $\angle B$ must equal 70° (together they form a straight line). $\angle D$ is vertical to $\angle B$, which means that it must also equal 70°. $\angle C$ is vertical to $\angle A$, so it must equal 110°.

The four angles $\angle E$, $\angle F$, $\angle G$, and $\angle H$ are in exactly the same proportion as the angles above. The little angles are both 70°. The big angles are both 110°.

Try the following problem.

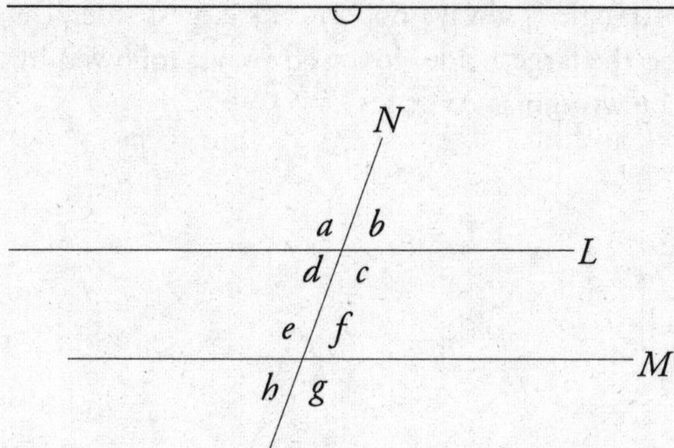

1. In the figure above, line L is parallel to line M. Line N intersects both L and M, with angles a, b, c, d, e, f, g, and h as shown. Which of the following lists includes all the angles that are supplementary to $\angle a$?

   A. Angles b, d, f, and h
   B. Angles c, e, and g
   C. Angles b, d, and c
   D. Angles e, f, g, and h
   E. Angles d, c, h, and g

Here's How to Crack It

An angle is supplementary to another angle if the two angles together add up to 180°. Because $\angle a$ is one of the eight angles formed by the intersection of a line with two parallel lines, we know that there are really only two angles: a big one and a little one. $\angle a$ is a big one. Thus only the small angles would be supplementary to it. Which angles are those? The correct answer is (A). By the way, if you think back to the last chapter and apply what you learned there, could you have plugged in on this problem? Of course you could have. After all, there are variables in the answer choices. Sometimes it is easier to see the correct answer if you substitute real values for the angles instead of just looking at them as a series of variables. Just because a problem involves geometry doesn't mean that you can't plug in on it.

$a = 100°$ $b = 80°$ L
$d = 80°$ $c = 100°$
$e = 100°$ $f = 80°$ M
$h = 80°$ $g = 100°$

TRIANGLES

A triangle is a three-sided figure whose inside angles always add up to 180°. The largest angle of a triangle is always opposite its largest side. Thus, in triangle *xyz* below, *xy* would be the largest side, followed by *yz*, followed by *xz*. On the ACT, "triangle *xyz*" will be written as Δxyz.

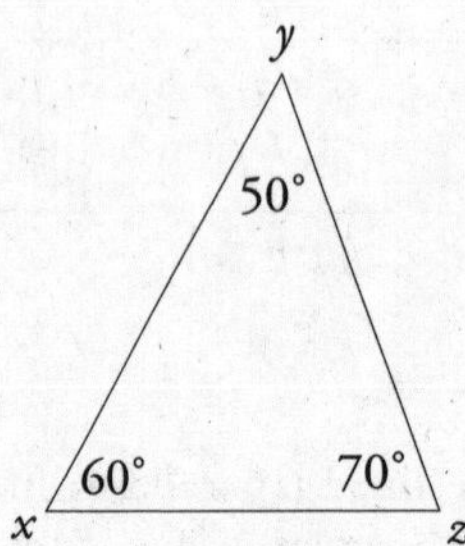

The ACT likes to ask about certain kinds of triangles in particular.

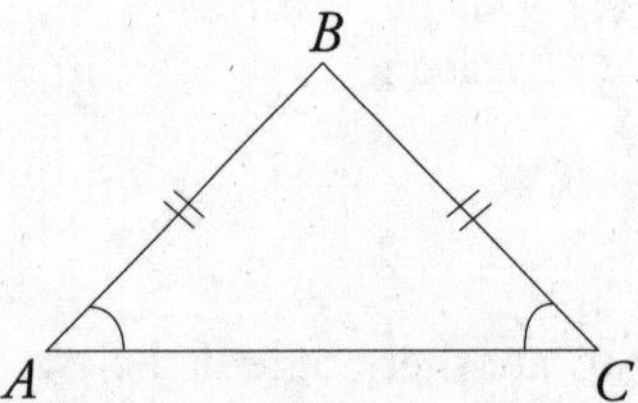

An **isosceles** triangle has two equal sides. The angles opposite those sides are also equal. In the isosceles triangle above, if $\angle A = 50°$, then so does $\angle C$. If $\overline{AB} = 6$, then so does $\overline{BC}$.

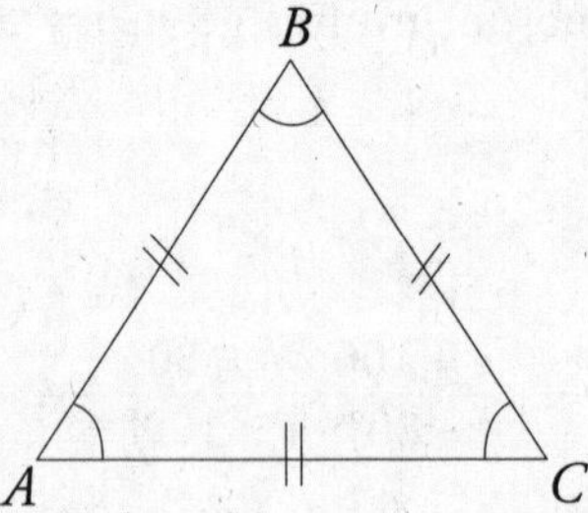

An **equilateral** triangle has three equal sides and three equal angles. Because the three equal angles must add up to 180°, all three angles of an equilateral triangle are always equal to 60°.

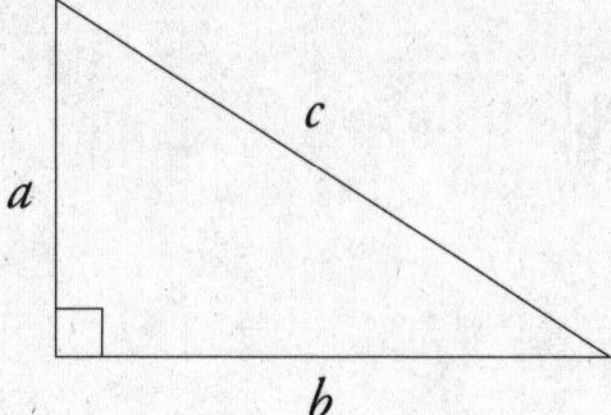

A **right triangle** has one inside angle that is equal to 90°. The longest side of a right triangle (the one opposite the 90° angle) is called the **hypotenuse.**

Pythagoras, a Greek mathematician, discovered that the sides of a right triangle are always in a particular proportion, which can be expressed by the formula $a^2 + b^2 = c^2$, where a and b are the shorter sides of the triangle, and c is the hypotenuse. This formula is called the **Pythagorean theorem**.

There are certain right triangles that the test writers at ACT find endlessly fascinating. Let's test out the Pythagorean theorem on the first of these.

$$3^2 + 4^2 = c^2$$
$$9 + 16 = 25$$
$$c^2 = 25, \text{ so } c = 5$$

The ACT writers adore the 3-4-5 triangle and use it frequently, along with its multiples, such as the 6-8-10 triangle and the 9-12-15 triangle. Of course, you can always use the Pythagorean theorem to figure out the third side of a right triangle, as long as you have the other two sides, but because ACT problems almost invariably use "triples" like the ones we've just mentioned, it makes sense just to memorize them.

The ACT has three commonly used right-triangle triples.

3-4-5 (and its multiples)

5-12-13 (and its multiples)

7-24-25 (not as common as the other two)

Don't Get Snared

Pythagoras's *Other* Theorem

Pythagoras also developed a theory about the transmigration of souls. So far, this has not been proven, nor will it help you on this exam.

- Is this a 3-4-5 triangle?

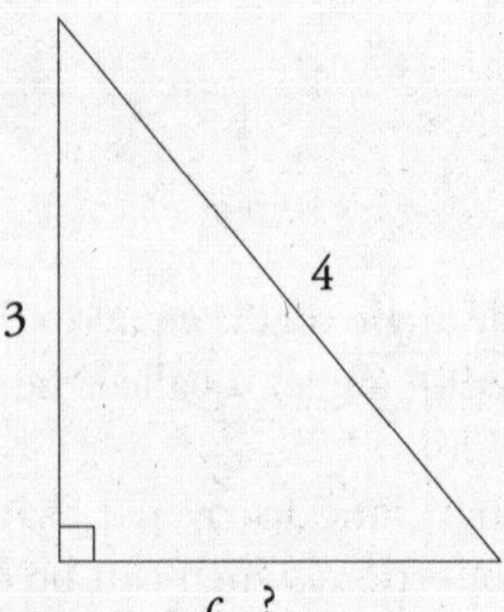

No, because the hypotenuse of a right triangle must be its *longest* side—the one opposite the 90° angle. In this case, we must use the Pythagorean theorem to discover side c: $3^2 + c^2 = 16$. $c = \sqrt{7}$.

- Is this a 5-12-13 triangle?

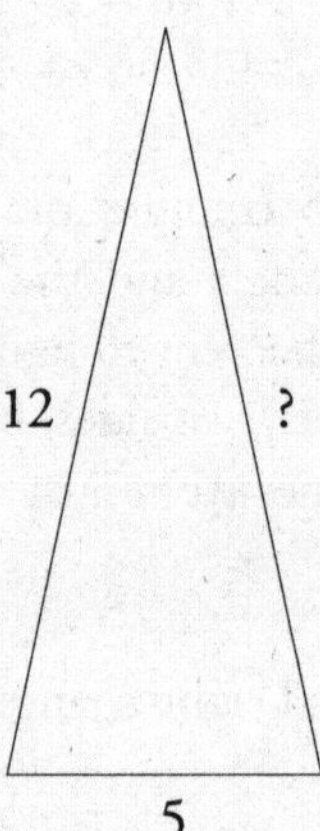

No, because the Pythagorean theorem—and triples—apply only to *right* triangles. We can't determine definitively the third side of this triangle based on the angles.

The Isosceles Right Triangle

As fond as the ACT test writers are of triples, they are even fonder of two other right triangles. The first is called the **isosceles right triangle.** The sides and angles of the isosceles right triangle are always in a particular proportion.

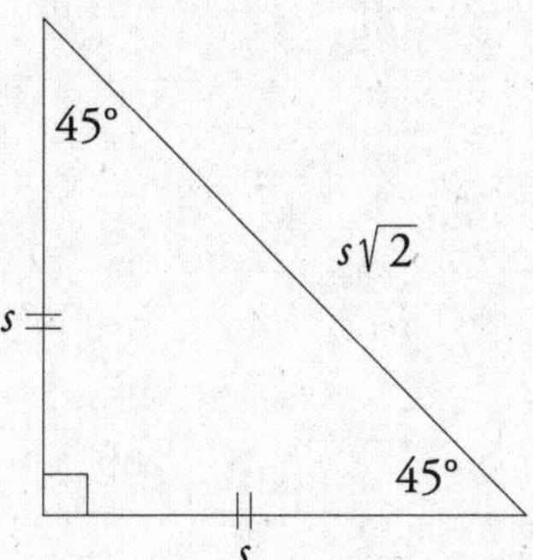

You could use the Pythagorean theorem to prove this (or you could just take our word for it). Whatever the value of the two equal sides of the isosceles right triangle, the hypotenuse is always equal to one of those sides times $\sqrt{2}$. Here are two examples.

Be on the Lookout...

for problems in which the application of the Pythagorean theorem is not obvious. For example, every rectangle contains two right triangles. That means that if you know the length and width of the rectangle, you also know the length of the diagonal, which is the hypotenuse of both triangles created by the diagonal.

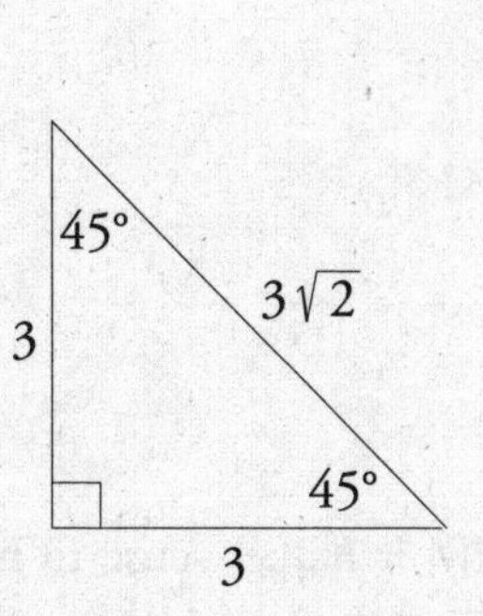

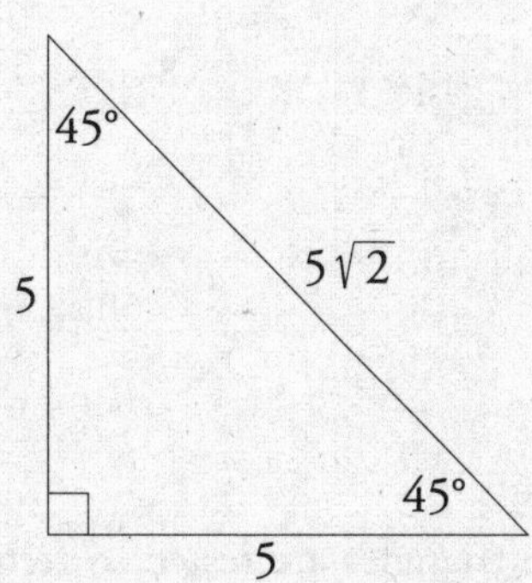

The 30-60-90 Triangle

The other right triangle tested frequently on the ACT is the **30-60-90 triangle**, which also always has the same proportions.

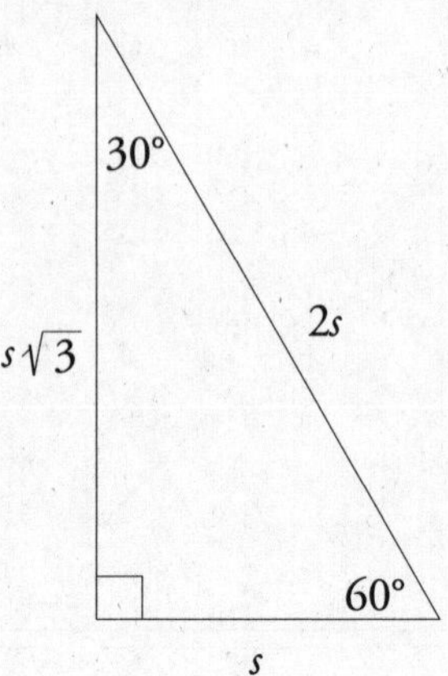

You can use the Pythagorean theorem to prove this (or you can just take our word for it). Whatever the value of the short side of the 30-60-90 triangle, the hypotenuse is always twice as large. The medium side is always equal to the short side times $\sqrt{3}$. Here are two examples.

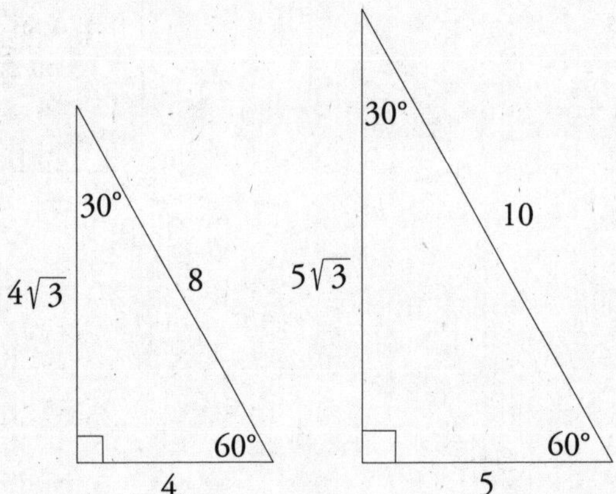

Because these triangles are tested so frequently, it makes sense to memorize the proportions, rather than waste time deriving them each time they appear.

Don't Get Snared

- In the isosceles right triangle below, are the sides equal to $3\sqrt{2}$?

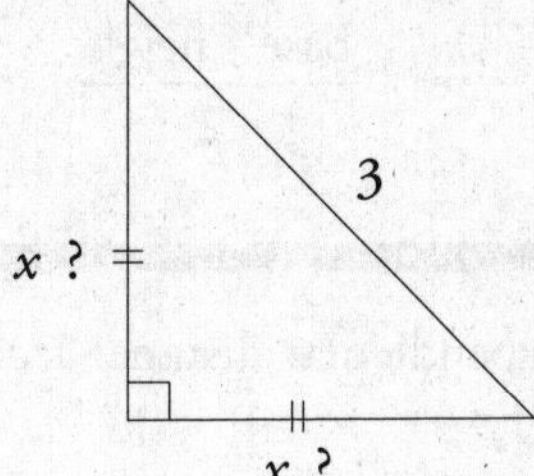

No. Remember, in an isosceles right triangle, hypotenuse = the side × $\sqrt{2}$. In this case, 3 = the side × $\sqrt{2}$. If we solve for the side, we get $\frac{3}{\sqrt{2}}$ = the side.

For arcane mathematical reasons, we are not supposed to leave a radical in the denominator, but we can multiply top and bottom by $\sqrt{2}$ to get $\frac{3\sqrt{2}}{2}$.

- In the right triangle below, is x equal to $4\sqrt{3}$?

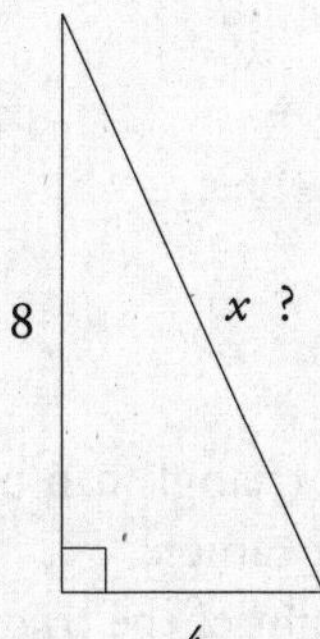

No. Even though it is one of ACT's favorites, you have to be careful not to see a 30-60-90 where none exists. In the triangle above, the short side is half of the *medium* side, not half of the hypotenuse. This is some sort of right triangle all right, but it is not a 30-60-90. The hypotenuse, in case you're curious, is really $4\sqrt{5}$.

Area

The **area** of a triangle can be found using the following formula:

$$\text{area} = \frac{\text{base} \times \text{height}}{2}$$

Height is measured as the perpendicular distance from the base of the triangle to its highest point.

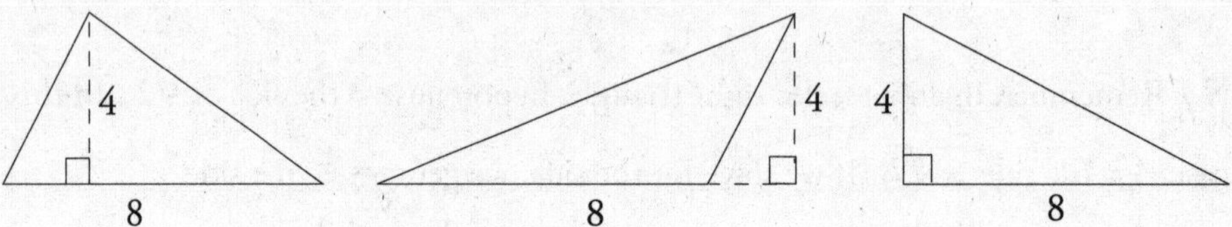

In all three of the above triangles, the area is

$$\frac{8 \times 4}{2} = 16$$

Don't Get Snared

- Sometimes the height of a triangle can be *outside* the triangle itself, as we just saw in the second example.
- In a right triangle, the height of the triangle can also be one of the sides of the triangle, as we just saw in the third example. However, be careful when finding the area of a *non-right* triangle. Simply because you know two sides of the triangle does not mean that you have the height of the triangle.

Similar Triangles

Two triangles are called similar if their angles have the same degree measures. This means their sides will be in proportion. For example, the two triangles below are similar.

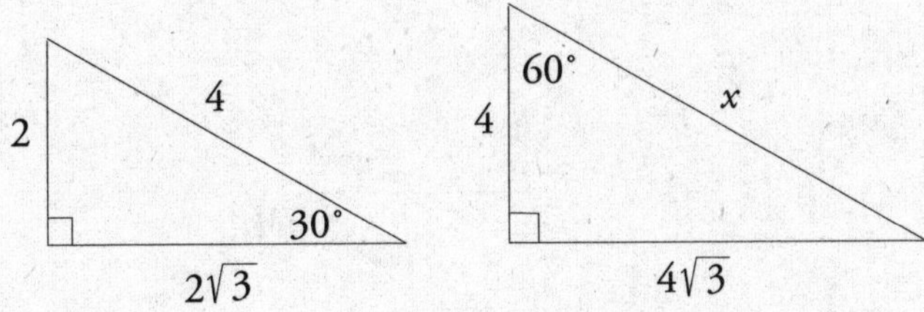

Because the sides of the two triangles are in the same proportion, you can find the missing side, x, by setting up a proportion equation.

	small triangle		big triangle
$\frac{\text{short leg}}{\text{hypotenuse}}$	$\frac{2}{4}$	=	$\frac{4}{x}$

$$x = 8$$

ACT Triangle Problems

Most of the triangle problems on the ACT combine *several* of the triangle concepts we've just reviewed. Be flexible, and look for clues as to which concepts are being tested. See the next page for some triangle problems as they might appear on the ACT.

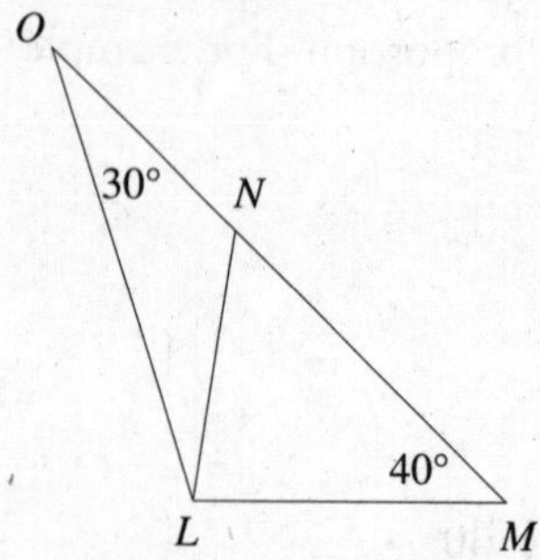

1. In the figure above, O, N, and M are colinear. If the length of $\overline{ON}$ and $\overline{NL}$ are the same, and the measure of $\angle LON$ is 30° and $\angle LMN$ is 40°, what is the measure of $\angle NLM$?

A. 40°
B. 80°
C. 90°
D. 120°
E. 150°

Third Side Rule

It is impossible for the third side of a triangle to be longer than the total of the other two sides. Nor can the third side of a triangle be shorter than the difference between the other two sides. Imagine a triangle with sides a, b, and c. $c < a + b$ and $c > a - b$.

Here's How to Crack It

We saw this problem at the beginning of the chapter and managed to solve it without using any geometry. Now let's solve it geometrically. Because $\overline{ON}$ is equal to $\overline{NL}$, we know that ΔONL is isosceles. If $\angle O = 30°$, then so does $\angle OLN$, and therefore $\angle ONL$ is equal to 120°. Because this angle and $\angle LNM$ add up to a straight line, $\angle LNM$ must be equal to 60°. $\angle LNM$ plus $\angle LMN$ add up to 100°, meaning that the angle we are looking for (NLM) is equal to 80° and the answer is B. Alternatively, in ΔOLM, $\angle OLM$ must equal 110°, and $\angle OLN$ makes up 30°, leaving 80° for $\angle NLM$. The answer is (B).

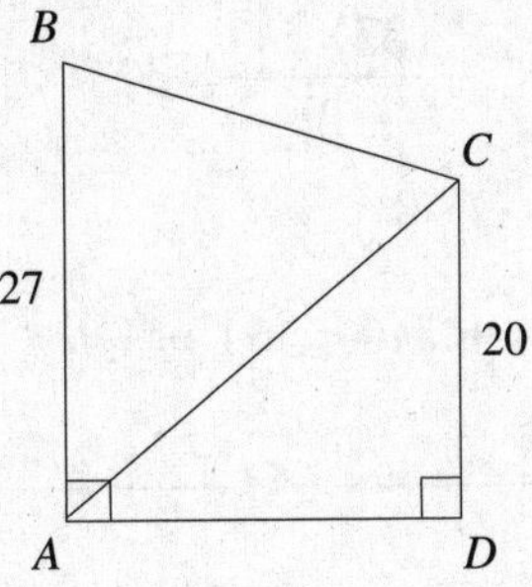

2. In the figure above, if $\overline{AB} = 27, \overline{CD} = 20$, and the area of $\Delta ADC = 240$, what is the area of polygon $ABCD$?

F. 420
G. 480
H. 540
J. 564
K. 1,128

Here's How to Crack It

Again, we saw this problem at the beginning of the chapter and managed to eliminate three of the five answer choices by using POE. Now let's solve it geometrically. The polygon in question is made up of two triangles. We are told that the area of ΔADC is 240.

$$\text{The formula for the area of a triangle} = \frac{\text{base} \times \text{height}}{2}$$

We don't know the base of this triangle, but we do know the height and the total area. Can we figure out the base? Of course.

$$\frac{(b)(20)}{2} = 240$$

$$b = 24$$

Now let's look at the other triangle. We need to find its area because the sum of the areas of the two triangles equals the area of the polygon for which we are looking. If we turn the polygon on its side so that $\overline{BA}$ is on the bottom, we have the base of the ΔABC. Do we know the height? Yes! The base of ΔADC also happens to be equal to the height of ΔABC: 24.

All that's left is to plug the base and height into the area formula to get the area of ΔABC.

$$\frac{(27)(24)}{2} = 324$$

The area of the polygon is 324 + 240 = 564, or (J).

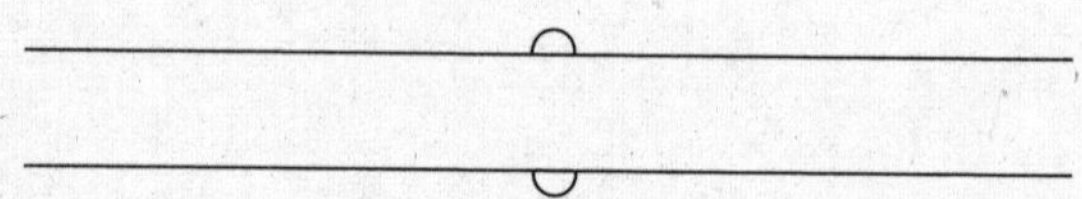

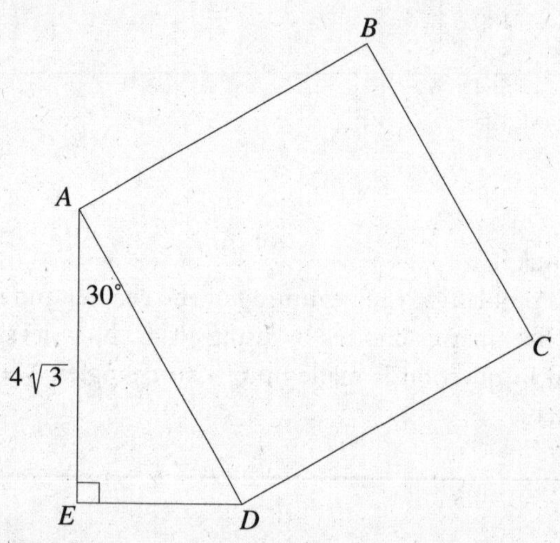

3. In the figure above, square $ABCD$ is attached to ΔADE as shown. If $\angle EAD$ is equal to 30° and $\overline{AE}$ is equal to $4\sqrt{3}$, then what is the area of square $ABCD$?

A. $8\sqrt{3}$
B. 16
C. 64
D. 72
E. $64\sqrt{2}$

Here's How to Crack It

The triangle in this diagram is a 30-60-90. Because angle A is the short angle, the side opposite that angle is equal to 4 and the hypotenuse is equal to 8. Because that hypotenuse is also the side of the square, the area of the square must be 8 times 8, or 64. This is (C). If you forgot the ratio of the sides of a 30-60-90 triangle, go back and review it. You'll need it.

POE Pointers

If you didn't remember the ratio of the sides of a 30-60-90 triangle, could you have eliminated some answers using POE? Of course. Let's see if we can use the diagram to eliminate some answer choices.

The diagram tells us that $\overline{AE}$ has length $4\sqrt{3}$. Remember the important approximations we gave you earlier in the chapter? A good approximation for $\sqrt{3}$ is 1.7. So $4\sqrt{3}$ = approximately 6.8. We can now use this to estimate the sides of square *ABCD*. Just using your eyes, would you say that $\overline{AD}$ is longer or shorter than $\overline{AE}$? Of course it's a bit longer; it's the hypotenuse of ΔADE. You decide and write down what you think it might be. To find the area of the square, simply square whatever value you decided the side equaled. This is your answer.

Now all you have to do is see which of the answer choices still makes sense. Could the answer be (A)? $8\sqrt{3}$ equals roughly 13.6. Is this close to your answer? No way. Could the answer be (B), which is 16? Still much too small. Could the answer be (C), which is 64? Quite possibly. Could the answer be 72? It might be. Could the correct answer be $64\sqrt{2}$? An approximation of radical 2 = 1.4, so $64\sqrt{2}$ equals 89.6. This seems rather large. Thus, on this problem, by using POE we could eliminate (A), (B), and (E).

FOUR-SIDED FIGURES

The interior angles of any four-sided figure (also known as a quadrilateral) add up to 360°. The most common four-sided figures on the ACT are the rectangle and the square, with the parallelogram and the trapezoid coming in a far distant third and fourth.

Your Friend the Triangle
Because a quadrilateral is really just two triangles, its interior angles must measure twice those of a triangle: 2(180) = 360.

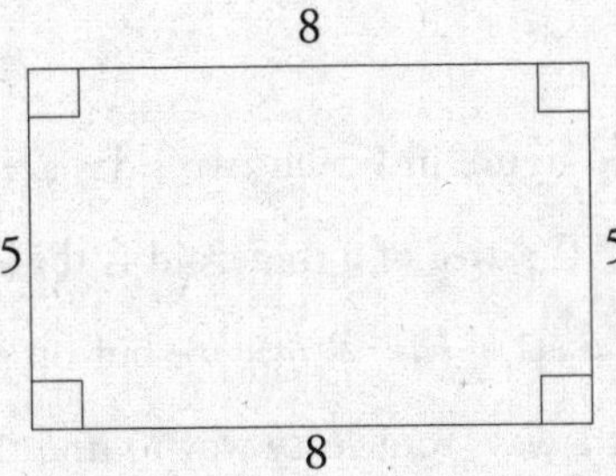

A **rectangle** is a four-sided figure whose four interior angles are each equal to 90°. The area of a rectangle is *base* × *height*. Therefore, the area of the rectangle above is 8 (*base*) × 5 (*height*) = 40. The perimeter of a rectangle is the sum of all four of its sides. The perimeter of the rectangle above is 8 + 8 + 5 + 5 = 26.

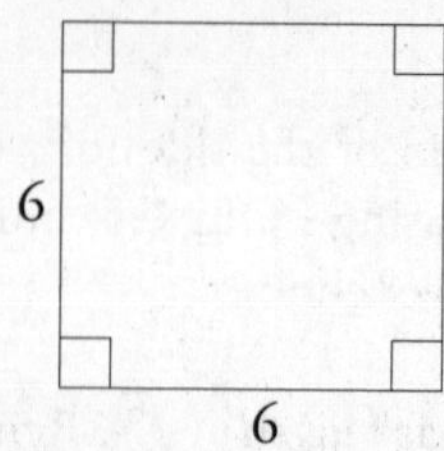

A **square** is a rectangle whose four sides are all equal in length. You can think of the area of a square, therefore, as **side squared.** The area of the above square is 6 (*base*) × 6 (*height*) = 36. The perimeter is 24, or 4*s*.

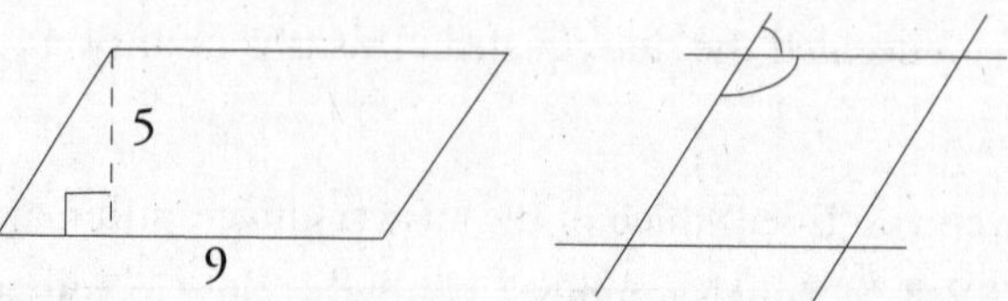

A **parallelogram** is a four-sided figure made up of two sets of parallel lines. We said earlier that when parallel lines are crossed by a third line, eight angles are formed but that in reality there are only two—the big one and the little one. In a parallelogram, 16 angles are formed, but there are still, in reality, only two.

Doh, I'm in a Square!
To help you remember the area of a four-sided figure (a square, a rectangle, or a parallelogram), imagine that Bart and Homer Simpson are stuck inside of it. To get its area, just multiply **B**art times **H**omer, or (*b*)(*h*), or the base times the height.

The area of a parallelogram is also *base* × *height,* but because of the shape of the figure, the height of a parallelogram is not necessarily equal to one of its sides. Height is measured by a perpendicular line drawn from the base to the top of the figure. The area of the parallelogram above is 9 × 5 = 45.

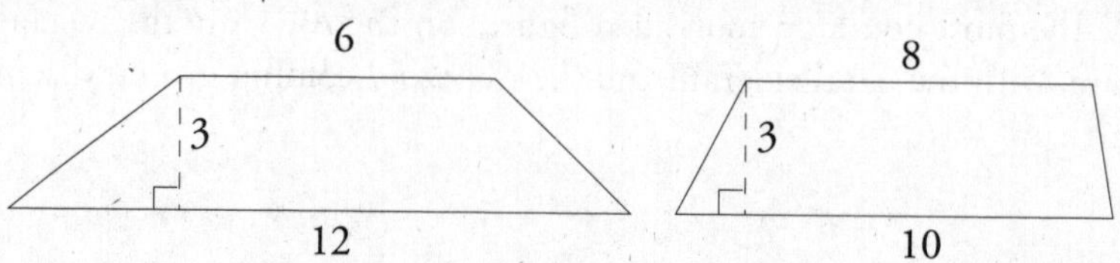

A **trapezoid** is a four-sided figure in which two sides are parallel. Both of the figures above are trapezoids. The area of a trapezoid is the *average of the two parallel sides* × *the height*, or $\frac{1}{2}$ (*base* 1 + *base* 2)(*height*), but on ACT problems involving trapezoids, there is almost always some easy way to find the area without knowing the formula (for example, by dividing the trapezoid into two triangles and a rectangle). In both trapezoids above, the area is 27.

CIRCLES

The distance from the center of a circle to any point on the circle is called the **radius.** The distance from one point on a circle through the center of the circle to another point on the circle is called the **diameter.** The diameter is always equal to twice the radius. In the circle on the left below, AB is called a **chord**. CD is called a **tangent** to the circle.

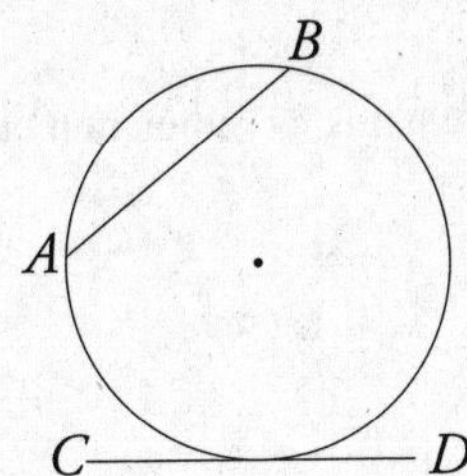

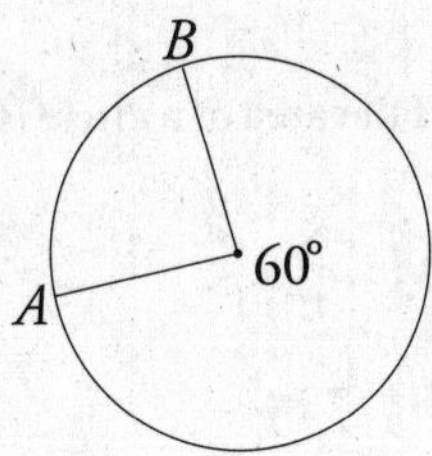

The curved portion of the right-hand circle between points A and B is called an **arc.** The angle formed by drawing lines from the center of the circle to points A and B is said to be **subtended** by the arc. There are 360° in a circle, so that if the angle we just mentioned equaled 60°, it would take up $\frac{60}{360}$ or $\frac{1}{6}$ of the degrees in the entire circle. It would also take up $\frac{1}{6}$ of the area of the circle and $\frac{1}{6}$ of the outer perimeter of the circle, called the **circumference.**

The formula for the **area** of a circle is πr^2.

The formula for the **circumference** is $2\pi r$.

In the circle below, if the radius is 4, then the area is 16π, and the circumference is 8π.

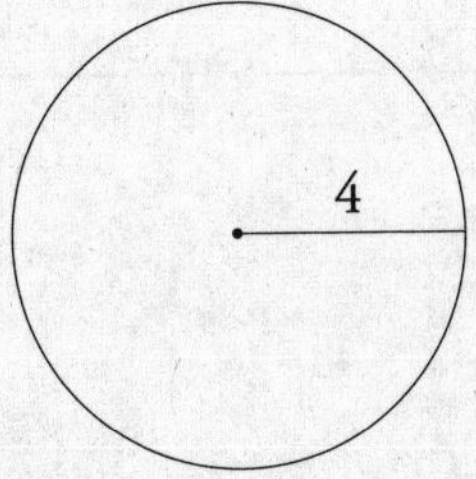

The key to circle problems on the ACT is to look for the word or phrase that tells you what to do. If you see the word *circumference,* immediately write down the formula for circumference, and plug in any numbers the problem has given you. By solving for whatever quantity is still unknown, you have probably already answered the problem. Another tip is to find the radius. The radius is the key to many circle problems.

---

1. If the area of a circle is 16 meters, what is its radius in meters?

A. $\frac{8}{\pi}$

B. 12π

C. $\frac{4\sqrt{\pi}}{\pi}$

D. $\frac{16}{\pi}$

E. $144\pi^2$

Here's How to Crack It

As soon as you see the word *area,* start thinking $\pi r^2 = 16$. The problem is asking for the radius, so you have to solve for r. If you divide both sides by π, you get

$$r^2 = \frac{16}{\pi}$$

$$r = \sqrt{\frac{16}{\pi}}$$

$$= \frac{4}{\sqrt{\pi}}$$

$$= \frac{4\sqrt{\pi}}{\pi}$$

The correct answer is (C).

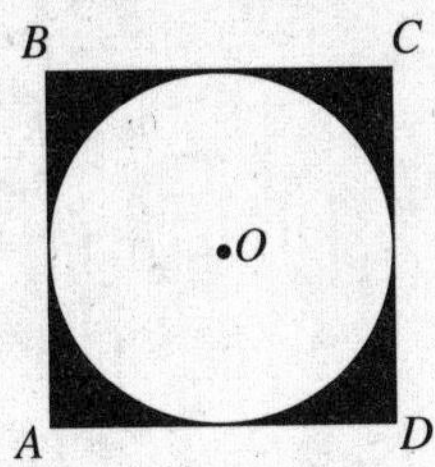

2. In the figure above, the circle with center O is inscribed inside square $ABCD$ as shown. If a side of the square measures 8 units, what is the area of the shaded region?

F. $8 - 16\pi$
G. 8π
H. 16π
J. $64 - 16\pi$
K. 64π

Geometry Hint
If there isn't a diagram, draw one yourself.

Here's How to Crack It

Because the side of the square measures 8 units, the area of the square is 64 square units. Hold that thought.

Before we do any more real math, let's take a moment to look at the diagram. What portion of the entire square would you say is shaded? Could it be as much as $\frac{1}{2}$? No, so we're looking for an answer that is less than half of 64—in other words, less than 32. Most of the answer choices are in terms of π, but a rough approximation of π is 3. Let's go through the choices and see if there are any we can eliminate.

F. $8 - 16(3) = -40$. This is clearly crazy. You can't have a negative area.
G. $8(3) = 24$. Let's hold onto this one.
H. $16(3) = 48$. No, we need an answer less than 32.
J. $64 - 16(3) = 16$. Let's hold onto this one, too.
K. $64(3) = 192$. This is larger than the entire square. No way.

You can use POE to eliminate three of the choices. If you're running out of time, or don't remember how to do the problem geometrically, guess and move on.

To solve the problem the way ACT expects you to, you must find the area of the circle and subtract it from the area of the square. What is left over is the shaded region. The formula for the area of a circle is πr^2. Do we know the radius of this circle? Sure. Because the circle is inscribed in the square, the side of the square has the same measure as the diameter of the circle. In other words, the radius of the circle is 4, and the area of the circle is 16π. Subtracting the area of the circle from the area of the square, we get $64 - 16\pi$, which is (J).

Geometry Drill

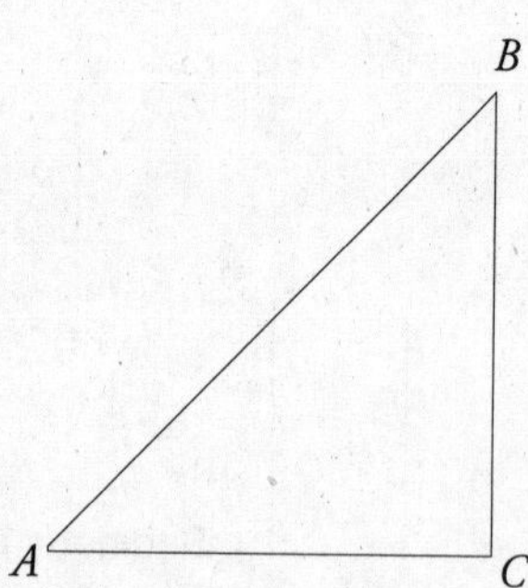

1. In ΔABC above, $\angle A = \angle B$, and $\angle C$ is twice the measure of $\angle B$. What is the measure, in degrees, of $\angle A$?

   A. 30
   B. 45
   C. 50
   D. 75
   E. 90

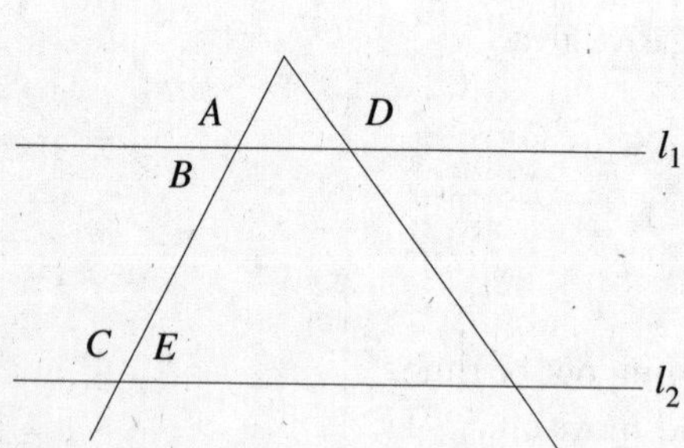

2. In the figure above, $l_1 \parallel l_2$. Which of the labeled angles must be equal to each other?

   F. A and C
   G. D and E
   H. A and B
   J. D and B
   K. C and B

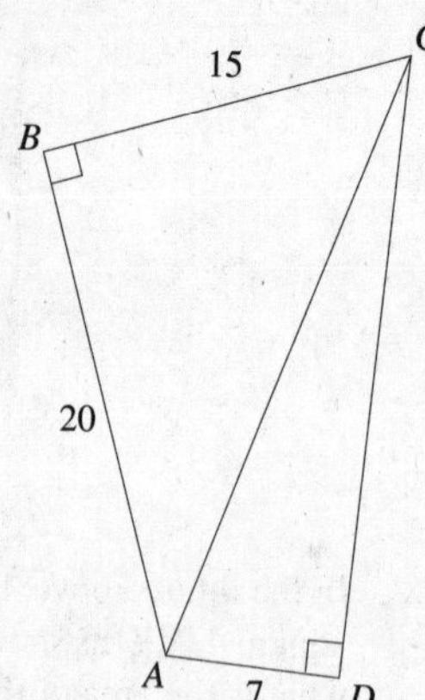

3. In the figure above, right triangles ABC and ACD are drawn as shown. If $\overline{AB} = 20$, $\overline{BC} = 15$, and $\overline{AD} = 7$, then $\overline{CD} = $?

   A. 21
   B. 22
   C. 23
   D. 24
   E. 25

4. If the area of circle A is 16π, then what is the circumference of circle B if its radius is $\frac{1}{2}$ that of circle A ?

   F. 2π
   G. 4π
   H. 6π
   J. 8π
   K. 16π

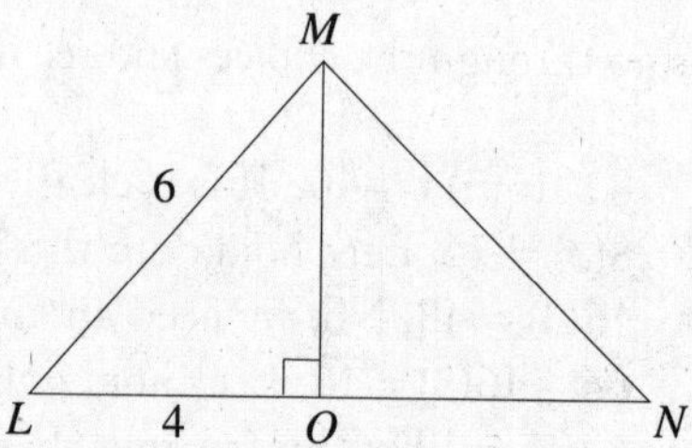

5. In the figure above, $\overline{MO}$ is perpendicular to $\overline{LN}$, $\overline{LO}$ is equal to 4, $\overline{MO}$ is equal to $\overline{ON}$, and $\overline{LM}$ is equal to 6. What is $\overline{MN}$?

   A. $2\sqrt{10}$
   B. $3\sqrt{5}$
   C. $4\sqrt{5}$
   D. $3\sqrt{10}$
   E. $6\sqrt{4}$

Summary

- If there is no diagram included in a problem, you should draw your own.
- There are several things to know about angles and lines.
    - A line is a 180° angle.
    - When two lines intersect, four angles are formed, but in reality there are only two distinct measures.
    - When two parallel lines are cut by a third line, eight angles are formed, but in reality there are still only two (a large one and a small one).
- There are several things to know about triangles.
    - A triangle has three sides and three angles; the sum of the angles equals 180°.
    - An isosceles triangle has two equal sides and two equal angles opposite those sides.
    - An equilateral triangle has three equal sides and three equal angles; each angle equals 60°.
    - A right triangle has one 90° angle. In a right triangle problem you can use the Pythagorean theorem to find the lengths of sides.
    - Some common right triangles are 3-4-5, 6-8-10, 5-12-13, and 7-24-25.
    - ACT test writers also like the isosceles right triangle, in which the sides are always in the ratio $s : s : s\sqrt{2}$, and the 30-60-90 triangle, in which the sides are always in the ratio $s : s\sqrt{3} : 2s$.
    - Similar triangles have the same angle measurements and sides that are in the same proportion.
    - The area of a triangle is equal to $\frac{(\text{base} \times \text{height})}{2}$, with height measured perpendicular to the base.

- Four-sided objects are called quadrilaterals and have four angles, which add up to 360°. There are several important things to remember.
    - The area of a rectangle, a square, or a parallelogram can be found using the formula *base* × *height* = *area,* with height measured perpendicular to the base.
    - The perimeter of any object is the sum of the lengths of its sides.
    - The area of a trapezoid is equal to the average of the two bases times the height.
- For any circle problem, you need to know four basic things:
    - radius
    - diameter
    - area (πr^2)
    - circumference (πd or $2\pi r$)
- Don't forget that you can plug in on geometry questions that have variables in the answer choices.

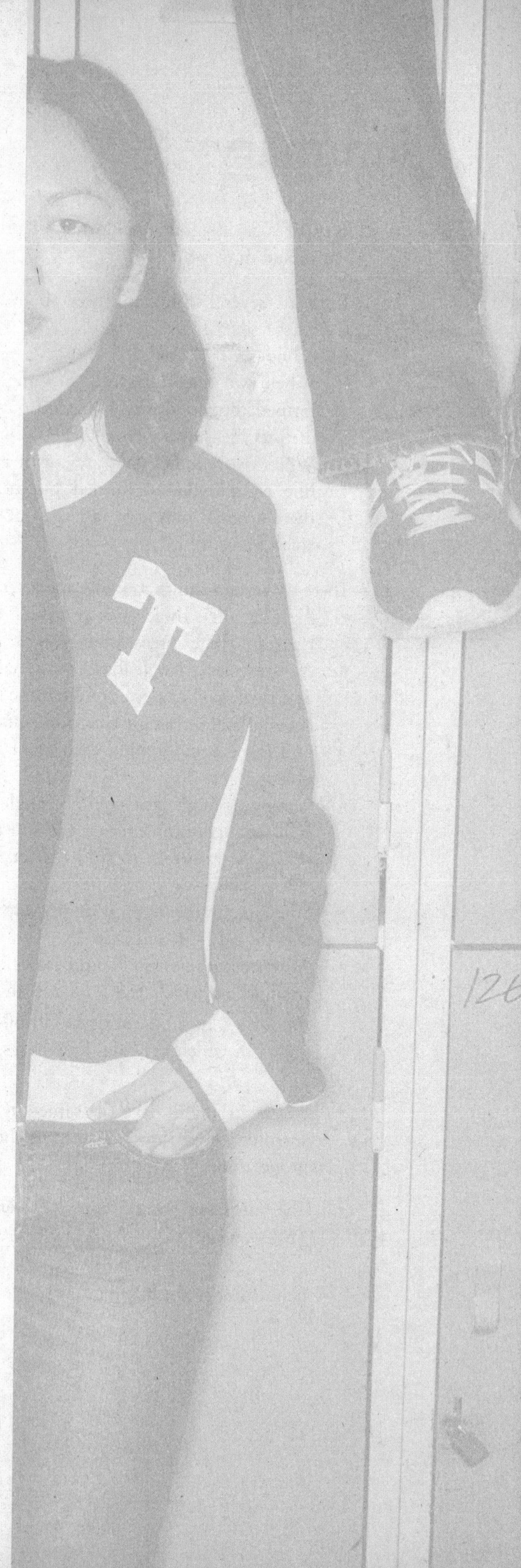

Chapter 14
Graphing and Coordinate Geometry

Out of the 23 geometry questions you can expect to see on the ACT Math test, 9 deal with coordinate geometry. Many of these questions will involve visualizing points on a line or within the coordinate plane; luckily for us, our graphing calculators can handle most of the work. While we discuss how to mathematically attack all the coordinate geometry problems the Math test will throw at us, we also show you how to use your calculator to simplify your approach.

GRAPHING REVIEW

Graphing Inequalities

Here's a simple inequality

$$3x + 5 > 11$$

As you know from reading the algebra chapter of this book, you solve an inequality the same way that you solve an equality. By subtracting 5 from both sides and then dividing both sides by 3, you get the expression

$$x > 2$$

An Open Circle
On the number line, a hollow circle means that point is *not* included in the graph.

This can be represented on a number line as shown below.

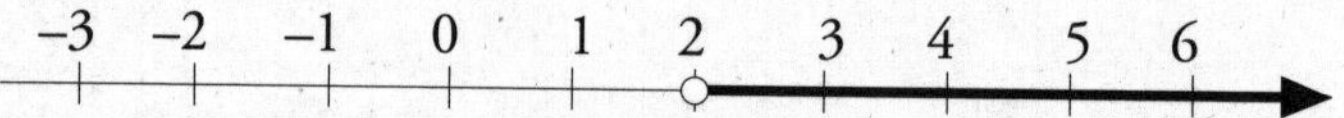

The open circle at 2 indicates that x can include every number greater than 2, but not 2 itself or anything less than 2.

A Solid Dot
On the number line, a solid dot means that point is included in the graph.

If we had wanted to graph $x \geq 2$, the circle would have to be filled in, indicating that our graph includes 2 as well.

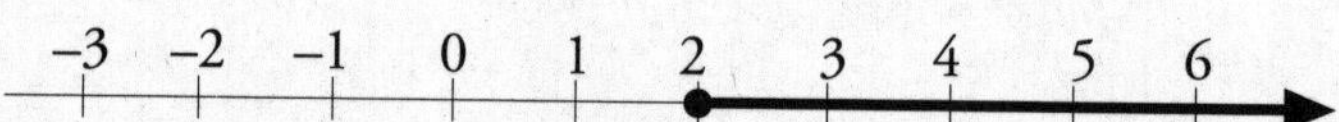

An ACT graphing problem might look like the one on the following page.

1. Which of the following represents the range of solutions for inequality $-5x - 7 < x + 5$?

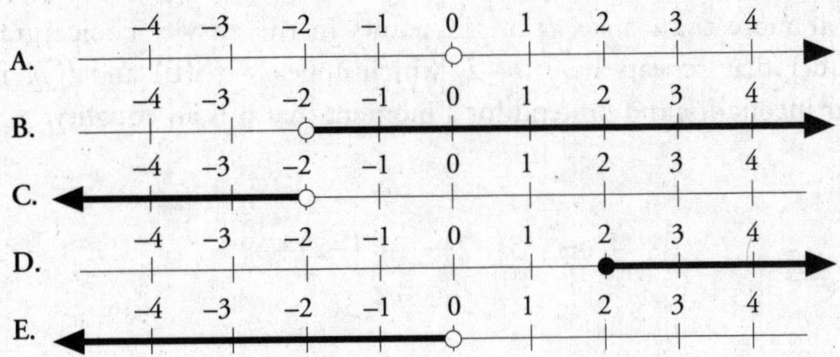

Here's How to Crack It

The ACT test writers want you first to simplify the inequality and then figure out which of the answer choices represents a graph of the solution set of the inequality. To simplify, isolate x on one side of the inequality.

$$\begin{array}{rcl} -5x - 7 & < & x + 5 \\ -x & & -x \\ \hline -6x - 7 & < & 5 \\ +7 & & +7 \\ \hline -6x & < & 12 \end{array}$$

Now divide both sides by –6. Remember that when you multiply or divide an inequality by a negative, the sign flips over.

$$\frac{-6x}{-6} < \frac{12}{-6}$$

$$x > -2$$

Which of the choices answers the question? If you chose (B), you're right.

Flip Flop

Remember that when you multiply or divide an inequality by a negative, the sign flips.

POE Pointers

You could have done this (and most other inequality graphing problems) just as easily by Working Backward. Look at the possible answer choices. The ACT test writers tend to surround the correct answer with at least one *almost* correct answer. Why don't we begin by checking to see if any numbers appear more than once as origin points in the answer choice graphs? The only number that repeats here is –2, which appears in (B) and (C). Let's plug –2 into our inequality and pretend for a moment that it is an equality.

$$\text{Does } -5(-2)-7=(-2)+5?$$
$$10-7=3?$$

Yes. Now, to decide whether the answer is (B) or (C), just pick a number that is in one answer but not the other. For example, in (C), –4 is part of the solution set but is not included in (B). By plugging –4 into the inequality, we will see if (C) is correct. If it isn't, then the answer is (B).

$$-5(-4)-7<(-4)+5$$
$$20-7<1$$
$$13<1$$

Is this true? No, so the answer must be (B).

Graphing in Two Dimensions

More complicated graphing questions concern equations with two variables, usually designated x and y. These equations can be graphed on a Cartesian grid, which looks like this.

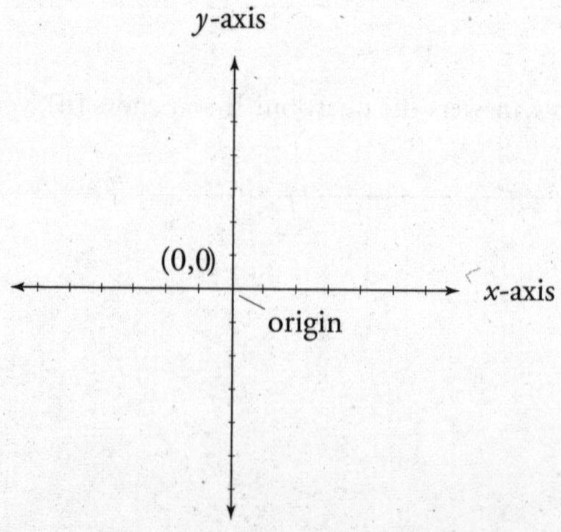

Every point (x,y) has a place on this grid. For example, the point A (3,4) can be found by counting over on the x-axis 3 places to the right of (0,0)—known as the **origin**—and then counting on the y-axis 4 places up from the origin, as shown below. Point B (5,–2) can be found by counting 5 places to the right on the x-axis and then down 2 places on the y-axis. Point C (–4,–1) can be found by counting 4 places to the left of the origin on the x-axis and then 1 place down on the y-axis.

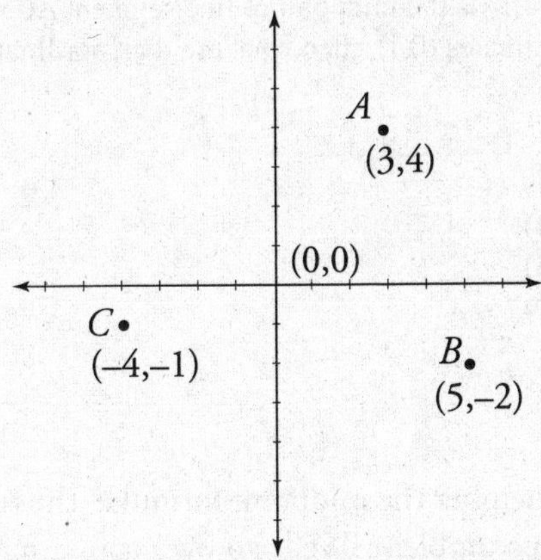

The grid is divided into four quadrants, which go counterclockwise.

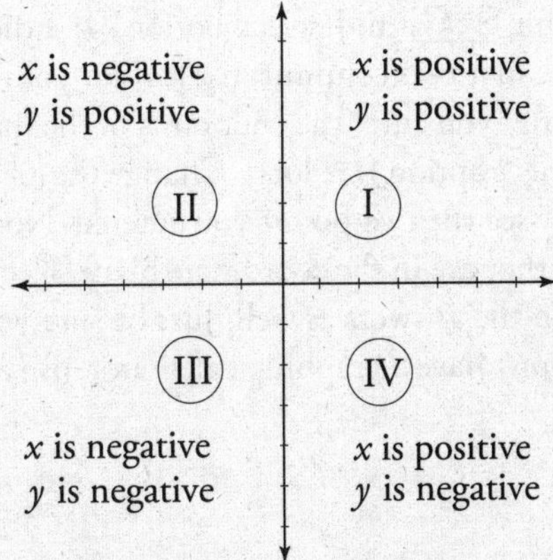

- In the first quadrant, x and y are both positive.
- In the second quadrant, x is negative but y is positive.
- In the third quadrant, x and y are both negative.
- In the fourth quadrant, x is positive but y is negative.

Note: This is when your graphing calculator (if you have one) will really get a chance to shine. Practice doing all the ACT coordinate geometry questions on your calculator now and you'll blow them away when you actually take the test.

Graphic Guesstimation

A few questions on the ACT might involve actual graphing, but it is more likely that you will be able to make use of graphing to *estimate* the answers to questions that the ACT test writers think are more complicated.

1. Point B (4,3) is the midpoint of line segment AC. If point A has coordinates (0,1), then what are the coordinates of point C?

A. (–4,–1)
B. (4,1)
C. (4,4)
D. (8,5)
E. (8,9)

Here's How to Crack It

You may or may not remember the midpoint formula: The ACT test writers expect you to use it to solve this problem. We'll go over it in a moment, along with the other formulas you'll need to solve coordinate geometry questions. However, it is worth noting that by drawing a rough graph of this problem, you can get the correct answer without the formula.

On your TI-83, you can plot independent points to see what the graph should look like. To do this, hit [STAT] and select option [1: Edit]. Enter the x- and y-coordinate points in the first two columns; use [L1] for your x-coordinates and [L2] for the y-coordinates. After you enter the endpoints of the line, hit [2nd][Y=] to access the [STAT PLOT] menu. Select option [1: Plot1]. Change the [OFF] status to [ON] and hit [GRAPH]. You should now see the two points you entered. Now you can ballpark the answers based on where they are in the coordinate plane. Keep in mind that you can also plot all the points in the answers as well. Just be sure you keep track of all the x- and y-values. If you don't have a graphing calculator, use the grid we've provided on the next page.

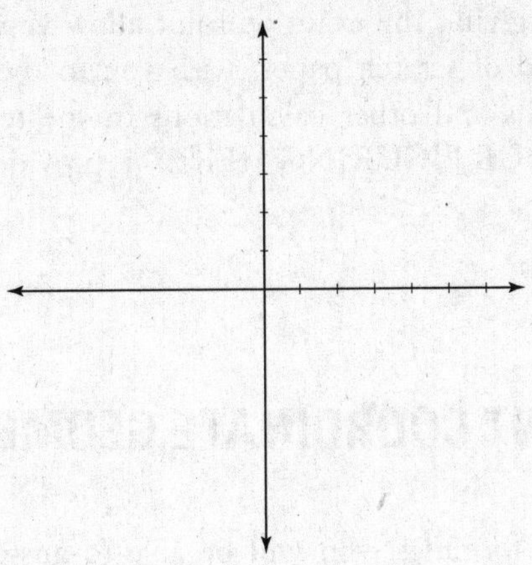

B is supposed to be the midpoint of a line segment *AC*. Draw a line through the two points you've just plotted and extend it upward until *B* is the midpoint of the line segment. It should look like this:

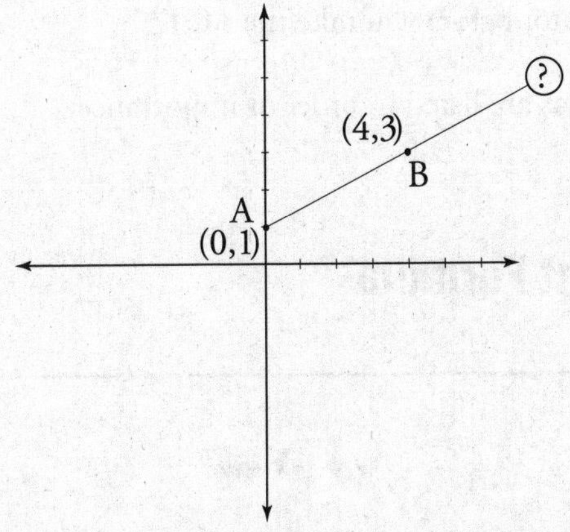

The place where you stopped drawing is the approximate location of point *C*. Now let's look at the answer choices to see if any of them are in the ballpark.

- **A.** (–4,–1): These coordinates are in the wrong quadrant.
- **B.** (4,1): This point is way below where it should be.
- **C.** (4,4): This point does not extend enough to the right.
- **D.** (8,5): Definitely in the ballpark. Hold on to this answer choice.
- **E.** (8,9): Possible, although the *y*-coordinate seems a little high.

Which answer choice do you want to pick? If you said (D), you are right.

By the way, the folks giving the exam will not allow you to bring graphing paper (or any other kind of scratch paper) with you to the real test, so get used to making your graphs and other calculations in the test booklet. A full column, labeled "DO YOUR FIGURING HERE," is provided on every page of the Mathematics test.

THE IMPORTANT COORDINATE GEOMETRY FORMULAS

By memorizing a few formulas, you will be able to answer virtually all of the coordinate geometry questions on this test. Remember, too, that in coordinate geometry you almost *always* have a fallback—just graph it out.

And always keep your graphing calculator handy on these types of problems. Graphing calculators are great for solving line equations and giving you graphs you can use to ballpark. Be sure you know how to solve and graph an equation for a line on your calculator before you take the ACT.

The following formulas are listed in order of importance:

The *y*-Intercept Formula

$$y = mx + b$$

To Find the *x*-intercept
Set y equal to zero and solve for x.

By putting (x,y) equations into the formula above, you can find two pieces of information that ACT likes to test: the **slope** and the ***y*-intercept**. Most graphing calculators will put an equation into y-intercept form at the touch of a button.

The **slope** is a number that tells you how sharply a line is inclining, and it is equivalent to the variable m in the equation above. For example, in the equation $y = 3x + 4$, the number 3 (think of it as $\frac{3}{1}$) tells us that from any point on the line, we can find another point on the line by going up 3 and over to the right 1.

In the equation $y = -\frac{4}{5}x - 7$, the slope of $-\frac{4}{5}$ tells us that from any point on the line, we can find another point on the line by going up 4 and over 5 to the left.

The ***y*-intercept**, equivalent to the variable b in the equation above, is the point at which the line intercepts the y-axis. For example, in the equation $y = 3x + 4$, the line will strike the y-axis at a point 4 above the origin. In the equation $y = 2x - 7$, the line will strike the y-axis at a point 7 below the origin. A typical ACT $y = mx + b$ question might give you an equation in another form and ask you to find either the slope or the y-intercept. Simply put the equation into the form we've just shown you.

---

1. What is the slope of the line based on the equation $5x - y = 7x + 6$?

A. –2
B. 0
C. 2
D. 6
E. –6

Here's How to Crack It

Isolate y on the left side of the equation. You can have your graphing calculator do this for you, or you can do it by hand by subtracting $5x$ from both sides.

$$\begin{array}{rcl} 5x - y &=& 7x + 6 \\ -5x & & -5x \\ \hline -y &=& 2x + 6 \end{array}$$

We aren't quite done. The format we want is $y = mx + b$, not $-y = mx + b$. Let's multiply both sides by –1.

$$(-1)(-y) = (2x+6)(-1)$$
$$y = -2x - 6$$

The slope of this line is –2, so the answer is (A).

The Slope Formula

You can find the slope of a line, even if all you have are two points on that line, by using the slope formula.

The Slippery Slope
A line going from bottom left to upper right has a positive slope.
A line going from top left to bottom right has a negative slope.

$$\text{slope} = \frac{\text{change in } y}{\text{change in } x} \text{ or } \frac{y_1 - y_2}{x_1 - x_2}$$

---

1. What is the slope of the straight line passing through the points (–2,5) and (6,4) ?

A. $-\frac{1}{16}$

B. $-\frac{1}{8}$

C. $\frac{1}{5}$

D. $\frac{2}{9}$

E. $\frac{4}{9}$

Here's How to Crack It

Find the change in y and put it over the change in x. The change in y is the first y-coordinate minus the second y-coordinate. (It doesn't matter which point is first and which is second.) The change in x is the first x minus the second x.

$$\frac{y_1 - y_2}{x_1 - x_2} \quad \frac{5 - 4 = 1}{-2 - 6 = -8}$$

The correct answer is (B).

If you take a look at the formula for finding slope, you'll see that the part on top ("change in y") is how much the line is rising (or falling, if the line points down and has a negative slope). That change in position on the y-axis is called the *rise.* The part on the bottom ("change in x") is how far along the x-axis you move and called the *run.* So the slope of a line is sometimes referred to as "rise over run."

In the question we just did, then, the rise was 1 and the run was –8, giving us the slope $-\frac{1}{8}$. Same answer, different terminology.

Midpoint Formula

If you have the two endpoints of a line segment, you can find the midpoint of the segment by using the midpoint formula.

$$\left(x[m], y[m]\right) = \left(\frac{x_1 + x_2}{2}, \frac{y_1 + y_2}{2}\right)$$

It looks much more intimidating than it really is.

To find the midpoint of a line, just take the *average* of the two *x*-coordinates and the *average* of the two *y*-coordinates. For example, the midpoint of the line segment formed by the coordinates (3,4) and (9,2) is just

$$\frac{(3+9)}{2} = 6 \text{ and } \frac{(4+2)}{2} = 3$$

$$\text{or } (6,3)$$

Remember the first midpoint problem we did? Here it is again.

1. Point *B* (4,3) is the midpoint of line segment *AC*. If point *A* has coordinates (0,1), then what are the coordinates of point *C* ?
   A. (–4,–1)
   B. (4,1)
   C. (4,4)
   D. (8,5)
   E. (8,9)

The Shortest Distance Between Two Points Is…a Calculator?

If you want to draw a line between two points on your TI-83, you can use the Line function. To access this, you'll want to press [2nd] [PRGM] to access the [DRAW] menu. From there, select option [2: Line]. The format of the line function is Line (X1, Y1, X2, Y2); for example, if you wanted to view the line that passes through the points (–2, 5) and (6,4), you would enter Line (–2, 5, 6, 4). Hit [ENTER] to see your line.

Here's How to Crack It

You'll remember that it was perfectly possible to solve this problem just by drawing a quick graph of what it ought to look like. However, to find the correct answer using the midpoint formula, we first have to realize that, in this case, we already *have* the midpoint. We are asked to find one of the endpoints.

The midpoint is (4,3). This represents the average of the two endpoints. The endpoint we know about is (0,1). Let's do the *x*-coordinate first. The average of the *x*-coordinates of the two endpoints equals the *x*-coordinate of the midpoint. So $\frac{(0+?)}{2}=4$. What is the missing *x*-coordinate? 8. Now let's do the *y*-coordinate. $\frac{(1+?)}{2}=3$. What is the missing *y*-coordinate? 5. The answer is (D).

If you had trouble following that last explanation, just remember that you already understood this problem (and got the answer) using graphing. Never be intimidated by formulas on the ACT. There is usually another way to do the problem.

The Distance Formula

We hate the distance formula. We keep forgetting it, and even when we remember it, we feel like fools for using it because there are much easier ways to find the distance between two points. We aren't even going to tell you what the distance formula is. If you need to know the distance between two points, you can always think of that distance as being the hypotenuse of a right triangle. Here's an example.

1. What is the distance between points *A* (2,2) and *B* (5,6) ?

A. 3
B. 4
C. 5
D. 6
E. 7

Here's How to Crack It

Let's make a quick graph of what this ought to look like.

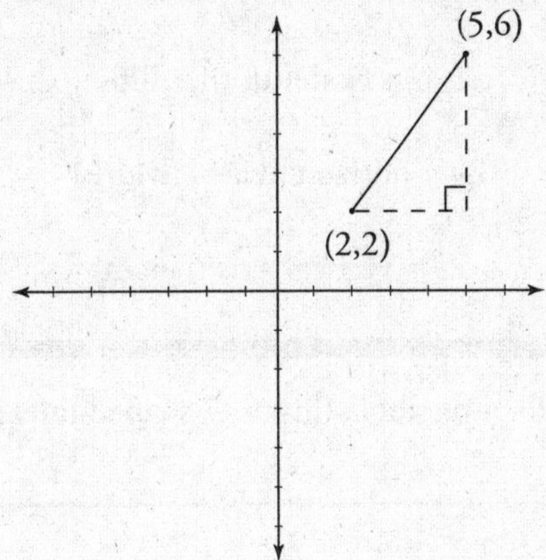

If we extend lines from the two points to form a right triangle under the line segment *AB*, we can use the Pythagorean theorem to get the distance between the two points. What is the length of the base of the triangle? It's 3. What is the length of the height of the triangle? It's 4. So what is the length of the hypotenuse? It's 5. Of course, as usual, it is one of the triples of which ACT is so fond. The answer is (C). You could also have popped the points into your calculator and had it calculate the distance for you.

Circles, Ellipses, and Parabolas, Oh My!

You should probably have a *vague* idea of what the equations for these figures look like; just remember that there are very few questions concerning these figures, and when they do come up, you can almost always figure them out by graphing.

The standard equation for a circle is shown below.

$$(x - h)^2 + (y - k)^2 = r^2$$

(h,k) = center of the circle

r = radius

The standard equation for an ellipse (just a squat-looking circle) is shown on the next page.

$$\frac{(x-h)^2}{a^2}+\frac{(y-k)^2}{b^2}=1$$

(h,k) = center of the ellipse

$2a$ = horizontal axis (width)

$2b$ = vertical axis (height)

The standard equation for a parabola (just a U-shaped line) is shown below.

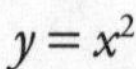

$$y = x^2$$

1. If the equation $x^2 = 1 - y^2$ were graphed in the standard (x,y) coordinate plane, the graph would represent which of the following geometric figures?

   A. square
   B. straight line
   C. circle
   D. triangle
   E. parabola

Here's How to Crack It

If you're familiar with what the equations of the various elements in the answer choices are supposed to look like, you may be able to figure out the problem without graphing at all. (However, that's why you bought a graphing calculator in the first place....) Let's consider what we know about the equations of geometric figures. If an equation has only x and y, we know that the graph of the equation is a straight line. (Think back to the $y = mx + b$ problems we did earlier.) However, in this equation, both x and y are squared, so we can rule out (B). There is no equation for a square, so we can rule out (A). Similarly, there's no equation for a triangle, so (D) is out. If only one of the variables were squared, this might be a parabola, but in this problem both are squared, which means we can eliminate (E). We are left with (C).

Graphing Circles on Your Calculator

To draw a circle on your TI-83, you first need to alter the Zoom settings. Press [ZOOM] and select option [5: ZSquare]. Next, hit [2nd] [PRGM] to access the [DRAW] menu. Select option [9: Circle]. All you need to do is enter the coordinates of the circle's center and the value of its radius. If, for instance, you were trying to graph a circle with a center of (2,3) and a radius of 5, your screen would say the following: Circle (2,3,5). Hit [ENTER] to see the resulting graph. You can draw as many circles as you like, but to clear the graph you need to press [2nd][DRAW] and select option [1: ClrDraw].

Estimating Note

Of course, we could also just plug some numbers into the equation and plot them out on a homemade (x,y) axis in the scratchwork column of the test booklet. Let's try this on the grid below.

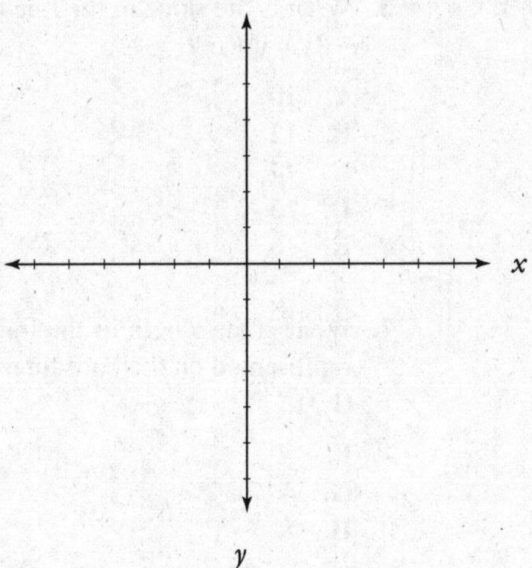

The easiest way to start is to let one of the variables equal 0. If $x = 0$, then y must equal 1. So one point of this equation is (0,1). If we let $y = 0$, then x must equal 1. So another point of this equation is (1,0). Plot out some other points of the equation. How about (–1,0) and (0,–1)? What kind of geometric figure does it appear that we have? If you said a circle, you are correct.

Graphing and Coordinate Geometry Drill

1. Which of the following represents the solution of the inequality $-3x - 6 > 9$?

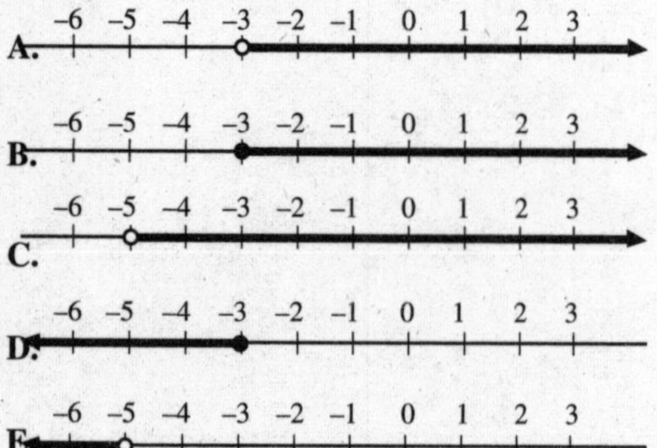

2. What is the midpoint of the line segment whose endpoints are represented on the coordinate axis by the points (3,5) and (–4,3) ?

   F. (–2,–5)

   G. $(-\frac{1}{2},4)$

   H. (1,8)

   J. $(4,-\frac{1}{2})$

   K. (3,3)

3. What is the slope of the line represented by the equation $10x + 2x = y + 6$?

   A. 10
   B. 12
   C. 14
   D. 15
   E. 16

4. What is the length of the line segment whose endpoints are represented on the coordinate axis by the points (–2,–1) and (1,3) ?

   F. 3
   G. 4
   H. 5
   J. 6
   K. 7

5. What is the slope of the line that contains the points (6,4) and (13,5) ?

   A. $-\frac{1}{8}$

   B. $-\frac{1}{9}$

   C. $\frac{1}{7}$

   D. 1

   E. 7

Summary

- In graphing an inequality, solve for the variable and look for the number-line graph that expresses the equation. Remember, you can often work backward on inequality graphing questions. Remember to flip the inequality when you divide or multiply by a negative.
- Graphing on an (x,y) axis is most useful as a way to estimate the correct answers to coordinate geometry questions.
- Most coordinate geometry questions can be solved by putting them into the format $y = mx + b$, where m is the slope of the line and b is the y-intercept.
- Some coordinate geometry questions can be solved by using the slope formula.

$$\text{slope} = \frac{\text{change in } y}{\text{change in } x}$$

- Other coordinate geometry questions can be solved using the midpoint formula.

$$(x[m], y[m]) = \frac{x_1 + x_2}{2}, \frac{y_1 + y_2}{2}$$

- You can always find the distance between two points by drawing a line between them and making it the hypotenuse of a right triangle.
- Every once in a while, ACT asks a question based on the equations of circles, ellipses, and parabolas. If you need a very high score, it might help to memorize these equations, but remember, these questions can frequently be done by using graphing to estimate the correct answer.

Chapter 15
Trigonometry

How much does ACT care about trigonometry? Because only four of the questions on the ACT Math test deal with trig, it doesn't seem to be all that important. Still, we'll spend some time reviewing what little content you need to ace these questions. You can expect two of the trigonometry questions on the test to be straightforward, so we'll start with the basic trig relationships. From there, we'll move on to the content that is likely to appear on any tougher trig questions.

SIDES OF A RIGHT TRIANGLE—RELATIONSHIPS

The easier trigonometry questions on this test involve the relationships between the sides of a right triangle. In the right triangle below, the angle x can be expressed in terms of the ratios of different sides of the triangle.

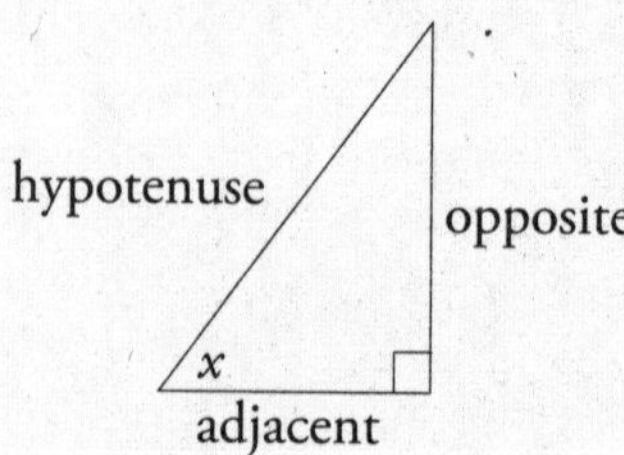

The **sine** of angle $x = \dfrac{\text{length of side opposite angle } x}{\text{length of hypotenuse}}$

The **cosine** of angle $x = \dfrac{\text{length of side adjacent angle } x}{\text{length of hypotenuse}}$

The **tangent** of angle $x = \dfrac{\text{length of side opposite angle } x}{\text{length of side adjacent angle } x}$

There is a very handy acronym to remember all this.

SOHCAHTOA

Sine is Opposite over Hypotenuse. Cosine is Adjacent over Hypotenuse. Tangent is Opposite over Adjacent. So in the triangle on next page, the sine of angle θ [*theta*, a Greek letter] would be $\frac{4}{5}$. The cosine of angle θ would be $\frac{3}{5}$. The tangent of angle θ would be $\frac{4}{3}$.

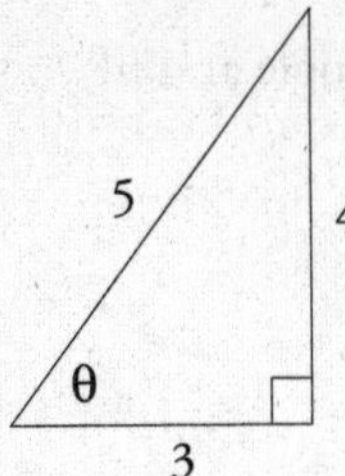

Sine, cosine, and tangent are often abbreviated as sin, cos, and tan, respectively.

YOU'RE ALMOST DONE

There are three more relationships to memorize. They involve the reciprocals of the previous three.

$$\text{The cosecant} = \frac{1}{\text{sine}}$$

$$\text{The secant} = \frac{1}{\text{cosine}}$$

$$\text{The cotangent} = \frac{1}{\text{tangent}}$$

Let's try a few problems.

31. What is sin θ, if $\tan\theta = \frac{4}{3}$?

A. $\frac{3}{4}$

B. $\frac{4}{5}$

C. $\frac{5}{4}$

D. $\frac{5}{3}$

E. $\frac{7}{3}$

Helpful Trig Identities

$$\sin^2\theta + \cos^2\theta = 1$$

$$\frac{\sin\theta}{\cos\theta} = \tan\theta$$

Here's How to Crack It

It helps to sketch out the right triangle and fill in the information we know.

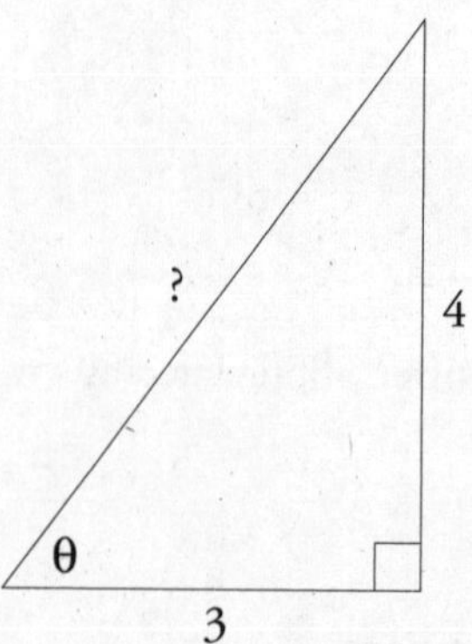

What kind of right triangle is this? That's right—a 3-4-5. Now, we need to know the sine of angle θ: opposite over hypotenuse, or $\frac{4}{5}$, which is (B).

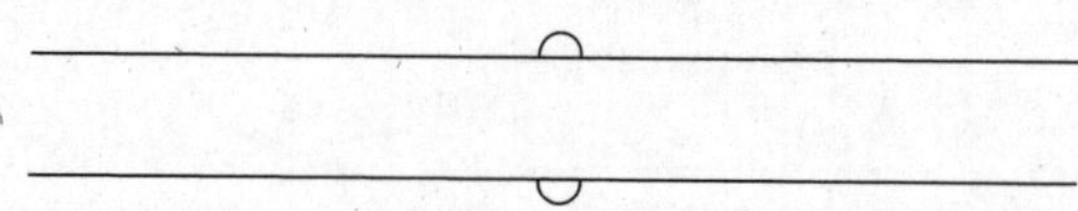

43. For all θ, $\dfrac{\cos\ \theta}{\sin^2\theta + \cos^2\theta} =$

A. $\sin\theta$
B. $\csc\theta$
C. $\cot\theta$
D. $\cos\theta$
E. $\tan\theta$

Here's How to Crack It

$\text{Sin}^2\theta + \cos^2\theta$ always equals 1. $\dfrac{\cos\theta}{1} = \cos\theta$. The answer is (D).

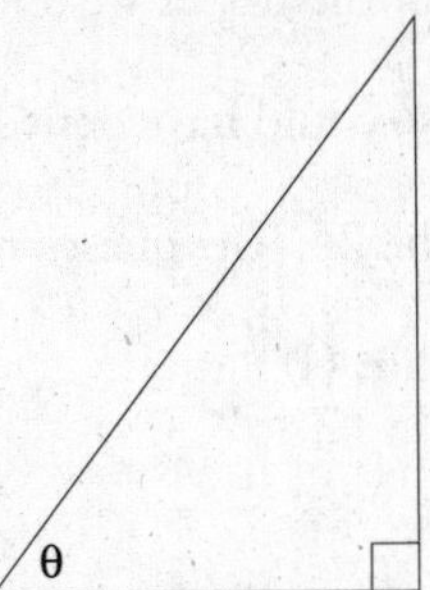

50. In a right triangle shown above, sec θ is $\frac{25}{7}$. What is sin θ ?

F. $\frac{3}{25}$

G. $\frac{5}{25}$

H. $\frac{7}{25}$

J. $\frac{24}{25}$

K. $\frac{25}{7}$

Here's How to Crack It

The secant of any angle is the reciprocal of the cosine, which is just another way of saying that the cosine of angle θ is $\frac{7}{25}$.

Secant $\theta \frac{1}{\cos\theta}$ so $\frac{1}{\cos\theta} = \frac{25}{7}$, which means that $\cos\theta = \frac{7}{25}$. Are you done? No! Cross off (H) because you know it's not the answer.

Cosine means adjacent over hypotenuse. Let's sketch it.

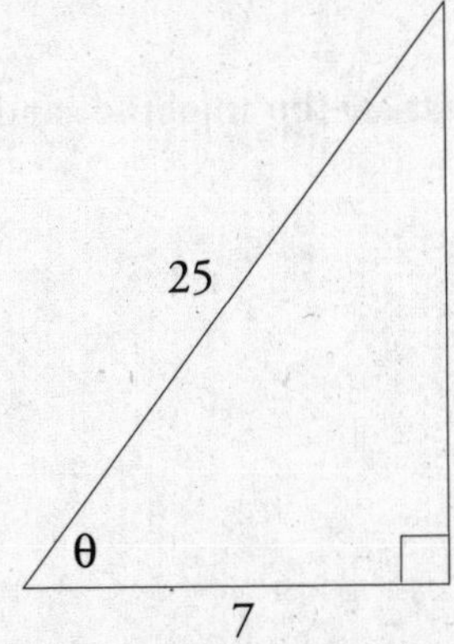

As you can see, we now have two sides of a right triangle. Can we find the third side? If you said this was one of the triples we told you about before, you are absolutely correct, although you also could have derived this by using the Pythagorean theorem. The third side must be 24. The question asks for sin θ. Sine = opposite over hypotenuse, or $\frac{24}{25}$, which is (J).

HARDER TRIGONOMETRY

When graphing a trig function, such as sine, there are two important **coefficients,** A and B: A{*sin* (Bθ)}.

The two coefficients A and B govern the **amplitude** of the graph (how tall it is) and the **period** of the graph (how long it takes to get through a complete cycle), respectively. If there are no coefficients, then that means A = 1 and B = 1 and the graph is the same as what you'd get when you graph it on your calculator.

- Increases in A increase the amplitude of the graph. It's a direct relationship.

That means if A = 2, then the amplitude is doubled. If A = $\frac{1}{2}$, then the amplitude is cut in half.

- Increases in B decrease the period of the graph. It's an inverse relationship.

That means if B = 2, then the period is cut in half, which is to say the graph completes a full cycle faster than usual. If B = $\frac{1}{2}$, then the period is doubled.

You can add to or subtract from the function as a whole, and also to or from the variable, but neither of those actions changes the shape of the graph, only its position and starting place.

Here's the graph of sin *x*. What are the amplitude and period?

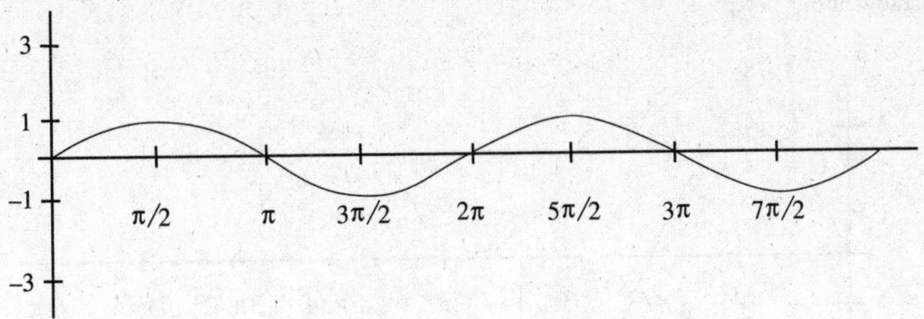

The simple function sin θ goes from –1 to 1 on the *y*-axis, so the amplitude is 1, while its period is 2π, which means that every 2π on the graph (as you go from side to side) it completes a full cycle. That's what you see in the graph above.

The graph below is also a sine function, but it's been changed. What is the function graphed here?

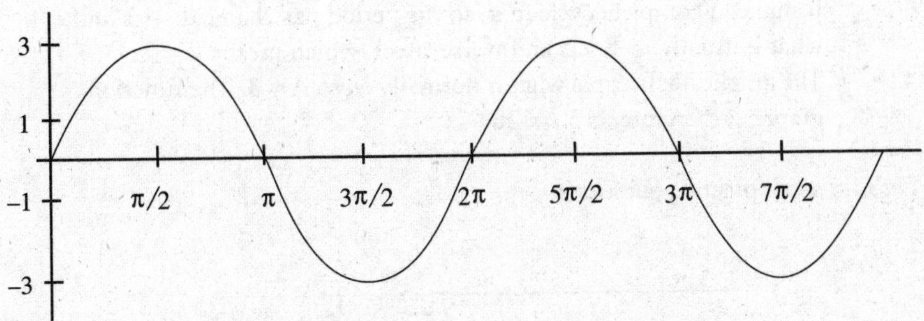

You have three things to check when looking at this graph: Is it sin or cos, is the period changed, and is the amplitude changed?

- This is a sin graph because it has a value of 0 at 0. Cos has a value of 1 at 0.
- It makes a complete cycle in 2π, so the period isn't changed. In other words, B = 1.
- The amplitude is triple what it normally is, so A = 3. The function graphed, therefore, is 3 sin θ.

How about here?

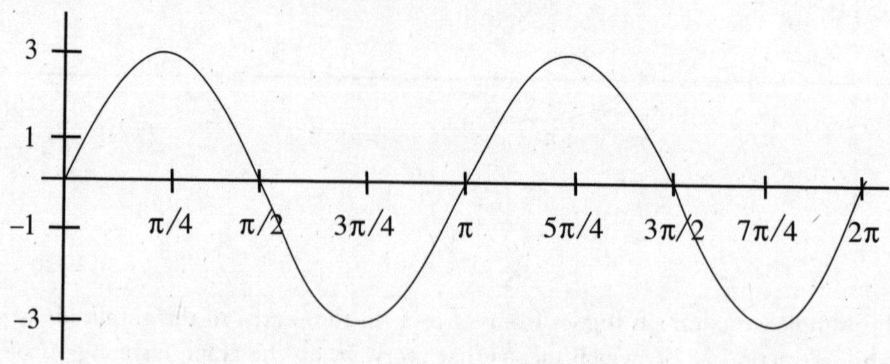

Once again, there are three things to check.

- This is a sin graph because it has a value of 0 at 0. Cos has a value of 1 at 0.
- It makes a complete cycle in π, so the period has changed—it's half of what it usually is. B has an inverse effect, which means B = 2.
- The amplitude is triple what it normally is, so A = 3. The function graphed, therefore, is 3 sin 2θ.

Let's try some practice questions.

49. As compared with the graph of $y = \cos x$, which of the following has the same period and three times the amplitude?

A. $y = \cos 3x$

B. $y = \cos \frac{1}{2}(x + 3)$

C. $y = 3 \cos \frac{1}{2}x$

D. $y = 1 + 3 \cos x$

E. $y = 3 + \cos x$

Here's How to Crack It

Recall that the coefficient on the outside of the function changes the amplitude and the one on the inside changes the period. Because the question states that the period isn't changed, you can eliminate (A), (B), and (C). The amplitude is three times greater, you're told; because there's a direct relationship between (A) and amplitude, you want to have a 3 multiplying the outside of the function. That leaves only (D) as a possibility.

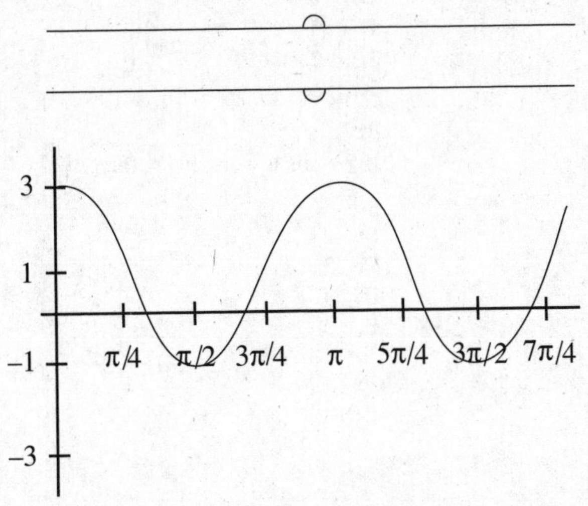

52. Which of the following equations describes the equation graphed above?

F. $2 \cos x$
G. $1 + 2 \cos x$
H. $\cos 2x$
J. $1 + \cos 2x$
K. $1 + 2 \cos 2x$

Here's How to Crack It

At first it looks like this graph has an amplitude of 3, but if you look closer, you'll see that though the top value is 3, the bottom value is –1, which means that the whole graph has been shifted up. Because (F) and (H) don't add anything to the function (which is how you move a graph up and down), they're out. The period of this graph is half of what it usually is, so B = 2, which eliminates (G). Because the amplitude is changed also, you can eliminate (J). The answer is (K).

Trigonometry Drill

1. In ΔABC below, the $\tan\theta$ equals

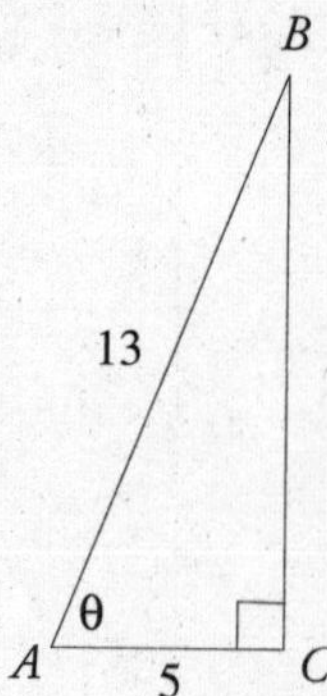

A. $\frac{5}{12}$
B. $\frac{12}{13}$
C. $\frac{17}{12}$
D. $\frac{12}{5}$
E. 3

2. If the cotangent of an angle θ is 1, then the tangent of angle θ is

F. –1
G. 0
H. 1
J. 2
K. 3

3. If $x + \sin^2\theta + \cos^2\theta = 4$, then $x = ?$

A. 1
B. 2
C. 3
D. 4
E. 5

Summary

- There are only four trigonometry questions on the ACT. At least two will deal with right triangles, and they are relatively easy if you know a few formulas.

- SOHCAHTOA will help you remember most of the formulas.

$$\text{sine} = \frac{\text{opposite}}{\text{hypotenuse}};\ \text{cosine} = \frac{\text{adjacent}}{\text{hypotenuse}};$$

$$\text{tangent} = \frac{\text{opposite}}{\text{adjacent}}$$

- The cosecant $= \frac{1}{\text{sine}}$, the secant $= \frac{1}{\text{cosine}}$, and the cotangent $= \frac{1}{\text{tangent}}$.

- $\sin^2\theta + \cos^2\theta = 1$.

- $\frac{\sin\theta}{\cos\theta} = \tan\theta$.

- For trig graphs, focus on the amplitude and the period: A{*sin* (Bθ)}. The amplitude is directly related to the size of A, while the period is inversely related to the size of B.

Part IV
How to Crack the ACT Reading Test

Chapter 16
Introduction to the ACT Reading Test

Reading on the ACT is not the same as reading for school. When you're reading for school, you have to *understand* what you've read and be able to discuss it. On the ACT, you only have to understand enough of the passage to answer the questions. You don't need to discuss the passage later. In fact, you'll just forget it. Therefore, rather than reading to remember, you'll want to direct your reading to find the right answers. This chapter shows you how to do just that.

OVERVIEW: CRACKING AND PACING THE READING TEST

The ACT Reading Test Format
You read 4 passages and answer 40 questions in 35 minutes.

The ACT Reading test presents 4 passages with 10 questions each. That's 40 questions total. You get 35 minutes for the whole section, which means you have about 9 minutes to cover each passage and the questions that follow it, *if* your pacing strategy requires you to work all 4 passages

The passages are edited pieces of books and magazines, and according to ACT, they're "typical of what a college freshman might be required to read...." And the questions? ACT says they test your ability to "understand" the passages.

But That's Not Really True

No one ever achieved a great insight by spending eight or nine pressured minutes reading an isolated fragment of a book or an article. Serious writers don't intend their works to be read in fragments or in so hurried a fashion as reading tests require. (Imagine that you were asked to read a *fragment* of the history of the relations between the United States, Germany, and Japan during the twentieth century. Suppose, in particular, that you're asked to read only about their cooperative relations in the years 1985–1990. You'd be missing the history of their relationships during the years 1940–1945—World War II—which means you'd be missing a rather important piece of the story.)

Furthermore, serious readers take time to think about the things they read. How far would Albert Einstein have gotten if someone had interrupted his reading after 35 minutes to announce that he should "close his book because time is up"? As a college student, you'll be asked not only to read but also to think about what you read—and then to reread—and then to think some more. Any professor will tell you that understanding takes thought, and thought usually takes time.

When you take the ACT Reading test, you're not asked to understand. You're not asked to do anything you'll ever do in college. You're just asked to take a "reading test."

The ACT Reading Test: Cracking the System

You'll raise your reading score if you're "wise" to the test and if you think strategically. We're first going to show you how ACT reading questions are built. Then we'll show you how to use that knowledge to select correct answers. You'll learn to implement the techniques covered below.

1. Attack the passages in the order that best suits you.
2. See through the camouflage that hides correct answer choices.
3. Identify incorrect answer choices and eliminate them quickly.
4. Answer questions without really reading the passage.
5. Put all of these techniques together to approach every passage and question with a step-by-step strategy that leads systematically to the correct answers.

READING TEST TRIAGE: ORDERING THE PASSAGES

The Reading test has four passages, one each from the following fields:

- Prose Fiction (excerpts from short stories and novels)
- Social Sciences (history, economics, psychology, political sciences, and anthropology)
- Humanities (art, music, architecture, and dance)
- Natural Sciences (biology, chemistry, physics, and physical sciences)

Students differ in their abilities to tackle these different passage types, and it's important that you decide which passages are easiest and hardest for you. That way you can decide which passages to do first (the easier ones) and which to do last or never (the harder ones). The passages are always in the same order.

Prose Fiction Passages

The prose fiction passage is almost the opposite of the natural science passage. It tells a fictitious story and is supposed to be packed with hints and suggestions about characters and their motivations.

> Allen's grandmother was readying herself to leave. She was, in fact, putting the final touches on her makeup which, as always, looked to Allen as though someone had thrown it on her face with a shovel. As Mrs. Mandale placed her newly purchased bracelet over her wrist, a look of troubled ambivalence came over her. "Perhaps this bracelet isn't right for me," she said. "I won't wear it."
>
> Waiting now for 30 minutes, Allen tried to be tolerant. "It is right for you," he said. "It matches your personality. Wear it." The bracelet was a remarkable illustration of poor taste. Its colors were vulgar and the structure lacked any sign of thoughtful design. The truth is, it did match his grandmother's personality. All that she did and enjoyed was tasteless and induced in Allen a quiet hopelessness.

Fiction Passages
Most prose fiction passages are primarily concerned with the following five things:

- Who
- What
- When
- Where
- Why

Prose fiction questions often require that you "read between the lines" and draw inferences about the way characters feel or behave.

1. Allen most likely encouraged his grandmother to wear her bracelet because he:

A. found it colorful and approved of its appearance.
B. found its appearance pathetic and wished his grandmother to look pretty.
C. was impatient with his grandmother for spending time worrying about the bracelet.
D. felt the bracelet matched his grandmother's bright personality.

Some people have an ability for these kinds of passages and questions. Others find them unclear and confusing. If you find literature passages easiest, do them first. If you find them most difficult, do them last or never.

For the record, the answer is (C). Allen has been waiting and is trying "to be tolerant."

Social Science and Humanities Passages

Social science and humanities passages are sort of a cross between natural science and prose fiction. Often, the author has views about the subject he or she is discussing, and you might be asked to draw inferences about them. You might also be asked questions about details.

Religion is so fundamental a part of human existence that one might easily forget to ask how it started. Yet it had to start somewhere and there had to be a time when human beings or their apelike ancestors did not entertain notions of the supernatural. Hence the historian should want to probe the origins of religious belief.

It is doubtful that morality played a part in the beginnings of religious belief. Rather, religion is traceable to a far more fundamental human and animal characteristic. Storms, floods, famine, and other adversities inspired *fear* in the hearts of primitive peoples as well they should have. Curiously, humankind early took the position that it might somehow subject such catastrophes to its control. Specifically, it believed it might control them by obedience and submission and by conforming its behavior to their mandates. Worship, ritual, sacrifice of life, and property became means through which early peoples sought to cajole the powers and avoid the blights and miseries the peoples dreaded. As Petronius, in Lucretius's tradition remarked, "It was fear that first made the gods."

11. According to the passage, natural disasters contributed to the development of religion by:

A. motivating human beings to acquire some command over their environment.
B. making human beings distinguish themselves from animals.
C. causing human beings to sacrifice their lives and goods.
D. providing a need for ritual and tradition.

12. The author believes that the origins of religion:

F. are extremely easy to ascertain and understand.
G. should not be questioned by historians because religion is fundamental to civilized life.
H. are directly tied to apelike subhuman species.
J. should be the subject of serious historical inquiry.

The correct answer to 11 is (A) and the answer to 12 is (J).

Mark Twain had magnificent style, and with *The Adventures of Huckleberry Finn*, he built the gateway to American fiction. *Huckleberry Finn* treats extraordinarily serious themes, and it reflects the author's coming of age. Although they don't represent truly mature works, other Twain Mississippi River stories, published before Huck Finn, afford Americans a clear, collective picture of pre–Civil War life in the Mississippi Valley.

With the coming and going of the Civil War, however, Twain adopted a revised agenda, which was reflected in the style and subject matter of his writing. The postwar era demanded that he address himself to the nation's social squalor. His work was more intellectualized, artificial, and at times angry. The author himself had faced several personal tragedies in series, and these too might have contributed to the metamorphosis.

21. According to the passage, which of the following statements is true of *The Adventures of Huckleberry Finn*?

A. It appeared after the publication of other Mark Twain stories describing life on the Mississippi River.
B. It was the first full-length book that Mark Twain published.
C. It would have been quite different if Mark Twain had not suffered personal tragedy.
D. It had no serious themes and addressed no serious issues.

22. In the author's opinion, *The Adventures of Huckleberry Finn*:

F. should not be read by children.
G. contributed less to American literature than did Twain's postwar writings.
H. is less adult in its subject matter than were Twain's postwar writings.
J. reveals that Mark Twain had grown since writing his early Mississippi River stories.

Our answers here are (A) for 21 and (J) for 22.

Natural Science Passages

Natural science passages are filled with lots of details and technical descriptions.

> It is further noteworthy that the terrestrial vertebrate's most significant muscles of movement are no longer located lateral to the vertebral column as they are in the fish but rather in ventral and dorsal relation to it. This trend in terrestrial evolution is highly significant and means that the terrestrial vertebrate's principal movements are fore and back, not side to side. The trend is well documented in the whale, an aquatic animal whose ancestors are terrestrial quadrupeds. The whale, in other words, has "returned" to the sea secondarily after an ancestral stage on the land. Unlike the fish, and in accordance with its ancestry, it propels itself by moving the tail up and down, not side to side. In a sense, the whale moves itself by bending up and down at the waist. Indeed, that very analogy is recalled by the mythical mermaid figure who seems to represent a humanlike line returned to the water secondarily like the whale.

The questions usually track the text pretty closely and require you to make few inferences.

31. Which of the following best represents a general trend associated with mammalian evolution?

- **A.** Enhancement of bodily movement from right to left and left to right
- **B.** Minimization of muscle groups oriented lateral to the vertebral column
- **C.** The development of propulsive fins from paired limbs
- **D.** Secondary return to the sea

Some people have a flair for the ACT's natural science passages, and some people find them extremely tedious and difficult. (And, by the way, it isn't necessarily good science students who do well with these passages nor poor science students who have trouble with them.) If among all of the passage types you find natural science the easiest, you should make it a rule to address the natural science passage first. If you find natural science passages the most difficult, however, save them for last.

The answer to 31 is (B).

Reading Test Triage

If you have a knack for particular passage types, great. Do them first. If not, look at the topics, as well as the questions and answer choices. Some will be straightforward, while others will look more complicated. Use your time wisely.

TIME, TIME AGAIN

After working through the chapters in this book, you will have a good idea of which types of passages are easiest for you and which are hardest. When you take the Reading test, you should do the easiest (for you) passages first. Why? Because many people run out of time on the ACT Reading test. It's better to run out of time and have to guess on the passages that are the most difficult. You'll get more points at the beginning by working the easier passages first, and you'll lose fewer points by guessing on the hardest passage as time runs out.

For more great titles by The Princeton Review
Reading Smart

How to Tell Which Passages You Find Easy and Hard

What do you do if you dislike all of the passages equally or show no particular—or, for that matter, consistent—knack for certain passage types? The subject matter of the passages may be dull, but in the end, you should base your ordering of the passages on

- **the user-friendliness of the topics themselves**
  "Wait a minute!" you say. "I thought you said that if I show no particular knack for certain passage types..." True, but...
  Let's say you notice that a social science or humanities passage is historical in nature. Chances are that events will be presented in chronological order, making the passage easy to navigate. Or let's say you've recently learned about lasers in physics class and, lo and behold, the natural sciences passage is about lasers. Chances are that you'll be able to eliminate answers or even answer some of the questions based on what you've learned. You don't have to love a topic to take advantage of familiarity with it. In fact, being too enamored of a topic can work against you. Remember, you get points for answering questions correctly, not for understanding the passages, and certainly not for reading over them with great interest.
- **the user-friendliness of the questions and answer choices**
  Many students who dislike all the passages find this an especially helpful guideline. Look at the questions. Do many of them direct you to particular lines in the passage, refer to dates, refer to proper nouns, or refer to italicized words? If so, a passage with several such questions will usually be much easier to manage. Look at the answer choices. Are they relatively straightforward, or do they resemble miniature novels? A passage with several longwinded questions and/or answer choices will always take more time to complete.

Take a quick look at the Reading in practice test 1. Try glancing at each passage—looking at either the topic or the questions and answer choices—and ask yourself which one looks easiest to you and which one you definitely want to leave for last. Ordering passages takes a little time at the beginning, but it can save you a lot of time (and gain you points) in the end.

Now that we've talked about the ordering of the passages and questions, let's talk about the whole point of this book—finding right answers.

THE RIGHT ANSWER MIGHT BE CAMOUFLAGED

Look at these two phrases.

"rationally conceived idea"

"concept born of reason"

The two phrases don't have a single word in common, but if you think about it, you'll probably agree that they mean the same thing. Lots of ACT reading questions test your ability to see that one sentence or phrase means more or less the same as another even though the wording is quite different. They test whether you can see that a sentence has been *paraphrased*, which means reworded.

Correct Answer Choices May Be Disguised

Look for answer choices that reword parts of the passage.

Read This Passage; It's Very Short

Regardless of personal religious belief, no true student of history can emerge from study without a scholarly appreciation for the significant role of religion in the development of human civilization.

Now that you've read the passage, answer this question.

11. Which of the following represents the author's belief regarding religion and the study of history?

- **A.** Many historians develop a deep suspicion of totalitarian societies and the way in which they abuse human rights.
- **B.** Most historians have a profound distaste for ancient documents and torn papers.
- **C.** True historians develop an appreciation for the role of religion in the course of human development.
- **D.** Few historians develop insight into the manner in which political leaders gain power.

It's pretty easy to see that (C) is right, and that (A), (B), and (D) are wrong. Choice (C) features the author's words and accurately reflects his meaning. Choices (A), (B), and (D) are extreme and have nothing whatsoever to do with anything in the passage. This question is pretty straightforward. The wrong answers are clearly wrong, and the right answer is clearly right.

Many ACT Questions Aren't so Easy

ACT questions won't always provide you with a correct answer that reprints the author's own words. Instead, the author's statements will be camouflaged by *rewording*. That means you must be on the lookout for answer choices that don't seem right because the author's sentences have been reworded. Let's take the question we just answered and turn it into an ACT question by rewriting the answer choices.

11. Which of the following represents the author's belief regarding the role of religion in the study of history?

A. Few historians have gained a complete appreciation for the development of religion.
B. Historians should not allow their personal religious beliefs to affect the historical conclusions with which they emerge.
C. Serious historians regard religious belief as an important force in man's social evolution.
D. A true student of religious history should not ignore a general study of human development.

Answer choice (C) is still the correct answer, but that's not so easy to spot anymore. Unless you're on the lookout for camouflage, you might not appreciate the similarity between these two statements:

1. …no true student of history can emerge from study without a scholarly appreciation for the significant role of religion in the development of human civilization.	*and*	2. Serious historians regard religious belief as an important force in man's social evolution.

These two statements don't have a single word in common. Yet, when you think about it,

"serious historians"	*is camouflage for*	"true student of history"
"important force"	*is camouflage for*	"significant role"
"man's social evolution"	*is camouflage for*	"development of human civilization"

Answer choice (C) presents the author's statements—camouflaged.

See Through the Camouflage

You'll raise your ACT score if you learn first to recognize camouflage and then to see through it. So let's practice. Each of the very short readings below comes from an ACT-type passage. We want you to

- read each one
- think carefully about what it means
- *with that meaning in mind* consider the meaning of each answer choice
- determine which one constitutes the author's statements, camouflaged

Let's try one.

The human condition is unequal, distributing its gifts and penalties according to a wildly haphazard scheme. A person is not what he deserves to be but simply what he is.

12. According to the passage, it is true that the human condition:

F. is a precious gift and should not be treated haphazardly.
G. does not allocate its burdens and benefits according to merit.
H. will become more predictable as human beings learn to appreciate it.
J. is sometimes unjust due to fundamental aspects of human nature.

Here's How to Crack It

What does the author say? The author says that life's pleasures and hardships are not given out fairly—according to what people deserve. Instead, they're given out randomly. The author is saying that you don't get what you deserve. You just get what you get.

With that in mind, let's look at the answer options and see which one makes the same statement in a different way.

What do the choices mean?

Answer choice (F) means that life is a very valuable thing and that people should not be careless with it. That's not what we're looking for.

Answer choice (G) says just what the author has said—in different words. Think about it.

"allocate"	*is camouflage for*	"distributing"
"burdens and benefits"	*is camouflage for*	"gifts and penalties"
"merit"	*is camouflage for*	"deserves"

Answer choice (H) means that people who appreciate life will find that it offers fewer surprises. The author did not say that.

Answer choice (J) means that human nature is the cause of life's unfairness. Interesting, but that's not what the author wrote.

Only (G) comes close to expressing the author's meaning. That's why it's right.

Try another.

Poverty, deformity, illness, loss, weakness, and mistreatment impose themselves relentlessly on individual lives. That circumstance begs the historian to ask why humans have for the most part accepted the situation so peaceably.

13. The passage indicates that persistent poverty and illness:

A. are caused partially by humanity's overriding concern with acceptance and peace.
B. are due in some part to a faulty understanding of history.
C. should make historians question the role of the individual in human affairs.
D. should provoke historical inquiry into humanity's willingness to tolerate adversity.

Here's How to Crack It

What does the author say? The author says, first of all, that people have always had a lot of trouble in their lives. He then says that historians should try to figure out why they're so willing to put up with it.

What do the choices mean?

Answer choice (A) means that people have trouble because they're too concerned with peace. Ridiculous, but more important, it's not what the author wrote.

Answer choice (B) means that people have trouble because they don't understand history. Not so ridiculous, but the author made no such statement.

Answer choice (C) means that all of this trouble should make historians try to figure out the place of individuals in society. Whatever that means, it's not what we're looking for.

Now look at answer choice (D). It's just what the doctor ordered. It's the author's statement—camouflaged. Think about it.

"should provoke historical inquiry"	*is camouflage for*	"begs the historian to ask"
"willingness to tolerate adversity"	*is camouflage for*	"why humans...accepted the situation so peaceably"

So answer choice (D) is right.

Here's another one.

Religious belief allows the unlucky, on some very important level, to treat their misery as insignificant in the grand scheme of things, for they look to something higher: the approval of their god and the faith that they will not in the end be forsaken.

14. The passage states that religious belief helps people by:

F. allowing them to accept the idea that they have been forsaken.
G. providing them with faith that they will overcome their difficulties.
H. diminishing the importance they might place on their day-to-day pain.
J. emphasizing that spiritual strength is more significant than luck.

Here's How to Crack It

What does the author say? The author says that religious belief helps people whose lives are difficult. It causes them to focus on the wish to please their god, which means that they place relatively little importance on the troubles they face in their lives.

What do the choices mean?

Answer choice (F) means that religious believers don't mind being forsaken. Sorry, not what we're looking for.

Answer choice (G) means that religion helps people believe they'll get over their problems. Sounds good, but it's not the meaning we're after.

Answer choice (H) means that religious believers don't think their troubles are so important. That's what the author said! Choice (H) represents the author's statements camouflaged. Think about it:

"diminishing the importance"	*is camouflage for*	"treat...as insignificant"
"pain"	*is camouflage for*	"misery"

Answer choice (J) means that religious believers think spiritual strength is more important than luck. The author doesn't say anything like that. Only (H) reflects the author's meaning. That's why it's right.

Summary

- There are always 4 passages and 40 questions on the ACT Reading test. The passages are always in this order: prose fiction, social science, humanities, and natural science.
- Spend the first minute of the test determining which passage will be hardest for you—this is the one to leave until last. Playing to your strengths early in the test will gain you the most points.
- Be wary of camouflaged answers. ACT test writers rarely use a direct quote from the passage in the correct answer.
- Don't forget to always guess your Letter of the Day if there are questions that you can't answer or don't get to in time.

Chapter 17
Distracters

The ACT test writers are good at writing wrong answers that look right. To get you to pick these wrong answers, they utilize certain distracting techniques. This chapter shows you how to be on the lookout for deceptive answers that track the language of the passage very closely, for switches that say the opposite of the correct answer, for extreme answer choices, and for answers that sound too nice. They are usually incorrect.

GET WISE TO DISTRACTERS: USE PROCESS OF ELIMINATION

You'll raise your ACT Reading score if you're good at spotting not only right answers but also the wrong ones. In the standardized test business, wrong answers are called "distracters," and that's a perfect name for them. Distracters are designed to misdirect your thinking—to break your concentration, distract you, and throw you off course. Even if you have a pretty good grasp of the passage and the question you're trying to answer, distracters can make you lose sight of both. But if you're wise to distracters, you can quickly eliminate them and rapidly make your way to the right answer.

FOUR KINDS OF DISTRACTERS

You should know about the four kinds of distracters that show up on the ACT Reading test. We're going to show you how each one operates so you'll know how to use them to your advantage.

Distracter 1: Deceptive Answers

Many distracters steal words directly from the passages and use them to create a statement that does *not* reflect the content of the passages. These distracters use the authors' words but distort their meanings, so we call them *deceptive answers.*

Read this statement.

> *Tom loves going to the movies with Mary.*

It's easy to write a bunch of sentences that do not reflect the statement's meaning, even though they use the words "Tom," "love," "movies," and "Mary." For example, consider this

> *Tom fell in love with Mary at the movies.*

or this

> *Tom and Mary love movies.*

or this

> *Tom and Mary generally enjoy seeing movies about love.*

If you think about *meaning,* not one of these statements resembles the one with which we started. Each distorts the original by taking its words and rearranging them. Yet they all sort of "sound like" the original because they use the same words.

Each one of the deceptive answers we just read would make a good ACT distracter. Suppose you've just read an ACT passage that contains the statement we worked with: "Tom loves going to the movies with Mary." Now imagine that you get a question like this

1. According to the passage, which of the following statements is true regarding Tom and Mary?

A. Tom fell in love with Mary at the movies.
B. Tom enjoys viewing motion pictures with Mary as his companion.
C. Tom and Mary generally enjoy seeing movies about love.
D. Both Tom and Mary love going to the movies.

Notice that (A), (C), and (D) use words that come straight from the passage. *They're all wrong.* Which one is right? Answer choice (B): It presents the author's meaning—in camouflage.

Use Process of Elimination (POE)
Look for the following four types of distracters on the ACT Reading test:

- deceptive answers
- the switch
- extremes
- answer choices that sound too nice

Don't Let Deceptive Answers Snare You

Don't be fooled by answer choices that misuse words and phrases from the passage.

Look at these four excerpts from ACT-like passages. Each one is followed by five statements. Three of the five are deceptive answer distracters. The other two accurately reflect the author's meaning; they *don't* distort. For each passage, decide which three statements are deceptive answers and which two are not.

Read this natural science excerpt.

As an explanation for the age and origin of the solar system, the nebular hypothesis lost ground at the turn of the twentieth century over questions about the distribution of angular momentum.

What does the author say?

- The nebular hypothesis was intended to explain the age and origin of the solar system.
- It lost influence at the beginning of the twentieth century.
- It happened because people raised questions about the distribution of angular momentum, and the nebular hypothesis did not provide adequate answers.

Now evaluate these statements.

	Deceptive Answer	Not a Deceptive Answer
31. According to the nebular hypothesis, the solar system was created by distributions of angular momentum.	☐	☐
32. The nebular hypothesis came under question at the beginning of the twentieth century.	☐	☐
33. The nebular hypothesis was challenged because of issues related to angular momentum.	☐	☐
34. Knowledge about the solar system's angular momentum was first distributed in the twentieth century.	☐	☐
35. The nebular hypothesis was poorly understood until the twentieth century, when theories of angular momentum gained ground.	☐	☐

Important
Distortions are often words in the passage that are used out of context. Eliminate them.

Statements 31, 34, and 35 are deceptive. They distort the author's meaning. The words come straight from the passage, but the meanings definitely do not. The author does not say

- the nebular hypothesis states that distributions of angular momentum created the solar system
- someone first distributed knowledge about angular momentum in the twentieth century
- people didn't understand the nebular hypothesis until the twentieth century

Statements 32 and 33 are not deceptive answers. They do not distort. The author does say

- the nebular hypothesis was questioned (lost ground) at the beginning of the twentieth century
- the nebular hypothesis was questioned because of concerns relating to angular momentum

Read this social science excerpt.

With revolutionary improvements in health care technologies, modern medicine's expansive arsenal has undoubtedly created an improved state of national health. Although the incidence of degenerative disease is on the rise, that is primarily because degenerative diseases are characteristic of old age and the population is living, on average, longer than did its parents and grandparents.

What does the author say?

- There has been great progress in medicine.
- It's true that there's more degenerative disease around than there used to be.
- That's because degenerative diseases usually affect the elderly, and people are living long enough to *get* these diseases.

Now evaluate these statements.	**Deceptive Answer**	**Not a Deceptive Answer**
11. Modern medicine has increased the individual's average life span.	☐	☐
12. Revolutionary health care techniques have produced degeneration in the state of national health.	☐	☐
13. Few people doubt that degenerative disease tends to increase longevity.	☐	☐
14. Today's health care technologies have bettered the national health.	☐	☐
15. With today's tools and techniques the physician can cure degenerative diseases that once caused early death.	☐	☐

Statements 12, 13, and 15 are deceptive answers. They distort the author's meaning. The words are familiar, but they've been rearranged to say something that has nothing to do with the passage. The author does not say

- modern medicine has had a negative effect on health care
- most people think degenerative disease makes for longer life
- modern medicine allows physicians to cure degenerative diseases

Statements 11 and 14 are not deceptive answers. They do not distort. The author does say

- modern medicine has increased the average life span
- modern medicine has improved the national health

Read this prose fiction excerpt.

Mrs. Mandale's physician repeatedly reminded his patient of her diabetes and had ordered her on several occasions to lose weight. Hence, Allen found himself taking his grandmother once each week to her weight-watching group.

Mrs. Mandale was not among the heavier women in her group. She never announced her weight, however, because, "a true lady did not discuss such personal matters." The group was one of Mrs. Mandale's few pleasures, but she feared walking unaccompanied in the city at night and asked that Allen take her each week to "group." She pointed out that she had done much for him, that her very health was involved, and that he should be willing to extend himself for her.

Half-and-Half
Beware of answer choices that are half good, half bad. They're also deceptive. If an answer is half bad, it's all wrong.

What does the author say?

- Allen's grandmother has diabetes.
- For that reason, her doctor ordered her to lose weight.
- To lose the weight, she participates in a weight-watching group.
- She's not one of the heavier women in the group.
- Even so, she won't reveal her weight, because she thinks true ladies shouldn't discuss such personal issues.
- The weight-watching group is one of Mrs. Mandale's few pleasures.
- The weight-watching group is conducted at night, and Mrs. Mandale does not like to walk in the city by herself at night.
- Mrs. Mandale thinks she's done a lot for Allen so she asks him to take her to her weight-watching group each week.

Now evaluate these statements.

	Deceptive Answer	Not a Deceptive Answer
1. Mrs. Mandale is willing to reveal her weight only because she weighs less than others in her weight-watching group.	☐	☐
2. The doctor recommends that Allen's grandmother not walk alone at night.	☐	☐
3. Mrs. Mandale finds her weight reduction group more enjoyable than most of her other activities.	☐	☐
4. Mrs. Mandale thinks that other women in her weight-watching group are not as ladylike as she is.	☐	☐
5. Mrs. Mandale believes she has been a positive force in her grandson's life.	☐	☐

Statements 1, 2, and 4 are deceptive answers. They distort the author's meaning. The key words come straight from the passage, but the statements are distortions. The author does not say

- Mrs. Mandale is willing to reveal her weight
- the doctor advised Mrs. Mandale against walking alone at night
- Mrs. Mandale believes herself to be more of a lady than the other women in the group

Statements 3 and 5 are not deceptive answers. They do not distort. The author does say

- the weight-watching group is one of the few pleasures Mrs. Mandale has
- Mrs. Mandale thinks she has done a lot for her grandson

Read this humanities excerpt.

Before the Civil War, Frances Ellen Watkins Harper was the best known of black abolitionist writers. Her greatest true novel, *Iola Leroy,* or *Shadows Uplifted,* appeared in 1892. The work was transitional: It treats both the pre–Civil War and post–Civil War periods. Although it describes the evils of slavery, its principal purpose was considerably different from some of the earlier novels for which Mrs. Harper became famous. In *Iola Leroy,* Mrs. Harper wished to promote justice and interracial tolerance. For that reason, the novel treats some issues with more idealism than realism.

Referring to her own novel, Mrs. Harper wrote: "I have woven a story whose mission will not be in vain if it awakens in the hearts of our countrymen a stronger sense of justice and a more Christlike humanity."

What does the author say?

- Mrs. Harper was a black abolitionist writer—the most famous of her time.
- Her greatest earlier novels dealt primarily with the evils of slavery.
- Her best novel was *Iola Leroy,* which was also called *Shadows Uplifted.*
- Dealing with the periods before and after the Civil War, *Iola Leroy* portrays the evils of slavery; Mrs. Harper primarily intended the novel to promote justice and tolerance among races.
- Because that was her purpose, she sometimes treated issues not in a realistic manner, but in an idealistic manner.

Now evaluate these statements. | **Deceptive Answer** | **Not a Deceptive Answer**

Now evaluate these statements.	Deceptive Answer	Not a Deceptive Answer
21. *Iola Leroy* depicts situations occurring before and after the Civil War.	☐	☐
22. Frances Ellen Watkins Harper was not well known as an abolitionist until the appearance of her first true novel, *Iola Leroy*.	☐	☐
23. Although best known as abolitionist literature, Mrs. Harper's prewar novels usually concerned justice, not slavery.	☐	☐
24. Mrs. Harper was well known before the Civil War but in the postwar period her fame diminished considerably.	☐	☐
25. Frances Ellen Watkins Harper opposed slavery before the war and attempted to improve relations among blacks and whites after the war.	☐	☐

Statements 22, 23, and 24 are deceptive answers. They distort the author's meaning. The words come right out of the passage, but the meanings have nothing to do with it. The author definitely does not say

- *Iola Leroy* was Mrs. Harper's *first* true novel, or that Mrs. Harper was not well known until that novel appeared
- Mrs. Harper's prewar novels concerned justice and not slavery
- Mrs. Harper lost fame after the Civil War

Statements 21 and 25 are not deceptive answers. They do not distort. The author does indicate that

- *Iola Leroy* concerned both the pre–Civil War and post–Civil War periods
- Mrs. Harper was an abolitionist before the war and that her postwar novel *Iola Leroy* was intended to improve relations among the races

Distracter 2: Switches

Some ACT distracters take the truth and switch it around. We call this "the switch." Don't let it fool you. For instance, read this.

> **1.** Professor Thorne generally explains a technological discovery first in terms of its history and then in terms of the science up on which it was founded.

We've learned that Professor Thorne discusses history *first* and science *second.*

Now look at this statement.

> **2.** Professor Thorne generally explains a technological discovery first in terms of the science on which it was founded, and then in terms of its history.

Statement 2 looks like Statement 1, but it's backward. Professor Thorne is doing things in the wrong order: science first and history second. Statement 2 takes the truth and turns it around. That's the essence of "the switch."

But the ACT Test Writers Get Sneaky

When the ACT test writers throw a switch into the answer choices, they don't always write something like Statement 2, which takes the author's statement and literally reverses the order of its words. Sometimes they *change* the wording and at the same time, turn the meaning upside down. Read Statement 1 again, and then look at Statement 3 below.

Use Process of Elimination (POE)

Sometimes it's easier to find the correct answer by eliminating the wrong answer choices. If you can eliminate answer choices with distracters such as deceptive answers, switches, or extremes, as well as answer choices that are too nice, you'll increase your chance of getting the right answer.

> **3.** After Professor Thorne describes the scientific aspects of a technological breakthrough, he explains the historical context in which the breakthrough was made.

It's not so easy to see at first, but Statement 3 is a switch. It doesn't use the words *first*, or *then*, and it begins with the word "after." But think about what it says. Professor Thorne discusses history *after* discussing science. That would mean that he discusses science first and history second. That's opposite to what you're told in the passage.

Now read this.

> **4.** Irrespective of population, every state elects two members to the United States Senate. The most populous state and the least populous state thus have equal representation in that important legislative body. In contrast, the House of Representatives is population-based and the number of representatives elected by any state depends on the number of citizens residing in that state.

Here's a switch.

5. Representation in the United States Senate is dependent on state population.

From Statement 4, we learned

- representation in the Senate is *not* based on population
- representation in the House *is* based on population

Statement 5 is exactly opposite to the original. It's a switch.

Eliminate the Switch

Let's say you're looking at a question. You spot two deceptive answers and eliminate them. That leaves you with two choices, and you aren't sure which is right. One thing you should do is determine whether one of them is a switch. If it is, then the *other* one is right. Here are two passage excerpts—each one followed by two to three questions. For each question, determine which answer choice is the switch.

The Switch

Look out for

- changes in the wording in the answer choices
- a "flip" in the meaning of the sentence

Read this social sciences excerpt.

Twenty or thirty thousand years ago, *Homo Sapiens* were uncommon animals, wandering alone or in small groups in a constant search for food. Primitive humans lived by the hunt, and modern nutritionists like to observe that with meat as a dietary staple, they were seldom iron-deficient as are many farm-based populations today. But the absence of iron deficiency was perhaps the only advantage to the hunting lifestyle of the time. The hunter, it should be remembered, may find himself the hunted, and by anything approaching our own standards today, primitive human life was unstable and incessantly hazardous.

In this regard, however, the advent of agriculture improved the human condition. Between ten and twenty thousand years ago, human beings discovered the use of herding and of growing, which apparently served as inspiration to man's mechanical facilities. Relatively crude weapons of hunt were replaced by more refined farming implements. To be sure, farming is subject to the uncertainties of weather and climate, but it ultimately allows humans a greater degree of control over their food supply and relieves them from the dangers of the hunt.

11. In terms of the tools and implements made by primitive man, the passage suggests that:

A. farming tools were less sophisticated than hunting weapons.
B. [Already eliminated]
C. agriculture is associated with more advanced tool-making skills.
D. [Already eliminated]

Look at (A). It says farming tools are less sophisticated than hunting weapons. Now look at the passage, lines 16–17. It says that hunting implements were crude and that farming implements were more refined. Choice (A) has it backward—it's a switch. Eliminate it.

12. According to the passage, a life based on agriculture:

F. [Already eliminated]
G. provides humans with more iron than is provided by hunting.
H. [Already eliminated]
J. offers a greater degree of certainty than does a hunting lifestyle.

Look at (G). It says that agriculture provides more iron than does hunting. The author does discuss iron deficiency, but she says that hunters were *not* iron deficient, and that farmers *are*. Choice (G) is a switch. Eliminate it.

Read this natural science excerpt.

In certain critical respects the magnificence of science lies not in its discovery of what is true but in its identification of that which is not. Pivotal points in scientific learning are those at which some long-held assumption is openly examined and exposed as a falsehood. Copernicus, Kepler, Galileo, and ultimately Newton established that the sun, not the earth, is the fixed center of the solar system and that the earth orbits the sun, thus invalidating the views of Aristotle and Ptolemy, which were largely unquestioned before that time.

Toward the turn of the last century, Michelson, Morley, Lorentz, and Einstein successfully challenged a host of assumptions about the absolute quality of space and time. Then, in the 1920s, theories put forward by Heisenberg, Schrodinger, and Dirac together created the science of quantum mechanics and thus destroyed time-honored views about position and velocity. Even Einstein had difficulty accepting Heisenberg's theory, which dealt a lethal blow to the cherished notion, advocated especially by LaPlace, that science could aspire to complete knowledge of the state of the universe and thus predict its future.

In 1929, Hubble, versed in the writings of Olbers one hundred years before him, showed that the universe was finite but expanding and more or less did away with the prevailing belief that the universe had to be either finite and static or infinite.

31. According to the passage, Ptolemy differed from Copernicus in that:

A. Ptolemy envisioned a stationary earth and Copernicus did not.
B. [Already eliminated]
C. [Already eliminated]
D. Ptolemy postulated that the earth followed an orbit about the sun and Copernicus did not.

Look at (D). It says that Ptolemy imagined the earth orbiting the sun and that Copernicus did not imagine the earth orbiting the sun. Now look at lines 5–9 of the passage. They tell us that Copernicus (and others) did *not* believe in a fixed earth. They thought the earth orbited the sun. That view invalidated Ptolemy's view. In other words, Ptolemy thought otherwise. He thought the earth was fixed and that the sun orbited the earth. Choice (D) is a switch. Eliminate it.

32. According to the passage, Heisenberg's theory:

F. [Already eliminated]
G. challenged traditional beliefs about position and velocity.
H. described a universe that could be understood and predicted.
J. [Already eliminated]

Look at (H). It says that Heisenberg's principle makes the universe seem predictable. Now read the passage, lines 16–19. They say that Heisenberg's theory *dealt a blow* to the idea that science could attain complete knowledge of the universe and predict its future. Heisenberg's principle *destroyed* the belief that science might completely understand the state of the universe. That means (H) is a switch. Eliminate it.

Sometimes the Switch Involves a Sneaky Word Substitution

Sometimes the switch involves the substitution of a wrong word (or name) for a right one. The answer choice looks correct but isn't because one word doesn't belong. Recall the natural science passage and look at the question on the next page.

33. The Aristotelian conception of the solar system was:

A. inconsistent with Newtonian and Galilean insights.
B. at odds with Copernican and Ptolemic views.
C. [Already eliminated]
D. [Already eliminated]

Look at (B). It indicates that Aristotle's views were different from those of Ptolemy and Copernicus. Now look at lines 5–9 of the passage. They tell us that Copernicus, Kepler, Galileo, and Newton challenged the views of Aristotle and Ptolemy. In other words, Aristotle and Ptolemy believed one thing and the other four, including Copernicus, believed another. "Copernican" belongs in the answer choice, but "Ptolemic" does not. Answer choice (B) is a switch. Eliminate it.

Sometimes the Switch Gives You a Simple Shortcut to the Right Answer

If the answer choices happen to feature two statements that are basically opposites, then one of them is usually right (and the other, of course, is the switch). That means you can focus on these two and ignore the other two answer options unless neither of the first two is correct.

For instance, consider the natural science excerpt we just read, and look at the following answer choices:

34. Blah, blah, blah...:

F. important in that it shows certain propositions to be true.
G. important in that it shows certain propositions to be false.
H. less precise than most scientists believe.
J. extremely misleading to those who fail to question its premises.

Notice that (F) and (G) are opposites. Without even looking at the question, you can conclude that one of them will probably be the right answer. Why? Because the ACT test writers are predictable that way. They tend not to present opposing statements unless one of them is right. In this case, answer choices (H) and (J) are wrong, and you can eliminate them.

Now let's look at the question.

---

34. In the first paragraph, the author makes the point that natural science can be:

F. important in that it shows certain propositions to be true.
G. important in that it shows certain propositions to be false.
H. less precise than most scientists believe.
J. extremely misleading to those who fail to question its premises.

Here's How to Crack It

You know that either (F) or (G) is probably right, so focus on these two. In the first sentence of the paragraph, the author states, "In certain critical respects the magnificence of science lies not in its discovery of what is true but in its identification of that which is not." Answer choice (G) makes the same statement—in camouflage. Answer choice (F) is the switch. Answer choice (G) is correct.

Distracter 3: Extremes

If an answer choice indicates that something is *always* so, *invariably* so, or *never* so, then it's usually wrong. We call such choices *extremes,* and you should be very suspicious of them.

Words like *completely, perfectly,* and *absolutely* also signal an extreme choice.

Extremes tend to be wrong because they're usually *debatable,* and the ACT test writers know that. Think about these statements:

Patients who are chronically depressed never enjoy their lives.

Never? *Ever?* It's pretty hard to prove the truth of such a statement.

It's one thing to say that depressed patients *have difficulty* enjoying their lives or that they *tend not* to enjoy their lives. But to say they *never* enjoy their lives just can't be correct.

Extreme Answer Choices

Look out for answer choices that are too extreme to be the correct answer. These are answer choices to eliminate. These answer choices include words such as *always, completely,* and *absolutely.*

A political leader should seek to make peace at all costs.

All costs? No matter what? That's pretty tough to defend. Such a statement is too one-sided to constitute a right answer on the ACT.

In order to lead a productive life, a citizen must devote all of his energy to his work.

All of his energy? Come on. That statement is too easy to dispute, and the ACT test writers know it. They can't call it correct.

Extreme statements are easy to write and they're very useful to standardized test writers. When a standardized test writer has trouble thinking of a wrong answer choice for one of the questions, he or she often constructs an extreme.

Without reading any passage, consider this question and determine which answer choice is an extreme statement.

---

31. The author's claim that "cause is relative only to perspective" introduces his argument that:

A. mental well-being depends on physical strength.
B. how something is perceived depends on its nature.
C. psychological health requires a perfect upbringing.
D. psychiatric condition depends on numerous factors, environmental and internal.

Here's How to Crack It

Answer choice (C) is extreme. The idea that anything has to be "ideal" or "perfect" or "absolutely precise" or "completely objective" or "totally honest" is usually contrary to ACT philosophy. Eliminate it.

Look at this question and determine which answer choice or choices are extremes.

---

32. The author believes that practicing psychiatrists:

F. cannot possibly help patients unless they are completely objective.
G. are hopelessly confused over the genesis of mental illness.
H. are scientists notwithstanding the uncertainties that surround psychiatry.
J. should, for the time being, treat mental disease in terms of environment.

Here's How to Crack It

Answer choices (F) and (G) are extremes. The phrases "cannot possibly," "completely objective," and "hopelessly confused" should tip you off.

Read this next question and determine which answer choice or choices are extremes.

---

33. According to information presented in the third paragraph, an individual organism will not survive to reproductive age unless:

A. all of its compensatory mechanisms are in ideal balance.
B. it has adequate homeostatic and feedback responses.
C. it is capable of complete adaptation to every form of stress.
D. other individuals of the same species fail to reproduce.

Here's How to Crack It

Answer choices (A) and (C) are extremes. "Ideal balance," "complete adaptation," and "every...stress" are the tip-off phrases.

Distracter 4: Choices That Sound Too "Nice"

Some distracters will appeal to you simply because they sound "nice," even though they have little to do with the question or the passage. Such distracters might draw on something you already know, or on the surface they might just seem reasonable and correct. Think, for instance, about statements like the following:

Ultimately, the voting public knows its own best interest.

Structure is important, but it should not be imposed in such a way as to stifle creativity.

The ideal society is one that allows for individual difference, but at the same time creates a people united in interest.

All people have a right to live and die with dignity.

These thoughts are so "nice" and "sensible" as to seem practically beyond challenge. Some students read them and think, "This must be right." Sometimes these kinds of statements do represent the correct answer. But at other times they don't. When you find yourself drawn to such an answer choice, you should check back with the question and ask yourself whether the answer choice is just a sweet and easy sentiment or whether it really *answers* the question you are asked.

Too Nice
Don't automatically fall for answer choices that sound too "nice." Check to see if the statement was actually made in the passage. If not, eliminate that answer choice.

For example, look at this prose fiction excerpt and consider the question that follows:

"And then the men!" said Jonathan, "the men coming aboard drunk, and having to be pounded sober!..." "Well, what can you do?" he went on. "If you don't strike, the men think you're afraid of them...." Jonathan Tinker was plainly part of the horrible tyranny that we all know exists on shipboard; and his listener respected him the more that, though he had heart enough to be ashamed of it, he was too honest not to own it.

1. Jonathan's listener respected him because he believed:

A. [Already eliminated]
B. Jonathan did not attempt to conceal his participation in maritime abuse.
C. Jonathan had a good heart and basically cared for his men.
D. [Already eliminated]

Here's How to Crack It

Look at (C). What could be more correct than a good heart and an honest concern for other people? Answer choice (C) is tempting, but it isn't right. Nice or not, the author does not state that the listener's respect for Jonathan had anything to do with a good heart or a concern for his men. Read the last two lines of the passage. The listener respected Jonathan because he had the honesty to "own" his acts. He acknowledged his participation in the tyranny.

Read this social studies excerpt.

The thought that older citizens might be denied health care on the basis of cost effectiveness is very troublesome and probably not acceptable to modern American society. Yet there is precedent for such policies in other westernized nations. In Sweden, for example, where the overwhelming majority of health care is funded by the government, patients over the age of 55 are not eligible for long-term life-saving renal dialysis. The nation has made a decision to invest a certain amount of its resources in renal dialysis, and it does not consider it sensible to provide the service to kidney patients over a certain age. Because Sweden is founded largely on egalitarian principles, a citizen over 55 is not permitted access to renal dialysis even if he is willing to pay for it on his own. The society does not believe that wealth should play a role in longevity. Recently, the United States has inaugurated a number of systems aimed at controlling health care costs and avoiding waste. These include requirements that patients obtain a second opinion before undergoing surgery and utilize review systems aimed at shortening hospital stays. To date, however, no agency or insurer in the United States premises its willingness to pay for health care on the age or the youth of the patient.

11. In Sweden, which of the following measures is designed to promote egalitarianism?

A. [Already eliminated]
B. The Swedish government denies certain life-saving medical resources to older citizens.
C. [Already eliminated]
D. The Swedish government attempts to provide the same health care to all citizens regardless of wealth or age.

Here's How to Crack It

Look at (D). Very, very attractive. What could be nicer than equal health care for all? But look at lines 4–14. In Sweden, we are told, citizens over 55 are denied access to renal dialysis. (D) is wrong, and (B) is right.

Summary

- ACT test writers love distracting answers. They try to get you to you to pick one of their wrong answers by taking you off track.
- Be careful of deceptive answers, switches, and extreme answer choices, as well as answers that are too good to be true.
- Don't forget to always guess your Letter of the Day if there are questions that you can't answer or don't get to in time.

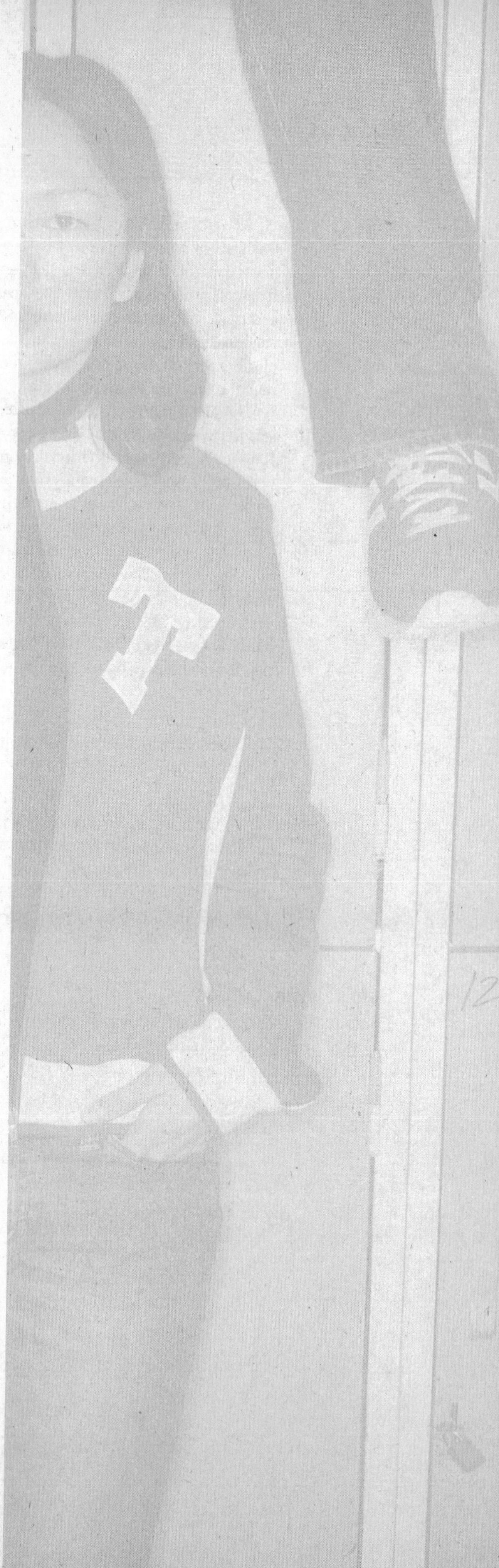

Chapter 18
The Four-Step System

The best way to beat the ACT system is to use a different one. The four-step system outlined in this chapter provides a way to look at the questions and passages methodically to maximize your points. Start by identifying any significant words in the questions. Scan the passage for these words, skim the passage and jot down notes, and then go back to the questions. We call this the loop.

Now that you've learned how to recognize right and wrong answer choices, we're going to teach you a four-step process that systematically leads you to the correct answers. We take time to explain each step slowly, so we can be sure you learn it. Because of that, you might at first think our system is lengthy or cumbersome. It isn't. It's streamlined and efficient. When we're all through, you'll see how speedily it works. (Think about how long it takes to tie a shoe. Now think about how long it would take to tell—not show—someone how to tie a shoe.)

We'll begin by answering the following simple question:

Why Are ACT Passages Hard to Follow?

You know how to read. So why is it so tough to read an ACT passage? It's tough, first of all, because the passage is pulled out of the middle of some larger work; you're reading it out of context. It's also tough to read an ACT passage because you don't know why you're reading it. You don't know what you're looking for or what you're supposed to "understand."

Stop thinking about the ACT for a second and suppose someone offers you a $20 per hour job. She points from her office window to a building sitting on a nearby lot. Then she hands you a key and says, "Check the place out and come back with a report."

That sounds easy enough, except for one thing.

You Don't Know What You're Looking For

What are you supposed to "check out?" The landscaping? The driveway? Are you looking for chipped paint? Leaky pipes? Broken windows?

You have no idea. So you roam around the place. An hour goes by and you roam back to your boss's office. She asks,

"Are there any mice in the basement?"

You tell her you don't know.

"In a whole hour you couldn't look in the basement and see if there were any mice?"

Of course you could have, but you didn't know she wanted you to. You had a simple job, and you blew it. Why? Because you never really knew what the job was. You didn't know what you were supposed to do.

The same sort of thing holds true for ACT reading passages. The passages are usually tough to read because you don't know what you're supposed to look for. They become much easier if you solve that problem. Having said that, we're ready to tell you about the first two steps of our system.

Step 1: Find the Lead Words and Phrases

Step 1 should take you about 30 seconds, and here's what it's all about. Before you read the passage, look at the questions (but not the answer choices) and underline any lead words they contain. Look, for instance, at the following question. (We'll help you ignore the answer choices by turning them all into "blah, blah, blah.")

11. Jeremy Bentham probably would have said that lawyers:

- **A.** blah, blah, blah…
- **B.** blah, blah, blah…
- **C.** blah, blah, blah…
- **D.** blah, blah, blah…

The question has some pretty ordinary words like "probably," "would," "have," and "that." We might find those words in a lot of different questions. The lead words special to this question are "Jeremy Bentham" and "lawyers." So when we say "lead words," we mean the words, phrases, or names that stand out and tell you what the question's about. Look at this question and underline the lead words or phrases.

12. The author states that the common law differs from the civil law in that:

- **F.** blah, blah, blah…
- **G.** blah, blah, blah…
- **H.** blah, blah, blah…
- **J.** blah, blah, blah…

There are of course some ordinary words like "author," "states," "from," "differs." This question's lead phrases are "common law" and "civil law."

Try three more.

21. According to the passage, Peters differs from Jefferson in that:

- **A.** blah, blah, blah…
- **B.** blah, blah, blah…
- **C.** blah, blah, blah…
- **D.** blah, blah, blah…

22. As discussed in the passage, the integrative movement produced:

- **F.** blah, blah, blah…
- **G.** blah, blah, blah…
- **H.** blah, blah, blah…
- **J.** blah, blah, blah…

33. According to the passage, edema and hypoproteinemia:

A. blah, blah, blah…
B. blah, blah, blah…
C. blah, blah, blah…
D. blah, blah, blah…

Identify the Lead Words
As you read each question, underline the key words or phrases that tell you the focus of the question.

- In question 21, the lead words are "Peters" and "Jefferson."
- In question 22, the lead phrase is "integrative movement."
- In question 33, the lead words are "edema" and "hypoproteinemia."

By the way, when you find lead words, don't worry about their meaning. You don't have to know who Peters is or what *edema* means. Your job at step 1 is to see that some name, word, or phrase is the focus of a question. Its meaning doesn't matter.

Some Questions Don't Have Lead Words

When you follow step 1, you're going to notice that some questions don't really have any lead words. Look at these three.

1. It can be most reasonably inferred that the author believes that:

A. blah, blah, blah…
B. blah, blah, blah…
C. blah, blah, blah…
D. blah, blah, blah…

2. Which of the following conclusions is drawn by the passage?

F. blah, blah, blah…
G. blah, blah, blah…
H. blah, blah, blah…
J. blah, blah, blah…

3. The author's discussion would best support which of the following statements?

A. blah, blah, blah…
B. blah, blah, blah…
C. blah, blah, blah…
D. blah, blah, blah…

As you can see, none of these three questions offers any critical words. "Writer," "opinion," "support," and "conclusion" are pretty ordinary. We might find them in lots of different questions. What do you do with these questions when you're pursuing step 1? You ignore them. Among the ten questions that follow a passage, usually 8 or 9 will offer you lead words. Those are the questions you're looking for when you follow step 1.

Take a look at the following ten questions (we've deleted the answer choices completely). Figure out which have lead words and which do not. We will revisit these questions as we cover the various techniques for the Reading test.

21. Which of the following conclusions is drawn by the passage?

22. As discussed in the passage, Quentin Bell believes that historians and critics:

23. The author expresses the idea that:

24. According to the passage, academicism and mannerism:

25. It can be most reasonably inferred that the author believes that:

26. According to the passage, Renoir differs from Daleur in that:

27. According to the passage, Cezanne's work is characterized by:

28. According to the sixth paragraph, the author implies that:

29. In the author's view, the phrase "modern sculpture" means sculpture that:

30. According to the author, subjectivism affected Rodin in which of the following ways?

Questions 22, 24, 26, 27, 29, and 30 have lead words: "Quentin Bell," "academicism," "mannerism," "Renoir," "Daleur," "Cezanne," "modern sculpture," "subjectivism." Questions 21, 23, 25, and 28 are more general. They don't have lead words. If you were to encounter these ten questions while pursuing step 1, you'd focus on 22, 24, 26, 27, 29, and 30. You'd ignore 21, 23, 25, and 28.

Step 2: Scan the Passage for Lead Words

Step 2 of our system should take you about 30 seconds. In step 2, you *scan* the passage very quickly looking for the same lead words you noticed in step 1. You don't read the passage; you scan it. That means you pass your eyes over all of it, trying only to spot the lead words. Every time you see a lead word, underline it.

Here's part of the humanities passage followed by five of the questions we just reviewed with good lead words. We want you to

- First follow step 1: Look at the questions and notice the lead words.
- Then follow step 2: Scan the passage and underline those same lead words wherever you see them.

Refer Back to the Passage for the Lead Words
Now that you have identified the lead words in the question, you can look for them in the passage.

At step 2, you should also underline any words or phrases that seem to be very much like the lead words you find in the questions. For instance, if a question uses the phrase "modern art forms," and the phrase "modern styles of art" appears in the passage, you should underline it.

Rodin was surely a great artist, but he was not an innovator as was Cezanne; prevailing tides of subjectivism came over him. Rodin's mission was to reinvest sculpture with the integrity it lost when Michelangelo died. Rodin succeeded in this mission. His first true work, *The Age of Bronze* (1877), marked the beginning of the end of academicism, mannerism, and decadence that had prevailed since Michelangelo's last sculpture, the *Rondanini Pieta.*

Yet it is largely Cezanne, not Rodin, who was artistic ancestor to Picasso, Gonzalez, Brancusi, Archipenko, Lipchitz, and Laurens, and they are unquestionably the first lights in the "new art" of sculpture. This "new art," of course, is the sculpture we call "modern." It is modern because it breaks with tradition and draws little on that which preceded it.

When I speak of "modern" sculpture, I do not refer to every sculptor nor even to every highly talented sculptor of our age. I do not exclude, necessarily, the sculptors of an earlier time. Modern sculpture, as far as I am concerned, is any that consciously casts tradition aside and seeks forms more suitable to the senses and values of its time. Renoir and Daumier are, in this light, modern sculptors notwithstanding the earlier time at which they worked. Daleur and Carpeaux are not modern, although they belong chronologically to the recent era.

Professor Quentin Bell argues that historians and critics name as "modern" those sculptors in whom they happen to be interested and that the term when abused in that way has no historical or artistic significance. That, I think, is not right. The problem is that Professor Bell thinks "modern" means "now," when in fact it means "new."

22. As discussed in the passage, Quentin Bell believes that historians and critics:

A. blah, blah, blah...
B. blah, blah, blah...
C. blah, blah, blah...
D. blah, blah, blah...

24. According to the passage, academicism and mannerism:

F. blah, blah, blah...
G. blah, blah, blah...
H. blah, blah, blah...
J. blah, blah, blah...

26. According to the passage, Renoir differs from Daleur in that:

A. blah, blah, blah…
B. blah, blah, blah…
C. blah, blah, blah…
D. blah, blah, blah…

27. According to the passage, Cezanne's work is characterized by:

A. a return to subjectivism.
B. a pointless search for form.
C. excessively personal expressions.
D. rejection of the impressionistic philosophy.

29. In the author's view, the phrase "modern sculpture" means sculpture that:

F. blah, blah, blah…
G. blah, blah, blah…
H. blah, blah, blah…
J. blah, blah, blah…

30. According to the author, subjectivism affected Rodin in which of the following ways?

A. blah, blah, blah…
B. blah, blah, blah…
C. blah, blah, blah…
D. blah, blah, blah…

In the first question, you see the name Quentin Bell (whoever he is). In the second, you notice the words "academicism" and "mannerism" (whatever they mean). In question 26, the lead words are "Renoir" and "Daleur." In question 27, "Cezanne" is a great lead word. In question 29, the lead phrase is "modern sculpture." For question 30, you should notice the words "subjectivism" and "Rodin."

So Your Underlined Passage Should Look Something Like This

Rodin was surely a great artist, but he was not an innovator as was Cezanne; prevailing tides of subjectivism came over him. Rodin's mission was to reinvest sculpture with the integrity it lost when Michelangelo died. Rodin succeeded in this mission. His first true work, *The Age of Bronze* (1877), marked the beginning of the end of academicism, mannerism, and decadence that had prevailed since Michelangelo's last sculpture, the *Rondanini Pieta*.

Yet it is largely Cezanne, not Rodin, who was artistic ancestor to Picasso, Gonzalez, Brancusi, Archipenko, Lipchitz, and Laurens, and they are unquestionably the first lights in the "new art" of sculpture. This "new art," of course, is the sculpture we call "modern." It is modern because it breaks with tradition and draws little on that which preceded it.

When I speak of "modern" sculpture, I do not refer to every sculptor nor even to every highly talented sculptor of our age. I do not exclude, necessarily, the sculptors of an earlier time. Modern sculpture, as far as I am concerned, is any that consciously casts tradition aside and seeks forms more suitable to the senses and values of its time. Renoir and Daumier are, in this light, modern sculptors notwithstanding the earlier time at which they worked. Daleur and Carpeaux are not modern, although they belong chronologically to the recent era.

Professor Quentin Bell argues that historians and critics name as "modern" those sculptors in whom they happen to be interested and that the term when abused in that way has no historical or artistic significance. That, I think, is not right. The problem is that Professor Bell thinks "modern" means "now," when in fact it means "new."

Let's Do It Again

Here's another short passage followed by four questions. Follow steps 1 and 2 just as you did before.

Such relatively reliable insights as we have into the nature of Halley's comet's nucleus derive largely from the work done by the Giotto imaging team. Named for the spacecraft from which six key photographs of the comet were taken at distances ranging from 14,430 to 2,730 kilometers, the team forged a single composite photograph under the directorship of H. Use Keler. As the photograph is normally held, north is up and the sun is at the left.

Discernibility of detail varies at different points in the photograph. The greatest resolution, 100 meters, is found in the upper left portion of the image and the poorest resolution, 400 meters, is found at the lower right. This circumstance and other of the photograph's features largely reflect the "instructions" that were given to the Giotto camera, which had been systematically programmed to track the brightest feature in its visual field. This, for example, explains why the greatest detail in the composite photograph is of the nucleus's uppermost aspect; it was photographed when the comet was closest to Giotto.

The Giotto photographs have allowed investigators to conclude that the surface of the nucleus is rough. This conclusion emanates from the observation that the border area between light and dark portions of the comet is irregular. In addition, the light side reveals a large crater and a hill. The most noticeable of the comet's features relate to the movement of dust away from selected portions of the comet's nucleus toward the sun. The resulting dust jets are brightly colored and likely arise from points and places that lack surface crust, which then would expose the deeper lying ices to the sun.

35. According to the passage, the nuclear surface of Halley's comet is believed to be:

A. blah, blah, blah…
B. blah, blah, blah…
C. blah, blah, blah…
D. blah, blah, blah…

36. As described in the passage, Giotto's camera was specifically programmed to:

F. blah, blah, blah…
G. blah, blah, blah…
H. blah, blah, blah…
J. blah, blah, blah…

37. As used in the passage, the word *resolution* (line 11) means:

A. blah, blah, blah…
B. blah, blah, blah…
C. blah, blah, blah…
D. blah, blah, blah…

38. The passage indicates that H. Use Keler:

F. blah, blah, blah…
G. blah, blah, blah…
H. blah, blah, blah…
J. blah, blah, blah…

For question 35, the lead phrases are "Halley's comet" and "nuclear surface." For question 36, it's "Giotto's camera." For question 37, it's "resolution." For question 38, it's "H. Use Keler."

Your Underlined Passage Should Look Something Like This

Such relatively reliable insights as we have into the nature of Halley's comet's nucleus derive largely from the work done by the Giotto imaging team. Named for the spacecraft from which six key photographs of the comet were taken at distances ranging from 14,430 to 2,730 kilometers, the team forged a single composite photograph under the directorship of H. Use Keler. As the photograph is normally held, north is up and the sun is at the left.

Discernibility of detail varies at different points in the photograph. The greatest resolution, 100 meters, is found in the upper left portion of the image and the poorest resolution, 400 meters, is found at the lower right. This circumstance and other of the photograph's features largely reflect the "instructions" that were given to the Giotto camera, which had been systematically programmed to track the brightest feature in its visual field. This, for example, explains why the greatest detail in the composite photograph is of the nucleus's uppermost aspect; it was photographed when the comet was closest to Giotto.

The Giotto photographs have allowed investigators to conclude that the surface of the nucleus is rough. This conclusion emanates from the observation that the border area between light and dark portions of the comet is irregular. In addition, the light side reveals a large crater and a hill. The most noticeable of the comet's features relate to the movement of dust away from selected portions of the comet's nucleus toward the sun. The resulting dust jets are brightly colored and likely arise from points and places that lack surface crust, which then would expose the deeper lying ices to the sun.

How Steps 1 and 2 Help You

If you were actually to read a passage from beginning to end, you'd never know, as you read, which words or lines you're supposed to understand. Furthermore, when you then went to look at questions about Renoir, H. Use Keler, or the Giotto camera, you'd have to start hunting through the passage to find those words and to figure out what they're all about. By following steps 1 and 2, you help yourself in two important ways.

1. You avoid wasting time trying to read and comprehend the whole passage.
2. You identify those places in the passage likely to provide answers to the questions you're going to be asked. It's *those* portions of the passage that you'll read carefully when the time comes to answer questions.

Here's What We Mean

Below is a small piece of the sculpture passage with our underlining in it. There's also a question you've seen before, except this time it has answer choices. Read the question carefully and look at the answer choices. Then take a look back at the sentence and read *it* very carefully. Think about what it means and figure out which answer choice expresses the same thing—in camouflage. That's the right answer.

Professor Quentin Bell argues that historians and critics name as "modern" those sculptors in whom they happen to be interested and that the term when abused in that way has no historical or artistic significance.

22. As discussed in the passage, Quentin Bell believes that historians and critics:

A. should be open-minded to new and innovative art forms.
B. misuse art and fail to understand its history.
C. are generally uninterested in modern art.
D. attach the phrase "modern art" to those sculptors that intrigue them.

The correct answer to this question is (D), and reading the whole passage definitely would *not* help you answer it any more quickly or accurately. The answer is wholly contained in a single sentence. The author says that Professor Quentin Bell (whoever he is) thinks historians and critics give the name "modern" to the sculptors in whom they happen to be interested. Choice (D) expresses that same thought—in camouflage.

You Won't *Always* Find the Answer in a Single Sentence

When you're looking for an answer, you might have to go to the underlined words and "read around" a little. You might have to read the sentences that appear immediately before and after the one that has your mark. Sometimes you'll have to read a whole paragraph.

Here again is the short passage about comets. It's followed by two questions you've already seen, except this time they have answer choices. Follow steps 1 and 2, and then answer the questions.

Such relatively reliable insights as we have into the nature of Halley's comet's nucleus derive largely from the work done by the Giotto imaging team. Named for the spacecraft from which six key photographs of the comet were taken at distances ranging from 14,430 to 2,730 kilometers, the team forged a single composite photograph under the directorship of H. Use Keler. As the photograph is normally held, north is up and the sun is at the left.

Discernibility of detail varies at different points in the photograph. The greatest resolution, 100 meters, is found in the upper left portion of the image and the poorest resolution, 400 meters, is found at the lower right. This circumstance and other of the photograph's features largely reflect the "instructions" that were given to the Giotto camera, which had been systematically programmed to track the brightest feature in its visual field. This, for example, explains why the greatest detail in the composite photograph is of the nucleus's uppermost aspect; it was photographed when the comet was closest to Giotto.

The Giotto photographs have allowed investigators to conclude that the surface of the nucleus is rough. This conclusion emanates from the observation that the border area between light and dark portions of the comet is irregular. In addition, the light side reveals a large crater and a hill. The most noticeable of the comet's features relate to the movement of dust away from selected portions of the comet's nucleus toward the sun. The resulting dust jets are brightly colored and likely arise from points and places that lack surface crust, which then would expose the deeper lying ices to the sun.

Reminder

Underline key words or phrases that resemble the critical words in the question. If you don't find the answer, read the sentences surrounding the underlined portion of the passage.

31. According to the passage, the nuclear surface of Halley's comet is believed to be:

A. smooth, because the interface of light and dark shows high resolution.
B. rough, because a visible border area is irregularly shaped.
C. smooth at some points and rough at others, depending on the relative degrees of light and dark.
D. undetectable, because even the most sophisticated instruments have limitations.

32. As described in the passage, the Giotto camera was specifically programmed to:

F. send "instructions" to Halley's comet regarding detail and resolution.
G. identify the portions of the comet that had relatively low light intensity.
H. detect areas of Halley's comet that bordered on light and dark.
J. photograph those areas of Halley's comet that gave off the most light.

Here's How to Crack It

The first question concerns the "nuclear surface" of "Halley's comet." That precise phrase does not appear in the passage, but the phrase "surface of the nucleus" shows up on line 21. That sentence and the one immediately following it give you the answer to the first question.

> The Giotto photographs have allowed investigators to conclude that the surface of the nucleus is rough. This conclusion emanates from the observation that the border area between light and dark portions of the comet is irregular.

These two sentences are telling you that Halley's comet has light and dark areas and that the border between these areas is irregular. When scientists noticed this they concluded that the surface of the nucleus was rough. You don't have to understand *why* that observation led to that conclusion. You just have to realize that these two sentences are telling you it did. Once you realize that, you know that the correct answer is (B).

The second question refers to "the Giotto camera." So when we first scanned the passage, we underlined the word "Giotto" everywhere it appeared. Look at the sentence that specifically mentions the "Giotto camera." What does it say?

> This circumstance and other of the photograph's features largely reflect the "instructions" that were given to the Giotto camera, which had been systematically programmed to track the brightest feature in its visual field.

The Giotto camera was systematically programmed to track the brightest feature in its visual field. Among the answer options, (J) is best. "Brightest feature" is camouflage for "areas...that gave off the most light."

Step 3: Skim and Scribble

Step 3 should take you about 60 seconds. In step 3, you skim the passage, and in the margin of each paragraph, you scribble a few words that describe its main idea. When we say "skim," we mean you should read fast—so fast that you're uncomfortable and not at all sure you comprehend the passage in detail. (Remember, you're not trying to understand the passage. You're trying to earn a high score on the ACT.) As you speed through each paragraph, you should

- direct a little more attention to the first two sentences than to the remainder
- ask yourself, "What, basically, is this paragraph about?"

Then, in two or three words, scribble an answer in the margin. Here are three paragraphs from a humanities passage. Let's skim and scribble.

artist > period

If we were to start fresh in the study of sculpture or any art, we might observe that the record is largely filled by works of relatively few great contributors. Next to the influences of these great geniuses, time periods themselves are of little significance. The study of art and art history are properly directed to the achievements of outstanding individual artists, not the particular decades or centuries in which any may have worked.

movements

Nonetheless, when we study art in historical perspective we select a convenient frame of reference through which diverse styles and talents are to be compared. Hence we write of "movements" and attempt to understand each artist in terms of the one to which he "belongs." Movements have limited use, but we should not talk of realism, impressionism, cubism, or surrealism as though they genuinely had lives of their own to which the artist was answerable. We regard the movement as the governing force and the artist as its servant. Yet it is well to remember that the movements do not necessarily present themselves in orderly chronological series and the individual artist frequently weaves her way into one and out of another over the course of a single career.

artist switch styles

Great artists are not normally confined by the "movements" that others may name for them. Rather, they transcend the conventional structure working now in one style, then in another, and later in a third. Picasso's work, for example, echoes many of the artistic movements, and other artists, too, moving from one style through another. Indeed, artists are people, and any may decide to alter her style for no more complex a reason than that which makes most people want to "try something new" once in a while.

Skim the Passage
As you read the passage, underline key phrases in the passage or jot down notes next to each paragraph. Don't try to memorize information in the passage, just know the lay of the land.

Paragraph 1

The first paragraph seems to be about the fact that individual artists are more important than the time periods in which they work.

artist > periods

That's enough.

Paragraph 2

The second paragraph has something to do with artistic "movements." What should you scribble?

movements

Paragraph 3

The third paragraph tells us that great artists don't really conform to movements. They vary their styles over time. So for paragraph 3, you scribble

artists switch styles

Enough said, and enough scribbled.

With enough practice, skim and scribble should take you about one minute per passage.

Use Trigger Words

When you're skimming a passage, pay attention to words that signal a change in direction. In line 1 of the second paragraph, for instance, we see the word "nonetheless," which means the author is about to criticize, negate, or "take something away" from thoughts previously expressed. "Nonetheless" is what we call a *trigger word.* Trigger words tell you the author is about to "go somewhere," and you should watch where he's going. Sometimes a trigger word means the author is reaching some sort of conclusion (*therefore, hence*).

Trigger words help you figure out what a paragraph is all about. The "nonetheless" at the beginning of the second paragraph indicates that the author's going to say something that opposes what he said in the first paragraph. He says there's some purpose in thinking of art in terms of "movements," even though he has already said the individual artist is more important than the time periods in which they work.

Look for Trigger Words

Here are 15 trigger words and/or phrases:

• *Despite* • *However* • *In spite of* • *Nonetheless* • *On the other hand* • *On the contrary* • *Yet* • *Notwithstanding* • *But* • *Ironically* • *Rather* • *Unfortunately* • *Therefore* • *Hence* • *Consequently*

Try Another Skim and Scribble

Here are four paragraphs from the comet passage. Skim and scribble. See if you can do it in one minute.

On the other hand, the Giotto photographs reveal virtually nothing of the interior of the comet's nucleus or its rotational period. For instance, it is not known, even, whether the interior of the nucleus had a density greater than or less than 1 gram per cubic centimeter, which is the density of water. Hans Rickman attempted to estimate the comet's density, hoping, with good reason, that this information would ultimately lead to better understanding of the nuclear interior. Rickman recognized that if he could gain estimates of the comet's mass and volume he would be able to derive an estimate of density from the simple physical formulas relating mass, volume, and density: He would divide the volume into the mass and arrive at an estimate.

The comet's overall dimensions were already known to an approximation, and on this basis Rickman took the volume as 500–550 cubic kilometers. He then employed a rather ingenious method of estimating the nuclear mass. Rickman considered the fact that the comet was losing gas at all times and that the expulsion produced a thrust. He then reasoned, according to simple law, that mass times the thrust due to expelled gas had to equal the product [rate at which mass was lost by expulsion of gas and dust] and the velocity of the expelled substance. Rickman then derived estimates of these values from the comet's motion and from the rate at which the comet visibly produced water. Rickman arrived at a value of 0.1 to 0.3 grams per cubic centimeter for the density of Halley's nucleus.

Using an analogous technique, R. Z. Sagdeev and colleagues arrived at a value of 0.2 to 1.5 grams per cubic centimeter. Stanton J. Peale, however, wrote that he had little confidence in the estimates of mass and volume that had been used in connection with the density calculations. He believed that little could be said about the nuclear density except that it was approximately equal to 1 gram per cubic centimeter.

Zdenek Sekanina and Stephen M. Larson studied the rotational period by first processing images of 1920 photographs in an attempt to improve the image of spiral dust features. They assumed that the spiral dust characteristics were caused by emission from distinct parts of the nuclear surface and that these areas were visible when rotation brought them into sunlight and were invisible in the dark of the cometary night. On these premises, the pair estimated that Halley has a rotation period of 2.2 days, and some spacecraft data have seemed to confirm the figure. However, Robert L. Millis and David G. Schleicher estimated a rotational period of 7.4 days by resorting to filters that allowed them to explore fluorescence of CN, C, and C_2 emissions and the continuum emission from dust particles. Other investigators have reported additional approximations of Halley's rotational period but the issue remains, for the time being, clouded.

Look for Trigger Words

What are trigger words? Trigger words are words that signal a change in a sentence. Some of the most common trigger words are *but*, *although*, *despite*, and *however*.

The first paragraph has something to do with the inside of the comet. Maybe it's about density, too. So we scribble

interior, density

The second paragraph seems to provide details about what someone named Rickman did to calculate the density of the comet's interior.

Rickman, details, density

The third paragraph concerns what other scientists said and did in response to Rickman's work.

other people

The last paragraph has something to do with calculating the comet's rotational period.

rotational period

Our Steps So Far

- **Step 1—Notice Critical Words:** Look quickly at the questions. Notice critical words. Ignore questions that don't have critical words.
  Approximate Time: 30 seconds
- **Step 2—Scan and Underline:** Scan the passage and underline critical words.
  Approximate Time: 30 seconds
- **Step 3—Skim and Scribble:** Read the passage at racing speed, giving special attention to the first two or three sentences of each paragraph. For each paragraph, scribble in the margin a few words that describe the main subject.
  Approximate Time: 60 seconds

So that's what we're talking about. It doesn't take long. Steps 1 through 3 together should take maybe one and a half to two minutes.

After Steps 1, 2, and 3

After you've spent about two minutes completing the three steps, go back to the questions.

The entire humanities passage about modern sculpture is on the next page. It's underlined and scribbled, and it includes ten questions. Even though we've already completed steps 1 to 3 for you, you should run through them again yourself so you're familiar with the underlining and scribbling. After you do that, we'll discuss step 4, which is called "practice the loop."

artist > period

If we were to start fresh in the study of sculpture or any art we might observe that the record is largely filled by works of relatively few great contributors. Next to the influences of these great geniuses, time periods themselves are of little significance. The study of art and art history are properly directed to the achievements of outstanding individual artists, not the particular decades or centuries in which any may have worked.

movements

Nonetheless, when we study art in historical perspective we select a convenient frame of reference through which diverse styles and talents are to be compared. Hence we write of "movements" and attempt to understand each artist in terms of the one to which he "belongs." Movements have limited use, but we should not talk of realism, impressionism, cubism, or surrealism as though they genuinely had lives of their own to which the artist was answerable. We regard the movement as the governing force and the artist as its servant. Yet it is well to remember that the movements do not necessarily present themselves in orderly chronological series and the individual artist frequently weaves her way into one and out of another over the course of a single career.

artists switch styles

Great artists are not normally confined by the "movements" that others may name for them. Rather, they transcend the conventional structure working now in one style, then in another, and later in a third. Picasso's work, for example, echoes many of the artistic movements, and other artists too, moving way from one style through another. Indeed, artists are people, and any may decide to alter her style for no more complex a reason than that which makes most people want to "try something new" once in a while.

Rodin and Cezanne

In studying modern sculpture one is tempted to begin a history with Auguste Rodin (1840–1917), who was a contemporary of Cezanne. Yet the two artists did not, in artistic terms, belong to the same period. Their strategies and objectives differed. Although Rodin was surely a great artist, he did not do for sculpture what Cezanne did for painting. In fact, although Cezanne was a painter, he had a more lasting effect on sculpture than did Rodin.

Cezanne vs. Impressionism

Cezanne's work constitutes a reaction against impressionism and the confusion he thought it created. He searched persistently for the "motif." Cezanne strived for clarity of form and was able to convert his personal perceptions into concrete, recognizable substance. He is justly considered to have offered the first glimmer of a new art—a new classicism.

Rodin not innovator; recalled Michelangelo

Rodin was surely a great artist, but he was not an innovator as was Cezanne; prevailing tides of subjectivism came over him. Rodin's mission was to reinvest sculpture with the integrity it lost when Michelangelo died. Rodin succeeded in this mission. His first true work, *The Age of Bronze* (1877), marked the beginning of the end of academicism, mannerism, and decadence that had prevailed since Michelangelo's last sculpture, the *Rondanini Pieta*.

Yet it is largely Cezanne, not Rodin, who was artistic ancestor to Picasso, Gonzalez, Brancusi, Archipenko, Lipchitz, and

Cezanne influenced "modern" sculpture

Laurens, and they are unquestionably the first lights in the "new art" of sculpture. This "new art," of course, is the sculpture we call "modern." It is modern because it breaks with tradition and draws little on that which preceded it.

"modern" does not necessarily mean "recent"

When I speak of "modern" sculpture, I do not refer to every sculptor nor even to every highly talented sculptor of our age. I do not exclude, necessarily, the sculptors of an earlier time. Modern sculpture, as far as I am concerned, is any that consciously casts tradition aside and seeks forms more suitable to the senses and values of its time. Renoir and Daumier are, in this light, modern sculptors notwithstanding the earlier time at which they worked. Daleur and Carpeaux are not modern, although they belong chronologically to the recent era.

Bell wrong; "modern" ≠ now "modern" = new

Professor Quentin Bell argues that historians and critics name as "modern" those sculptors in whom they happen to be interested and that the term when abused in that way has no historical or artistic significance. That, I think, is not right. The problem is that Professor Bell thinks "modern" means "now," when in fact it means "new."

21. Which of the following conclusions is drawn by the passage?

A. Cezanne had greater influence on modern sculpture than did Rodin.
B. Rodin made no significant contribution to modern sculpture.
C. Daumier should not be considered a modern sculptor.
D. Carpeaux should be considered a modern sculptor.

22. As discussed in the passage, Quentin Bell believes that historians and critics:

F. have no appreciation for the value of modern art.
G. abuse art and its history.
H. should evaluate works of art on the basis of their merit without regard to the artist's fame.
J. attach the phrase "modern art" to those sculptors that intrigue them.

23. The author expresses the idea that:

A. art should never be studied in terms of movements.
B. true artists are seldom understandable in terms of a single movement.
C. lesser artists do not usually vary their styles.
D. great artists are always nonconformists.

24. According to the passage, academicism and mannerism:

F. were readily visible in Rodin's earliest work.
G. are partially manifest in the *Rondanini Pieta.*
H. characterized the work of artists who followed Michelangelo.
J. were primarily part of the Bronze Age.

25. It can be most reasonably inferred that the author believes that:

A. Rodin was more innovative than Cezanne.
B. Cezanne was more innovative than Rodin.
C. Modern art is more important than classical art.
D. Cezanne tried to emulate impressionism.

26. According to the passage, Renoir differs from Daleur in that:

F. Daleur had no inspiration and Renoir was tremendously inspired.
G. Renoir's work was highly innovative and Daleur's was not.
H. Daleur was a sculptor and Renoir was not.
J. Renoir revered tradition and Daleur did not.

27. According to the passage, Cezanne's work is characterized by:

A. a return to subjectivism.
B. a pointless search for form.
C. excessively personal expressions.
D. rejection of the impressionistic philosophy.

28. According to the sixth paragraph, the author implies that:

F. mannerism reflects a lack of integrity.
G. Rodin disliked the work of Michelangelo.
H. Rodin embraced the notion of decadence.
J. Rodin should have resisted the appeal of subjectivism.

29. In the author's view, the phrase "modern sculpture" means sculpture that:

A. postdates the *Rondanini Pieta*.
B. is not significantly tied to work that comes before it.
C. shows no artistic merit.
D. genuinely interests contemporary critics.

30. According to the author, subjectivism affected Rodin in which of the following ways?

F. It ended his affiliation with mannerism.
G. It caused him to lose his artistic integrity.
H. It limited his ability to innovate.
J. It caused him to become decadent.

Questions That Point

With the passage underlined and scribbled, go back to the questions, but don't go necessarily to question 21. Go first to the questions that point you to an answer. Look at questions 21–30 on the last passage. Questions 22, 24, 26, 27, 28, 29, and 30 point to the answer. Questions 22, 24, 26, 27, 29, and 30 have lead words. For those questions, we've already underlined the relevant sections of the passage and we know where to look.

- Question 28 sends us directly to the relevant paragraph.
- Questions 21, 23, and 25 don't point anywhere. We'll save them for last.

Now we're ready to answer questions.

Step 4: Practice the Loop

Step 4 should take you about 40 seconds per question if you're trying to finish all 4 passages.

- Go to the first question that points to an answer. Read it carefully. If it's relatively clear, make sure you remember the question before you go back to the passage. If the question is confusing, reword it so that you know what you're looking for.
- Return to the appropriate portion of the passage (either you've underlined it or the question sends you there).
- Read it carefully. Whenever possible, try to formulate your own answer to the question and jot it down.
- Go back to the question and pick the answer choice that most resembles your answer.

Practice the Loop

Once you've practiced using these techniques, you can put them together and form "the loop." Read the question, go to the passage, underline the appropriate words or phrases that relate to the question, and then go to the answer choices. As you read each answer choice, watch out for the distracters. If you're stuck, then take another pass through the loop.

Now suppose something strikes you as correct. Be suspicious. Ask yourself if you're falling for a deceptive answer, a switch, or something too "nice." If you consider those possibilities and still think the answer is right, choose it and go to the next question.

Now suppose you're uncertain about the answer and when you come back to the question, nothing strikes you as right. Fine. Try to eliminate answers that are wrong. Look for a deceptive answer, a switch, an extreme statement, and eliminate it. (In the process, the right answer might strike you, in which case you'll choose it and move on.)

If you don't settle on an answer, take a second pass through the loop.

- Come back to the question. Sometimes you've missed a clue in the question.
- Go back to the appropriate portion of the passage.
- Read it again. Understand it as best you can.
- Look at the choices that still remain (some were eliminated a few seconds earlier, during your first pass through the loop).

If one of the choices now strikes you as correct, choose it. If nothing strikes you as correct, see if you can eliminate it, and then guess among whatever answer choices remain.

We'll start with question 22 because question 21 doesn't point.

---

22. As discussed in the passage, Quentin Bell believes that historians and critics:

F. have no appreciation for the value of modern art.
G. abuse art and its history.
H. should evaluate works of art on the basis of their merit without regard to the artist's fame.
J. attach the phrase "modern art" to those sculptors that intrigue them.

Here's How to Crack It

We go to the relevant part of the passage, which we've already underlined.

> Professor Quentin Bell argues that historians and critics name as "modern" those sculptors in whom they happen to be interested and that the term when abused in that way has no historical or artistic significance.

- Read it carefully and try to understand it. Formulate an answer in your own words and write it down.
- Go back to the question and pick the answer choice that best matches what you came up with on your own.

In this case, one might easily answer this question by saying that Professor Bell argued that historians and critics use the word "modern" to describe anything in which they happen to be interested. Hey, that sounds a lot like (J), and thus, (J) is the correct response.

Suppose, however, that you couldn't come up with an answer of your own. Don't panic. Just start eliminating answer choices that are wrong. Answer choice (F) is an extreme statement ("no" appreciation). Eliminate it.

Choice (H) is very "nice" and very irrelevant. Eliminate it.

You're left with (G) and (J), but you're not sure which is right.

So take a second pass through the loop.

- Go back to the relevant part of the passage and read it again.
- Return to the question and try to choose again between choices (G) and (J).

Still not sure? Try to eliminate one of the choices. Answer choice (G) is a deceptive answer. (The author uses the word *abuse* but doesn't say that anyone abuses art or its history.) Eliminate (G). That leaves (J), so that's the answer you choose.

Altogether, you've spent 30 to 50 seconds answering question 22.

Use the loop to answer question 24.

---

24. According to the passage, academicism and mannerism:

F. were readily visible in Rodin's first true work.
G. are partially manifest in the *Rondanini Pieta.*
H. characterized the work of artists who followed Michelangelo.
J. were primarily part of the Bronze Age.

Here's How to Crack It

Go to the pertinent part of the passage.

> Rodin was surely a great artist, but he was not an innovator as was Cezanne; prevailing tides of subjectivism came over him. Rodin's mission was to reinvest sculpture with the integrity it lost when Michelangelo died. Rodin succeeded in this mission. His first true work, *The Age of Bronze* (1877), marked the beginning of the end of academicism, mannerism, and decadence that had prevailed since Michelangelo's last sculpture, the *Rondanini Pieta.*

- Read it carefully and try to answer it yourself. Jot down your answer.
- Go back to the question and find the answer choice that best matches what you jotted down.

Maybe you're not sure of the answer, but you realize that (F) and (J) are deceptive answers and eliminate them. You're left with (G) and (H).

Now you take a second pass through the loop.

- Read the question again. Any new insight?
- Go back to the relevant part of the passage and read it again.
- Return to the question.

The last sentence tells us that academicism, mannerism, and decadence were around *since Michelangelo produced his last sculpture.* Answer choice (H) says the same thing—in camouflage. Choose (H) and move on.

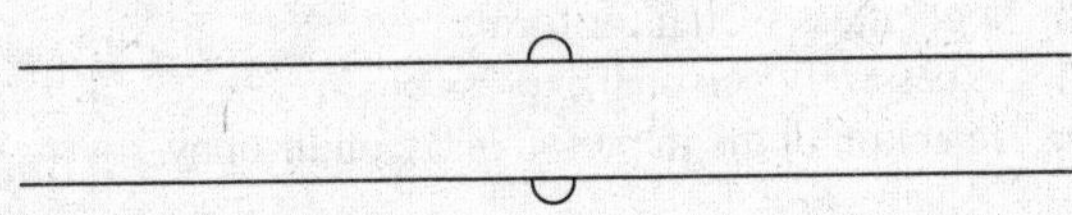

26. According to the passage, Renoir differs from Daleur in that:

F. Daleur had no inspiration and Renoir was tremendously inspired.
G. Renoir's work was highly innovative and Daleur's was not.
H. Daleur was a sculptor and Renoir was not.
J. Renoir revered tradition and Daleur did not.

Here's How to Crack It

Read the important part of the passage carefully.

> When I speak of "modern" sculpture, I do not refer to every sculptor nor even to every highly talented sculptor of our age. I do not exclude, necessarily, the sculptors of an earlier time. Modern sculpture, as far as I am concerned, is any that consciously casts tradition aside and seeks forms more suitable to the senses and values of its time. Renoir and Daumier are, in this light, modern sculptors notwithstanding the earlier time at which they worked. Daleur and Carpeaux are not modern although they belong chronologically to the recent era.

- First, try to answer the question yourself. This one's fairly easy to answer on your own. The author clearly states that he views Renoir as modern and Daleur as not modern. Thus, (G) is the correct response.
- If you couldn't come up with your own answer, start eliminating bad answer choices.
- Choice (F) is a statement in the extreme. Eliminate it.
- Choice (H) is a switch. (The passage tells you that "Renoir and Daumier are modern sculptors." That means Renoir was a sculptor.) Eliminate it.
- Take a second pass. The author writes that modern sculpture is any that "casts tradition aside…." Then he writes that Renoir is a modern sculptor and Daleur is not. That means Renoir casts tradition aside and Daleur does not. Choice (G) says the same thing in camouflage, so (G) is right. ((J) is a deceptive answer.)

Now use the loop to answer questions 27 to 30. When you're done, you can read on and compare your reasoning with ours.

---

27. According to the passage, Cezanne's work is characterized by:

A. a return to subjectivism.
B. a pointless search for form.
C. excessively personal expressions.
D. rejection of the impressionistic philosophy.

Here's How to Crack It

Go to the pertinent part of the passage.

> Cezanne's work constitutes a reaction against impressionism and the confusion he thought it created. He searched persistently for the "motif." Cezanne strived for clarity of form and was able to convert his personal perceptions into concrete, recognizable substance. He is justly considered to have offered the first glimmer of a new art—a new classicism.

- What does the passage tell us? Well, it says that Cezanne rejected impressionism and created a new style called "new classicism." That sounds a lot like (D).
- Not sure? Let's look at the other answer choices and see what we can eliminate.
- Answer choice (B) is extreme (and ridiculous). Eliminate it. With our eye on (A), (C), and (D), we take a second pass. The first sentence tells us that Cezanne reacted against impressionism. Choice (D) says the same thing—in camouflage.

Question 28: (J) is right.

- Choices (F), (G), and (H) are deceptive answers.

Question 29: (B) is right.

- Choices (A) and (D) are deceptive answers. (C) is a statement in the extreme.

Question 30: (H) is right.

- Choices (F), (G), and (J) are deceptive answers.

What If You *Can't* Settle on an Answer?

Simple. You guess. If you've taken two (or maybe three) passes through the loop and you still can't decide on an answer, look at the choices still remaining, take a guess, and move on. Remember: Having eliminated one or two choices, you've raised the odds that your guess will be right.

Three More Examples

We held questions 21, 23, and 25 for last because they don't point. Now it's time to answer them. For questions that don't point, you

- use the answer choices to tell you what the question is about
- use your scribbles to get you to the right part of the passage

---

Here are the answer choices for question 21.

A. Cezanne had greater influence on modern sculpture than did Rodin.
B. Rodin made no significant contribution to modern sculpture.
C. Daumier should not be considered a modern sculptor.
D. Carpeaux should be considered a modern sculptor.

Apparently, this question has a lot to do with the phrase "modern sculpture."

For Paragraph 8, we scribbled

"modern" does not necessarily mean "recent"

So you go to Paragraph 8. From there on, you follow the loop.

The correct answer is (A).

- Answer choice (B) is extreme.
- Answer choices (C) and (D) are both switches.

Let's look at question 23. Here are the answer choices.

A. art should never be studied in terms of movements.
B. true artists are seldom understandable in terms of a single movement.
C. lesser artists do not usually vary their styles.
D. great artists are always nonconformists.

Apparently, the question has something to do with movements and style. It calls our attention to Paragraphs 2 and 3 where we scribbled

(2) *movements*

(3) *artists switch styles*

It turns out that the answer is in Paragraph 3. It's (B).

- Answer choices (A) and (D) are extreme.
- Answer choice (C) is a distortion.

Lastly, look at question 25. Here are the answer choices.

A. Rodin was more innovative than Cezanne.
B. Cezanne was more innovative than Rodin.
C. Modern art is more important than classical art.
D. Cezanne tried to emulate impressionism.

This question appears to be focusing on the differences between Rodin and Cezanne.

For Paragraph 6, we scribbled

Rodin not innovator

Read Paragraph 6 again. From there on, follow the loop. The best answer is (B).

- (A) is the switch.
- (C) and (D) are deceptive answers.

Steps 1–4
Step 1—Find the Critical Words
Approximate Time: 30 seconds
Step 2—Scan the Passage for Critical Words
Approximate Time: 30 seconds
Step 3—Skim and Scribble
Approximate Time: 60 seconds
Step 4—Practice the Loop
Approximate Time: 40 seconds per question

Special Question Type: State of Mind

When you take the ACT, you'll probably get a few questions that ask you to describe attitudes or states of mind. Often, the answer choices are just one word.

Some Question Types Do Not Require You to Go Through the Loop
Why? The answer is not found in the passage. These question types are: Fact vs. Opinion, State of Mind, Vocab-in-Context, Except/Not/Least, and Roman Numeral

1. The author's attitude toward…blah, blah, blah…is best described as:

A. skeptical.
B. approving.
C. concerned.
D. hopeful.

In a literature passage, these questions pertain not to the author, but to some character. Read this final paragraph of a prose fiction passage and look at the question that follows it.

So they parted with a shake of the hand, Jonathan Tinker saying that he believed he should go down to the vessel and sleep aboard, if he could sleep, and murmuring at the last moment the hope of returning the compliment, while the contributor walked homeward, weary to the flesh, but, in spite of his sympathy for Jonathan Tinker, very elated in spirit. The truth is, and however disgraceful to human nature, let the truth be told, he had recurred to his primal satisfaction in the man as calamity capable of being used for such and such literary ends, and, while he pitied him, rejoiced in him as an episode of real life quite as striking and complete as anything in fiction.

1. As final response to his conversation with Jonathan Tinker, the contributor experienced a feeling of

A. worry.
B. amusement.
C. gratification.
D. disappointment.

Here's How to Crack It

If this kind of item throws you, it's probably because you start thinking about the distracters and lose sight of the question.

- Think about the person and the situation about which you're being asked.
- Turn the item into four true/false questions by saying to yourself: TRUE/FALSE "This guy was ________."
  Then fill in the blank with each of the answer choices.
- When you hit a statement that's true, you've got the ACT answer.

Let's try it.

- We think about the contributor as he is described in the last paragraph, and we say to ourselves (very quickly):
  TRUE/FALSE "This guy was worried."
  TRUE/FALSE "This guy was amused."
  TRUE/FALSE "This guy was gratified."
  TRUE/FALSE "This guy was disappointed."

Answer choices (A), (B), and (D) yield statements that sound false. There's nothing in the paragraph to suggest that this guy was worried or disappointed, and he's not particularly amused, either. (He didn't, for example, "chuckle," or "grin.") The paragraph tells us that the contributor experiences "satisfaction" and that he "rejoices." Answer choice (C) yields a statement that seems true.

Many decisions of the United States Supreme Court are inconsistent with the precedents by which they are theoretically balanced. It is true that the court has some freedom to overrule its own precedents, but in such cases it is expected to announce, forthrightly, that it has determined a particular precedent to be erroneous, and that such precedent is renounced.

Contrary to what should be so, however, there are a great many occasions on which the Supreme Court does in fact disavow its own precedents without acknowledging that it has done so. Instead, the Court contrives some implausible distinction between the precedent and the case before it and purports, dishonestly, to abide by a precedent it has in fact determined to repudiate.

11. In this passage, the author's attitude toward the United States Supreme Court is best described as one of:

A. criticism.
B. disbelief.
C. appreciation.
D. surprise.

Here's How to Crack It

- We consider what the author has said about the Supreme Court's attitude toward precedent. She objects to the dishonesty through which the court sometimes avoids precedent while pretending to honor it.
- We make four true/false questions.
  TRUE/FALSE "This woman is critical."
  TRUE/FALSE "This woman is in a state of disbelief."
  TRUE/FALSE "This woman is appreciative."
  TRUE/FALSE "This woman is surprised."

The correct answer is (A). The author thinks that if the Supreme Court decides not to abide by a precedent, it should do so honestly. Contrary to what should be so, the author explains, the court rejects precedents while pretending to honor them. She's making a criticism.

Special Question Type: Vocab-in-Context

On the ACT, you will encounter a couple of questions that ask you to define words or phrases that are used in the context of specific parts of the passages.

Many artists have spoken of seeing things differently while drawing, and have often mentioned that drawing puts them into a somewhat altered state of awareness. In that different subjective state, artists speak of feeling transported, "at one with their work," able to grasp relations that they ordinarily cannot see.

21. In line 79, the word *transported* is used to mean:

A. moved from one place to another.
B. engaged in artistic endeavor.
C. in an altered state of consciousness.
D. dreaming.

Here's How to Crack It

Go to the relevant section of the passage and read a couple of lines above and a couple of lines below where you see the word *transported.*

- Draw a line through the word *transported*, and based on your understanding of the lines surrounding it, try to replace it with a word or phrase of your own. In this case, the word *different* or the phrase from the passage, "altered state of awareness," would fit well, so the correct answer is (C).
- Having trouble coming up with your own word? No problem; just go to the answer choices and eliminate those that don't work.
- Answer choice (A) says "moved from one place to another," which is the primary definition of *transported* but has nothing to do with the passage. Eliminate it. Answer choice (B) says "engaged in artistic endeavor." This seems a little suspicious because the whole paragraph is about art. In essence, this is a deceptive answer choice. Eliminate it. Finally, (D) says *dreaming.* It's not a terrible answer choice, but does the passage actually tell us that artists go to sleep while working? No? Well, then, eliminate it.

Special Question Type: Except/Not/Least

If questions contain the words *except*, *not*, or *least*, you should leave them until you have answered all other questions. If you have time to return to them, your job is to identify the answers that are not supported by the passages.

In Scotland, bees are carried in carts to the Highlands and set free. In France and Poland, bees are carried from pasture to pasture and along rivers in barges so that they can collect the honey from the vegetation that grows along the rivers' banks. In Egypt they are taken up the Nile and floated slowly home again.

13. The passage mentions transportation of bees by river in all of the following countries EXCEPT:

A. Scotland.
B. France.
C. Egypt.
D. Poland.

Here's How to Crack It

- Skip this question until you have done all the others with the exception of any roman numeral questions. By the time you return to it, you probably will have read most of the passage.
- Look for a lead word in the question. Here, you're interested in the transportation of bees by river, so go back to the passage and see what the passage says on this subject.
- The passage says that bees are transported by river in France, Poland, and Egypt. Because you are looking for the answer choice that is not true, you can eliminate (B), (C), and (D), leaving only the correct answer, which is (A).

Special Question Type: Roman Numeral

A few questions on the ACT will provide you with three statements preceded by roman numerals (and not just in the Reading test). On these questions, your job is to determine which of the statements, according to the passages, are true.

---

16. According to the passage, bees:

I. are attracted to pastures.
II. are attracted to cultivated fields.
III. are attracted to vegetation that grows along river banks.

F. I only
G. II only
H. III only
J. I and III only

Here's How to Crack It

- You should leave roman numeral questions for last.
- Look at both the question and the roman numeral statements for lead words.
- Take each roman numeral and check, one at a time, to see if the passage makes that statement.
- If you use the last passage and check it for mention of "pastures," you will find that bees do, in fact, like pastures. Because roman numeral I appears to be true, you can quickly eliminate (G) and (H) because they omit roman numeral I.
- Now all you need to do is make a second pass to check and see if the passage states that bees like vegetation that grows along river banks. According to the passage, bees collect honey from these plants, so both roman numerals I and III are true. Thus, (J) is the correct answer.

Summary

- By following a straightforward, four-step system, you can avoid wrong answers and find the right ones more easily.
- The first step is to find the critical words and phrases in the questions.
- The second step is to locate those critical words and phrases in the answer choices.
- Third, skim the passage and scribble a few words that describe the main idea of each paragraph. You aren't reading for comprehension but rather for a general idea.
- Last, practice the loop. Use the techniques to go through the questions as quickly and accurately as possible.
- Be aware of special question types, including Vocabulary-in-Context questions, EXCEPT/NOT/LEAST questions, and roman numeral questions.
- Don't forget to guess your Letter of the Day if there are questions that you can't answer or don't reach in time.

Part V
How to Crack the ACT Science Reasoning Test

Chapter 19
Introduction to the ACT Science Reasoning Test

The ACT Science Reasoning test always comes fourth, after the Reading test and before the optional essay. It really should be called the ACT Science *Reading* test because you aren't required to know any science at all; you just have to read about science and answer questions.

There are three types of passages on the Science test: charts and graphs, experiments, and fighting scientists. To maximize your score on the test, you should do the easiest passages first and the more difficult passages last.

THE SCIENCE REASONING TEST

The ACT Science Reasoning Test Format
You read 7 passages and answer 40 questions in 35 minutes.

Remember that tough biology test for which you had to memorize dozens of facts about photosynthesis? When you sat down to take the test, you either knew the answers or you didn't. Well, that's not the case on the science portion of the ACT. Even though the word *science* appears in the title, this test doesn't resemble the science tests you've had in high school. The ACT Science Reasoning test presents you with science-based reading passages and requires that you answer questions about them. Sounds just like the Reading test, doesn't it? That's because it *is* just like the Reading test. Rather than test your knowledge of science, it's supposed to test your ability to "think about science."

Of course, a little science knowledge doesn't hurt. If a passage is about photosynthesis, you'll undoubtedly do better if you know something about photosynthesis. But remember, the information you need to answer each question is contained within the passage itself. So if science has never been your strength, don't worry. In this chapter, we're going to show you techniques that will help you master scientific reasoning, even if you don't know anything about photosynthesis, bacteria, the periodic table, or quantum mechanics.

What Does the Science Reasoning Test Look Like?

The Science Reasoning test has seven passages, each of which is followed by five to seven questions. The passages cover material drawn from biology, chemistry, physics, and the physical sciences (including geology, astronomy, and meteorology). They vary in organization and difficulty, as well as in the scientific reasoning skills they test.

Sound intimidating? It really isn't—all you need is the ability to answer questions strategically.

You've already developed some of these skills during science lab in school. Others you can borrow from what you learned in the ACT Reading section. (If you had any trouble mastering those skills, this is a good time to review them and make them stick.) The only additional skill you'll need is a basic understanding of math to help you read and interpret charts, figures, and graphs. You are not allowed to use a calculator on the Science Reasoning test. Luckily, you won't need one.

> **Do You Need to Be a Science Whiz?**
> Not at all. This test is more like a Reading test whose sole subject matter is science. What you *do* need is an understanding of the scientific method and of how to interpret charts, graphs, and tables. The topics on the test vary widely—no one has taken all these classes in school. If you haven't learned anything about genetics, or if you can't remember what you did learn, don't panic. You are not the only one. Remember that this is an open book test—everything you need to answer the questions is right there in the passage. Just find the information for each passage and you'll do fine.

You'll have 35 minutes to answer 40 questions. That's about five minutes per passage! It's like a car race: You have to move fast but you don't want to crash. In this section, we teach you how to do exactly that.

What Are the Passages Like?

All of the passages fall within three basic categories.

1. Charts and Graphs (aka Data Representation)— 15 questions, 3 passages

These passages provide you with one or more charts, tables, graphs, or illustrations, and are intended to test your ability to understand and interpret the information that's presented. There are three charts and graphs passages per test, and each one has five questions. (Chapter 20 covers charts and graphs.)

2. Experiments (aka Research Summaries)— 18 questions, 3 passages

These passages describe several experiments—and their results—to see whether you can follow the procedures in each experiment (or experiments) and interpret them. There are three experiments passages per test, each with six questions. (Chapter 22 covers experiments.)

Level of Difficulty
Just like on the ACT Reading test, the passages here are not organized in order of difficulty. Prioritize the passages. Before you read a passage, take a good look at the layout. Can you identify the passage type? Do easy passages right away, more difficult passages later.

3. Fighting Scientists (aka Conflicting Viewpoints)— 7 questions, 1 passage

These passages present (usually) two or three conflicting views on a research hypothesis. Typical topics include: "Is There Life on Mars?", "Where Did the Dinosaurs Go?", and "What's Fire?" Frequently, the fight is over something that has already been resolved (such as "What's Fire?"). You will be asked about the conflict and the evidence supporting each view. The ACT test writers may also ask you to figure out what kind of evidence might actually resolve the conflict. There will be only one fighting scientists passage per test, and it will have seven questions. (Chapter 23 covers fighting scientists.)

What Are the Questions Like?

The questions on the ACT Science Reasoning test fall into three general categories.

1. Look It Up (Understanding)

These questions test your ability to paraphrase specific parts of the passage. They're like the questions that you see on the Reading test, and they usually require that you focus on one sentence, paragraph, or chart. You might be asked to think about what happened in the passage and what the underlying assumptions are behind it. You may have to look up a value on a chart.

2. Why? (Analysis)

These questions call for a deeper understanding of the information in the passage, meaning that you may have to consider more than one part of the passage. You'll be required to recognize relationships between different pieces of information in the passage. For instance, you might be asked to put two thoughts together and figure out why something happened, or predict what's *going* to happen.

3. What If? (Generalization)

These questions require that you see things in perspective and look at "the bigger picture." You're asked to understand how events described in the passage may relate to situations not described in the passage. For instance, a passage may describe an experiment and the results. One question might ask you to predict the result if the experiment was performed under different conditions. Or suppose a passage describes an experimental finding. A question might ask you to assess the impact of the finding on the "real world."

Here's Our Step-by-Step Game Plan for Tackling Science Reasoning Passages

We have a step-by-step game plan for reading ACT science passages and answering questions about them. We'll outline the plan first, and then discuss each step in detail.

> To Read or Not to Read
>
> Because most of the questions on charts and graphs and experiments passages have nothing to do with the introduction, you don't want to spend any time on it unless you have to. The ACT test writers are trying to waste your time with the introductions—don't let 'em! Just skip those complicated, detailed introductions unless you can't answer a question—then go look at them. From time to time, there is a question that can be answered only by reading the introduction. They're not common though. Fighting scientists passages are different. Often the introductions are critical. So, read the entire passage (quickly!), including any introductions.

Step 1. Scan the Passage

Before you read the passage, take a quick look at the format. Your first task is to identify the passage type. Is it a charts and graphs, experiments, or fighting scientists passage? Count the questions. Here's why.

- Charts and graphs passages always have five questions.
- Experiments passages always have six questions.
- Fighting scientists passages always have seven questions.

If there are tables, illustrations, or graphs, familiarize yourself with their content. This should only take you about 20 seconds. (Remember, time is limited.) If there are experiments, skim the experiments and jot down key words in the margin. For instance, if the first experiment varied the temperature, jot down "temperature change." If the next experiment kept the temperature the same but varied the material used, jot down "material change." Little notes to jog your memory can be very helpful when you get to the questions and can keep you from having to read the entire experiment again.

Step 2. Look at Each Question and Identify Its Type

Once you've scanned the passage, you should move on to the questions. To which category does each question belong? Identify each as either an understanding, analysis, or generalization question. Why? Because knowing the question type will help you eliminate distracters and zero in on the right answer.

Step 3. Guesstimate

Some of the questions will require you to do some pretty simple calculations. Sometimes you can come up with the right answer choice by "guesstimating," which means making a rough estimate. (Remember this from Chapter 14, on geometry?) This technique works particularly well on problems that require you to interpret graphs.

Use Process of Elimination (POE)
Sometimes it's easier to find the correct answer by eliminating the wrong answer choices. Each time you eliminate a wrong answer choice, you increase your chance of selecting the correct answer.

Step 4. Use Process of Elimination (POE)

As on all tests on the ACT, you should use POE to eliminate incorrect answer choices. Once you have eliminated a couple of answer choices, you'll be able to spend a little time on the remaining choices and make a pretty good guess.

Time Management
Because you must complete 7 passages in 35 minutes, you need to budget your time accordingly. Don't forget that you're getting the same number of points for correctly answering easy as well as hard questions. Use the "triage" rule. Don't waste time struggling with a hard question when you can move on and answer an easy question. You can always come back to the question if you have time.

Don't Forget to Pace Yourself

To improve your score on the Science Reasoning test, you have to pace yourself. That means you'll have to answer the questions strategically. Remember the "triage" rule? (If not, review Chapter 2.) It applies to the Science Reasoning test as well. At the beginning of the test, take a quick look at all the passages and try to pick the order in which you want to do them based on what looks easiest. As you work on each of the passages, apply the "triage" rule to the questions. Does a question seem difficult or confusing? Then don't waste your time on it. You can always come back to that question later.

Which questions are the easiest? Those that simply require going back to the passage and looking up something tend to be easier. So do questions that ask you to project what will happen based on a trend established in the passage. In contrast, questions about assumptions underlying an experiment or hypothesis tend to be far more difficult.

The "triage" rule, as applied to both the passages and the questions, should allow you to move through the Science Reasoning test much more efficiently. While you want to move through the passages in an efficient manner and at a good pace, you cannot afford to rush yourself. If you have to guess on some questions, that's fine. Your objective is to get as many questions correct as possible, not to spend the same amount of time on each question and each passage.

Know Your Strengths and Weaknesses

After practicing all three passage types, you may find that you are best at charts and graphs passages. Or perhaps you really like the fighting scientists. Whatever you like best, make sure to do the passages that are easiest *for you* first. Leave the passages that give you the most trouble for last. The ACT Science Reasoning test always comes at the end when you're already tired. By prioritizing the passages, you give yourself the best chance to get the most points that you can.

One More Note

Some questions are fairly long themselves. They're like "mini passages" and usually accompany experiments and fighting scientists passages. These take a lot of time to do, so work these questions only after you've done all of the easy questions. Don't let tough, time-consuming questions delay you from moving on to the next passage, however. Use POE, guess, and move on. Once you have finished all of the questions for a passage, whether by guessing or working on them, don't go back to that passage. You're done with it.

Now that we've outlined our general step-by-step strategy, we'll show you how to apply that strategy to the three passage types that you'll see on the ACT Science Reasoning test.

Summary

- There are always 7 passages and 40 questions on the ACT Science Reasoning test. There are always three charts and graphs passages, three experiments passages, and one fighting scientists passage. The passages are not in any particular order.
- Spend the first minute of the test determining which passages will be hardest for you—these are the ones to leave until last. Playing to your strengths early in the test will gain you the most points.
- You don't need to know any science to do well on the Science Reasoning test. You just need to be able to read passages that are about science topics.
- Use the Process of Elimination and guesstimation to eliminate incorrect answers.

Chapter 20
Charts and Graphs

There are always three charts and graphs passages on the ACT. Each passage has five questions associated with it. Rather than reading in detail, scan the passages and the charts or graphs and then go straight to the questions. Keep track of variables, units, and trends in the charts. Use POE to eliminate incorrect answers. These passages tend to be shorter and more straightforward.

Step 1: Scan the Passage

You'll notice that the text is pretty skimpy on a charts and graphs passage. (Some passages contain only three sentences.) Because charts, tables, or graphs make up the major part of the passage, you'll need to examine them carefully. This just means using some of the skills you've developed in everyday life.

What do you do when you have to take a bus to a place you've never been? You look at a bus map. To understand the map, you have to figure out how it's designed and what the signs and symbols mean. Well, the same rule applies to the graphs, tables, and charts you'll see on the ACT.

What Is a Variable?
A variable is a quantity ("thing") that has some type of value. There are two types of variables you'll need to know for the ACT: independent variables and dependent variables.

In a charts and graphs passage, the ACT test writers are focusing on your ability to read charts and graphs. No big surprise there, but what that means is that they are not focusing on your ability to read the introduction. On this kind of passage, you want to skip the introduction. If you get into trouble doing the questions, then come back and give the intro a closer look, but otherwise, keep moving. Don't let them waste your time. Time is precious on the Science Reasoning test.

Scanning a Graph: Look at the Variables and Units

When you see a graph, table, or chart, you should ask yourself the following two questions:

1. What are the variables? (sunlight? temperature? number of plants?)
2. How are they measured? (in grams? quarts? meters?) Keep in mind that values can also be represented as percentages.

Let's look at an example.

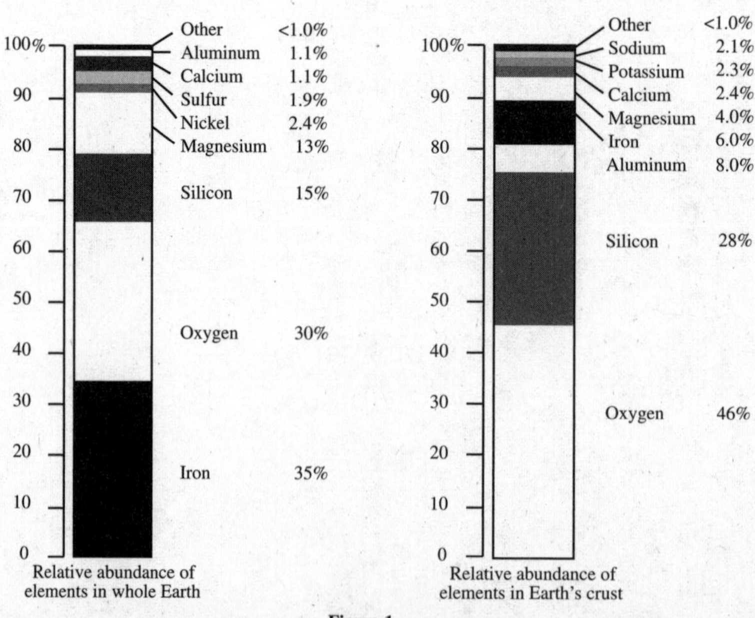

Figure 1

Relative abundance by weight of elements in the whole Earth and in the Earth's crust

We see two bar graphs that describe the composition of the whole earth compared with that of the earth's crust.

1. What are the variables?
2. How are they measured?

Do you see the numbers on either side of the bar graphs? They tell you the values are given in percentages (%). The graph on the left describes the percent (by weight) of an element in the whole earth. The one on the right describes the percent (by weight) of an element in the earth's crust.

Now let's see if you can work with a slightly more complicated graph.

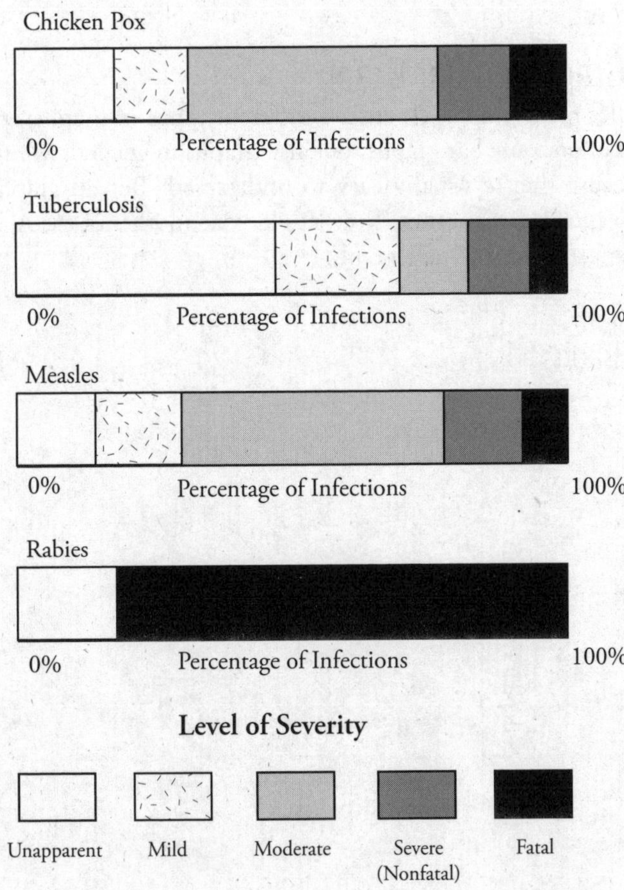

Watch Out!
Sometimes the ACT test writers will attempt to trick you by giving you the answer choices in the wrong units. You may have to convert between units on the test. For example, if the passage discusses the rate of a machine in miles per hour, the answer choices may be given in miles per minute. This may happen only once or twice on a test, but because it can happen, you need to be aware and stay focused.

Scan the Bar Graphs

1. What are the variables?
    - There are four diseases: chicken pox, tuberculosis, measles, and rabies.
    - Did you notice the small boxes under the bar graphs? They make up a key that gives you more information about the variables. The graph is about diseases, and the key describes levels of severity.
    - Now how many levels are there?
    - There are five levels: unapparent, mild, moderate, severe (nonfatal), and fatal.

2. How are they measured?
    - The values are in percentages, just as before.

Not Every Graph Is a Bar Graph

The ACT is filled with graphs. There are different types of graphs, so you must learn how to read not only bar graphs, but also graphs in general. We started with bar graphs because they're usually easy to understand. But all graphs illustrate how one variable relates to another. Now let's look at another of the ACT test writers' favorite graphs: the coordinate graph.

Coordinate Graphs

What Are the Four Types of Coordinate Graphs?

- linear graphs
- graphs with curves
- scatter diagrams
- flat lines

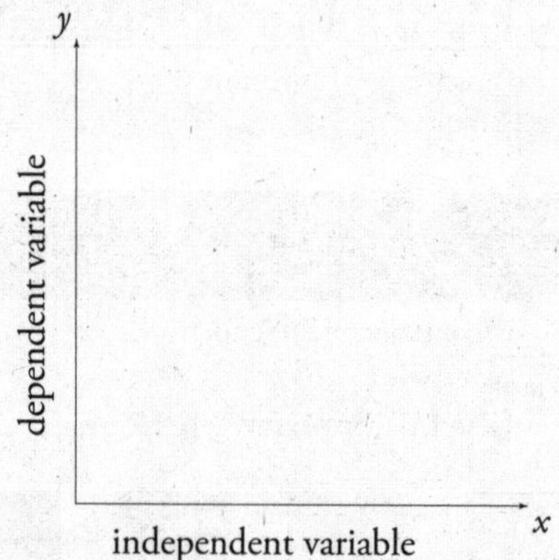

Look at the coordinate graph above. It has a horizontal axis (x-axis) and a vertical axis (y-axis). The x-axis shows the independent variable, the thing that's being manipulated (or changed purposely). The y-axis contains the dependent variable, the thing that is affected when the independent variable is changed.

Now let's look at what happens when we put some points on the graph.

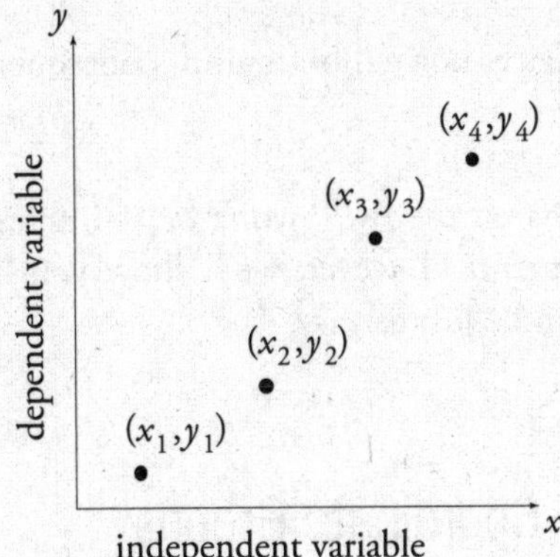

Every point on the graph represents a value for both the independent variable (*x*-variable) and the dependent variable (*y*-variable). In other words, each point represents an (*x*,*y*) pair. Don't forget that. Whenever you see a point on a graph, you should remember that it has both an *x*-component and a *y*-component.

Now let's look at what happens when we take the same graph and indicate that the graph represents an experiment performed by Dr. Frankenstein.

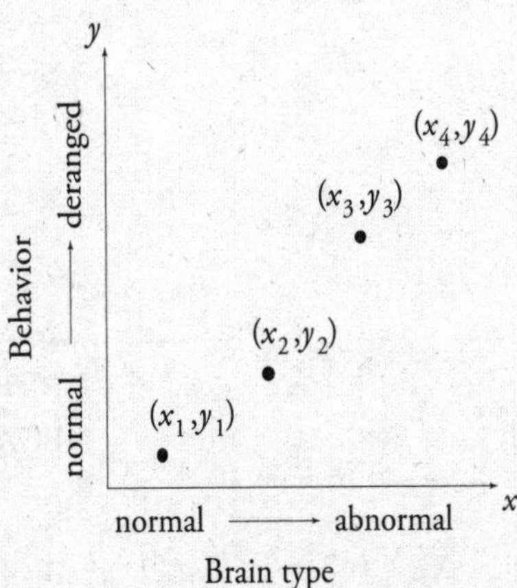

Dr. Frankenstein's Experiment

Take a look at the axes. The variables are brain type and behavior. The brain type is an independent variable and is represented along the *x*-axis. The brain type affects the monster's behavior, which is represented along the *y*-axis.

When building his monster, Dr. Frankenstein can use the brain of either a normal person or a psychopath. In this experiment (x_1,y_1) represents a normal brain (the independent variable) with a normal behavior (dependent variable). The point (x_4,y_4) represents a psychopath's brain and the associated tendency toward deranged behaviors.

Let's look, for example, at point (x_2,y_2) on the graph. When the monster is given this brain type (x_2), what type of behavior does he exhibit? Does he behave normally, or is he deranged?

Point (x_2,y_2) represents a fairly normal brain and, consequently, a reasonably well-behaved individual.

Unfortunately, most graphs on the ACT won't be as interesting as the one about Dr. Frankenstein's experiment. However, we'll show you how interpreting even the most boring graphs can be just as easy.

Know Four Kinds of Coordinate Graphs

On the ACT, you will see four kinds of coordinate graphs. Just remember to look at what the variables are, how they're measured, and how they're related.

Linear Graphs

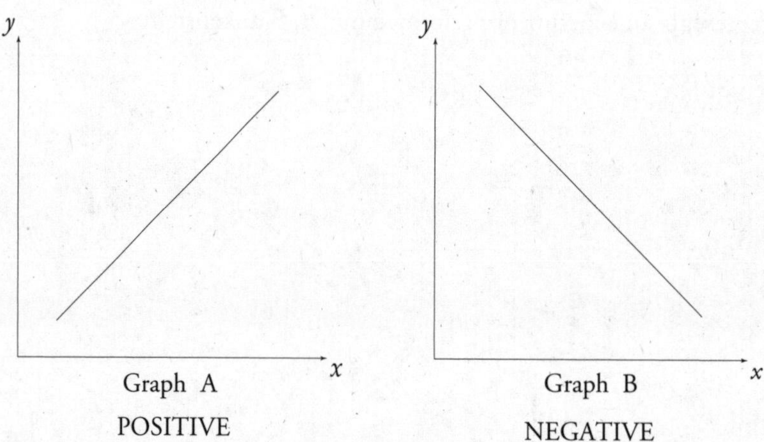

Graph A
POSITIVE

Graph B
NEGATIVE

The graphs above show a linear relationship. *Linear* is a fancy word meaning that the points follow a straight line. A positive linear relationship occurs when an increase in x (as you move to the right along the x-axis) leads to an increase in y (Graph A). A negative, or an inverse, relationship occurs when an increase in x leads to a decrease in y (Graph B).

Let's see if you can recognize the relationship on the next page.

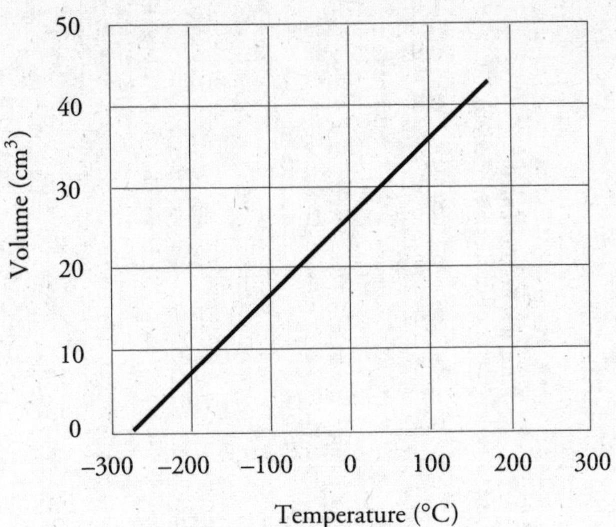

Does the graph show a positive or a negative linear relationship between temperature and volume?

If you answered positive, you're right. If, for some reason, you forget which graph shows a positive relationship, just remember that positive means that the line is pointing upward to the right.

Graphs with Curves

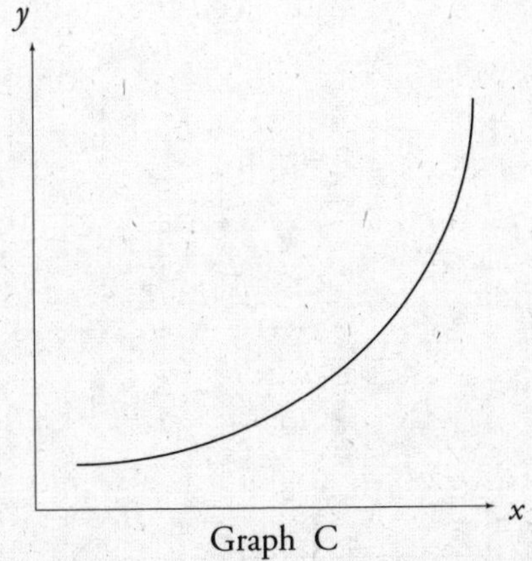

Graph C

Another common graph displays a curve, as shown in Graph C. The curve above means that for every increase in x, the y-values become larger. The changes in y are exponential and become greater the more x increases. If a graph is curved, that means that the amount y changes with each change in x is different at different points on the graph. Let's look at another example.

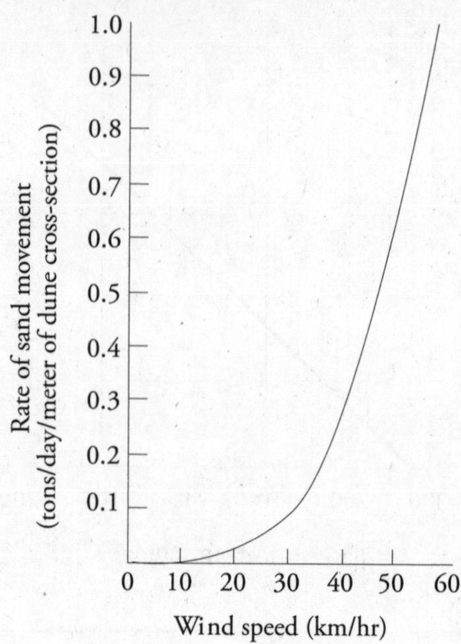

When the wind speed is 40 km/hr, what is the rate of sand movement?

The answer is 0.3. Now let's see what happens when the wind speed is 50 km/hr. The rate of sand movement increases to 0.6. Did you notice that the rate of sand movement doubled? Now what happens when the wind speed is 60 km/hr? The rate of sand movement increases even more. As you pick larger values for wind speed, the rate of sand movement will shoot up in value.

Scatter Diagrams

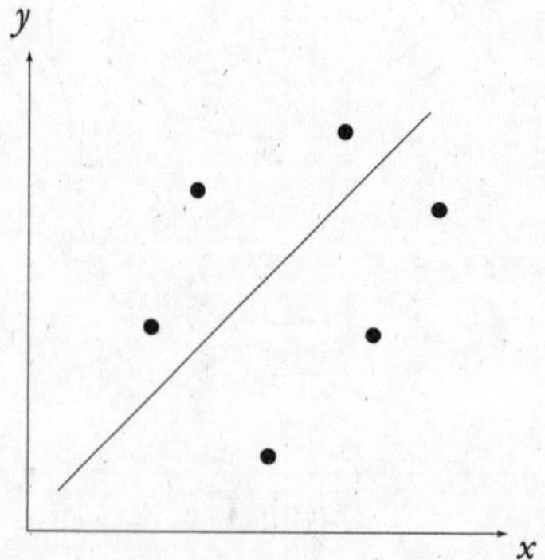

The ACT test writers expect you to understand a scatter diagram. See the line that runs through the center of the graph? It's called a "best-fit" line. It tells you that if you took the average of all the points on the graph and lined them up, they would form the straight line above. Therefore, the graph tells you two things: (1) what the points would look like if they were averaged and lined up (a straight line), and (2) how they *really* look on the graph (scattered).

Flat Lines

Every so often, the ACT will plot data on a graph in which there is no relationship between the variables. That is to say, the two elements plotted on the graph have no effect on each other. When this occurs, the result is a flat line. A line with no slope accurately graphs data in which there is no change. For example

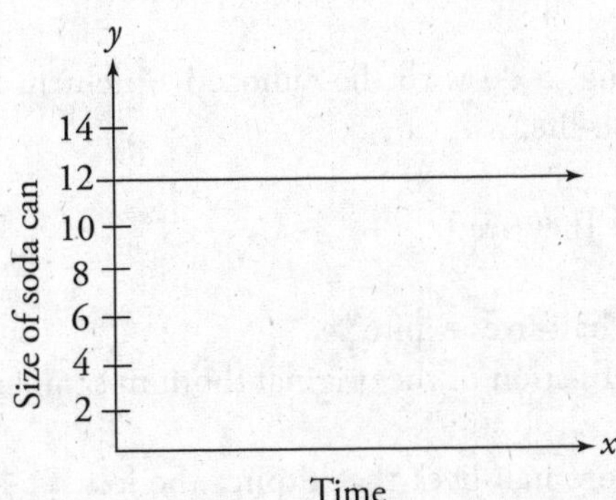

Here, the graph displays the effect of time on the size of a soda can. Does time actually affect the size of the can? Of course not. As a result, we get a line with no slope.

Now that we have tackled scanning graphs, let's see if we can apply the same technique to scanning tables and illustrations.

Scanning a Table: Look at the Variables

Just as you did with graphs, look at the table or chart to figure out what the variables are. You want to know what's being compared with what. As you read the chart, take the time to understand how these variables are related to each other (don't skimp on this part). Let's look at the example on the following page.

Number of half-lives expired for radioactive thorium	Remaining fraction of original thorium sample
0	1
1	$\frac{1}{2}$
2	$\frac{1}{4}$
3	$\frac{1}{8}$
4	$\frac{1}{16}$

This table has something to do with the radioactive element thorium, which has something called a "half-life."

What are the variables? They are

A. the number of half-lives expired
B. the remaining fraction of the original thorium sample

As you can see, the more half-lives that expire, the less we have of the original thorium sample.

Scanning an Illustration: Look at the Variables

Instead of a chart or graph, sometimes the ACT test writers will give you an illustration. Sometimes these illustrations will have text within the picture, but usually they will not have a specific explanation accompanying them. The ACT test writers want to see if you can follow a flow chart or interpret a diagram. Look at the example on the next page.

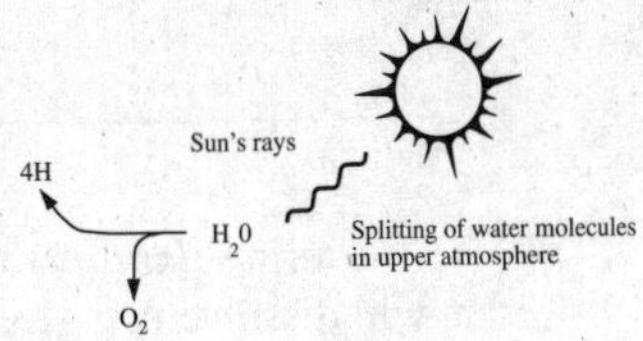

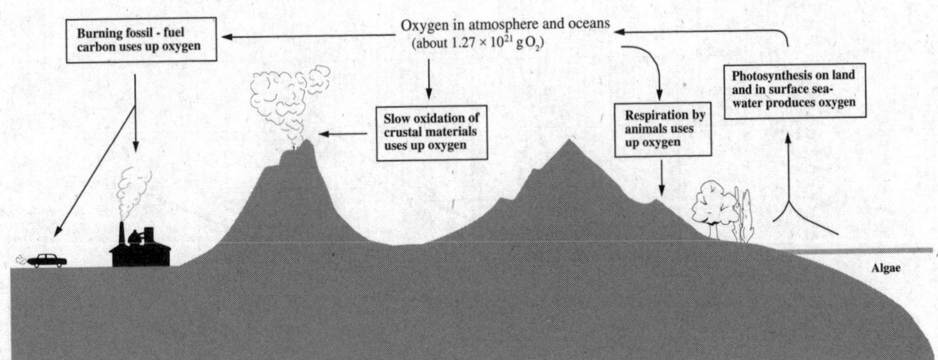

The Cycle of Oxygen Through the Atmosphere

The figure above illustrates the oxygen cycle. Based on this figure, which of the processes releases oxygen into the atmosphere? Look at the arrows associated with each box. The information inside every box is the variable. Which of the boxes has an arrow that shows that oxygen is released into the atmosphere? The box labeled "photosynthesis on land and in surface seawater produces oxygen."

Now what if the ACT test writers ask you what kinds of living organisms produce oxygen? According to this diagram, the answer is algae and plants on land. The direction of the arrow indicates that oxygen is moving from algae and the ground to the atmosphere. All the other arrows are pointing away from the atmosphere.

Step 2: Identify the Question Type

Now that you know how to scan the various charts, graphs, and illustrations, let's go right to the questions. Remember that there are only three basic question types, each addressing a different skill.

Question Type 1: Look It Up

The majority of these questions test your ability to understand the figures. They want you to explain, describe, and identify some of the basic scientific concepts or assumptions that underlie the information provided in the figures. Some questions involve only one figure in the passage, while others require two or more. So for "Look It Up" questions, identify the piece of information needed.

Know the Three Question Types

- Look It Up
- Why?
- What If?

Here's an example.

The term *solubility* refers to the amount of a substance (solute) that will dissolve in a given amount of a liquid substance (solvent). The solubility of solids in water varies with temperature. The graph below displays the water solubility curves for six crystalline solids.

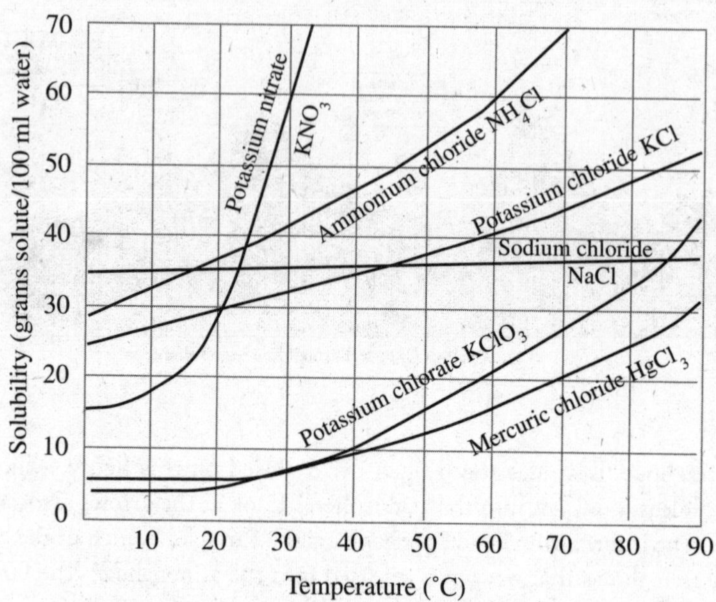

1. Which of the following factors affects the degree to which KCl is soluble in water?

 A. Only the quantity of KCl added to 100 ml of water
 B. The temperature of the solution
 C. Only the amount of solvent present in the solution
 D. The weight of KCl

Here's How to Crack It

This question requires that you understand the variables—what's being compared with what. The variables are

- the solution's temperature; and
- solubility, or the mass of solute that will dissolve in 100 ml of water

The graph shows you that for KCl, the solubility varies with the solution's temperature. That's why the answer is (B).

Translating Tables to Graphs

Sometimes you will be given a question that asks, "Which of the following graphs would best represent the results in the passage?" If you're given a table, you might have to translate the information into a graph.

Luckily, we've just learned a few things about graphs and tables. Now we have to learn how to read a table and translate this information into a graph. To make a graph, draw both axes and label the axes *x* and *y*. Remember, the *x*-axis is the independent variable, and the *y*-axis is the dependent variable. After you have drawn your axes, you can begin to plot some points on the graph.

Let's see if we can translate the information in the table about radioactive thorium into a graph.

Number of half-lives expired for radioactive thorium	Remaining fraction of original thorium sample
0	1
1	$\frac{1}{2}$
2	$\frac{1}{4}$
3	$\frac{1}{8}$
4	$\frac{1}{16}$

What If You Just Don't Understand the Table, Graph, or Chart?

Sometimes the ACT includes tables, graphs, or charts that seem utterly incomprehensible. Don't get stuck on them. Just see if you can figure out the variables and then go to the questions. Perhaps there's only one question relating to that particular table, graph, or chart. Don't panic. Most of the time you aren't required to understand the entire passage; you just need to search for the information you need to answer each question.

The first thing to do is draw your axes.

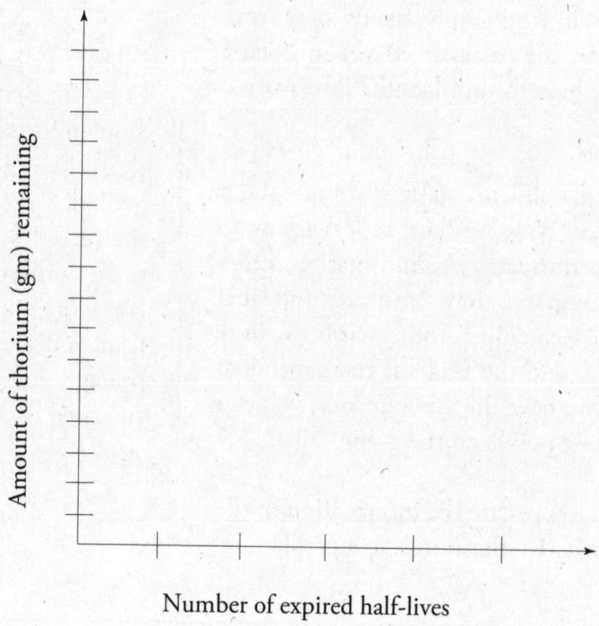

What is the independent variable? It's the number of expired half-lives. Label your *x*-axis with the numbers 0 through 4. Now, what is the dependent variable? It's the amount of thorium left after each expired half-life. Label the *y*-axis with the numbers $\frac{1}{16}$ to 1. Now you can plot the values on the graph and connect the dots!

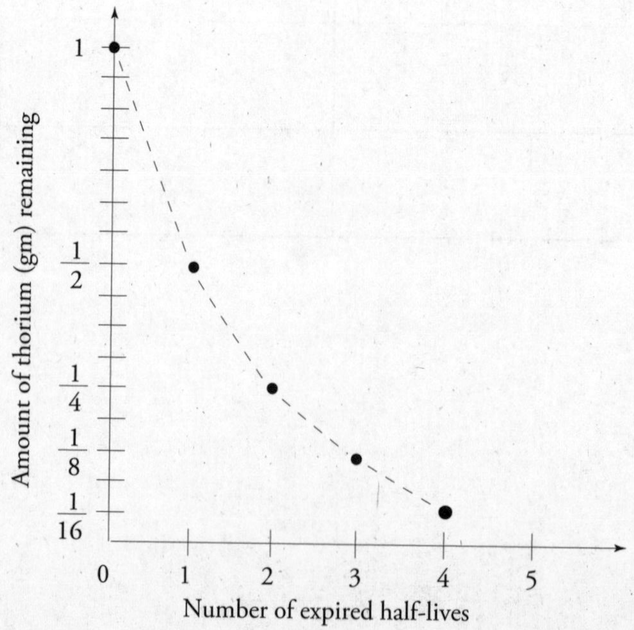

Now let's see if you can translate a table into a graph.

An investigator conducted a study to determine the relationship between temperature and pH of the enzyme chymotrypsin. Her findings are listed in the table below.

What's Chymotrypsin?
Who knows? Who cares? You don't need to understand it to answer the question. You just need to be able to read a chart.

Temp. (C°)	pH level
47	2
42	5
37	7
32	4
27	3

Chymotrypsin acidity: temperature dependence

Use the space in the margin to draw a graph that represents the relationship between temperature and pH in this experiment.

This Is What Your Graph Should Look Like

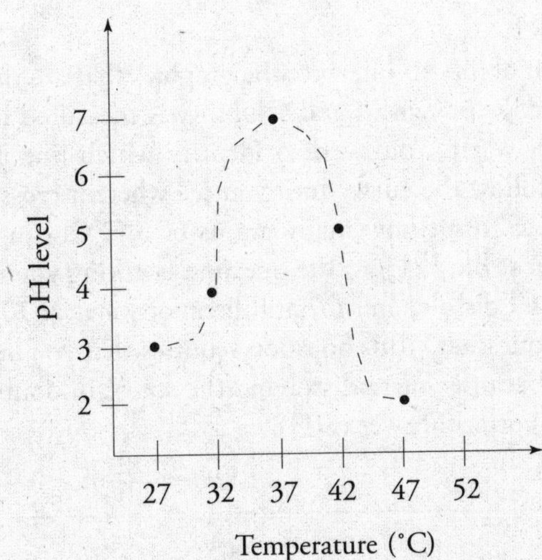

Did you label your axes? Temperature is the independent variable, and pH is the dependent variable. Now here's where it can get a little tricky. You should have labeled your *x*-axis with the units increasing as you move to the right. If you plotted your numbers differently, you probably got the wrong answer. Are you ever going to have to draw a graph on the ACT? No, but you will have to recognize which of the graphs in the answer choices best represents the information in the chart or passage. These questions are fairly easy if you practice how to read the axes, and look at the points (or lines) on the graphs.

Question Type 2: Why?

For this type of question, you're supposed to have a slightly deeper understanding of the passage. The question will usually require you to look at several pieces of information to get the right answer. Basically, you're being asked to figure out how different pieces of information are related to one another.

Draw on More Than One Piece of Information

Here's an example using the previous passage about solubility. Don't forget to refer to the graph on page 320.

---

2. How many grams of NH_4Cl can be dissolved in 200 milliliters of water at 70°C ?

F. 70 grams
G. 90 grams
H. 140 grams
J. 180 grams

Here's How to Crack It

The passage tests your ability to interpret the graph. What are the units? Temperature is measured in degrees Celsius and solubility is measured in grams of solute per 100 milliliters of water. You need to identify which line represents NH_4Cl on the graph. Then follow the curve until you see where it crosses 70°C. You can then look at the *y*-axis to see how many grams of NH_4Cl can dissolve in water. The answer is 70 grams. But hold it. The question is asking you to determine how many grams of NH_4Cl dissolve in *200* milliliters of water at 70°C. (This is what makes it an analysis question.) This question requires that you double the number of grams of NH_4Cl because you're dissolving the solute in double the amount of water. Therefore, the correct answer is (H).

Question Type 3: Generalization

In this type of question, you need to go beyond the information given. You may be presented with a new situation and be asked to apply the concepts provided in the passage.

Step Back and Look at the Big Picture

Here's an example using the same passage about solubility.

---

3. Based on the passage, what can you conclude about the relationship between solubility and temperature?

   A. The solubility of a substance has little to do with the concentration of the solvent or the temperature.
   B. Temperature is a dependent variable in the study.
   C. For any given solution, a temperature increase allows for more solute to be dissolved in a solvent.
   D. An increase in temperature will always lead to a decrease in solubility.

Here's How to Crack It

This is a What If? question, which means you're supposed to look at the "big picture." The ACT test writers want you to make a generalization not just about the six solids on the graph, but about substances in general. What are some of the trends you notice among all the solutes? As the temperature increases, the number of grams that can be dissolved in water increases (more stuff can be added). This means that higher temperatures allow for more solute to be dissolved in water. Therefore, (C) is the correct answer.

Answer choice (A) is clearly wrong because solubility and temperature are related (just look at the graph). Is temperature an independent variable or a dependent variable? Well, an independent variable is one with which you can play around. Therefore, temperature is the independent variable, so (B) is wrong. Answer choice (D) is incorrect because it is opposite—an increase in temperature leads to an increase rather than a decrease in solubility.

Step 3: Guesstimate

Interpolation

Sometimes the ACT test writers will give you a graph and ask you to predict the position of an unplotted point. This means that you may have to make a guess about where a point will lie on the graph based on the data you already have. The word for this is **interpolation**, and it's a skill you'll need for analyzing graphs. It's not too difficult to develop. The values that they want you to guess are within the range of points on the graph. Let's look at the graph below.

Interpolation
To estimate values on a graph between two known values

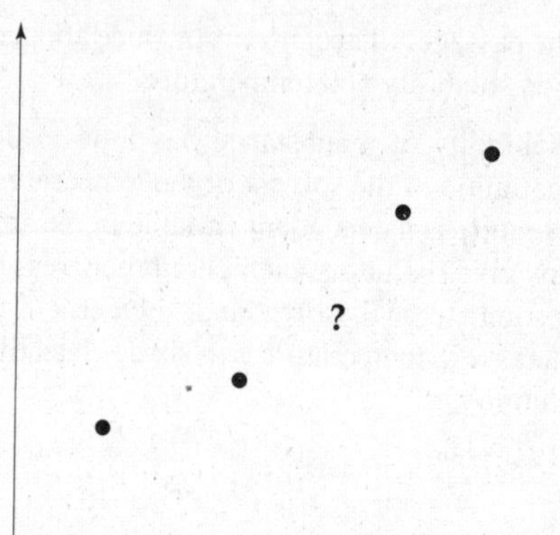

What if the ACT test writers asked you to predict the value of y if you were given a value x on the graph? Based on the position of the other points (the **trend**), you would predict the point would be located where the question mark is.

Let's try an example.

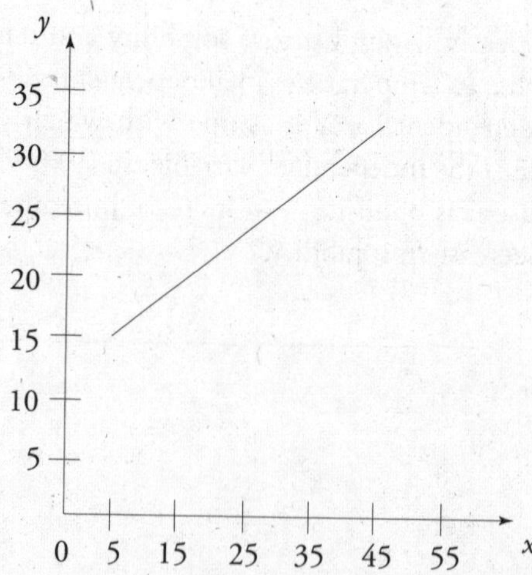

If x is 10, what is the value of y?

We're not sure! The ACT test writers didn't give you a value of 10 on the x-axis. What should you do? First, determine where 10 would lie on the x-axis. This is the first step in guesstimating. Remember, guesstimating will help you approximate an answer. Because 10 falls between 5 and 15, you can guesstimate where x and its corresponding y-value lie on the graph. Can you make a guess as to the value of y on the graph? Move across the x-axis to the approximate position of 10, and then move up from the x-axis until you reach the line. From there, draw a horizontal line to the y-axis. What is the value of y? It's about 17 or 18. Piece of cake, right?

Let's Do It Again

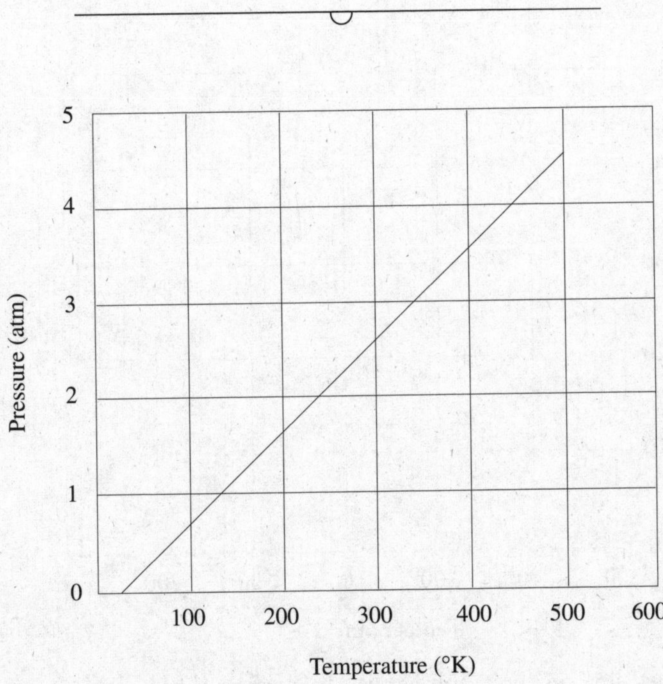

1. Based on the graph above, what is the atmospheric pressure when the temperature is 350°K?

A. 2.0 atm
B. 2.5 atm
C. 3.0 atm
D. 3.5 atm

Here's How to Crack It

Once again, the ACT test writers didn't give a value of 350°K for x. But you do know that 350°K is half way between 300°K and 400°K. So what do you do next? Guesstimate. Move across the x-axis until you reach the midpoint between 300°K and 400°K. Then move up until you reach the line and move across to the y-axis. What is the approximate value of y? The answer is 3.0 atm, (C).

Extrapolation

The ACT test writers want to test another skill. Sometimes they want you to extend the line on a graph.

Extrapolation
To project or expand known data into an area not known

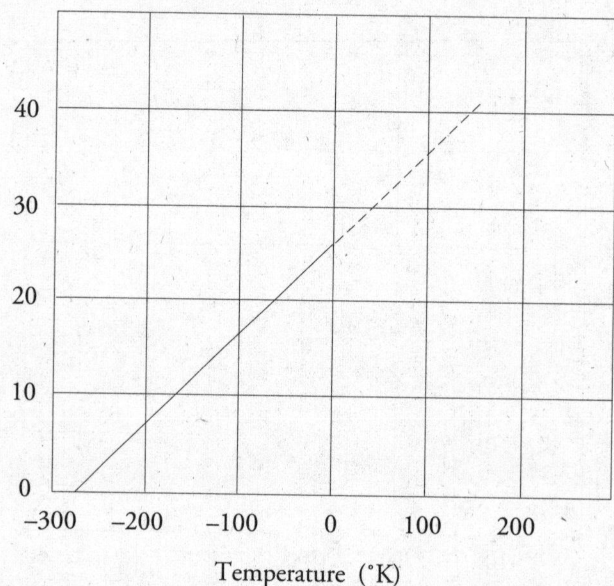

See the dashed line on the graph above? This shows that if you continued the experiment and picked values of x that were outside of the range given by the solid line, you would get the dashed line shown above. This is called **extrapolation.** Let's look at an example.

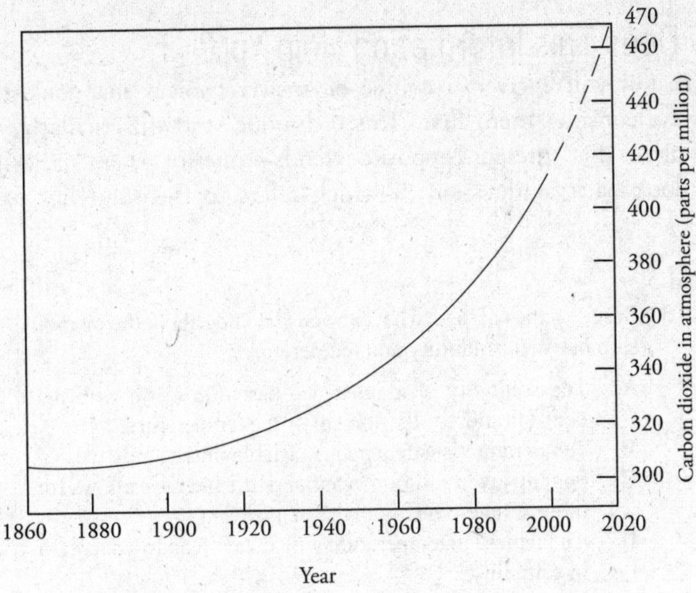

Estimated CO_2 concentration in the atmosphere up to the year 2020

What will be the CO_2 concentration in the atmosphere in the year 2020?

This is a graph of the concentration of CO_2 in the atmosphere since 1860. Notice that the graph gives values of CO_2 concentration all the way up to the year 2020. But we're barely in the twenty-first century! So how did they arrive at these values? They "projected" the CO_2 concentration level based on previous trends in the data. Therefore, the CO_2 concentration will be about 470 parts per million. That's extrapolation. You'll probably need this skill to answer several questions.

Step 4: Use Process of Elimination

Often the ACT test writers will give you several answer choices that look a lot alike. Why's that? They are attempting to disguise the correct answer choice. Test writers usually write the question first, then the correct answer, and finally the incorrect answers. Because they don't want the correct answer to be too obvious, they often surround it with several similar (but wrong) answers.

So How Does This Information Help You?

Use POE

If two answer choices are opposites, start with them first.

It means that if you're given a couple of answer choices that look alike, you should always consider them first. This technique works particularly well with answer choices that present opposite trends—one of them is usually correct. Let's look back at question 3, which refers to the solubility passage on page 320.

3. Based on the passage, what can you conclude about the relationship between solubility and temperature?

A. The solubility of a substance has little to do with the concentration of the solvent or the temperature.
B. Temperature is a dependent variable in the study.
C. For any given solution, a temperature increase allows for more solute to be dissolved in a solvent.
D. An increase in temperature will always lead to a decrease in solubility.

Did you notice that (C) and (D) are opposites? So which answer choices should you consider first? Answer choices (C) and (D).

Charts and Graphs Drill 1

The kinetic molecular theory provides new insights into the movement of molecules in liquids. It states that molecules are in constant motion and collide with one another. When the temperature of a liquid increases, there will be an increase in the movement of molecules and in the average kinetic energy. The figure below depicts the distribution of the kinetic energy of two volumetrically identical samples of water at different temperatures (T).

Water has attractive intermolecular forces that keep the molecules together. When enough heat is added to water, it will weaken these forces and allow some molecules to evaporate and escape the liquid as a gas. The activation energy (Ea) is the minimum energy necessary for molecules to escape the liquid and undergo a phase change.

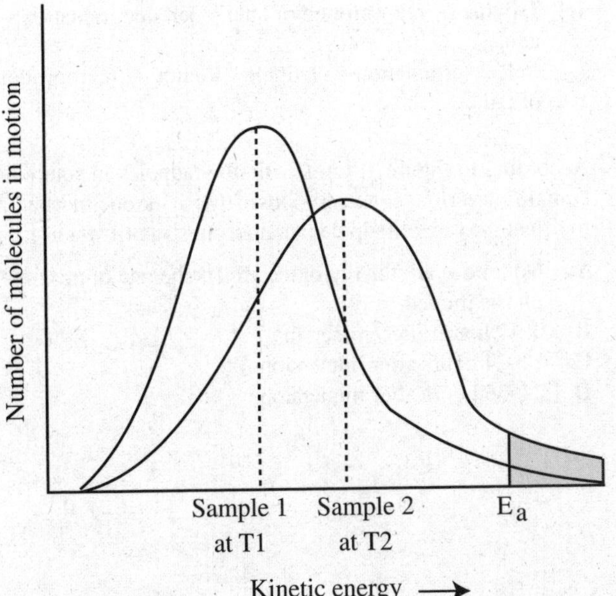

Distribution of Kinetic Energy for Two Samples of Water

Figure 1

1. Which of the following statements best describes the changes observed in the graph?

- **A.** At T1, Sample 1 has a lower kinetic energy than does Sample 2.
- **B.** At T2, Sample 1 has a lower kinetic energy than does Sample 2.
- **C.** An increase in temperature leads to a decrease in kinetic energy.
- **D.** Water never undergoes a phase change.

2. Assume that water undergoes a phase change to a gas. Which of the following statements would be true?

- **F.** The attractive intermolecular forces of the escaping molecules are weak.
- **G.** The average kinetic energy of the water remains the same.
- **H.** The rate of movement of the gas molecules decreases.
- **J.** The gas will undergo no further phase changes.

3. Suppose a third sample of water is heated to a higher temperature than Sample 2. It is then found that a greater number of molecules escaped the liquid in Sample 3 than in Sample 2. Would these results be consistent with the results depicted in Figure 1?

- **A.** Yes, an increase in temperature leads to a decrease in the number of escaping molecules in the liquid.
- **B.** Yes, as the temperature increases, it leads to more molecules escaping the liquid.
- **C.** No, the temperature reading of Sample 2 would be five times as high as that of the third sample.
- **D.** No, the average kinetic energy of the water will decrease.

4. It can be inferred from the passage that when a substance undergoes a phase change from a liquid to a gas it will:

- **F.** evaporate.
- **G.** condense.
- **H.** disintegrate.
- **J.** remain the same.

5. Given the samples at T1 and T2, and the kinetic energies measured and shown in Figure 1, which temperature produces the highest single kinetic energy measurement?

- **A.** Both T1 and T2
- **B.** T2
- **C.** T1
- **D.** Neither T1 nor T2

Charts and Graphs Drill 2

Amphibians are unique organisms that undergo drastic physical changes during the transformation from an immature organism into an adult form. This process, called metamorphosis, begins with the determination of cells at the tadpole stage. A study was conducted using tadpoles to determine the influence of thyroxine (a hormone) on metamorphosis.

As shown in the graph below, tadpoles were placed in solutions containing various concentrations of thyroxine. Increased levels of thyroxine correlated with increased rates of tail reabsorption and the appearance of adult characteristics such as lungs and hind legs.

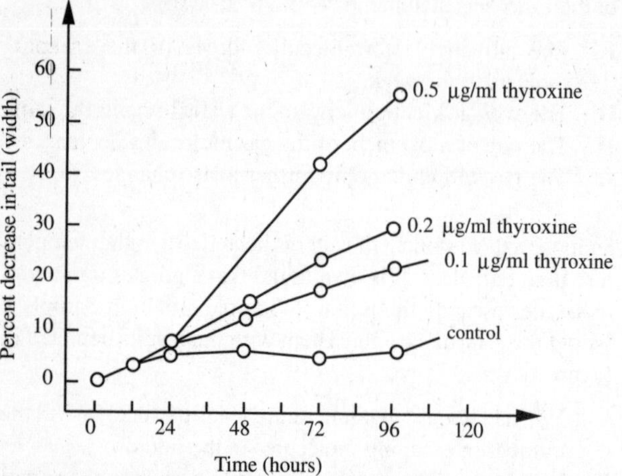

Decrease in tail width in relation to varying levels of thyroxine solutions

Figure 1

1. Suppose that a tadpole was immersed in a 0.3 μg/ml solution for 72 hours. What would be the expected approximate decrease in tail width?

   A. 22%
   B. 30%
   C. 41%
   D. 50%

2. Which of the following generalizations about tadpoles is supported by the results of the study?

   F. They will not undergo metamorphosis if they are not given thyroxine.
   G. Metamorphosis in a normal tadpole takes at least five days.
   H. The most rapid disappearance of the tail is associated with the immersion of tadpoles in the most dilute thyroxine solution.
   J. Temperature plays a major role in metamorphosis.

3. After four days, the tadpoles are checked for development. In all samples other than the control, which of the following concentrations of thyroxine would the tadpoles be likely to show the LEAST development?

   A. 0.5 μg/ml
   B. 0.2 μg/ml
   C. 0.1 μg/ml
   D. All of the tadpoles would show the same development.

4. Based on the information in the passage, which of the following would be a correct order of the stages of tadpole development?

   F. Tadpole → adult → reabsorption of tail → cell determination
   G. Tadpole → cell determination → reabsorption of tail → adult
   H. Tadpole → reabsorption of tail → cell determination → adult
   J. Cell determination → tadpole → adult → reabsorption of tail

5. According to Figure 1, immersing the tadpoles in solutions containing various concentrations of thyroxine does not begin to affect the rate of tadpole metamorphosis until when?

   A. No time at all; the thyroxine affects the rate of metamorphosis immediately.
   B. 0–12 hours after immersion
   C. 12–24 hours after immersion
   D. 24–36 hours after immersion

Charts and Graphs Drill 3

Each element is arranged in the periodic table according to its atomic number, which represents the number of protons in the nucleus. In every neutrally charged atom, the number of electrons equals the number of protons. The table below lists some of the properties of row 2 elements in the periodic table. *Electronegativity* is a measure of the relative strength with which the atoms attract outer electrons. Within a row of the periodic table, the electronegativity tends to increase with increasing atomic number, due to the tighter bonding between protons and electrons. The highest value for electronegativity is 4.0.

Element	Atomic number	Atomic radius	Electro–negativity	Characteristic
Li	3	1.52	1.0	metal
Be	4	1.13	1.5	metal
B	5	0.88	2.0	non-metal
C	6	0.77	2.5	non-metal
N	7	0.70	3.0	non-metal
O	8	0.66	3.5	non-metal
F	9	0.64	4.0	non-metal

Table 1

1. Which of the following graphs best represents the relationship between atomic number and atomic radius for row 2 elements?

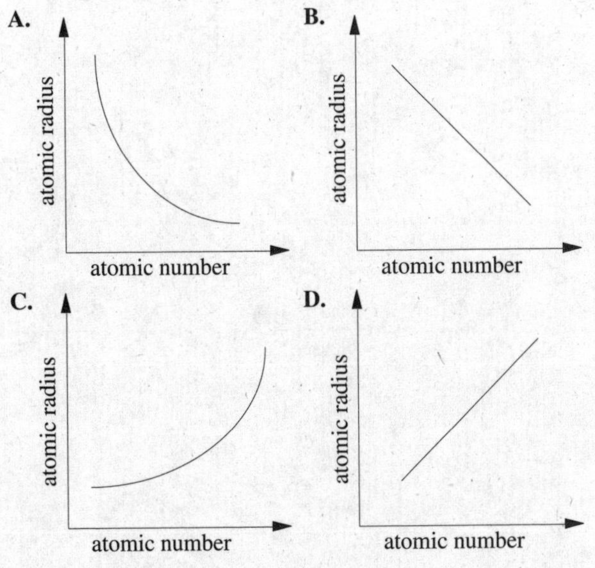

2. What conclusion could be appropriately drawn from the data regarding electronegativity in Table 1 ?

   F. An element with high electronegativity has an even atomic number.
   G. An element with high electronegativity will be a metal.
   H. An element with high electronegativity will have little tendency to attract outer electrons.
   J. An element with high electronegativity will be a non-metal.

3. What generalization can one make concerning the relationship between two properties of elements?

   A. As the atomic radius decreases, the electronegativity decreases.
   B. As the atomic radius decreases, the electronegativity increases.
   C. All metals have higher electronegativity values than non-metals.
   D. The atomic radius of F is larger than that of N.

4. Which of the following is true regarding the comparative electronegativity of fluorine (F) and lithium (Li)?

   F. The electronegativity of F is greater than Li because F has fewer electrons in its outer shell.
   G. The electronegativity of F is greater than Li because F electrons are more tightly bound.
   H. The electronegativity of Li is greater than F because Li has a greater metallic character.
   J. The electronegativity of Li is greater than F because Li has a greater metallic character.

5. Generally speaking, ionization energy follows the same trends as does electronegativity. Elements with a high electronegativity also have a high ionization energy. Which of the following is a correct order of elements with INCREASING ionization energies?

   A. Li, N, F
   B. F, N, Li
   C. B, N, Be
   D. Be, O, Li

Summary

- There are three charts and graphs passages on the Science Reasoning test. They are identified easily because they do not have summaries of research or experiments. Instead, most of the information is presented in one or more charts or graphs.
- Look at the variables and units presented in the chart or graph. Scan the charts and graphs and look for trends in the information presented. Then, go directly to the questions.
- Use Guesstimation and POE to narrow down the answer choices. Often eliminating incorrect answers is easier than only searching for the correct answer.
- Do the easiest questions first and leave the difficult questions for last. When you've finished all the questions on one passage, go on to another.
- Don't forget to always guess your Letter of the Day for questions that you have no idea how to do.

Chapter 21
Experiments

There are always three experiments passages on the ACT and each has six questions. Rather than read in detail, scan the experiments, looking for changes in the experiments, and look at any charts; then go straight to the questions. Jot down notes about the overall experimental objective and note what is changing from experiment to experiment; these changes are what the ACT usually asks questions about. Use the Process of Elimination to eliminate incorrect answers.

Experiments passages are easy to spot. They usually contain an introductory paragraph followed by a number of experiments and six questions. Like charts and graphs passages, they may include graphs, tables, illustrations, or charts.

Step 1: Scan the Passage

Identify the Research Objective

Have you ever heard of the *scientific method*? That's a fancy name for the steps an investigator takes in conducting a study. One of the key steps is to state the **objective.** The objective is a statement that tells you the purpose of the study. For every experiment described on the ACT, there will always be an objective.

Example #1

Let's look at an example.

An investigator was interested in observing whether a chemical reaction occurs when compounds are mixed with water. Chemical reactions are known to produce heat. Three compounds were observed in order to determine whether, based on the release of heat, a reaction took place. A thermometer was placed in each test tube to record any change in temperature.

Test tubes	Temperature Change?	
	Yes	No
1. Powdered bleach + H_2O	x	
2. Salt + H_2O		x
3. Sugar + H_2O		x

Experiments

Look for three things on an experiments passage.

- Identify the objective. (*What* were they studying?)
- Identify the method of research. (*How* did they study it?)
- Identify the results. (*What* did they find?)

How Do You Spot the Objective?

The objective is to determine whether heat was released in any of the reactions listed in the table. Notice that the objective tells you exactly what the investigator wants to know: Did a reaction take place?

Where do you usually find the objective of the study? The objective is usually found in the beginning or at the end of the introductory paragraph. Once you find the objective of the study, underline it. Knowing the objective of the study will keep you focused throughout your reading of the passage.

Your Underlined Passage Should Look Like This

<u>An investigator was interested in observing whether a chemical reaction occurs when compounds are mixed with water.</u> Chemical reactions are known to produce heat. Three compounds were observed in order to determine whether, based on the release of heat, a reaction took place. A thermometer was placed in each test tube to record any change in temperature.

Example #2

A laboratory experiment was conducted to determine whether the lack of sunlight influences photosynthesis (production of glucose). Eight potted *Salvia* flowers were randomly selected and divided into two groups and labeled Group A and Group B. The plants were then subjected to differing light conditions and examined one week later.

Group A

These plants were exposed to sunlight for the duration of the study. At the end of the study, these plants were green in appearance and produced glucose.

Group B

These plants were kept in the dark. At the end of the study, they were yellow in appearance and did not produce glucose.

What Is the Objective of the Study?

The objective of the study is to determine whether the lack of sunlight influences photosynthesis in plants.

<u>A laboratory experiment was conducted to determine whether the lack of sunlight influences photosynthesis (production of glucose).</u> Eight potted *Salvia* flowers were randomly selected and divided into two groups and labeled Group A and Group B. The plants were then subjected to differing light conditions and examined one week later.

So what should you do once you realize you've been given an experimental reasoning passage? Identify the objective and don't answer the questions until you're sure you understand it. Test takers often make careless mistakes when they read the passage too quickly and lose sight of the objective.

Write, Write, Write!
Don't forget to take notes on each step within the experiment. You don't have to write a lot—just jot down key changes.

Follow the Procedure and Identify the Variables

It's a good idea to make some brief notes on each experiment. These notes should highlight the differences between experiments in a passage. (Why else would the ACT test writers include two or more experiments if the experiments weren't different in some way?) Often these notes will refer to the procedure in the experiment. This might seem like a waste of time, but it's not. By noting what each experiment does differently, you will be able to quickly assess which experiment any given question is asking about.

The ACT test writers also want to see whether you can identify the variables in the experiments. Generally, there will be two or more variables that are important in the passage—you're supposed to identify the relationship between them.

So whenever you read an experimental reasoning passage, you should do two things.

1. Follow the procedure used in the experiments.
2. Identify the variables.

Let's take some notes using the experiment about photosynthesis.

> A laboratory experiment was conducted to determine whether the lack of sunlight influences photosynthesis (production of glucose). Eight potted *Salvia* flowers were randomly selected and divided into two groups and labeled Group A and Group B. The plants were then subjected to differing light conditions and examined one week later.

Group A

> These plants were exposed to sunlight for the duration of the study. At the end of the study, these plants were green in appearance and produced glucose.

Group B

> These plants were kept in the dark. At the end of the study, they were yellow in appearance and did not produce glucose.

Look at each of the study groups and follow the procedure.

What happened in Group A? What happened in Group B?

Just refer back to the appropriate sections of the passage. Group A plants, with sun, were green and made glucose. Group B plants, without sun, turned yellow and didn't make glucose (undergo photosynthesis). For experimental reasoning passages on the test, you should scribble a few key words next to each experiment. That way, you'll come away with not only a better understanding of the key points in the paragraph, but you'll also leave out extraneous information.

Here's What the Scribbles Should Look Like

A laboratory experiment was conducted to determine whether the lack of sunlight influences photosynthesis (production of glucose). Eight potted *Salvia* flowers were randomly selected and divided into two groups and labeled Group A and Group B. The plants were then subjected differing light conditions and examined one week later.

Group A

These plants were exposed to sunlight for the duration of the study. At the end of the study, these plants were green in appearance and produced glucose.

sun
green
glucose

Group B

These plants were kept in the dark. At the end of the study, they were yellow in appearance and did not produce glucose.

no sun
yellow
no glucose

Study the Results

The results are the conclusion of the study. When you examine the results, make sure you underline them or scribble some notes in the margin. Once you've completed this step, try to identify any similarities or differences between the results. Do you notice any trends in the data?

Example #3

For example, let's look at a passage about the effects of gibberellins (a plant hormone) on plants.

Dr. Keller examined the influence of gibberellins (a plant hormone) on a crop of dwarf tomato plants for 180 days.

	Amount of gibberellins (ml)	Average height of tomato plants (cm)
Sample 1	0	10.0
Sample 2	2	13.5
Sample 3	4	15.7
Sample 4	6	16.0
Sample 5	8	16.0

What was the trend in the experiment?

The average plant height increased with the addition of the hormone until the plants reached a certain height, at which point they grew no further.

Here's What the Scribbles Should Look Like

Plant height = more with gibb. then leveled off.

What are the variables?

Look at the chart. The variables are the amount of gibberellins and the height of the tomato plants.

Example #4

Let's read a passage about catalysts and apply the same technique.

An investigator was interested in observing whether a chemical reaction occurs when compounds are mixed with water. Chemical reactions are known to produce heat. Three compounds were observed in order to determine whether, based on the release of heat, a reaction took place. A thermometer was placed in each test tube to record any change in temperature.

Test tubes	Temperature Change?	
	Yes	No
1. Powdered bleach + H_2O	x	
2. Salt + H_2O		x
3. Sugar + H_2O		x

What was the procedure in this experiment?

The investigator took a bunch of test tubes and filled them with different mixtures to see if chemical reactions took place.

Here's What the Scribbles Should Look Like

Powdered bleach + H_2O = Reaction

Salt + $H_2O \neq$ Reaction

Sugar + $H_2O \neq$ Reaction

What are the variables?

In this case, all you have to do is to look at the chart. The variables are the reactants and the presence or absence of a reaction. Did you need to take a lot of notes for this experiment? Nope. Why not? The key information was already laid out for you in a simple table.

So How Do You Scan Experiments Passages?

1. Look for the objective.
2. Follow the procedure and identify the variables.
3. Study the results.

Step 2: Identify the Question Type

You'll see the same categories of questions as those for data representation.

Question Type 1: Look It Up (Understanding)

The ACT test writers want to know whether you understand the experiment. For instance, do you know the variables? (We now know how to tackle those questions.) If you removed one of the variables in the study, would it change the results? What happened in the experiment?

Let's look at an example using the study about gibberellins on page 339.

1. Which of the following graphs would best represent the effect of gibberellins on dwarf tomato plants in the study?

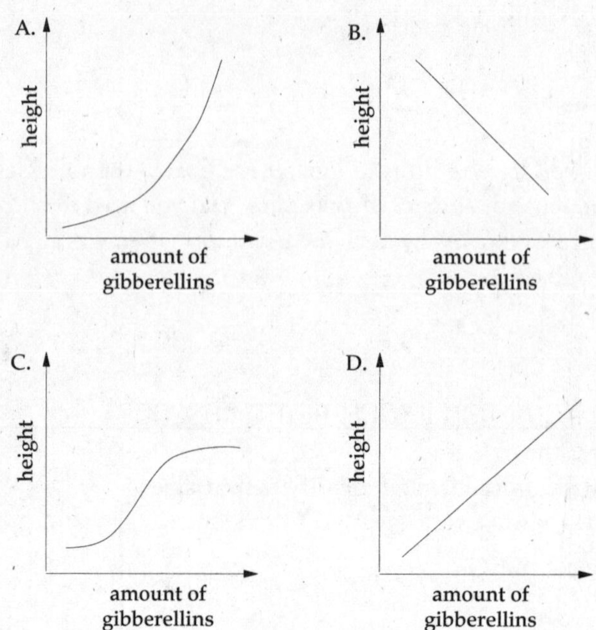

Here's How to Crack It

Remember our technique on how to translate charts into graphs? (If not, review Chapter 20.) Well, we can also use it in this section of the test. Let's go back to the chart.

We can use this information to find the correct graph. The graph that illustrates the same trend as the chart is (C). Look at the numbers in the chart and notice that the height increases up to Sample 5 and then it remains constant, as the amount of gibberellins increases further. You just need to look at the chart to find the answer.

Know How to Identify Controls

The ACT test writers will sometimes ask you to identify the control of the study. A **control** is simply a standard of comparison. What does a control do? It enables the investigator to be certain that the outcome of the study occurs because of changes in the independent variable and nothing else. So a control is something they don't mess with during the experiment. Let's look at an example.

What Is a Control?
A control is a variable (or group) that remains constant throughout the study.

Say the principal of your school thinks that students who eat breakfast do better on standardized tests than those who don't eat breakfast. He takes a group of ten students from your class and gives them free breakfast every day for a year. When the school year is over, he administers the ACT and they all score brilliantly!

Did they do well because they ate breakfast every day? How do you know whether the principal's theory is right? Maybe he just got lucky and picked the best test takers in the class to participate in the study.

The best way to be sure that eating breakfast made a difference in this case is to pick students in the class who *never* eat breakfast and to follow them for a year as well. Have *them* take the ACT and see how they score. What if they do just as well as the group that ate breakfast? Then we'll know that eating breakfast doesn't make a difference.

The group that didn't eat breakfast was the control group. They were not "exposed" to the variable of interest—breakfast.

Let's read the photosynthesis experiment again.

> A laboratory experiment was conducted to determine whether the lack of sunlight influences photosynthesis (production of glucose). Eight potted *Salvia* flowers were randomly selected and divided into two groups and labeled Group A and Group B. The plants were then subjected to differing light conditions and examined one week later.

Group A

> These plants were exposed to sunlight for the duration of the study. At the end of the study, these plants were green in appearance and produced glucose.

Group B

> These plants were kept in the dark. At the end of the study, they were yellow in appearance and did not produce glucose.

Which of the plants served as the control(s) in this study?

The plants in group A served as controls. Why? Because these plants were exposed to sunlight throughout the study. The experimental group was subjected to the factor being investigated—no sunlight. Here's another example using the gibberellin experiment.

Dr. Keller examined the influence of gibberellins (a plant hormone) on a crop of dwarf tomato plants for 180 days.

	Amount of gibberellins (ml)	Average height of tomato plants (cm)
Sample 1	0	10.0
Sample 2	2	13.5
Sample 3	4	15.7
Sample 4	6	16.0
Sample 5	8	16.0

1. Which of the following samples served as the control(s) in the study?

A. Sample 1
B. Sample 2
C. Sample 4
D. Samples 1 and 2

Here's How to Crack It

Let's find the control in this study. A control in this case is something that is *not* exposed to the hormone. In this case, the control is the first sample. The first measure of the sample was collected *before* the hormone was added to the crop (the chart tells you that the amount of gibberellins found in Sample 1 plants is 0). So the correct answer is (A).

Know How to Identify Assumptions

Another common Look It Up question on the Science Reasoning test asks you to identify the assumption in the argument.

What is an assumption? An **assumption** is a sort of simple logic that everyone takes for granted. Suppose one says

Brenda's car is in the driveway; now I can stop by and see her.

What is the assumption in this statement? The assumption is

Brenda is home when her car is in the driveway.

Yet Brenda could be at a neighbor's house or out of town. For the ACT, an assumption is an unwritten belief that, if false, would make the conclusion of the study invalid.

Here's an assumption question that refers to the passage on photosynthesis.

What Is an Assumption?
Assumptions are facts or statements that are taken for granted.

---

2. Which of the following was NOT assumed in the design of the experiment?

F. Each plant requires the same amount of water.
G. The plants are genetically identical.
H. The plants are naturally green all season.
J. The plants will be exposed to sunlight.

Here's How to Crack It

Think about it for a moment. What are some of the things you would have to assume about the study for the results to be acceptable? A major assumption is that the plants are genetically identical. If they weren't, then the findings could be invalid. For example, if a bunch of different plants were used, the experimenter couldn't be sure if the differences in the results were because of the lack of sunlight or to the variety of the plants themselves. The researcher also assumed that water was not a factor and that the plants don't turn yellow on their own. The only answer that contains something not assumed is (J).

Question Type 2: Why? (Analysis)

Remember the Why? questions that came with charts and graphs passages? (If not, review Chapter 20.) They required you to integrate two or more pieces of information. Well, that's how it works on experiments questions as well. The only difference is that they may also ask you to compare the results of the data with the ideas presented in the passages. Here are some of the types of questions they may ask.

> Can you think of another way to test the same relationship between the independent and dependent variables?

> If the experiment were repeated many times and gave different results, what would that mean in terms of the conclusion of the study?

Let's look at an example that refers to the passage on photosynthesis.

---

3. Suppose the Group B plants were placed in the dark for only two days and continued to produce glucose. What would these results mean in terms of the objective of the study?

   A. Plants require sunlight to produce glucose.
   B. Plants are able to make glucose under any conditions.
   C. Photosynthesis occurs in all plants.
   D. Photosynthesis is not completely inhibited by the lack of sunlight for two days.

Here's How to Crack It

The ACT test writers want to see if you can relate these new results to the original ones. The Group B plants did not undergo photosynthesis if they were placed in the dark for one week. However, the plants did undergo photosynthesis if they were put in the dark for two days. This must mean that two days wasn't enough time to halt photosynthesis. Therefore, the correct answer is (D).

Question Type 3: What If? (Generalization)

Sometimes you'll be asked how the knowledge gained from the experiment might be applied to new situations. As usual, we're supposed to look at the "bigger picture." Here are some sample questions.

> Given the results of the study, can we predict the outcome of some future experiments?

> How do these results influence our understanding of the world?

Let's look at a What If? question that refers to the passage about gibberellins.

---

4. Suppose 20 milliliters of gibberellins was given to a similar crop of tomato plants for 180 days. What would happen to the height of these plants relative to the height of the plants in the initial experiment?

F. The new plants would be taller than the plants in the experiment.
G. The new plants would be shorter than the plants in the experiment.
H. The new plants would die.
J. The new plants would have the same height as Samples 4 and 5 in the experiment.

Here's How to Crack It

Let's look back at the experiment and review the results. The tomato plants grew when the hormone was added, but eventually leveled off. What would happen if we added even more hormone to the plants? Based on the results of the experiment, their height should remain the same. The correct answer is (J).

Experiments Drill 1

It has been observed that plants exhibit phototropism (bending toward light) when placed in the presence of a light source. The actual part of the plant that bends toward the light source is not the tip of the plant but rather a region farther down the stem. Four flowering plants were exposed to sunlight in order to determine the site of light detection and the response of these plants.

Experiment 1

When light struck Plant 1 from the side, a region a few millimeters down from the tip bent as it grew until the tip pointed directly toward the light source.

Experiment 2

Plant 2 was also placed in the presence of sunlight, but the tip of the plant was covered with a dark cap. The plant failed to bend toward the light source.

Experiment 3

Plant 3 was exposed to the same conditions as was Plant 2, except a clear cap replaced the dark cap. This plant bent toward the light source.

Experiment 4

When a flexible dark collar was placed around the bending region of Plant 4, the plant still bent toward the light source.

1. The results of Experiments 1 and 2 indicate that:

A. the plant requires both sunlight and nutrition in order to bend.
B. the tip of the plant detects the light source.
C. the light-proof cap assists the plant in its bending action.
D. it is the amount of sunlight that causes the bending of the plant.

What Type of Question Is This?____________________

Experiments Drill 1 (cont.)

2. Which of the following plant(s) served as the control(s) in the experiment?

   F. Plant 1 only
   G. Plant 3 only
   H. Plants 1 and 3 only
   J. Plants 2 and 3 only

What Type of Question Is This? ____________________

3. Based on the results of Experiments 1–4, it can be concluded that:

   A. the strength of the sun's rays correlated with the bending of the plant.
   B. flowering plants are unaffected by sunlight.
   C. the tip of the plant must transmit information about light direction to the lower bending region.
   D. flowering plants respond to light quite differently than do non-flowering plants.

What Type of Question Is This? ____________________

4. Suppose the tip of the flowering plant is cut off in the presence of a light source, and a new tip does not grow. What will be the response of the plant?

   F. The plant will not bend toward the light.
   G. The plant will exhibit phototropism.
   H. The plant will die.
   J. The plant will produce flowers.

What Type of Question Is This? ____________________

Experiments Drill 2

Stratification (the horizontal layering of particles) causes settling sediments to form distinct rock formations that contain different types of fossils. Breaks in the sequence of layers may be due to erosion by wind or water. A geologist studied the bedding of different rock formations in an area in order to establish the stratigraphic succession of rock formations and their fossil assemblage.

Study 1

On her expedition, the geologist found rock formations with the order and content shown below.

Rock	Fossil assemblage
1. Limestone	All kinds of marine animal fossils
2. Black shale	Small marine animal fossils only
3. Coal	Plant fossils

Study 2

The geologist examined the rock formation in another location 10 miles away and discovered rock formations with the order and content shown below.

Rock	Fossil assemblage
1. Black shale	Small marine animal fossils
2. Coal	Plant fossils
3. Sandstone	Rare vertebrate bones

Study 3

At a third site 20 miles away, the geologist discovered another rock sequence.

Rock	Fossil assemblage
1. Limestone	All kinds of marine animal fossils
2. Coal	Plant fossils
3. Sandstone	Rare vertebrate bones

The following table gives the types of fossilized organisms normally found in a variety of rock formations.

Rock	Types of fossilized organisms
1. Sandstone	Ancient fish skeletons and shark teeth
2. Coal	Tree stumps, ferns, twigs, and green algae
3. Black shale	Snails, clams, oysters, and periwinkles
4. Limestone	Annelids, sponges, clams, and radiolarians

Experiments Drill 2 (cont.)

1. Which of the following findings would NOT be consistent with the types of fossils normally found in the black shale formation?

   A. Periwinkles
   B. Clams
   C. Oysters
   D. Sponges

What Type of Question Is This? ________________

2. Based on the information presented in the studies, it could be inferred that the remains of ancient pine needles would be found in which of the following types of rocks?

   F. Limestone
   G. Black shale
   H. Coal
   J. Sandstone

What Type of Question Is This? ________________

3. Given the sequence of rock formation in Studies 1 and 2, what might have been the ordered sequence of rock formations in the area at one time?

   A. Limestone, coal, black shale, and sandstone
   B. Limestone, black shale, coal, and sandstone
   C. Coal, sandstone, black shale, and limestone
   D. Black shale, limestone, sandstone, and coal

What Type of Question Is This? ________________

4. The sequence of rock formations in Study 3 is similar but not identical to the sequence of rock formations in Studies 1 and 2. Which of the following factors could be responsible for differences among the three sites?

   F. Weathering
   G. Extreme heat
   H. A mild rainstorm
   J. Cohesion

What Type of Question Is This? ________________

Experiments Drill 3

Consider a massless spring hanging vertically from a stationary wooden block. When a mass is attached to the spring, it causes the spring to vibrate. This is an example of simple harmonic motion in which a force leads to the displacement of the spring.

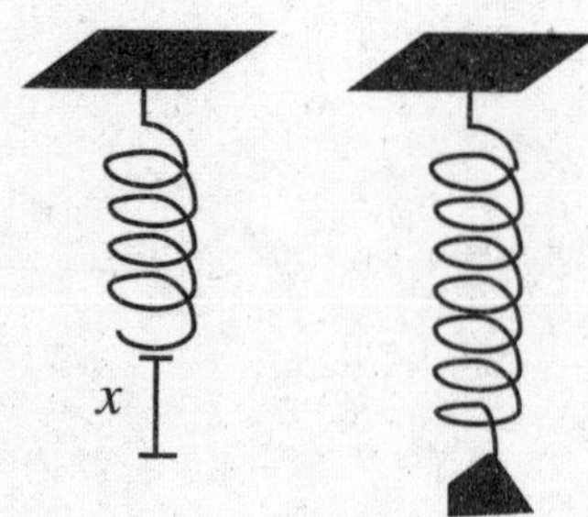

The equation for Hooke's spring law is $F = -kx$. The force (F) is proportional to the displacement (x), where k is called the proportionality constant pertaining to a given spring. The negative sign signifies that the force exerted by the spring is in the opposite direction of the displacement. Several trials were done to observe the relationship between force and the displacement of an object. The results are tabulated in the chart below.

Trial	Mass (gm)	k	x (cm)	F (lb.)
1	2	2.0	4	8
2	3	2.0	6	12
3	4	2.0	8	16
4	5	2.0	10	20

Table 1

1. From the trials above, it can be concluded that the displacement of an object depends on the:

   A. length of the spring.
   B. force according to Hooke's law.
   C. density of air.
   D. height of the wooden block.

What Type of Question Is This?__________________

Experiments Drill 3 (cont.)

2. If a downward force of 9 pounds was placed on the mass, the approximate displacement would be:

   F. 2.5 centimeters.
   G. 3.0 centimeters.
   H. 4.5 centimeters.
   J. 18.0 centimeters.

What Type of Question Is This? ____________________

3. When the weight of the mass attached to the spring is doubled:

   A. the displacement remains the same and the force is doubled.
   B. the displacement is halved and the force is doubled.
   C. the displacement is quadrupled and the force is quadrupled.
   D. the displacement is doubled and the force is doubled.

What Type of Question Is This? ____________________

Summary

- There are three experiments passages on the Science Reasoning test. They are identified by the inclusion of two, three, or more experiments. They may also show some information in chart or graph form.
- First, scan the passage and identify the research objective (what the researcher is trying to test in the experiments). Then, follow the procedures and identify what the researcher is changing from experiment to experiment—this is usually what the questions will relate to.
- Take notes on each experiment identifying what changed from one to the next.
- Use Guesstimation and POE to narrow down the answer choices. Often eliminating incorrect answers is easier than finding the correct answer.
- Do the easiest questions first and leave the difficult questions for last. When you've finished all the questions on one passage, go on to another passage.
- Don't forget to guess your Letter of the Day on questions that you don't know how to do.

Chapter 22
Fighting Scientists

The third type of passage on the Science Reasoning Test is called "fighting scientists." There will be only 1 of these passages and it will be accompanied by 7 questions. Two, three, or possibly more conflicting views on a scientific phenomenon will be presented. Make a plan of the order in which you will read the scientists, and work one theory at a time before tackling the questions that require comparing and contrasting all the theories.

Think of it as a debate. Each debater proposes a hypothesis and then supports that hypothesis with facts, opinions, and assumptions. The ACT test writers want you to evaluate and compare the arguments made by each debater, but they don't care who wins the debate. We don't care either, but we do want you to answer correctly seven questions about the debate. In order to do that, you must understand each viewpoint and how it agrees and disagrees with the others. Some questions will ask about just one theory, but most of the questions will ask you to compare and contrast two or more. That's a lot to keep track of. Wouldn't it be easier to navigate this passage if you had a plan?

FOLLOW A PLAN

The fighting scientists passage has a lot in common with the Reading test, and you might recognize some of the same strategies we taught you to employ for Reading. Remember when we asked you how you would fare if your boss assigned you the task of checking out an empty building? How well do you do when you don't know what you're looking for? Not very well. How well would you fare if you dived right into a passage on the Reading test if you didn't know what you're looking for? Right. So how can you succeed on the fighting scientists passage if you don't know what you're looking for?

Step 1: Make a Map

Your first task is to map the order in which you will read the scientists. Just as on the Reading test, you should look at the questions first. In the fighting scientists section, the questions help you determine which hypothesis to read and which questions to answer first.

Let's try this with the questions on the next page. Read each question and mark it with a "1" if it asks about Hypothesis 1, a "2" if it asks about Hypothesis 2, and a "B" if it asks about both hypotheses.

1. Hypotheses 1 and 2 agree that the dinosaurs:

2. The basis of Hypothesis 1 is that a meteorite striking Earth was the primary cause of the dinosaurs' demise. Which of the following discoveries would best support this case?

3. Suppose a geologist discovered that the fossilized bones of dinosaurs contained traces of radioactive iridium. How would this evidence influence the two hypotheses?

4. The authors of the two hypotheses would disagree over whether the extinction of the dinosaurs was:

5. If current climatic changes turn out to be as dramatic as those described by the author of Hypothesis 2, which of the following would he say is most likely to occur?

6. Studies have shown that climatic conditions are interdependent. As conditions become less favorable for life in one locale, they improve in another. If fossil evidence were found which showed that this happened at the K-T boundary, how would it affect Hypothesis 2?

7. Both Hypothesis 1 and 2 would be supported by evidence showing that:

You should have a "B" next to questions 1, 3, 4, and 7. Question 2 should have a "1" next to it, and questions 5 and 6 should have a "2" next to them. What does this tell us? We're reading Hypothesis 2 first!

Step 2: One Side at a Time

In order to compare and contrast multiple hypotheses, you need to understand each viewpoint and how it agrees and disagrees with the others. Reading and working the questions for one scientist at a time will give you the firm grasp of each theory you need.

Once the questions have provided a map, read the introduction to identify the disagreement.

> Approximately 65 million years ago (at the boundary between the Cretaceous and Tertiary periods, known as the K-T boundary), the dinosaurs became extinct.
>
> Here are two of the hypotheses that have been presented to explain their disappearance.

What will the hypotheses debate? They will debate what caused the extinction of the dinosaurs.

Next, read Hypothesis 2. You don't need to comprehend everything in the passage or remember every point of fact or argumentation, and until you read the other hypothesis, you have no basis for comparison. You do need to grasp the argument each is making, so as you read Hypothesis 2, find and underline the scientist's main point.

Hypothesis 2

This event at the K-T boundary was neither sudden nor isolated. It was a consequence of minor shifts in the earth's weather that spanned the K-T boundary. Furthermore, its effect was not as sweeping as some have suggested. While the majority of dinosaurs disappeared, some were able to adapt to the changing world. We see their descendants every day—the birds.

Alterations in the earth's *jet stream* (a steady, powerful wind that blows from west to east, circling the globe) shifted rains away from the great shallow seas that extended across much of what is now North America. As these late-Cretaceous seas began to dry up, a chain reaction of extinctions was set into motion. First affected was plant life. Next, animals that fed on plants began dying off. Ultimately, the lack of prey caused the demise of the dinosaurs. It was the mobility of the winged dinosaurs that saved them, allowing them to move to more favorable locations as conditions in their ancestral homes deteriorated.

What Are They Fighting About?

Some of the scientific theories you'll read about in a fighting scientists passage were settled a long time ago. In reading a passage arguing that Earth is the center of the universe, you may think, "Wait, Earth is NOT the center of the solar system—why in the world are they arguing about this?" For the ACT, the arguments presented are what count. Even though an argument may have been disproved a long time ago, it's still possible to evaluate it scientifically, and that's all you're being asked to do on this test.

What is the main point of Hypothesis 2?

According to Hypothesis 2, the extinction of dinosaurs was caused by a chain reaction prompted by changes in the weather.

Your Underlined Version Should Look Like This

Hypothesis 2

<u>This event at the K-T boundary was neither sudden nor isolated. It was a consequence of minor shifts in the earth's weather that spanned the K-T boundary</u>. Furthermore, its effect was not as sweeping as some have suggested. While the majority of dinosaurs disappeared, some were able to adapt to the changing world. We see their descendants every day—the birds.

Alterations in the earth's *jet stream* (a steady, powerful wind that blows from west to east, circling the globe) shifted rains away from the great shallow seas that extended across much of what is now North America. As these late-Cretaceous seas began to dry up, a chain reaction of extinctions was set into motion. First affected was plant life. Next, animals that fed on plants began dying off. Ultimately, the lack of prey caused the demise of the dinosaurs. It was the mobility of the winged dinosaurs that saved them, allowing them to move to more favorable locations as conditions in their ancestral homes deteriorated.

Did you notice that we didn't underline the details of the theory in the second paragraph? It's not that they are unimportant, but until we dive into the questions, we don't know what to pay attention to other than the main point. As we work the questions for Hypothesis 2, we'll gain a deeper understanding of the details of the theory.

Without further ado, let's go to the questions about Hypothesis 2.

---

5. If current climatic changes turn out to be as dramatic as those described by the author of Hypothesis 2, which of the following would he say is most likely to occur?

A. A rapid extinction of most of Earth's life, beginning with sea dwellers such as krill (a microscopic crustacean) and progressing through the food chain
B. A gradual and complete extinction of Earth's life forms that moves through the food chain from the bottom up
C. An extinction of most life forms on Earth that is gradual and simultaneous, affecting predators as well as prey at roughly the same rates
D. A progressive extinction that begins with vegetation and eventually reaches to the top of the food chain, affecting most dramatically those life forms least suited to relocation

Here's How to Crack It

The main point of Hypothesis 2 is that changes in the weather prompted a chain reaction of extinctions through the food chain until the dinosaurs were affected. We need to look for an answer that would predict a similar result from today's climactic changes. Use POE as you make your way through the answer choices.

(A) is tempting because it mentions a progression "through the food chain," but the word "rapid" contradicts the first sentence of Hypothesis 2: "The event at the K-T boundary was neither sudden nor isolated." (B) looks good, until we go back to the passage to confirm it and see that some dinosaurs survived, those that evolved into birds. Because of the word "complete," we have to eliminate it. (C) is out because of the word "simultaneous," which we know from evaluating choice (A) is contradicted by the passage. The answer must be (D), and it paraphrases nicely what we underlined as the main point.

---

6. Studies have shown that climatic conditions are interdependent. As conditions become less favorable for life in one locale, they improve in another. If fossil evidence were found which showed that this happened at the K-T boundary, how would it affect Hypothesis 2?

F. It would strengthen the hypothesis by supporting one of the argument's assumptions.
G. It would weaken the hypothesis, because the area of improving climatic conditions should have provided a means for the survival of the dinosaurs well into the Tertiary period.
H. It would weaken the hypothesis by introducing additional evidence that the author could not have anticipated.
J. It would have no bearing on the hypothesis because the mobility of the winged dinosaurs would render such shifts irrelevant.

Here's How to Crack It

We've learned a lot about Hypothesis 2. We read it and underlined the main point, and then evaluated some of the nuances of the argument to eliminate wrong answers for question number 5. When you consider the import of this new fossil evidence, you should draw upon the deeper understanding you've gained. The correct answer to question 5 reminded us that those *least* suited to relocation are more impacted by the changes in weather. The author stated explicitly that some dinosaurs survived and evolved into birds. Those two facts together allow us to realize this new evidence would make Hypothesis 2 more credible. Eliminate (G), (H), and (J), and select (F) as the correct answer.

Step 3: The Other Side

Now it's time to read Hypothesis 1, but we know more than we did before reading Hypothesis 2 and thus should read more proactively. When you read the second theory, you should look for and underline the following:

- the main idea
- how this hypothesis disagrees from the first
- how this hypothesis agrees with the first

Differentiate Between Theories
Questions on the fighting scientists passages often ask about the areas of agreement as well as disagreement between the scientists' theories. Make sure you know what both the similarities and differences are.

Hypothesis 1

For many years, scientists have speculated about the cause of the extinction of the dinosaurs. Fossil records confirm that dinosaurs as well as other life forms were suddenly wiped out. The natural cause of extinction is the inability of an organism to adapt to environmental changes, yet the extinction of all life forms is unlikely. Chemical analysis of clay found from this era attributes the sweeping extinction of dinosaurs to the collision of a huge meteorite with Earth. These fossil records confirm the presence of a high concentration of iridium, a rare heavy metal that is abundant in meteorites. It is believed that a meteorite hit the earth and created a huge crater, which threw up a dust cloud that blocked the sun for several months. This event led first to the destruction of much plant life and eventually all other life forms that consumed plants and/or herbivores, including the dinosaurs.

Write, Write, Write
Underlining and taking notes in the margins helps you keep track of the differences between the scientists.

What is the main point? Hypothesis 1 believes a meteorite struck Earth and wiped out the dinosaurs.

How do the two hypotheses differ? Hypothesis 2 believes the extinction was gradual; Hypothesis 1 believes it was sudden.

How do they agree? Both hypotheses mention the food chain.

If you didn't come up with those points, look at the underlined portions of the passage below.

Hypothesis 1

For many years, scientists have speculated about the cause of the extinction of the dinosaurs. <u>Fossil records confirm that dinosaurs as well as other life forms were suddenly wiped out.</u> The natural cause of extinction is the inability of an organism to adapt to environmental changes, yet the extinction of all life forms is unlikely. <u>Chemical analysis of clay found from this era attributes the sweeping extinction of dinosaurs to the collision of a huge meteorite with Earth.</u> These fossil records confirm the presence of a high concentration of iridium, a rare heavy metal that is abundant in meteorites. It is believed that a meteorite hit the earth and created a huge crater, which threw up a dust cloud that blocked the sun for several months. <u>This event led first to the destruction of much plant life and eventually all other life forms that consumed plants and/or herbivores, including the dinosaurs.</u>

Fighting Scientists

In a fighting scientists passage, you're given two or more opinions about a scientific phenomenon. Your job is to identify the differences between or among the viewpoints and the information the scientists use to support their points of view.

Now let's do the one question on Hypothesis 1 before we tackle the questions on both.

2. The basis of Hypothesis 1 is that a meteorite striking Earth was the primary cause of the dinosaurs' demise. Which of the following discoveries would best support this case?
   F. The existence of radioactive substances in the soil
   G. The presence of other rare metals common to meteorites in the clay beds of the ocean from that period
   H. Fossil records of land-dwelling reptiles that roamed Earth for an additional 10 million years
   J. Evidence of dramatic changes in sea levels 65 million years ago

Here's How to Crack It

What type of evidence would support Hypothesis 1? Any evidence that shows that dinosaurs were wiped out as a result of the impact of a meteorite. Would the presence of radioactive substances in the soil support Hypothesis 1? It could support the passage only if the radioactive elements were from meteorites (like iridium). Answer choice (F) did not specify that. Would the fact that some land-dwelling reptiles survived past this period support Hypothesis 1? No, so (H) is out. We can also get rid of (J) because it supports Hypothesis 2. What about (G)? What if other rare metals that are known to be found in meteorites were discovered? Would this support Hypothesis 1? Yes. The correct answer is (G).

Step 4: Compare and Contrast

We are now armed with a clear understanding of each hypothesis's main point, how the two differ, and how they agree.

1. Hypothesis 1 and 2 agree that the dinosaurs

    I. vanished because of a meteorite impact with the earth.
    II. became extinct due to disruptions in their food chain.
    III. became extinct due to some external force other than predation

A. I only
B. I and II only
C. II and III only
D. III only

Here's How to Crack It

We've already identified the area in which the two agree: the impact on the food chain. We can also eliminate choices that support only one of the theories. Statement 1 supports only Hypothesis 1, so it's out. Eliminate all answer choices with Statement 1 and we're left with (C) and (D) only. Because Statement II is in both answer choices, we know it must be correct. Of course, we'd identified the food chain as a point of agreement. Now let's check Statement III. Do both hypotheses state that dinosaurs became extinct because of some external force? Yes, so the correct answer is (C).

3. Suppose a geologist discovered that the fossilized bones of dinosaurs contained traces of radioactive iridium. How would this evidence influence the two hypotheses?

A. It would support both hypotheses.
B. It would support Hypothesis 2 and weaken Hypothesis 1.
C. It would support Hypothesis 1 and weaken Hypothesis 2.
D. It would not support Hypothesis 1 or Hypothesis 2.

Here's How to Crack It

Which of the hypotheses would be supported if a geologist found fossil bones that contained traces of radioactive iridium? Hypothesis 1 of course! The passage states that radioactive iridium is abundant in meteorites. If dinosaurs were exposed to the dust of meteorites, their bones would contain this metal. Hypothesis 2 didn't mention anything about iridium, so (C) is the correct answer.

4. The authors of the two hypotheses would disagree over whether the extinction of the dinosaurs was:

F. a natural process.
G. rapid.
H. the result of a disruption on the food chain of the late-Cretaceous period.
J. preventable.

Here's How to Crack It

The two hypotheses disagreed about the cause of the extinction, but they also disagreed on the pace. Hypothesis 1 believed it was sudden, whereas Hypothesis 2 believed it was gradual. Thus, (G) is the correct answer. Be careful with (H), because that's an issue on which both *agree.*

7. Both Hypothesis 1 and 2 would be supported by evidence showing that:

A. pterodactyls (winged dinosaurs) survived well into the Tertiary period, adapted to changes in the earth's environment, and eventually evolved into a non-dinosaur life form.
B. blockage of the sun's rays by particles measurable only on the microscopic scale can still have a significant effect on rates of photosynthesis.
C. even apparently minor degradation of the plant population in a given ecosystem can have far-reaching effects on the animal population within that ecosystem.
D. iridium is extremely likely to remain trapped in an ocean's bed when that ocean dries up.

Here's How to Crack It

On what point do the hypotheses agree? Look for an answer choice that provides evidence about the food chain. Eliminate any answer choice that supports only one hypothesis. (A) is out because Hypothesis 1 never mentioned relocation or winged dinosaurs. (B) looks good because it mentions photosynthesis, so keep it. (C) looks much better because it explicitly mentions the effects of plants on animals. (D) is incorrect because Hypothesis 2 never mentioned iridium and Hypothesis 1 never mentioned the ocean drying up. The test writers are trying to distract you with a switch, but you won't fall for it when you take the passages one at a time and learn each thoroughly before working the questions on both. The correct answer is (C).

Fighting Scientists Drill 1

How did the continents take on their current shape? Two differing views are presented below.

Scientist 1

According to a theory based on plate tectonics, the land surface of Earth once comprised a single continent, termed *Pangaea,* which was surrounded by a single vast ocean. Pangaea broke apart because the surfaces of Earth floated on massive plates above the deeper mantle of the ocean's basin. Horizontal movement of the plates began to split up the land about 137 million years ago during the Jurassic period. The continents and the ocean basins moved along convection currents in the mantle, resulting in a continuous degeneration of Earth's physical features. The movement of these rigid plates produced zones of tectonic activity along their margins such as earthquakes, volcanoes, and mountain formations. Fossil records as well as geological evidence show similarities between widely displaced continents. For instance, the coastlines of South America and Africa contain similar rock formations and appear to fit together like a jigsaw puzzle.

Scientist 2

The continents and the ocean basins of Earth are permanent, fixed features of the planet. The hypothesis of plate tectonics is flawed because there is insufficient evidence to support it. The force of gravity is stronger than any known tangential force that can act on Earth's crust. The layers of crust that support the continents and ocean basins are strong enough to preserve Earth's physical features and are too strong to permit horizontal drift. Tectonic activity has always been present, but the hypothesis of plate tectonics explains such activity only in one late period of ancient history. In addition, it is not clear what kind of force could allow the continents, composed largely of granite, to move through areas of dense, iron-rich rock that comprise the ocean basins. Any geological evidence that supports such a theory may be because of the existence of similar conditions on different continents.

1. Which of the following statements is the most inconsistent with the beliefs of Scientist 1?

A. Continents were once part of a large land mass.
B. Continents split up and drifted apart.
C. Ocean basins have not changed for millions of years.
D. Geological evidence shows similarities between widely displaced continents.

2. Scientist 1 studied the fossils along the coast of South America and Africa and found identical fernlike plants on rocks of the same age. What claim could Scientist 2 make to refute the findings of Scientist 1?

F. The dating and comparison of plant fossils is an exact science.
G. The soil and climate conditions along the two coasts must have been very similar at the time the fossils were created.
H. The ferns were extremely large.
J. Ferns will only thrive in their original habitat.

3. A new zone of tectonic activity has been discovered in the large land mass of Eurasia. This zone shows geological evidence of having been active for several thousand years. Which scientist is supported by this finding and why?

A. Scientist 1, because it proves that tectonic activity occurs on the planet.
B. Scientist 1, because it shows that Pangaea and Eurasia are the same land mass.
C. Scientist 2, because it proves that tectonic activity occurs in land masses and not solely in the ocean basin and along coastlines.
D. Scientist 2, because it shows that the continents are made out of granite.

4. Both Scientist 1 and Scientist 2 are experts in plate tectonics. To what discipline of science do these scientists belong?

F. Physics
G. Geology
H. Biology
J. Chemistry

5. Which of the following claims would be supported by both scientists?

I. Tectonic activity has always been a factor in the geology of land masses.
II. The continents and the ocean basins are fixed features of the planet.
III. Continental drift occurred in the Jurassic period.

A. I only
B. II only
C. I and II only
D. II and III only

Fighting Scientists Drill 2

How did life on Earth originate? Two differing views are presented.

Hypothesis 1

In 1953, a graduate student attempted to recreate the conditions of primeval Earth in a sealed glass apparatus that he filled with methane, ammonia, hydrogen, and water. Sparks were released into the glass to simulate lightning, and heat was applied to the water. The result was the formation of organic compounds, known as amino acids, which are the building blocks of proteins. Since that time, others have shown how DNA may have been synthesized under various conditions as well. RNA, which is DNA's partner in the translation of genetic information into protein products, has been found to have the ability to reproduce itself under certain conditions. Thus, the origins of life are to be found in the "primordial soup" of the ancient earth that provided conditions for the simplest forms of organic matter to form and develop increasingly sophisticated means of organization. With the ability of compounds to make copies of themselves comes the opportunity for evolution by the mechanisms of heredity and mutation.

Hypothesis 2

Previous assumptions about the makeup of the "primordial soup" are inaccurate. It is not at all clear that methane and ammonia were present on the primeval earth or that conditions were as favorable as in the graduate student's experiment. The ability of RNA to reproduce itself is also limited to particular conditions that the primeval earth is unlikely to have provided. There is a possibility that, given enough time, random events could alone have resulted in the development of entire single-celled organisms, but some have likened that possibility to the chance that a tornado whirling through a junkyard could result in the formation of a 747 jetliner. During much of the time when the "primordial soup" was to have existed, Earth was a regular target of meteors that kept oceans boiling and the atmosphere inhospitable to organic development. Clearly much more research is needed before this theory can be widely accepted.

1. Which of the following statements about the conditions on primeval Earth could be used to support Hypothesis 2?

A. Atmospheric conditions were too unstable to support the gases essential to the theories of the "primordial soup."
B. Organic molecules were able to thrive under primeval Earth conditions.
C. The origin of life began in the "primordial soup."
D. The atmosphere contained methane, ammonia, hydrogen, and water.

2. To accept Hypothesis 1, one must assume that:

F. Earth was bombarded by meteors during that time period.
G. the conditions in the glass were analogous to the conditions on primeval Earth.
H. proteins are the building blocks of amino acids.
J. Earth lacked hydrogen in the atmosphere.

3. Which of the following shows how, according to Hypothesis 1, the building blocks of life were formed?

A. Methane + Ammonia + Hydrogen + Water →Primordial Soup → Amino Acids
B. Meteors → Primordial Soup → Amino Acids
C. Amino Acids → Primordial Soup → DNA → Methane + Ammonia + Hydrogen + Water
D. Primordial Soup → proteins → Amino Acids

Fighting Scientists Drill 3

Will Earth experience another ice age?

Hypothesis 1

Scientists have long speculated whether glaciation will ever take place again. Given that glaciation is an unusual event, it is highly unlikely that such a phenomenon will ever repeat itself. Glaciation usually takes place under periods of extremely cool temperatures. However, it appears that the temperature on Earth has been milder and more stable than at any other period. In fact, it would take a 5°C drop in the average surface temperature in order for glaciation to occur. In addition, there would have to be a significant increase in precipitation.

Hypothesis 2

Although Earth has not experienced glaciation in a long time, the event, no matter how rare, can occur if the right conditions are met. Two factors that are critical to the growth of glaciers are precipitation and temperature. There are a number of areas, specifically land masses in the polar regions, that are currently cold enough to produce glaciers but do not have sufficient snowfall to develop glacier systems. However, if enough events occur simultaneously, they could bring on an ice age. For instance, if there is an increase in the level of snowfall in the winter in these polar regions, this could eventually lead to glaciation. On the other hand, the level of pollution in the atmosphere is also sufficient to gradually cool Earth. Under these conditions, it is quite clear that glaciation is only a matter of the right combination of events at the right time.

1. Which of the following discoveries would most clearly favor Hypothesis 2?

A. Canada has more snowfall this year than any other year.
B. When snow falls, it sticks to the ground.
C. The more pollution in the air, the more the temperature drops.
D. Earth's bodies of waters are becoming more polluted.

2. Which of the following statements is the strongest argument a supporter of Hypothesis 2 would use to counter Hypothesis 1?

F. The temperature around polar regions fluctuates.
G. The precipitation rate has been increasing in the Swiss Alps.
H. Just because ideal conditions are rare does not mean they will not occur in the future.
J. The temperature in the North Pole has gone up 2°C.

3. If Hypothesis 2 is correct and glaciation can take place in the future, what regions would be most affected?

I. Heavily polluted regions
II. Polar regions
III. Humid regions

A. I only
B. II only
C. I and II only
D. II and III only

4. According to Hypothesis 2, what conditions could cause glaciation?

F. Low levels of pollution leading to high precipitation
G. High levels of pollution leading to a blanketing effect that blocks out the sun and decreases the temperature dramatically
H. A lack of snowfall and low temperatures
J. A 5°C drop in the average surface temperature

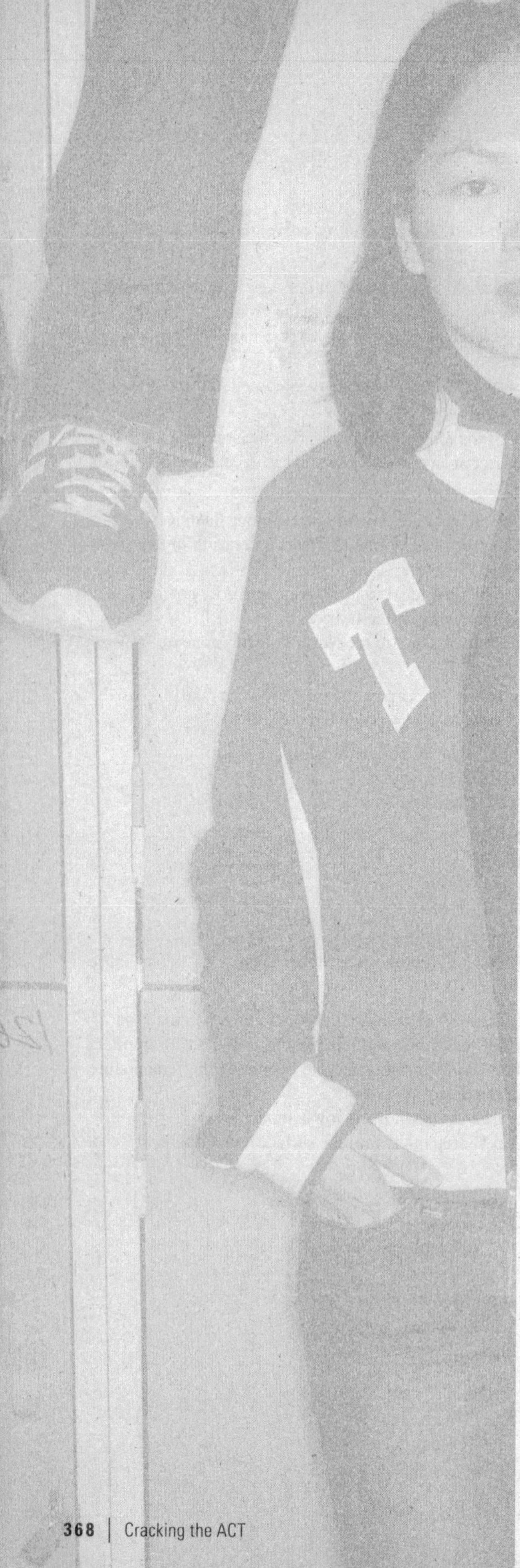

Summary

- There is one fighting scientists passage on the Science Reasoning test. In this passage, two, three, or more scientists present their differing views on a scientific subject.
- Don't pick a side. The ACT test writers want you to evaluate and compare the arguments presented, not decide which one is correct. Even if you know something about the topic, answer the questions using only what is presented in the passage.
- First, use the questions to make a map of the order in which you will read the theories and answer questions on each, one at a time.
- Leave the questions on more than one theory for last.
- Don't forget to guess your Letter of the Day if there are questions that you don't know how to do.

Part VI
How to Crack the ACT Writing Test

Chapter 23
The Essay

The ACT includes an optional Essay section. Some schools are requesting an essay while others are not. We recommend that you take the essay when you take the ACT because you can't take the essay on its own later if you find that you need it; you'd have to take the whole ACT over again. The essay follows a predictable format, so preparation and practice help a lot.

THE KIND-OF OPTIONAL ESSAY

The ACT includes an "optional" essay component, but if you've already started to skip this section, stop for a moment. Although most students would not voluntarily choose to spend an extra half hour on a Saturday morning writing an essay for a standardized test, we **do** recommend that you write the essay. Why? There are two reasons.

- First, some schools require that you take the essay portion. You wouldn't want to have to take the entire test over again if you discover that your dream school wants an essay and you had decided not to write one.
- Second, writing the essay can make your college application look more attractive. Your essay score will appear on every score report you send to colleges, regardless of whether or not the school requires an essay. Every school to which you apply will see that you took the initiative to write the essay, which is a good thing.

Plus, it's not that difficult to get a good score on the essay, especially if you follow the guidelines in this chapter. An impressive score is an impressive score, optional or not.

OK, OK, I'LL WRITE THE ESSAY... WHAT DO I HAVE TO DO?

The ACT essay will provide you with a prompt "relevant" to high school students—basically it's a topic on which the ACT test writers believe almost any typical high school student will have some opinion. Here's an example of a sample prompt.

> The Children's Internet Protection Act (CIPA) requires all school libraries receiving certain federal funds to install and use blocking software to prevent students from viewing material considered "harmful to minors." However, some studies conclude that blocking software in schools damages educational opportunities for students, both by blocking access to web pages that are directly related to the state-mandated curriculums and by restricting broader inquiries of both students and teachers. In your view, should the schools block access to certain Internet websites?
>
> In your essay, take a position on this question. You may write about either one of the two points of view given, or you may present a different point of view on this question. Use specific reasons and examples to support your position.

Your job is to write an essay in which you take some sort of position on the prompt and develop your position through the use of appropriate supporting examples. You've probably written an essay like this in your high school English class. The only difference is that on the ACT you have a mere 30 minutes to read the prompt, brainstorm some examples, organize the essay, write it, and proofread it. You may be thinking that there's no way that you can write a great essay in such a short amount of time on a topic you've never seen before, and that is indeed true. But that's okay, because the ACT essay graders don't expect a perfect essay; they don't want to penalize you for minor spelling and grammar mistakes. Instead, graders will focus on the major components of your essay.

WHAT THE GRADERS ARE GRADING

If you think you have a tough job writing an essay in only 30 minutes, have some sympathy for the graders. They have to grade each essay in a matter of minutes. Imagine how you would feel if you spent an entire day grading thousands of essays on the same topic. By essay number 50 or so, you probably wouldn't care much if a student used "except" instead of "accept."

ACT Graders vs. English Teachers

The graders who grade for ACT aren't like your English teachers. They don't have the time to focus on the little details of each essay, and frankly, they don't care about your grade the way your English teacher does. So, don't sweat the small stuff. Focus on the big picture for the ACT: good thesis, organization, strong examples, and neatness.

ACT graders focus on the big picture. Your essay will be read by two graders, each of whom will assign it a score from 1 to 6 (for a total essay score from 2 to 12) based on how closely it adheres to the standards below. The essays are graded **holistically**, meaning the graders don't keep track of all the good things and bad things in an essay on a checklist or score sheet. Each reader simply reads the entire essay, and based on his or her overall impressions of the essay assigns it a grade.

According to the ACT guidelines, essay graders will base your score on your ability to do the following:

1. Take a position on the prompt To score well on the ACT essay, you need a clear thesis statement. Essay graders will look for one when determining your score.

2. Maintain focus on topic Once you come up with a thesis, stick to it. Avoid digressions in your essay—or even worse, changing or countering your thesis halfway through the paper.

3. Support your ideas Good essays support their thesis statements with supporting examples. There is no magic number of examples. However, you do need to show that you understand the issue in the prompt, that you have a position on that issue, that you have a reason for that position, and that you can support that reason with evidence. You have to address the other side of the issue, but you don't want to argue it as strongly as your own side. Address the other issues and then point out why your examples are better.

4. Organize your ideas This is one of the most important criteria. You must write an organized essay, meaning it needs to contain an introduction, body paragraphs, and a conclusion.

5. Use language clearly and effectively The graders will look at stylistic issues, but those issues are not as important as the issues above. As a rule of thumb, graders will take issue with your grammar and language only if it detracts from their ability to identify the previous criteria.

HOW TO GET A GOOD SCORE

The way to get a good score on the essay is to make the graders' job easy: Show that you have a thesis, a clear essay structure, and some relevant examples. By following the guidelines presented here, you'll be able to write a clear, effective essay in the limited time available. Let's look at each step in the process. Be sure to practice each step individually, and then try to put all the steps together.

Step 1: Work with the Prompt

Our first task is to read the prompt. Here's the one we saw earlier.

> The Children's Internet Protection Act (CIPA) requires all school libraries receiving certain federal funds to install and use blocking software to prevent students from viewing material considered "harmful to minors." However, some studies conclude that blocking software in schools damages educational opportunities for students, both by blocking access to web pages that are directly related to the state-mandated curriculums and by restricting broader inquiries of both students and teachers. In your view, should the schools block access to certain Internet websites?
>
> In your essay, take a position on this question. You may write about either one of the two points of view given, or you may present a different point of view on this question. Use specific reasons and examples to support your position.

After reading the prompt, you must decide what side of the argument you will dfend. Even if you don't have a strong opinion either way, you still must pick a side. Although it is possible to write an essay that examines both sides of the issue at length, it is difficult to do that on the ACT because of the time limit. It's much easier to pick one side and defend it.

Key Words and Phrases

When reading the prompt, underline the key words and phrases. What are some of the key words in the prompt on the previous pages?

____

____

Some of the key words we see in the prompt are "school libraries," "blocking software," "prevent students," "harmful to minors," "damages educational opportunities," and "Internet websites." By identifying key words before you start to write, you can focus your essay and find the most pertinent examples.

On your test booklet, jot down something like this:

Pro	Con

Decide which side you wish to defend—there is no right or wrong answer, so just pick the side that you think will be easier to support. Next, brainstorm two or three reasons why you chose the side you did. Fill them in under the appropriate heading.

Pro	**Con**
____________________	____________________
____________________	____________________
____________________	____________________
____________________	____________________

At this point, you should have something that looks like this

✓ Pro	Con
• Internet contains many offensive/objectionable sites	________
• Dangerous spyware and adware can harm computers	________
• School computers should be used only for school work	________
	________

Of course, your reasons or examples may differ. The actual examples that you come up with do not matter, as long as they are related to the prompt. Now that you have your examples, you're halfway done. But before you move on, you need to think of an example or two for the other side of the argument. To get a top score on the essay, you have to consider both sides of the issue. So let's brainstorm an example or two for the opposing side.

Now you should have something like this

✓ Pro	✓ Con
• Internet contains many offensive/objectionable sites	• Restricting access is a form of censorship
• Dangerous spyware and adware can harm computers	• Students are deprived of opportunities to learn about certain topics
• School computers should be used only for school work	

If you're having trouble coming up with appropriate examples, the prompt usually contains some good ideas.

Step 2: Structure Your Essay

Good ACT essays have a clear, logical structure. Your essay must contain an introductory paragraph, body paragraphs, and a conclusion. Although what you write in each paragraph of any given type will change, the structure of each paragraph should be fairly consistent.

Let's look at an introductory paragraph first.

Introductions

Your introductory paragraph should accomplish two major things.

1. Frame the discussion You must tell the reader exactly what the topic of the essay will be. Introduce the topic by restating or, better yet, paraphrasing the prompt.

2. State your thesis Establish which side of the issue you are on and why.

Use the lines below to write your introduction, and then compare it with the sample paragraph that follows.

Here's our sample.

The Internet has brought many changes to our world. Computers are used in businesses, homes, and of course, schools. However, with increased use of computers comes increased dangers. A new law, the Children's Internet Protection Act, requires schools to use blocking programs to restrict students' Internet access. Although some parents, students, and teachers believe that this law is a bad one, the dangers from the Internet make it clear that schools should block student access to certain Internet sites.

The First Impression
The introduction should be general. Specific examples belong in the body paragraphs and should support the thesis statement that you include in the introduction.

Notice that this introduction accomplishes the two basic goals mentioned previously. It paraphrases the prompt—expanding on it a bit by discussing the impact of the Internet and computers on everyday life—and introduces the question of whether schools should block student access to certain sites. Then the paragraph clearly states the author's position; in this case, the author agrees that schools should block student access.

That is all that is required in an introductory paragraph. Don't try to do too much with the first paragraph. Many writers make the mistake of trying to explain why they chose a particular side, but you should save that for the body paragraphs.

Body Paragraphs, Part I: Supporting Your Position

Body paragraphs are where you will give the reasons or support for your position. A good body paragraph will contain three major things.

1. A good transition/topic sentence Transition sentences contribute to the flow and organization of the essay. Using transitions will help the grader follow your argument. Topic sentences show the grader that you are focused on your thesis.

2. A relevant example Each body paragraph should discuss one and only one example. Otherwise, the paragraph becomes muddled and hard to follow. If you are using only one example, however, you'll want to break it up into logical paragraphs.

3. An explanation of how the example supports your position It's not enough simply to throw a couple of examples into your essay and expect the grader to know what to make of them. Your job as a writer is to show the grader why the examples you chose support your position. Let's try to write a body paragraph. Using the lines below and one of the examples you've chosen (or one of ours) from the Pro/Con list, write a body paragraph. Then, compare it with the sample paragraph that follows.

Here's our sample.

One convincing reason that schools should block access to certain Internet sites is that the Internet contains many offensive or objectionable sites. For example, there are sites on the Internet that contain racist and sexist jokes and content. Other sites might display material that is inappropriate for children. Because there is no censorship, there is no telling what sites a student can visit. This sort of material has no place in a school. If students see violent or offensive sites, they might be influenced. They could insult or hurt other students. For this reason, it is a good idea for schools to block access to certain sites.

Let's examine this body paragraph. The paragraph starts with a good topic sentence. The first sentence repeats the thesis, making it easy for the reader to follow the argument. Next, the author brings in an example—the presence of objectionable sites on the Internet. The following sentences expand on the example, presenting different sites that are inappropriate for a school setting. Finally, and most important, the last sentences tell the grader why the example supports the point—objectionable sites could lead students to insult or harm other students. Also, the last sentence again mentions the thesis. This helps the essay stay focused and makes the argument more forceful.

Practice writing body paragraphs for your remaining examples. For each one, try to start with a transition or topic sentence that restates the thesis. Then, present your example. Finally, state how your example supports your position. Try to end your body paragraph by restating the thesis again.

Writing to Your Grader

We're not talking about writing personal letters here. Rather, we're referring to modifying your writing style to make it fit what the grader wants to see. You do this all the time. When you get a new English teacher, you figure out how that teacher wants you to write your essays, and you tweak your style a little to meet expectations. You should do the same thing for the ACT graders. Figure out what they want to see and write that type of essay. It will help you get a better score.

Body Paragraphs, Part II: Attacking the Other Position

To get a good score on the ACT, you'll also have to write another type of body paragraph—one that discusses the "con," or opposite, side of the argument. This paragraph is similar to the supporting paragraph in structure. The only difference is that you will now attack the example and state why it is not an important consideration. Take a look at our sample paragraph first, and then try to write your own body paragraphs using one of the examples from the other side of the example.

Some people believe that it is wrong for schools to restrict access to certain Internet sites. These people think that restricting access is the same thing as censorship. However, this argument is incorrect. The school is not trying to control what students think or write. It is only trying to control what sorts of things a student can or cannot do at a school computer. This is well within the rights of the school. After all, schools can impose dress codes and dictate what classes students can take. It doesn't make sense to say that a school can determine what books a student reads or what clothes he or she wears, but cannot restrict access to certain Internet sites. Thus, this argument is not convincing.

The purpose of this paragraph is to look at the opposing side of the argument and then show the grader why the opposing side is wrong. The topic sentence clearly states the opposing position, and the next sentence gives a reason that some might consider the opposing side valid. The most important part of this paragraph comes in the third sentence. You must clearly indicate to the grader that you do not agree with this side. If you don't, your essay might seem to support both sides of the issue. Next, attack the opposing side by showing that the reason stated is inadequate, insufficient, or just plain wrong.

If you're having trouble attacking the other position, try one of the three techniques below.

1. The example is true, but... State the example, and then look for ways in which it could still be true but not relevant to the argument.

Example: Although it is true that restricting Internet access is a form of censorship, this is not relevant to the argument. The issue is whether students should be allowed to view the content at school.

2. The example is true, but not as important as... In this case, acknowledge that the example is relevant, but not as important as some other factor. A good way to attack a position is to compare the con example with the pro example and then state why the pro example is a more important consideration.

Example: It may be true that restricting Internet access is a form of censorship, but there is a more important consideration in this argument. Isn't it more important to keep the students safe than to worry about censorship?

3. The example is flawed because... Try to attack the actual example.

Example: Some people believe that restricting access to the Internet is a form of censorship. But this is flawed because the school isn't dictating what a student can think or write. It is only stating that students cannot view this material at school.

Now try it on your own. Use the lines on the next page to write a body paragraph attacking one side of the argument.

After you've written your body paragraphs, it's time to wrap things up.

Conclusions

Conclusions have only one purpose. Without looking below, try to guess what that purpose is.

1. A conclusion should restate the thesis If you said the conclusion should conclude the essay, give yourself a prize. The conclusion should restate the thesis and sum up the essay. Go ahead and use the lines provided to write a conclusion paragraph. Then, compare your conclusion with the sample one.

Here's our sample.

As this essay has shown, it is important and necessary for schools to block student access to certain Internet sites. The Internet has many potential dangers for a student, from objectionable sites to harmful computer viruses and bugs. A school that doesn't restrict access to the Internet puts itself at risk for far more serious issues.

This conclusion gets the job done. The first sentence restates the thesis and the next sentence repeats some of the major arguments of the essay. The final sentence of the conclusion is a good place to get a little sentimental or philosophical. It's the last thing the grader will see, so it's a nice touch.

Putting It All Together

The trick now is to string all of these individual paragraphs into a focused and coherent essay that addresses both sides of the issue, yet still clearly supports only one perspective. At first this seems like a daunting task, but if you practice using the outline below, you'll master it in no time.

Your essay should conform to the following outline:

I. Introduction paragraph
   A. Paraphrase the prompt
   B. State your thesis
II. Con body paragraph
   A. Topic sentence
   B. Con example
III. Pro body paragraph
   A. Topic sentence
   B. Pro example
IV. Pro body paragraph II
   A. Topic sentence
   B. Pro example II
V. Conclusion
   A. Restate thesis

Here's what the essay looks like in its entirety.

The Internet has brought many changes to our world. Computers are used in businesses, homes, and, of course, schools. However, with increased use of computers comes increased dangers. A new law, the Children's Internet Protection Act, requires schools to use blocking programs to restrict students' Internet access. Although some parents, students, and teachers believe that this law is a bad one, the dangers from the Internet make it clear that schools should block student access to certain Internet sites.

Some people believe that it is wrong for schools to restrict access to certain Internet sites. These people think that restricting access is the same thing as censorship. However, this argument is incorrect. The school is not trying to control what students think or write. It is only trying to control what sort of things a student can or cannot do at a school computer. This is well within the rights of the school. After all, schools can impose dress codes and dictate what classes students can take. It doesn't make sense to say that a school can determine what books a student reads or what clothes he or she wears, but cannot restrict access to certain Internet sites. Thus, this argument is not convincing.

One convincing reason that schools should block access to certain Internet sites is that the Internet contains many offensive or objectionable sites. For example, there are sites on the Internet that contain racist and sexist jokes and content. Other sites might display material that is inappropriate for children. Because there is no censorship, there is no telling what sites a student can visit. This sort of material has no place in a school. If students see violent or offensive sites, they might be influenced. They could insult or hurt other students. For this reason, it is a good idea for schools to block access to certain sites.

Another good reason to restrict student access to the Internet is the presence of dangerous computer viruses, spyware, and other harmful computer programs. These programs can infect a computer via the Internet and affect the hardware of the system and all the computers that are attached to it. A student who visits certain restricted sites puts the entire computer network at risk. One infected computer can wipe out or ruin all the other computers in the school. Thus, it would be a very wise move for schools to restrict access to certain dangerous Internet sites.

As this essay has shown, it is important and necessary for schools to block student access to certain Internet sites. Although some people think restricting sites is censorship, the Internet has many potential dangers for a student, from objectionable sites to harmful computer viruses and bugs. A school that doesn't restrict access to the Internet puts itself at risk for far more serious issues.

Now it's your turn. Using the following prompt, write an essay. Don't time yourself; just focus on structuring your essay according to the guidelines.

In recent years, many schools have adopted a "Great Books"–based curriculum. These schools require students to study certain designated classic books of Western civilization, arguing that familiarity with these "Great Books" is essential to education. However, opponents of this curriculum argue that forcing teachers and students to use only the "Great Books," most of which are written by white, European authors, results in a biased view on the world. In your opinion, should schools adopt a "Great Books"–based curriculum?

In an essay, take a position on this question. You may write on either one of the views presented, or on a different point of view relevant to the question. Use examples and reasons to support your position.

Step 3: Proofread

After you finish your essay, spend one or two minutes proofreading your essay if you have time. You don't have to catch every single grammatical and spelling mistake, but try to make sure there are no glaring errors. You can also edit as you go, but a quick review at the very end never hurts.

If you do find an error, erase it completely or cross it out with a single line and then neatly write the correction above it. Although you won't be graded on neatness, it is important. A neatly written essay makes for a happy grader, and a happy grader is a good thing.

OTHER THINGS TO KEEP IN MIND

Here are some other factors to consider when writing your essay. These factors are not nearly as crucial as the ones discussed earlier, but they can help boost your essay grade.

1. Length ACT graders tend to reward longer essays. Try to write at least five paragraphs spanning one and a half to two pages. If your writing tends to be small, you may want to practice writing larger, especially because it will also make your essay a bit neater and easier to read. If your handwriting is large, make sure you write an extra page to compensate.

2. Sentence structure Varying your sentence structure helps to improve the rhythm of your essay. If you write a really long sentence with lots of modifiers and dependent clauses, it sometimes helps to follow it with a shorter, more direct sentence. It really works. Don't try to be too fancy, though. The longer the sentence is, the more opportunity there is to confuse the reader or to make a grammatical mistake.

3. Diction Diction refers to word choice. You certainly want to sprinkle some nice vocabulary words throughout your paper. But make sure to use and spell them correctly. If you're uncertain about the meaning or spelling of a word, it's best just to pick a different word. Using a big word incorrectly makes a worse impression than using a smaller word correctly.

4. Neatness Make sure you indent each new paragraph. Align your essay using the lines on the paper. Don't go over the lines or write down the side of the page. Avoid messy cross-outs. Although the grader should not take these kinds of things into consideration when determining your grade, a neat, legible essay will be easier to read. Your grader will read hundreds, if not thousands of essays. A neat essay will make the grader happier.

PRACTICE ESSAY PROMPTS

Here are four sample essay prompts on which to practice. After you finish each essay, read it over—or better yet, have someone else read it—and use the Essay Checklist on page 395 to see how well your essay conforms to the ACT's grading standards. When you practice writing essays, it's best to limit your time to 30 minutes to experience how short the alloted time really is.

Practice Prompt #1

New laws are being proposed that would require schools to accommodate students who wish to transfer to a different school if the school falls below a certain level on statewide standardized tests. Supporters of this law believe that it is a student's right to transfer to a new school if his or her current school is not fulfilling its duties. Opponents argue that this law is impractical—what would happen if all the students requested transfers?—and unfairly weights test scores without considering other factors at a school. In your opinion, should students be allowed to transfer if schools score below a certain level on standardized tests?

In an essay, take a position on this question. You may write on either one of the views presented or on a different point of view relevant to the question. Use examples and reasons to support your position.

Practice Prompt #2

Colleges reward professors, who have significant research and teaching experience, with tenure. Once tenured, a professor holds his or her job without review and with little danger of being fired or replaced. Some people believe that high school teachers should be tenured as a reward for dedicated service. These people argue that tenure will attract highly qualified candidates to the profession and also allow teachers to do their jobs without fear of losing them. Opponents of this plan believe that tenure only leads to poor teaching. Without any fear of losing their jobs, teachers will not care as much about their students. In your opinion, should high school teachers receive tenure?

In an essay, take a position on this question. You may write on either one of the views presented, or on a different point of view relevant to the question. Use examples and reasons to support your position.

Practice Prompt #3

Many communities are considering adopting curfews for high school students. Some educators and parents favor curfews because they believe it will encourage students to focus more on their homework and make them more responsible. Others feel curfews are up to families, not the community, and that students today need freedom to work and participate in social activities in order to mature properly. Do you think that communities should impose curfews on high school students?

In an essay, take a position on this question. You may write on either one of the views presented or on a different point of view relevant to the question. Use examples and reasons to support your position.

Practice Prompt #4

> In response to articles examining sensitive topics such as dating and partying, many schools are considering censoring their newspapers. Some schools believe that these topics are inappropriate for student-run papers, while others believe that, as long as what is printed is true, student papers should have the same freedoms as regular newspapers do. What is your opinion on this topic?
>
> In an essay, take a position on this question. You may write on either one of the views presented or on a different point of view relevant to the question. Use examples and reasons to support your position.

Summary: An Essay Checklist

Now look at your essays and see if you applied the strategies presented in this chapter.

- The Introduction
  Did you
  - start with a topic sentence that paraphrases or restates the prompt?
  - clearly state your position on the issue?
- Body Paragraph 1
  Did you
  - start with a transition/topic sentence that discusses the opposing side of the argument?
  - give an example of a reason that one might agree with the opposing side of the argument?
  - clearly state that the opposing side of the argument is wrong or flawed?
  - show what is wrong with the opposing side's example or position?
- Body Paragraphs 2 and 3
  Did you
  - start with a transition/topic sentence that discusses your position on the prompt?
  - give one example or reason to support your position?
  - show the grader how your example supports your position?
  - end the paragraph by restating your thesis?
- Conclusion
  Did you
  - restate your position on the issue?
  - end with a flourish?
- Overall
  Did you
  - write neatly?
  - avoid multiple spelling and grammar mistakes?
  - try to vary your sentence structure?
  - use a few impressive-sounding words?

Part VII
Drill Answers and Explanations

Chapter 24
Drill Answers and Explanations

Sentence Structure and Punctuation Drill (Chapter 6)

1 B Did you notice as you were reading that the passage begins with a list of nice things about the town of Roskilde? Lists often mean parallel construction. Because this is a list of things, or nouns, we need to check if everything on the list is presented in the same way. The list is composed of the gingerbread houses of Roskilde with their neatly thatched roofs, the gardens filled with flowers, blooms, and the happy smiles on the fresh-faced inhabitants. Which one of these seems a little out of place? Each of them begins with "the" except for the third item on the list. And come to think of it, the third item is a lot longer. Is "blooms" by itself a nice thing about Roskilde, or does it really belong with the gardens back in the previous item on the list?

Let's look at the answer choices. We see several ways to connect the two nouns. Different constructions of the nouns in the answer choices indicate that this could be a parallel construction problem (or possibly a misplaced modifier). Answer choice (A) implies that there are four items on the list, but that these items are not set up the same way. Let's get rid of it. Choice (D) is essentially just the same, but even worse; there is no comma after "blooms." Choice (C) splits the sentence in two. Can the second half of the sentence stand on its own? No way. Answer choice (B) puts the blooms back in the garden, and it clears up all problems of parallel construction. The correct answer is (B).

2 H The answer choices here provide an immediate clue: One of the choices breaks up the sentence into two pieces, while the others leave it intact. Changes in punctuation may mean a comma splice. They don't always, of course, but we should still check. Can the clauses on both sides of the punctuation stand alone? Yes, they can. Aha! This is definitely a comma splice. We are now probably giving serious thought to (H), which splits the sentence in two.

However, because there is more than one way to fix a comma splice, we should check the other answer choices just to see if any of them are better than (H). Choice (G) takes the comma splice and removes the comma, turning it into a run-on sentence. This is no better. Choice (J) merely inserts another pause after "the Vikings," which does not help matters. The correct answer is (H).

3 C Here the sentence, which is partially underlined, contains a *list* of actions: *The Vikings a) once wandered* and *b) may have travel.* Are the two verbs in the same tense? No. What did we really need here? If you said "traveled," you are absolutely correct.If you missed this as you were reading it the first time, the answer choices provided great clues. Each was just another form of a verb. Anytime you see verb changes in the answer choices, you should immediately think of parallel construction. Each choice is in a different tense. Just read through them until you get a match with "wandered." The correct answer is (C).

4 H Punctuation again! Three of the choices break up the sentence; one doesn't. Let's see which is better this time. Again, we ask ourselves, can the clauses on both sides of the punctuation stand by themselves? This time, the answer is no. The clause that begins "Where the Viking ships..." is dependent. This is a sentence fragment. We need to combine the two thoughts. Our only option is (H).

5 B The answer choices here give us a choice of nouns. This could be a parallel construction problem or a misplaced modifier. Because there is no list in this case, let's check for a misplaced modifier. How does the sentence begin?

Until 20 years ago used only by the fishermen who still play their trade in the fiord,…

This is a long modifying phrase. The noun that comes next in the sentence must be what is being modified. Are "tourists" what the fishermen used until 20 years ago? No! This is a misplaced modifier. We can eliminate (A) and (C). In (D), the shore must share itself. Can a shore do something like that? Nope. In choice (B), the construction indicates that the fishermen and the tourists must do the sharing. The correct answer is (B).

6 F We can spot the *type* of error ACT is looking for this time by going straight to the answer choices. This is one of those construction shift questions. Let's move "in the traditional manner" around in the sentence and find the best fit. You say it was just fine where it was? You're right. The answer is (F).

7 B More punctuation! Again, our choices either put the sentence together or break it apart. Can the two phrases on either side of the punctuation stand on their own? The answer this time is yes. We have another run-on sentence. There is only one choice that breaks up the two clauses: The correct answer is (B).

8 J More of the same. Can "who one hopes was only a boy at the time," stand on its own? No. We are down to (H) and (J). The correct answer is (J). How do you decide between "who" and "whom"? To find out, make sure you check out the Grammar and Usage chapter.

9 C In the underlined portion, the semicolon breaks up two independent clauses. Of course, that is acceptable behavior for a semicolon, but only if there is no conjunction between them. Thus, we can get rid of (A). Looking at the answer choices, none of the alternatives gets rid of the conjunction. Therefore, we cannot break the two clauses into two separate sentences. This allows us to eliminate (D). When you have two independent clauses linked by a conjunction, what kind of punctuation is required? If you said a comma, you were absolutely right. The correct answer is (C).

10 F Notice that the underlined portion contains two commas. When do we need two commas in a sentence? When we want to set off a clause or phrase that describes a noun in more detail but is not vital to the meaning of the sentence (a nonrestrictive element). Let's remove the phrase "a true adventurer" from the sentence. Do we lose any vital information? No. Therefore, the correct answer is (F). If you weren't sure how to correct the underlined portion, you could have looked at your answer choices. Answer choice (G) has three commas. Do they make the sentence any clearer? No. The comma after the word "true" is unnecessary. Answer choice (H) is incorrect because a colon should come after a complete thought and precede a list of related details. Answer choice (J) supplies only *one* comma. Remember, nonrestrictive elements need a *pair* of commas.

11 B Because the wording is exactly the same in each of the answer choices, it is easy to see that this question can only concern punctuation. Choice (D) creates an incomplete sentence: "My romantic picture of the West;". Because this cannot stand alone, we can cross off (D). The phrase "complete with cowboys and Indians" is supposed to be a parenthetical description of the author's vision of what the West would be like. As the underlined sentence stands, it is unclear where the main clause ends and the parenthetical thought begins, so cross off (A). If there had been a pair of parentheses in one of the answer choices, that could well have been the correct answer, but there were no parentheses in any of the choices. What is another way to surround a parenthetical thought? If you suggested dashes, you were correct. Now, look at the difference between (B) and (C). In choice (B), there are *two* dashes surrounding the parenthetical thought. In (C), there is only *one* at the beginning of the phrase. The correct answer is (B).

12 H Again, we can be pretty sure that this is a question about punctuation. Let's look at the entire sentence. It begins with a long introductory phrase, followed by an independent clause. Do we need any punctuation between a long phrase and a clause? Sure. We need a comma. The only answer choice that correctly positions the comma between the phrase and the clause is (H).

13 D If you look at the answer choices, you'll realize that this question is concerned with proper use of the apostrophe. Whose back is it? It is the mule's back. We need the possessive form here. Thus, (A) is immediately gone. Choice (C) uses the pronoun "our." Does this agree with the first part of the sentence? It could, but look at "back." Do "mules" have only one "back?" Nope. So (C) is out. In (B), "mules" gives the impression that she is riding more than one mule at the same time. The correct answer is (D).

14 J This sentence contains an independent clause followed by a list of related details, so the best punctuation mark to connect the two is the colon. A period or semicolon would be inappropriate because the sentence does not contain two independent clauses. So (F) and (G) are eliminated. A comma would not be sufficient: The related details should be set off in order to separate the hue from its description. So (H) is eliminated. The best answer to this question is (J).

15 C Here we have a series of items that need commas. Eliminate (D) because it doesn't have any commas. The original sentence, (A), is missing a comma after the word "shale." In (B), the adjective "freshwater" is split from the noun "shale." Commas should be placed after "limestone" and "shale." Therefore, the correct answer is (C).

16 G Does the sentence require the word "its" or "it's"? If you use the word "it's," the sentence would be the same as: *It is* imposing peaks. This is clearly wrong. "Its" refers to the Grand Canyon. Thus, (F) is wrong. A comma is unnecessary after the word "its" in (J) because it would break up the thought of the sentence. Two down and two to go. Is an apostrophe needed after the word "its"? Definitely not. There is no such word as "its'." Therefore, the correct answer is (G).

Grammar Drill (Chapter 7)

1 B Looking at the answer choices, you might notice that there are two potential errors to check: pronoun agreement and tense. Why? Because the answers contained two different pronouns and two different verb tenses. Let's check pronouns first. In the original underlined portion of the sentence, "one" is a pronoun. Does it agree with the other pronouns in the same sentence? Not really. The author begins the passage by addressing "you." It is confusing and incorrect to change to "one" in the same sentence. Which answer choice uses "you" correctly? The correct answer is (B).

2 H Checking the answer choices, we see that the question seems to revolve around verb tense. The sentence is describing something that happened yesterday, so we can expect that the sentence should be in some form of the past tense. Two events take place in this sentence. The author woke up, and the alarm clock failed to go off. Which of these two events happened first, thus causing the other? If you said that the failure of the alarm clock took place before the author woke up, you were absolutely correct. When two events occur in the past, but one occurs before the other, the sentence requires the past perfect. The correct answer is (H).

3 D The answer choices here offer us the choice of the adverb "previously" or the adjective "previous." To decide which is correct, we need to know to what "previously" (or "previous") is referring. The word being modified here is "evening," which we all know is a noun. The correct modifier of a noun is an adjective. This eliminates (A) and (B). Now, does an adjective normally precede or follow the noun it modifies? The correct answer is (D).

4 G The answer choices here indicate that we have to consider either of two errors: tense or subject-verb agreement. Let's check subject-verb agreement first. Find the subject of the sentence. If you said the subject was "each," you were absolutely correct. "Of the first three taxis I saw" is modifying "each." Now check the verb. "Each…were." In our review, we said that the word *each* is always singular—but the verb in this case is plainly plural. Aha! We have found the error. Check the answer choices to see which ones are singular. Our only remaining choices are (G), "was," and (J), "is." In what general tense is this passage written? Check the tense of the verbs in surrounding sentences. The correct answer is (G).

5 A Clearly this question is testing our understanding of the "who/whom" issue. Remember that the difference between the pronouns "who," and "whom" lies in whether they are being used as subjects or objects in the clause or phrase that contains them. "Who finally picked me up" is a clause modifying the taxi driver. What is the subject of the clause? If you said "who" you are absolutely correct. Thus, "who" is fine just the way it is. We can eliminate (B) and (C), both of which contain "whom." Now let's see what the difference is between (A) and (D). Again, it comes down to tense. Is this passage being told in the present tense? No. The correct answer is (A).

6 J The answer choices are offering you a variety of options having to do with "and" or "but." This is an idiom question. Try making up your own sentence using the idiomatic expression in question: *My sister Jane is not only stupid....* How would you finish this sentence? Or put it this way: What would be *the next word* in the sentence after "stupid"? *My sister Jane is not only stupid,* but *she is also a pain.* Choices (F) and (G) bite the dust. The answer is either (H) or (J). In the sentence you just made up, did you use "she" or "her" after the "but"? Chances are you used "she." "But she is also a pain" is a clause. Because "she" is the subject of the clause, we have to use the subject form, "she," instead of the object form, "her." The same is true for the sentence in the passage. The correct answer is (J).

7 C This question is about the proper use of the superlative. The answer choices (including "worser" and "worst") give you a pretty good indication that this is the case. If you are discussing two bad options, you would have to decide which of them was *worse.* If you are discussing three or more bad options, you would have to decide which of them was *the worst.* The correct answer is (C).

Rhetorical Skills Drill (Chapter 8)

1 C The underlined portion and the answer choices all contain sentence connectors. This is a transition question. Do we need an *also*, a *but*, or a *thus*? It seems pretty clear we need a *but.* The answer is (C).

2 F Several of the answer choices here seem to use similar words. We should consider redundancy immediately. Choices (G) and (H) are clearly redundant. Answer choice (J) ("famousness") is not a word. Thus, the best answer is (F).

3 D The underlined portion and the answer choices all seem to contain similar words, so again we should consider redundancy. There is no need to say both "initially" and "for the first time" in the same sentence. Choices (B) and (D) are the only choices that avoid redundancies. Choice (B) is awkward and incorrectly phrased, so (D) is correct.

4 J At first this might strike you as an idiom question. In fact, style questions often resemble idiom questions. The metaphor of an actor sharpening his or her skills is effective, but how far do we want to take it? Is it necessary to say "to a knife edge" to get the point across? The answer is (J): OMIT the underlined portion.

5 D As with all organization questions, we should try to spot either the beginning sentence or any pair of sentences we can link together. There is a certain cause and effect visible between Sentence 1 and Sentence 4. Which of the answer choices puts them next to each other in that order? Two of them do. The answer would seem to have to be (C) or (D). Because both choices put Sentence 2 first, the question becomes "where does Sentence 3 belong?" Well, the paragraph begins by saying *Playhouse 90* was a training ground. It is most logical to put the list of future stars after the introductory sentence, so (D) is the best answer.

6 G We see more sentence connectors, so we are again prepared for transition. "(Blank) the frantic pace, accidents happened frequently." Let's try out the words in the answer choices. Could "despite" fill in the blank? No. We want a causal word. Answer choice (G), "Due to," is the correct answer.

7 C How do we change the tone of Paragraph 3 with one word? Well, "accidents" sounds a little drastic. Which choice minimizes the sound of that word? If you said (C), "mishaps," you are absolutely correct.

8 G Summary questions always take a while. Answer choice (F) merely repeats the first half of the first sentence of the passage, entirely missing *Playhouse 90.* Answer choice (G) seems really good. Answer choice (H) concentrates on the third paragraph only. Answer choice (J) concentrates solely on the three actors and writers mentioned. Are they the primary focus of the passage? Not really. The answer is (G).

9 A Organization of paragraphs requires an overview of the entire passage. As always, try to find one paragraph you feel you can label as first or last, and proceed from there. Because the first paragraph is the best introduction to the passage as a whole, the correct answer is (A).

Basics Drill (Chapter 10)

1 D Answer choice (C) does not equal 54, so we can eliminate it right away. Answers (A), (B), and (E) all equal 54, but each of these choices includes a factor that is not prime. The correct answer is (D).

2 H First, ballpark the answer choices. There are 2 negative signs in the question (not including the one inside the absolute value symbols), which means your answer must be positive. Eliminate (F) and (G). Next, you can find that the absolute value of –6 is 6. From here, use your calculator to do the heavy lifting. Just be sure you enter the data correctly; your equation should be (–)5 × 4 × 6/–3, which comes out to 40.

3 D Work smarter here, not harder. If you're given a list of possible factors/divisors, simply use your calculator to test each answer choice. (D) is the only choice that does not come out to an integer.

4 F Again, put your calculator to work. You should have entered (–2)^3 + 3^(–2) + (8≠9), which yields –7.

5 C Use the "carat" function, with carefully placed parentheses, to apply a fractional exponent: Enter 27^(2/3) to get 9.

6 F $(xy)^3$ equals x^3y^3. Anything to the zero power equals 1, so z disappears from the numerator. The correct answer is (F).

7 C To make this expression an integer, we need an even numerator. Why? Because it is going to be divided by 2. How can we ensure that the numerator of this fraction is even? The value a must be odd. The correct answer is (C). Another, perhaps simpler, way to approach this question is to plug in numbers and see what happens. Use the answer choices to help you decide what numbers to try. First, let's try 2, which is positive and even. If we put 2 in for a, we get $\frac{9}{2}$, which isn't an integer, so we can cross out (E) and (B). Try 0 next, because that's an easy number to work with. $\frac{11}{2}$ isn't an integer; 0 doesn't work, so (D) is out too. We're down to (A), negative, and (C), odd. Let's try 3 for a. That gives $\frac{8}{2}$, which is 4, which is an integer. So a doesn't have to be negative, but it does have to be odd. (C) is the answer.

8 G Just count on your fingers. Is 0 even? Yes. The correct answer is (G). Note: If you chose J, it's because you read "between –4 and 4" as "between –4 and 4, inclusive"—that is, including –4 and 4 themselves. Sometimes a math test is actually a vocabulary test.

9 C As in question 3, we can use our calculator to test the answer choices. For 4,7*W*6 to be divisible by 6, the quotient must be an integer. Plug each answer choice in for *W* and see which answer choice makes this happen. Using (C), you'll find that $\frac{4{,}746}{6} = 791$.

10 J Ignore your instinct to start doing the math and pick up your calculator. You're given an equation and a series of possible answers; just test each choice until you get $\frac{1}{3}$. Using (J), type 9^(–1/2) into your calculator. It should come out to .333, which is the same as $\frac{1}{3}$. You can always hit [MATH] [1:Frac] [ENTER]] Í to make sure you have the right fraction.

Arithmetic Drill (Chapter 11)

1 C A ratio is a $\frac{\text{part}}{\text{part}}$. Because the only actual number of students that we have is a whole, we will need to convert the ratio into a fraction. If the ratio is $\frac{4}{5}$, then the whole is 9. The equation we need is $\frac{4}{9} = \frac{x}{27}$. $x = 12$, and the answer is (C).

2 J First, let's do some quick elimination. The average of the first 5 tests is 88. Because the sixth test is less than 88, the final average must also be less than 88. Scratch (K). Now let's get to work. Let's use the average pie to think about what information we are given. The first bite-size piece tells us that Linda had 5 scores with an average of 88. It sounds like we are missing the total, so multiply 5 × 88 to get 440. What does the next piece say? Linda forgot the test on which she scored an 82, so we'll have to tack that onto the total. 440 + 82 = 522. What is the question asking us to find? We need an average, which means we must have the total and the number of things. Our new total is 522, and because we added on the test Linda forgot, our number of tests is now 6. Divide 522 by 6 to arrive at 87.

3 E Percent translation should do the trick. Because we are taking percentages, let's start with the original amount. What happens with the 490 tons of grain? We lost both 3 percent and 5 percent of the original; because we aren't asked to take a percent of the remaining grain, we can combine the percentages and do one calculation: What is 8% of 490? Punch (8/100) x 490 into your calculator to get 39.2. Subtract that from 490, circle (E), and move on.

4 F First, let's convert these numbers into improper fractions. $5\frac{1}{3}$ equals $\frac{16}{3}$. $6\frac{1}{4}$ equals $\frac{25}{4}$. Clearly, when we subtract the second number from the first, the result will be negative. Cross off (J) and (K) because they are both positive. Your calculator can easily subtract mixed numbers—as long as you enter them correctly. In order to do so, add each integer to the attached fraction prior to subtracting by using parentheses. Your equation should look like this: $(5 + (\frac{1}{3})) - (6 + (\frac{1}{4}))$. After hitting enter, you should get –.91667. Can you eliminate anything? Definitely (J) and (K); if you know your common fractions, you can strike (G) as well. Ballpark the remaining two answers by figuring out which fraction is closer to –1. (F) it is.

5 D This is straight calculator work! Just be sure you enter 1,245/.05 and NOT 1,245/.5, or your answer will be off by a significant amount.

Algebra Drill (Chapter 12)

1 A If $x = -3$, then the first term of the numerator $(x + 3)$ equals 0. 0 times any number equals 0, so the correct answer is (A).

2 H If we factor the equation, we get $(x - 3)(x - 1) = 0$. x could be either 3 or 1. Because we are being asked for the larger value, the correct answer is (H). Note that you could have worked backward on this question, starting with (K), because the question wants you to find the "largest value."

3 D Because this question contains two equations with two different variables, this is a simultaneous equations question. Let's get rid of the fraction in the second equation. Multiply the entire equation by 2. We get

$$x + 2y = 8$$
$$x - 2y = 20$$

If we add the two equations together, we get $2x = 28$, or $x = 14$. The correct answer is (D).

4 G If we factor, we get $\frac{(x+9)(x-3)}{(x+9)}$

The $(x + 9)$s cancel out, so the correct answer is (G). Note that you could have plugged in on this question. Also, you could have used the denominator to help you factor the numerator.

5 A The correct translation of the equation is $3x - 2 = 5(3) + 4$. Thus, the correct answer is (A).

6 G "A certain number" sounds pretty cosmic to us. This is a Plugging In question. Let's pick a number of books. Because we will be dividing by 5 and by 3, a good number might be 15. $\frac{2}{5}$ of 15 = 6. If 6 are gone, then 9 remain to be given out. In the afternoon, $\frac{1}{3}$ of 9 are given out: This equals 3. If 3 are given out in the afternoon, that leaves 6. The question asks for the fraction of books that remains. Every fraction is a part over a whole. The part is 6; the whole is 15. $\frac{6}{15}$ reduces to $\frac{2}{5}$. The correct answer is (G).

Geometry Drill (Chapter 13)

1 B Let's say $\angle A$ equals $x°$. $\angle B$ also equals $x°$. $\angle C$ is therefore $2x°$. We have a total of $4x°$. Because there are 180° in a triangle, $4x = 180$. x equals 45, and therefore, the correct answer is (B). Note that you could have worked backward on this problem.

2 F When two parallel lines are cut by a third line, there are really only two angles formed—a big one and a little one. We need to find an answer choice with two big angles or two little angles. Remember, any answer choice with $\angle D$ in it must be wrong because this angle is not formed by two parallel lines being cut by a third. The correct answer is (F).

3 D You could use the Pythagorean theorem to solve this question, but you will be done much faster if you know the triples that ACT likes to use. The triangle on the left is a multiple of a 3-4-5 triangle: 15-20-25. The triangle on the right is a 7-24-25 triangle. The correct answer is (D).

4 G The radius of circle A is 4. If circle B has a radius that is half of circle A, its radius is 2. Therefore, the circumference is 4π. The correct answer is (G).

5 A This time we have to use the Pythagorean theorem because all we know about ΔLMO is that it is a right triangle. Using the Pythagorean theorem, we find that $\overline{MO}$ is equal to $\sqrt{20}$ or $2\sqrt{5}$. ΔMON is an isosceles right triangle, so the hypotenuse is equal to the side times $\sqrt{2}$. The correct answer is (A).

Graphing and Coordinate Geometry Drill (Chapter 14)

1 E We can immediately cross off (B) and (D) because the equation does not contain a greater-than-or-equal-to sign. If you chose (C), you forgot that the sign flips when you multiply or divide an inequality by a negative number. The correct answer is (E).

2 G If you don't remember the formula for finding a midpoint, just make a rough graph. Which quadrant should the answer be in? If you said the second, you are correct. The x-coordinate should be negative, the y-coordinate should be positive. Which answer choices are possible? There's only one. The correct answer is (G).

3 B We need to put this into the standard $y = mx + b$ form. In this case, the equation becomes $y = 12x - 6$. The slope is 12, and the answer is (B).

4 H Forget the distance formula. Instead, try sketching out a graph. Make the line between the two points the hypotenuse of a right triangle. It turns out to be a 3-4-5 triangle. The correct answer is (H).

5 C Just use the slope formula—the difference in y over the difference in x. The correct answer is (C).

Trigonometry Drill: Answers and Explanations (Chapter 15)

1 D This is a 5-12-13 triangle. The tangent of an angle is opposite over adjacent. The correct answer is (D).

2 H The cotangent of an angle is the reciprocal of the tangent. If the tangent is 1, then so is the cotangent. The correct answer is (H).

3 C $\sin^2\theta + \cos^2\theta$ always equals 1. Therefore, x must equal 3. The correct answer is (C).

Charts and Graphs Drill 1 (Chapter 20)

1 B This is a Look It Up question on which you can use POE. As you were reading the question, did you notice that (A) and (B) were the same except that the words "T1" and "T2" were switched? The answer choices are opposites, and one of them will probably be correct. Let's try (A) and (B) first. At T1, Sample 1 has a greater number of molecules in motion. The introduction clarifies that this corresponds to an increase in kinetic energy. The graph contradicts (A), so the answer appears to be (B). Now let's check the other two choices. Does an increase in temperature lead to a decrease in kinetic energy? No. The passage states that an increase in temperature leads to an increase in kinetic energy. So we can eliminate (C). Now let's look at (D). Is it true that water never undergoes a phase change? No; in fact, the text accompanying the graph says just the opposite. So we can eliminate (D). Also, remember to be cautious of extreme language such as "never." The correct answer is (B).

2 F This is a Why? question because it requires a greater understanding of the passage than does question 1. The question refers to the second paragraph, which mentions phase changes. What happens during a phase change? Two things happen: (1) Increased kinetic energy weakens the attractive intermolecular forces in the water, and (2) Some molecules escape the liquid as a gas. Now that we have reviewed this information, it's pretty easy to eliminate (G) and (H). Now let's look at (J). Did we read anything in the passage that told us about other phase changes? No. This answer is beyond the realm of the passage and can be eliminated. So the correct choice is (F), and again we've reached it by using POE.

3 B This is a What If? question. The ACT test writers want to see if you can predict what will happen if you raise the temperature of water higher than that of Sample 2. What answer choices should you eliminate? Decide whether the correct answer should begin with a yes or a no. How do we do that? Just check the graph with the results for Samples 1 and 2. When you increase the temperature, will the sample have more or less kinetic energy? It will have more. That means we can rule out (D). We can eliminate (C) because the temperature reading of Sample 2 is lower than the third sample. Now compare (A) with (B) to see which one is correct. Does an increase in temperature lead to greater or fewer numbers of molecules escaping the liquid? Greater. Thus, the correct answer is (B).

4 F This is a Why? question. The passage states that when a substance goes from the liquid to the gas phase, it will evaporate. When a substance has reached the temperature at which it undergoes the phase change, it will evaporate. That's how molecules will escape. Therefore, the answer is (F).

5 C This is a Look It Up question. When you look at the figure, which line goes the highest? Which has the highest kinetic energy at any one point? Well, the curve for T1 goes higher than the curve for T2. T2 has the highest average kinetic energy, but that's not what this question asks us to find. Therefore, (A) and (B) can be eliminated. (D) is a nonsensical answer choice. (C) is the best answer.

Charts and Graphs Drill 2 (Chapter 20)

1 B This is a Why? question. Do we see a solution of thyroxine that is 0.3 μg/ml? No. The ACT test writers want you to "guesstimate" where 0.3 μg/ml would fall on the table. This value would have to lie somewhere between 0.2 μg/ml and 0.5 μg/ml. The question requires that you make a guess within the values given. What do we call this skill? Interpolation! Now if we move across the x-axis to the value of 72 hours, and we move up to the range of values between 0.2 μg/ml and 0.5 μg/ml, we see that the y-values range from about 23 percent to 37 percent. The only one that falls in that range is (B)—30 percent.

2 G This is a What If? question. Notice that they want to know what is true for tadpoles in general. Let's start with (F). This is a ridiculous answer choice. We know that all normal tadpoles undergo metamorphosis. If you're not sure, take a look at the graph. The control group in the graph represents normal tadpoles. They do have some decrease in tail width, although not a lot, in 120 hours or 5 days. (Notice that you needed to know that 5 days is the same as 120 hours.) Thus, (F) is incorrect. You can also rule out (H) because the figure clearly shows that high concentrations of thyroxine solutions lead to the greatest decrease in tail width. The passage doesn't mention anything about temperature, thus (J) is out. The correct answer is (G). We see that the control sample shows some reduction in tail size in 120 hours, so it must take longer for the process to be complete.

3 C This is a Look It Up question. You must realize that as the tadpole develops, the tail is reabsorbed—or it shrinks. The graph compares percent decrease in tail width to hours. At 96 hours (4 days), the tadpoles showing the lowest percent decrease in tail width would be the least developed. Therefore, the answer must be (C), the tadpoles in 0.1 μg/ml.

4 G This is also a Look It Up question. Thyroxine affects the metamorphosis of the tadpole by influencing the process of cell determination from tadpole cells into mature adult cells. You don't have to understand this process—just realize that it occurs between tadpole and adult stages. Begin with (F), (G), and (H), because you need a tadpole to start the process. Using POE, the correct answer can be only (G).

5 C Take a look at the figure provided. When do the lines start to differentiate from one another (showing different rates of tail reabsorption)? We can see that by 24 hours, the tadpoles placed in the various thyroxine solutions have each had a larger percent of their tails reabsorbed than the tadpoles in the control group. (D) can be eliminated. Now look between 0 and 24 hours. At 0 hours and at 12 hours, the percent decrease in tail width is the same for all the tadpoles. Therefore, the change in metamorphosis rate must occur between 12 and 24 hours, so (C) is correct.

Charts and Graphs Drill 3 (Chapter 20)

1 A Finally, a question about drawing a graph! This question was easy because you only needed to look at the *x*- and *y*-axes (a typical Look It Up question). The atomic number of the elements was the independent variable, and the atomic radius was the dependent variable. What happens to the atomic radius as you increase the atomic number? It gets smaller. That means we can eliminate (C) and (D). Now we have to decide if it's a linear relationship or an exponential one. Just check the numbers. Notice that the numbers decrease by a smaller amount each time—so it's a curve, not a straight line. Thus, the correct answer is (A).

2 J This question requires that you integrate information from two parts of the table, so it's a Why? question. You should look at relationships between electronegativity and one of the other properties of elements. Let's start with (G) and (J). Why? They are opposites (the switch again), so they can't both be true. If an element has a high electronegativity, is it a metal or a non-metal? It's a non-metal, so eliminate (G). Now we can check the other answer choices. Must an element with a high electronegativity have an even or an odd atomic number? Let's check. If you look at the two highest electronegative elements, O and F, one is even and one is odd. So (F) is not true. As for (H), we know that elements with high electronegativity pull their outer electrons (the passage defines electronegativity as a measure of that strength). Therefore, we can eliminate (H). The correct answer is (J).

3 B This question asks you to make a generalization about trends in the chart, with regard to the bigger picture. Let's take a moment to think about the answer choices. If we want to make generalizations about elements, would an answer that refers to specific elements be the correct one? Probably not. So we can probably eliminate (D). But let's look at (D) more closely to be sure. Is the atomic radius of F larger than that of N? No. Do all metals have high electronegativity values? No. Now notice that (A) and (B) state opposite trends. Use the chart to determine which is correct. As the atomic radius decreases, electronegativity increases. Thus, the correct is (B).

4 G This is a Why? question because you have to integrate the information on the chart and information in the passage. The first part is easy. Look at the chart to tell you which has a greater electronegativity, Li or F. F, of course! So we can get rid of (J). Now why is the electronegativity of F greater than that of Li? We have to choose between (F) and (G). Can you determine which one of these is correct by using the information in the chart? NO. Go back to the introduction and skim for information about electronegativity. The passage says specifically that within a row of the periodic table, the electronegativity tends to increase with increasing atomic number, due to the tighter bonding between protons and electrons. Its not the number that's important, but rather how tightly bound they are. F has a higher atomic number than Li and more electrons than Li, so, F's electrons are more tightly bound than Li's. Therefore, the best answer is (G).

5 A This is a Why? question. You must take new information given in the question and apply it to the chart given in the passage. Fortunately, this is very easy. Be careful; the question asks for increasing order of ionization energies. Because it follows the same trend as electronegativity, just find the answer that lists elements with increasing electronegativities. The answer can only be (A).

Experiments Drill 1 (Chapter 21)

1 B This is a Look It Up question, and it directs your attention to Experiments 1 and 2. In Experiment 1, the plant bends when exposed to sunlight. In Experiment 2, the light-proof cap inhibits the influence of sunlight in such a way that prevents the bending of the plant. Clearly, the cap prevented sunlight from having any effect. So we can eliminate (C). The passage doesn't give any information on the amount of sunlight (D) or the influence of nutrition (A). The only answer that correctly addresses the effect of the cap on the plant tip is (B). It was the tip of the plant that was covered by the cap; therefore, the tip of the plant must somehow perceive sunlight.

2 F Here is a Look It Up question about the control of the study. The control sample is Plant 1. Nothing was done to this plant. Plants 2, 3, and 4 were all manipulated to some degree to determine the influence of sunlight on phototropism. Plant 1 is left as is in the sunlight. Therefore, the answer is (F).

3 C This is a Why? question that requires more than one piece of information, so you need to look at the results of all of the experiments. Did you notice that when the tip was covered, the plant didn't bend? Actually, it's not the tip that bends but a region farther down from the tip. That means there must be some sort of communication between the tip of the plant and that region for this response to take place. Therefore the answer is (C). (B) is incorrect because plants *do* respond to sunlight—they bend. The passage does not give any information about differences between flowering plants and non-flowering plants, (D) or the strength of the sun's rays, (A).

4 F This is a What If? question. Did you notice that the question begins with the word *suppose*? That's a hint that you're supposed to predict the outcome of a similar study. You already know that the initial communication for phototropism occurs in the tip of the plant. If the tip is cut off, the most likely reaction would be that the plant will no longer be able to send information to the lower bending region, and, therefore, the plant will not bend. If you followed all the results of the study, then this should have been a logical follow-up based on the results. The answer to this question is (F).

Experiments Drill 2 (Chapter 21)

1 D This is a Look It Up question. You need to find the types of fossilized organisms that are found in the black shale layer. You should therefore look at the table. What types of fossilized organisms are found in the black shale layer? There are snails, clams, oysters, and periwinkles. You can eliminate any of these answer choices because you're looking for the wrong answer choice. The only one that is not found in this layer is sponges. So the answer is (D).

2 H This is a Why? question. Pine needles are not mentioned in any of the studies, but if you look at the data in each study, you will notice that plant fossils occur in only one kind of rock: coal. Thus the correct answer is (H).

3 B This is a Why? question. You're supposed to observe the results of Studies 1 and 2 and figure out

the correct sequence of the rock formations. Did you notice that the layers of Studies 1 and 2 overlap? The ordering of the layers must have been limestone, black shale, coal, and sandstone. The only one with the correct sequence is (B).

4 F This is a Look It Up question. The ACT test writers want you to read the part of the passage that mentions that the rock formations can be altered by various types of erosions. Which of the answer choices is an example of erosion? The correct answer is the term "weathering," which refers to the break-up of rock formations by physical or chemical means. Answer choice (J) is ridiculous because it has nothing to do with the passage. In addition, a mild rainstorm or extreme heat would not be sufficient to wear away rock formations. So the correct answer is (F).

Experiments Drill 3 (Chapter 21)

1 B This is a Why? question. You can use the table to help you answer this question. Displacement changes according to what other variable? Force. As force changes, the displacement also changes. You could have looked at the formula $F = -kx$, which shows that force is related to displacement (x). None of the other factors listed will affect the displacement. So the answer to this question is (B).

2 H This is a Why? question that requires you to predict the displacement that would result from a hypothesized value of force. This is an example of interpolation. We're looking for a value that is going to fall within the range of values provided. What do we do? Guesstimate using the chart. The displacement from a force of 8 pounds is 4 pounds and from 10 pounds would be 5. The only answer choice in that range is (H), 4.5; (H) is the correct answer.

3 D This is a Why? question. Where in the chart do we look to see what happens when the weight of the mass is doubled? Only trials 1 and 3 do this. Between Trials 1 and 3, the displacement and the force are both doubled, so (D) is correct.

Fighting Scientists Drill 1 (Chapter 22)

1 C This is a Look It Up question. What are the beliefs of Scientist 1? His main point is that Pangaea (one continent) existed 137 million years ago. Now let's start by looking at each of the answer choices. Were the continents once part of one large land mass? Yes. We read that in the passage. What about (B)? Did the continents break up and drift apart? Definitely. Does the statement that the ocean basins remained fixed agree with the theory? No. If so, how would the continents drift apart? So (C) is inconsistent. (D) is not inconsistent with the theory of Scientist 1. So the correct answer choice is (C).

2 G This is a Why? question. Scientist 2 needs to show how what Scientist 1 said fits with Scientist 2's hypothesis. It will also probably be something which disagrees with Scientist 1's argument. Answer choice (F) states that the techniques used to date and compare fossils are accurate. This is an argument Scientist 1 makes but that Scientist 2 doesn't mention. Cross it out. Answer choice (G) says that the soil and climate conditions were once the same—a nice paraphrase of what Scientist 2 says at the end of the argument. Keep (G) for now. Answer choice (H) supports Scientist 1 because extremely large ferns would have a hard time floating thousands of miles across the ocean. You can eliminate (J) because it doesn't support either scientist. Scientist 2 would infer that these ferns grew well in both places; (G) has to be right.

3 C This is a Why? question, and it's kind of tricky. Either scientist could use this information to support his theory if he could come up with a valid reason. Answer choice (A) says that Scientist 1 is supported because the finding shows tectonic activity. But we already knew about that and besides, that's a point on which the scientists agree. So eliminate (A). Answer choice (D) also gives us information that was already stated in Scientist 2's statement, so this choice is weak. Choice (B) is ridiculous because neither scientist believes that Pangaea exists today, so cross it out. At this point, (C) is looking pretty good. Scientist 2 could soundly reason that tectonic activity in a solid land mass demonstrates that this geological phenomenon does not lead to continental drift. The best answer is (C).

4 G This is a Look It Up question. The passage tells us about the formation of land masses, tectonic plates, and other geological evidence—namely fossils. You must be able to add this together and determine that the scientists know something about geology. So only (G) can be correct.

5 A This is a Look It Up question. You must know what each scientist supports. Let's go through the choices one by one. Statement I is supported by both scientists because both believe that tectonic activity exists and changes geological formations. (Scientist 1 thinks it's more important than does Scientist 2, but that doesn't matter here.) So Statement I is correct and we're down to (A) and (C). Let's keep checking. Only Scientist 2 supports Statement II and only Scientist 1 supports Statement III. Therefore, (A) must be the correct answer.

Fighting Scientists Drill 2 (Chapter 22)

1 A This is a Why? question because we're asked to find an answer that supports the argument. To do this, we must understand the argument. What's the main point of Hypothesis 2? The debater believes that the chance of RNA reproducing as the graduate student described is extremely small. Look for an answer choice that supports this argument. Answer choice (A) states that conditions in the atmosphere were too unstable to support the necessary gases. Does this statement support Hypothesis 2? Yes. How? Because it weakens Hypothesis 1. So (A) is correct. Answer choices (B), (C), and (D) are wrong because they support Hypothesis 1.

2 G This is a Look It Up question, and we're looking for an assumption in the argument. What does Scientist 1 believe? That the experiment shows how the first organic compounds were made. Is (F) an assumption in this argument? No. It refers to Hypothesis 2. What about (G)? Yes. The scientist assumed that the experiment mimicked the conditions of primeval Earth. So (G) is correct. Answer choice (H) states that proteins are the building blocks of amino acids. That's wrong; as stated in Hypothesis 1, amino acids are the building blocks of proteins. So get rid of (H). Answer choice (J) is incorrect because Earth had to have hydrogen in order to form organic compounds.

3 A This is a Look It Up question. What does Hypothesis 1 say about amino acids? The passage tells us that amino acids are the building blocks of life, so let's start with the answer choices that list amino acids last. We can quickly eliminate (C). We can also eliminate (B) because the meteor theory was part of Hypothesis 2, not Hypothesis 1. And we're down to (A) and (D). We can also find in the passage that amino acids are the building blocks of proteins, so amino acids should be before proteins in the list. So by POE and understanding the passage, we arrive at the correct answer, (A).

Fighting Scientists Drill 3 (Chapter 23)

1 C This is a Why? question. We are looking for an answer that supports Hypothesis 2. Hypothesis 2 states that an increase in precipitation or an increase in pollution would lead to a significant drop in temperature. Answer choice (A) states that there is more snow in Canada this year, but we don't know if that's enough snow for glaciation. So we can eliminate it. Let's look at (B). If snow didn't stick to the ground, would there be an ice age? Answer choice (B) is silly; eliminate it. What about (C)? If there is a drop in temperature for every increase in the pollution rate, could that lead to glaciation? Yes. Let's look at (D). If the water became more polluted, would that necessarily lead to the next ice age? We're not sure. The passage states that pollution in the air, not necessarily in the water, leads to a decrease in temperature. So the correct answer is (C).

2 H This is a Why? question. For this question we're looking for an answer that could disprove Hypothesis 1. What is the main point of Hypothesis 1? The debater says that it is highly unlikely that Earth will experience another ice age. Why? Because he believes that the necessary conditions will not be met in the future. What is the best way to disprove this point? Just indicate that the conditions could change in the future and then the chance for glaciation could increase. Which choice states that? Answer choice (H). Now let's look at (F). A fluctuation in temperature would not necessarily mean that the temperature was low enough for glaciation to occur. We therefore can eliminate this choice. Even if there was more snowfall in the Swiss Alps, we are not given an indication of how long it lasted. So you can get rid of (G). Now, if the temperature went up 5°C in the North Pole, it would be warmer, not colder, so (J) is out. So the correct answer choice is (H).

3 C This is a Look It Up question because you are being asked to identify the regions in which glaciation would take place. Let's start with Statement II, because it appears in the most answer choices. Based on the passage, would glaciation take place in polar regions? The passage tells us that polar regions would be one of the first locations in which glaciation would take place. Now that you can

eliminate answer choices that don't include Statement II, you can eliminate (A). What about heavily polluted regions? Yes. The passage refers to the other possible cause of a temperature drop—pollution. We can eliminate (B) and (D) because they don't include Statement II. Therefore, (C) must be correct.

4 G This is also a Look It Up question. According to Hypothesis 2, there are two conditions that are critical to glaciation: temperature and precipitation. Answer choice (F) is incorrect because pollution doesn't cause precipitation. Answer choice (G) sounds good because it states that pollution leads to a major drop in temperature (it has one of the conditions). What about (H)? You can eliminate (H) because glaciation needs both low temperatures and high precipitation. (J) supports Hypothesis 1, not Hypothesis 2, so we can eliminate it. The best answer is (G).

Part VIII
The Princeton Review ACT Practice Exam 1 and Answers and Explanations

Practice Exam 1

ENGLISH TEST

45 Minutes—75 Questions

DIRECTIONS: In the five passages that follow, certain words and phrases are underlined and numbered. In the right-hand column, you will find alternatives for the underlined part. In most cases, you are to choose the one that best expresses the idea, makes the statement appropriate for standard written English, or is worded most consistently with the style and tone of the passage as a whole. If you think the original version is best, choose "NO CHANGE." In some cases, you will find in the right-hand column a question about the underlined part. You are to choose the best answer to the question.

You will also find questions about a section of the passage, or about the passage as a whole. These questions do not refer to an underlined portion of the passage, but rather are identified by a number or numbers in a box.

For each question, choose the alternative you consider best and fill in the corresponding oval on your answer document. Read each passage through once before you begin to answer the questions that accompany it. For many of the questions, you must read several sentences beyond the question to determine the answer. Be sure that you have read far enough ahead each time you choose an alternative.

PASSAGE I

I Am Iron Man

[1] The term "Iron Man" has many connotations, including references to a song, a comic book icon, even a movie. [2] Yet only one definition of the term truly lives up to its name: the Ironman Triathlon held annually in Hawaii[1] a picturesque setting for a challenging race. [3] This grueling race demands amazing physical prowess and the ability to swim, bike, and run a marathon, all in less than 12 hours with no break. [4] Very few individuals are up to the task. [2]

Otherwise,[3] Gordon Haller is a notable exception. Growing up in the 1950s, Haller developed an interest in many sports catgorized as endurance athletics, and welcomed their[4] grueling physical demands. As he pursued a degree in physics he drove a

1. A. NO CHANGE
   B. Hawaii,
   C. Hawaii, being
   D. Hawaii, it is

2. If the writer were to delete Sentence 4, the essay would primarily lose details that:
   F. emphasize how difficult the race truly is.
   G. mourn how few athletes are able to visit Hawaii in order to compete in the race.
   H. highlight that most athletes prefer the run to the swimming or biking components of the race.
   J. suggest that women are not truly competitive in the race.

3. A. NO CHANGE
   B. As a result,
   C. In addition,
   D. However,

4. F. NO CHANGE
   G. athletics and welcomed their
   H. athletics, and welcomed there,
   J. athletics and, welcomed there

GO ON TO THE NEXT PAGE.

taxi to pay the bills, but competitive training proved[5] his passion. So when he heard about the race in 1978, the first year it was held, he immediately signed up.

The race somewhat[6] originated in an amusing way. The members of two popular sports clubs, the Mid-Pacific Road Runners of Honolulu, and the Waikiki Swim Club[7] of Oahu, had a long-standing and good-natured debate going over who made better athletes: runners or swimmers. However, some local bikers thought both clubs were wrong, while claiming[8] that they, in fact, deserved the title. Wanting to settle the dispute once and for all, when[9] they decided to combine three separate races already held annually on the island[10] into one massive test of endurance. Thus, the Waikiki Roughwater Swim of 2.4 miles, the Around-Oahu Bike race of 112 miles, and the Honolulu Marathon of 26.2 miles were all combined to form the Ironman Triathlon.

Haller was one of only fifteen competitors to show up that February morning to start the race. He quickly scanned the few pages of rules and instructions, and while reading those pages[11] on the last page he discovered a sentence that would become the race's famous slogan: "Swim 2.4 miles! Bike 112 miles! Run 26.2 miles! Brag for the rest of your life!" Haller took that to

5. A. NO CHANGE
   B. verified
   C justified
   D. certified

6. The best placement for the underlined word would be:
   F. where it is now.
   G. before the word *in*.
   H. before the word *amusing* (changing *an* to *a*).
   J. before the word *way*.

7. A. NO CHANGE
   B. Runners, of Honolulu, and the Waikiki Swim Club
   C. Runners of Honolulu and the Waikiki Swim Club
   D. Runners, of Honolulu, and the Waikiki Swim Club,

8. F. NO CHANGE
   G. and while claiming
   H. they claimed
   J. claiming

9. A. NO CHANGE
   B. and
   C. where
   D. DELETE the underlined portion.

10. The best placement for the underlined phrase would be:
   F. where it is now.
   G. before the word *Wanting* (revising the capitalization accordingly).
   H. before the word *once*.
   J. after the word *endurance* (ending the sentence with a period).

11. A. NO CHANGE
   B. and
   C. and while perusing those pages
   D. and in those sheets of paper

GO ON TO THE NEXT PAGE.

heart, and at the end of the day, he had became [12] the first Ironman champion in history. [13]

In the approximately thirty years since that very first race, the Ironman has become a tradition in Hawaii and now boasts approximately 1,500 entrants every year. The competitors who [14] complete the race don't have to be the first across the finish line to claim success: just finishing is a victory unto itself.

12. **F.** NO CHANGE
G. become
H. became
J. becamed

13. Which of the following true statements, if added here, would most effectively and specifically emphasize Haller's achievement as described in this essay?

A. Twelve other people also finished the race that day.
B. There were points in the race when Haller thought he couldn't possibly finish.
C. No women raced this year, but that was soon to change.
D. Haller's amazing physical strength had enabled him to do what no one else in the past had accomplished.

14. Which of the following alternatives to the underlined portion would be LEAST acceptable?

F. The individuals
G. That
H. The athletes
J. The people

Question 15 asks about the preceding passage as a whole.

15. If the writer were to delete the final paragraph of this essay, the essay would primarily lose information that:

A. discusses the level of interest the race attracts in the present day.
B. describes the way the current race is different from the race that Haller ran in 1978.
C. describes how the victors respond when they cross the finish line.
D. explains why 1,500 people would be willing to compete in such a difficult race.

GO ON TO THE NEXT PAGE.

PASSAGE II

New Beginnings

[1]

As a junior in high school, I am very concerned about college. I'm trying to do everything right: <u>when I keep</u> [16] my grades up, participate in a few extracurricular activities, prepare for standardized tests, even perform community service. I spend most days thinking about the <u>future hoping</u> [17] that I'm on the right path, I do my best at everything I can.

16. F. NO CHANGE
    G. I keep
    H. I am keeping
    J. I have kept

17. A. NO CHANGE
    B. future, hoping
    C. future. Hoping
    D. future praying

[2]

[1] I'm interested in a career in <u>nursing,</u> [18] I decided to try to secure a spot as a volunteer at the local hospital. [2] I accepted his offer immediately, thinking to myself that here <u>lies</u> [19] all the opportunities I could ever want! [3] It would be the best of both worlds: helping people while gaining valuable on-the-job experience! [4] So I put on a nice <u>pair of slacks, a blouse,</u> [20] and some comfortable shoes—don't all nurses wear comfortable shoes?—and went to visit the business office. [5] Fortunately, the hospital director was quite willing to let me help out, and he said I could start that summer as soon as I finished my finals. [21]

18. F. NO CHANGE
    G. nursing, therefore,
    H. nursing, so
    J. nursing, but

19. A. NO CHANGE
    B. lays
    C. lay
    D. lie

20. F. NO CHANGE
    G. pair, of slacks, a blouse,
    H. pair, of slacks, a blouse
    J. pair of slacks a blouse

21. For the sake of the logic and coherence of this paragraph, Sentence 2 should be placed:
    A. where it is now.
    B. after Sentence 3.
    C. after Sentence 4.
    D. after Sentence 5.

[3]

The director gave me a brief tour of various departments as he told me about the primary focus of each, an <u>expert himself in every facet of hospital administration,</u> [22] until we stopped right in front of the maternity ward. "This is where you're going to work," he said, ushering me through the brown double doors.

22. F. NO CHANGE
    G. expert, himself in every facet of hospital administration,
    H. expert, himself, in every facet of hospital administration
    J. expert himself in every facet of hospital administration

GO ON TO THE NEXT PAGE.

Walking into the ward, my ears were immediately overwhelmed. Women yelled and newborns wailed. Nurses rushed around to adjust medical instruments that screamed for attention. I felt suspicious in the center of so much action and wondered if I had been too hasty in seeking out such a difficult service project.

[4]

Apparently my fear must have shown clearly on my face as I looked around because the director said, "Don't worry. You'll get used to the pace up here. You are going to help in the nursery." With that, we walked down the busy hallway past the numerous delivery rooms and into the most peaceful room I've ever seen. The pastel colors provided a quiet backdrop to the humming of machines and soft coos of sleeping infants. A whispering nurse, the one in charge of the nursery, welcomed me, thanked me for volunteering, and asked me to start folding some baby blankets and placing it in the appropriate drawer. The director gave me a questioning look, which I returned with a quiet nod. [29] I got right to work.

23. A. NO CHANGE
B. my ears immediately felt overwhelmed, women
C. I was overwhelmed by the sounds. Women
D. hearing and overwhelmed. Women

24. Which choice would be most consistent with the figurative description provided elsewhere in this paragraph?
F. NO CHANGE
G. beseiged
H. weak
J. defenseless

25. Which of the following alternatives to the underlined portion would be LEAST acceptable?
A. face while
B. face when
C. face at the same time that
D. face since

26. Given that all the choices are true, which one provides the most vivid description of the hospital hallway?
F. NO CHANGE
G. down a hallway filled with bright blue and pink balloons, beautiful flowers, and jubilant fathers
H. past a nurses' station and a handful of expectant fathers
J. under the yellowing ceiling of the dated hospital

27. A. NO CHANGE
B. nurse the one in charge of the nursery,
C. nurse the one in charge of the nursery
D. nurse, the one in charge of the nursery

28. F. NO CHANGE
G. place them
H. placed them
J. placing these

29. If the writer were to delete the phrase "which I returned with a quiet nod" from the preceding sentence and end the sentence with a period, the sentence would primarily lose:
A. a detail that expresses the narrator's ease while in the nursery.
B. a specific description of the narrator's anger towards the director.
C. information that indicates the narrator will quit the hospital as soon as the director leaves.
D. nothing at all, because this information had already been provided earlier in the passage.

GO ON TO THE NEXT PAGE.

Question 30 asks about the preceding passage as a whole.

30. Upon reviewing the essay and realizing that some key information has been left out, the writer composes the following sentence incorporating that information:

> Soon enough, I showed up for my first day at the hospital.

This sentence would most logically be placed before the first sentence in Paragraph:

F. 1.
G. 2.
H. 3.
J. 4.

PASSAGE III

Give a Snake a Break

Throughout much of history, snakes have had <u>a reputation for being more deadly then</u> [31] they actually are. Negative associations abound: a "snake in the grass" is a seemingly innocent person intent on causing harm. [32] A "snake charmer" uses flattery to distract you from his shady intent. Nearly every <u>reference to a snake that is popular in modern society</u> [33] bears this negative connotation. Despite this perception, the snake, <u>with its</u> [34] ugly, slimy appearance, is one of the most unjustly maligned creatures on the planet.

31. **A.** NO CHANGE
B. a reputation for being more deadly than
C. a reputation as the most deadly than
D. the deadliest reputation then

32. Given that all the following statements are true, which one provides the most relevant information at this point in the essay?
F. "Snake oil" refers to fake medicine that promises impossible results.
G. Most snakes are passive creatures that will never cause you injury.
H. Snakes are carnivorous reptiles that can be found on every continent except Antarctica.
J. Pet snakes have becomes increasingly common over the last decade.

33. **A.** NO CHANGE
B. reference that is popular about a snake
C. famous reference they have about a snake
D. popular reference to a snake

34. **F.** NO CHANGE
G. who's
H. sporting it's
J. with its'

GO ON TO THE NEXT PAGE.

Snakes are only rarely dangerous to humans. Their fangs, so [35] intimidating when the snakes are hissing, are designed not to attack people but to hold small prey; small rodents, birds, [36] insects, etc. Only exceptionally large snakes, like pythons or anacondas, pose a real threat. Most of the time, the typical snake you encounter in your backyard is more afraid of you than you are of it and will gladly avoid any contact with you.

Poisonous snakes—such as rattlesnakes, vipers, and cobras—are most frightening to people, but they attack if they are only provoked. [37] While certainly venomous, these snakes pose a threat mainly to smaller animals. Of the 5 million snake bites that occur each year to humans around the world, only about 2.5 percent prove fatal. [38] Prompt treatment with one of the available antivenoms do much [39] to ensure the victim's survival. Although you may get an infection at the wound site, you can be effectively treated, seeing as [40] you are still shaken from the encounter, you will survive.

Why put up with snakes at all? Even if they don't normally kill humans, most people still considering them a nuisance and avoiding [41] them like the plague. Individuals who dislike snakes for this reason do not appreciate the great service snakes do for humanity. The typical diet of a snake includes small rodents like rats, mice, gophers, and prairie dogs, as well as lizards, birds, fish, and insects. We may not like snakes, if they [42] were mysteriously wiped out of existence, however, we would be

35. **A.** NO CHANGE
B. fangs being
C. fangs, so they are
D. fangs, they are

36. **F.** NO CHANGE
G. prey,
H. prey:
J. prey

37. **A.** NO CHANGE
B. they will provoke and attack them.
C. they will attack humans only if provoked.
D. if provoked, they will attack them.

38. The writer is considering deleting the preceding sentence from this paragraph. If the writer made this deletion, the paragraph would primarily lose:

F. scientific proof that snakes are too dangerous to coexist with humans.
G. an example of the various locations where most fatalities take place.
H. a specific statistic to support a previous claim.
J. excessive detail that distracts the reader from the broader message of the passage.

39. **A.** NO CHANGE
B. can do much
C. are able to do much
D. have much ability

40. **F.** NO CHANGE
G. but because
H. and even if
J. however

41. **A.** NO CHANGE
B. consider them a nuisance and avoid
C. considering them a nuisance and avoid
D. considered them a nuisance to avoid

42. **F.** NO CHANGE
G. snake's if they
H. snakes, they
J. snakes; if they

GO ON TO THE NEXT PAGE.

virtually overrun with other vermin that would spread disease and filth.

So, next time you hear about someone putting down snakes, stand up for our legless friends. <u>These snakes in the grass help us more than we might think.</u> 43

43. The writer wants to provide a sentence here that will tie the conclusion of the essay to its beginning. Which choice does that best?

A. NO CHANGE
B. Snakes make excellent pets.
C. Let's reduce the incidence of snake bites around the world.
D. Wouldn't you rather see a snake in your yard than a rat?

Questions 44 and 45 ask about the preceding passage as a whole.

44. The writer is considering deleting the last sentence of the first paragraph of the essay. If the writer were to make this deletion, the essay would primarily lose a statement that:

F. adds a bit of sarcasm to a rather humorous introduction.
G. identifies the overall point of the entire passage.
H. summarizes the list of examples previously provided by the author.
J. provides a list of animals more useful than the snake.

45. Suppose the writer's goal had been to write an essay focusing on the various ways in which humans were threatened by snakes. Would this essay fulfill that goal?

A. Yes, because the author gives specific statistical evidence that proves snake bites happen around the world.
B. Yes, because the essay focuses on many of the negative stereotypes associated with snakes.
C. No, because the essay primarily focuses on the fact that snakes are not harmful to humans.
D. No, because the essay points out that snakes feed primarily on rodents and other small animals.

PASSAGE IV

Zora Neale Hurston, Independent Woman

Zora Neale Hurston proves to be a study in contrasts: a black writer reaching a white audience, a woman struggling in a man's profession, an independent thinker living in a conformist era. <u>Now,</u> 46 almost 50 years since her death, her hard work and fabulous novels still have much to teach the modern audience.

46. Which of the following alternatives to the underlined portion would be LEAST acceptable?

F. Presently,
G. Currently,
H. Instantly,
J. At the present,

She overcame the challenges she <u>faced and</u> 47 demonstrated that perseverance makes anything possible.

47. Which of the following alternatives to the underlined portion would be LEAST acceptable?

A. faced, and in so doing,
B. faced and, thus,
C. faced that
D. faced, an action that

GO ON TO THE NEXT PAGE.

Hurston ascribed much of her deeply individualistic personality to the experience of growing up in Eatonville, Florida. The town was unique in that it was particularly hot in the summer, but mild at other times of the year. Hurston always said growing up in a community totally separate from the larger white society allowed her a freedom that independence not available to everyone in the south.

[1] Hurston began her undergraduate studies at Howard University, but her obvious intelligence and talent soon earned her a scholarship to Barnard College in New York City. [2] Moving north in the 1920s thrust her into the midst of the Harlem Renaissance, a black cultural movement that spawned exceptional achievements in literature, books, poems, and plays, art, and music. [3] Interacting with the likes of Langston Hughes, W.E.B. DuBois, Billie Holiday, and Duke Ellington, Hurston developed her skills as a writer and published numerous short stories and poems. [55] [4] The most influential work that came to define her career grew out of her attempt to capture the black experience. [5] That novel, called *Their Eyes Were Watching God*, traced three generations of a family living in

48. **F.** NO CHANGE
G. personally individualistic
H. freely independent
J. truly egotistical

49. Given that all the choices are true, which one most effectively identifies why Eatonville has a history unlike any other city in the United States?

A. NO CHANGE
B. a fairly representative small town, founded in the mid-nineteenth century.
C. the first all-black town to be incorporated in the country.
D. not yet in existence at the start of the Civil War.

50. **F.** NO CHANGE
G. and was
H. it featured
J. and

51. **A.** NO CHANGE
B. intelligence, and talent
C. intelligence, and talent,
D. intelligence and talent,

52. **F.** NO CHANGE
G. 1920s, thrust
H. 1920s, thrust,
J. 1920s; thrust

53. **A.** NO CHANGE
B. literature, written records of stories once transmitted orally,
C. literature, which includes all forms of written expression,
D. literature,

54. **F.** NO CHANGE
G. developed up
H. develops up
J. develops

55. At this point, the writer is considering adding the following true statement:

> Billie Holiday's music evokes such feeling and melancholy that it's no wonder she became so popular.

Should the writer add this sentence here?

A. Yes, because it provides an interesting detail about one of the other Harlem Renaissance artists.
B. Yes, because music was an important influence on Hurston's work.
C. No, because it doesn't clearly identify which of Billie Holiday's songs were popular.
D. No, because it distracts the reader from the main point of this paragraph.

GO ON TO THE NEXT PAGE.

Eatonville. [6] Her interesting (56) representation of the southern dialect caused her Harlem Renaissance contemporaries to belittle the work for what they saw as its propagation of inaccurate

56. Which choice would most clearly indicate that the dialect referenced in the passage was a realistic representation of the actual way language was spoken in Eatonville?

F. NO CHANGE
G. unusual
H. authentic
J. fascinating

stereotypes. [7] Hurston, however, remained true to it, (57) convinced that the accuracy of her representation would ultimately prevail over

57. A. NO CHANGE
B. her project,
C. that thing,
D. which,

the political pressures her peers sought to inflict upon her. [58]

58. The writer has decided to divide this paragraph into two. The best place to add the new paragraph break would be at the beginning of Sentence:

F. 4, because it would indicate that Hurston's writing was most strongly influenced by Langston Hughes.
G. 4, because it would signal the essay's shift in focus to one of Hurston's novels.
H. 5, because all the remaining sentences in the paragraph provide a detailed summary of the plot of Hurston's novel.
J. 5, because it would indicate that the essay is now going to focus on social conditions in Eatonville.

History has shown that Hurston was right. However, modern (59) critics admire her authentic and skillful representation of the language as well as her realistic portrayal of daily life in the early twentieth century. She is universally applauded, as one of the best writers of her era, (60) ranked with Toni Morrison, Maya Angelou, and Alice Walker as one of the most important African-American writers of all time.

59. A. NO CHANGE
B. Modern
C. Thus, modern
D. In addition, modern

60. F. NO CHANGE
G. applauded as one of the best writers of her era and
H. applauded as one of the best writers of her era
J. applauded, as one of the best writers of her era, she is

PASSAGE V

Jimmy Carter, Humanitarian

[1]

Everyone has heard of Jimmy Carter. As president of the United States from 1977 to 1981. He (61) oversaw a particularly turbulent time in American history. Americans taken hostage in the Middle East, serious inflation woes, major gasoline shortages around the country, and a tenuous relationship with a potential

61. A. NO CHANGE
B. 1981 but he
C. 1981, and he
D. 1981, he

GO ON TO THE NEXT PAGE.

enemy—the Soviet Union—are hardly the stuff of pleasant memories. [62]

[2]

Yet even though Carter held Americas most, powerful office, [63] he will probably be remembered more for the work he [64] has done since he left the White House. His record on humanitarian issues around the world sets him apart as a caring, dedicated person who wants to see the underprivileged, those of low economic or social status, [65] benefit from the great wealth, power, and generosity of this country.

[3]

One of the major issues Carter has focused on throughout his career is peace in the Middle East. He questioned [66] a national energy policy designed to reduce American dependence long before it was popular to do so on foreign oil, [67] and brokered a peace treaty between Israel and Egypt. Likewise, he was among the first to insist publicly on basic human rights for everyone around the world, founding [68] a non-profit organization, The Carter Center, to work towards that end. In his opinion, this includes extending modern health care to developing nations in order to contain disease and improve quality of life around the world, in many different countries. [69]

62. F. NO CHANGE
G. enemy the Soviet Union—
H. enemy the Soviet Union
J. enemy—the Soviet Union

63. A. NO CHANGE
B. held America's most,
C. held America's most
D. held Americas, most

64. F. NO CHANGE
G. himself
H. him
J. itself

65. A. NO CHANGE
B. underprivileged, who may not have many resources,
C. underprivileged
D. underprivileged, who have less than others in society,

66. F. NO CHANGE
G. promoted
H. purchased
J. rejected

67. The best placement for the underlined portion would be:
A. where it is now.
B. after the word *designed*.
C. after the word *dependence*.
D. after the word *was*.

68. Which of the following alternatives to the underlined portion would NOT be acceptable?
F. world, and he found
G. world, and he founded
H. world, so he founded
J. world and founded

69. A. NO CHANGE
B. world.
C. world, both east and west of the United States.
D. world, including countries on every continent except Antarctica.

GO ON TO THE NEXT PAGE.

[4]

[1] Carter works actively to improve the standard of living <u>at home here in the United States</u> [70] as well. [2] He and his wife Roslyn are enthusiastic supporters of Habitat for Humanity. [3] This volunteer-based organization devotes itself to building affordable but quality housing for those who otherwise might not be able to buy a home. [4] However, Carter does not <u>focus abroad all his efforts.</u> [71] [5] Community workers come together on their own free time to construct, paint, and landscape simple homes, working side-by-side with the families that will occupy the residences. [72]

[5]

For all these reasons, Carter deserves respect for dedicating his career to public service. Everyone can <u>agree for</u> [73] his impressive philanthropy and acknowledge <u>his obvious devotion to all of humanity.</u> [74]

70. **F.** NO CHANGE
G. at home, not just abroad,
H. at home, within the area over which he was president,
J. at home,

71. **A.** NO CHANGE
B. focus all his efforts abroad.
C. focus all abroad his efforts.
D. focus all his abroad efforts.

72. For the sake of the logic and coherence of this paragraph, Sentence 4 should be placed:
F. where it is now.
G. before Sentence 1.
H. after Sentence 2.
J. after Sentence 5.

73. **A.** NO CHANGE
B. agree to
C. agree by
D. agree with

74. Which choice would best help this sentence to summarize key points made in the essay?
F. NO CHANGE
G. he should have been president for a second term.
H. he has the right to express his opinions as much as any other American.
J. he clearly didn't want the hostages to be harmed.

Question 75 asks about the preceding passage as a whole.

75. Upon reviewing notes for this essay, the writer comes across the following true statement:

> Habitat does more than build houses: it builds communities.

If the writer were to use this sentence, the most logical place to add it would be at the end of Paragraph:
A. 1
B. 2
C. 3
D. 4

END OF TEST 1

STOP! DO NOT TURN THE PAGE UNTIL TOLD TO DO SO.

MATHEMATICS TEST

60 Minutes—60 Questions

DIRECTIONS: Solve each problem, choose the correct answer, and then darken the corresponding oval on your answer sheet.

Do not linger over problems that take too much time. Solve as many as you can; then return to the others in the time you have left for this test.

You are permitted to use a calculator on this test. You may use your calculator for any problems you choose, but some of the problems may best be done without using a calculator.

Note: Unless otherwise stated, all of the following should be assumed:

1. Illustrative figures are NOT necessarily drawn to scale.
2. Geometric figures lie in a plane.
3. The word *line* indicates a straight line.
4. The word *average* indicates arithmetic mean.

DO YOUR FIGURING HERE.

1. On a level field, a telephone pole 24 feet tall casts a shadow 6 feet long, and at the same time of day, another nearby telephone pole casts a shadow 18 feet long. How many feet tall is the second telephone pole?

A. 6
B. 12
C. 24
D. 36
E. 72

2. The membership fees for WebFilms consist of a monthly charge of $14 and a one-time new-member fee of $16. Sherwood made a credit card payment of $100 to pay his WebFilms fees for a certain number of months, including the new-member fee. How many months of membership did Sherwood include in his credit card payment?

F. 4
G. 6
H. 7
J. 12
K. 14

3. If $y = -6$, what is the value of $\frac{y^2 - 4}{y - 2}$?

A. –8
B. –4
C. 4
D. 9
E. 28

GO ON TO THE NEXT PAGE.

4. A school offered its students an optional field trip. If 15 or fewer students went on the field trip, the charge for each student would be $11.50. If more than 15 students chose to go on the field trip, the charge for each student would be $10.25. 18 students opted to go on the tour, but each pre-paid $11.50. The students agreed to put the extra amount toward dinner on the trip. How much total money will be put toward dinner on the trip?

   F. $12.50
   G. $14.75
   H. $21.75
   J. $22.50
   K. $33.00

5. A 16-piece orchestra wants to choose one of its members to speak at performances. They decide that this member CANNOT be one of the 4 soloists in the group. What is the probability that Itzhak, who is NOT a soloist, will be chosen as the speaker?

   A. 0
   B. $\frac{1}{16}$
   C. $\frac{1}{12}$
   D. $\frac{1}{4}$
   E. $\frac{1}{3}$

6. What is the perimeter, in feet, of a rectangle with width 8 feet and length 17 feet?

   F. 25
   G. 34
   H. 50
   J. 136
   K. 272

7. Passes to the Renaissance Faire cost $9 when purchased online and $12 when purchased in person. The group sponsoring the fair would like to make at least $4,000 from sales of passes. If 240 passes were sold online, what is the minimum number of tickets that must be sold in person in order for the group to meet its goal?

   A. 153
   B. 154
   C. 290
   D. 334
   E. 445

DO YOUR FIGURING HERE.

GO ON TO THE NEXT PAGE.

DO YOUR FIGURING HERE.

8. For what value of q is the equation $\frac{9}{q} = \frac{6}{10}$ true?

F. 3
G. 5
H. 13
J. 15
K. 19

9. If $-9(y - 13) = 16$, then $y = ?$

A. $-\frac{133}{9}$

B. $-\frac{29}{9}$

C. $-\frac{16}{9}$

D. $-\frac{1}{3}$

E. $\frac{101}{9}$

10. In the figure below, F, G, H, and J are collinear. $\overline{FG}$, $\overline{GK}$, and $\overline{HK}$ are line segments of equivalent length, and the measure of $\angle JHK$ is 120°. What is the degree measure of $\angle GFK$?

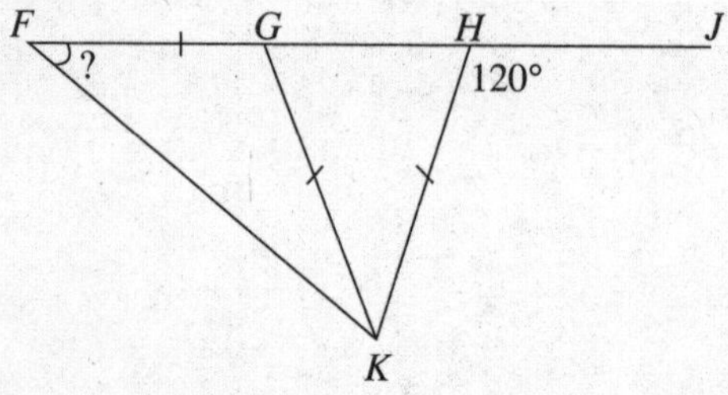

F. 30°
G. 45°
H. 60°
J. 120°
K. 150°

11. If $f(x) = 7x^2 - 9x + 4$, then $f(-3) = ?$

A. –32
B. –2
C. 32
D. 40
E. 94

GO ON TO THE NEXT PAGE.

DO YOUR FIGURING HERE.

12. What is the least common multiple of 25, 16, and 40?

F. 27
G. 32
H. 320
J. 400
K. 16,000

13. While working on a problem on his calculator, Tex had meant to multiply a number by 3, but he accidentally divided the number by 3. Which of the following calculations could Tex then do to the result on the screen in order to obtain the result he originally wanted?

A. Multiply by 3
B. Multiply by 9
C. Divide by 3
D. Divide by 9
E. Add the original number

14. The 8-sided figure below is divided into 12 congruent isosceles right triangles. The total area of the 12 triangles is 96 square centimeters. What is the perimeter, in centimeters, of the figure?

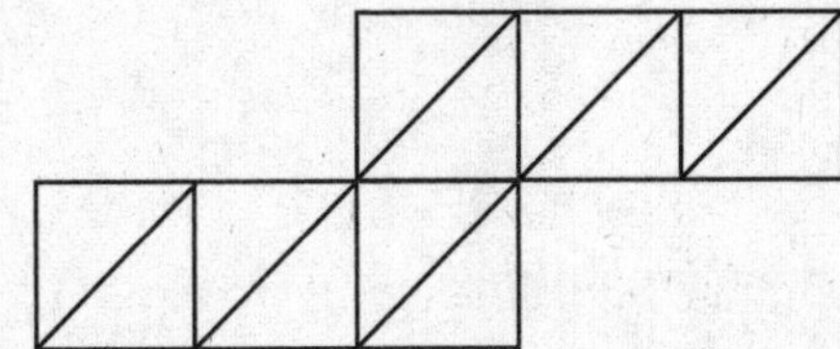

F. 8
G. $20 + 4\sqrt{2}$
H. 48
J. $40 + 8\sqrt{2}$
K. 56

15. In ΔXYZ, $\angle Y$ is a right angle and $\angle Z$ measures less than 52°. Which of the following phrases best describes the measure of $\angle X$?

A. Greater than 38°
B. Equal to 38°
C. Equal to 45°
D. Equal to 142°
E. Less than 38°

GO ON TO THE NEXT PAGE.

16. Among the following arithmetic operations, which could the emoticon ☺ represent given that the equation $(8 ☺ 2)^3 - (4 ☺ 1)^2 = 48$ is true?

DO YOUR FIGURING HERE.

I. Subtraction
II. Multiplication
III. Division

F. I only
G. III only
H. II and III only
J. I and III only
K. I, II, and III

17. Which of the following equations represents the linear relation shown in the standard (x,y) coordinate plane below?

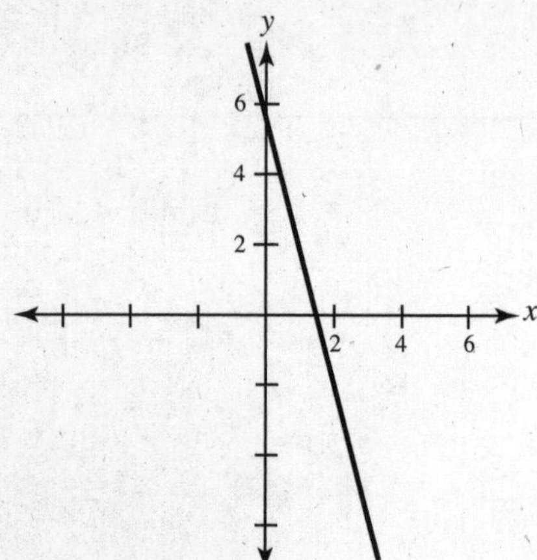

A. $y = -5x$
B. $y = -6x$
C. $y = -2x + 2$
D. $y = -5x + 6$
E. $y = -2x + 6$

18. An integer, x, is subtracted from 6. That difference is then multiplied by 3. This product is 15 more than half the original integer. Which of the following equations represents this relationship?

F. $3(6 - x) = \frac{x}{2} + 15$

G. $3(6 - x) + 15 = \frac{x}{2}$

H. $3(6 - x) = 15 - \frac{x}{2}$

J. $x - 6 \times 3 = \frac{15}{2}$

K. $6 + 3 = \frac{x}{2} + 15$

GO ON TO THE NEXT PAGE.

DO YOUR FIGURING HERE.

19. The employees of two factories, X and Y, are comparing their respective production records. Factory X has already produced 18,000 units and can produce 120 units per day. Factory Y has produced only 14,500 units but can produce 155 units per day. If d represents the number of days (that is, days during which each factory is producing its maximum number of units), which of the following equations could be solved to determine the number of days until X's total production equals Y's total production?

A. $18{,}000 + 120d = 14{,}500 + 155d$
B. $18{,}000 + 155d = 14{,}500 + 120d$
C. $(18{,}000 + 120)d = (14{,}500 + 155)d$
D. $(120 + 155)d = 18{,}000 - 14{,}500$
E. $(120 + 155)d = 18{,}000 + 14{,}500$

20. A ramp used to access the side entrance to the DPC Candy Store, which is located 7 meters above the ground, covers 24 meters along the level ground from the edge of the building. How many meters long is the ramp?

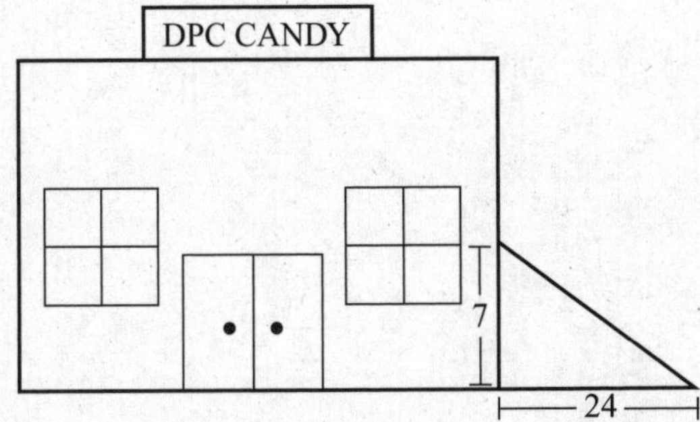

F. 13
G. 14
H. 17
J. 23
K. 25

21. The expression $9(y + 3) - 2(4y - 4)$ is equivalent to:

A. $y - 1$
B. $y + 15$
C. $y + 18$
D. $y + 23$
E. $y + 35$

22. If $a + 3b = 27$ and $a - 3b = 9$, then $b = ?$

F. 3
G. 9
H. 14
J. 18
K. 36

GO ON TO THE NEXT PAGE.

DO YOUR FIGURING HERE.

23. When $(2x + 4)^2$ is written in the format $ax^2 + bx + c$, where a, b, and c are integers, what is the value of $a + b - c$?

A. –20
B. 4
C. 20
D. 32
E. 36

24. What is the area, in square meters, of the figure below?

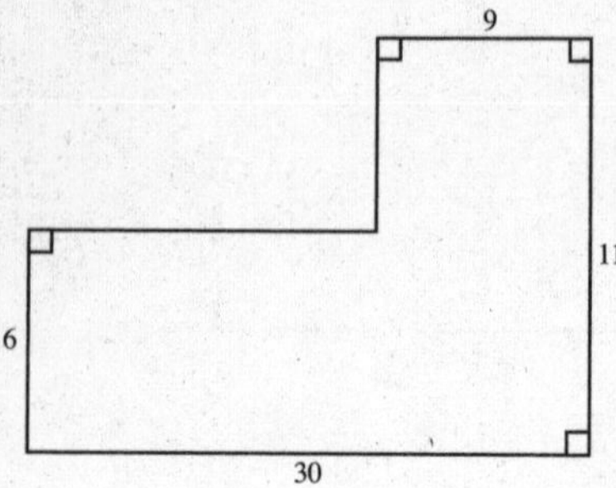

F. 336
G. 330
H. 225
J. 82
K. 56

25. The table below gives the values of two functions, g and h, for various values of x. One of the functions expresses a relationship that can be expressed by the formula $a + bx$, where a and b are real number coefficients. What is the value of that function for $x = 0$?

x	$g(x)$	$h(x)$
–3	4	
–2	2	3
–1	1	6
0		
1	1	
2		15
3		18

A. 0
B. 0.5
C. 1
D. 2
E. 9

GO ON TO THE NEXT PAGE.

26. What is the slope of the line represented by the equation $10y - 16x = 13$?

DO YOUR FIGURING HERE.

F. -16
G. $\frac{13}{10}$
H. $\frac{8}{5}$
J. 10
K. 16

27. What is the sum of the 2 solutions of the equation $x^2 + 5x - 24 = 0$?

A. -24
B. -8
C. -5
D. 0
E. 5

28. Two similar triangles have perimeters in the ratio 5:6. The sides of the larger triangle measure 12 in, 7 in, and 5 in. What is the perimeter, in inches, of the smaller triangle?

F. 18
G. 20
H. 22
J. 24
K. 32

29. In early November in Winnipeg, Manitoba, the temperatures for each of nine consecutive days were –9°C, 3°C, –7°C, 2°C, 5°C, 1°C, 0°C, –8°C, –7°C. What was the median of the temperatures in these nine days in early November?

A. –7°C
B. 0°C
C. 1.5°C
D. 3°C
E. 5°C

30. When asked the price, in dollars, of his fancy calculator, Albert responded, "If you take the square root of the price, then add $\frac{3}{8}$ the price, the result is 66." What is the price, in dollars, of Albert's calculator?

F. 169
G. 144
H. 121
J. 13
K. 12

GO ON TO THE NEXT PAGE.

31. The kinetic energy, KE, of an object travelling at v velocity can be modeled by the equation $KE = \frac{1}{2}mv^2$, where m is the mass of the object. If an object is moving at a velocity of 9, and it has a kinetic energy of 120, about how great is the object's mass?

A. Between 0 and 1
B. Between 1 and 2
C. Between 2 and 3
D. 6
E. 13

DO YOUR FIGURING HERE.

32. Let x, y, and z be distinct positive integers. What is the fourth term of the geometric sequence below?

$$2xz, 2x^2yz, 2x^3y^2z, \ldots$$

F. $2x^2yz$
G. $2x^4y^3z$
H. $2x^3yz^2$
J. $4x^3y^2z$
K. $4x^4y^3z^2$

GO ON TO THE NEXT PAGE.

DO YOUR FIGURING HERE.

Use the following information to answer questions 33–35.

A recent survey of book critics asked 30 critics how many stars out of a possible 5 they gave to a recent novel from a popular author. The 30 critics' responses are summarized by the histogram below.

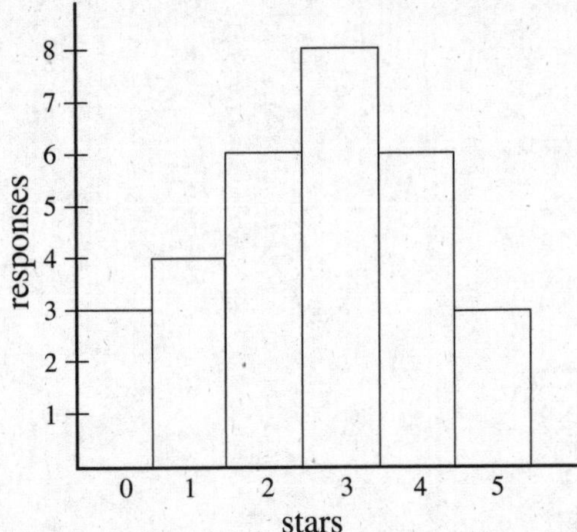

33. What fraction of the critics gave the book a one-star review?

A. $\frac{1}{2}$

B. $\frac{3}{8}$

C. $\frac{17}{50}$

D. $\frac{3}{10}$

E. $\frac{2}{15}$

34. The group that took the survey wants to show the data in a circle graph (pie chart). What should be the measure of the central angle of the portion for one-star reviews?

F. 15°
G. 24°
H. 30°
J. 48°
K. 60°

GO ON TO THE NEXT PAGE.

35. To the nearest hundredth, what is the average star review for the 30 reviews?

A. 2.00
B. 2.33
C. 2.50
D. 2.63
E. 3.00

DO YOUR FIGURING HERE.

---

36. For all $x > 8$, $\dfrac{(x^2 + 7x + 12)(x - 2)}{(x^2 + 2x - 8)(x + 3)} = ?$

F. $\dfrac{-3(x-2)}{(x+3)}$

G. $\dfrac{-2(x-2)}{(x+3)}$

H. $\dfrac{(x-2)}{(x+2)}$

J. $\dfrac{11}{4}$

K. 1

37. A rock band, The Young Sohcahtoans, is trying to design a t-shirt logo. The measurements they have chosen are represented on the figure below. The angle to the right of the logo "TYS" has a degree measure of 35°, and the side of the figure has a measure of 10 in. Which of the following expressions gives the measure, in inches, of the diagonal top side of the figure?

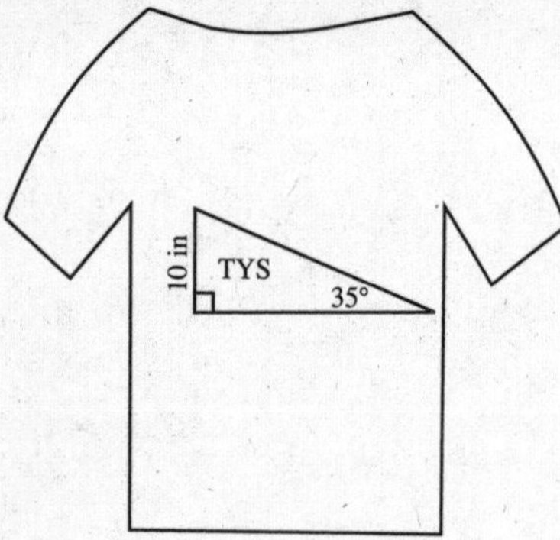

A. 10tan35°

B. 10cos35°

C. 10sin35°

D. $\dfrac{10}{\sin 35°}$

E. $\dfrac{10}{\cos 35°}$

GO ON TO THE NEXT PAGE.

DO YOUR FIGURING HERE.

38. The endpoints of the diameter of a circle O are A and C. In the standard (x,y) coordinate plane, A is at (4,3) and C is at (–9,–2). What is the y-coordinate of the center of the circle?

F. –5

G. $\frac{-5}{2}$

H. $\frac{1}{2}$

J. 1

K. 2

39. On a sonar map in the standard (x,y) coordinate plane, the Yellow Submarine and the Sandwich Submarine are located at the points (–7,4) and (–2,6), respectively. Each unit on the map represents an actual distance of 5 nautical miles. Which of the following is closest to the distance, in nautical miles, between the two submarines?

A. 5
B. 19
C. 27
D. 30
E. 67

40. All of the following statements about rational and/or irrational numbers must be true EXCEPT:

F. the sum of any two rational numbers is rational.
G. the product of any two rational numbers is rational.
H. the sum of any two irrational numbers is irrational.
J. the product of a rational and an irrational number may be rational or irrational.
K. the product of any two irrational numbers is irrational.

41. For the imaginary number i, which of the following is a possible value of i^n if n is an integer less than 5 ?

A. 0
B. –1
C. –2
D. –3
E. –4

GO ON TO THE NEXT PAGE.

42. The table below gives the values of $f(x)$ for selected values of x in the function $f(x) = (x + 4)^2 - 1$, where x and y are both real numbers.

DO YOUR FIGURING HERE.

x	$f(x)$
–7	8
–5	0
–3	0
–1	8
0	15
1	24

For the equation above, which of the following values of x gives the greatest value of $f(x)$?

F. –4
G. –5
H. –6
J. –7
K. –8

43. The volume of the right circular cylinder shown below is 64π cubic inches. If its height is 4 in, what is its radius in inches?

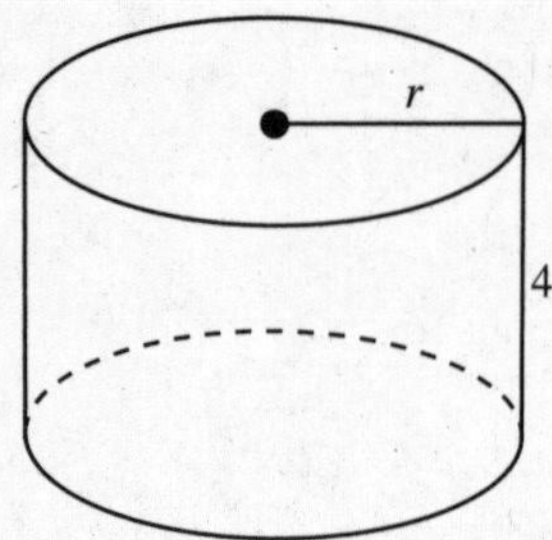

A. 2
B. 4
C. 8
D. 10
E. 16

GO ON TO THE NEXT PAGE.

DO YOUR FIGURING HERE.

44. Line segments $\overline{GH}$, $\overline{JK}$, and $\overline{LM}$ are parallel and intersect line segments $\overline{FL}$ and $\overline{FM}$ as shown in the figure below. The ratio of the perimeter of ΔFJK to the perimeter of ΔFLM is 3:5, and the ratio of $\overline{FH}$ to $\overline{FM}$ is 1:5. What is the ratio of $\overline{GJ}$ to $\overline{FG}$?

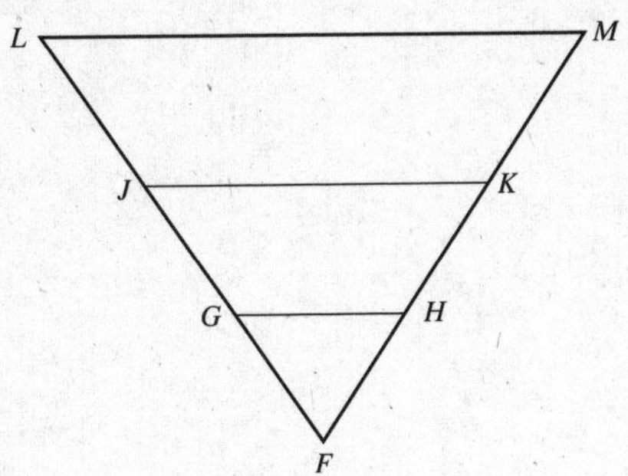

F. 1:5
G. 1:3
H. 1:2
J. 2:1
K. 5:3

45. Avi is trying to draw a map of his most recent bike ride. He chose to place Market Street on the x-axis and Broad Street on the y-axis. He rode 60 m at an angle of 60° relative to Market Street, then rode 100 m at an angle of 45° relative to Market Street, and finally rode 35 m directly north on Broad Street. How many meters north of Market Street did Avi ride?

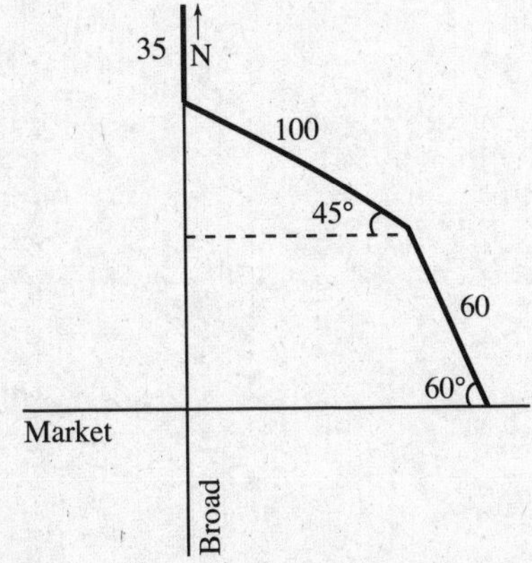

A. 35

B. 115

C. 195

D. $50\sqrt{2} + 30\sqrt{3}$

E. $35 + 50\sqrt{2} + 30\sqrt{3}$

GO ON TO THE NEXT PAGE.

DO YOUR FIGURING HERE.

46. In the standard (x,y) coordinate plane, what is the area of the circle $(x - 3)^2 + (y + 2)^2 = 25$?

F. 5π
G. 10π
H. 25π
J. 125π
K. 225π

47. In the standard (x,y) coordinate plane below, the base of a right triangle lies along the x-axis and is bisected by the y-axis. The vertex of the angle opposite the base is on the graph of the parabolic function $f(x) = 2x^2 - 4$. Let b represent any value of x such that $-\sqrt{2} < x < 0$. Which of the following is an expression in terms of b for the area, in square coordinate units, of any such right triangle?

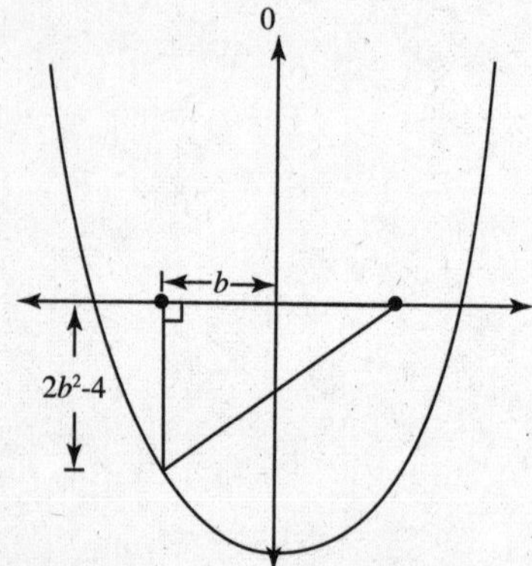

A. $4b^4 - 16b^2 + 16$
B. $4b^3 - 8b$
C. $2b^3 - 4b$
D. $2b^2 + b - 4$
E. $b^2 - 4b + 4$

48. Which of the following expressions must be an even integer if x is an integer?

F. $x + 5$

G. $\frac{x}{4}$

H. x^4

J. $4x$

K. 5^x

GO ON TO THE NEXT PAGE.

DO YOUR FIGURING HERE.

49. Which of the following ranges of consecutive integers contains the value of the expression $\log_9(9^{\frac{7}{3}})$?

A. 0 and 1
B. 1 and 2
C. 2 and 3
D. 5 and 6
E. 7 and 8

Use the following information to answer questions 50–52.

The employees at Belinda's Paint Store are having a competition to see who can create the most new accounts over a period from January to June in a certain year. Data is missing because one of the employees began to erase it from the white board, thinking that the competition was over. The numbers in the chart below have been confirmed with the assistant manager's personal records.

	Month					
Employee	Jan.	Feb.	Mar.	Apr.	May	June
Don	64					
Maura	31	25		27	29	24
Cameron	23	19	22	17	20	22
Belinda	78	92	83	86		90

50. Which of the following is closest to the percent decrease in Cameron's new accounts from January to February?

F. 4.0%
G. 17.4%
H. 19.4%
J. 20.0%
K. 21.1%

51. At the beginning of the year, Maura wanted to average 30 new accounts per month for the first four months of the year. How many new accounts did she need to create in March in order to reach this goal?

A. 25
B. 27
C. 29
D. 31
E. 37

GO ON TO THE NEXT PAGE.

52. Additional records are uncovered that show that Don's sales decreased 5% each month from January to May because his responsibilities in the store mounted and he could not seek out new accounts as frequently. Which of the following is closest to the number of new accounts Don created in May?

DO YOUR FIGURING HERE.

F. 44
G. 52
H. 56
J. 72
K. 84

---

53. The amplitude of the trigonometric function shown below is defined as the average of the absolute values of the maximum value of $f(x)$ and the minimum value of $f(x)$. The trigonometric function graphed below can be described by the equation $f(x) = a\sin(bx + c)$, where a, b, and c are real numbers. Which of the following values describes the amplitude of this function?

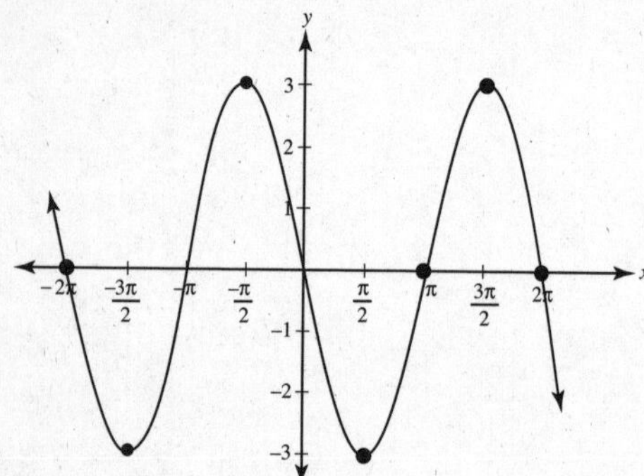

A. 1
B. 2
C. 3
D. π
E. 2π

GO ON TO THE NEXT PAGE.

DO YOUR FIGURING HERE.

54. A group of die-hard baseball fans has purchased a house that gives them a direct view of home plate, although their view of the rest of the field is largely impeded by the outfield wall. The house is 30 meters tall, and their angle of vision from the top of the building to home plate has a tangent of $\frac{7}{6}$. What is the horizontal distance, in meters, from home plate to the fans' house?

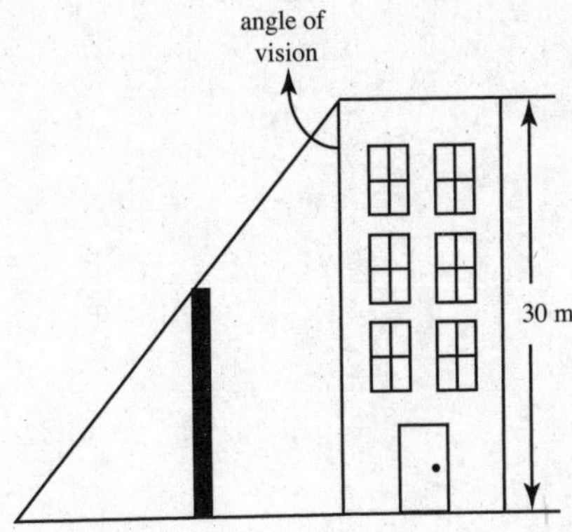

F. 35.0
G. 32.0
H. 25.7
J. 5.0
K. 4.3

55. Given the equation $|y^2 - 11| - 2 = 0$, which of the following is a solution but NOT a rational number?

A. $11\sqrt{13}$
B. $4\sqrt{13}$
C. $2\sqrt{13}$
D. $\sqrt{13}$
E. 3

GO ON TO THE NEXT PAGE.

56. Below is the graph that a specialty automobile manufacturer uses to plot the speed tests done on his new cars. The speed is recorded in units of $\frac{m}{s}$ and is conducted for a period of 9 seconds. A certain order of 3 of the following 6 actions describes the results of the speed test depicted in the graph below. Which order is it?

DO YOUR FIGURING HERE.

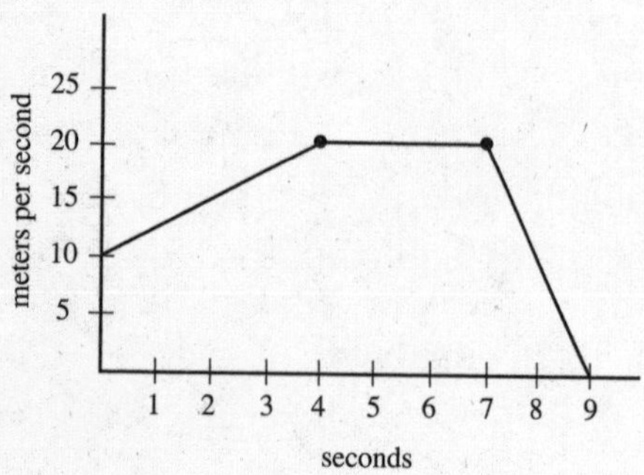

I. Constant speed for 1 second
II. Constant speed for 3 seconds
III. Speed increase for 4 seconds
IV. Speed increase for 9 seconds
V. Speed decrease for 2 seconds
VI. Speed decrease for 7 seconds

F. IV, II, VI
G. III, II, V
H. I, III, V
J. III, I, VI
K. V, I, II

57. As shown in the figure below, a compass has marks for every 10° and "North" and "South" are the endpoints of a line segment. If the point of the needle of this compass travels 42 mm as it moves in a clockwise direction from "East" to "North," how long is the needle to the nearest tenth of a millimeter?

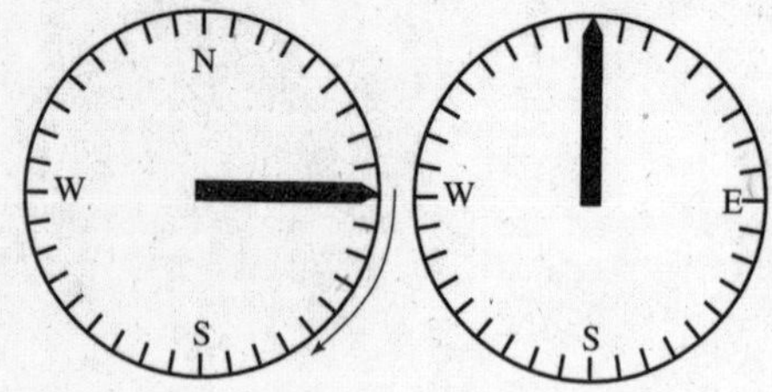

A. 6.7
B. 8.9
C. 13.4
D. 14.0
E. 17.8

GO ON TO THE NEXT PAGE.

DO YOUR FIGURING HERE.

58. For θ, an angle whose measure is between 270° and 360°, $\cos\theta = \frac{5}{13}$. Which of the following equals $\tan\theta$?

F. $\frac{-5}{12}$

G. $\frac{-5}{13}$

H. $\frac{5}{13}$

J. $\frac{5}{12}$

K. $\frac{12}{13}$

59. Consider all values a and b such that the product $ab = 8$. For how many values does there exist a positive integer c that satisfies both $2^a = c$ and $c^b = 256$?

A. Infinitely many
B. 6
C. 4
D. 2
E. 0

60. A sphere is inscribed in a cube with a diagonal of $3\sqrt{3}$ ft. In feet, what is the diameter of the sphere?

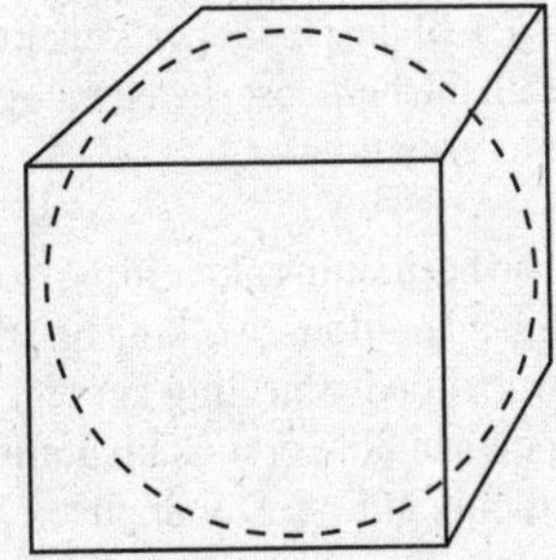

F. $3\sqrt{3}$

G. 2

H. $2\sqrt{2}$

J. 3

K. $3\sqrt{3}$

END OF TEST 2

STOP! DO NOT TURN THE PAGE UNTIL TOLD TO DO SO.

DO NOT RETURN TO A PREVIOUS TEST.

READING TEST

35 Minutes—40 Questions

DIRECTIONS: There are four passages in this test. Each passage is followed by several questions. After reading a passage, choose the best answer to each question and fill in the corresponding oval on your answer document. You may refer to the passages as often as necessary.

Passage I

PROSE FICTION: This passage is adapted from the novel *A Well-Worn Jacket* by Antonia Duke (©2008 by Antonia Duke).

Monique was enjoying this afternoon more than she had anticipated. Often, the tryouts for the spring musical tested the limits of her patience and nerves, with one hopeful girl after the next taking turns strutting onto the tarnished wooden stage, delivering a competent but uninspired version of some Rodgers & Hammerstein number, and then being politely excused by Mrs. Dominguez as the next name on the list was called.

However, this was to be Monique's third straight year in the musical, and the confidence that her seniority afforded her around the more nervous newcomers allowed her to bask in the radiance of her own poise.

She had already sung her audition song an hour ago, commencing the day's ceremonies. This year, Monique used "God Bless the Child," a choice she found to be quite sophisticated since Billie Holiday's version of it was familiar mostly to adults, and even then, mostly to adults of the previous generation. More importantly, it required a reserved performance, which Monique felt showcased her maturity, especially because most of the other auditioners chose songs that would show their enthusiasm, even if it meant their technical mastery would not be on full display.

Normally, the first audition slot was dreaded by most. Mrs. Dominguez would ask if anyone wanted to volunteer to "get it over with," but no one would make a sound. Then, she would call the first name off her list and the room would drop into an uncomfortably solemn silence as the first student walked nervously up to the stage. Monique often imagined during those moments that she was witness to a death-row inmate taking his inexorable march toward a quick curtain.

But not this year. Monique had decided to make a show of her own self-confidence by volunteering to go first. Such a defiantly fearless act, she had figured, would probably instill even more fear into her competition because they would realize that Monique had something they clearly lacked. Mrs. Dominguez had seemed neither surprised nor charmed by Monique's decision to go first. Although she was annoyed by Monique's escalating arrogance, she also acknowledged that Monique was one of the more talented actors and was probably correct in assuming herself a shoo-in.

At this late stage of the afternoon, Monique felt like a monarch, sitting in the back of the auditorium with her royal court of friends and admirers. They took care to sit far enough away from Mrs. Dominguez that they would not be caught in the act of belittling the other students' auditions.

To Monique, the endless parade of aspirants who sang their hearts out for three minutes each were like jesters performing for her amusement. As Mrs. Dominguez read Esperanza Solito's name off her list, Monique and her entourage prepared themselves for a special treat.

Esperanza was one of the most awkward students at Thornton High. Her caramel-colored face was usually hidden behind thick tortoise shell glasses. Her wavy black hair exploded off her scalp like a snapshot of an atom bomb. She wore clothing that looked like it had spent years in a musty attic. Understanding her debased position on the social totem pole, Esperanza scurried through the high school's hallways with her eyes looking narrowly at the back of the person walking in front of her, trying to disappear within the herd lest she be recognized by any malicious onlookers as easy prey.

Esperanza had been sitting alone in the front row, paying little attention to the other auditions, working on geometry homework until her name was called. Shuffling her feet towards the center of the stage, Esperanza did not look up until she was there, and even then looked only at Mrs. Dominguez.

"Whenever you're ready," Mrs. Dominguez said politely, sensing the potential for this audition to devolve into a painful target of ridicule.

As Esperanza began the opening notes to "The Star Spangled Banner," Monique and her friends looked at each other in total disbelief. Clearly, they thought, Esperanza had no theater pedigree, or she would never stoop to singing such a trite, formulaic song. Standing perfectly still, Esperanza moved methodically through the tune with little flair or emotion. However, the

GO ON TO THE NEXT PAGE.

expectant smiles of mockery were quickly vanishing from the faces of all who listened.

Anticipating a tentative, mousy voice that would befit such a quirky presence as Esperanza's, the audience instead heard an unusually smooth, rich tone with full command of the multiple registers that the national anthem's melody requires. At the climactic "rocket's red glare," Esperanza's voice filled the room with a calm resonance that forced one's heart to lift within one's chest as though some reluctant patriotism was determined to find its way out. The final phrase of the song, so often soaked in vibrato by melodramatic singers, was gently performed, with a touch that felt like a mother tucking in her baby to sleep.

Although Monique was loath to admit it and Esperanza was reluctant to want it, Esperanza had just set herself apart from the herd.

1. It can reasonably be inferred from the passage that Monique believed the song she chose for her audition:

A. would be the most inspiring Rodgers & Hammerstein numbers she could choose.
B. was the most sophisticated song in Billie Holiday's repertoire.
C. would likely be more recognizable to Monique's parents than to her friends.
D. would allow Monique to more effectively showcase her enthusiasm.

2. The passage initially portrays Monique and her friends as:

F. concerned and nervous.
G. confused and surprised.
H. friendly and inclusive.
J. aloof and disparaging.

3. According to the narrator, what did Esperanza do prior to singing "The Star Spangled Banner"?

A. Looked only at Mrs. Dominguez
B. Walked confidently up to the stage
C. Watched the other auditions carefully
D. Finished her geometry homework

4. The main purpose of the statement in line 29 is to:

F. inform the reader that students' fears of going first were largely a thing of the past.
G. present reasons for why this year's audition was the strangest yet.
H. suggest that Monique's imagination no longer involved the same imagery.
J. offer a contrast created by Monique's choice of audition slot.

5. It can be reasonably inferred from the passage that Esperanza Solito:

A. was teased more than anyone else at her school.
B. was not sitting near Monique and her friends during the auditions.
C. had her audition immediately after Monique's audition.
D. had previously explained her stage fright to Mrs. Dominguez.

6. According to the passage, Monique figured that volunteering to perform "God Bless the Child" as the first audition of the day would:

F. bolster her confidence in her performance.
G. make the other auditioners feel they could not compete with her.
H. guarantee her a part in the play.
J. impress and charm Mrs. Dominguez.

7. According to the passage, when Esperanza Solito got to the climax of "The Star Spangled Banner," she:

A. raised her voice to emphasize the lines.
B. demonstrated her patriotism.
C. had a sudden bout of nerves.
D. could be heard throughout the auditorium.

8. The passage states that Mrs. Dominguez suspected Esperanza's audition could be:

F. vulnerable to ridicule.
G. one of the most awkward.
H. a special treat.
J. neither surprising nor charming.

9. Which of the following details is used in the passage to describe how Monique and her friends responded to hearing Esperanza's audition?

A. Their decision to sit comfortably behind Mrs. Dominguez
B. Their preconceived notions about Esperanza's voice
C. Their fading facial expressions of mockery
D. Their fondness for patriotic songs

10. The passage most strongly suggests that Esperanza's choice of audition material was:

F. good for a mousy voice.
G. often partly sung with vibrato.
H. an impressive, original choice.
J. something Monique's friends had anticipated.

GO ON TO THE NEXT PAGE.

Passage II

SOCIAL SCIENCE: This passage is adapted from the article "Information Stupor-highway" by Cal Jergenson (©2005 by Cal Jergenson).

Think about a remote control. Something so simple in function is seemingly capable of invisible magic to most of us. Only those with an engineering and electronics background probably have any real idea of *why* a remote control works. The rest of us just assume it *should*. And the longer a given technology exists, the more we take it for granted.

Consider for a moment a split screen showing modern remote control users versus the first remote control users: the original users would be cautiously aiming the remote directly at the television, reading the names of the buttons to find the right one, and deliberately pressing the button with a force that adds nothing to the effectiveness of the device. The modern users would be reclined on a sofa, pointing the remote any which way, and instinctively feeling for the button they desired, intuiting its size, shape, and position on the remote.

Humans are known for being handy with tools, so it is no surprise that we get so comfortable with our technology. However, as we become increasingly comfortable with how to *use* new technologies, we become less aware of how they *work*. Most people who use modern technology know nothing of its underlying science. They have spent neither mental nor financial resources on its development. And yet, rather than be humbled by its ingenuity, we consumers often become unfairly demanding of what our technology should do for us.

Many of the landmark inventions of the twentieth century followed predictable trajectories: initial versions of each technology (television, video games, computers, portable phones, etc.) succeeded in wowing the general public. Then, these wondrous novelties quickly became commonplace. Soon, the focus of consumer attitudes towards these inventions changed from awed gratitude to discriminating preference.

Televisions needed to be bigger and have a higher resolution. Video games needed to be more realistic. Computers needed to be more powerful yet smaller in size. Cell phones needed to be smaller yet capable of performing other tasks such as taking pictures, accessing the Internet, and even playing movies.

For children of the last twenty years born into this modern life, these technological marvels seem like elements of the periodic table: a given ingredient that is simply part of the universe. Younger generations don't even try to conceive of life without modern conveniences. They do not appreciate the unprecedented technology that is in their possession; rather, they complain about the ways in which it fails to live up to ideal expectations. "The videos that my phone can record are too pixelated." "My digital video recorder at home doesn't allow me to program it from my computer at work." "It's taking too long for this interactive map to display on my portable GPS." "My robotic vacuum cleaner never manages to get the crumbs out of the cracks between the tiles."

If it sounds as though we're never satisfied, we aren't. Of course, our fussy complaints do actually motivate engineers to continually refine their products. After all, at the root of our tool-making instinct is the notion that "there must be a better way." Thus, the shortcomings of any current version of technology are pinned on the limitations of its designers, and the expectation is that someone, somewhere is working on how to make the existing product even better.

The most dangerous extension of this mindset is its effect on our outlook on solving global climate problems. The firmly substantiated problem of global warming threatens to quickly render the planet Earth inhospitable to most humans.

The solution? If you ask most people, you will hear that the solution resides in creating more efficient versions of our current technologies and devising alternative forms of energy than those that burn fossil fuels.

Blindly confident that the creativity of human problem-solvers can wriggle us out of any dilemma, most people feel guiltless in continuing to live their lives with the assumption that someone else is working on these problems.

Unfortunately, having no real scientific perspective on the problems to be solved or the complexity of global weather patterns, most people are unduly optimistic about humanity's ability to think its way out of this problem. In a culture completely spoiled by the idea that technology can achieve whatever goal it is tasked to perform, the idea that a global climate crisis may be beyond the reach of a clever technological solution is unthinkable.

Hence, the idea that we, as a culture, may need to reexamine our lifestyles and consumer habits is too alien to take seriously. In contemporary society, the leaders who are most able to communicate the state of the world do not dare suggest to the public the unpopular ideas that "times will be rough," "sacrifices must be made," or "we may have to take some steps backwards."

As a result, the human race will continue defiantly with the status quo and, ultimately, blame technology when problems arise. At that point, we'll all be searching for the "rewind" button on the remote control.

GO ON TO THE NEXT PAGE.

11. The passage states that original users of remote controls likely did all of the following EXCEPT:

A. use more strength pressing the button than is necessary.
B. aim the remote directly at the television.
C. feel instinctively for the desired button.
D. read the names of the buttons carefully.

12. In the passage, the author answers all of the following questions EXCEPT:

F. How do most people think the global climate crisis should be solved?
G. What was the most significant invention of the twentieth century?
H. What idea underlies humanity's tool-making instinct?
J. How do consumer attitudes about new technology change?

13. The descriptions offered by the author in the second paragraph (lines 7–15) are used to illustrate the concept that:

A. consumer behavior toward new forms of technology changes over time.
B. modern humans do not pay enough attention to instructions.
C. the first consumers of new technology used new devices with ease and comfort.
D. remote controls have become far more effective over the years.

14. The principal tone of the passage can best be described as:

F. nostalgic.
G. critical.
H. sympathetic.
J. frightened.

15. As it is used in line 78, the word *alien* most nearly means:

A. extraterrestrial.
B. repetitive.
C. unusual.
D. hilarious.

16. The author uses the statement "these technological marvels seem like elements of the periodic table" (lines 38–39) most nearly to mean that:

F. children learn technology while they learn chemistry.
G. consumers regard many technological inventions as unremarkable.
H. space exploration gives us most of our technology.
J. consumers complain when modern conveniences break down.

17. The phrase *the status quo* (lines 84–85) most likely refers to:

A. reexamining the scope and complexity of technology.
B. making sacrifices to combat the global climate crisis.
C. blaming technology for the problems we encounter.
D. our current pattern of lifestyles and consumer habits.

18. One form of consumer behavior the author describes is a discriminating preference for:

F. less realistic video games.
G. needing to understand technology.
H. more powerful computers.
J. wanting to make sacrifices.

19. Among the following quotations from the passage, the one that best summarizes what the author sees as a potential danger is:

A. "the shortcomings of any current version of technology" (line 54).
B. "devising alternative forms of energy" (line 64).
C. "the complexity of global weather patterns" (lines 71–72).
D. "our outlook on solving global climate problems" (line 59).

20. The last paragraph differs from the first paragraph in that in the last paragraph the author:

F. makes a prediction rather than making an observation.
G. refutes a scientific theory.
H. quotes experts to support his opinions.
J. uses the word "we" instead of "I."

GO ON TO THE NEXT PAGE.

Passage III

HUMANITIES: The following passage is adapted from the article "Conquering Jazz" by Patrick Tyrrell (©2006 by Patrick Tyrrell).

From the time I started playing instruments, I have been intrigued and slightly mystified by the world of jazz. I'm not talking about adventurous, atonal, confusing jazz that normal music listeners have a hard time following. I'm talking about the lively, accessible, beautiful jazz that came of age in the swinging 1920s and 1930s: the simultaneously hip and regal symphonic swing of Duke Ellington and Count Basie; the carnival of contrapuntal melodies that inexplicably harmonize with each other in New Orleans' jazz; the buoyant, atmosphere-touching saxophone solos of Charlie Parker and the young John Coltrane.

The one thing I had always heard about jazz but could never accept was that jazz was an improvised form of music. How could this be?

The trademark of beautiful jazz is the complexity of the music. All the instrumentalists are capable of dizzying arrays of notes and rhythms. The soloists find seemingly impossible transitions from one phrase to the next that are so perfect one would think they had spent weeks trying to devise *just* the right route to conduct safe passage. To think they spontaneously craft these ideas seems preposterous.

My first nervous jabs into the world of jazz came during college. I was in a rock band, but my fellow guitarist and bandmate, Victor, also played in a jazz ensemble. At our practices, I would sometimes show off a new chord I had just "invented" only to have him calmly and confidently name it, "Oh, you mean C-sharp diminished?" Often, in between our band's simplistic rock songs, I would look over and see him playing chord shapes on his guitar I had never seen before. Were we playing the same instrument?

Of course, rock music, as well as most early classical music, operates within a much simpler harmonic world than does jazz. There are 12 tones in Western music: A-flat, A, B-flat, B, C, D-flat, D, E-flat, E, F, G-flat, and G. There are major chords, which sound happy, and minor chords, which sound sad. Essentially, rock music requires only that you learn the major and minor chord for each of the 12 tones. If you do, you can play 99 percent of all the popular radio songs from the 1950s onward.

Jazz uses the same twelve tones as do rock and classical, but it employs a much more robust variety of chords. Major sevenths, augmented fifths, flat ninths, and diminished chords all add to the depth and detail of the music. These often bizarre-sounding chords toss in subtle hints of chaos and imbalance, adding a worldly imperfection to otherwise standard chord values. Jazz starts sounding better the older you get, just as candy starts tasting too sweet and a bit of bitterness makes for a more appealing flavor.

For the most part, Victor's elliptical personality prevented him from ever giving me straightforward explanations when I asked him to divulge the "magician's secrets" of jazz. But I did learn that jazz is only *partly* improvised. The musicians aren't inventing the structure of songs spontaneously, just the specific details and embellishments. A sheet of jazz music doesn't look like a sheet of classical music. There aren't notes all over the page dictating the "ideas." There are just chord names spaced out over time, dictating the "topic of conversation."

There's a legendary book in the jazz world known as "The Real Book." It's a collection of a few hundred classic songs. Open it up in any room full of jazz musicians, and they could play in synchrony for a week. For years, I wanted my own copy, but I had always been too afraid to buy it, afraid that I wouldn't know how to use the book once I had it. Then, at age 30, more than a decade since Victor and I had gone our separate ways, I bought myself a copy. I resolved to learn how to play all the chords on guitar and piano. For the next few months, I quietly plucked away at these strange, new combinations. F-sharp minor-7 flat-5? Each chord was a cryptic message I had to decode and then understand. It felt like being dropped off alone in a country where I didn't speak the language.

But I made progress. Chords that initially took me twenty seconds to figure out started to take only a few. My left hand was becoming comfortable in its role of supplying my right hand with a steady bass line. Meanwhile, to my amazement, my right hand began to improvise melodies that sounded undeniably *jazzy*.

It seemed like the hard work of figuring out the exotic jazz chords had sent new melodic understanding straight to my hand, bypassing my brain entirely. I felt like a witness to performances by detached hands; I couldn't believe that I was the one creating these sounds. I'm sure this feeling will not last, but for now I'm enjoying the rare and miraculous feeling of improvising music that I still consider beyond my abilities.

21. Which chord, if any, does the author eventually conclude is the most confusing jazz chord to play?

A. The passage does not indicate any such chord.
B. C-sharp diminished
C. Major sevenths
D. F-sharp minor-7 flat-5

GO ON TO THE NEXT PAGE.

22. As it is used in line 47, "magician's secrets" most nearly means:

F. information on how to play jazz.
G. forbidden bits of knowledge.
H. instances of harmless trickery.
J. the true nature of a private person.

23. As portrayed by the author, Victor responds to the author's *invented* chord with what is best described as:

A. amazement.
B. jealousy.
C. confusion.
D. nonchalance.

24. The author states that "The Real Book" was something he explored for a few:

F. years.
G. months.
H. weeks.
J. days.

25. The details in lines 40–44 primarily serve to suggest the:

A. aspects of jazz's complexity that more mature listeners enjoy.
B. lack of depth and detail found in rock and classical music.
C. confusion and awkwardness of standard jazz chord values.
D. unpleasantly bitter taste of candy that develops with age.

26. In the context of the passage, the author's statement in lines 68–71 most nearly means that:

F. he was so overworked that his hands could still move, but his thoughts were turned off.
G. he had accidentally trained his hands to resist being controlled by his brain.
H. it was easier to decode the exotic jazz chords by pointing at them with his hands.
J. his hand was capable of playing music that his mind was incapable of fully comprehending.

27. The author implies that F-sharp minor-7 flat-5 is an example of a chord that he:

A. had little trouble decoding now that he had "The Real Book."
B. had previously only seen during his travels abroad.
C. knew how to play on guitar but not on a piano.
D. initially found confusing and struggled to understand.

28. The passage supports which one of the following conclusions about Victor?

F. He played music with the author until the author turned 30 years old.
G. He gave his copy of "The Real Book" to the author as a gift.
H. He was at one time a member of multiple musical groups.
J. He invented a chord and named it C-sharp diminished.

29. The passage is best described as being told from the point of view of someone who is:

A. reviewing the chain of events that led to his career in jazz.
B. discussing reasons why jazz is less complicated than it seems.
C. relating his impressions of jazz music and his attempts to play it.
D. highlighting an important friendship that he had in college.

30. Assessing his early and later experiences with "The Real Book," the author most strongly implies that it was:

F. pleasantly strange to begin with but annoyingly familiar by the end.
G. initially difficult to decipher, but ultimately manageable following diligent practice.
H. almost impossible to understand because its pages didn't look like sheets of classical music.
J. very useful as a learning tool, but not useful for more profound study.

GO ON TO THE NEXT PAGE.

Passage IV

NATURAL SCIENCE: This passage is adapted from the article "Fair-Weather Warning" by Julia Mittlebury (©2007 by Julia Mittlebury).

Could the sun be causing epidemics? Take cholera, for example, an often fatal disease caused by the bacterium *Vibrio cholerae* (*V. cholerae*). Every so often, coastal areas suffer massive outbreaks of cholera due to infected food or water. Where do these outbreaks come from?

The bacterium that causes cholera is found in areas that contain the copepod, a certain type of crustacean. The copepod depends on zooplankton for nourishment, and these zooplankton in turn depend on phytoplankton for their nourishment. Phytoplankton use photosynthesis to feed on sunlight. Although one might need to go to the bottom of the food chain, the evidence shows that an increase in sunlight might mean an increase in the potential for cholera.

Interested in this correlation, Rita Calwell and her fellow researchers at the University of Maryland are studying ways to use satellite measurements of sea temperatures, sea height, and chlorophyll concentrations in order to predict when conditions favoring a cholera outbreak are more likely. As sea temperatures rise, photosynthetic organisms such as phytoplankton become more abundant. As sea levels rise, the phytoplankton, zooplankton, copepods, and, by extension, the cholera bacterium are all brought closer to the shore. This increases the likelihood of food and water contamination.

By monitoring the cholera food chain in reverse, Calwell and her colleagues believe they can predict the emergence of cholera 4 to 6 weeks in advance. Calwell's model predicted the rate of infection during one recent cholera outbreak in Bangladesh with 95 percent accuracy. Unfortunately, because this field of study is so new and its insights are so speculative, local public health officials have not yet begun to base any preventative measures on these satellite-based forecasts.

Just up the road from Calwell and the University of Maryland, Kenneth Linthicum is leading similar efforts at the NASA Goddard Space Flight Centre in Greenbelt, Maryland. He has designed a model to analyze the spread of Rift Valley fever, a mosquito-spread virus that killed about 100,000 animals and 90,000 people back in December 1997.

Scientists observed that prior to the outbreak, the equatorial region of the Indian Ocean saw a half-degree increase in surface temperature. Although half of a degree sounds like only a slight difference, the temperature of an ocean does not change easily. Warmer ocean water in this region corresponds with strong and prolonged rains, increased cloud cover, and warmer air over equatorial parts of Africa. These characteristics favor the proliferation of mosquitoes and help keep them alive long enough for the virus to become easily transmittable.

In September 2007, Linthicum and his team became alerted to similar environmental changes. Over the next few months, they warned local health officials in Kenya, Somalia, and Tanzania that conditions were ripe for a mosquito-based outbreak. As a result, only 300 lives were lost, an almost miraculous improvement from the devastation of the 1997 outbreak. While it is impossible to know if this outbreak would have been as far-reaching as that of 1997, it seems likely that the advance warning succeeded in saving thousands, if not tens of thousands, of lives.

Similarly, a study by David Rogers at Oxford University has helped to predict outbreaks of sleeping sickness, a parasitic disease caused by West African tsetse flies. Here, Rogers first calibrated regional levels of photosynthesis to the size of a vein in the wings of the flies. The vein size is a good measure of how numerous and robust the tsetse fly population is. Today, by reading the photosynthetic levels from satellite data, even researchers outside of West Africa can predict potential epidemics in the region.

This type of research is encouraging to many in the disease prevention field, because traditional methods involve slow, costly research. The newfound ability to cull massive amounts of meteorological data from satellites and to run that data through computer models has been much more efficient.

The goal of these models is to study the relationships between disease data and climate data. However, to do so requires decades', if not centuries', worth of high quality data to identify correlating factors with accuracy. Currently, the climatic data is much more reliable than the disease data. Nevertheless, excitement about the potential usefulness of satellite-based predictions is persuading health agencies to compile and integrate their disease data more efficiently to give easier access to those trying to discover climate-disease links.

It may still take a good deal of time and energy before this technology is ready for practical application. Critics claim that the number of variables underlying the spread of disease are too numerous and varied for a climate-based approach ever to be reliable. Fluctuations in the immunity of local populations, human and animal migrations, and the resistance to drugs used to commonly treat certain diseases could confuse climate-based models. Advocates respond, though, that these non-climatic factors can similarly be incorporated into their research as long as the relevant data is collected, and the resulting models will have even better accuracy.

GO ON TO THE NEXT PAGE.

31. According to Calwell, scientists may be able to predict cholera outbreaks more than a month in advance by:

A. noticing increased activity in a known food chain.
B. using accurate climatic models derived from weather in Bangladesh.
C. measuring the decline of zooplankton with falling sea temperatures.
D finding connections between chlorophyll levels and diseased marine life.

32. According to the passage, levels of sunlight can influence cholera because:

F. phytoplankton feed on sunlight and contaminate the water.
G. the *V. cholerae* bacterium increases its photosynthetic rate.
H. sunlight promotes the growth of organisms upon which copepods depend.
J. many epidemics are caused by direct, prolonged exposure to sunlight.

33. According to the passage, the use of satellite data has aided the attempts of Oxford University researchers to predict outbreaks of sleeping sickness by providing information about:

A. the number of West African parasites.
B. which areas globally have the most photosynthesis.
C. the health and number of tsetse flies.
D. which flies have the biggest veins.

34. The passage states that Linthicum is conducting similar efforts to Calwell's in that Linthicum:

F. studies the climatic triggers of cholera.
G. works at the University of Maryland.
H. managed to save thousands of lives in 2007.
J. uses satellite data to build predictive models.

35. According to the passage, the use of satellite data to predict potential epidemics is encouraging because:

A. computer number-crunching is quicker and less expensive than traditional research methods.
B. it allows scientists to control the photosynthetic levels in West Africa.
C. satellites do not make the same mathematical errors that human forecasters often do.
D. there is already a large supply of long-term disease data available from satellites.

36. As it is used in line 44, the word *favor* most nearly means:

F. errand.
G. task.
H. promote.
J. request.

37. It can reasonably be inferred that the phrase *similar environmental changes* (line 48), refers to:

A. the beginning of the rainy season in Kenya.
B. the amount of bacteria circulating in the jet stream.
C. the proliferation of mosquitoes throughout central Africa.
D. warmer ocean water influencing rain and cloud cover.

38. The passage states that climatic satellite data has helped to do all of the following EXCEPT:

F. measure sea height.
G. predict tsete fly populations.
H. forecast disease outbreaks.
J. raise the ocean temperature.

39. The phrase *confuse climate-based models* (line 85–86) refers directly to the fact that:

A. current models do not account for non-climate related factors.
B. drug resistance sometimes results in disorientation.
C. epidemics sometimes vanish more quickly than they arise.
D. researchers are not used to non-climate data.

40. It can reasonably be inferred from the passage that the information about the use of satellite-based data is presented primarily to:

F. demonstrate the various kinds of data that must be collected.
G. analyze the data's potential use in disease-prevention.
H. illustrate how few scientists do on-the-ground research.
J. show how West African tsete fly populations have been predicted.

END OF TEST 3

STOP! DO NOT TURN THE PAGE UNTIL TOLD TO DO SO.

DO NOT RETURN TO A PREVIOUS TEST.

SCIENCE TEST

35 Minutes–40 Questions

Directions: There are seven passages in this test. Each passage is followed by several questions. After reading a passage, choose the best answer to each question and fill in the corresponding oval on your answer document. You may refer to the passages as often as necessary.

You are NOT permitted to use a calculator on this test.

Passage I

Two ways to measure the quality of soil are *bulk density* and the *soil organic matter test*, SOM (a measure of the active organic content). High quality soil provides structure to plants and moves water and nutrients, so plants grow in larger quantities, leading to higher crop yields at harvest.

Bulk density is measured as the dry weight of a sample of soil divided by the volume of the sample. A bulk density measure above 1.33 g/cm^3 negatively affects soil quality. Figure 1 shows the bulk density levels for 5 different years at Fields A and B.

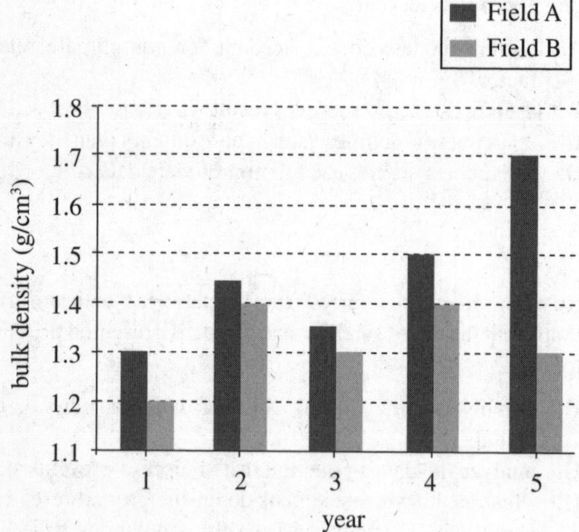

Figure 1

Table 1 shows how soil quality varies with SOM. Table 2 shows the average SOM of each field for each of the 5 years.

Table 1

SOM	Soil quality rating
<0.25	poor
0.25 to 0.50	fair
0.51 to 0.75	good
>0.75	excellent

Table 2

Field	Average SOM
A	0.89
B	0.28

Figure 2 shows the total crop yield at each field at the end of the 5 years.

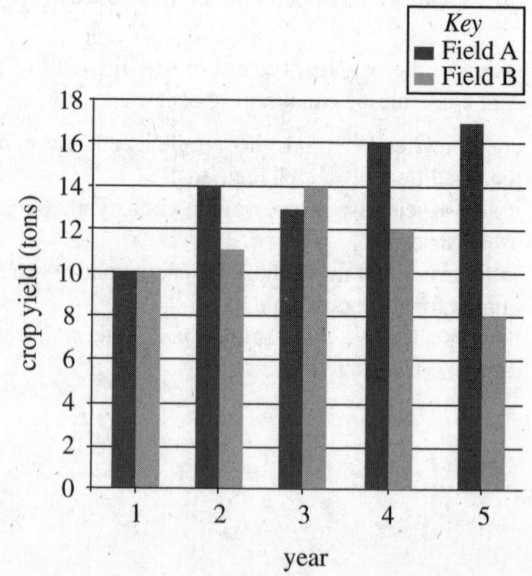

Figure 2

GO ON TO THE NEXT PAGE.

1. Which set of data best supports the claim that Field A has *lower* soil quality than Field B ?

   A. Figure 1
   B. Figure 2
   C. Table 1
   D. Table 2

2. If 8 tons or fewer in crop yields were considered a failed harvest, in which year and in which field would there have been a failed harvest?

   F. Field A in Year 1
   G. Field A in Year 3
   H. Field B in Year 4
   J. Field B in Year 5

3. Suppose a new crop rotation for Field B included legumes and other deep-rooted and high-residue crops. The SOM of this field will most likely change in which of the following ways? The SOM will:

   A. decrease, because soil quality is likely to increase.
   B. decrease, because soil quality is likely to decrease.
   C. increase, because soil quality is likely to increase.
   D. increase, because soil quality is likely to decrease.

4. Based on Figures 1 and 2, consider the average bulk density and the average crop yields for Fields A and B over the study period. Which site had the lower average crop yield, and which site had the higher average bulk density?

	Lower crop yield	Higher bulk density
F.	Field A	Field A
G.	Field B	Field B
H.	Field A	Field B
J.	Field B	Field A

5. As soil quality improves, the number of earthworms increases. Students hypothesized that more earthworms would be found in Field B. Are the data presented in Table 2 consistent with this hypothesis?

   A. Yes; based on SOM, Field B had a soil quality rating of fair and Field A had a soil quality rating of poor.
   B. Yes; based on SOM, Field B had a soil quality rating of excellent and Field A had a soil quality rating of fair.
   C. No; based on SOM, Field B had a soil quality rating of poor and Field A had a soil quality rating of fair.
   D. No; based on SOM, Field B had a soil quality rating of fair and Field A had a soil quality rating of excellent.

GO ON TO THE NEXT PAGE.

Passage II

Ferric oxide (Fe_2O_3) is more commonly known as rust. This is produced in a reaction between iron, a common metal, and water, H_2O.

$$2Fe + 3\,H_2O \longrightarrow Fe_2O_3 + 3H_2$$

Table 1 shows the amount of Fe_2O_3 produced over time from 15 g Fe submerged in different liquids: 100 mL distilled water, a salt solution made from dissolving 20 g of salt in 100 mL of distilled water, and a sugar solution made from dissolving 20 g of sugar in 100 mL of distilled water.

Table 1

Solution	g Fe_2O_3 produced			
	Day 2	Day 4	Day 6	Day 8
Distilled water	0.34	0.40	0.59	0.72
Salt solution	0.56	0.81	1.23	1.84
Sugar solution	0.00	0.05	0.11	0.19

The distilled water trial was repeated four times, but for each trial, the water was buffered to different pH levels and a total volume of 100 mL (see Figure 1).

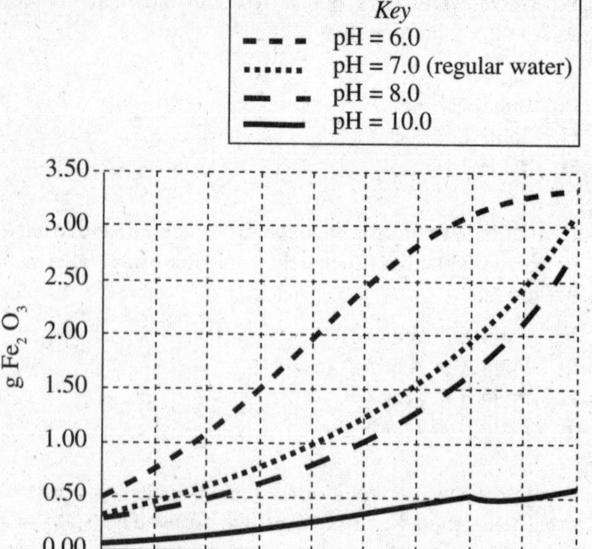

Figure 1

6. Based on Table 1, if the amount of Fe_2O_3 produced on Day 9 had been measured for the salt solution, it would most likely have been:

   F. less than 0.56 g.
   G. between 0.59 g and 0.72 g.
   H. between 1.23 g and 1.84 g.
   J. greater than 1.84 g.

GO ON TO THE NEXT PAGE.

7. In the experiments shown in Table 1 and Figure 1, by measuring the rate at which Fe_2O_3 was formed every day, the experimenters could also measure the rate at which:

A. H_2O was produced.
B. H_2 was produced.
C. Fe was produced.
D. FeO was produced.

8. Consider the amount of Fe_2O_3 produced by the salt solution on Day 2. Based on Table 1 and Figure 1, the water buffered to pH = 10.0 produced approximately the same amount of Fe_2O_3 on which of the following days?

F. Day 1
G. Day 3
H. Day 6
J. Day 10

9. According to Table 1, what was the amount of Fe_2O_3 produced by the sugar solution from the time the amount was measured on Day 6 until the time the amount was measured on Day 8 ?

A. 0.08 g
B. 0.11 g
C. 0.19 g
D. 0.30 g

10. Based on Table 1, which graph best shows how the amount of Fe_2O_3 produced by the sugar solution changes over time?

F.

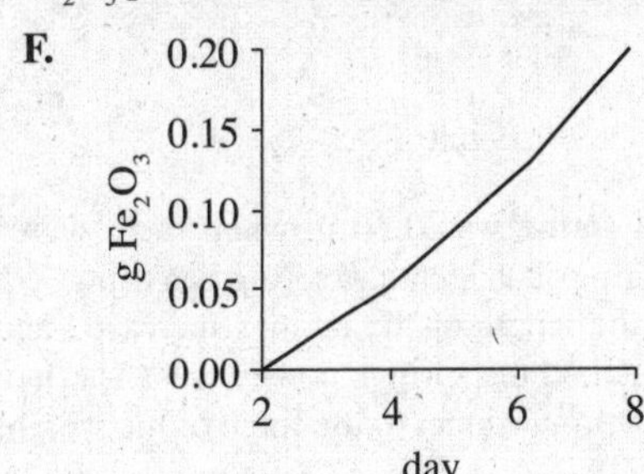

G.

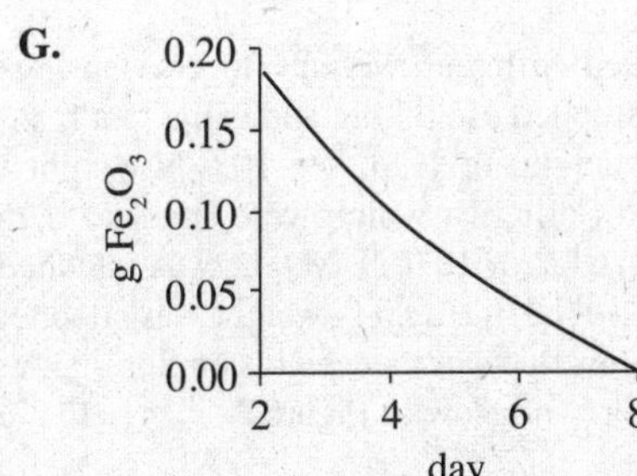

H.

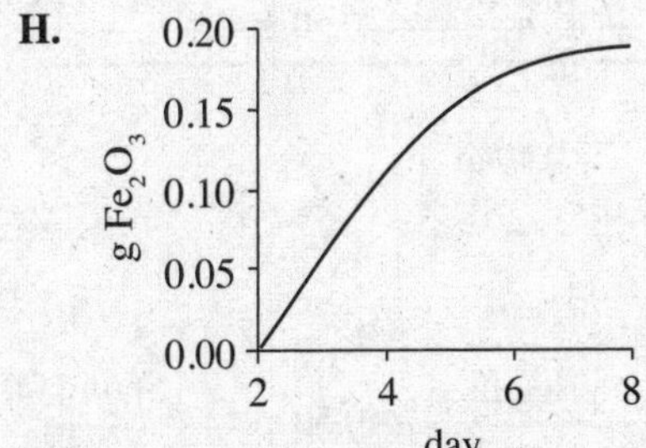

J.

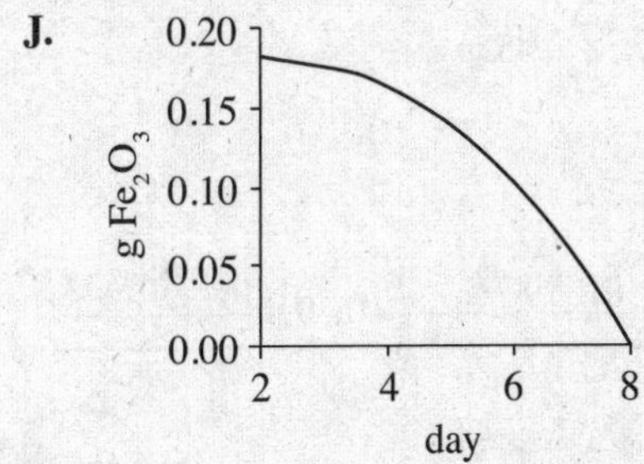

GO ON TO THE NEXT PAGE.

Passage III

Some physics students conducted experiments to study forces and springs. They used several identical springs attached to a horizontal board, shown below in Figure 1.

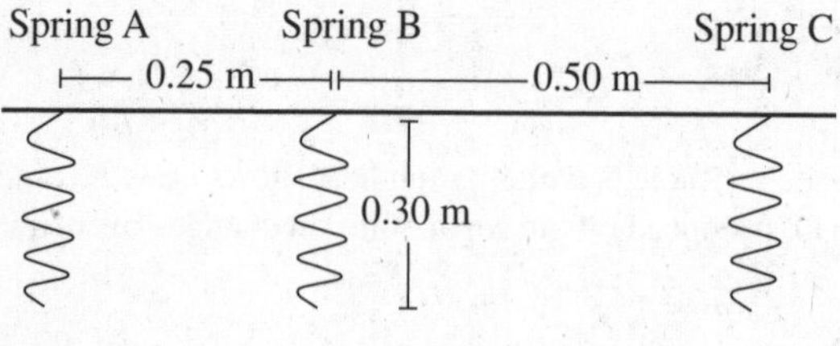

Figure 1

The length of each spring was 0.30 m when there were no weights attached. The springs had identical spring constants. When weights were attached, the length of the springs increased as the force of the weights stretched the springs downwards. The length the springs stretched was proportional to the force of the weight.

Experiment 1

The students attached different weights to two springs at once. When the springs stopped oscillating and came to a rest, the students measured their length. In Trial 1, a 10.0 N weight was attached to Spring A and Spring B, which were attached 0.25 m apart on the board. In Trial 2, a 15.0 N weight was attached to Spring A and Spring B. In Trial 3, a 20.0 N weight was attached to Spring A and Spring B. The effects of the weights on Springs A and B for the three trials are shown below in Figure 2.

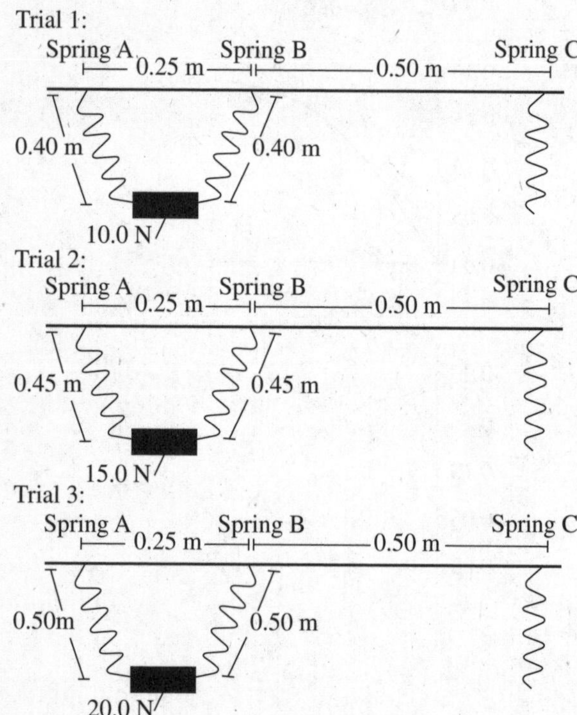

Figure 2

Experiment 2

The students attached a 0.25 m board with a high friction surface to Spring B and Spring C (see Figure 3). The students then placed a 5.0 N weight at different locations along the board. Because of the high friction surface, the weights stayed in place when the board was at an angle.

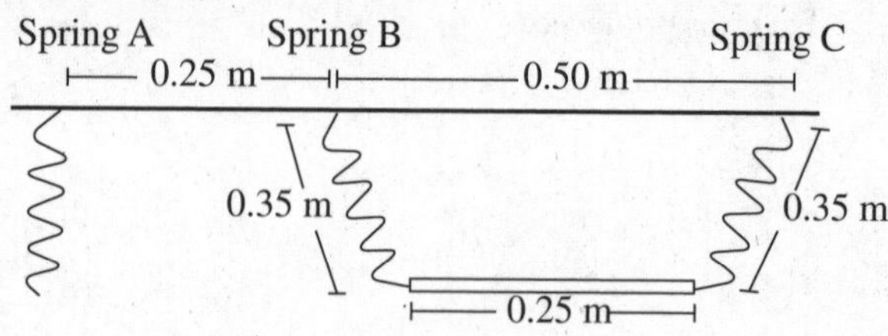

Figure 3

In each of these 3 trials, a 5.0 N weight was placed at various distances along the board from the attachment with Spring B (see Figure 4). In Trial 4, the weight was placed so its center was 0.075 m along the board from the attachment with Spring B. In Trial 5, the weight was placed so its center was 0.125 m along the board from the attachment with Spring B. In Trial 6, the weight was placed so its center was 0.200 m along the board from the attachment with Spring B. The effects of the weight position on the lengths of Springs B and C for the 3 trials are also shown in Figure 4.

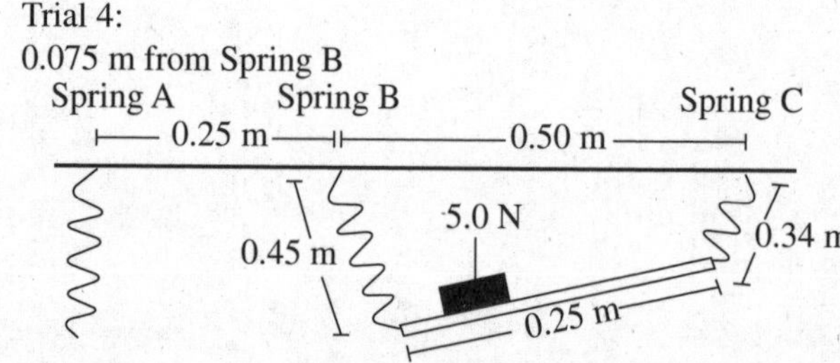

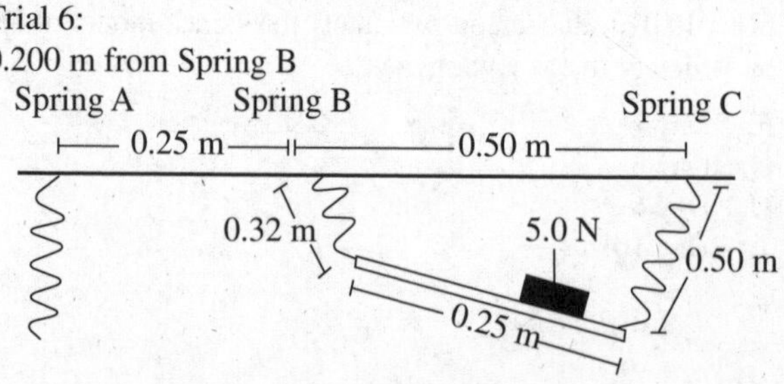

Figure 4

GO ON TO THE NEXT PAGE.

11. In a new study, suppose the students had placed a 10.0 N weight on Spring A only. Which of the following drawings most likely represents the results of this experiment?

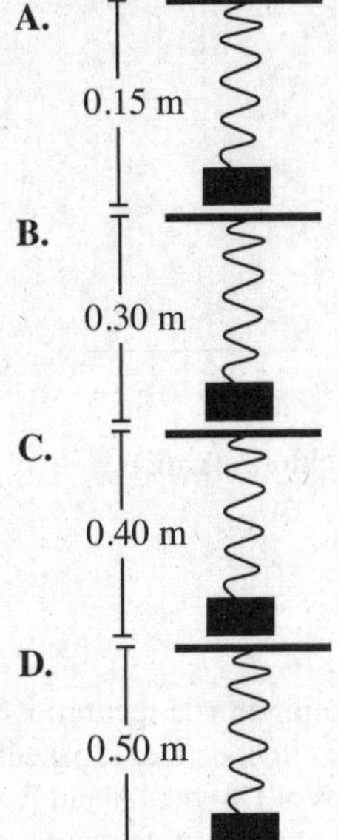

12. In Experiment 2, as the distance between the 5.0 N weight and the attachment of the board to Spring B increased, the force exerted on Spring B:

F. increased only.
G. decreased only.
H. increased, then decreased.
J. decreased, then increased.

13. Which of the following statements is most likely the reason that the students used identical springs in Trials 1–3 ?

A. To ensure that the springs stretched similarly when a weight was attached
B. To ensure that the springs did not share the weight evenly
C. To compensate for the effects of oscillation on the results of the experiment
D. To compensate for the weight of the board exerted on each of the springs

14. Based on the results of Trials 1 and 5, the weight of the board used in Experiment 2 was:

F. 0 N.
G. 2.5 N.
H. 5.0 N.
J. 10.0 N.

15. In which of the following trials in Experiment 2, if any, was the force exerted by the weight and the board equally distributed between Springs B and C ?

A. Trial 4
B. Trial 5
C. Trial 6
D. None of the trials

16. Assume that when a spring is stretched from its normal length, it stores the energy to return to its normal state as potential energy. Assume also that the greater the force of the weight stretching the spring, the more the spring will stretch. Was the potential energy stored by Spring C higher in Trial 5 or Trial 6 ?

F. In Trial 5, because the force of the weight on Spring C was greater in Trial 5.
G. In Trial 5, because the force of the weight on Spring C was less in Trial 5.
H. In Trial 6, because the force of the weight on Spring C was greater in Trial 6.
J. In Trial 6, because the force of the weight on Spring C was less in Trial 6.

GO ON TO THE NEXT PAGE.

Passage IV

Sodium chloride, or salt, is used to de-ice roads and sidewalks during the winter because it lowers the freezing point of water. Water with sodium chloride freezes at a lower temperature than water alone, so putting sodium chloride on icy sidewalks and roads can cause the ice to melt. Sodium chloride is highly effective as a de-icer and is given a *de-icer proof* of 100. Distilled water is ineffective as a de-icer and is given a de-icer proof of 0.

Different proportions of sodium chloride and distilled water were combined to create mixtures with de-icer proofs between 0 and 100.

Table 1

De-icer proof	Volume of distilled water	Volume of sodium chloride
100	0 ml	50 ml
80	10 ml	40 ml
60	20 ml	30 ml
40	30 ml	20 ml
20	40 ml	10 ml
0	50 ml	0 ml

Experiment 1

A 125 g cube of ice, frozen from distilled water, was submerged in 500 mL of each de-icing mixture listed in Table 1. After 300 seconds, the portion of the cube that had not been melted was removed and weighed. The de-icing rate was calculated by determining the weight of ice melted per second. By doing this, it was possible to determine de-icer proof for a solution based on the rate at which ice was melted.

Experiment 2

The addition of magnesium chloride to a de-icer changes its de-icer proof. Different amounts of magnesium chloride were added to 500 mL samples of sodium chloride. Each de-icing mixture was tested under the same conditions as Experiment 1 and the measured de-icing rate was used to calculate the de-icer proof. The results are shown in Figure 1.

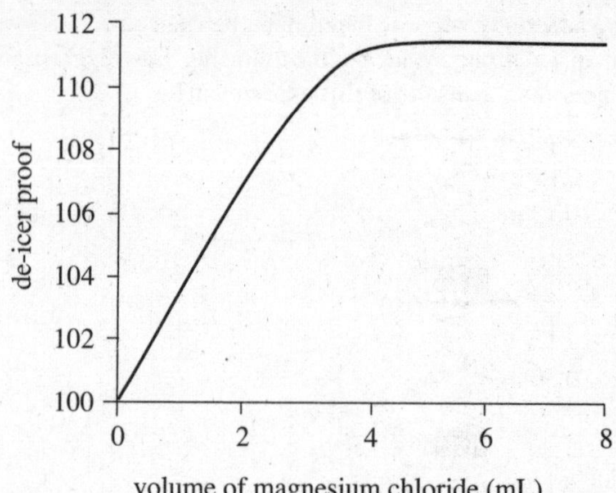

Figure 1

Experiment 3

The *temperature rating* (TR) is the minimum de-icer proof of a de-icing solution for a de-icer to have any effect on ice. 125 g cubes of ice were submerged in 500 mL samples of De-icers A and B and the samples were then placed in freezers at different temperatures. Table 2 shows the de-icer proof determined for each de-icer at each freezer temperature and the known TR for that temperature.

Table 2

Freezer temperature	TR	Proof of: De-icer A	Proof of: De-icer B
−10°C	24.1	90.3	70.1
−25°C	36.9	78.9	64.9
−50°C	49.7	68.8	59.7
−75°C	52.3	56.6	51.7

17. Suppose a trial had been performed in Experiment 3 with a freezer temperature of −30°C. At this temperature, which of the following sets of proofs would most likely have been determined for De-icer A and De-icer B ?

	De-icer A	De-icer B
A.	68.8	59.7
B.	70.1	70.5
C.	75.5	61.8
D.	78.9	64.9

GO ON TO THE NEXT PAGE.

18. Based on Table 1, if 1 mL distilled water were added to 4 mL sodium chloride, the proof of this mixture would be:

F. 4.
G. 8.
H. 40.
J. 80.

19. Based on Experiment 3, as temperature decreases, the minimum proof for a de-icer to be effective:

A. increases only.
B. decreases only.
C. increases, then decreases.
D. decreases, then increases.

20. Which of the following expressions is equal to the proof for each de-icer mixture listed in Table 1 ?

F. $\dfrac{\text{volume of sodium chloride}}{\text{volume of water}} \times 100$

G. $\dfrac{\text{volume of water}}{\text{volume of sodium chloride}} \times 100$

H. $\dfrac{\text{volume of sodium chloride}}{(\text{volume of water} + \text{volume of sodium chloride})} \times 100$

J. $\dfrac{\text{volume of water}}{(\text{volume of water} + \text{volume of sodium chloride})} \times 100$

21. Based on Table 1 and Experiment 2, if 6 mL magnesium chloride were added to a mixture of 10 mL distilled water and 40 mL sodium chloride, the proof of the resulting de-icer would most likely be:

A. less than 60.
B. between 60 and 80.
C. between 80 and 112.
D. greater than 112.

22. Which of the 2 de-icers from Experiment 3 would be better to use to melt ice if the temperature were between –10°C and –75°C ?

F. De-icer A, because its proof was lower than the TR at each temperature tested.
G. De-icer A, because its proof was higher than the TR at each temperature tested.
H. De-icer B, because its proof was lower than the TR at each temperature tested.
J. De-icer B, because its proof was higher than the TR at each temperature tested.

GO ON TO THE NEXT PAGE.

Passage V

Comets originate from regions of our solar system that are very far from the sun. The comets are formed from debris thrown from objects in the solar system: they have a nucleus of ice surrounded by dust and frozen gases. When comets are pulled into the earth's atmosphere by gravitational forces and become visible, they are called *meteors*. Meteors become visible about 50 to 85 km above the surface of Earth as air friction causes them to glow. Most meteors vaporize completely before they come within 50 km of the surface of Earth.

The Small Comet debate centers on whether dark spots and streaks seen in images of the Earth's atmosphere are due to random technological noise or a constant rain of comets composed of ice. Recently, images were taken by two instruments, UVA and VIS, which are located in a satellite orbiting in Earth's magnetosphere. UVA and VIS take pictures of the aurora borealis phenomenon, which occurs in the magnetosphere. The UVA and VIS technologies provide images of energy, which cannot be seen by the human eye.

The pictures taken by VIS and UVA both show dark spots and streaks. Scientists debate whether these spots and streaks are due to a natural incident, such as small comets entering the atmosphere, or random technological noise. The layers of Earth's atmosphere are shown in Figure 1.

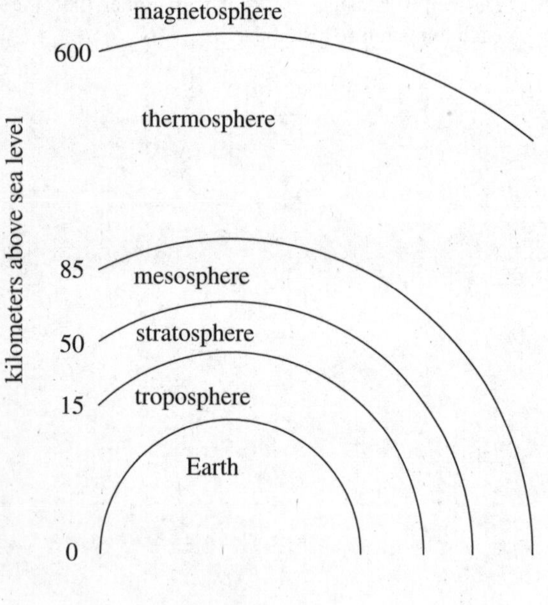

Figure 1

Two scientists debate whether there is a constant rain of comets burning up in Earth's magnetosphere.

Scientist 1

Small comets are pulled into Earth's atmosphere by gravitational effects and burn up in the magnetosphere. They are about 20 to 30 feet in diameter and burn up in the magnetosphere because they are much smaller than the comets that become meteors. Comets with larger radii will burn up in portions of the atmosphere much closer to Earth. About 30,000 small comets enter the Earth's magnetosphere every day. The dark spots and streaks on UVA and VIS images occur when the small comets begin to boil in the magnetosphere, releasing krypton and argon and creating gaseous H_2O, which interacts with hydroxyl, OH^-, radicals. Images taken by these instruments at different points in time show the same frequency of dark spots and streaks and give conclusive evidence in favor of the Small Comet theory. If the spots and streaks were due to random technological noise, then the frequency of their appearance would fluctuate.

Scientist 2

The dark spots and streaks in the UVA and VIS images are due to technological noise, not small comets. If the small comet theory were true, and 20 small comets bombarded Earth's atmosphere per minute, there would be a visible bright object at least twice every five minutes. This is because, as objects enter the Earth's mesosphere, they burn up, creating large clouds of ice particles. As the ice particles vaporize, they have a brightness in the sky approximately equal to that of Venus. Because comets rarely enter Earth's atmosphere, such bright flashes are rare occurrences, far less than two times every five minutes, so the Small Comet theory cannot be correct. Further, since comets originate from regions of space beyond the orbit of the farthest planet, they contain argon and krypton. If the Small Comet theory were true and Earth were bombarded by 30,000 comets per day, there would be 500 times as much krypton in the atmosphere as there actually is.

23. According to Scientist 2, which of the following planets in our solar system is most likely the closest to the region of space where comets originate?

A. Jupiter
B. Venus
C. Neptune
D. Saturn

GO ON TO THE NEXT PAGE.

24. Based on Scientist 1's viewpoint, a comet that burns up in the thermosphere would have a diameter of:

F. 5–10 ft.
G. 10–20 ft.
H. 20–30 ft.
J. greater than 30 ft.

25. Which of the following generalizations about small comets is most consistent with Scientist 1's viewpoint?

A. No small comet ever becomes a meteor.
B. Some small comets become meteors.
C. Small comets become meteors twice every five minutes.
D. All small comets become meteors.

26. During the *Perseids*, an annual meteor shower, more than 1 object burning up in the atmosphere is visible per minute. According to the information provided, Scientist 2 would classify the Perseids as:

F. typical comet frequency in the magnetosphere.
G. unusual comet frequency in the magnetosphere.
H. typical meteor frequency in the mesosphere.
J. unusual meteor frequency in the mesosphere.

27. Given the information about Earth's atmosphere and Scientist 1's viewpoint, which of the following altitudes would most likely NOT be an altitude at which small comets burn up?

A. 750 km
B. 700 km
C. 650 km
D. 550 km

28. Suppose a study of the dark holes and streaks in the UVA and VIS images revealed krypton levels 500 times greater than normal levels. How would the findings of this study most likely affect the scientists' viewpoints, if at all?

F. It would strengthen Scientist 1's viewpoint only.
G. It would strengthen Scientist 2's viewpoint only.
H. It would weaken both Scientists' viewpoints.
J. It would have no effect on either Scientist's viewpoint.

29. Scientist 1 would most likely suggest enhanced imaging technology that can take pictures of objects in the atmosphere be used to look at what region of the atmosphere to search for small comets?

A. The region between 15 km above sea level and 50 km above sea level.
B. The region between 50 km above sea level and 85 km above sea level.
C. The region between 85 km above sea level and 600 km above sea level.
D. The region between above 600 km above sea level.

GO ON TO THE NEXT PAGE.

Passage VI

A cotton fiber is composed of one very long cell with two cell walls. During a 2-week period of cell life called elongation, cotton fibers grow 3 to 6 cm. The level of hydrogen peroxide in cotton fiber cells during elongation is very high. Scientists wanted to study whether the level of hydrogen peroxide affected the length of the cotton fiber.

The amount of hydrogen peroxide is controlled by an enzyme called *superoxide dismutase* (SOD). This enzyme turns superoxide into hydrogen peroxide. Four identical lines of cotton fiber plants were created. Each line was able to express only one of three types of superoxide dismutase. The gene for SOD1 was incorporated into L1, the gene for SOD2 was incorporated into L2, and the gene for SOD3 was incorporated into L3.

Experiment

Five cotton plants of each line were grown in nutrient solution until cotton fibers completed the elongation period. The average length of cotton fibers and the average concentration of hydrogen peroxide were determined. This information is shown in Table 1.

Table 1

Line	At the end of elongation period:		
	Average elongation period length (days)	Average amount of hydrogen peroxide (μmol/mg)	Average cotton fiber length (cm)
L1	8	2.1	3.6
L2	4	0.2	1.4
L3	20	5.6	5.9
L4	12	2.3	4.5

Next, because the scientists had determined the average elongation period, they measured the amount of hydrogen peroxide and the length of the cotton fibers halfway through their elongation period. This information is shown in Table 2.

Table 2

Line	At the midpoint of elongation period:		
	Day of elongation period	Average amount of hydrogen peroxide (μmol/mg)	Average cotton fiber length (cm)
L1	4	4.1	2.7
L2	2	5.3	1.0
L3	10	12.4	2.0
L4	6	8.7	3.2

Finally, the scientists measured the amount of hydrogen peroxide and the length of cotton fibers on the first day of the elongation period. This information is shown in Table 3.

Table 3

Line	On the first day of elongation period:		
	Day of elongation period	Average amount of hydrogen peroxide (μmol/mg)	Average cotton fiber length (cm)
L1	1	1.2	0.2
L2	1	6.0	0.5
L3	1	5.7	0.1
L4	1	1.9	0.2

30. For L2, as the elongation period moved from the first day to the end, the amount of hydrogen peroxide:

F. increased only.
G. decreased only.
H. increased, then decreased.
J. decreased, then increased.

31. Which of the following is a dependent variable in the experiment?

A. The point in time during the elongation period
B. The type of superoxide dismutase the plant could express
C. The length of the cotton fiber
D. The type of cotton plant

GO ON TO THE NEXT PAGE.

32. A cotton fiber is one very long cell with two cell walls. A cotton fiber is a special kind of what type of cell?

F. Prokaryotic
G. Animal
H. Plant
J. Bacterial

33. One plant had an average cotton fiber length of 0.5 cm, and the average amount of hydrogen peroxide in its fibers was 5.9 μmol/mg. Which of the following most likely describes this plant?

A. It was from L1 and at the end of its elongation period.
B. It was from L1 and at the midpoint of its elongation period.
C. It was from L2 and at the beginning of its elongation period.
D. It was from L2 and at the end of its elongation period.

34. The scientists used one of the four lines of cotton plants as a control. Which line was most likely the control?

F. L1
G. L2
H. L3
J. L4

35. Suppose the data for all the plants were plotted on a graph with the time of the elongation period on the *x*-axis and the average length of the cotton fiber on the *y*-axis. Suppose also that the best-fit line for these data was determined. Which of the following would most likely characterize the slope of this line?

A. The line would have a positive slope.
B. The line would have a negative slope.
C. The line would have a slope equal to zero.
D. The line would have no slope, because the line would be vertical.

GO ON TO THE NEXT PAGE.

Passage VII

Convection is a heat transfer process caused by moving liquid or gas currents from a hot region to a cold region. As a liquid or gas cools, it gets more dense. An example of a convection process is a cup of hot coffee: the liquid towards the top is cooled by the air, so it becomes more dense and sinks to the bottom of the cup; the hotter liquid towards the bottom of the cup is less dense, so it rises towards the top. See Figure 1, below.

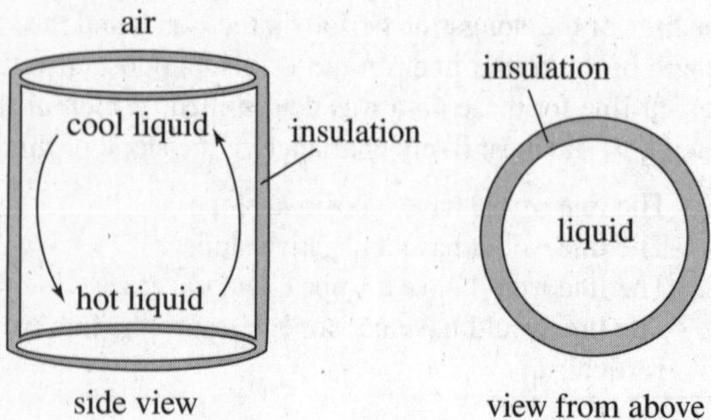

Figure 1

The temperature of the liquid at the hot end of the insulated system is higher than the temperature at the cool end of the system. The difference (ΔT) between the hot liquid at the bottom and the cold liquid at the top changes depending on the starting temperature of the system. Table 1 gives ΔT for 500 mL water in an insulated container with a height of 6.0 cm and a cross-sectional area of 4.0 cm^2 when the container is heated to different temperatures.

Table 1

Heated temperature (°C)	ΔT (°C)
80	1
100	4
120	10
140	19

Figure 2 shows how ΔT changes with cross-sectional area for 500 mL 100°C water in a container with a height of 6.0 cm. Figure 3 shows how ΔT changes with height for 500 mL 100°C water in a container with a cross-sectional area of 4.0 cm^2.

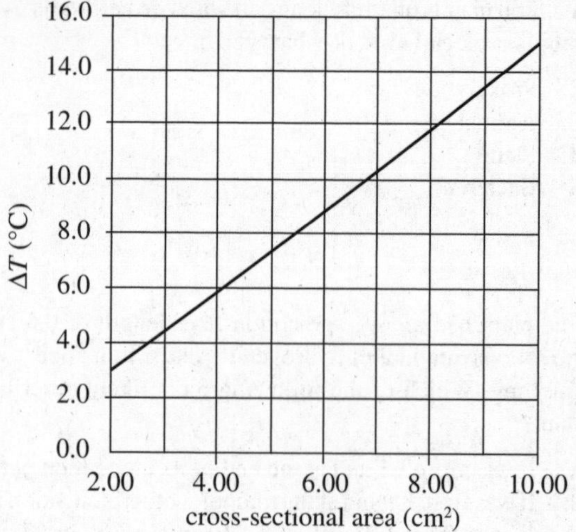

Figure 2

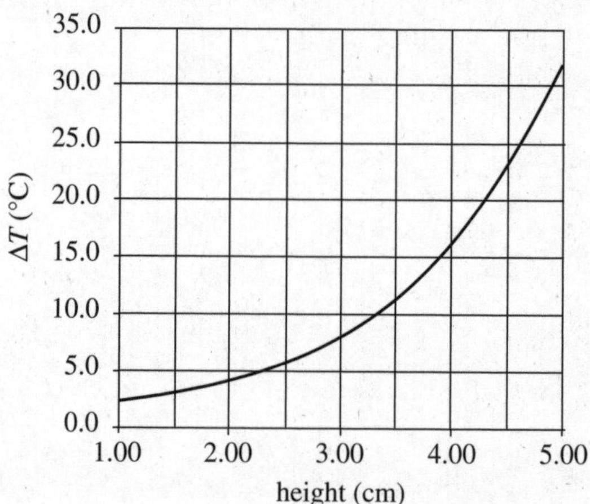

Figure 3

36. System 1 and System 2 are two convection systems. Based on Figure 2, if System 1 were the same height as System 2, but had two times the cross-sectional area and the systems were heated to the same temperature, the ratio of ΔT for System 1 to ΔT for System 2 would be:

F. 1:1
G. 1:2
H. 2:1
J. 3:1

GO ON TO THE NEXT PAGE.

37. For the systems described in the passage, if the containers were metal containers rather than insulated containers, heat would be transferred from the water to the container by which of the following heat transfer process?

I. Convection
II. Conduction
III. Radiation

A. I only
B. II only
C. I and III only
D. I and II only

38. Which of the following systems, if all were heated to the same temperature, would have the highest ΔT ?

F.

G.

H.

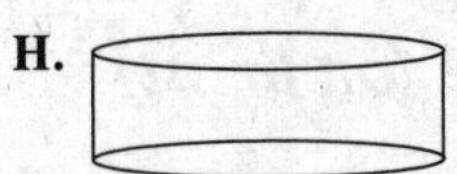

J.

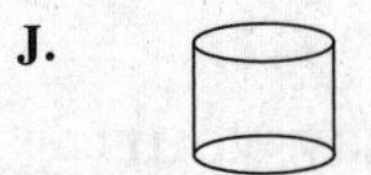

39. Based on the information in Table 1, if an insulated container of 500 mL of water with a height of 6.0 cm and a cross-sectional area of 4.0 cm² were heated to 120°C, which of the following pairs could represent the temperatures of the liquid at the top and bottom ends of the container?

	Bottom end	Top/Exposed to air end
A.	140°C	120°C
B.	140°C	110°C
C.	115°C	115°C
D.	120°C	110°C

40. The data in the passage supports the hypothesis that ΔT increases as which of the following increases?

F. Amount of insulation
G. Volume of liquid
H. Radius of the container
J. Air temperature

END OF TEST 4

STOP! DO NOT RETURN TO ANY OTHER TEST.

DIRECTIONS

This is a test of your writing skills. You will have thirty (30) minutes to write an essay. Before you begin planning and writing your essay, read the writing prompt carefully to understand exactly what you are being asked to do. Your essay will be evaluated on the evidence it provides of your ability to express judgments by taking a position on the issue in the writing prompt; to maintain a focus on the topic throughout your essay; to develop a position by using logical reasoning and by supporting your ideas; to organize ideas in a logical way; and to use language clearly and effectively according to the conventions of standard written English.

You may use the unlined pages in this test booklet to plan your essay. These pages will not be scored. ***You must write your essay on the lined pages in the answer folder.*** Your writing on those lined pages will be scored. You may not need all the lined pages, but to ensure you have enough room to finish, do NOT skip lines. You may write corrections or additions neatly between the lines of your essay, but do NOT write in the margins of the lined pages. ***Illegible essays cannot be scored, so you must write (or print) clearly.***

If you finish before time is called, you may review your work. Lay your pencil down immediately when time is called.

DO NOT OPEN THIS BOOK UNTIL YOU ARE TOLD TO DO SO.

ACT Assessment Writing Test Prompt

Schools in some states have changed their school calendars so that they are now year-round schools. Advocates of year-round schooling argue that the traditional summer break is a waste of students' time that could otherwise be spent learning. Opponents charge that today's students are already overburdened with the stresses of school and need the summer to get a much-needed break. In your view, should the traditional three-month summer vacation from school be maintained?

In your essay, take a position on this question. You may write about either one of the two points of view given, or you may present a different point of view on this question. Use specific reasons and examples to support your position.

ACT Diagnostic Test Form

Use a No. 2 pencil only. Be sure each mark is dark and completely fills the intended oval. Completely erase any errors or stray marks.

1. YOUR NAME: ______________________________ (Print) Last First M.I.

SIGNATURE: ______________________________ DATE: ____/____/____

HOME ADDRESS: ______________________________ (Print) Number and Street

______________________________ City State Zip

E-MAIL: ______________________________

PHONE NO.: ______________________________ (Print)

SCHOOL: ______________________________

CLASS OF: ______________________________

IMPORTANT: Please fill in these boxes exactly as shown on the back cover of your tests book.

2. TEST FORM

____

3. TEST CODE

0	0	0	0
1	1	1	1
2	2	2	2
3	3	3	3
4	4	4	4
5	5	5	5
6	6	6	6
7	7	7	7
8	8	8	8
9	9	9	9

4. PHONE NUMBER

0	0	0	0	0	0	0
1	1	1	1	1	1	1
2	2	2	2	2	2	2
3	3	3	3	3	3	3
4	4	4	4	4	4	4
5	5	5	5	5	5	5
6	6	6	6	6	6	6
7	7	7	7	7	7	7
8	8	8	8	8	8	8
9	9	9	9	9	9	9

5. YOUR NAME

First 4 letters of last name				FIRST INIT	MID INIT
A	A	A	A	A	A
B	B	B	B	B	B
C	C	C	C	C	C
D	D	D	D	D	D
E	E	E	E	E	E
F	F	F	F	F	F
G	G	G	G	G	G
H	H	H	H	H	H
I	I	I	I	I	I
J	J	J	J	J	J
K	K	K	K	K	K
L	L	L	L	L	L
M	M	M	M	M	M
N	N	N	N	N	N
O	O	O	O	O	O
P	P	P	P	P	P
Q	Q	Q	Q	Q	Q
R	R	R	R	R	R
S	S	S	S	S	S
T	T	T	T	T	T
U	U	U	U	U	U
V	V	V	V	V	V
W	W	W	W	W	W
X	X	X	X	X	X
Y	Y	Y	Y	Y	Y
Z	Z	Z	Z	Z	Z

6. DATE OF BIRTH

MONTH	DAY		YEAR	
JAN				
FEB				
MAR	0	0	0	0
APR	1	1	1	1
MAY	2	2	2	2
JUN	3	3	3	3
JUL		4	4	4
AUG		5	5	5
SEP		6	6	6
OCT		7	7	7
NOV		8	8	8
DEC		9	9	9

7. SEX

MALE
FEMALE

8. OTHER

1 A B C D E
2 A B C D E
3 A B C D E

OpScan *i*NSIGHT™ forms by Pearson NCS EM-255315-1:654321 Printed in U.S.A.

THIS PAGE INTENTIONALLY LEFT BLANK

The Princeton Review Diagnostic ACT Form

Completely darken bubbles with a No. 2 pencil. If you make a mistake, be sure to erase mark completely. Erase all stray marks.

ENGLISH

1	A	B	C	D
2	F	G	H	J
3	A	B	C	D
4	F	G	H	J
5	A	B	C	D
6	F	G	H	J
7	A	B	C	D
8	F	G	H	J
9	A	B	C	D
10	F	G	H	J
11	A	B	C	D
12	F	G	H	J
13	A	B	C	D
14	F	G	H	J
15	A	B	C	D
16	F	G	H	J
17	A	B	C	D
18	F	G	H	J
19	A	B	C	D
20	F	G	H	J
21	A	B	C	D
22	F	G	H	J
23	A	B	C	D
24	F	G	H	J
25	A	B	C	D
26	F	G	H	J
27	A	B	C	D
28	F	G	H	J
29	A	B	C	D
30	F	G	H	J
31	A	B	C	D
32	F	G	H	J
33	A	B	C	D
34	F	G	H	J
35	A	B	C	D
36	F	G	H	J
37	A	B	C	D
38	F	G	H	J
39	A	B	C	D
40	F	G	H	J
41	A	B	C	D
42	F	G	H	J
43	A	B	C	D
44	F	G	H	J
45	A	B	C	D
46	F	G	H	J
47	A	B	C	D
48	F	G	H	J
49	A	B	C	D
50	F	G	H	J
51	A	B	C	D
52	F	G	H	J
53	A	B	C	D
54	F	G	H	J
55	A	B	C	D
56	F	G	H	J
57	A	B	C	D
58	F	G	H	J
59	A	B	C	D
60	F	G	H	J
61	A	B	C	D
62	F	G	H	J
63	A	B	C	D
64	F	G	H	J
65	A	B	C	D
66	F	G	H	J
67	A	B	C	D
68	F	G	H	J
69	A	B	C	D
70	F	G	H	J
71	A	B	C	D
72	F	G	H	J
73	A	B	C	D
74	F	G	H	J
75	A	B	C	D

MATHEMATICS

1	A	B	C	D	E
2	F	G	H	J	K
3	A	B	C	D	E
4	F	G	H	J	K
5	A	B	C	D	E
6	F	G	H	J	K
7	A	B	C	D	E
8	F	G	H	J	K
9	A	B	C	D	E
10	F	G	H	J	K
11	A	B	C	D	E
12	F	G	H	J	K
13	A	B	C	D	E
14	F	G	H	J	K
15	A	B	C	D	E
16	F	G	H	J	K
17	A	B	C	D	E
18	F	G	H	J	K
19	A	B	C	D	E
20	F	G	H	J	K
21	A	B	C	D	E
22	F	G	H	J	K
23	A	B	C	D	E
24	F	G	H	J	K
25	A	B	C	D	E
26	F	G	H	J	K
27	A	B	C	D	E
28	F	G	H	J	K
29	A	B	C	D	E
30	F	G	H	J	K
31	A	B	C	D	E
32	F	G	H	J	K
33	A	B	C	D	E
34	F	G	H	J	K
35	A	B	C	D	E
36	F	G	H	J	K
37	A	B	C	D	E
38	F	G	H	J	K
39	A	B	C	D	E
40	F	G	H	J	K
41	A	B	C	D	E
42	F	G	H	J	K
43	A	B	C	D	E
44	F	G	H	J	K
45	A	B	C	D	E
46	F	G	H	J	K
47	A	B	C	D	E
48	F	G	H	J	K
49	A	B	C	D	E
50	F	G	H	J	K
51	A	B	C	D	E
52	F	G	H	J	K
53	A	B	C	D	E
54	F	G	H	J	K
55	A	B	C	D	E
56	F	G	H	J	K
57	A	B	C	D	E
58	F	G	H	J	K
59	A	B	C	D	E
60	F	G	H	J	K

The Princeton Review Diagnostic ACT Form

Completely darken bubbles with a No. 2 pencil. If you make a mistake, be sure to erase mark completely. Erase all stray marks.

READING

1 A B C D
2 F G H J
3 A B C D
4 F G H J
5 A B C D
6 F G H J
7 A B C D
8 F G H J
9 A B C D
10 F G H J
11 A B C D
12 F G H J
13 A B C D
14 F G H J
15 A B C D
16 F G H J
17 A B C D
18 F G H J
19 A B C D
20 F G H J
21 A B C D
22 F G H J
23 A B C D
24 F G H J
25 A B C D
26 F G H J
27 A B C D
28 F G H J
29 A B C D
30 F G H J
31 A B C D
32 F G H J
33 A B C D
34 F G H J
35 A B C D
36 F G H J
37 A B C D
38 F G H J
39 A B C D
40 F G H J

SCIENCE REASONING

1 A B C D
2 F G H J
3 A B C D
4 F G H J
5 A B C D
6 F G H J
7 A B C D
8 F G H J
9 A B C D
10 F G H J
11 A B C D
12 F G H J
13 A B C D
14 F G H J
15 A B C D
16 F G H J
17 A B C D
18 F G H J
19 A B C D
20 F G H J
21 A B C D
22 F G H J
23 A B C D
24 F G H J
25 A B C D
26 F G H J
27 A B C D
28 F G H J
29 A B C D
30 F G H J
31 A B C D
32 F G H J
33 A B C D
34 F G H J
35 A B C D
36 F G H J
37 A B C D
38 F G H J
39 A B C D
40 F G H J

I hereby certify that I have truthfully identified myself on this form. I accept the consequences of falsifying my identity.

Your signature

Today's date

The Princeton Review
Diagnostic ACT Form

ESSAY

Begin your essay on this side. If necessary, continue on the opposite side.

Continue on the opposite side if necessary.

The Princeton Review
Diagnostic ACT Form

Continued from previous page.

PLEASE PRINT YOUR INITIALS

First	Middle	Last

Continued from previous page.

PLEASE PRINT YOUR INITIALS

First	Middle	Last

Continued from previous page.

PLEASE PRINT YOUR INITIALS

First	Middle	Last

Chapter 26
Practice Exam 1: Answers and Explanations

English		Math		Reading		Science	
1. B	40. H	1. E	40. K	1. C	40. G	1. A	40. H
2. F	41. B	2. G	41. B	2. J		2. J	
3. D	42. J	3. B	42. K	3. A		3. C	
4. G	43. A	4. J	43. B	4. J		4. J	
5. A	44. G	5. C	44. J	5. B		5. D	
6. H	45. C	6. H	45. E	6. G		6. J	
7. C	46. H	7. B	46. H	7. D		7. B	
8. J	47. C	8. J	47. C	8. F		8. J	
9. D	48. F	9. E	48. J	9. C		9. A	
10. F	49. C	10. F	49. C	10. G		10. F	
11. B	50. J	11. E	50. G	11. C		11. D	
12. H	51. A	12. J	51. E	12. G		12. G	
13. D	52. F	13. B	52. G	13. A		13. A	
14. G	53. D	14.K	53. C	14. G		14. H	
15. A	54. F	15. A	54. F	15. C		15. B	
16. G	55. D	16. G	55. D	16. G		16.H	
17. C	56. H	17. D	56. G	17. D		17. C	
18. H	57. B	18. F	57. B	18. H		18. J	
19. D	58. G	19. A	58. F	19. D		19. A	
20. F	59. B	20. K	59. C	20. F		20. H	
21. D	60. G	21. E	60. J	21. A		21. C	
22. F	61. D	22. F		22. F		22. G	
23. C	62. F	23. B		23. D		23. C	
24. G	63. C	24. H		24. G		24. J	
25. D	64. F	25. E		25. A		25. A	
26. G	65. C	26. H		26. J		26. J	
27. A	66. G	27. C		27. D		27. D	
28. G	67. C	28. G		28. H		28. F	
29. A	68. F	29. B		29. C		29. D	
30. H	69. B	30. G		30. G		30. G	
31. B	70. J	31. C		31. A		31. C	
32. F	71. B	32. G		32. H		32. H	
33. D	72. G	33. E		33. C		33. C	
34. F	73. D	34. J		34. J		34. J	
35. A	74. F	35. D		35. A		35. A	
36. H	75. D	36. K		36. H		36. H	
37. C		37. D		37. D		37. B	
38. H		38. H		38. J		38. F	
39. B		39. H		39. A		39. D	

ENGLISH TEST

1. B This sentence needs a comma after the complete idea and before the incomplete one. This brief pause clarifies that the incomplete idea is modifying Hawaii. Choices (C) and (D) introduce additional words that are unnecessary or create an error.

2. F In Sentence 4, the writer provides additional support for how difficult the race is. If deleted, the passage would lose this emphasis, as choice (F) describes. Choices (G), (H), and (J) all introduce extraneous details that have not been provided by the passage.

3. D This sentence requires a contrast to the previous paragraph. Only choice (D) provides that with *however*.

4. G As written, this sentence incorrectly places a comma after the word *athletics*, which is not needed since an incomplete idea follows. This eliminates choices (F) and (H). Choice (J) is not correct because it places a comma after the word *and*, and uses the incorrect pronoun *there* to refer to sports' *physical demands*, which requires the possessive.

5. A. This sentence is correct as written, because *proved* as it is used means *became*. All the other options are synonyms of a different definition of *proved* and thus change the intended meaning of the sentence.

6. H The word *somewhat* is referring to the *amusing way* in which the race started. Therefore, *somewhat* needs to be before the word *amusing* to correctly modify it, choice (H).

7. C This sentence is providing the names of two sports clubs and the island on which they functioned. There is no need to separate anything here with a comma because it is a list of only two items, so that eliminates choices (A), (B), and (D). Only (C) correctly removes the commas.

8. J *Claiming* describes the bikers and does not require a conjunction, eliminating choices (F) and (G). Choice (H) would create a comma splice.

9. D The phrase before the comma is incomplete, and the word *when* introduces a second incomplete idea, leaving the sentence without any complete ideas. Therefore, the only possible answer is to delete the underlined portion, or (D).

10. F The underlined phrase refers to the three separate races that were eventually combined into the single race of the Triathlon. Therefore, it should remain where it is now, choice (F).

11. B As written, the underlined section is redundant because it references the pages he is reading, although they were just mentioned a few words before. This redundancy can be eliminated by selecting choice (B).

12. H You can never join the helping verb *had* with the simple past tense *became*. This eliminates choice (F). Choice (G) is the present tense of the verb, and choice (J) is the incorrect form of the past tense,

so both of those can be eliminated as well. Only choice (H) provides the correct form of the simple past tense.

13. D Only choice (D) points out Haller's great achievement of winning the first Ironman. Choices (A) and (C) detract from his achievement by focusing on other competitors, and choice (B) discusses a moment of doubt Haller has.

14. G Choices (F), (H), and (J) all provide specific, plural phrases that could represent the competitors to whom the sentence is referring. Choice (G) is a singular, ambiguous *that* that cannot refer to the competitors.

15. A The final paragraph discusses how many compete in the race today, as well as how popular the race has become since its inception. This most closely aligns with choice (A).

16. G The underlined portion is incorrect as written because the *when* makes the second part of the sentence incomplete. Therefore, choice (F) can be eliminated. Whenever there is a list, all the elements of that list must be parallel. None of the other items in the sentence as written end in *–ing*, so that eliminates choice (H). Nor are any of them in the past tense, which eliminates (J). Only (G) matches the others, and thus must be the correct answer.

17. C As written, this sentence contains two complete ideas with no punctuation in between, which eliminates choice (A). Simply adding a comma does not fix the problem, so choice (B) cannot be correct. Changing *hoping* to *praying* does not help either, so choice (D) cannot be correct. Only choice (C), which separates the sentence into two by introducing a period, offers a viable solution.

18. H A conjunction is needed to join the two halves of the sentence together, eliminating (F) and (G) (note: *therefore* is an adverb, not a conjunction). *But* is not the right conjunction to use because the two clauses do not disagree with each other. That eliminates choice (J). The only choice left is (H).

19. D The subject of this sentence, *all the opportunities*, comes after the verb. However, the verb still must agree with it. Since the subject is plural, choices (A) and (B) are inappropriate because those are singular forms of the verb. Choice (C) is incorrect because the verb *lay* refers to placing an item down, like a book on the table, which is inappropriate in this context. The only acceptable choice is (D).

20. F In a list, there should be a comma after every item, including the one before the *and*. The first item in this list is *a nice pair of slacks*, so the first comma is needed after that expression but nowhere inside of it. This eliminates all the answer choices except (F).

21. D Sentence 2 refers to the narrator's acceptance of the volunteer position. This must logically follow the sentence that contains the director's offer of the position, Sentence 5.

22. F The phrase *an expert himself in every facet of hospital administration* is an additional descriptive detail that is not essential to the sentence. Therefore, it should have a comma on both sides of it. The correct answer is (F).

23. C The phrase preceding the comma at the beginning of this sentence must refer to the first noun following the phrase. As written, that noun is *my ears*, which cannot be correct because ears do not walk anywhere. Only choice (C) corrects the misplaced modifier by making *I* the subject.

24. G In an earlier sentence in this paragraph, the narrator describes herself as *overwhelmed* by all the noise in the hospital. Therefore, as the sounds continue, she becomes more overwhelmed, or *beseiged*, as in choice (G).

25. D The underlined section of the sentence refers to how the narrator's face revealed her fear at the same time that she looked around the ward. Choice (D) changes this meaning, so it is therefore the LEAST acceptable option.

26. G This question calls for a vivid description of the hallway. Only choice (G) provides this, by giving specific details about all the family members and colorful decorations. Choice (F) just describes the hallway as busy, which is not particularly vivid. Choices (H) and (J) don't specifically refer to the hallway at all.

27. A The phrase *the one in charge of the nursery* provides an extra detail that is not essential to the meaning of the sentence. As such, it needs to be set off by commas on both sides. Only choice (A) gives us this option.

28. G The pronoun *it* should be referring to the blankets. However, *it* is singular, so choice (F) can be eliminated. *Them* is the appropriate pronoun to use, so choice (J) can be eliminated as well. Finally, *placing* doesn't match *start* as it needs to. Therefore, choice (H) can be eliminated and choice (G) must be the answer.

29. A The final paragraph expresses the narrator's comfort in the nursery, especially as compared to the maternity ward. Therefore, when she gives the hospital director a nod, she is acknowledging the fact that she enjoys the new atmosphere. This most closely aligns with choice (A). At no point in the passage does the narrator express anger or the intention to quit, so choices (B) and (C) cannot be correct. Finally, nowhere else in the passage is the narrator nodding, so choice (D) can be eliminated as well.

30. H This new information acts as an introduction to the narrator's first day working at the hospital. This most logically should be inserted at the beginning of Paragraph 3, in which the actual activities of her first day are described.

31. B In this sentence, the author is making a comparison between the reputation snakes have and the reputation they deserve. Such a comparison will always be separated by the word *than*, which eliminates choices (A) and (D). Choice (C) can be eliminated because it changes the meaning of the sentence to imply that snakes have the deadliest reputation, which was not stated.

32. F At this point in the essay, the author is identifying numerous negative associations related to the snake. Only choice (F) adds to this list. Choices (G), (H), and (J) do not contain anything particularly negative in their portrayals of the snake.

33. D As written, the phrase *that is popular* refers to *a snake*, which is incorrect. The phrase should refer to the *reference*. The only choice which provides this concisely is choice (D).

34. F Choice (G) contains the word *who's*, which is the contraction for *who is* and is inappropriate in this sentence. Choice (H) contains the word *it's*, a contraction for *it is* and likewise inappropriate. Choice (J) contains the word *its'*, which is never correct. The only remaining choice is (F).

35. A This sentence is correct as written. The phrase following *fangs* is an unnecessary descriptive piece added to the sentence, which should be set off with commas. It is not necessary to introduce any additional words, because that would make the sentence a run-on.

36. H The word *prey* is followed by a list of the items that fall into this category. A colon is needed before such a list, which makes choice (H) correct.

37. C As written, the phrase *they are provoked* is ambiguous. Does it refer to the snakes or the people? Only choice (C) clarifies this ambiguity in a concise way.

38. H The statistic quoted acts as support for the preceding sentence, arguing that snakes normally do not pose much threat to humans. Therefore, choice (H) is the correct response.

39. B The underlined phrase needs a verb consistent with the singular subject of *Prompt treatment*. Only choice (B) is consistent and concise.

40. H As underlined, the transition in this sentence is neither parallel nor logical, because the second half of the sentence is a separate idea that does not follow from the first. Only choice (H) provides a parallel transition.

41. B As written, this sentence is not a complete thought. It needs verbs, and without helping verbs like *was* or *is*, the words *considering* and *avoiding* can't stand alone. Choices (A) and (C) don't fix the problem. Choice (D) incorrectly changes the sentence to past tense, as well as combines two clauses. Only choice (B) gives two present tense verbs, "consider" and "avoid," to fix the fragment in the original sentence.

42. J As written, this sentence has complete ideas joined incorrectly. Two complete thoughts cannot be joined by a comma, which eliminates choices (F) and (H). Nor can two complete thoughts have no punctuation between them, so choice (G) must also be incorrect. Only choice (J) correctly uses a semi-colon between the two thoughts.

43. A The opening paragraph referred to all the common derogatory phrases associated with snakes. Therefore, since choice (A) refers to the *snake in the grass* referenced in that paragraph, it would achieve the writer's aim of referencing the opening paragraph. All the other choices refer to items mentioned elsewhere in the passage, not in the first paragraph.

44. G The final sentence of the first paragraph refers to the snake as *unjustly maligned* despite its *ugly, slimy appearance.* The essay goes on to describe some of the misconceptions people have about snakes. Therefore, this sentence sets up the main idea of the passage as a whole, as choice (G) suggests.

45. C Choice (C) is correct because the author takes a positive view of snakes: they do not hurt humans to the degree commonly believed, and they help society by keeping the population of undesirable rodents and other pests in check.

46. H The underlined portion needs a word to indicate the present day. All the choices do this except choice (H), which changes the meaning.

47. C Choice (C) changes the meaning to indicate that the challenges showed anything was possible, whereas the original meaning of the sentence indicates that Hurston's perseverance is what made anything possible. Therefore, choice (C) is not acceptable.

48. F The underlined portion is correct as is, because it is the only choice that accurately reflects Hurston as an individualistic person, in keeping with the description of her provided in the previous paragraph. All the other choices change the meaning of the phrase in ways not supported by the passage.

49. C This question calls for something historical in nature that makes Eatonville unique. Only choice (C) provides this. Choice (A) doesn't make the town unique, as many cities share a similar climate. Likewise, choices (B) and (D) discuss the town's founding but do not indicate that the town is different from any other community founded in the same era.

50. J This sentence needs a simple conjunction to join the two items listed, *freedom* and *independence.* For this reason, choice (J) is the answer. Choice (F) makes no sense in the context of the sentence, because what follows *that* is not a separate clause. Choice (G) incorrectly introduces an unnecessary verb. Choice (H) makes the sentence two complete ideas linked incorrectly.

51. A The underlined portion is correct as written, choice (A). This list of two items is essential to the meaning of the sentence, so it should not be set off with commas. Only information that could be removed without altering the meaning requires commas.

52. F This sentence is correct as written. Choices (G) and (H) introduce a comma into the sentence that incorrectly separates the subject from the verb. Choice (J) incorrectly introduces a semi-colon, which can only be used to connect two complete thoughts.

53. D The correct choice is (D), because it correctly eliminates the redundancy in the underlined passage. The term *literature* means *books, poems, and plays,* so there is no need to repeat it, as choice (A) does. The same applies to choices (B) and (C), so they are likewise incorrect.

54. F This sentence needs a verb in the past tense. This eliminates choices (H) and (J). Choice (G) cannot be correct, because *developed* does not require a preposition to follow it. Therefore, the correct answer must be choice (F).

55. D This additional information relating to Billie Holiday is not relevant at this point in a passage dedicated to Hurston. It provides interesting but superfluous detail, which most closely aligns with choice (D).

56. H This question wants a word that indicates the novel accurately reflects the actual dialect spoken. Choice (H) does this, because if something is authentic, it is true to the original. Choices (F), (G), and (J) positively comment on the dialect, but tell us nothing about how accurate it is.

57. B As written, the underlined *it* is ambiguous. The sentence needs to clearly identify what *it* is referring to. This eliminates both choices (A) and (C). Choice (D) cannot work, because *which* does not refer to Hurston's work. Therefore, choice (B) must be correct.

58. G Sentence 4 identifies one of Hurston's novels, and the following sentences provide additional information about the plot of that novel and the critical reception it received. Choice (G) most closely aligns with this summary. Choice (F) is incorrect because nothing in the remaining sentences indicates one specific influence. Choice (H) is incorrect because only one of the subsequent sentences provides a plot detail. Finally, choice (J) is incorrect because the remaining sentences focus on the novel, not Eatonville specifically.

59. B As written, the underlined portion is incorrect because the transition it uses indicates the sentence disagrees with the one that came before it. Therefore, choice (A) can be eliminated. However, choices (C) and (D) are incorrect as well, because there is no direct cause and effect relationship between the two sentences. Choice (B) is the best choice because no transition is necessary at all.

60. G The phrase *as one of the best writers of her era* is essential to the meaning of the sentence, which means it cannot be set off by commas. It does, however, need an *and* after it to join the two halves of the sentence together. Thus, choice (G) must be correct.

61. D As written, this sentence is incomplete and cannot be ended with a period. This eliminates choice (A). There is also no need to introduce a conjunction, because that does not fix the problem. Therefore, the correct answer must be (D).

62. F The phrase *Soviet Union* is extra information that is not essential to the meaning of the sentence. As such, it should have a dash on both sides of it, which only choice (F) provides.

63. C The word *Americas* is being used as a possessive, because it owns the *powerful office* that follows. Therefore, it should have an apostrophe before the *s*. This eliminates choices (A) and (D). The phrase *most powerful* is modifying the word *office* and does not need a comma. Therefore, choice (C) must be correct.

64. F The underlined portion is correct as written. A pronoun in the subject case is needed here, because it is the subject of the verb in the idea that follows.

65. C The phrase *underprivileged* indicates that these individuals are not as fortunate as others in a given society. As such, it would be redundant to specify this again. Only choice (C) eliminates this redundancy.

66. G This sentence indicates that Carter supported a national energy policy. Only choice (G) aligns with this information.

67. C The phrase *on foreign oil* refers to what America depended upon. Therefore, it should be as close as possible to the word *dependence*, or choice (C).

68. F All the answer choices refer to the creation of the Carter Center. However, choice (F) changes the meaning to imply that Carter discovered the Center, rather than started it.

69. B The phrase *around the world* already refers to many different countries, so it would be redundant to specify those countries. Therefore, the correct answer is choice (B).

70. J The first words in this phrase, *at home*, indicate that Carter works within the United States. There is no need to identify this again, making the sentence redundant. Therefore, the correct answer is choice (J).

71. B As written, the placement of *abroad* incorrectly modifies the verb *focus*, which changes the intended meaning of the sentence. The word *abroad* refers to where Carter expends his efforts, or choice (B).

72. G Sentence 4 functions as a transition between the previous paragraph and this paragraph. As such it should come first, as choice (G) suggests.

73. D The correct preposition needs to be *with* in order to maintain the intended meaning of the sentence: someone concurring with Carter. Choices (A) and (C) use prepositions that never work with *agree*. Choice (B) changes the meaning to taking on an obligation.

74. F This essay intends to identify some of the positive humanitarian goals Carter has sought to achieve in his career. Choice (F) most closely aligns with this goal. Choices (G) and (J) focus on his politics while ignoring his humanitarian interests, so they can be eliminated. Choice (H) comments on a right as an American, which has nothing to do with the rest of the passage.

75. D The new sentence references Habitat for Humanity, which was discussed in Paragraph 4. Therefore, it would most logically be added to the end of that paragraph, or choice (D).

MATHEMATICS TEST

1. E Set up a proportion with the information you have and the information you are looking for:

$$\frac{\text{height}}{\text{length of shadow}} = \frac{24\text{ ft}}{6\text{ ft}} = \frac{x\text{ ft}}{18\text{ ft}}$$

Do the cross-multiplication to find that $x = 72$ feet, answer choice (E).

2. G Remember that Sherwood's \$100 payment covers both his one-time new-member fee and a few months of a membership. Since the new-member fee is \$16, this means that Sherwood put \$100 – \$16 = \$84 toward his monthly fees. Since each month costs \$14, Sherwood paid for \$84 ÷ \$14 = 6 months of membership.

3. B Although this looks like a problem in which you'll need to factor, you actually can just substitute the y value: $\frac{y^2-4}{y-2} = \frac{(-6)^2-4}{(-6)-2} = \frac{(36)-4}{-8} = \frac{32}{-8} = -4.$

4. J Because the group ended up with more than 15 students, they overpaid. Figure out the total amount they should have paid and subtract it from the amount that they did pay: (18)(\$11.50) – (18)(\$10.25) = \$22.50.

5. C When you are finding a probability, you need to figure out a basic part/whole relationship. In this case, there are 16 members in the orchestra, but only 12 of them are eligible to become speakers, so the "whole" (the denominator) must be 12. If you chose (B), you forgot to omit the 4 soloists. The likelihood that Itzhak would be chosen for this person is therefore $\frac{1}{12}$, because he represents one possibility out of the twelve eligible for the speaker-position.

6. H In order to find the perimeter of a rectangle, remember that there are four sides. In this case the four sides add up as follows: 8 ft + 8 ft + 17 ft + 17 ft = 50 ft. If you chose (F), you may have only added two sides of the rectangle, and if you chose (J), be careful—this is the area!

7. B Work slowly through this problem. The group has sold 240 passes online at \$9 each. This means that they have already made (240)(\$9) = \$2160. In order to reach their goal, they will need \$4000 – \$2160 = \$1840. Since the question asks how many in-person tickets they will need to sell, you can approximate how many tickets will get them \$1840 by dividing: \$1840 ÷ \$12 = 153.333. Since there is no such thing as 0.333 tickets, you have to round up to get 154 tickets, answer choice (B).

8. J Do basic cross-multiplication here. $\frac{9}{q} = \frac{6}{10}$ becomes (9)(10) = 6q, so $q = \frac{(9)(10)}{6} = \frac{90}{6} = 15$.

9. E Make sure you keep all your negative signs straight and distribute properly. The original equation is $-9(y - 13) = 16$. First, distribute the (–9) to find $(-9y + 117) = 16$. Subtract the 117 from both sides to find $(-9y) = -101$. Divide each side by the (–9) to find $y = 11.2 = \frac{101}{9}$.

10. F Because Points F, G, H, and J are collinear, you can figure out $\angle GHK$ by subtracting 180° – $\angle JHK$ = 180° – 120° = 60°. Segments $\overline{GK}$ and $\overline{HK}$ are equivalent, so angles $\angle GHK$ and $\angle HGK$ are congruent, and $\angle HGK$ = 60°. Again because they are collinear, $\angle HGK + \angle FGK$ = 180°, so $\angle FGK$ = 120°. Isolate this triangle to find $\angle GFK$. Because of the two congruent sides, $\angle GFK \cong \angle GKF$, so $\angle FGK + \angle GFK + \angle GKF = \angle FGK + 2(\angle GFK)$ = 120° + 2($\angle GFK$) = 180°, and $\angle GFK$ = 30°.

11. E To find the answer, substitute (–3) for x throughout the equation $f(x) = 7x^2 - 9x + 4$. Once you've done this, you will find the following: $7(-3)^2 - 9(-3) + 4 = 7(9) + 27 + 4 = 63 + 27 + 4 = 94$. If you chose any of the other answers, you may not have distributed the negative properly.

12. J Use the answer choices and work backwards. Find the smallest number that divides evenly by 16, 25, and 40. This is 400: 400 ÷ 16 = 25; 400 ÷ 25 = 16; and 400 ÷ 40 = 10. If you chose (K), be careful—this is a common multiple of all three numbers, but it is not the *least* common multiple.

13. B In order to cancel the original mistake, Tex will need to multiply by 3. Then, to get the number he wants, he will need to multiply by another 3. In total, he will be multiplying by 9, as in choice (B).

14. K There are 12 triangles, and the area of the whole figure is 96 cm^2, so each of the triangles has an area of 8 cm^2. Because each of the triangles is right isosceles, the base and height of each triangle are equivalent, so to find the length of each of these, use the area formula: $A = \frac{1}{2} = bh = \frac{1}{2}b^2$. Solve for b:$b = \sqrt{2A}$. The area of each triangle is 8, so you can find the base: $b = \sqrt{2A} = \sqrt{2(8)} = \sqrt{16}$ = 4. You don't need to find the hypotenuse of the triangle, because this problem asks for the perimeter of the figure, so count up the sides (there are 14) to find that the perimeter is 56 cm.

15. A The sum of the measures of all angles in a triangle is 180°. $\angle Y$ is described as a right angle, which means its measure is 90°. The other two angles, therefore, will have to add up to 90° to complete the 180° in the triangle. If $\angle Z$ measures less than 52°, then $\angle X$ must be *greater* than 90° – 52° = 38°. It cannot be *equal* to this value (as in choice [B]), because $\angle Z$ is described as *less than* 52°.

16. G Try the different operations listed. You will find that the only operation that makes the statement true is division. Replace all the emoticons with division signs: $(8 \div 2)^3 - (4 \div 1)^2 = (4)^3 - (4)^2 = 64 - 16 = 48$.

17. D First, identify a point on the graph. The easiest place to start is with the intercepts. The x-intercept is unclear, but the y-intercept passes through (0, 6), eliminating choices (A), (B), and (C). Between the latter two choices, you can solve for the x-intercept, to find that in choice (D), $x = \frac{6}{5}$ and in choice (E), $x = 3$. Although the exact x-intercept is unclear on the graph, it is definitely less than 2, so you can eliminate (E).

18. F Translate the English in this problem into the math of the answer choices. The problem reads, "An integer, x, is subtracted from 6. That difference is then multiplied by 3." This translates into the following: $(6 - x) \bullet 3$ or $3(6 - x)$. The second part of the problem reads, "This product is 15 more than half the original integer." Therefore $3(6 - x)$ will equal "15 more than half the original integer": $15 + \frac{1}{2}x$ or $\frac{1}{2}x + 15$. Therefore, $3(6 - x) = \frac{1}{2}x + 15$.

19. A Find the total production of each company after d days. Factory X starts with 18,000 units and can produce 120 units per day, so its production after d days will be $18{,}000 + 120d$. Factory Y starts with only 14,500 units, but it can produce 155 units per day, so its production after d days will be $14{,}500 + 155d$. Since you are looking for the number of days after which the total production of each factory will be equal, set the two equations equal to one another: $18{,}000 + 120d = 14{,}500 + 155d$. That's all there is to it—you don't have to solve this!

20. K Use the Pythagorean theorem to find the length of the hypotenuse: $a^2 + b_2 = c^2$, where c is the hypotenuse. $c = \sqrt{a^2 = b^2} = \sqrt{7^2 + 24^2} = \sqrt{50{,}625} = 25$. Note that this is 7:24:25, a Pythagorean triple. If you remember a few of the basic triples, you can save yourself a lot of figuring.

21. E Make sure you are distributing properly: $9(y + 3) - 2(4y - 4) = 9y + 27 - 8y + 8 = y + 35$.

22. F Set up a system of equations to find a:

$$a + 3b = 27$$

$$\underline{a - 3b = 9}$$

$$2a = 36$$

If $2a = 36$, then $a = 18$. Use this value to find the value of b:

$$18 - 3b = 9$$

$$3b = 18 - 9$$

$$3b = 9$$

$$b = 3$$

23. B Make sure you FOIL the equation properly: $(2x + 4)^2 = 4x^2 + 8x + 8x + 16 = 4x^2 + 16x + 16$. In this case $a = 4$, $b = 16$, and $c = 16$, so $a + b - c = 4 + 16 - 16 = 4$. If you chose (C), you may have forgotten to FOIL. If you chose (E), you may done $a + b + c$ rather than $a + b - c$.

24. H Split the figure into two rectangles and find the area of each. See the figure below:

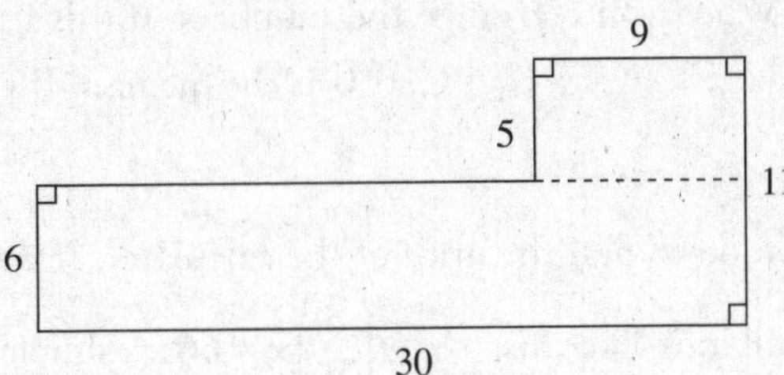

The smaller rectangle has sides of length 9 and 5, so its area by the formula $A = lw$ is 45. The larger rectangle has sides 30 and 6, so by the same formula, its area is 180. Add the two areas together to get $180 + 45 = 225$. If you chose (J), be careful—this is the perimeter.

25. E Look carefully at the values for each function. If a function can be graphed as $ax + b$, it is a linear function, and it will increase at constant increments. Function g decreases then increases in value. In fact, note the symmetry—this is a parabolic function, and can be graphed according to $ax^2 + bx + c$. Note that all the values in h increase by 3, so this is the function you want to work with. Since $h(-1) = 6$, $h(0)$ must equal 9.

26. H Put the equation into the slope-intercept form, $y = mx + b$. The m in this equation is the slope of the line. From the equation given, $10y - 16x = 13$, isolate the y term to get $10y = 16x + 13$, and divide through by 10 to get $y = \frac{16}{10}x + \frac{13}{10}$. Reduce to $y = \frac{8}{5}x + \frac{13}{10}$. The m term in this equation is $\frac{8}{5}$.

27. C First, simplify the expression: $x^2 + 5x - 24 = (x + 8)(x + 3)$. Now that you have the two expressions, find the solutions by setting each quantity equal to 0. If $x + 8 = 0$, then $x = -8$. If $x - 3 = 0$, then $x = 3$. Now find the sum of the solutions: $-8 + 3 = -5$. If you chose (E), you may have simplified correctly but found the roots incorrectly. If you chose (A), you found the product, not the sum.

28. G The perimeter of the larger triangle is 12 in + 7 in + 5 in = 24 in. Since you know the ratio of the perimeters, you do not have to find each side of the smaller triangle; you can set up the following ratio:

$$\frac{5}{6} = \frac{x}{24}$$

$$\frac{5(24)}{6} = x$$

$$x = 20 \text{ in}$$

29. B To find the median of a list of numbers, those numbers must be listed in order. Make sure you rearrange the numbers given before you find the median. If you didn't rearrange the numbers, you may have picked (E). When you rearrange the numbers in this list, they are in this order: –9°C, –8°C, –7°C, -7°C, 0°C, 1°C, 2°C, 3°C, 5°C. 0°C is the median. If you picked (A), be careful—this is the mode.

30. G You can set up an equation to find the price of the calculator. If we call the price of the calculator x, then the equation will look like this: $\sqrt{x}+\left(\frac{3}{8}\right)x=66$. A simpler tactic is to try out the answer choices to see which works in this equation. You will find this to be $144: \sqrt{144}+\left(\frac{3}{8}\right)144=66$.

31. C You need to solve for m in the equation given. The equation as written is $KE=\frac{1}{2}mv^2$. Once you've solved for m, the equation should look like this: $m=\frac{2KE}{v^2}$. Once you have this equation, substitute the values from the problem: $m=\frac{2KE}{v^2}=\frac{2(120)}{9^2}=\frac{240}{81}\approx$ 2.97, between 2 and 3. If you chose (B), you may have forgotten to apply the $\frac{1}{2}$.

32. G A "geometric sequence" is one in which all subsequent numbers have a fixed ratio to one another. In order to figure out this ratio, look at how the numbers change. The first term $2xz$ is multiplied by xy to become the second term $2x^2yz$. This second term is multiplied again by xy to become $2x^3y^2z$. Multiply this term by xy to find the answer: $2x^4y^3z$. Note, process of elimination may be more effective here. Throughout the sequence given, neither 2 nor the z has changed, so you can eliminate (H), (J), and (K). The exponents have increased, not decreased, so you can eliminate (F).

33. E Use the histogram. Four critics gave the book a one-star review. There are thirty total critics, so the relationship you need is $\frac{4}{30}=\frac{2}{15}$.

34. J There are 360° in a circle, and, as the histogram shows, one-star reviews make up $\frac{2}{15}$ of all the reviews. As a result, the one-star reviews will make up $\frac{2}{15}$ of the whole circle: $\frac{2}{15}\times 360° = 48°$.

35. D Make sure you count every review. There are thirty of them, and the sum of the thirty reviews is 79. To find the average, divide $\frac{79}{80}$ to get 2.63, rounded to the nearest hundredth.

36. K Simplify the expression by factoring.

$$\frac{(x^2+7x+12)(x-2)}{(x^2+2x-8)(x+3)}=\frac{(x+3)(x+4)(x-2)}{(x+4)(x-2)(x+3)}=\frac{(x+4)(x-2)(x+3)}{(x+4)(x-2)(x+3)}=1.$$

37. D The logo in the t-shirt is a right triangle. You are given the 35° angle, so you need to determine which side you have and which side you need to find relative to this angle. On the figure, you have the 10-inch side, which is *opposite* this angle. You're looking for the top diagonal side of the triangle, which in this case is the *hypotenuse* of the triangle. Sine is the function that requires *opposite* and *hypotenuse* by the following formula: $\sin\theta=\frac{opp}{hyp}$. By this equation, $hyp=\frac{opp}{\sin\theta}$ and the top side $=\frac{10}{\sin 35°}$.

38. H The center of the circle will be the midpoint of the diameter. Use the midpoint formula to find the midpoint of the points (4,3) and (–9,–2): $\left(\frac{x_1+x_2}{2},\frac{y_1+y_2}{2}\right)$. Insert the points to find $\left(\frac{4+(-9)}{2},\frac{3+(-2)}{2}\right)$. If you chose (J), be careful—you may have forgotten to divide by 2, and if you chose (G), you mixed up the *x*- and *y*-coordinates.

39. H Use the distance formula to find the distance between the two points (–7,4) and (–2,6): $d=\sqrt{(x_2-x_1)^2+(y_2-y_1)^2}=\sqrt{(-7-(-2))^2+(4-6)^2}=\sqrt{(-5)^2+(-2)^2}=\sqrt{29}$.

This value is approximately 5.385, but if you chose (F), you didn't complete the problem. Every unit on the map is equal to 5 nautical miles, and the problem is asking for the value in nautical miles. Multiply 5.385 by 5 nautical miles to find 26.92 nautical miles, which is closest to answer choice (H).

40. K On a "must be" question, the relationships must be true in all cases. If there is one case in which a relationship is not true, that answer choice is incorrect. Because this is an EXCEPT question, the incorrect relationship will be the correct answer. Answer (K) is often true, but not always. If you multiply $\sqrt{2}$, an irrational number, by itself, you get a rational number: 4.

41. B Because *i* is defined as the square root of negative one ($\sqrt{-1}$), its range of possibility when raised to certain powers is limited. $i=\sqrt{-1}$, $i^2=\sqrt{-1}$, $i^3=-\sqrt{-1}$, $i^4=1$. If you continue the pattern, you will find that these are the only possible values for *i* raised to any power (including negative powers). Choice (B) is the only answer choice that lists one of these values.

42. K Note the symmetry in the chart. The equation given shows that this graph is a parabola, but even if you haven't made that deduction, the values in the chart show a general trend in the data. When x is –3 and –5, $y = 0$; when x is –1 and –7, $y = 8$. According to this data, you can infer that values less than –7 and greater than –1 will be greater than 8. Therefore, –8 will have a greater value than the others listed in the answer choices. If you have trouble reading the chart, you can always try out the values in the equation and see which gives you the greatest $f(x)$.

43. B The formula for the volume of a right circular cylinder is $V = \pi r^2 h$. This question asks for the radius and gives V and h, so solve the equation for r: $r = \sqrt{\frac{V}{\pi h}}$. Substitute the values that you know to find r: $r = \sqrt{\frac{64\pi}{\pi(4)}} = \sqrt{16} = 4$. If you chose (E), you may have forgotten to take the square root of the radius. If you chose (C), you may have forgotten to include the height in your calculation.

44. J First, consider the relationships that you know. The ratio of the perimeter of ΔFLM to ΔFLM is 3:5, and the ratio of $\overline{FG}$ to $\overline{FG}$ is 1:5. Because all traingles share $\angle F$ and the lines are parallel, the three triangles are similar, which means all their sides—and therefore the perimeters—are proportional. From the proportions given, you can determine that the ratio of ΔFGH to ΔFLM to ΔFLM is 1:3:5; therefore, the ratio of $\overline{FG}$ to $\overline{FG}$ to $\overline{FG}$ is also 1:3:4. Based on this ratio, you can substitute values for each of the segments to figure out the ratio of $\overline{GJ}$ to $\overline{FG}$. You can say that $\overline{FG} = 1$, $\overline{FG} = 3$, and $\overline{FG} = 5$. This enables you to calculate $\overline{GJ} = \overline{FG} - \overline{FG} = 3 - 1 = 2$. The ratio of $\overline{GJ}$ to $\overline{FG}$ is therefore 2:1. If you chose (H), make sure you read the question carefully—you may have switched the segments.

45. E You need to find the distance along the y-axis that Avi traveled in total. Isolate each part of Avi's ride. Note that each of these legs can be made into the hypotenuse of a right triangle. The first part of the ride creates a special 30-60-90 triangle, and the second part of the trip creates a special 45-45-90 triangle. See the figures below:

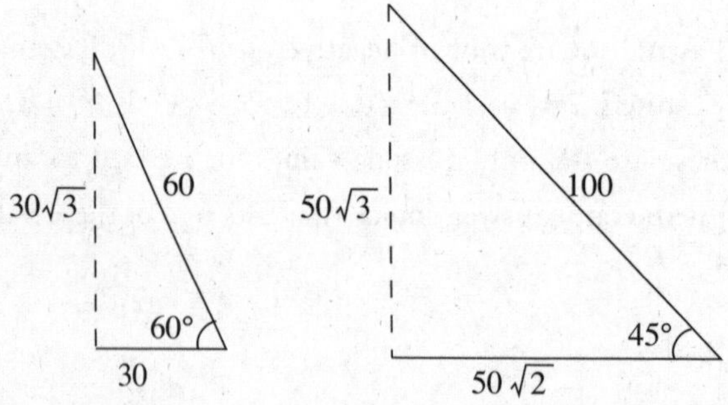

Therefore, the vertical height of the first part of the ride is $30\sqrt{3}$, and the vertical height of the second part of the ride is $50\sqrt{2}$. Don't forget to add the 35 m he rode along Broad St. at the end, to get a full vertical distance of $35 + 50\sqrt{2} + 30\sqrt{3}$. Answer choice (C) is the amount of the actual ride—read carefully; you just want the distance he traveled along the y-axis.

46. H The formula for a circle to which this problem is referring is $(x - h)^2 + (y - k)^2 = r^2$. In other words, the 25 in the equation $(x - 3)^2 + (y + 2)^2 = 25$ is the r^2. If $r^2 = 25$, then $r = 5$. With the radius, you can find the area of the circle with the basic formula $A = \pi r^2$. In this problem, since $r = 5$, the area will be $A = \pi(5)^2 = 25\pi$.

47. C Nearly everything you need is written on the figure. The only real piece of information you need from the text of the problem is that the y-axis bisects the base of the triangle. This tells you that the base of this triangle is $2b$. The height, according to the figure, is $2b^2 - 4$. With the base and height, you have all you need to find the area of the triangle with the standard formula $A = \frac{1}{2}bh$. Substitute the expressions to find $A = \frac{1}{2}(2b)(2b^2 - 4) = (b)(2b^2 - 4) = 2b^3 - 4b$. If you chose (B), you may have forgotten to divide by two.

48. J Because of the words "must be," the expression given must produce an even number in every instance. If you can find one instance in which an expression produces an odd number, you can eliminate that expression and answer choice. Since x can be any integer, there are many combinations you can try. In Choice (F), x could be 4, in which case $x + 5 = 4 + 5 = 9$, which is not even. In choice (G), x could be 1, which would make $\frac{x}{4} = \frac{1}{4}$,which is not even (nor is it an integer). If $x = 1$, choice (H) gives $x^4 = 1$, which is not even, and in choice (K), 5 raised to any integer power will always be odd. Only (J) generates an even number with every integer. This is because the product of an even number multiplied by either an even or an odd number will always be even.

49. C First, bring the exponent to the front of the expression: $\log_9(9^{\frac{7}{3}}) = \frac{7}{3}\log_9 9$. Once you're done, you can simplify the log portion of the expression. By the rules of logarithms, $\log_9 9$ can be rewritten as either $9^x = 9$ or $\frac{\log_9}{\log_9}$. As both expressions show, $\log_9 9 = 1$, which means you're left with $\frac{3}{4}$, between 2 and 3.

50. G In order to find the percent change, use the formula: % change $= \frac{\textit{difference}}{\textit{original}} \times 100\%$. In this case, Cameron's sales decreased from 23 to 19. In other words, he started at 23 (the original number), and he decreased to 19 (a difference of 4). Therefore, % change $= \frac{4}{23} \times 100 \approx 17.4\%$. If you chose (K), you may have calculated the increase from 19 to 23 rather than the decrease from 23 to 19.

51. E Maura wanted an average of 30 new accounts over the course of 4 months. This means that over the course of these four months, she had to create a total of 120 new accounts. Write this in an equation: Total = Jan. + Feb. + Mar. + Apr. Substitute what you know. 120 = 31 + 25 + Mar. + 27. The total accounts needed in March will therefore be 120 – 31 – 25 – 27 = 37.

52. G Don had 64 sales in January, and this value decreases by 5% each month. Do the calculations as follows, and don't round until you're done! February accounts = (64) – (0.05)(64) = 60.8. March accounts = (60.8) – (0.05)(60.8) = 57.76. April accounts = (57.76) – (0.05)(57.76) = 54.872. May accounts = (54.872) – (54.872)(0.05) = 52.1284 ≈ 52 accounts.

53. C You can disregard the long equation of the function given in the problem. All you need to answer this question is the graph. As the problem says, the amplitude of this function is the "average of the absolute values" of the minimum and maximum values of $f(x)$. Pull this information from the graph. The graph goes up to $y = 3$ and down to $y = -3$. Take the average of the absolute values of these: $\frac{|3|+|3|}{2} = 3$. If you chose (E), be careful—this is the period.

54. F Start with the tangent relationship. The problem says that the tangent of the angle of vision is $\frac{7}{6}$. From SOHCAHTOA, you know that the tangent relationship is defined as $\tan\theta = \frac{opp}{adj}$, or, in terms of this problem, the tangent of the angle of vision is $\frac{\text{horizontal distance}}{\text{height of the building}}$. Set up a proportion: $\frac{7}{6} = \frac{\text{horizontal distance}}{\text{height of the building}}$. Fill in what you know: $\frac{7}{6} = \frac{\text{horizontal distance}}{30}$. Cross multiply to find that the horizontal distance from home plate to the building is 35 m. If you chose (H), you may have found the opposite relationship.

55. D If you chose (E), be careful—3 is a solution to this equation, but it is rational. This question asks for a solution that is NOT rational. To find the solutions, solve the equation for y. First, isolate the absolute value expression $|y^2 - 11| = 2$. Remember as you're solving this equation that you will have to create two different equations as you're removing the absolute value sign: $y^2 - 11 = 2$ and $y^2 - 11 = -2$. Solve each of these equations to find that $y^2 = 13$ and $y^2 = 9$, and therefore $y = \pm 3$ and $y = \pm\sqrt{13}$. The irrational solutions are $\pm\sqrt{13}$.

56. G A positive slope indicates speed increase; a 0 slope indicates a constant speed; a negative slope indicates a speed decrease. The speed increases for 4 seconds, then remains constant for 3 seconds, then decreases to 0 in 2 seconds. This is best described by answer (G). Note, if you're not sure how to read the graph, recall that the problem says the entire test takes 9 seconds. Therefore, whether speeds are increasing or decreasing, the times during which they do so will have to add to 9 seconds.

57. B Because the compass is a circle, it has a degree measure of 360°. "East" starts at 90° from "North," so the point of the needle will need to travel 270° to get back to "North" in a clockwise direction. In other words, the point of the needle will have to travel across $\frac{3}{4}$ of the circle as it goes from "East" to "North" in a clockwise direction. The problem states that the point of the needle travels 42 mm, so if you apply the ratio to this problem, you can say that 42 mm is $\frac{3}{4}$ of the circumfer-

ence of the circle. Use this to find the full circumference: $42 = \frac{3}{4}C$ and $C = 56$ mm. Use this value to find the length of the needle, which is just the radius of this circle: $C = 2\pi r$. Solve the equation for r to find its value: $r = \frac{C}{2\pi} = \frac{56\text{mm}}{2\pi} \approx 8.9$. If you chose (A), you may have assumed the circumference of the circle was 42 mm. If you chose (E), you may have found the diameter of the circle.

58. F From 270° to 360°, the cosine function has a range of values from 0 to 1. In other words, it is always positive. Sine, by contrast, has a range of values from –1 to 0—it's always negative. Because the problem is asking for a tangent value from 270° to 360°, you know it must be negative because $\tan\theta = \frac{\sin\theta}{\cos\theta}$. Therefore, you can eliminate answers (J) and (K). Then, because $\cos\theta = \frac{5}{13}$, the adjacent side, opposite side, and hypotenuse relative to the angle θ form the Pythagorean triple 5:12:13, respectively. You know that $\tan\theta = \frac{opp}{adj}$, and within the range from 270° to 360°, tangent is negative, so $\tan\theta = \frac{-5}{12}$.

59. C Since you need a and b such that $ab = 8$, your four possible pairs are $a = 1, b = 8$; $a = 2, b = 4$; $a = 4, b = 2$; $a = 8, b = 1$. Keep your work organized as you figure:

a	b	2^a	c	c^b
1	8	2	2	256
2	4	4	4	256
4	2	16	16	256
8	1	256	256	256

As this small chart demonstrates, there are four values of c that work in both expressions. If you chose (D), you may have forgotten that both $a = 1, b = 8$ and $a = 8$ and $b = 1$ are distinct and valid pairs.

60. J The formula for the length of the diagonal of a rectangular prism is $a^2 + b^2 + c^2 = d_2$ where a, b, and c represent the edges of the rectangular prism and d represents its diagonal. In the case of a cube, $a = b = c$, so the equation can be rewritten as follows: $3a^2 = d^2$. In this problem, $d = 3\sqrt{3}$, so $3a^2 = (3\sqrt{3})^2$. Therefore, $3a^2 = (9)(3)$ and $a = 3$. Therefore, the length of the edge of this cube is 3. Look at the figure—you can see from the figure that the length of the diameter of the sphere is equivalent to the length from one side of the figure to another, an edge. The diameter of the sphere is equivalent to an edge of the cube, so the diameter is 3, answer choice (J).

READING TEST

1. C Choice (C) is correct because the third paragraph states that "God Bless the Child" was *familiar mostly to adults.* Because of this, it is more likely that the song would be familiar to Monique's parents, who must be adults, than it would be to her friends, who are presumably high school students and not yet adults. Choice (A) is incorrect because the passage never identifies "God Bless the Child" as a Rodgers & Hammerstein number. Choice (B) is incorrect because the passage does not support the extreme claim that "God Bless the Child" is the *most* sophisticated Billie Holiday song. Choice (D) is incorrect because Monique's song choice is presented as a contrast to the overly enthusiastic choices of her peers.

2. J Choice (J) is correct because the passage initially describes Monique and her friends as *aloof,* because they isolate themselves in the auditorium and Monique acts like a monarch with a royal court, and *disparaging,* because they are anxious to belittle the other students during their auditions. Choice (F) is incorrect because, although the passage describes that most students are nervous about going first, this does not describe how Monique and her friends are presented. Choice (G) is incorrect because, although Monique and her friends react to Esperanza's song choice with *disbelief,* that is not how they are initially portrayed in the passage. Choice (H) is incorrect because Monique and her friends are portrayed as being unfriendly and excluding.

3. A Choice (A) is correct because the passage states that Esperanza did not look up until she got to center stage and then *looked only at Mrs. Dominguez.* Choice (B) is incorrect because the passage says she shuffled her feet on her walk to the stage, which is not a confident stride. Choice (C) is incorrect because the passage states she was *paying little attention to the other auditions.* Choice (D) is incorrect because the passage only states that she was *working* on her geometry homework, not that she finished it.

4. J The question is asking for the rhetorical effect of the statement *But not this year.* The previous paragraph establishes that students generally dread the first audition slot and relates the tense manner in which Monique used to view the first slot. The paragraph that follows this phrase explains that Monique had decided to embrace the first slot as a means of surprising her peers. Choice (J) is correct because it identifies the statement in question as a contrast between the status quo and Monique's surprising decision. Choice (F) is incorrect because the passage provides no evidence that most students have resolved their fears of going first, only that Monique has. Choice (G) is incorrect because the passage never establishes the extreme claim that this year's audition was the *strangest yet.* Choice (H) is incorrect because the passage does not go on to describe any different imagery Monique associates with the uncomfortable first slot but rather to say she is no longer uncomfortable with it at all.

5. B The passage describes in the sixth paragraph that Monique and her friends are *sitting at the back of the auditorium.* In the ninth paragraph the passage states that *Esperanza had been sitting alone in the first row.* Together, these facts justify choice (B). Choice (A) is incorrect because it makes the extreme claim that Esperanza is the *most* teased student, for which there is no evidence in the passage. Choice (C) is incorrect because the passage does not say that Monique and Esperanza auditioned consecutively, and the seventh paragraph implies that there was *an endless parade* of students who auditioned in between them. Choice (D) is incorrect because, although Mrs. Dominguez is sensitive to possible ridicule meeting Esperanza's audition, there is no evidence of a conversation taking place beforehand.

6. G Choice (G) is correct because the passage states that Monique figured going first would *instill fear into her competition because they would realize that Monique had something they clearly lacked.* Choice (F) is incorrect because, although going first is evidence of Monique's self-confidence, the passage does not say Monique chose to go first to increase her self-confidence. Choices (H) and (J) are incorrect because Monique's stated motivation for going first is to intimidate her rivals, not to increase her chances of getting a part or to gain any favor with Mrs. Dominguez.

7. D The passage states that at the *climactic* moment of "rockets' red glare," *Esperanza's voice filled the room with a calm resonance.* This makes choice (D) correct. Choice (A) is incorrect because it is not supported in the passage. Choice (B) is incorrect because the detail about singing in multiple registers describes the song as a whole, not necessarily the climax. Choice (C) is incorrect because the passage contradicts it by saying that Esperanza was *calm.*

8. F When Mrs. Dominguez tells Esperanza she can begin to audition, the passage states that Mrs. Dominguez was *sensing the potential for* the *audition to devolve into a painful target of ridicule.* This makes answer choice (F) correct. Choice (G) is incorrect because this is how Esperanza is described in relation to Thornton High. Choice (H) is incorrect because this is what is anticipated by Monique and her friends. Choice (J) is incorrect because this relates to how Mrs. Dominguez viewed Monique's decision to audition first.

9. C Choice (C) is correct because the passage states that, once Esperanza was moving *methodically through the tune, the expectant smiles of mockery were quickly vanishing from the faces of all who listened.* Choice (A) is incorrect because the decision of where to sit was based on wanting to make comments about all the auditions and came before Esperanza's audition. Choice (B) is incorrect because their preconceived notions are described prior to Esparanza's audition, not as a reaction to the audition. Choice (D) is incorrect because the passage states that Monique and her friends were critical of Esperanza's song choice and even the resulting patriotism they felt is described as *reluctant.*

10. G Esperanza sings "The Star Spangled Banner" for her audition. The twelfth paragraph explains that *the final phrase of the song* is *often soaked in vibrato*. This makes choice (G) correct. Choice (F) is incorrect because the passage states that Monique and her friends anticipated a "mousy" voice from Esperanza, but says nothing about "The Star Spangled Banner" being well suited to that type of voice. Choice (H) is incorrect because, although Esperanza's performance is ultimately impressive, the passage says that the song is *trite* and *formulaic*. Choice (J) is incorrect because when Esperanza begins singing her song, *Monique and her friends looked at each other in total disbelief.*

11. C The third paragraph asks the reader to consider a contrast between an original user of a remote and a modern user. Choices (A), (B), and (D) are details provided to describe the original user. Choice (C) is a detail provided to describe the modern user. Hence, choice (C) is correct.

12. G Choice (G) is correct because the author lists several important inventions of the twentieth century but does not identify any of them as the *most significant*. Choice (F) is incorrect because the author states that most people think the solution is new clean energy technology. Choice (H) is incorrect because the author attributes the root of tool-making to the mindset of *There's got to be a better way*. Choice (J) is incorrect because the author describes how consumers go from *awed gratitude to discriminating preference*.

13. A The point that an example is used to illustrate is often found right before the example. In this case, the end of the first paragraph states that *the longer a given technology exists, the more we take it for granted*. The comparison between different users of remote controls is designed to illustrate this idea. Choice (A) best summarizes this concept and so is correct. Choice (B) is incorrect because the author never stresses a need to read instructions. Choice (C) is incorrect because modern users are described as using remote controls with ease and comfort. Choice (D) is incorrect because, while likely true, there is no support in the passage for the idea that remote controls have become *far more effective* than they were.

14. G The passage focuses on the technology around us that often goes unappreciated, ultimately warning us that our unrealistic faith in technology may lead us into global climate trouble. Words and phrases like *spoiled*, *unduly optimistic*, and *unfairly demanding* indicate the author's attitude that most modern humans are somewhat in the wrong. Choice (G) is the safest match for this tone, which makes it the correct answer. Choice (F) is incorrect, because although the passage does look backwards in time at certain spots, it is primarily focused on how the present is rather than a wish to return to the past. Choice (H) is incorrect because the author seems to be calling attention to the *dangerous extension of* our *mindset*, rather than sympathizing with it. Choice (J) is incorrect because the majority of the passage does not indicate the author's fear. The various references to shock and awe for new technology indicate amazement but not fright. The possible doomsday scenario towards the end of the passage does sound scary, but it functions only to demonstrate that modern humans have some problematic attitudes towards technology.

15. C The context for this sentence explains that, because we are spoiled by technology, we typically believe it can fix any problem. The notion that we might need to fix ourselves is unthinkable. Choice (C) is the correct answer because it best expresses that the suggestion that we need to change our own habits would be *unlike* our normal assumptions about technology. Choice (A) is incorrect because extraterrestrial literally means "not from earth," and the context does not suggest the idea is *that* exotic. Choice (B) is incorrect because the passage indicates this idea is seldom heard within our culture, so the notion that it is a repetitive idea is not supported. Choice (D) is incorrect because, although we do not take the idea in question seriously, it is because we are not accustomed to hearing the idea, not because the idea itself is funny.

16. G The point of this paragraph is that children born into a society that already possesses impressive technology do not tend to appreciate how impressive it is that this technology is human-made. They accept it as a given, much as one accepts the elements of the periodic table as the given substances found in the universe. Choice (G) is correct because it best expresses this idea. Choice (F) is incorrect because the passage does not suggest that children are literally learning about technology side-by-side as they learn about the periodic table. Choice (H) is incorrect because the reference to the *universe* does not provide any support for such an extreme claim as *most technology* comes from space exploration. Choice (J) is incorrect because it confuses the point of this paragraph, which is that children tend *not* to be impressed by the technology around them.

17. D The penultimate paragraph discusses how people in our culture assume that technology will solve our problems and do not want to hear about needing to change or reassess their lifestyle. Because leaders with public voices are too afraid to tell the public otherwise, the final paragraph says that we will continue as we have been. Hence, choice (D) is correct. Choice (A) is incorrect because it misses the correct meaning of the phrase, and *scope* and *complexity* were discussed in relation to assessing the global climate problem, not technology. Choice (B) is incorrect because this describes specifically what the passage explains we will *not* be doing. Making sacrifices would mean *changing* the status quo. Choice (C) is incorrect because the passage is saying that if we ever find ourselves in a disastrous situation as a result of maintaining our current lifestyles and habits, *then* we would blame technology. This would be a result of following the status quo but not the idea to which the phrase itself refers.

18. H *Discriminating preference* is used at the end of the seventh paragraph to foreshadow the ever-evolving demands of consumers for new technology. The eighth paragraph lists some of them. The passage states that *computers needed to become more powerful*. This makes choice (H) correct. Choice (F) is incorrect because the eighth paragraph contradicts that idea. Choice (G) is incorrect because the passage repeatedly suggests that most users of technology are happily oblivious to *how* it works. Choice (J) is incorrect because the second to last paragraph portrays this idea as something the public does not want to hear.

19. D The first half of the passage discusses the modern mindset towards technology. Then it says that the *most dangerous extension of this mindset* is how it relates to our ability to solve global climate problems. The second half of the passage explains why our attitude towards technology may worsen the situation. Choice (D) is correct because it precisely identifies the reason the author finds our overconfidence in technology to be potentially dangerous. Choice (A) is incorrect because this phrase refers to the flaws we consumers find with existing technology that we hope will be fixed. This is not directly relevant to the global warming problem with which the author associates the most danger. Choices (B) and (C) are incorrect because they refer to things that indirectly relate to the author's central concern. However, the author does not consider *devising new forms of energy* or *the complexity of global weather* to be dangerous in and of themselves.

20. F The passage ends with a severe prediction that humanity may ruin its habitat, all the while blaming technology for failing to rescue it. This makes choice (F) correct. Choice (G) is incorrect because the last paragraph does not contain any refutation of a theory. Choice (H) is incorrect because the last paragraph does not include an expert opinion. Choice (J) is incorrect because both paragraphs use "we."

21. A Choice (A) is correct because, although the author discusses having great difficulty and confusion in learning jazz chords, he does not ever identify one that is *most* confusing. Choices (B), (C), and (D) are incorrect because they are never identified as the *most* confusing chords.

22. F In the context of the passage as a whole, the author discusses Victor as a source of knowledge about jazz. The author states he did not get *straightforward explanations* from Victor but that he *did learn* some things. Choice (F) is correct because, given the context of the passage, it refers to the most likely subject matter the author would be trying to get from Victor. Choice (G) is incorrect because the idea that knowledge about jazz would be *forbidden* is too strong. There is no evidence that the author was being purposefully excluded from learning about jazz. Choice (H) is incorrect because there is no context to support the idea that the author was asking about literal magic tricks. Choice (J) is incorrect because there is no context to support the idea that the author was trying to learn more about Victor as a person, nor does the passage ever describe Victor as *private*.

23. D Upon seeing the author's *invented* chord, Victor *calmly* informs the author of the chord's proper name. Choice (D) is correct because nonchalance indicates a relaxed, unimpressed manner, which is how Victor responds. Choice (A) is incorrect because Victor would not be amazed by a chord for which he already knows the technical name. Choice (B) is incorrect because Victor would not be jealous that the author could play a chord that was already familiar to Victor. Choice (C) is incorrect because Victor does not show confusion; he shows immediate recognition of what chord the author is playing.

24. G In the tenth paragraph, the author states that *for the next few months, I quietly plucked away* at the music found in "The Real Book." Hence, choice (G) is correct and choices (F), (H), and (J) are incorrect.

25. A The passage describes the more complex chord types of jazz and describes the effects of using them as introducing *subtle hints of chaos and imbalance, adding a worldly imperfection*, and becoming more enjoyable as one's age starts making things like candy taste too sweet and "imperfections" like bitterness make *for a more appealing flavor.* Choice (A) provides the best summary for these ideas. Choice (B) is incorrect because the description of jazz's complexity is not intended to be a critical comment about fundamental flaws in rock and classical music. Just because jazz's unique chords add *detail and depth to the music*, that doesn't mean the author thinks that other styles of music necessarily lack detail and depth. Choice (C) is incorrect because the passage does not specify anything about the confusion and awkwardness of *standard jazz chord values*; it describes what elements jazz chords add to *standard chord values.* Choice (D) is incorrect because the context explains that candy starts tasting unpleasantly *sweet* the older one gets.

26. J The end of the passage describes the author beginning to develop an ability to play jazz, but his newfound ability is still mentally surprising. Choice (J) summarizes this context best and is therefore correct. Choice (F) is incorrect because the passage does not support the idea that the author was *overworked.* Choice (G) is incorrect because, although the author is surprised by what his hands can do musically, there is no context to support that the author is actually losing the ability to *control* his hands. Choice (H) is incorrect because there is no information to support the idea that the author *pointing* at chords was part of his learning process.

27. D Choice (D) is correct because the tenth paragraph describes the author's initial attempts to work through the *strange, new combinations* he found in "The Real Book." He mentions F-sharp minor-7 flat-5 while speaking of chords that he *had to decode and then understand.* Choice (A) is incorrect because the context of this paragraph suggests that the author did indeed have some trouble with these unfamiliar chords. Choice (B) is incorrect because the remark about not knowing the language of a foreign country has no literal relation to this specific chord or the author's previous travels (about which we know nothing). Choice (C) is incorrect because the passage provides no evidence that the author knew how to play this chord on guitar.

28. H The fifth paragraph identifies Victor as a member of the author's rock band as well as a member of a jazz ensemble. This makes choice (H) correct. Choice (F) is incorrect because the passage states that at age 30, it had been *over a decade* since the author and Victor had gone their separate ways. Choice (G) is incorrect because the passage states that the author bought his own copy of "The Real Book." Choice (J) is incorrect because the passage does not say that Victor invented this chord, rather that he told the author the name of the chord the author presumed to have invented.

29. C The passage begins with the author's love for jazz. It transitions into his own experiences learning how to play jazz and culminates with his early successes in doing so. Choice (C) is correct because it encompasses the various points of focus throughout the passage. Choice (A) is incorrect because the passage only occasionally refers to a chain of events and never establishes that the author has a jazz career. Choice (B) is incorrect because the author does not try to show that jazz is uncomplicated; he describes the hard work he put into learning its complexity. Choice (D) is incorrect

because the central focus of the passage is the author's learning of jazz. Although the author's friendship with Victor relates to jazz, it is not the central focus of the author's discussion.

30. G In the last few paragraphs, the author describes the process by which he struggled to learn jazz. He begins by seeing jazz as *a cryptic message to decode* but later describes himself as *becoming comfortable* and possessing a *new melodic understanding.* These details make choice (G) correct. Choice (F) is incorrect because the author never says that the book becomes annoyingly familiar by the end. Choice (H) is incorrect because the author identifies a difference between jazz sheet music and classical sheet music, but this detail does not enter his discussion of his experiences with "The Real Book." Choice (J) is incorrect because the author has not suggested that he has moved on to other learning tools or more profound study.

31. A The third and fourth paragraphs discuss Calwell's work. Paragraph 4 explains that *by monitoring the cholera food chain in reverse,* Calwell is able to make predictions. This makes choice (A) correct. Choice (B) is incorrect because climatic models were used to predict an outbreak in Bangladesh, not derived from studying its weather. Choice (C) is incorrect because, in addition to being too narrow a description of Calwell's method, the decline of zooplankton and falling sea temperatures would each suggest a reduced risk of a potential cholera outbreak. Choice (D) is incorrect because chlorophyll measurements are used to forecast growing populations of plankton on which copepods feed.

32. H The first few paragraphs explain the food chain that allows the cholera bacterium to grow. The bacterium grows around copepods, which feed on zooplankton, which feed on phytoplankton, which feed on sunlight. Hence, sunlight influences cholera by influencing the food chain on which the cholera bacterium depends. This makes choice (H) correct. Choice (F) is incorrect because the passage never says that phytoplankton *contaminate* the water. Choice (G) is incorrect because the passage does not state that *V. cholerae* uses photosynthesis at all. Choice (J) is incorrect because there is no support for this broad generalization about sunlight causing many epidemics. The first sentence of the passage is a rhetorical question, and the way in which the passage describes sunlight facilitating outbreaks has nothing to do with *direct, prolonged exposure.*

33. C The eighth paragraph explains that researchers at Oxford *calibrated regional levels of photosynthesis to the size of a vein in the wings of the flies.* The vein size measures *how numerous and robust the tsetse fly population is.* Therefore, the satellite data that measures photosynthesis is used to tell researchers how big the veins of tsetse flies are and hence how strong and prevalent their population is. This makes choice (C) correct. Choice (A) is incorrect because the passage does not say that the satellite data can be used to determine the total number of *parasites* in West Africa. Choice (B) is incorrect because measuring photosynthesis is done to gauge the size of tsetse fly populations in West Africa, not to find the global area with the *most* photosynthesis. Choice (D) is incorrect because the point of the data is not to find the flies with the biggest veins but to estimate the size of veins in tsetse flies.

34. J The passage as a whole is presenting ways in which satellite data is being used to predict disease outbreaks, and both Calwell and Linthicum are offered as examples of those efforts. Hence, choice (J) is correct. Choice (F) is incorrect because Linthicum is studying Rift Valley fever, not cholera. Choice (G) is incorrect because Linthicum works at NASA in Greenbelt, Maryland. Choice (H) is incorrect because this does not indicate a similarity between Linthicum and Calwell since the passage never indicates that Calwell may have saved thousands of lives.

35. A The ninth paragraph states that satellite data is more efficient than the traditional method of doing research for the reasons discussed in choice (A). Thus, choice (A) is correct. Choice (B) is incorrect because the passage does not indicate that scientists can *control* photosynthetic levels, just that they can measure them. Choice (C) is incorrect because the passage does not discuss the types of *mathematical errors* that human forecasters make. Choice (D) is incorrect because the tenth paragraph contradicts this idea by indicating there is not a lot of reliable disease data available.

36. H The context of this word discusses conditions that would encourage or help mosquito populations to grow. *Promote* means to encourage or help, so choice (H) is correct. Choices (F) and (G) are incorrect because the weather is not performing an errand or a task for the mosquitoes. Similarly, choice (J) is incorrect because weather conditions would not *request* the growth of mosquito populations. The three incorrect answer choices relate more to the sense of *doing someone a favor* than to how the word is used in this context.

37. D The sixth paragraph explains the weather conditions that facilitate the growth and spread of mosquito populations, which include increased rain, more clouds, and warmer air. The environmental changes Linthicum is studying are those that would precede a growth in mosquito populations. Hence, choice (D) is correct. Choice (A) is incorrect because the beginning of the rainy season in Kenya is not identified as the precursor to mosquito population growth. Choice (B) is incorrect because the passage never mentions bacteria in the jet stream. Choice (C) is incorrect because the environmental changes Linthicum is monitoring are those that precede mosquito population growth, not the population growth itself.

38. J While it is true that satellite data has *measured* increases in ocean temperature, the passage never suggests or states that satellite data has actually *helped to* raise the ocean temperature. For this reason, choice (J) is correct. Choice (F) is incorrect because it is mentioned in the Calwell research. Choice (G) is incorrect because it is mentioned as part of the Oxford study. Choice (H) is incorrect because it is mentioned several times throughout the passage and represents the main point of the passage.

39. A The context for this phrase is that fluctuations in certain variables would make climate-based models inaccurate predictors. The variables are labeled as *non-climatic factors* in the following sentence. This makes choice (A) the correct answer. Choice (B) is incorrect because there is no discussion of the effects of drug resistance. Choice (C) is incorrect because it does not address the source of confusion which is a failure to incorporate certain variables into the model. Choice (D) is incorrect because it implies—without any textual evidence—that researchers are unfamiliar with non-climate data, although the passage suggests only that they are not currently using it in their models.

40. G With the examples of Calwell, Linthicum, and Rogers, the author presents researchers who are using satellite-based data to predict disease outbreaks. The passage ends by assessing the value of these efforts. This makes choice (G) the correct answer. Choice (F) is incorrect because the passage does not itemize which satellite data *must* be collected, nor is the type of data the primary focus. Choice (H) is incorrect because the author does not stress that a small number of scientists do research by traditional methods. Choice (J) is incorrect because it is too narrow a purpose for an author who also discussed applications relating to predicting cholera and Rift Valley fever.

SCIENCE TEST

1. A Higher bulk density means lower soil quality. Figure 1 shows that Field A consistently has a higher bulk density, so Choice (A) is the correct answer. Table 1 does not contain any information about Field A or B, eliminating choice (C). Figure 2 and Table 2 show that the crop yields and average SOM for Field A are higher, which goes against what the question looks to prove, eliminating choices (B) and (D).

2. J Figure 2 shows that Field B had a harvest of approximately 8 tons in Year 5. Of the values given in the figure, this is the only one that has a harvest less than or equal to 8 tons, thus making it a failed harvest.

3. C Table 1 shows that as the SOM increases, the soil quality increases. Eliminate choices (A) and (D) because both show an inverse, rather than a direct, relationship. With the new information provided in the question, you can infer that legumes and *deep-rooted and high-residue crops* will increase the amount of organic matter in the soil, and thus lead to an increase in the soil organic matter (SOM) rating. Only choice (C) provides this relationship.

4. J Figure 1 shows that Field A had a higher bulk density every year; therefore, regardless of the actual values, it can be assumed that the average bulk density was higher for Field A. Figure 2 shows that Field B had the lower crop yield in every year but Year 3. Therefore, it can be assumed that Field B has a lower average crop yield than Field A. The only choice that is correct for both parts of the question is choice (J).

5. D Use Table 1 to judge the average SOM for Field A and Field B given in Table 2. Field A's average SOM of 0.89 rates as excellent and Field B's average SOM of 0.28 rates as fair. This means the hypothesis is not consistent with the data presented, so the correct answer is choice (D).

6. J Based on Table 1, the salt solution increased the amount of rust every day. On Day 8, the sample had 1.84 g of rust, so on Day 9 the amount of rust must be higher than 1.84 g, choice (J).

7. B The formula shows that when rust is produced, H_2 is also produced, so choice (B) is the only possible correct answer.

8. J Table 1 shows that the salt solution produced 0.56 g Fe_2O_3 on Day 2. Figure 1 shows that the water buffered to pH = 10.0 had less than 0.50 g Fe_2O_3 until day 9, so the only correct answer is choice (J).

9. A Table 1 shows that the sugar solution produced 0.11 g Fe_2O_3 on Day 6 and 0.19 g on Day 8. The amount produced from Day 6 to Day 8, then, would have been 0.19 – 0.11 = 0.08 g.

10. F Table 1 shows that the sugar solution had 0.00 g Fe_2O_3 on Day 2 and shows a steady increase. Choices (G) and (J) show the amount of Fe_2O_3 produced decreasing as time passes, so they cannot be correct. Choice (H) shows a big increase in Fe_2O_3 between Day 2 and Day 6, then a small increase between Day 6 and Day 8. Table 1 shows that the biggest increase in Fe_2O_3 was between Day 6 and Day 8, 0.08 g, so choice (H) cannot be correct. Only choice (F) shows 0.00 g on Day 1 and steady increases in g Fe_2O_3 produced, so this must be the correct answer.

11. D Based on Experiment 1, shown in Figure 2, you can see that a 10.0 N weight shared between two springs caused Spring A to stretch to 0.40 m, so a 10.0 N weight on Spring A alone must cause it to stretch further. Choice (D) is the best answer.

12. G Based on Experiment 2, shown in Figure 4, you can see that as the weight moved farther from Spring B, Spring B stretched less as the force on Spring B decreased. Choice (G) is the correct answer.

13. A Because the students were attaching weights to two springs at once in Trials 1–3, it was important to use identical springs so that the effects on each spring would be the same. If they had used different springs there would be no way of determining the relationship between the length of the spring and the weight. Choice (A) best describes this reason. Choice (B) does not make much sense, for the same reasons, so it should be eliminated. Choice (D) must be eliminated because it discusses the weight of the board, which is not used in Trials 1–3. Choice (C) discusses oscillation, which is only mentioned in the passage to state that the students waited until oscillation ceased before measuring. Once you are left with choices (A) and (C), choice (A) is clearly the better answer.

14. H Experiment 2, Trial 5 shows the 5.0 N weight at exactly the midpoint of the board, and the springs stretched to 0.40 m. Experiment 1, Trial 1 has springs stretched to 0.40 m and a weight of 10.0 N. So the board in Experiment 3 must weight 10.0 N – 5.0 N = 5.0 N, choice (H).

15. B Experiment 2, Trial 5 is the only trial in Experiment 2 where the springs are stretched the same amount, choice (B).

16. H If potential energy is highest when the springs are stretched the most, then the correct answer must be the trial wherein the spring was stretched the most, so you can eliminate choices (F) and (G) right away. Now, you need to find the answer that gives the correct reason for this phenomenon. Spring C was stretched the most because the force of the weight was greater, choice (H).

17. C Based on Table 2, you know that the proofs for both de-icers decrease as temperature decreases, so you know that the proof at –30°C for each de-icer must be *less than* the proof at –25°C and *greater than* the proof at –50°C. Knowing this, you can eliminate choice (A) right away because the proofs are the same as the proofs at –50°C. You can eliminate choice (D) because the proofs are the same as the proofs at –25°C. Choice (B) shows the proof for De-icer B greater than the proof for De-icer A, but Table 2 shows that De-icer A always has a greater proof than De-icer B, so choice (B) cannot be correct. This leaves the correct answer, choice (C).

18. J You can see from Table 1 that when 10 mL distilled water is added to 40 mL sodium chloride, the proof is 80. The proof changes based on the relative proportions of distilled water and sodium chloride. Choices (F) and (G) can be eliminated because proofs that small must be from de-icers that have almost all water. Because the proportions of water to sodium chloride are the same as in the problem, choice (J) is the correct answer.

19. A The passage tells you that TR is the minimum proof for a de-icer to be effective at a particular temperature. Table 2 shows that as temperature decreases, TR increases only, so choice (A) is the correct answer.

20. H Based on Table 1, you can see that when the amount of sodium chloride is 0, the proof is 0, so you can eliminate choice (J). You can also eliminate choices (F) and (G), because Table 1 shows proof values when the volume of distilled water or sodium chloride is 0, but those formulas would have you divide by 0, which isn't possible. This leaves you with choice (H), which a quick check of proofs of 0 and 100 will show you is correct.

21. C Table 1 shows you that a mixture of 10 mL distilled water and 40 mL sodium chloride produces a de-icer with a proof of 80. Figure 1 shows you that adding magnesium chloride increases the proof of a 100 proof de-icer, but that no matter how much magnesium chloride is added the proof never goes above 112. Based on this, you can eliminate choices (A) and (B) because they indicate that the proof would decrease and choice (D) because it indicates that the proof would exceed 112. The correct answer is choice (C).

22. G The passage tells you that TR is the minimum proof for a de-icer to be effective, so the better de-icer will be one that has a proof higher than the TR for each temperature, so you should eliminate choices which state that the better de-icer will have a proof lower than the TR, choices (F) and (H). Based on Table 2, you can see that only De-icer A had a proof higher than the TR for each temperature, so choice (G) is the correct answer.

23. C Scientist 2 says that small comets originate from regions of the solar system beyond the farthest planet's, Neptune's (remember, Pluto is no longer classified as a planet!), orbit, choice (C),

24. J Scientist 1 says that small comets have a diameter of 20–30 ft and burn up in the magnetosphere. Since larger comets burn up in the parts of the atmosphere closer to the earth, a comet that burns up in the thermosphere must have a diameter of greater than 30 ft, choice (J).

25. A Scientist 1 states that small comets are too small to be meteors. Scientist 1 also states that small comets burn up in the magnetosphere, but the passage says that meteors burn up between 50 and 85 km above Earth's surface, in the mesosphere. The correct choice, therefore is that no small comet ever becomes a meteor, choice (A).

26. J The passage states that visible objects burning up in the atmosphere are called meteors, so you should eliminate choices that do not call the objects meteors, choices (F) and (G). Second, Scientist 2 tells you that meteors are seen "far less" often than twice every five minutes, so to see bright objects every minute is not typical, eliminating choice (H). This leaves the correct answer, choice (J).

27. D Scientist 1 says that all small comets burn up in the magnetosphere. Figure 1 shows the magnetosphere is above 600 km, so the answer is choice (D). The other values given in the answer choices represent altitudes above the magnetosphere.

28. F Scientist 1's viewpoint is that the dark spots are not mere noise; a change in the atmospheric conditions around these spots would support that viewpoint. Scientist 1 also states that the comets release krypton as they burn up, so the discovery of krypton around the spots confirms Scientist 1's viewpoint, choice (F). The other choices can be eliminated because none state that Scientist 1's viewpoint was strengthened.

29. D Scientist 1 states that small comets all burn up in the magnetosphere. According to this hypothesis, only enhanced imaging technology that could take pictures of the magnetosphere would be useful for seeing small comets. Therefore, only enhanced imaging technology that could record data above 600 km above sea level would be effective, choice (D).

30. G In Tables 1, 2, and 3, the amount of hydrogen peroxide decreases consistently from the first day (Table 3) to the end of the elongation period (Table 1), choice (G).

31. C The dependent variable of the experiment is a variable that the experimenter is not intentionally manipulating or changing (which is the independent variable) or controlling (control groups or variables); it's the variable that the experimenter is trying to understand or predict. In this experiment, the experimenter manipulated the type of plant, the type of superoxide dismutase, and the point in time that measurements were taken. The length of the cotton fiber was neither intentionally changed nor controlled (represented as L1, L2, and L3). The introduction indicates that the *scientists wanted to study whether the level of hydrogen peroxide affected the length of the cotton fiber.* Choice (C) is the correct answer.

32. H Only plant cells have cell walls, so the correct answer is choice (H). Choice (F), prokaryotic, refers to unicellular life forms without a membrane-bound nucleus; cotton plants are not unicellular, so choice (F) cannot be correct. Animal cells, choice (G), do not have cell walls, so this choice can be eliminated. Bacteria, choice (J), are also unicellular and cotton plants are not bacteria, so choice (J) cannot be correct. In addition, you could use "cotton" as the clue; because of the answer choices, "Plant" is the best approximation of what cotton is.

33. C Take the information given, length of cotton fiber and amount of hydrogen peroxide, and find the most similar line and point in time. The correct answer is choice (C), L2 at the beginning of its elongation period.

34. J The only cotton plant line which did not have its genetic structure altered was L4, so this was the control.

35. A The *x*-axis will move in a positive direction, so determine how the average lengths change. For all the data, the lengths increase with increasing elongation periods. Thus you can conclude that the line will have a positive slope, as choice (A) suggests.

36. H Figure 2 shows that there is a linear relationship between cross-sectional area and ΔT. You can also see that as cross-sectional area increases, ΔT increases. If System 1 has a larger cross-sectional area than System 2, it must have a larger ΔT, so you can eliminate choices (F) and (G). The question tells you that System 1 has twice the cross-sectional area of System 2, so choice (H) is the correct answer. A quick check of Figure 2 confirms this: when cross-sectional area is 4 cm^2, ΔT is 6°C and when cross-sectional area is 8 cm^2, ΔT is 12°C.

37. B This question requires you to apply your outside knowledge. Radiation is heat transfer through electromagnetic waves in empty space. Convection, as discussed in the passage, is heat transfer through moving currents. Conduction is heat transfer through direct contact between particles, the only correct answer for the process in which water touching the metal container transfers heat to the metal container, choice (B).

38. F Figure 2 shows that ΔT increases with cross-sectional area. Figure 3 shows that ΔT increases with height. The best answer, therefore, will have a large height and a large cross-sectional area. Choice (F) is the best answer because it has larger values for both than any other choice.

39. D Table 1 shows that for water in the setup described, ΔT should be 10°C. Find the differences in temperature in the answer choices given. Choice (A) has a difference of 20°C. Choice (B) has a difference of 30°C. Choice (C) has a difference of 0°C. Only choice (D) has the appropriate ΔT of 10°C.

40. H The passage gives relationships between ΔT and only three variables: cross-sectional area, length, and starting temperature. None of these are possible choices, but radius is linked to cross-sectional area. As radius increases, area increases. Figure 2 shows that as cross-sectional area increases, ΔT increases, so the correct answer is choice (H). Insulation, amount of liquid, and air temperature are not discussed in the passage.

WRITING TEST

To grade your essay, see the Essay Checklist on the following page. The following is an example of a top-scoring essay for the prompt given in this test. Note that it's not perfect, but it still follows an organized outline and has a strong introductory paragraph, a concluding paragraph, and transitions throughout.

Today's high school student is presented with many opportunities to cheat. The Internet is a ready source of resources for the unscrupulous, even including papers already written on just about any topic imaginable. But the problem of cheating reaches farther than just homework assignments—students today also have chances to cheat during exams in school, as teachers cannot possibly monitor the behavior of every student in a classroom simultaneously. Because the pressure to get great grades and get into a good college is so high, the pressure to cheat is very high. Nevertheless, it is critically important that schools do not give up in the fight against cheating because cheating is unfair to the students who play by the rules, because the consequences of being caught only increase later in life, and because one of the purposes of school is to teach students values.

Contrary to popular belief, not every student cheats. In all likelihood, the percentage of students cheating regularly is much lower than 50 percent. But the damage these students do to the students who don't cheat is very real and very severe. Colleges are choosing students based on their GPA and their class rank (in part—there are obviously other factors). When students cheat, they get higher grades that they don't deserve. As these cheaters move up the class rank, they are pushing down students who deserve to be higher, hurting those students' college opportunities. Cheaters will often say "Who cares if I cheat—it doesn't hurt anyone else's grades." Maybe not, but the damage done is even worse—it's hurting other people's futures.

Because it's hard for teachers in high school to keep an eye on every student, cheaters believe that they won't get caught, and for a while they are probably going to be right. Cheaters learn tricks that work well in the high school environment. The problem is, though, that they will keep on cheating through life and eventually will get caught. Colleges and businesses take this sort of behavior much more seriously, and so the cost of being caught cheating becomes much higher. If the cheater gets caught in high school and learns not to continue this behavior in the future, it will be embarrassing, but the real cost will be much easier for him or her to bear. So, schools should work hard to catch cheating during high school and should treat it seriously.

Finally, schools have a responsibility to set an example to their students. Part of the school's job, whether students like it or not, is to teach them the values of right and wrong. If schools are perceived by the student body to be giving up in the face of cheating, that not only sends us the message that this sort of devious behavior is acceptable (which we know is not true), it also ruins the reputation of the administration in our eyes. We will no longer take the school seriously on any matter, which will have a long-term damaging effect on the school community.

Clearly, cheating is wrong. There is no disagreement on this point, even from those who cheat. Just as clearly, schools have to do their very best to prevent cheating from occurring. Of all the reasons given, the first is the most important: These people are stealing college opportunities from their classmates.

Essay Checklist

1. The Introduction
   Did you
   - o start with a topic sentence that paraphrases or restates the prompt?
   - o clearly state your position on the issue?

2. Body Paragraph 1
   Did you
   - o start with a transition/topic sentence that discusses the opposing side of the argument?
   - o give an example of a reason that one might agree with the opposing side of the argument?
   - o clearly state that the opposing side of the argument is wrong or flawed?
   - o show what is wrong with the opposing side's example or position?

3. Body Paragraphs 2 and 3
   Did you
   - o start with a transition/topic sentence that discusses your position on the prompt?
   - o give one example or reason to support your position?
   - o show the grader how your example supports your position?
   - o end the paragraph by restating your thesis?

4. Conclusion
   Did you
   - o restate your position on the issue?
   - o end with a flourish?

5. Overall
   Did you
   - o write neatly?
   - o avoid multiple spelling and grammar mistakes?
   - o try to vary your sentence structure?
   - o use a few impressive-sounding words?

SCORING YOUR PRACTICE EXAM

Step A

Count the number of correct answers for each section and record the number in the space provided for your raw score on the Score Conversion Worksheet below.

Step B

Using the Score Conversion Chart on the next page, convert your raw scores on each section to scaled scores. Then compute your composite ACT score by averaging the four subject scores. Add them up and divide by four. Don't worry about the essay score; it is not included in your composite score.

Score Conversion Worksheet		
Section	Raw Score	Scaled Score
1	______/75	________
2	______/60	________
3	______/40	________
4	______/40	________

SCORE CONVERSION CHART

Scaled Score	Raw Scores			
	Test 1 English	Test 2 Math	Test 3 Reading	Test 4 Science
36	75	59–60	40	39–40
35	72–74	57–58	--	38
34	71	56	39	37
33	70	54–55	38	--
32	69	53	37	36
31	68	51–52	--	35
30	66–67	50	36	34
29	65	49	35	33
28	64	47–48	34	32
27	62–63	45–46	33	31
26	60–61	42–44	32	29–30
25	58–59	40–41	31	27–28
24	56–57	38–39	30	26
23	53–55	35–37	29	24–25
22	51–52	33–34	27–28	22–23
21	47–50	32	26	20–21
20	44–46	30–31	24–25	18–19
19	41–43	28–29	22–23	17
18	39–40	26–27	21	15–16
17	37–38	22–25	19–20	14
16	34–36	18–21	17–18	13
15	31–33	14–17	15–16	12
14	29–30	10–13	13–14	11
13	27–28	08–09	11–12	10
12	25–26	07	09–10	09
11	23–24	05–06	08	08
10	20–22	04	06–07	07
09	17–19	--	--	05–06
08	15–16	03	05	04
07	12–14	--	04	--
06	10–11	02	03	03
05	07–09	--	--	02
04	06	01	02	--
03	04–05	--	--	01
02	02–03	--	01	--
01	00–01	00	00	00

Part IX
The Princeton Review ACT Practice Exam 2 and Answers and Explanations

Practice Exam 2

ENGLISH TEST

45 Minutes—75 Questions

DIRECTIONS: In the five passages that follow, certain words and phrases are underlined and numbered. In the right-hand column, you will find alternatives for each underlined part. In most cases, you are to choose the one that best expresses the idea, makes the statement appropriate for standard written English, or is worded most consistently with the style and tone of the passage as a whole. If you think the original version is best, choose "NO CHANGE." In some cases, you will find in the right-hand column a question about the underlined part of the passage. You are to choose the best answer to the question.

You will also find questions about a section of the passage or the passage as a whole. These questions do not refer to an underlined portion of the passage, but rather are identified by a number or numbers in a box.

For each question, choose the alternative you consider best and blacken the corresponding oval on your answer document. Read each passage through once before you begin to answer the questions that accompany it. For many of the questions, you must read several sentences beyond the question to determine the answer. Be sure that you have read far enough ahead each time you choose an alternative.

PASSAGE I

Crocheting Makes a Good Hobby

Crocheting is the art of making fabric by twisting yarn or thread with a hook. Although many associate it by [1] older women, crocheting can be a fun hobby for people of both genders [2] and all ages. Once you start crocheting, you won't be able to put down the hook; you'll have a hobby for life. [3]

1. A. NO CHANGE
   B. to
   C. by
   D. with

2. F. NO CHANGE
   G. for people of both genders, masculine and feminine,
   H. for male and female people of both genders
   J. for people of both genders, both males and females,

3. At this point, the author is considering adding the following true statement:

   Irish nuns helped save lives with crocheting when they used it as a way to make a living during the Great Irish Potato Famine of 1846.

   Should the writer add this sentence here?

   A. Yes, because it is essential to know when crocheting became internationally prominent and how it did so.
   B. Yes, because the reference to the Great Irish Potato Famine demonstrates that the author is conscious of historical events.
   C. No, because the reference to the Great Irish Potato Famine is not relevant to the main topic of this essay.
   D. No, because many people who left Ireland in 1846 brought crocheting with them to the United States and Australia.

GO ON TO THE NEXT PAGE.

Time-honored and easily taught[4] to all, crocheting is an easy hobby to pick up. Instructional books are readily available, and once you've learned a few basic stitches. Picking[5] up the more advanced ones is a snap. Once you learn how to crochet, you can purchase store-bought books that detail crocheting patterns[6] that tell you exactly how to make the projects that interest you. Even if you want to try several projects, the supplies required for it's[7] completion are minimal; all you need are a crochet hook, yarn, and a pair of scissors. You don't need to worry about making a big investment, either; fifteen dollars will buy you no fewer than[8] three starter kits!

[1] As you grow more proficient, you can expand your supplies by purchasing hooks of different types[9] to vary the size of your stitches. [2] Crochet hooks are available in all sizes, ranging,[10] from very small to very large, with everything in between. [3] Some are so big that you need to use two strands of yarn. [4] Other hooks are very tiny, so small that you must use thread. [5] These hooks are suitable for making smaller, more delicate things such as lace doilies, tablecloths, and bedspreads. [6] These hooks make big stitches, so you can finish a project with them very quickly. [7] It is best to start with hooks that are medium in size; these are the easiest to manipulate and require only one strand of yarn. [11]

4. F. NO CHANGE
G. teaches
H. taughted
J. teached

5. A. NO CHANGE
B. stitches; picking
C. stitches, picking
D. stitches since picking

6. F. NO CHANGE
G. buy books and other pamphlets at craft and book stores detailing certain specific patterns
H. buy pattern books
J. acquire store-bought pattern books

7. A. NO CHANGE
B. its
C. its'
D. their

8. F. NO CHANGE
G. fewer then
H. less than
J. less then

9. A. NO CHANGE
B. types;
C. types:
D. types,

10. F. NO CHANGE
G. sizes, ranging
H. sizes; ranging
J. sizes ranging,

11. For the sake of the logic and coherence of this paragraph, Sentence 6 should be placed:

A. where it is now.
B. after Sentence 1.
C. after Sentence 3.
D. after Sentence 7.

GO ON TO THE NEXT PAGE.

Because it seems like there are a million hooks to keep track of, crocheting makes a good hobby because it requires only time and patience, not attention or tremendous investment. You can crochet while watching television, listening to music, or visiting with other people. It is fun and relaxing and allows you to express your creative side in an easy way. Also, you have finished a project, you have a cherished keepsake. Whether you have made an afghan to keep you warm on cold winter nights or a lace tablecloth to add a touch of elegance to your dining room, your creation is sure to be cherished for a long time to come.

12. Given that all the choices are true, which one provides the most effective transition from the preceding paragraph to this one?
   - F. NO CHANGE
   - G. Because it can take a long time to finish a project,
   - H. With such a simple and inexpensive set of materials,
   - J. No longer a field dominated primarily by older women,

13.
   - A. NO CHANGE
   - B. Also, finally you
   - C. Also, despite the fact you
   - D. Also, once you

14.
   - F. NO CHANGE
   - G. at
   - H. of
   - J. within

Question 15 asks about the preceding passage as a whole.

15. Suppose the writer's goal had been to write an essay that demonstrates the commercial potential of crocheting. Would this essay successfully accomplish that goal?
   - A. Yes, because it gives examples of end products of crocheting and shows the different kinds of materials needed to produce a wide range of products.
   - B. Yes, because it discusses the supplies necessary to create crocheted products, and it shows the usefulness of many of them during the cold winter months.
   - C. No, because it does not mention the market value of crocheted products or how one might go about selling them.
   - D. No, because it describes other industries and hobbies that would be more commercially successful.

PASSAGE II

Seurat's Masterpiece

[1] How can I describe the wonder I felt the first time I saw my favorite painting, Georges Seurat's *A Sunday on La Grande Jatte*? [2] I had admired the work for years in art books, but I never thought I saw the actual painting, which was housed in Chicago, many miles from where I lived. [3] I finally got my

16.
   - F. NO CHANGE
   - G. would see
   - H. had seen
   - J. was seeing

GO ON TO THE NEXT PAGE.

chance to when I met someone else who loved the painting as much as I did. [4] We both had three days off at the same time, so we decided to make a road trip to Chicago so we could see the painting in all it's grandeur. [5] We packed our bags, jumped in the car, and headed on our way toward Chicago. [20]

[1] The first thing that struck me as we entered the room where the painting was displayed; was the size of the painting. [2] A common size for canvases is 24 by 36 inches. [3] It was enormous! [4] It covered a large part of an even larger wall. [5] The painting's size amazed me since it was painted with dots, a technique called pointillism. [6] To create a painting of such magnitude using this technique seemed an almost impossible task. [7] Seurat had done it, though, and had made it look easy! [23]

17. **A.** NO CHANGE
B. at the moment
C. just to
D. DELETE the underlined portion.

18. **F.** NO CHANGE
G. our
H. its
J. its'

19. **A.** NO CHANGE
B. jumped in the car, and had headed
C. jumped in the car, and head
D. had jumped in the car, and headed

20. Upon reviewing this paragraph and noticing that some information has been left out, the writer composes the following sentence, incorporating the information:

> Her name was Lisa; she lived in my dorm, and a mutual friend had introduced us to each other, knowing how much both of us loved art.

For the sake of the logic of this paragraph, this sentence should be placed after Sentence:

F. 2.
G. 3.
H. 4.
J. 5.

21. **A.** NO CHANGE
B. displayed:
C. displayed,
D. displayed

22. **F.** NO CHANGE
G. task and difficult to complete.
H. task, difficult to complete.
J. task, overwhelming in its difficulty.

23. Which of the following sentences is LEAST relevant to the development of this paragraph and therefore could be deleted?

A. Sentence 2
B. Sentence 4
C. Sentence 5
D. Sentence 6

GO ON TO THE NEXT PAGE.

Even more impressive, however, was the beauty of the painting. Viewed from a distance, the colors looked muted, capturing the idyllic mood of a summer day in the park.
24

24. Given that all of the choices are accurate, which provides the most effective and logical transition from the preceding paragraph to this one?

F. NO CHANGE
G. One thing that struck me was
H. Many art critics have written about
J. The debate rages on over

When I approached the painting, though, its colors exploded into myriad hues, illustrating the artist's skill in combining colors to create a mood. Even the parts of the painting that appeared white from a distance were vibrantly multicolored when viewed up close. [26] The effect was incredible;
25

25. Which of the following alternatives to the underlined portion would NOT be acceptable?

A. As I approached the painting, though,
B. However, as I approached the painting,
C. I approached the painting, though,
D. However, when I approached the painting,

26. If the writer were to delete the phrase "from a distance" from the preceding sentence, the paragraph would primarily lose:

F. an essential point explaining the author's love of the painting.
G. the first part of the contrast in this sentence, which the author uses to describe viewing the painting.
H. a further indication of the length of the road trip taken by the author and her friend.
J. nothing, because the information provided by this phrase is stated more clearly elsewhere in the paragraph.

he sat and stared at the painting in wonder for a good portion of the afternoon. [28]
27

27. A. NO CHANGE
B. one
C. they
D. we

28. At this point, the writer is considering adding the following true statement:

> The Art Institute of Chicago contains many other famous paintings, among them Edvard Munch's *The Scream* and Grant Wood's *American Gothic.*

Should the writer make this addition here?

F. Yes, because it gives additional details essential to understanding the collection at the museum.
G. Yes, because it demonstrates a contrast between the author's favorite painting and those in this sentence.
H. No, because it provides information that is not relevant at this point in the paragraph and essay.
J. No, because it is contradicted by other information presented in this essay.

My friend and I saw many other sights, on our trip to Chicago, but the best part by far was being able to see our favorite work of art. The image is forever imprinted in my mind
29

29. A. NO CHANGE
B. sights, which
C. sights;
D. sights

GO ON TO THE NEXT PAGE.

at the museum gift shop, even when I'm not looking at the souvenir print I bought.
30

30. The best placement for the underlined portion would be:

F. where it is now.
G. after the word *image*.
H. after the word *looking*.
J. after the word *bought* (ending the sentence with a period).

PASSAGE III

The Language of Cats

Many people believe that language is the domain of human beings. However, cats have developed an intricate language not for each other, but for the human beings who have adopted them as pets.
31 32

31. A. NO CHANGE
B. developed, an intricate language
C. developed an intricate language,
D. developed; an intricate language

32. Which choice would most clearly and effectively express the ownership relationship between humans and cats?

F. NO CHANGE
G. like to have cats around.
H. often have dogs as well.
J. are naturally inclined to like cats.

When communicating with each other, cats' "talk" is a complex system of nonverbal signals. In particular, their tails, rather than any kind of "speech," provide cats' chief means of expression. They also use physical contact to express their feelings. With other cats, cats will use their voices only to express pain. [35]
33 34

33. A. NO CHANGE
B. a complicated system of nonverbal signals is used by cats to "talk."
C. cats "talk" with a complex system of nonverbal signals.
D. "talking" is done by them with a system of complex nonverbal signals.

34. F. NO CHANGE
G. having provided
H. has provided
J. were provided by

35. If the preceding sentence were deleted, the essay would primarily lose:

A. a redundant point made elsewhere in the essay.
B. another description of the ways in which cats communicate nonverbally.
C. an exception to the general trend described in this paragraph.
D. a brief summary of the information contained in the essay up to this point.

Next, incredibly, all of that changes when a human walks into the room. Cats use a wide range of vocal expressions when they communicate with a person, from affectionate mews to
36

36. F. NO CHANGE
G. (Do NOT begin new paragraph) Incredibly,
H. (Begin new paragraph) Next incredibly,
J. (Begin new paragraph) Incredibly,

GO ON TO THE NEXT PAGE.

menacing hisses. Since <u>cats verbal expressions</u> [37] are not used to communicate with other cats, it is <u>logical and reasonable</u> [38] to conclude that cats developed this "language" expressly to communicate with their human owners.

This fact is demonstrated more <u>clear since</u> [39] observing households that have only one cat. An only cat is usually very vocal, since the only creature around with whom the cat can communicate is its owner. Cats with other feline companions, though, are much quieter. If they want to have a conversation, they need only go to their fellow cats and communicate in their natural way. [40]

Since cats learned to meow for the sole purpose of communicating with human beings, owners should take the time to learn what their different meows mean. If an owner <u>knows, to</u> [41] name just a few examples, which meow means the cat is hungry, which means the cat wants to be petted, and which means the cat wants to have a little "conversation," the bond between cat and owner will grow deeper. [42] Certainly, after a time, owners will see that communicating with their pets, not just cats, is every bit as important to forging good relationships <u>as to communicate</u> [43] with other humans. Once, as an owner, you know that the cat is not just

37. A. NO CHANGE
B. cat's verbal expressions
C. cats' verbal expressions
D. cats verbal expressions,

38. F. NO CHANGE
G. logical and well-reasoned
H. logical to a startling degree
J. logical

39. A. NO CHANGE
B. clear when
C. clearly since
D. clearly when

40. At this point, the writer is considering adding the following true statement:

On the other hand, the natural way for most birds to communicate is vocally, by way of the "bird song."

Should the writer add this sentence here?

F. Yes, because it shows that cats are truly unique in communicating nonverbally.
G. Yes, because it adds a relevant and enlightening detail about another animal.
H. No, because it basically repeats information given earlier in the essay.
J. No, because it does not contribute to the development of this paragraph and the essay as a whole.

41. A. NO CHANGE
B. knows, to,
C. knows to,
D. knows to

42. If the writer wanted to emphasize that cats communicate vocally with their owners to express a large number of different emotions in addition to those listed in the previous sentence, which of the following true statements should be added at this point?

F. Many animals communicate hunger similarly to cats.
G. Cats will tell their owners when they feel pain, sadness, irritation, or love.
H. Cats communicate these emotions differently to other cats.
J. Humans have the easiest time communicating with other mammals.

43. A. NO CHANGE
B. as being communicative
C. as communicating
D. through communicating

GO ON TO THE NEXT PAGE.

making senseless noises without any rhyme or reason but is making an attempt to communicate, you can make an effort to communicate back. After all, your cat isn't meowing just for the sake of making noise; however, cats are less communicative than many other animals.

44. F. NO CHANGE
G. making senseless noises
H. senselessly making noises with no thought involved
J. making senseless noises, having no idea what they mean,

45. Which choice would best summarize the main point the essay makes about cats' communication with their human owners?
A. NO CHANGE
B. rather, there's a good chance your cat is trying to tell you something.
C. instead, your cat is probably trying to communicate with other cats by meowing.
D. on the other hand, it is better to have more than one cat so they can undergo a natural development.

PASSAGE IV

Visiting Mackinac Island

Visiting Mackinac (pronounced "Mackinaw") Island is like taking a step back to the past in time. Victorian houses' and a fort dating back to the War of 1812 surround the historic downtown, where horses and buggies still pull passengers down the road.

46. F. NO CHANGE
G. moving in a past-related direction
H. going back to the past, not the future,
J. stepping back

47. A. NO CHANGE
B. house's
C. houses
D. houses,

The only way to get to Mackinac Island is by boat or private plane, and you may not bring your car. Automobiles are outlawed on the little, isolated, Michigan, island, so visitors can see the sights only by horse, carriage, or by riding a bicycle, or on foot. Luckily, the island is small enough that cars are not necessary, Mackinac measures only a mile and a half in diameter.

48. F. NO CHANGE
G. your sweet self over to
H. yourself on down to
J. over to

49. A. NO CHANGE
B. isolated Michigan island
C. isolated Michigan island,
D. isolated, Michigan, island

50. F. NO CHANGE
G. by bicycle,
H. riding on a bicycle,
J. bicycle,

51. A. NO CHANGE
B. necessary, furthermore, Mackinac
C. necessary. Mackinac
D. necessary Mackinac

GO ON TO THE NEXT PAGE.

There are many things to see while visiting Mackinac Island. The majestic Grand Hotel is a popular tourist spot, as are the governor's mansion and Arch Rock, a towering limestone arch formed naturally by water erosion. [52] Fort Mackinac, where they still set off cannons every hour, is also a popular place to visit. Visible from parts of the island are Mackinac Bridge—the longest suspension bridge ever built—and a picturesque old lighthouse.

Shopping is also a favorite pastime on Mackinac Island. The island's biggest industry is tourism, [53] For the island's many tourists, the most popular item <u>of sale</u> (54) on Mackinac Island is fudge. The downtown streets are lined with fudge shops, <u>where</u> (55) tourists can watch fudge of all different flavors being made before lining up to buy some for themselves. These fudge shops are so <u>numerous and abundant</u> (56) that the local residents have even developed a special nickname for these tourists: <u>I call</u> (57) the tourists "fudgies."

Apart from sightseeing and shopping, Mackinac Island is a great place to just sit back and relax. In the summer, a gentle lake breeze floats through the air, <u>when it creates</u> (58) a beautiful, temperate climate. It is peaceful to sit in the city park and watch the ferries and private boats float into the harbor. The privacy of

52. If the writer were to delete the phrase "formed naturally by water erosion" (placing a period after the word *arch*), this sentence would primarily lose:

F. a detail describing the unique formation of the Arch Rock.
G. factual information concerning the geological formations of the tourist attractions on Mackinac Island.
H. a contrast to the governor's mansion, which was constructed by human hands.
J. nothing; this information is detailed elsewhere in this paragraph.

53. Given that all the following are true, which one, if added here at the end of this sentence, would provide the most effective transition to the topic discussed in the sentence that follows?

A. so there are many souvenir stores, T-shirt shops, and candy and ice cream parlors.
B. so Mackinac Island has not been negatively affected by outsourcing.
C. which is a big change from the island's eighteenth-century use in the fur trade.
D. but it's not a tourist attraction like many others with theme parks and chain restaurants.

54. **F.** NO CHANGE
G. for selling
H. for sale
J. of selling

55. Which of the following alternatives to the underlined portion would NOT be acceptable?

A. which
B. so
C. and
D. in which

56. **F.** NO CHANGE
G. abundantly numerous
H. numerous
J. of an abundance truly numerous

57. **A.** NO CHANGE
B. one calls
C. it calls
D. they call

58. **F.** NO CHANGE
G. creating
H. once it creates
J. as if it had created

GO ON TO THE NEXT PAGE.

the island's environs certainly don't give it the hustle-bustle quality of a city, but the relaxing atmosphere makes Mackinac Island the perfect place to visit to get away from the hectic pace of everyday life.

59. A. NO CHANGE
B. isn't giving
C. hasn't given
D. doesn't give

Question 60 asks about the preceding passage as a whole.

60. Suppose the writer had intended to write an essay on the difficulty the residents of Mackinac Island have had prohibiting automobile traffic from the historic island. Would this essay have successfully fulfilled that goal?

F. Yes, because the automobile has become such an essential part of American tourist travel that the residents are clearly threatened.
G. Yes, because this essay discusses the fact that automobiles are outlawed and goes on to detail many of the reasons this was possible.
H. No, because the essay focuses instead on other aspects of Mackinac Island, mentioning automobiles in only one part of the passage.
J. No, because this essay describes the ways the residents of Mackinac Island have sought to bring automobiles back to the island, not to outlaw them.

PASSAGE V

Fun with Karaoke

[1]

[1] Karaoke is one of the most popular forms of entertainment in the world. [2] What defies understanding, though, is why so many ordinary people insist on getting up on stage in public, humiliating themselves in front of both their friends; and peers. [3] Whether practiced at home, in a restaurant, or at a party, karaoke is a form of entertainment that provides people with a great time and a positive feeling. [4] It is understandable that people would enjoy singing in the

61. A. NO CHANGE
B. friends and peers.
C. friends, and peers.
D. friends and, peers.

62. Which of the following alternatives to the underlined portion would NOT be acceptable?

F. that has provided
G. , providing
H. , that is, providing
J. that having provided

GO ON TO THE NEXT PAGE.

privacy of their homes. [5] There are many different ways to respond to this question. [63]

[2]

Looking more closely, and you'll see a main reason for karaoke's success is its glitz and glamour. Karaoke provides people with a moment when they are more than just everyday folks—they are stars. Even though their performances may be heard only in dimly lit bars or busy restaurants, but karaoke singers are still performing as if in a true concert with such concert-hall staples, as microphones, lights, and applause. Even though the singers' voices are not spectacular, the audience has known that it's all for fun and responds anyway. And in the end, everyone would like to be a rock star. Karaoke is as close as many people will get to fame and stardom, but this is not the only reason for its enduring popularity.

[3]

There is another, more obvious reason why karaoke is so popular and singing in public is such fun. The average person allows his or her singing to be heard only in the shower or in the car as the radio plays. Karaoke, by contrast, allows the average person the opportunity to share that ordinarily solitary experience with other people. In lieu of how good or bad

63. For the sake of logic and coherence, Sentence 2 should be placed:
A. where it is now.
B. after Sentence 3.
C. after Sentence 4.
D. after Sentence 5.

64. F. NO CHANGE
G. Having looked
H. To look
J. Look

65. A. NO CHANGE
B. restaurants which
C. restaurants,
D. restaurants but

66. F. NO CHANGE
G. staples:
H. staples
J. staples;

67. A. NO CHANGE
B. is knowing
C. knew
D. knows

68. Given that all the choices are true, which one would most effectively conclude this paragraph while leading into the main focus of the next paragraph?
F. NO CHANGE
G. This is why AudioSynTrac and Numark Electronics were so successful in debuting the first singalong tapes and equipment back in the 1970s.
H. Japan's lasting influence on karaoke is obvious all the way down to its name—the Japanese word karaoke translates roughly to "empty orchestra."
J. Singing in front of people is more fun for many people than singing in the shower or in the car.

69. A. NO CHANGE
B. furthermore,
C. moreover,
D. as a result,

70. F. NO CHANGE
G. Regardless of
H. However
J. Because of

GO ON TO THE NEXT PAGE.

their voices are, people can experience the sheer joy of music shared with others, whose singing is mostly a private affair as well, through karaoke.
71

[4]

The effect karaoke has on people may also provide an explanation for its popularity: it helps bring people who are ordinarily shy out of their shells. [72] Karaoke helps them overcome stage fright, build their self-confidence, and conquer their fears. The singers may feel nervous or silly if they first take the stage, but when the audience breaks out into applause, the singers are sure to feel rewarded.
73

[5]

Whatever the reason, karaoke continues to grow in popularity. Last year, karaoke made no less than $7 billion in profit in Japan. Many dismiss it as a fad, but as long as karaoke is fun and leaves people feeling good, it will not disappear.
74

71. **A.** NO CHANGE
B. who
C. whom
D. who's

72. If the writer were to delete the clause "who are ordinarily shy" from the preceding sentence, the essay would primarily lose:

F. a detail that explains why karaoke is so popular in the international community.
G. a detail meant to indicate that karaoke is popular among those not normally inclined to sing in public.
H. information that emphasizes the possible psychological benefits of karaoke for the chronically shy.
J. an indication that karaoke may be used at some future time to help singers overcome stage fright.

73. **A.** NO CHANGE
B. when
C. unless
D. where

74. **F.** NO CHANGE
G. lesser than
H. fewer then
J. few than

Question 75 asks about the preceding passage as a whole.

75. Upon reviewing notes for this essay, the writer comes across some information and composes the following sentence incorporating that information:

> While different regions of the United States prefer different artists, the most popular karaoke requests are invariably for country artists, varying from the modern Carrie Underwood to the classic Johnny Cash.

For the sake of the logic and coherence of this essay, this sentence should be:

A. placed at the end of Paragraph 3.
B. placed at the end of Paragraph 4.
C. placed at the end of Paragraph 5.
D. NOT added to the essay at all.

END OF TEST 1

STOP! DO NOT TURN THE PAGE UNTIL TOLD TO DO SO.

MATHEMATICS TEST

60 Minutes—60 Questions

DIRECTIONS: Solve each problem, choose the correct answer, and then darken the corresponding oval on your answer sheet.

Do not linger over problems that take too much time. Solve as many as you can; then return to the others in the time you have left for this test.

You are permitted to use a calculator on this test. You may use your calculator for any problems you choose, but some of the problems may best be done without using a calculator.

Note: Unless otherwise stated, all of the following should be assumed:

1. Illustrative figures are NOT necessarily drawn to scale.
2. Geometric figures lie in a plane.
3. The word *line* indicates a straight line.
4. The word *average* indicates arithmetic mean.

DO YOUR FIGURING HERE.

1. Point X is located at –15 on the real number line. If point Y is located at –11, what is the midpoint of line segment XY ?

A. –13
B. –4
C. –2
D. 2
E. 13

2. Given triangle CDE (shown below) with a right angle at E, what is the length of leg DE ?

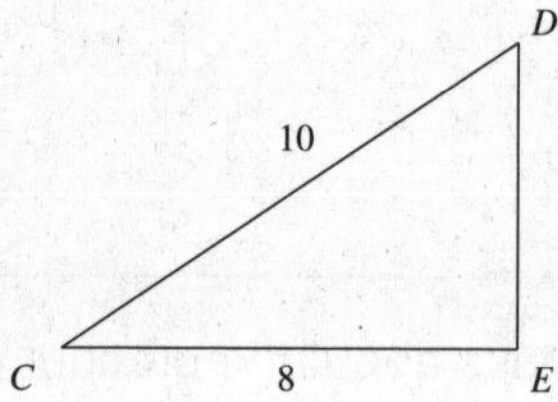

F. $\sqrt{2}$
G. 2
H. 6
J. $\sqrt{164}$
K. 16

3. Lucy is studying her ant farm. She needs to approximate the number of ants in the population, and she realizes that the number of ants, N, is close to 50 more than double the volume of the ant farm, V. Which of the formulas below expresses that approximation?

A. $N \approx \frac{1}{2}V + 50$

B. $N \approx \frac{1}{2}(V + 50)$

C. $N \approx 2V + 50$

D. $N \approx 2(V + 50)$

E. $N \approx V^2 + 50$

GO ON TO THE NEXT PAGE.

DO YOUR FIGURING HERE.

4. Lisa has 5 fiction books and 7 nonfiction books on a table by her front door. As she rushes out the door one day, she takes a book at random. What is the probability that the book she takes is fiction?

F. $\frac{1}{5}$

G. $\frac{5}{7}$

H. $\frac{1}{12}$

J. $\frac{5}{12}$

K. $\frac{7}{12}$

5. In the spring semester of her math class, Katie's test scores were 108, 81, 79, 99, 85, and 82. What was her average test score in the spring semester?

A. 534
B. 108
C. 89
D. 84
E. 80

6. Given parallel lines l and m, which of the following choices lists a pair of angles that must be congruent?

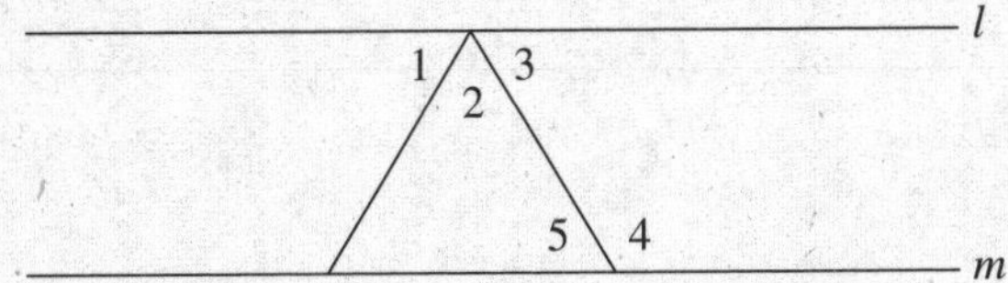

F. $\angle 1$ and $\angle 2$
G. $\angle 1$ and $\angle 3$
H. $\angle 2$ and $\angle 3$
J. $\angle 2$ and $\angle 5$
K. $\angle 3$ and $\angle 5$

7. Gregor works as a political intern and receives a monthly paycheck. He spends 20% of his paycheck on rent and deposits the remainder into a savings account. If his deposit is \$3,200, how much does he receive as his monthly pay?

A. \$ 4,000
B. \$ 5,760
C. \$ 7,200
D. \$ 8,000
E. \$17,000

GO ON TO THE NEXT PAGE.

DO YOUR FIGURING HERE.

8. Given parallelogram $ABCD$ below and parallelogram $EFGH$ (not shown) are similar, which of the following statements must be true about the two shapes?

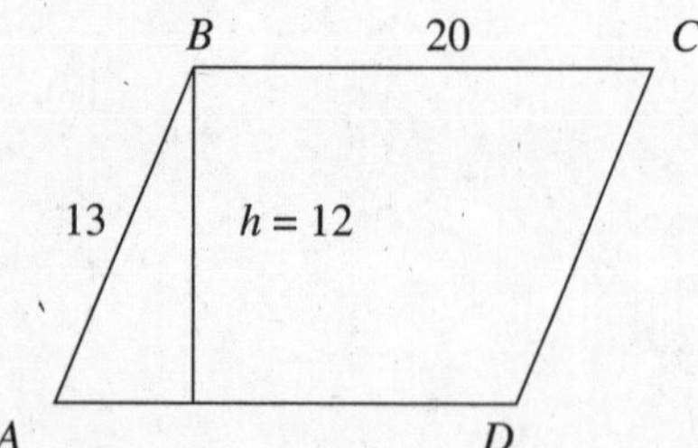

F. Their areas are equal.
G. Their perimeters are equal.
H. Side AB is congruent to side EF.
J. Diagonal AC is congruent to diagonal EG.
K. Their corresponding angles are congruent.

9. A size 8 dress that usually sells for \$60 is on sale for 30% off. Victoria has a store credit card that entitles her to an additional 10% off the reduced price of any item in the store. Excluding sales tax, what is the price Victoria pays for the dress?

A. \$22.20
B. \$24.75
C. \$34.00
D. \$36.00
E. \$37.80

10. Erin and Amy are playing poker. At a certain point in the game, Erin has 3 more chips than Amy. On the next hand, Erin wins 4 chips from Amy. Now how many more chips does Erin have than Amy?

F. –1
G. 1
H. 7
J. 11
K. 14

11. If $y = 4$, what does $|1 - y| = ?$

A. –5
B. –3
C. 3
D. 4
E. 5

12. $(3a + 2b)(a - b^2)$ is equivalent to:

F. $4a + b^2$
G. $3a^2 - 2b^3$
H. $3a^2 + 2ab + 2b^3$
J. $3a^2 - 3ab^2 + a^2 b^2$
K. $3a^2 - 3ab^2 + 2ab - 2b^3$

GO ON TO THE NEXT PAGE.

DO YOUR FIGURING HERE.

13. For all real values of y, $3 - 2(4 - y) = ?$

A. $-2y - 9$
B. $-2y + 8$
C. $-2y - 1$
D. $2y - 5$
E. $2y + 11$

14. What does $(y^3)^8 = ?$

F. y^{11}
G. y^{24}
H. $8y^3$
J. $8y^{11}$
K. $24y$

15. If the first day of the year is a Monday, what is the 260th day?

A. Monday
B. Tuesday
C. Wednesday
D. Thursday
E. Friday

16. If a square has an area of 64 square units, what is the area of the largest circle that can be inscribed inside the square?

F. 4π
G. 8π
H. 16π
J. 64
K. 64π

17. What is the product of the solutions of the expression $x^2 - 5x - 14 = 0$?

A. -14
B. -2
C. 0
D. 5
E. 7

18. Factoring the polynomial $x^{12} - 9$ reveals a number of factors for the expression. Which of these is NOT one of the possible factors?

F. $x^6 + 3$
G. $x^{12} - 9$
H. $x^3 + \sqrt{3}$
J. $x^3 - \sqrt{3}$
K. $x - \sqrt{3}$

GO ON TO THE NEXT PAGE.

DO YOUR FIGURING HERE.

19. What is the value of $\frac{2x+4}{3x}$ when $x = \frac{1}{6}$?

A. $4\frac{1}{3}$

B. 2

C. $\frac{26}{3}$

D. 12

E. 24

20. If you drive 60 miles at 90 miles an hour, how many minutes will the trip take you?

F. 15
G. 30
H. 40
J. 60
K. 90

21. The area of a trapezoid is found by multiplying the height by the average of the bases: $A = \frac{1}{2}h(b_1 + b_2)$. Given the side measurements below, what is the area, in square inches, of the trapezoid?

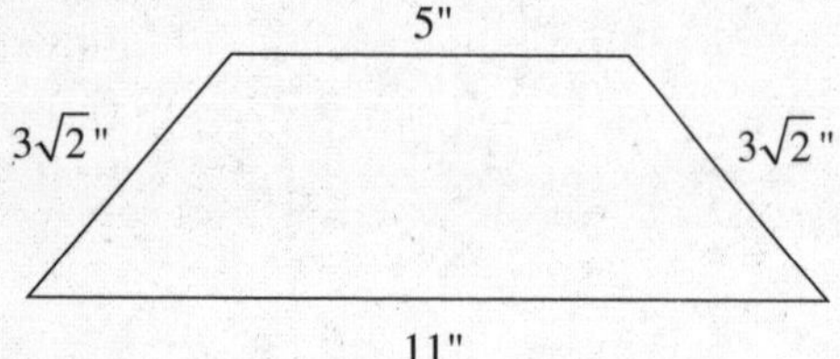

A. $15\sqrt{2}$
B. 22
C. 24
D. $24\sqrt{2}$
E. $30\sqrt{2}$

22. If $x = -\frac{2}{3}$ and $x = \frac{1}{4}$ are the roots of the quadratic equation $ax^2 + bx + c = 0$, then which of the following could represent the two factors of $ax^2 + bx + c$?

F. $(3x + 2)$ and $(4x - 1)$
G. $(3x + 1)$ and $(4x - 2)$
H. $(3x - 1)$ and $(4x + 2)$
J. $(3x - 2)$ and $(4x + 1)$
K. $(3x - 2)$ and $(4x - 1)$

GO ON TO THE NEXT PAGE.

DO YOUR FIGURING HERE.

23. In the rhombus below, diagonal $AC = 6$ and diagonal $BD = 8$. What is the length of each of the four sides?

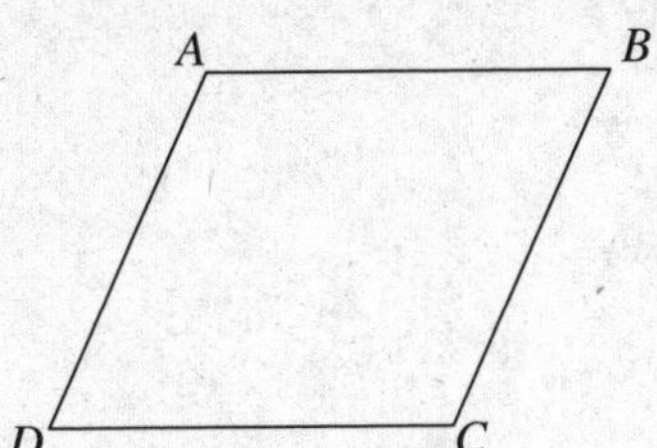

A. $\sqrt{7}$
B. $\sqrt{14}$
C. 5
D. 7
E. 10

24. A rectangular rug has an area of 80 square feet, and its width is exactly 2 feet shorter than its length. What is the length, in feet, of the rug?

F. 8
G. 10
H. 16
J. 18
K. 36

25. In the Cartesian plane, a line runs through points(1,–5) and (5,10). Which of the following represents the slope of that line?

A. $\frac{4}{15}$
B. $\frac{4}{5}$
C. 1
D. $\frac{5}{4}$
E. $\frac{15}{4}$

26. The equation of a circle in the standard (*x*,*y*) *coordinate plane is given by the equation* $(x + 5)^2 + (y - 5)^2 = 5$. What is the center of the circle?

F. $(-\sqrt{5}, \sqrt{5})$
G. $(-5, 5)$
H. $(\sqrt{5}, -\sqrt{5})$
J. $(5, -5)$
K. $(5, 5)$

GO ON TO THE NEXT PAGE.

27. The graph below shows a function, $f(x)$, in the coordinate plane. Which of the following choices best describes the *domain* of this function?

(Note: The domain is defined as the set of all values of x for which a function is defined.)

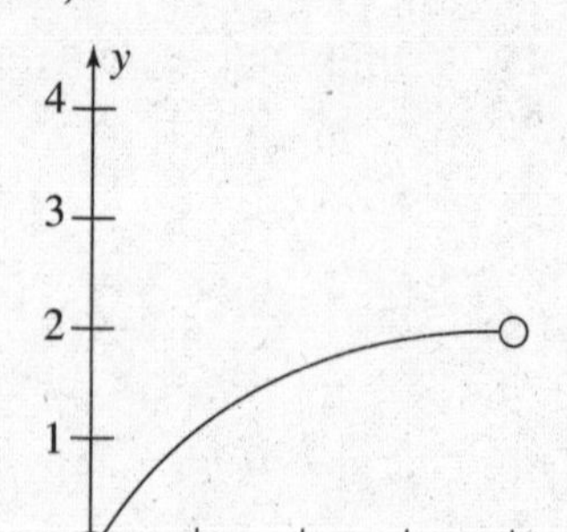

A. $\{0, 1, 2, 3, 4\}$
B. $\{0, 1, 2\}$
C. $\{x: 0 < x < 2\}$
D. $\{x: 0 < x < 4\}$
E. All real values of x

DO YOUR FIGURING HERE.

28. Amber decides to graph her office and the nearest coffee shop in the standard (x,y) plane. If her office is at point $(-1,-5)$ and the coffee shop is at point $(3,3)$, what are the coordinates of the point exactly halfway between those of her office and the shop? (You may assume Amber is able to walk a straight line between.)

F. $(1, -1)$
G. $(1, 4)$
H. $(2, -1)$
J. $(2, 4)$
K. $(2, 0)$

29. For a chemistry class, Sanjay is doing an experiment that involves periodically heating a container of liquid. The graph below shows the temperature of the liquid at different times during the experiment. What is the average rate of change of temperature (in degrees Celsius per minute) during the times in which Sanjay is applying heat to this container?

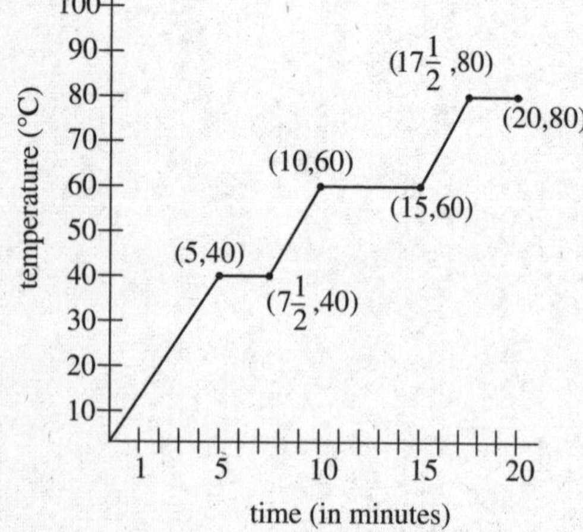

A. 4
B. 5
C. 8
D. 10
E. 20

GO ON TO THE NEXT PAGE.

DO YOUR FIGURING HERE.

30. If $\frac{a^x}{a^y} = a^5$, for $a \neq 0$, which of the following statements must be true?

F. $x \neq 0$ and $y \neq 0$

G. $x + y = 5$

H. $x - y = 5$

J. $xy = 5$

K. $\frac{x}{y} = 5$

31. What is the slope of the line given by the equation $8 = 3y - 5x$?

A. -5

B. $-\frac{5}{3}$

C. $-\frac{3}{5}$

D. $\frac{3}{5}$

E. $\frac{5}{3}$

32. When adding fractions, a useful first step is to find the least common denominator (LCD) of the fractions. What is the LCD for these fractions?

$$\frac{2}{3^2 \bullet 5}, \frac{13}{5^2 \bullet 7 \bullet 11}, \frac{2}{3 \bullet 11^3}$$

F. $3 \bullet 5 \bullet 7 \bullet 11$

G. $3^2 \bullet 5^2 \bullet 7 \bullet 11$

H. $3^2 \bullet 5^2 \bullet 11^3$

J. $3^2 \bullet 5^2 \bullet 7 \bullet 11^3$

K. $3^3 \bullet 5^3 \bullet 7 \bullet 11^4$

33. $\frac{1}{4} \bullet \frac{2}{5} \bullet \frac{3}{6} \bullet \frac{4}{7} \bullet \frac{5}{8} \bullet \frac{6}{9} \bullet \frac{7}{10} = ?$

A. $\frac{1}{720}$

B. $\frac{1}{360}$

C. $\frac{1}{120}$

D. $\frac{27}{49}$

E. 1

GO ON TO THE NEXT PAGE.

34. Dave is in Pikeston and needs to go to Danville, which is about 110 miles due south of Pikeston. From Danville, he'll head east to Rocketville, about 200 miles from Danville. As he sets out on his trip, a plane takes off from the Pikeston airport and flies directly to Rocketville. Approximately how far, in miles, does the plane fly?

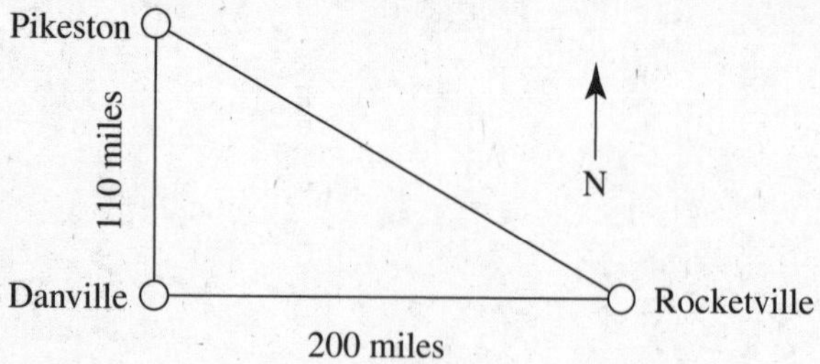

F. 310

G. $\sqrt{310}$

H. $\sqrt{27900}$

J. $\sqrt{30000}$

K. $\sqrt{52100}$

35. The figure below is a pentagon (5-sided figure). Suppose a second pentagon were overlaid on this pentagon. At most, the two figures could have how many points of intersection?

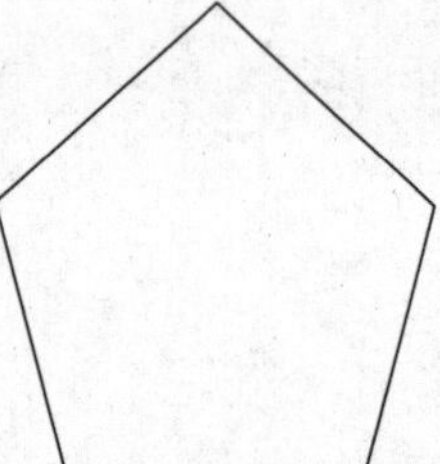

A. 1
B. 2
C. 5
D. 10
E. Infinitely many

36. MicroCorp will hold its annual company picnic next week and will assign 3 planning duties to its employees. One person selected will reserve a venue, another will arrange catering, and a third will plan activities. There are 10 employees eligible to fulfill these duties, and no employee can be assigned more than one duty. How many different ways are there for duties to be assigned to employees?

F. 7^3

G. 9^3

H. 10^3

J. $9 \cdot 8 \cdot 7$

K. $10 \cdot 9 \cdot 8$

DO YOUR FIGURING HERE.

GO ON TO THE NEXT PAGE.

37. In the (x,y)coordinate plane below, points $P(6,2)$ and $Q(1,4)$ are two vertices of ΔPQR. If $\angle PQR$ is a right angle, then which of the following could be the coordinates of R ?

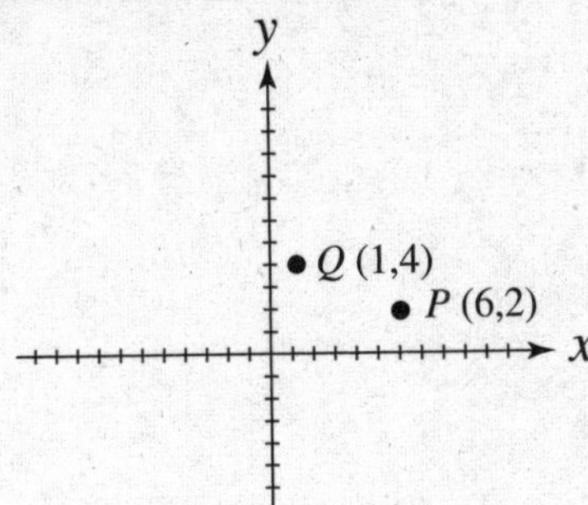

A. (4,–3)
B. (3, 0)
C. (2, 1)
D. (2, 4)
E. (3, 9)

DO YOUR FIGURING HERE.

38. If $y = 0.25(100 - y)$, then what is the value of y ?

F. 200
G. 75
H. 25
J. 20
K. 18

39. If $0° \leq x° \leq 180°$ and $4\cos^2 x = 1$, then $x° = ?$

A. 0°
B. 60°
C. 90°
D. 150°
E. 180°

40. Danielle's living room is a rectangle with the dimensions 16 feet by 18 feet. If she partially covers the bare floor with a circular throw rug with a diameter of 12 feet, what is the approximate area of bare floor, in square feet, that remains exposed?

(Note: Assume the rug lies completely flat and does not touch any wall.)

F. 113
G. 144
H. 175
J. 288
K. Cannot be determined without knowing the exact position of the rug

GO ON TO THE NEXT PAGE.

DO YOUR FIGURING HERE.

41. In the standard (x,y) coordinate plane, which of the following is the equation of the line perpendicular to the line $y = -2x + 2$ and that passes through the point $(0,-3)$?

A. $y = -2x - 3$

B. $y = -\frac{1}{2}x + 2$

C. $y = \frac{1}{2}x - 3$

D. $y = \frac{1}{2}x + 2$

E. $y = 2x - 3$

42. In the figure given below, what is $\sin \theta$?

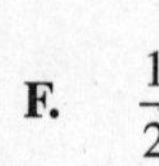

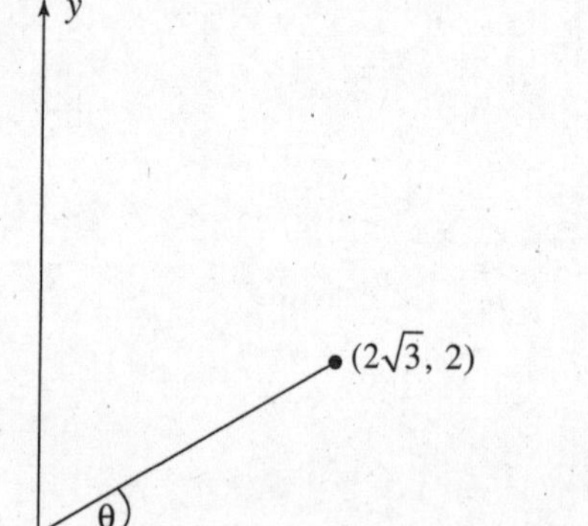

F. $\frac{1}{2}$

G. $\frac{\sqrt{3}}{3}$

H. $\frac{\sqrt{3}}{2}$

J. 1

K. $\sqrt{3}$

43. If $a = 5$ and $b = -\frac{1}{4}$, which of the following expressions will be the greatest?

A. $a + b$
B. $a - b$
C. $a \times b$
D. $a \div b$
E. $|a \times b|$

44. When $\frac{x}{3} - 1 = -\frac{13}{12}$, which of the following must be true?

F. $-12 < x < -3$
G. $-3 < x < 0$
H. $0 < x < 3$
J. $3 < x < 4$
K. $4 < x$

GO ON TO THE NEXT PAGE.

DO YOUR FIGURING HERE.

45. Which choice below is the complete solution set of $|2z-3| \geq 7$?

A. $z \geq 5$
B. $z \leq -2$ or $z \geq 5$
C. $-5 \leq z \leq 5$
D. $z \leq -6$ or $z \geq 2$
E. $z \leq -5$ or $z \geq 2$

46. Which trigonometric function (where defined) is equivalent to $\dfrac{\sin^2 x}{\cos x \tan x}$?

F. $\dfrac{\cos x}{\sin^2 x}$
G. $\dfrac{1}{\cos x}$
H. $\sin x$
J. $\dfrac{1}{\sin x}$
K. $\dfrac{1}{\sin^2 x}$

47. When $a \neq b$, the expression $\dfrac{ax-bx}{4a-4b} < 0$. Which of the following describes the complete set of x values that make this inequality true?

A. $x = -4$ only
B. $x = 4$ only
C. $x = -\dfrac{1}{4}$ only
D. $x < 0$
E. $x > 0$

GO ON TO THE NEXT PAGE.

DO YOUR FIGURING HERE.

48. The volume of a cone, which is derived by treating it as a pyramid with infinitely many lateral faces, is given by the formula $V = \frac{1}{3}\pi r^2 h$, where r is the radius of the base and h is the height. If the radius is halved and the height is doubled, what will be the ratio of the new volume to the old volume?

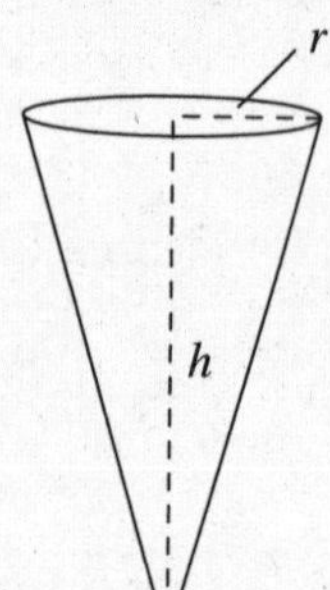

F. 4:1
G. 2:1
H. 1:1
J. 1:2
K. 1:4

49. Al bikes a trail to the top of a hill and back down. He bikes up the hill in m minutes, then returns twice as quickly downhill on the same trail. What is the total time, in hours, that Al spends biking up the hill and back down?

A. $\frac{m}{60}$

B. $\frac{m}{40}$

C. $\frac{m}{30}$

D. $\frac{3m}{2}$

E. $2m$

50. Pippin the guinea pig is running on her wheel when, due to a manufacturing error, the wheel breaks free of its axis. Pippin remains in her wheel, running in a straight line until the wheel has rotated exactly 15 times. If the diameter of the wheel is 10 inches, how many inches has the wheel rolled?

F. 75
G. 150
H. 75π
J. 150π
K. $1{,}500\pi$

GO ON TO THE NEXT PAGE.

DO YOUR FIGURING HERE.

51. A circle is inscribed in a square, as shown below. If x is the distance from the center of the circle to a vertex of the square, then what is the length of the radius of the circle, in terms of x ?

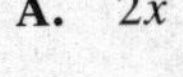

A. $2x$

B. $x\sqrt{2}$

C. x

D. $\dfrac{x\sqrt{2}}{2}$

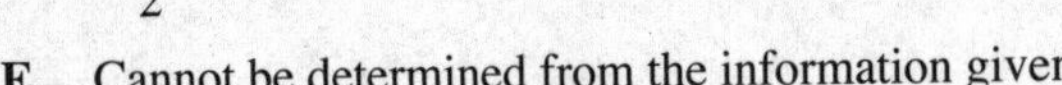

E. Cannot be determined from the information given

52. A function is defined for x and y such that $f_{(x,y)} = -2xy + y + x - 4$. So, for $x = 2$ and $y = 3$, $f_{(2,3)} = -2 \times 2 \times 3 + 3 + 2 - 4 = -12 + 1 = -11$. If x and y are to be chosen such that $f_{(x,y)} = f_{(y,x)}$, then which of the following restrictions must be placed on x and y ?

F. $x > 0$ and $y > 0$

G. $x < 0$ and $y < 0$

H. $x = y$

J. $xy < 0$

K. No restrictions are needed.

53. A pipe of radius 4 feet sends water to two smaller pipes of equal size. If each of the smaller pipes allows exactly half as much water to flow as the larger pipe, what is the radius of one of the smaller pipes?

A. 2

B. 2π

C. $2\sqrt{2}$

D. $4\sqrt{2}$

E. $2\pi\sqrt{2}$

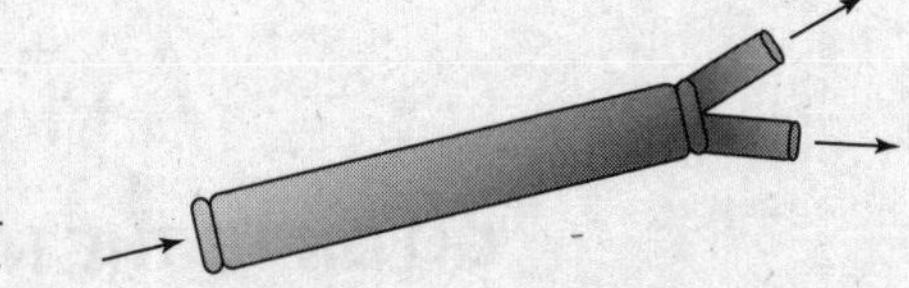

GO ON TO THE NEXT PAGE.

DO YOUR FIGURING HERE.

54. The cross-sectional view of a tent is shown below. If the tent is 6 feet wide at its base, then which of the following expressions could be used to calculate the height of the tent, in feet?

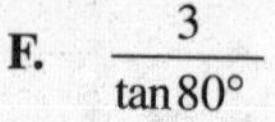

F. $\dfrac{3}{\tan 80^\circ}$

G. $3\tan 40^\circ$

H. $\dfrac{3}{\tan 40^\circ}$

J. $6\tan 40^\circ$

K. $3\tan 80^\circ$

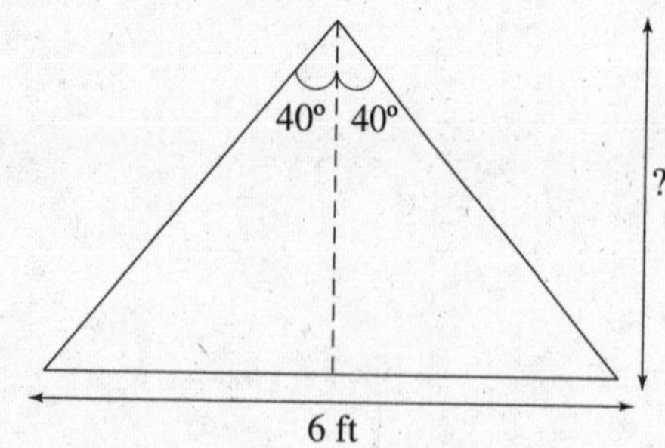

55. Two girls walk home from school. Starting from school, Susan walks north 2 blocks and then west 8 blocks, while Cindy walks east 3 blocks and then south 1 block. Approximately how many blocks apart are the girls' homes?

A. 7.1
B. 10.4
C. 11.4
D. 12.7
E. 16.0

56. For all integer values of a and b such that $a > 0$ and $b < 0$, which of the following must also be an integer?

F. 3^{a+b}

G. 3^{a-b}

H. 3^{ab}

J. 3^{-a}

K. $3^{\frac{a}{b}}$

GO ON TO THE NEXT PAGE.

57. If x and y are real numbers and $0 < x < y < \frac{y}{x}$, which of the following gives the set of all values which $\frac{y}{x}$ could have?

DO YOUR FIGURING HERE.

A. 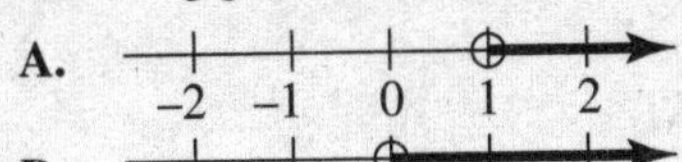
−2 −1 0 1 2

B. −2 −1 0 1 2

C. −2 −1 0 1 2

D. −2 −1 0 1 2

E. −2 −1 0 1 2

58. A circular running track is being built in a fenced-in athletic field 100 feet wide and 150 feet long. If a border of 10 feet is needed between the outside edge of the track and the fence, what is the radius of the largest track that can be built?

F. 40
G. 45
H. 65
J. 90
K. 110

59. If a sphere is cut by two different planes, dividing it into sections, how many sections is it possible to end up with?

A. 2 only
B. 2 or 4 only
C. 3 only
D. 3 or 4 only
E. 2, 3, or 4 only

60. For all real values of a and b, the equation $|a - b| = 5$ can be interpreted as "the positive difference of a and b is 5." What is the positive difference between the 2 solutions for a ?

F. b

G. $b + 5$

H. $2b$

J. $\sqrt{b^2 - 25}$

K. 10

END OF TEST 2

STOP! DO NOT TURN THE PAGE UNTIL TOLD TO DO SO.

DO NOT RETURN TO A PREVIOUS TEST.

READING TEST

35 Minutes—40 Questions

DIRECTIONS: There are four passages in this test. Each passage is followed by several questions. After reading a passage, choose the best answer to each question and fill in the corresponding oval on your answer document. You may refer to the passages as often as necessary.

Passage I

PROSE FICTION: The following passage is excerpted from the coming-of-age novel *The Year of the Unicorn* by Krista Prouty (©2008 by Krista Prouty).

It was always the same, every Christmas. My sister and I would wake up early, my parents would send us back to bed, and we would instead huddle in my room, discussing which gifts might be waiting for us downstairs. One year it was a bicycle that I wanted, and I can still remember telling my sister exactly what it would look like: pink, with silver streamers and a sparkly silver seat. Eventually we would hear our parents moving around downstairs and we would know that it was almost time. Once the scent of coffee made it to our rooms, we would hurl ourselves downstairs since that signified that our parents were not only awake but caffeinated and ready for gift-giving.

The year that I was nine, and Lily was six, the gift that I had been craving was the Barbie Dream House. Another girl from my school had one and I had been lucky enough to be allowed a glimpse of it after school one day. She was like a princess bestowing largesse; allowing one or two people over after school most days, demonstrating the various clever mechanisms, then sitting quietly, contentedly, while we gazed in wonder for a few minutes. Then, she sent us on our way. I knew that if I could only have a Dream House of my own, my life would be complete. It was a bigger gift than I usually requested but, logically, I felt, that meant I was all the more likely to have my wish granted.

One night I overheard my parents, after they thought Lily and I had gone to bed.

"Bill, what are we going to do about Christmas this year?" My mother's voice, quiet and unsettlingly uncertain, came from the kitchen.

"I don't know yet, Mel, but we'll figure something out. We always do, honey."

"I know. I just can't help but worry." Whatever my mother said next was drowned out by the running water—she must have been washing up after dinner. I crept back to my bedroom, a little bit troubled by what I had heard but, as is the way of children, soon forgot and went back to Barbie Dream House dreaming.

On the Christmas morning in question, Lily and I huddled in my room, waiting for the signal to appear. She wanted a new bike and kept asking me if Santa would get it for her, but all I could think about was my Dream House. Somehow, I had convinced myself that I was certain to get it, that life and the fates could not possibly be cruel enough to deny me this. I could see the wallpaper that was printed on the plastic walls, the darling matching furniture, and the ingenious hand-operated elevator. It would smell like new plastic. I inhaled deeply, imagining myself showing my gift off to friends and foes alike. Instead of new plastic, however, my nostrils quivered to the odor of freshly brewed coffee. It was time.

My eyes still full of the glories I expected, I barreled down the stairs, almost knocking Lily down in my haste. Both of my parents were standing in the kitchen, sipping coffee. I tore past them, even though I knew that they would expect me to stop and wait for them to walk into the living room with me. My longing was simply too exquisite to wait any longer. I burst through the double doors into our living room, words of joy and gratitude ready on my lips, only to find—there was no Dream House. Frantically, I began to paw through the boxes under the tree, certain that it had to be there, somewhere, blind to the movement of my parents and sister entering the room behind me, nervous smiles on both my parents' faces. Eventually I was forced to concede that the tree was not somehow harboring a Dream House under its limbs. I looked up at my parents, grief and confusion painted large on my features.

"Hold up a minute, honey. Santa brought you one more gift that wouldn't quite fit under the tree. Bill, go ahead—show her."

As I watched my father head towards a corner where a large blanket was draped over some bulky object, hope flickered back to life a bit. But the size was all wrong, as was the shape. Still smiling anxiously, my father pulled the blanket away from what appeared to be a huge dollhouse. If Barbie's Dream House was sleek and modern, this was awkward and old-fashioned. It had a peaked roof and a patio, with what looked like handmade furniture and wallpaper that looked suspiciously like the paper my parents had hung in Lily's room last fall. Slowly, realization dawned—my father had made it for me.

GO ON TO THE NEXT PAGE.

Looking back, I can only recall the rest of that day hazily, even though the events up until that moment are as clear today as they were at the time. I remember the feeling of devastation that I felt, as I realized that the other girls from school would not, in fact, be blown away by my Christmas gift. I tried to be as grateful as I could, understanding even then that my father had probably spent countless hours working on the house, but my disappointment was only too evident. I just couldn't understand why they had given me this crude approximation instead of my heart's desire. As an adult, I wish I could go back in time, whisper the reason to my younger self, try to be more appreciative of my father's efforts, but that is not the way of the world. I still have the house, though, and when I have children of my own, I will tell them the whole story, and I hope they will understand better than I did.

1. Which of the following statements does NOT describe one of the narrator's reactions to her Christmas gift?
   - **A.** She is devastated by the realization that the other children at school will not be impressed by this gift.
   - **B.** She wishes that her parents had bought her a real Barbie Dream House instead of a handmade one.
   - **C.** She despises the house for its old-fashioned appearance and lack of modern conveniences, such as an elevator.
   - **D.** She appreciates all the effort her father went to in order to give her this gift and tries to convey a sense of gratitude.

2. According to the passage, when the narrator smells coffee on Christmas morning, it means that:
   - **F.** her parents are ready to proceed with the Christmas festivities.
   - **G.** she and her sister should hurry to the kitchen for breakfast.
   - **H.** her father has finally finished preparing her Christmas gift.
   - **J.** it is time to burst into the living room in front of her parents.

3. The narrator would most likely agree with which of the following statements about owning a Barbie Dream House?
   - **A.** She would become a princess able to bestow largesse on other children.
   - **B.** She would, at least for the moment, be content with her life.
   - **C.** It would allow her to appreciate her parents' hard work and sacrifices.
   - **D.** She would then be able to pass it on to her own children someday.

4. What is the main point of the first paragraph?
   - **F.** The smell of coffee still reminds the narrator of the Christmases of her childhood.
   - **G.** The narrator's family had a specific ritual that was followed every Christmas morning.
   - **H.** Most years, the narrator and her sister would hurl themselves into their gifts without warning.
   - **J.** The narrator had once desperately wanted a pink and silver bicycle.

5. Which of the following statements most accurately expresses the narrator's feelings when she first sees the gift that her father made for her?
   - **A.** She is disappointed that it is not the exact gift that she had hoped to receive.
   - **B.** She gratefully acknowledges the long hours her father must have put into the gift.
   - **C.** She admires the traditional architecture of the house and its attractive wallpaper.
   - **D.** She looks forward to showing her new house off to all of the other girls at school.

6. The narrator's father can most accurately be characterized as:
   - **F.** ignorant and cruel.
   - **G.** thoughtful but lazy.
   - **H.** concerned and hard-working.
   - **J.** caring but inaccessible.

7. It can logically be inferred from the passage that the reason the narrator was not given the official Barbie Dream House for Christmas is because:
   - **A.** it is too costly a gift for her parents to buy that year.
   - **B.** she had already been given the pink and silver bicycle that she wanted.
   - **C.** her father had always wanted to make his daughter a dollhouse.
   - **D.** her parents do not wish for their daughter to be happy.

8. According to the passage, the reason why the narrator hopes to someday give her dollhouse to her children is that she:
   - **F.** wants them to be able to impress the other children at school as she once did.
   - **G.** knows that, by that time, it is likely to be worth a great deal of money.
   - **H.** remembers how much she appreciated the gift when it was given to her.
   - **J.** hopes that they will be better able to understand the meaning behind the gift than she was.

GO ON TO THE NEXT PAGE.

9. A reasonable conclusion that the narrator draws regarding her dollhouse is that:

A. it is far more beautiful than was the plastic Barbie Dream House that she had initially desired.
B. without an elevator, it is less valuable than it would otherwise have been.
C. it was given to her with the intention that she keep it to pass on to her own children someday.
D. constructing it must have been time-consuming and labor-intensive.

10. The main point of the last paragraph is that:

F. the narrator would have been much happier if she had been given a Barbie Dream House.
G. it is not fair to give one child a long-desired gift and not give the same to another child.
H. the disappointments suffered in childhood affect people well into adulthood.
J. the passage of time can alter the way events from the past are viewed.

Passage II

SOCIAL SCIENCE: This passage is adapted from T. H. Watkins' *The Great Depression* (©1993, Little, Brown and Co.; Blackside Inc.).

One of the most durable and well regarded of all the New Deal's programs came from President Roosevelt himself, who had his own share of inventiveness. If the president cared about the fate of people, he also cared about the fate of trees, having practiced the art of silviculture on his Hyde Park estate with such enthusiasm that on various official forms he was fond of listing his occupation as "tree farmer." It was in early March, 1933, that he proceeded to bring the two concerns together—enlisting young unemployed men in a kind of volunteer "army" to be put to work in the national forests, national parks, and on other federal public lands. When he went to Congress for authorization of the program, he called the new agency the Civilian Corps Reforestation Youth Rehabilitation Movement, but before sinking under the weight of an acronym like CCRYRM, it was soon changed to the Civilian Conservation Corps (known forever after as the CCC). Congress chose not to handle the details itself. It simply authorized the president to create the program and structure it as he saw fit by executive order; it was to last two years. Responsibility was divided up among the Labor Department, which was to screen and select the enrollees, the War Department, which would house and feed them in their nonworking hours, and the Departments of Agriculture and Interior, which would design and supervise projects in regional and national forests, national parks, and other public lands. The men would be paid $30 a month, anywhere from $23 to $25 of it to be sent to their families.

The CCC officially began on April 5, 1933, calling for an enrollment of 250,000 to be housed in 1,468 camps around the country. The cost for the first year was estimated at $500 million. The men had to be US citizens between the ages of seventeen and twenty-seven (later, twenty-four), out of school, out of work, capable of physical labor, over 60 inches but under 78 inches in height, more than 107 pounds in weight, and had to possess no fewer than "three serviceable natural masticating teeth above and below." They would serve terms of no more than nine months so that as many as possible could be accommodated over the course of time.

Among the earliest enrollees were some veterans who had returned to Washington, setting up camp and demanding payment of their bonuses for service during the war. While making it clear that he opposed the payments on economic grounds, FDR provided tents, showers, mess halls, and latrines, and, waiving the age restriction for them, invited the members of this new Bonus Army to join his new agency. What was more, Eleanor Roosevelt dropped by one rainy day for a visit, slogging through ankle-deep mud to meet and talk with the men. "Hoover sent the army," said one veteran of the previous summer's BEF disaster, "Roosevelt sent his wife." When it became clear that no bonus would be forthcoming, about twenty-five hundred of the men took Roosevelt up on his offer and joined the CCC.

In the summer of 1934, Roosevelt expanded the size of the CCC to 350,000 and would raise it to 500,000 in 1935. Congress continued to reauthorize it faithfully over the next seven years, and by the time it was closed out in 1942, the CCC had put more than three million young "soil soldiers" to work. In the national forests alone they built 3,470 fire towers, installed 65,100 miles of telephone lines, scraped and graded thousands of fire breaks, roads, and trails, and built 97,000 miles of truck trails and roads, spent 4.1 million man-hours fighting fires, and cut down and hauled out millions of diseased trees and planted more than 1.3 billion young trees in the first major reforestation campaign in the country's history. For the National Park Service, they built roads, campgrounds, bridges, and recreation and administration facilities; for the Biological Survey (a predecessor of today's Fish and Wildlife Service), they conducted wildlife surveys and improved wildlife refuge lands; and for the Army Corps of Engineers, they built flood control projects in West Virginia, Vermont, and New York State.

In return, the CCC, at its best, took at least some young men out of the urban tangle of hopelessness where so many resided, introduced them to the intricacies and healing joy of the outdoors, and clothed and fed them better than many had been for years. Moreover, the program taught more than a hundred thousand to read and write, passed out twenty-five thousand eighth-grade diplomas and five thousand high-school diplomas, gave structure and discipline to lives that had experienced little of either, strengthened bodies and minds, and for many provided a dose of self-esteem they had never known.

GO ON TO THE NEXT PAGE.

11. The main idea of the passage is that:
    - A. the CCC forced unemployed young men to work in the national forests, national parks, and on other federal public lands for no payment or bonus.
    - B. it was only after President Roosevelt created the CCC that veterans had suitable employment during the Great Depression.
    - C. research into the history of the New Deal shows that the idea for the CCC came from the Congress.
    - D. among the programs of the New Deal, the CCC employed young men to build public works projects on public lands in return for modest wages, food, clothing, and some education.

12. The main idea of the third paragraph (lines 37–49) is that:
    - F. President Hoover had dispatched the army to meet with disgruntled veterans, but President Roosevelt sent his wife, Eleanor, to meet with the Bonus Army.
    - G. when they realized President Roosevelt would not pay the bonus, many veterans abandoned the Bonus Army and accepted his invitation to join the CCC.
    - H. President Roosevelt supplied shelter and food to the veterans before paying the bonus the veterans demanded.
    - J. many of the veterans were above the age requirement of the CCC.

13. As it is used in line 7 to describe President Roosevelt, the term *tree farmer* most nearly means that Roosevelt:
    - A. had supported his family by growing trees before he entered politics.
    - B. believed in an agrarian economy over urban industrialization.
    - C. continued his successful business selling trees while in office.
    - D. had a great interest in trees and knew a good deal about them.

14. According to the passage, which of the following was a project the CCC performed for the National Park Service?
    - F. Building fire towers
    - G. Building campground facilities
    - H. Installing telephone lines
    - J. Conducting wildlife surveys

15. According to the passage, which of the following statements is true about the CCC?
    - A. The agency provided enrollees with academic instruction.
    - B. The agency provided enrollees with urban job training.
    - C. The agency accepted only men with six teeth.
    - D. The agency offered courses in nutrition and self-esteem.

16. Information in the fourth paragraph (lines 50–67) makes it clear that the CCC:
    - F. was voluntary and therefore did not pay members anything.
    - G. ran for more years and employed more men than was originally intended.
    - H. employed 4.1 million men.
    - J. battled fires in West Virginia, Vermont, and New York.

17. The passage most strongly suggests that before the 1930s, the national forests:
    - A. received no federal support or aid for projects to clear diseased trees.
    - B. included land reserved for wildlife refuges.
    - C. had never undergone a major reforestation campaign.
    - D. experienced more floods than forest fires.

18. According to the passage, when did the CCC change its name?
    - F. After President Roosevelt received authorization from Congress.
    - G. After Congress protested that CCRYRM was too difficult to say.
    - H. In the same year the size expanded to 500,000 men.
    - J. After the Bonus Army disbanded.

19. The passage states that the same year the CCC was authorized enrollees had to be:
    - A. over 78 inches in height.
    - B. in school.
    - C. between the ages of seventeen and twenty-seven.
    - D. between the ages of seventeen and twenty-four.

20. According to the passage, CCC programs in national parks and forests were:
    - F. conducted far from where the members were fed and housed.
    - G. under the control of the Departments of Agriculture and the Interior.
    - H. supervised by the Labor Department.
    - J. minimum-wage jobs.

GO ON TO THE NEXT PAGE.

Passage III

HUMANITIES: This passage is adapted from John Gattuso, ed., *Native American* (©1993, Houghton Mifflin Co.).

Northwest natives are carvers by tradition, but it was the natives of the far north, in what is now British Columbia and Alaska, who first carved totem poles. The history of these fascinating works is surprisingly brief, for it wasn't until the mid-18th century, when European explorers first encountered these remote tribes, that the unique sculptures began to appear. Although the natives were already expert carvers of canoes, tools, longhouses, and furniture, they lacked the iron tools necessary to fell a massive tree in one piece and carve its entire length.

With the iron axes they got in trade for their baskets, boxes, and pelts, the coastal tribes of the far north could take advantage of the trees that grew so tall and straight in their wet climate. Initially, the poles were made to stand against the front of a house, with figures facing out and a door cut through the base, so all would enter the house through the pole. In this case, the totem pole functioned as a family crest, recounting genealogies, stories, or legends that in some way identified the owner. Towards the end of the 19th century, the poles stood free on the beach or in the village outside the carvers' homes. Some villages were virtual forests of dozens, sometimes hundreds, of poles.

The family that carved the pole gave a potlatch with feasting, games, and much gift-giving. The guests, in return, raised the pole. These gatherings were costly and required a great deal of preparation and participation. The custom frustrated whites trying to "civilize" the Indians, especially missionaries who solved the problem by knocking the poles down. Employers, too, complained that their Indian workers were unreliable when a pole was being carved or a potlatch planned. Eventually, both the Canadian and United States governments banned potlatches, and pole carving nearly died out. The ban was lifted in the 1950s.

The Tlingit, on the southeastern coast of Alaska, and the Haidas and Tsimshian of western Canada are known for their pole carving. On a tour in 1899, a group of Seattle businessmen visited the Tlingit village of Tongas and, finding no one there, took one of the poles. They erected it in Seattle where, at a towering 50 ft., it became one of the city's most distinctive monuments. In 1938, Tlingit carvers copied the pole after the original was destroyed by fire, and it remains in Pioneer Square today.

Poles serve the important purpose of recording the lore of a clan, much as a book would. The top figure on the pole identifies the owner's clan, and succeeding characters (read from top to bottom) tell their stories. Raven, the trickster, might tell the story of how he fooled the Creator into giving him the sun, or Frog might tell how he wooed a human woman. With slight variations between villages, everyone knew these stories, and potlatch guests dramatized them at the pole-raising with masks, drumming, and songs. And so the legends were preserved from one generation to the next.

There is a story behind almost every image on the pole. For example, if an animal had the power to transform itself into other beings, the carver would portray it in all its forms. If Raven were sometimes bird, sometimes human, he would be carved with both wings and limbs, or have a human face with a raven's beak. Other images are used to describe the spirits' special abilities. Eyes are frequently used to suggest acuteness or skill. So, for example, if an eye appears in an animal's ear, it might indicate that that animal has a sharp sense of hearing. And human figures in unexpected places, like an ear or nose, might mean that the animal has great powers.

Learning to read totem poles is like learning to read a language. They speak of history, mythology, social structure, and spirituality. They serve many purposes and continue to be carved by the descendants of the original carvers.

Today, Haida, Tlingit, Tsimshian, Kwakiutl and other native craftsmen carve, predominantly for the tourist trade, small "souvenir" totem poles in wood and black slate (or argillite). They also carve extraordinarily beautiful masks, effigies, boxes, house posts, and fixtures…

21. Which of the following statements best expresses the main idea of the passage?

A. Many Native American tribes created totem poles with meaningful symbols, but these poles were less important than the canoes carved before the mid-18th century.
B. Although the Tlingit village was deserted, the Seattle businessmen who took the totem pole were not right to take it without permission.
C. The history of totem pole carving dates back to only the mid-18th-century, but these poles have played an important role in Native American culture since that time.
D. The ban issued by the Canadian and United States governments against potlatches was lifted in the 1950s, but interest in totem-pole carving had diminished by that time.

22. Which of the following questions is NOT answered in the passage?

F. In terms of geographical region, which were the first groups to carve totem poles?
G. What is the tallest totem pole in North America?
H. What is the predominant use of the small totem poles carved today?
J. What prevented Native American tribes from carving totem poles before the 18th century?

GO ON TO THE NEXT PAGE.

23. The passage suggests that one of the main purposes of totem poles is the way in which they:

A. demonstrate the artistic skill of the carvers.
B. function as landmarks in major North American cities.
C. document the history and mythology of various clans.
D. complement the festivities of the potlatch.

24. The main function of the sixth paragraph (lines 49–59) is to:

F. identify the origins of the stories behind every image on a totem pole.
G. describe and explain some of the images that might appear on a totem pole.
H. contrast the images on the totem poles of the Northwest natives with those of British Columbia and Alaska.
J. explain the role of the Raven in Native American mythology.

25. All of the following are used in the passage as illustrations of the role totem poles play in Native American culture EXCEPT the:

A. function of the top figure on the pole.
B. descriptions of the Raven and Frog as characters on the pole.
C. reference to the popularity of totem poles in the tourist industries of many tribes.
D. placement of the Tlingit totem pole in Seattle's Pioneer Square.

26. The second paragraph (lines 10–20) establishes all of the following about the totem poles carved by the coastal tribes of the far north EXCEPT that they were:

F. initially used as the entryways of houses.
G. fashioned from tall, straight trees.
H. used to identify the owners of the poles.
J. produced only by clans with family crests.

27. One of the main points of the fifth paragraph (lines 39–48) is that the various characters on a totem pole are meant to represent:

A. the owner of the totem pole.
B. the lore of the owner's clan.
C. Raven, the trickster, fooling the Creator.
D. Frog wooing a human woman.

28. According to the passage, which of the following places is home to the Tlingit?

F. Seattle
G. Western Canada
H. Pioneer Square
J. Alaska

29. The author most likely includes the information in lines 60–63 to suggest that:

A. totem poles are notable for reasons beyond physical beauty.
B. totem poles have replaced books for Native American tribes.
C. Native American tribes have no spoken or written language.
D. the descendants of the original carvers of totem poles carve copies of older poles.

30. Which of the following words best describes the attitude of the employers referred to in the third paragraph (lines 21–30) in reaction to potlatches?

F. Patient
G. Accepting
H. Irritated
J. Civilized

GO ON TO THE NEXT PAGE.

Passage IV

NATURAL SCIENCE: This passage is adapted from the article "The Pioneer Mission to Venus" by Janet G. Luhmann, James B. Pollack, and Lawrence Colin (©1994, *Scientific American*).

Venus is sometimes referred to as the Earth's "twin" because it resembles the Earth in size and in distance from the sun. Over its 14 years of operation, the National Aeronautics and Space Administration's *Pioneer Venus* mission revealed that the relation between the two worlds is more analogous to Dr. Jekyll and Mr. Hyde. The surface of Venus bakes under a dense carbon dioxide atmosphere, the overlying clouds consist of noxious sulfuric acid, and the planet's lack of a magnetic field exposes the upper atmosphere to the continuous hail of charged particles from the sun. Our opportunity to explore the hostile Venusian environment came to an abrupt close in October 1992, when the *Pioneer Venus Orbiter* burned up like a meteor in the thick Venusian atmosphere. The craft's demise marked the end of an era for the U.S. space program; in the present climate of fiscal austerity, there is no telling when humans will next get a good look at the earth's nearest planetary neighbor.

The information gleaned by *Pioneer Venus* complements the well-publicized radar images recently sent back by the *Magellan* spacecraft. *Magellan* concentrated on studies of Venus's surface geology and interior structure. *Pioneer Venus*, in comparison, gathered data on the composition and dynamics of the planet's atmosphere and interplanetary surroundings. These findings illustrate how seemingly small differences in physical conditions have sent Venus and the Earth hurtling down very different evolutionary paths. Such knowledge will help scientists intelligently evaluate how human activity may be changing the environment on the Earth.

Well before the arrival of *Pioneer Venus*, astronomers had learned that Venus does not live up to its image as Earth's near-twin. Whereas Earth maintains conditions ideal for liquid water and life, Venus's surface temperature of 450 degrees Celsius is hotter than the melting point of lead. Atmospheric pressure at the ground is some 93 times that at sea level on Earth.

Even aside from the heat and the pressure, the air on Venus would be utterly unbreathable to humans. The Earth's atmosphere is about 78 percent nitrogen and 21 percent oxygen. Venus's much thicker atmosphere, in contrast, is composed almost entirely of carbon dioxide. Nitrogen, the next most abundant gas makes up only about 3.5 percent of the gas molecules. Both planets possess about the same amount of gaseous nitrogen, but Venus's atmosphere contains some 30,000 times as much carbon dioxide as does Earth's. In fact, Earth does hold a quantity of carbon dioxide comparable to that in the Venusian atmosphere. On Earth, however, the carbon dioxide is locked away in carbonate rocks, not in gaseous form in the air. The crucial distinction is responsible for many of the drastic environmental differences that exist between the two planets.

The large *Pioneer Venus* atmospheric probe carried a mass spectrometer and gas chromatograph, devices that measured the exact composition of the atmosphere of Venus. One of the most stunning aspects of the Venusian atmosphere is that it is extremely dry. It possesses only a hundred thousandth as much water as Earth has in its oceans. If all of Venus's water could somehow be condensed onto the surface, it would make a global puddle only a couple of centimeters deep.

Unlike the Earth, Venus harbors little if any molecular oxygen in its lower atmosphere. The abundant oxygen in the earth's atmosphere is a by-product of photosynthesis by plants; if not for the activity of living things, Earth's atmosphere also would be oxygen poor. The atmosphere of Venus is far richer than the earth's in sulfur-containing gases, primarily sulfur dioxide. On Earth, rain efficiently removes similar sulfur gases from the atmosphere.

Pioneer Venus revealed other ways in which Venus is more primordial than Earth. Venus's atmosphere contains higher concentrations of inert, or noble, gases—especially neon and isotopes of argon—that have been present since the time the planets were born. This difference suggests that Venus has held on to a far greater fraction of its earliest atmosphere. Much of Earth's primitive atmosphere may have been stripped away and lost into space when our world was struck by a Mars-size body. Many planetary scientists now think the moon formed out of the cloud of debris that resulted from such a gigantic impact.

31. With regard to the possibility of returning to the planet Venus, information presented in the passage makes it clear that the author is:

A. cheerful and optimistic.
B. sarcastic and contentious.
C. doubtful and pragmatic.
D. uncertain and withdrawn.

32. Which of the following statements most accurately summarizes how the passage characterizes the state of scientific knowledge about Venus before the *Pioneer* mission?

F. The scientific community was hesitant to return to Venus after an earlier mission had ended in disaster.
G. Scientists saw Earth and Venus as near polar opposites in atmospheric conditions.
H. The common belief that Earth and Venus were "twins" had been eroding under the weight of scientific evidence.
J. Scientists knew little about the planet Venus because they were more interested in other planets.

GO ON TO THE NEXT PAGE.

33. Based on the passage, discoveries made in which two areas of study have caused scientists to re-evaluate their theories about Earth and Venus?

A. Water content and bedrock composition
B. Sulfuric gases and photosynthesis
C. Carbon dioxide and climate change
D. Atmosphere and surface temperature

34. The main point of the second paragraph (lines 17–27) is to:

F. account for the failure of the *Magellan* mission and to show the superiority of the *Pioneer* mission.
G. suggest that information from both the *Magellan* and *Pioneer* missions can bring the scientific community to a deeper understanding of Venus.
H. show that the *Magellan* had sent back information regarding the physical characteristics while the *Pioneer* had not.
J. hypothesize that the findings of the *Pioneer* mission will help scientists to approach problems more intelligently.

35. The passage indicates that if humans were to attempt to live on the planet Venus, survival would not be possible because:

A. of the mistaken belief that Venus and Earth are "twin" planets.
B. carbon dioxide is locked away in bicarbonate rocks, not in gaseous form.
C. the atmospheric pressure, heat, and air are not suitable for human life.
D. all of the water on Venus is condensed onto the surface.

36. According to the passage, some evidence gained before the *Pioneer Venus* mission suggesting that Earth and Venus are not near-twins stated that:

F. Venus produces no lead on or underneath its surface.
G. Earth was found to be much farther from the sun than was previously thought.
H. the atmosphere of Venus contains 78 percent nitrogen and 21 percent oxygen.
J. the surface temperature of Venus is 450 degrees Celsius and thus unlivable for humans.

37. As it is used in line 56, the word *harbors* most nearly means:

A. sails.
B. hides.
C. holds.
D. soaks.

38. According to the passage, "primordial" describes planets that:

F. are oxygen-poor due to a lack of activity by living things.
G. are not hospitable to humans because they have thick atmospheres and high surface temperatures.
H. have preserved many of the characteristics present when the planets were formed.
J. have been struck by large bodies which have altered the planets' atmospheres.

39. It can reasonably be inferred that the "activity of living things" described in line 59 directly refers to organisms on Earth that:

A. produce oxygen by their own natural processes and influence the contents of Earth's atmosphere.
B. remove sulfur gases from the atmosphere during heavy rainfall.
C. lock away carbon dioxide in carbonate rocks and maintain a reserve of the gas.
D. could easily live in oppressive atmospheres similar to the atmosphere of Venus.

40. According to the passage, the *Pioneer Venus* mission to Venus involved investigating details relating to the planet's:

F. surface geology and interior structure.
G. atmosphere as it has been changed by the influence of photosynthesis.
H. similarities to the planet Earth.
J. atmospheric contents.

END OF TEST 3

STOP! DO NOT TURN THE PAGE UNTIL TOLD TO DO SO.

DO NOT RETURN TO A PREVIOUS TEST.

SCIENCE TEST

35 Minutes–40 Questions

Directions: There are seven passages in this test. Each passage is followed by several questions. After reading a passage, choose the best answer to each question and fill in the corresponding oval on your answer document. You may refer to the passages as often as necessary.

You are NOT permitted to use a calculator on this test.

Passage I

Metallic *alloys*, solid mixtures of metal, are useful for coin production when they contain a high percentage of zinc. When electric current is applied to zinc in the presence of precious metal solutions of *silver nitrate*, *copper sulfate*, and *potassium gold cyanide*, the precious metals *plate* (form a coating) on the zinc surface.

- Silver nitrate, formed when silver dissolves in *nitric acid*, reacts with zinc to form solid silver and *zinc nitrate*.
- Copper sulfate, formed when copper dissolves in *sulfuric acid*, reacts with zinc to form solid copper and *zinc sulfate*.
- Potassium gold cyanide contains reactive gold ions.

A chemist performed experiments on precious metal plating.

Experiment 1

The chemist obtained 4 coin-like samples of a high percentage zinc alloy. All samples were circular, had a radius of 1 cm, and had the same thickness. The mass of each coin was recorded. Each coin was wired via a battery to a strip of either pure silver or copper metal. Coins wired to silver were placed in dilute nitric acid and coins wired to copper were placed in dilute sulfuric acid. Electric current of either 1,000 milliamperes (mA) or 2,000 mA was applied for 30 minutes to each sample. The coins were removed and the increase in mass from precious metal plating was recorded in milligrams. Results of the experiment are shown in Table 1.

Table 1

Coin sample	Precious metal solution		Increased mass from plating (mg)
	identity	electric current (mA)	
I	silver nitrate	1,000	2.0
II	silver nitrate	2,000	4.0
III	copper sulfate	1,000	1.2
IV	copper sulfate	2,000	2.4

Experiment 2

The chemist completely dissolved equal amounts of pure silver in 4 beakers of nitric acid. He then placed equivalent coin-like samples of zinc into the beakers for different lengths of time measured in minutes (mins). The coin surfaces developed a silver metal coating without any electric current applied. The concentrations of silver coating on the coin and zinc nitrate in the surrounding solution were determined in parts per billion (ppb) and recorded in Table 2.

Table 2

Coin sample	Time (mins)	Silver coating concentration (ppb)	Zinc nitrate concentration (ppb)
V	5	75	30
VI	15	125	55
VII	30	200	75
VIII	60	500	85

1. A comparison of the results for coin samples II and IV supports the hypothesis that zinc is plated more extensively when exposed to:

A. silver nitrate and a current of 1,000 mA than silver nitrate and a current of 2,000 mA.
B. copper sulfate and a current of 1,000 mA than copper sulfate and a current of 2,000 mA.
C. silver nitrate than when exposed to copper sulfate.
D. copper sulfate than when exposed to silver nitrate.

GO ON TO THE NEXT PAGE.

2. If the chemist were to repeat Experiment 1, but compress each coin sample to a radius of 0.5 cm to decrease the surface area exposed to the surrounding solution, how would the mass of precious metal plated most likely be affected?

F. The mass of precious metal plated would decrease for all coin samples.
G. The mass of precious meal plated would decrease for coin samples I and III and increase for coin samples II and IV.
H. The mass of precious metal plated would remain constant for all coin samples.
J. The mass of precious metal plated would increase for all coin samples.

3. According to the information in the passage, a zinc alloy coin sample exposed to which of the following conditions would result in the greatest concentration of zinc nitrate?

A. 10 minutes in a solution with a high initial concentration of silver nitrate
B. 10 minutes in a solution with a low initial concentration of silver nitrate
C. 6 minutes in a solution with a high initial concentration of silver nitrate
D. 6 minutes in a solution with a low initial concentration of silver nitrate

4. In Experiment 1, if the chemist had applied 1,580 mA to a 1 cm radius zinc alloy coin sample in a copper sulfate solution, approximately how much copper would have plated after 30 minutes?

F. 0.6 mg
G. 1.1 mg
H. 1.9 mg
J. 4.6 mg

5. In Experiment 1, which of the following variables was the same for all 4 zinc alloy coin sample trials?

A. Change in mass from plating
B. Electric current applied
C. Type of precious metal solution used
D. Initial radius of the sample

6. According to the passage, if a chemist wants to study the effect of plating zinc alloys with silver, the chemist should monitor the concentration of which of the following substances in the surrounding solution?

F. Potassium gold cyanide
G. Zinc nitrate
H. Copper sulfate
J. Sulfuric acid

GO ON TO THE NEXT PAGE.

Passage II

Organic compounds are molecules that frequently contain carbon (C), hydrogen (H), and oxygen (O) joined together by covalent bonds (symbolized by straight lines in chemical notation). As the number of bonds to o xygen atoms increases in a carbon chain, the overall molecule is increasingly oxidized. For example, aldehydes are more oxidized than alcohols, which are more oxidized than alkanes as shown in Table 1. The melting points of these compounds are listed in Table 2, and their *viscosities* (resistance to flow, or "stickiness,") are listed in Table 3.

Table 1

Carbons in the chain	Name prefix	Structure		
		alkane (suffix -ane)	alcohol (suffix -anol)	aldehyde (suffix -analdehyde)
4	but-	$H_3C-CH_2-CH_2-CH_3$	$H_3C-CH_2-CH_2-CH_2-OH$	$H_3C-CH_2-CH_2-CH_2=O$
5	pent-	$H_3C-CH_2-CH_2-CH_2-CH_3$	$H_3C-CH_2-CH_2-CH_2-CH_2-OH$	$H_3C-CH_2-CH_2-CH_2-CH_2=O$
6	hex-	$H_3C-CH_2-CH_2-CH_2-CH_2-CH_3$	$H_3C-CH_2-CH_2-CH_2-CH_2-CH_2-OH$	$H_3C-CH_2-CH_2-CH_2-CH_2-CH_2=O$
7	hept-	$H_3C-CH_2-CH_2-CH_2-CH_2-CH_2-CH_3$	$H_3C-CH_2-CH_2-CH_2-CH_2-CH_2-CH_2-OH$	$H_3C-CH_2-CH_2-CH_2-CH_2-CH_2-CH_2=O$
8	oct-	$H_3C-CH_2-CH_2-CH_2-CH_2-CH_2-CH_2-CH_3$	$H_3C-CH_2-CH_2-CH_2-CH_2-CH_2-CH_2-CH_2-OH$	$H_3C-CH_2-CH_2-CH_2-CH_2-CH_2-CH_2-CH=O$

GO ON TO THE NEXT PAGE.

Table 2

Carbons in the chain	Melting point (K)		
	alkane	alcohol	aldehyde
4	135	183	174
5	143	194	213
6	178	221	217
7	182	239	231
8	216	257	285

Table 3

Carbons in the chain	Viscosity (cP)		
	alkane	alcohol	aldehyde
4	0.01	3.0	0.4
5	0.24	5.1	0.5
6	0.29	5.4	0.8
7	0.39	5.8	1.0
8	0.54	8.4	1.2

7. Which organic compounds in Table 2 are solids at 215 K ?

A. All alkanes, alcohols, and aldehydes with 5 carbons or fewer
B. Alcohols and aldehydes with 6 or more carbons and octane
C. The 4- and 5-carbon alcohols and aldehydes, and all alkanes with 7 or fewer carbons
D. The 5-carbon pentane and pentanol compounds and the 4-carbon butane, butanol, and butanaldehyde.

8. According to Tables 1 and 3, which organic compound has the highest viscosity?

F. Octanol
G. Octanaldehyde
H. Hexanol
J. Butane

9. According to Table 3, how do the different types of 5-carbon molecules differ with respect to their viscosity?

A. The alkane has a higher viscosity than the aldehyde and the aldehyde has a higher viscosity than the alcohol.
B. The alkane has a higher viscosity than the alcohol and the alcohol has a higher viscosity than the aldehyde.
C. The alcohol has a higher viscosity than the alkane and the alkane has a higher viscosity than the aldehyde.
D. The alcohol has a higher viscosity than the aldehyde and the aldehyde has a higher viscosity than the alkane.

10. For each type of organic compound, what is the relationship between the length of the carbon chain to the melting point and viscosity? As the number of carbons in the chain increases, the melting point:

F. decreases and the viscosity decreases.
G. increases and the viscosity increases.
H. increases but the viscosity decreases.
J. decreases but the viscosity increases.

11. According to Table 2, the difference in melting point between an alkane and an alcohol with the same number of carbons is approximately how much?

A. 25 K
B. 35 K
C. 45 K
D. 65 K

GO ON TO THE NEXT PAGE.

Passage III

A mass suspended by a lightweight thread and swinging back and forth approximates the motion of a *simple gravity pendulum*, a system in which gravity is the only force acting on the mass, causing an acceleration of 9.8 m/sec^2. The time to complete one cycle of swinging back and forth is the *period* and is inversely related to gravitational acceleration.

Using the same type and length of thread, 2 cubes were suspended, lifted to the same starting angle, and let go. The amount of time required for each pendulum to complete one swinging cycle (1 period) was recorded with a timer capable of reading to the nearest 0.01 sec. The measured times were used to calculate acceleration.

Experiment 1

A cube of lead (11.3 grams) and a cube of tin (7.4 grams) were suspended from a 0.5 m length of thread. Both cubes had the same length. (Note: A cube's volume is proportional to its length cubed; its surface area is proportional to its length squared.) The cubes were set in motion from a fixed starting angle and the period for each was recorded.

Table 1

Trial	Measured period (sec)	
	lead cube	tin cube
1	1.48	1.51
2	1.45	1.47
3	1.46	1.42
4	1.49	1.45
5	1.39	1.53

The average periods were 1.46 sec and 1.48 sec for the lead and tin cubes respectively. The average accelerations were 9.3 m/sec^2 for lead and 9.1 m/sec^2 for tin.

Experiment 2

The same procedures used in Experiment 1 were repeated using a thread length of 1.0 m and the same fixed starting angle. Results were recorded in Table 2.

Table 2

Trial	Measured period (sec)	
	lead cube	tin cube
6	2.10	2.12
7	2.04	2.06
8	2.05	2.07
9	2.12	2.11
10	2.00	2.10

The average periods were 2.06 sec and 2.09 sec for the lead and tin cubes respectively. The average accelerations were 9.3 m/sec^2 for lead and 9.0 m/sec^2 for tin.

Experiment 3

Given the results of the first 2 experiments, the accuracy of the timer was tested. The procedures of Experiment 1 were repeated using only the lead cube. The trials were recorded on digital video at 100 frames per second. The video was then reviewed to obtain precise measurements of the period for each trial and results are shown in Table 3.

Table 3

Trial	Measured period (sec)
11	1.47
12	1.42
13	1.49
14	1.50
15	1.46

The average period recorded in Table 3 was 1.47 sec.

12. To demonstrate that a pendulum's acceleration is reduced by drag force from air resistance, which additional experiment can be performed in addition to those in the passage?

F. The cubes are suspended by 0.5 m and 1 m springs and set in motion by extending the spring 9.8 cm and letting go in a vacuum chamber with no air pressure.
G. The cubes are suspended by 0.5 m and 1 m threads and set in motion from the same starting angle in a vacuum chamber with no air pressure.
H. The cubes are suspended by 0.5 m and 1 m springs and set in motion by extending the spring 9.8 cm and letting go in a vacuum chamber at 1 atmosphere of pressure.
J. The cubes are suspended by 0.5 m and 1 m threads and set in motion from the same starting angle in a vacuum chamber at 1 atmosphere of pressure.

13. In Experiment 1, could a timer that reads to the nearest second be used to obtain similar results, and why?

A. No, because the period of both pendulums was between 1 and 2 seconds.
B. No, because the pendulums would have traveled farther in 1 second than they did in 1 period.
C. Yes, because the period of both pendulums was approximately 1.5 seconds.
D. Yes, because the pendulums would not have traveled as far in 1 second as they did in 1 period.

GO ON TO THE NEXT PAGE.

14. The results of the experiments indicate that forces other than gravity are acting on the pendulums because the calculated values of acceleration were:

F. the same for pendulums of different lengths.
G. the same for cubes of different mass.
H. lower than the expected 9.8 m/sec^2 from gravity alone.
J. greater than the expected 9.8 m/sec^2 from gravity alone.

15. Based on the passage, if a tin cube is suspended from a 2.0 m thread and set in motion multiple times from the same starting angle, the average measured period will most likely be:

A. less than 1.48 sec.
B. approximately 1.48 sec.
C. approximately 2.09 sec.
D. greater than 2.09 sec.

16. In Experiment 2, if an additional trial were conducted using the lead cube, the cube's measured period would most likely be nearest:

F. 1.90 sec.
G. 2.05 sec.
H. 2.15 sec.
J. 2.20 sec.

17. Experiments 1 and 2 were conducted using lead and tin cubes most likely to determine if a pendulum's period was altered by the material attached to the string and the cube's:

A. length.
B. surface area.
C. starting angle.
D. mass.

GO ON TO THE NEXT PAGE.

Passage IV

Accepted classification systems of life do not include *viruses*. Although viruses possess certain features of cellular organisms, including genetic material that codes for making new viral particles, they cannot *replicate* (make copies of) themselves without first infecting a living cell. Biologists agree that viruses originated from genetic material called *nucleic acid*, but it is difficult to prove any single theory regarding how this occurred. Three hypotheses of viral origin are presented here.

Coevolution Hypothesis

Some biologists argue that viruses evolved alongside other organisms over billions of years. They suggest that simple molecules of *ribonucleic acid* (RNA), a *nucleotide* that forms the genetic code for proteins, joined to form more complex sequences. These RNA sequences developed enzyme-like abilities including the ability to self-replicate and insert themselves into other nucleotide sequences. While some RNA sequences became incorporated into membrane-bound cells, others were packaged inside proteins as the first viral particles that could replicate after infecting cellular organisms (see Figure 1).

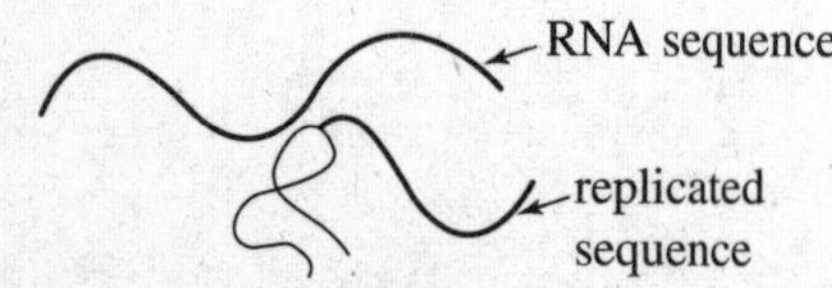

ancestral self-replicating RNA

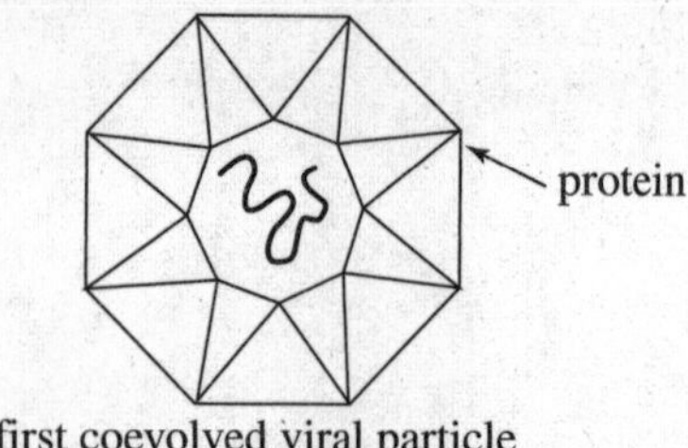

first coevolved viral particle

Figure 1

Cellular Origin Hypothesis

Some biologists claim that nucleotide sequences within *prokaryotic* (non-nucleated) and *eukaryotic* (nucleated) cellular organisms incorporated into a protein coating and escaped from the cell as a viral particle. Initially, DNA or RNA nucleotide sequences gained the code required for other cells to replicate them. Next, these sequences associated with proteins to form an outer *capsid*. Finally, the *virion* (viral particle) became capable of passing through the cell membrane and infecting other cells where it could be replicated. After the initial escape, viruses evolved independently from their initial host and ultimately could infect either prokaryotic or eukaryotic cells.

Regressive Evolution Hypothesis

An alternative explanation of viral origin is that viruses evolved from cellular organisms. Some cellular organisms, particularly certain bacteria, are *obligate intracellular parasites* because they must infect a host cell in order to reproduce. Regressive evolution suggests that some bacterial parasites gradually lost the structures required for survival outside of a cell. The result was a virus particle containing only nucleotides, a capsid (protein coating), and at times an outer membrane or envelope. This would account readily for viruses that contain complex *deoxyribonucleic acid* (DNA) similar to that found in bacteria and other cellular organisms (see Figure 2).

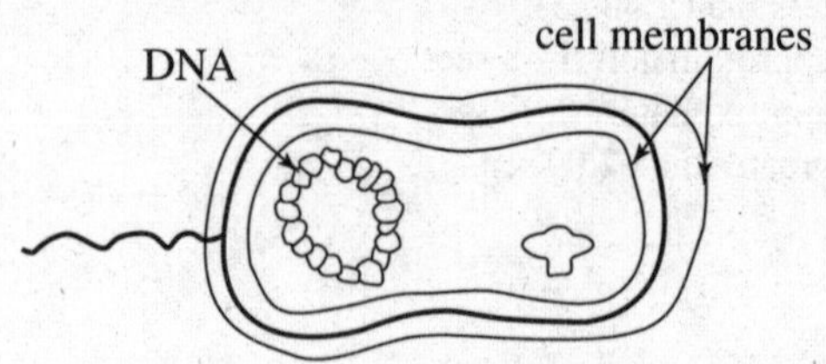

ancestral intracellular parasite bacteria

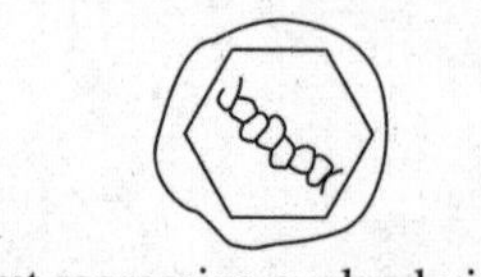

first regressive evolved virus

Figure 2

18. The development of which of the following is addressed in the passage by the Coevolution Hypothesis, but NOT by the Regressive Evolution Hypothesis?

F. Self-replication
G. Capsid
H. Deoxyribonucleic acid
J. Cell membrane transit

19. Supporters of all of the theories presented in the passage would agree with the conclusion that the first viruses:

A. evolved from bacteria.
B. could self-replicate outside a cell.
C. were enclosed within a membrane.
D. contained nucleic acid.

20. The Coevolution Hypothesis does NOT provide an explanation for the earliest virus particles possessing:

F. protein.
G. enzyme-like activity.
H. nucleotides.
J. DNA.

GO ON TO THE NEXT PAGE.

21. If the Cellular Origin Hypothesis is correct, which of the following conclusions can be made about modern T4 DNA viruses, which infect *Escherichia coli* bacteria, and modern PP7 RNA viruses, which infect *Pseudomonas aeruginosa* bacteria?

A. T4 and PP7 are more closely related to each other than to bacteria genetically.
B. T4 and PP7 are only distantly related genetically through a cellular organism.
C. T4 and PP7 both evolved from prokaryotic organisms.
D. T4 and PP7 both evolved from eukaryotic organisms.

22. The discovery of which of the following living organisms would provide the most support for the Regressive Evolution Hypothesis?

F. Extracellular parasites with DNA resembling a known virus
G. Extracellular parasites with unique RNA nucleotide sequences
H. Intracellular parasites with DNA resembling a known virus
J. Intracellular parasites with unique RNA nucleotide sequences

23. Supporters of all the theories presented would agree with which of the following conclusions about the origin of viruses?

A. Viral capsids contain a protein structure similar to the cell walls of modern bacteria.
B. The first viruses did not originate before the first cellular organisms.
C. RNA viruses are more advanced than DNA viruses.
D. The first virus contained DNA and was surrounded by an envelope similar to a cell membrane.

24. Which of the following questions is raised by the Coevolution Hypothesis, but is NOT answered in the passage?

F. Why were some RNA sequences packaged into protein structures and others incorporated into cell structures?
G. Why did obligate intracellular parasites lose their ability to survive outside of cells?
H. How could two different types of cellular organisms account for the origin of viruses?
J. How did virions develop the ability to pass through the cell membrane out of the cell?

GO ON TO THE NEXT PAGE.

Passage V

Wind causes *topsoil deflation*, a type of erosion that is affected by plant and organic cover as well as water content of the soil. Scientists performed 2 experiments using equal-sized fields containing the same volume of soil. The soil samples were primarily a mixture of sand and silt, but differed in the percentage of clay they contained. Soil X was composed of 5% clay and soil Y was composed of 40% clay. Large fans were used to simulate wind. Topsoil deflation was measured in kilograms per hectare (kg/ha) following 10 hours of wind.

Experiment 1

A mixture of compost and straw was used to represent plant and organic cover. The percentage of soil covered with the mixture was considered to approximate an equivalent percentage of natural vegetative cover. One field remained uncovered, and the other fields were covered with different percentages of compost and straw. The topsoil deflation from each field was recorded in Table 1.

Table 1

Soil	Topsoil deflation (kg/ha) by percentage of organic cover			
	0%	25%	50%	75%
X	105,000	68,000	46,000	20,000
Y	65,000	42,000	28,500	12,000

Experiment 2

Rainfall was simulated using a sprinkler system. Sprinklers were turned on for either 4 hours or 8 hours for fields of each kind of soil. Two additional fields composed of each type of soil were left unwatered. Afterward, soil samples were taken from all of the fields to determine their water content percentage, which was recorded in Table 2. Wind was applied as in Experiment 1 and topsoil deflation for all fields was recorded in Table 3.

Table 2

Soil	Water content of soil following various sprinkler times		
	0 hours	4 hours	8 hours
X	10%	13%	16%
Y	10%	14%	22%

Table 3

Soil	Topsoil deflation (kg/ha) following various sprinkler times		
	0 hours	4 hours	8 hours
X	89,250	66,000	14,000
Y	53,400	40,100	10,300

GO ON TO THE NEXT PAGE.

25. According to the results of Experiments 1 and 2, topsoil deflation will be minimized by:

A. decreased organic cover, increased amount of rainfall, and the use of either soil X or Y as topsoil.
B. decreased organic cover, decreased amount of rainfall, and the use of soil Y as topsoil.
C. increased organic cover, increased amount of rainfall, and the use of soil Y as topsoil.
D. increased organic cover, increased amount of rainfall, and the use of soil X as topsoil.

26. If Experiment 1 were repeated using a soil containing 10% clay with 0% organic cover, which of the following would be the most likely topsoil deflation amount?

F. 110,200 kg/ha
G. 99,800 kg/ha
H. 70,700 kg/ha
J. 60,200 kg/ha

27. To further investigate the effect of water content on erosion from topsoil deflation, the scientists should repeat Experiment:

A. 1, using a different type of topsoil.
B. 1, using plastic covers over the fields.
C. 2, using no sprinklers.
D. 2, using fields exposed to various amounts of rainfall.

28. What assumption in experimental design is most important to consider when applying the findings of Experiment 1 to a practical situation?

F. The quantity of topsoil deflation is independent of the percentage of clay present in the soil.
G. The presence of straw on the soil does not accurately simulate vegetation and organic cover.
H. Air movement from fans provides an accurate simulation of the wind responsible for topsoil deflation.
J. Compost is more effective than water content in the prevention of topsoil erosion.

29. In Experiment 2, the water content in the two soil types was similar after 4 hours of sprinkling, yet the topsoil deflation was significantly different. Which of the following statements provides the best explanation for these findings?

A. Topsoil erosion is independent of the water content found in the soil.
B. Fields are susceptible to topsoil deflation only when water completely evaporates from the topsoil.
C. Soil with a lower percentage of clay is more prone to erosion from topsoil deflation than one with a higher percentage of clay.
D. Water is trapped in the topsoil by wind and this increases the rate of topsoil deflation.

30. If Experiment 2 were repeated with soil containing 10% clay, which of the following values would be expected for water content and topsoil deflation in a field following 8 hours of water sprinkling?

F. water content of 17%; topsoil deflation of 13,400 kg/ha
G. water content of 21%; topsoil deflation of 9,700 kg/ha
H. water content of 15%; topsoil deflation of 10,900 kg/ha
J. water content of 14%; topsoil deflation of 101,000 kg/ha

GO ON TO THE NEXT PAGE.

Passage VI

The oceans of Earth are exposed to various climates and consequently have different physical properties. Deep oceans can be divided into zones based on temperature gradient and penetration of sunlight. Figure 1 shows the zones of a typical deep-water ocean, the depth of the zone boundaries in meters (m), and the overall pressure at those depths in kilopascals (kPa). Figure 2 shows the water temperature in degrees Celsius (°C) in warmer tropical oceans and cooler temperate oceans at varying depths. Sound waves are used to measure water temperature at depth, and readings from two different ocean regions are recorded in Table 1.

Zone of Ocean | Depth (m) | Total pressure (kPa)

surface | 0 | 101
epipelagic; continental shelf; mixed | 100 | 1,107
 | 140 | 1,509
 | 200 | 2,112
mesopelagic; thermocline
 | 1,000 | 10,153
bathypelagic; continental rise
 | 4,000 | 4.0×10^4
abyssopelagic; deep water; abyss
 | 6,000 | 6.0×10^4
hadopelagic

Figure 1

(Note: Figure is NOT drawn to scale)

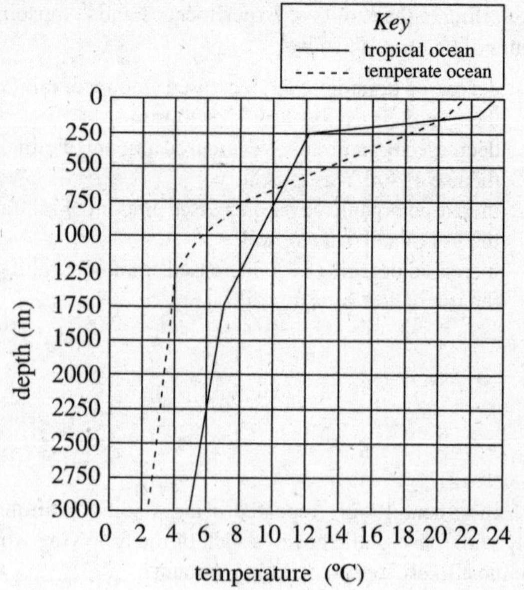

Figure 2

Table 1

Total pressure (kPa)	Depth (m)	Ocean temperature (°C)	
		Region 1	Region 2
101	0	24	21
200	9.8	22	20
300	19.8	14	11
400	29.7	11	9
500	39.7	10	8
600	49.6	9	8
700	59.6	7	6
800	69.5	5	3
900	79.5	4	2

31. According to Figure 1, the regions of several ocean zones overlap. Which of the following pairs of ocean zones share part of a common depth range?

 A. Bathypelagic and mesopelagic
 B. Bathypelagic and epipelagic
 C. Epipelagic and thermocline
 D. Epipelagic and mesopelagic

GO ON TO THE NEXT PAGE.

32. According to Figure 1, an oceanographic reading taken at a total pressure of 1,200 kPa is most likely from which of the following zones?

  F. Abyss
  G. Continental rise
  H. Mixed
  J. Continental shelf

33. According to Figure 2, a sonographic measurement of temperature would be unable to distinguish the difference between tropical and temperate oceans at which of the following depths?

  A. 250 m
  B. 500 m
  C. 625 m
  D. 750 m

34. According to Table 1, the relationship between depth and ocean temperature is best described by which of the following statements?

  F. The water temperature increased with increasing depth in Region 1 only.
  G. The water temperature decreased with increasing depth in Region 1 only.
  H. The water temperature increased with increasing depth in Region 2 only.
  J. The water temperature decreased with increasing depth in Region 2 only.

35. According to Figure 1 and Table 1, if water temperature measurements were taken at depths greater than 79.5, the total pressure at those depths would most likely:

  A. decrease to less than 101 kPa.
  B. increase to more than 900 kPa.
  C. stay at 900 kPa.
  D. increase to 101 kPa.

GO ON TO THE NEXT PAGE.

Passage VII

Although many forms of bacteria are helpful for human health, they can also cause illness and even death from severe infections. *Antibiotics* are a class of medicines used to combat bacterial infections. *Bacteriostatic* activity inhibits bacteria cell division and *bactericidal* activity kills bacterial cells. Both actions eliminate populations of bacteria over time. Several classes of bacteriostatic and bactericidal antibiotics are described in Table 1.

Table 1

Class	Example	Active against	Mechanism	Common uses
β-lactams	ampicillin	some gram-positive and gram-negative bacteria	disrupt cell wall synthesis; bactericidal	respiratory and skin infections
Tetracyclines	doxycycline	atypical gram-indeterminate bacteria	disrupt bacterial mRNA synthesis; mostly bacteriostatic	respiratory and genitourinary infections
Macrolides	azithromycin	gram-positive and atypical bacteria	disrupts bacterial protein synthesis; mostly bacteriostatic	atypical and respiratory infections
Aminoglycosides	gentamicin, streptomycin	gram-negative bacteria	disrupt bacterial protein synthesis; bactericidal	severe systemic infections
Quinolones	ofloxacin, gatifloxacin	broad spectrum of bacteria	disrupt bacterial DNA replication; bactericidal	respiratory, genitourinary, and gastrointestinal infections
Antifolates	sulfamethoxazole, trimethoprim	some gram-positive and gram-negative bacteria	disrupt bacterial DNA and RNA synthesis; mostly bacteriostatic	genitourinary and skin infections

GO ON TO THE NEXT PAGE.

The effectiveness of several antibiotics against a bacterium known to cause common skin infections was tested. Drugs were introduced to the bacterial culture by themselves or in combination with sulfamethoxazole (forming SMX compounds). The effectiveness of these antibiotics at eliminating the responsible bacterium is shown in Figure 1.

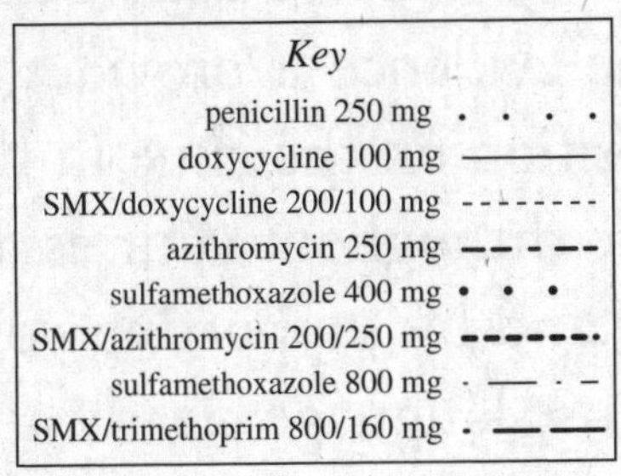

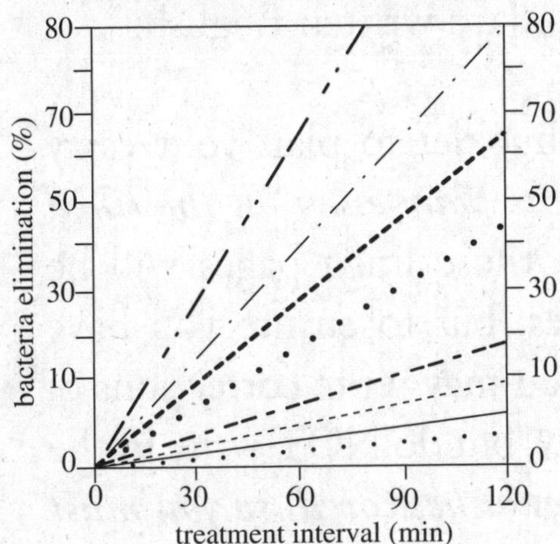

Figure 1

36. According to the information in Table 1 and Figure 1, what can be concluded about the use of sulfamethoxazole as an antibiotic for common skin infections?

F. Using sulfamethoxazole 800 mg is ineffective as an antibiotic.
G. Increasing the dosage of sulfamethoxazole decreases its overall effectiveness as an antibiotic.
H. As an antibiotic, the mechanism of action of sulfamethoxazole is unknown.
J. Compounding antibiotics with sulfamethoxazole increases their effectiveness against common skin infections.

37. According to Figure 1, if an investigator administered a sulfamethoxazole dose of 600 mg, 20% of the original bacteria would remain after a treatment interval:

A. greater than 120 min.
B. between 90 to 120 min.
C. between 60 to 90 min.
D. between 30 to 60 min.

38. After treatment of a bacterial culture similar to that in the passage with 250 mg of penicillin for 2 hours, the culture will probably contain:

F. less bacteria overall, but most will have survived.
G. less bacteria overall, and most will have been killed.
H. the same amount of bacteria overall, and most will have survived.
J. the same amount of bacteria overall, and most will have been killed.

39. Is the statement "antibiotics compounded with sulfamethoxazole are more effective against common skin infections than when administered alone" supported by the information shown in Figure 1, and why?

A. No, because penicillin is more effective against a common skin infection bacterium than sulfamethoxazole 400 mg.
B. No, because azithromycin is more effective against a common skin infection bacterium than SMX/azithromycin.
C. Yes, because sulfamethoxazole 800 mg is more effective against a common skin infection bacterium than SMX/azithromycin.
D. Yes, because SMX/doxycycline is more effective against a common skin infection bacterium than doxycyline.

40. According to the passage, the most effective antibiotic against bacteria is one that results in the:

F. lowest percentage of bacterial elimination in the shortest treatment interval.
G. lowest percentage of bacterial elimination in the longest treatment interval.
H. greatest percentage of bacterial elimination in the shortest treatment interval.
J. greatest percentage of bacterial elimination in the longest treatment interval.

END OF TEST 4

STOP! DO NOT RETURN TO ANY OTHER TEST.

DIRECTIONS

This is a test of your writing skills. You will have thirty (30) minutes to write an essay. Before you begin planning and writing your essay, read the writing prompt carefully to understand exactly what you are being asked to do. Your essay will be evaluated on the evidence it provides of your ability to express judgments by taking a position on the issue in the writing prompt; to maintain a focus on the topic throughout your essay; to develop a position by using logical reasoning and by supporting your ideas; to organize ideas in a logical way; and to use language clearly and effectively according to the conventions of standard written English.

You may use the unlined pages in this test booklet to plan your essay. These pages will not be scored. ***You must write your essay on the lined pages in the answer folder.*** Your writing on those lined pages will be scored. You may not need all the lined pages, but to ensure you have enough room to finish, do NOT skip lines. You may write corrections or additions neatly between the lines of your essay, but do NOT write in the margins of the lined pages. ***Illegible essays cannot be scored, so you must write (or print) clearly.***

If you finish before time is called, you may review your work. Lay your pencil down immediately when time is called.

DO NOT OPEN THIS BOOK UNTIL YOU ARE TOLD TO DO SO.

ACT Assessment Writing Test Prompt

Most schools have established honor codes or other rules to prevent students from cheating on exams and other school assignments. Many students admit to cheating, arguing that the practice has become so common—and is so rarely penalized—that it is the only way to survive in today's competitive academic world. Educators, however, feel that such behaviors only hurt the students, and that cheating in school is just the first step to more academic dishonesty, professional misconduct, and unethical business practices in the future. In your view, should high schools become more tolerant of cheating?

In your essay, take a position on this question. You may write about either one of the two points of view given or you may present a different point of view on this question. Use specific reasons and examples to support your position.

[illegible] Assessment Writing [illegible]

Many schools have established honor codes as one means to prevent students from cheating on exams and other school assignments. [illegible] educators [illegible] arguing [illegible] the practice [illegible] becoming common [illegible] [illegible] involved in [illegible] academic [illegible] Educators, however, feel that [illegible] the [illegible] of the [illegible] in school is the first step toward [illegible] dishonesty [illegible] in academic and medical [illegible] in [illegible] view [illegible] should become more significant [illegible]?

In your essay, take a position on this question. You may either support one of the two points of view given, or you may present a different point of view on this question. Use specific reasons and examples to support your position.

ACT Diagnostic Test Form

Use a No. 2 pencil only. Be sure each mark is dark and completely fills the intended oval. Completely erase any errors or stray marks.

1. YOUR NAME: ______ (Print) Last ______ First ______ M.I.

SIGNATURE: ______ DATE: ___/___/___

HOME ADDRESS: ______ (Print) Number and Street

______ City ______ State ______ Zip

E-MAIL: ______

PHONE NO.: ______ (Print)

SCHOOL: ______

CLASS OF: ______

IMPORTANT: Please fill in these boxes exactly as shown on the back cover of your tests book.

2. TEST FORM

______

3. TEST CODE

0	0	0	0
1	1	1	1
2	2	2	2
3	3	3	3
4	4	4	4
5	5	5	5
6	6	6	6
7	7	7	7
8	8	8	8
9	9	9	9

4. PHONE NUMBER

0	0	0	0	0	0	0
1	1	1	1	1	1	1
2	2	2	2	2	2	2
3	3	3	3	3	3	3
4	4	4	4	4	4	4
5	5	5	5	5	5	5
6	6	6	6	6	6	6
7	7	7	7	7	7	7
8	8	8	8	8	8	8
9	9	9	9	9	9	9

5. YOUR NAME

First 4 letters of last name				FIRST INIT	MID INIT
A	A	A	A	A	A
B	B	B	B	B	B
C	C	C	C	C	C
D	D	D	D	D	D
E	E	E	E	E	E
F	F	F	F	F	F
G	G	G	G	G	G
H	H	H	H	H	H
I	I	I	I	I	I
J	J	J	J	J	J
K	K	K	K	K	K
L	L	L	L	L	L
M	M	M	M	M	M
N	N	N	N	N	N
O	O	O	O	O	O
P	P	P	P	P	P
Q	Q	Q	Q	Q	Q
R	R	R	R	R	R
S	S	S	S	S	S
T	T	T	T	T	T
U	U	U	U	U	U
V	V	V	V	V	V
W	W	W	W	W	W
X	X	X	X	X	X
Y	Y	Y	Y	Y	Y
Z	Z	Z	Z	Z	Z

6. DATE OF BIRTH

MONTH	DAY		YEAR	
JAN				
FEB				
MAR	0	0	0	0
APR	1	1	1	1
MAY	2	2	2	2
JUN	3	3	3	3
JUL		4	4	4
AUG		5	5	5
SEP		6	6	6
OCT		7	7	7
NOV		8	8	8
DEC		9	9	9

7. SEX

MALE

FEMALE

8. OTHER

1	A	B	C	D	E
2	A	B	C	D	E
3	A	B	C	D	E

OpScan *i*NSIGHT™ forms by Pearson NCS EM-255315-1:654321 Printed in U.S.A.

THIS PAGE INTENTIONALLY LEFT BLANK

The Princeton Review Diagnostic ACT Form

Completely darken bubbles with a No. 2 pencil. If you make a mistake, be sure to erase mark completely. Erase all stray marks.

ENGLISH

1	A	B	C	D	21	A	B	C	D	41	A	B	C	D	61	A	B	C	D
2	F	G	H	J	22	F	G	H	J	42	F	G	H	J	62	F	G	H	J
3	A	B	C	D	23	A	B	C	D	43	A	B	C	D	63	A	B	C	D
4	F	G	H	J	24	F	G	H	J	44	F	G	H	J	64	F	G	H	J
5	A	B	C	D	25	A	B	C	D	45	A	B	C	D	65	A	B	C	D
6	F	G	H	J	26	F	G	H	J	46	F	G	H	J	66	F	G	H	J
7	A	B	C	D	27	A	B	C	D	47	A	B	C	D	67	A	B	C	D
8	F	G	H	J	28	F	G	H	J	48	F	G	H	J	68	F	G	H	J
9	A	B	C	D	29	A	B	C	D	49	A	B	C	D	69	A	B	C	D
10	F	G	H	J	30	F	G	H	J	50	F	G	H	J	70	F	G	H	J
11	A	B	C	D	31	A	B	C	D	51	A	B	C	D	71	A	B	C	D
12	F	G	H	J	32	F	G	H	J	52	F	G	H	J	72	F	G	H	J
13	A	B	C	D	33	A	B	C	D	53	A	B	C	D	73	A	B	C	D
14	F	G	H	J	34	F	G	H	J	54	F	G	H	J	74	F	G	H	J
15	A	B	C	D	35	A	B	C	D	55	A	B	C	D	75	A	B	C	D
16	F	G	H	J	36	F	G	H	J	56	F	G	H	J					
17	A	B	C	D	37	A	B	C	D	57	A	B	C	D					
18	F	G	H	J	38	F	G	H	J	58	F	G	H	J					
19	A	B	C	D	39	A	B	C	D	59	A	B	C	D					
20	F	G	H	J	40	F	G	H	J	60	F	G	H	J					

MATHEMATICS

1	A	B	C	D	E	16	F	G	H	J	K	31	A	B	C	D	E	46	F	G	H	J	K
2	F	G	H	J	K	17	A	B	C	D	E	32	F	G	H	J	K	47	A	B	C	D	E
3	A	B	C	D	E	18	F	G	H	J	K	33	A	B	C	D	E	48	F	G	H	J	K
4	F	G	H	J	K	19	A	B	C	D	E	34	F	G	H	J	K	49	A	B	C	D	E
5	A	B	C	D	E	20	F	G	H	J	K	35	A	B	C	D	E	50	F	G	H	J	K
6	F	G	H	J	K	21	A	B	C	D	E	36	F	G	H	J	K	51	A	B	C	D	E
7	A	B	C	D	E	22	F	G	H	J	K	37	A	B	C	D	E	52	F	G	H	J	K
8	F	G	H	J	K	23	A	B	C	D	E	38	F	G	H	J	K	53	A	B	C	D	E
9	A	B	C	D	E	24	F	G	H	J	K	39	A	B	C	D	E	54	F	G	H	J	K
10	F	G	H	J	K	25	A	B	C	D	E	40	F	G	H	J	K	55	A	B	C	D	E
11	A	B	C	D	E	26	F	G	H	J	K	41	A	B	C	D	E	56	F	G	H	J	K
12	F	G	H	J	K	27	A	B	C	D	E	42	F	G	H	J	K	57	A	B	C	D	E
13	A	B	C	D	E	28	F	G	H	J	K	43	A	B	C	D	E	58	F	G	H	J	K
14	F	G	H	J	K	29	A	B	C	D	E	44	F	G	H	J	K	59	A	B	C	D	E
15	A	B	C	D	E	30	F	G	H	J	K	45	A	B	C	D	E	60	F	G	H	J	K

The Princeton Review Diagnostic ACT Form

Completely darken bubbles with a No. 2 pencil. If you make a mistake, be sure to erase mark completely. Erase all stray marks.

READING

1	A	B	C	D	11	A	B	C	D	21	A	B	C	D	31	A	B	C	D
2	F	G	H	J	12	F	G	H	J	22	F	G	H	J	32	F	G	H	J
3	A	B	C	D	13	A	B	C	D	23	A	B	C	D	33	A	B	C	D
4	F	G	H	J	14	F	G	H	J	24	F	G	H	J	34	F	G	H	J
5	A	B	C	D	15	A	B	C	D	25	A	B	C	D	35	A	B	C	D
6	F	G	H	J	16	F	G	H	J	26	F	G	H	J	36	F	G	H	J
7	A	B	C	D	17	A	B	C	D	27	A	B	C	D	37	A	B	C	D
8	F	G	H	J	18	F	G	H	J	28	F	G	H	J	38	F	G	H	J
9	A	B	C	D	19	A	B	C	D	29	A	B	C	D	39	A	B	C	D
10	F	G	H	J	20	F	G	H	J	30	F	G	H	J	40	F	G	H	J

SCIENCE REASONING

1	A	B	C	D	11	A	B	C	D	21	A	B	C	D	31	A	B	C	D
2	F	G	H	J	12	F	G	H	J	22	F	G	H	J	32	F	G	H	J
3	A	B	C	D	13	A	B	C	D	23	A	B	C	D	33	A	B	C	D
4	F	G	H	J	14	F	G	H	J	24	F	G	H	J	34	F	G	H	J
5	A	B	C	D	15	A	B	C	D	25	A	B	C	D	35	A	B	C	D
6	F	G	H	J	16	F	G	H	J	26	F	G	H	J	36	F	G	H	J
7	A	B	C	D	17	A	B	C	D	27	A	B	C	D	37	A	B	C	D
8	F	G	H	J	18	F	G	H	J	28	F	G	H	J	38	F	G	H	J
9	A	B	C	D	19	A	B	C	D	29	A	B	C	D	39	A	B	C	D
10	F	G	H	J	20	F	G	H	J	30	F	G	H	J	40	F	G	H	J

I hereby certify that I have truthfully identified myself on this form. I accept the consequences of falsifying my identity.

____
Your signature

____
Today's date

The Princeton Review Diagnostic ACT Form

ESSAY

Begin your essay on this side. If necessary, continue on the opposite side.

Continue on the opposite side if necessary.

The Princeton Review
Diagnostic ACT Form

Continued from previous page.

PLEASE PRINT YOUR INITIALS

First	Middle	Last

The Princeton Review
Diagnostic ACT Form

Continued from previous page.

PLEASE PRINT YOUR INITIALS

First	Middle	Last

The Princeton Review
Diagnostic ACT Form

Continued from previous page.

PLEASE PRINT YOUR INITIALS

First	Middle	Last

Chapter 28
Practice Exam 2: Answers and Explanations

English		Math		Reading		Science	
1. D	40. J	1. A	40. H	1. C	40. J	1. C	40. H
2. F	41. A	2. H	41. C	2. F		2. F	
3. C	42. G	3. C	42. F	3. B		3. A	
4. F	43. C	4. J	43. B	4. G		4. H	
5. C	44. G	5. C	44. G	5. A		5. D	
6. H	45. B	6. K	45. B	6. H		6. G	
7. D	46. J	7. A	46. H	7. A		7. B	
8. F	47. C	8. K	47. D	8. J		8. F	
9. A	48. F	9. E	48. J	9. D		9. D	
10. G	49. C	10. J	49. B	10. J		10. G	
11. C	50. J	11. C	50. J	11. D		11. C	
12. H	51. C	12. K	51. D	12. G		12. G	
13. D	52. F	13. D	52. K	13. D		13. A	
14. F	53. A	14. G	53. C	14. G		14. H	
15. C	54. H	15. A	54. H	15. A		15. D	
16. G	55. A	16. H	55. C	16. G		16. G	
17. D	56. H	17. A	56. G	17. C		17. D	
18. H	57. D	18. K	57. A	18. F		18. F	
19. A	58. G	19. C	58. F	19. C		19. D	
20. G	59. D	20. H	59. D	20. G		20. J	
21. D	60. H	21. C	60. K	21. C		21. B	
22. F	61. B	22. F		22. G		22. H	
23. A	62. J	23. C		23. C		23. B	
24. F	63. C	24. G		24. G		24. F	
25. C	64. J	25. E		25. D		25. C	
26. G	65. C	26. G		26. J		26. G	
27. D	66. H	27. D		27. B		27. D	
28. H	67. D	28. F		28. J		28. H	
29. D	68. F	29. C		29. A		29. C	
30. J	69. A	30. H		30. H		30. F	
31. A	70. G	31. E		31. C		31. C	
32. F	71. A	32. J		32. H		32. J	
33. C	72. G	33. C		33. D		33. C	
34. F	73. B	34. K		34. G		34. G	
35. C	74. F	35. E		35. C		35. B	
36. J	75. D	36. K		36. J		36. J	
37. C		37. E		37. C		37. A	
38. J		38. J		38. H		38. F	
39. D		39. B		39. A		39. D	

ENGLISH TEST

1. D The verb *associate* requires the preposition *with*. None of the other choices are idiomatically correct.

2. F All the proposed substitutions essentially expand upon the word *genders* without adding any new information to the sentence. As a result, you can eliminate answers (G), (H), and (J) because they are all unnecessarily wordy.

3. C You can eliminate answers (A) and (B) right away because the proposed sentence is totally out of context with what you've read so far. Only (C) gives the correct reason why you shouldn't include the proposed sentence: the content of the sentence is irrelevant to the passage as a whole.

4. F Eliminate choices (H) and (J) immediately because these will not be correct under any circumstances. Only (F) uses the correct form of the past participle.

5. C Choices (A) and (B) contain punctuation that is used to separate independent clauses. Since *once you've learned a few basic stitches* is not an independent clause, neither answer choice can work. Instead, *once you've learned a few basic stitches* operates more as an introductory idea, which must be set off with a comma, as in choice (C).

6. H In this situation, (H) is the most concise answer that makes sense in the context. Notice all the other answer choices contain redundant words and phrases.

7. D This sentence is talking about the *completion of several projects*. Only answer choice (D) has the appropriate plural pronoun. If you picked (B), be careful: pronouns must agree in number.

8. F Since you can count the starter kits (there are three, as the passage says), use *fewer* rather than *less*. With that, you can eliminate choices (H) and (J). Next, you need to use *than*, which is a comparison word, rather than *then*, which is a word used to describe a sequence of events in time. Only choice (F) works in this sentence.

9. A No change is necessary here because no pause is needed after the word *types*. Choices (B) and (C) in particular use punctuation that is much too strong in this context.

10. G Use Process Of Elimination aggressively here. The idiomatic phrase *ranging from* should not be split up with a comma, so eliminate choices (F) and (J). Then, eliminate (H) because *ranging from very small to very large, with everything in between* is not an independent clause. Only (G) works in the context.

11. C This sentence talks about hooks that are *so big that you need to use two strands of yarn*, so it must be moved closer to other sentences that do the same. Only Sentence 3 works, because it talks about large hooks.

12. H Choices (F) and (G) don't make sense in the context. These are actually ideas with a negative slant and would be more appropriate in a sentence that was talking about some negative aspect of crocheting. Choice (J) might have worked better in the first paragraph. In this paragraph, however, choice (H) provides the most effective lead-in.

13. D As written, this sentence contains a comma splice in its use of a comma to separate two independent clauses, so eliminate (A). Choices (C) and (D) both contain words that turn the first part of the sentence into a dependent clause, but choice (C) suggests a contrast where none exists. Choice (D) is the best answer because it fixes the dependency problem and contains the appropriate transition word.

14. F Only choice (F) gives the idiomatically correct preposition. The others change the meaning of the sentence or use incorrect idioms.

15. C The essay is clearly in favor of crocheting, but it has not discussed the commercial potential of crocheting at all, so you can eliminate choices (A) and (B). Neither has it talked about the commercial potential of any other hobby, so you can eliminate choice (D).

16. G The verbs in this sentence are fairly complex, so use Process of Elimination aggressively. You can eliminate choices (F), (H), and (J) because all would be used in a situation in which the author *had seen* the painting. In the context of this sentence, however, the author is trying to suggest that she never believed that she *would see* the painting, so only (G) can work.

17. D This sentence may sound correct as written, but be careful. If you're going to use the *chance to* construction, you must complete the infinitive. In other words, in this situation, the sentence would have to read, *I finally got my chance to see the painting.* In this case, the only possible solution is to delete the underlined portion. Note that this is the most concise answer that works. Always give these deletions and omissions special consideration—they can often get some of the tangled logic out of the sentences as written.

18. H This sentence refers to the *grandeur* of the *painting.* In other words, you need the possessive pronoun *its* when describing the painting's grandeur. Only choice (H) works.

19. A The verbs in this sentence form a kind of list, so make sure all the verbs in the sentence are consistent (or "parallel") with one another. The verbs should read *packed, jumped,* and *headed.* Only choice (A) keeps all three verbs consistent with one another.

20. G The proposed insertion has the word *her* right at the beginning, which means that you need to find the sentence that contains its antecedent. Notice the clause in Sentence 3, *I met someone else who loved the painting as much as I did.* This *someone else* is the best available antecedent for *her* in the paragraph.

21. D There are dependent clauses on either side of this sentence, so you can't use either a colon or a semi-colon. Even a comma gives the sentence a pause where none is necessary. Only (D) gives the sentence its appropriate flow and does not break up the compound subject and its verb.

22. F Notice the word *impossible* directly before the underlined portion. Since this word is not underlined, it can't be changed, thus making choices (G), (H), and (J) redundant.

23. A Sentence 1 does talk about the size of the canvas, but Sentence 2 is out of context in this paragraph. This paragraph is about the author's impressions of the painting; the kind of technical detail presented in Sentence 2 is not part of these impressions.

24. F Remember that transitions are used to connect the ideas in paragraphs. The previous paragraph is about the author's impression of the painting, particularly relating to the size of the painting. The new paragraph goes on to present the author's impression of another element of the painting, which she finds *even more impressive*, as in choice (F). Choices (G), (H), and (J) might work in a different context, but they don't connect these paragraphs as well as (F).

25. C Notice that (A), (B), (D), and the underlined portion of the original sentence all contain the subordinating conjunctions *as* and *when*. The absence of any of these conjunctions in choice (C) creates a comma splice, and (C) is therefore NOT an acceptable substitution.

26. G *From a distance* is the first part of the contrast in this sentence, the second part of which is *up close*. If you were to delete the prepositional phrase *from a distance*, this contrast would be unclear.

27. D The subjects of these paragraphs have been the author and her friend, so of all the answer choices, only (D), which contains the first-person plural pronoun *we*, could work here.

28. H This essay has been about the author's love of a single painting, so there is no need to mention other paintings at this point in the essay; eliminate choices (F) and (G). You can also eliminate (J) because this information is not contradicted elsewhere in the passage.

29. D No pause is necessary between *sights* and *on our trip*, so eliminate all answer choices that suggest this pause with unnecessary punctuation.

30. J The only clear placement for the underlined portion is after the word *bought*, completing the phrase *bought at the museum gift shop*. The other answer choices make the sentence unclear.

31. A The clause *cats have developed* is not an independent clause, so a semi-colon can't be used after it. Eliminate choice (D). In fact, no pause is needed anywhere in this sentence, so any of the choices that introduce unnecessary commas can be deleted. Choice (A) is the only choice that does not contain unnecessary pauses.

32. F Make sure you read the question carefully. It's asking for something that expresses the *ownership* relationship between people and cats. Choice (H) can be eliminated because it talks about dogs, and choices (G) and (J) can be eliminated because they don't express the ownership relationship for which the question is asking.

33. C In this sentence, the phrase *When communicating with each other* is a misplaced modifier. As written it sounds like the "*talk*" is somehow *communicating with each other*. It is of course the *cats* that are communicating with each other, which means that only (C) fixes the misplaced modifier.

34. F First, since this question is testing changes in verb tense, identify the subject of the verb. In this case, the subject is the plural noun *tails*, which requires a plural verb. You can eliminate choice (H) immediately, and choice (G) makes the sentence incomplete. Choice (J) changes the meaning of the sentence and uses a wordy passive construction. Given the new mistakes in all the proposed substitutions, the best answer is (F), NO CHANGE.

35. C The paragraph has been discussing the ways that cats communicate nonverbally. The sentence gives an exception to this rule, which only choice (C) adequately describes.

36. J You'll want to begin a new paragraph here, because the focus of the essay changes with the introduction of the word *human*. Because this sentence is not describing a step in a process, and there's no first idea for which this can be the *next*, you can eliminate choice (H). Only choice (J) works.

37. C Use context. The previous sentence is describing plural cats, so this sentence should do the same. Only choice (C) gives the correct possessive form of the plural, *cats'*.

38. J Choices (F) and (G) are redundant. The word *logical* alone gets the point across here. Choice (H) modifies *logical*, but it does so unnecessarily—*to a startling degree* is not specific. Only choice (J) is concise while preserving the meaning of the sentence.

39. D *Clear* is an adjective, which modifies a noun; *clearly* is an adverb, which can modify a verb, an adjective, or another adverb. The word being modified here is *demonstrated*, which is a verb, so you'll need the adverb *clearly* and can eliminate choices (A) and (B). Choice (C) can't work because the subordinating conjunction *since* is not the appropriate transition between ideas in the sentence. Only choice (D) contains the correct adverb with the proper subordinating conjunction *when*.

40. J The information given is true and may be interesting, but in the context of this passage, it would be out of context. Remember, this is a passage about cats, so it is not at all likely that a sentence about birds will contribute to the main idea of the passage.

41. A The structure of this sentence is clumsy, but you can change only what appears in the underlined portion. In this instance, your most important clue is the comma after the word *examples*. This comma suggests that the infintive phrase *to name only a few examples* is being set off as unnecessary to the meaning of the sentence. The sentence as written is the only choice that does not contain a grammatical error.

42. G Of all the possibilities listed here, only choice (G) establishes any kind of link between *cats* and *their owners*. Other answer choices talk about *mammals*, but this question asks specifically about *cats*.

43. C The underlined portion must be parallel with the rest of the sentence. Early in the sentence, the author speaks of *communicating as every bit as important as forging good relationships*. A second *as* will be needed to complete the comparison, and any verb used will need the same conjugation as *forging*. (B) and (C) both meet these criteria, but of the two, (C) is more concise.

44. G Choice (G) is the most concise substitution that maintains the meaning of the sentence. Choices (F), (H), and (J) are redundant because they contain some form of the word *senseless* and other words that mean the same thing.

45. B Some of the transition words offered in the answer choices may seem similar, so it is best in this situation to compare what comes after those transition words. Again, you need an answer that ex-

presses the relationship between *cats* and their *owners*. Although the word *human* does not appear in it, choice (B) is the only one of the answer choices that talks about a relationship between cats and humans.

46. J Choices (F), (G), and (H) all give redundant constructions. Only choice (J) gives a concise construction and maintains the meaning of the sentence.

47. C The *houses* described here are not in possession of anything, so you can eliminate choices (A) and (B). You can also eliminate choice (D) because it introduces an unnecessary pause after the word *houses*.

48. F Only choice (F) maintains the meaning of the subject without introducing new, unnecessary information. Choice (J) might look appealing, but (F) is still more concise. Think of it this way: to say the same thing, (F) takes one word and (J) takes two. Go with the most concise choice that works.

49. C *Michigan island* is a compound noun in this case, so the adjective *isolated* should not be set off from *Michigan* with a comma. Eliminate choices (A) and (D). Then, notice the coordinating conjunction *so* directly after the underlined portion. If a coordinating conjunction is being used to link two independent clauses, it must be preceded by a comma. Only choice (C) works.

50. J All items in a list must be parallel. In this sentence, the list should read *by horse, carriage, or bicycle*. Choices (F), (G), and (H) are not within this parallel structure.

51. C As written, this sentence creates a comma splice. The clause that ends with the word *necessary* and the clause that begins with the word *Mackinac* are both independent, so of the different possible punctuation marks in the answer choices, only a period can be used to separate them.

52. F If the end of this sentence were deleted, the meaning of the sentence would not fundamentally change, but you would lose an interesting detail about Arch Rock, as choice (F) suggests. Choice (G) is misleading in that it suggests the geological descriptions of multiple tourist attractions, where the underlined portion gives the geological description of only one attraction. There is no contrast with the governor's mansion, so eliminate choice (H); the information is not detailed elsewhere in the passage, so eliminate choice (J).

53. A The next sentence discusses *fudge*, and only choice (A) contains any mention of stores that might sell this product. Choices (B), (C), and (D) are all true, as the question suggests, but none of them is relevant at this point in the passage.

54. H This question is testing the idiom *for sale*. The only viable alternative to this would be *on sale*, but that doesn't appear in the answer choices. Choices (F), (G), and (J) all suggest incorrect idioms.

55. A Choices (B), (C), and (D) are all grammatically correct while preserving the basic meaning of the sentence. Choice (A), *which*, is neither grammatically correct nor consistent with the meaning of the sentence. Therefore, choice (A) would NOT be an acceptable alternative.

56. H Only choice (H) removes the redundancy problem and maintains the meaning of the sentence.

57. D The pronoun in this portion of the sentence should refer back to the *local residents.* As such, it should be a third-person plural. Only choice (D) has the appropriate pronoun, *they.*

58. G Of all the answer choices, only choice (G) reduces the wordiness of the sentence while clarifying its meaning.

59. D The subject of this sentence is *privacy,* so the verb in the underlined portion must agree with a singular noun. Eliminate choice (A). Choices (B) and (C) change the meaning of the sentence by changing the tense of the auxiliary verbs. Only choice (D) maintains the meaning of the sentence and fixes the verb-conjugation problem.

60. H This passage discusses Mackinac Island as a tourist destination and mentions cars only in the beginning of this essay. If the writer's intention is to show the difficulties residents have with cars, this essay has not succeeded; its subject has been the island itself and its many tourist attractions.

61. B The two nouns *friends* and *peers* are not part of a list or separate ideas. Instead, they are both the objects of the prepositional phrase in *front of,* and they should thus not be separated with any punctuation.

62. J Choice (J) is grammatically incorrect because it makes the sentence unable to stand on its own (i.e., it changes the sentence from an independent to a dependent clause). It is therefore NOT an acceptable alternative to the underlined portion.

63. C Sentence 2 refers to something that *defies understanding,* and the word *though* suggests that something in a previous sentence does not defy understanding. Sentence 4 reads, *It is understandable that people would enjoy singing in the privacy of their homes.* Sentence 2 should follow this sentence because it describes, by way of a contrast, something that is not so understandable.

64. J Notice the other verb in this sentence, *see.* These verbs should be parallel; the basic subjects and verbs of each part of the sentence should read *look and you'll see.* Only choice (J) contains the parallel verb and maintains the meaning of the sentence.

65. C The *even though* at the beginning of this sentence operates as a subordinating conjunction, thus making everything up to *busy restaurants* part of a single dependent clause. Choices (A) and (C) set this dependent clause off with a comma correctly, but choice (A) has the coordinating conjunction *but.* A coordinating conjunction preceded by a comma can only be used to separate two independent clauses.

66. H The phrase *such staples as* should not be divided with any punctuation. Only choice (H) gives the appropriate absence of punctuation. In order to use a colon, the clause before the colon must be independent. This one is not, so you can eliminate choice (G).

67. D The verb in the underlined portion must be parallel with the other major verb in this sentence, *responds.* Only choice (D) establishes this parallelism. Choices (A) and (C) are in the wrong tense, and choice (B) makes for an awkward construction.

68. F The beginning of the next paragraph speaks of *another, more obvious reason*. The underlined portion, therefore, must contain a reason of some kind. Only choice (F) contains anything close, particularly in the final clause, *this is not the only reason for its enduring popularity*. The other answer choices do not link these two paragraphs, nor do they make sense in the larger context of the passage.

69. A This sentence should be in contrast with the previous sentence, and the sentence as written signals this contrast. The others give adverbs that suggest a comparison rather than a contrast.

70. G This sentence needs something that will suggest that the quality of people's voices doesn't matter. Only choice (G) does this with the word *regardless*. The prepositional phrase *in lieu of* suggests a substitution, but nothing is being substituted here; rather, the poor singing of many of karaoke's participants is being disregarded in consideration of other, more important things.

71. A Choice (D) gives the contraction *who is*, which does not work here, so you can eliminate that immediately. Choices (B) and (C) are not grammatically correct in this situation. The sentence as written contains the appropriate possessive pronoun and should therefore not be changed.

72. G The clause *who are ordinarily shy* is important in its modification of the word *people*. It would be incorrect to say that karaoke brings people in general out of their shells. The clause is necessary because it clarifies that the sentence is talking about people not normally inclined to perform in public.

73. B The word *first* indicates that the underlined portion will need to have something to do with time. Choice (D) suggests a place, so you can eliminate it. Choices (A) and (C) suggest a cause and effect that is not substantiated in the rest of the sentence. Only choice (B), *when*, gives the appropriate time word.

74. F If you are not sure how to use *less* and *fewer*, look at the second word in each underlined portion. *Then* refers to a sequence of events; *than* is a comparison word. In this sentence, the author is making a comparison, so you need *than*. Eliminate choice (H). Now choice (F) is the only choice that makes the sentence grammatically correct. As a general note, *less* is used with general quantities (e.g., less money) and *fewer* is used with quantities that can be counted (e.g., fewer dollars). This question actually tests an exception to the rule in which both adjectives can work depending on the context; if were you to expand this sentence, it would read *less money than $7 billion* rather than *fewer than 7 billion dollars*.

75. D This passage deals with the international popularity of karaoke. At no point does the passage discuss specific regions. Therefore, the proposed insertion would not be appropriate at any point in the passage.

MATHEMATICS TEST

1. A The midpoint of segment *XY* is the average of *X* and *Y*, so add them up and divide by 2: $\frac{-15+-11}{2}=\frac{-26}{2}=-13$.

2. H Use the Pythagorean theorem ($a^2 + b^2 = c^2$) to find the length of *DE*: $8^2 + (DE)^2 = 10^2$, so $64 + (DE)^2 = 100$, $(DE)^2 = 36$, $DE = \sqrt{36} = 6$. Also note that this is a Pythagorean triple with sides of 6, 8, and 10.

3. C The phrase *double the volume of the ant farm* means your equation must contain the expression $2V$, so eliminate choices (A), (B), and (E). The second sentence also says that the number of ants *is close to 50 more*, so your expression will have to contain the expression $2V + 50$; choice (C) is correct because it adds 50. Choice (D) is incorrect because, when the 2 is distributed, it becomes $2V + 100$.

4. J The probability that Lisa will take a fiction book can be defined as a fraction: the number of fiction books divided by the total number of books. Therefore, the probability of Lisa taking a fiction book is $\frac{5}{5+7}=\frac{5}{12}$: choice (J). (K) is the probability that she will take a nonfiction book; (G) is the ratio of fiction books to nonfiction books.

5. C To find the average, add up all the test scores and divide by the number of tests: $\frac{108+81+79+99+85+82}{6}=\frac{534}{6}=89$, choice (C). You can eliminate choices (A) and (B) because the average must be less than the highest test score.

6. K Angles 3 and 5 are alternate interior angles and therefore congruent. Angles 1 and 3 look congruent only because the triangle appears to be isosceles—the problem does not give any indication that it is, so eliminate choice (G).

7. A If p is Gregor's monthly pay, write an equation that represents Gregor's deposit. He spends 20% and deposits the rest, so $p - (0.2)p = 3200$ or $(0.8)p = 3200$. Divide through by the (0.8) to find that $p = 4000$. If you're not sure how to set up the equation, you could also try out the answer choices as possibilities for Gregor's monthly pay to see which gives a deposit value of $3200.

8. K By definition, similar polygons have equal corresponding angles, making choice (K) the correct response. Two similar polygons are really the same figure on different scales: smaller or larger versions of each other. Therefore, their dimensions are not necessarily the same, making choices (F), (G), (H), and (J) incorrect.

9. E Work through this word problem one step at a time. $60 × .30=$18, so the dress is discounted $18. $60 – $18 = $42, the sale price. Now calculate Victoria's second discount: $42 × .10 = $4.20. $42 – $4.20 = $37.80, the price Victoria pays. Choice (D) incorrectly discounts the dress 40%; this is wrong because Victoria gets 10% off the *reduced price*, not the original price.

10. J Erin begins with x chips, which means (according to the second sentence of the question) Amy has $x - 3$. When Erin wins 4 of Amy's chips, Erin's total increases to $x + 4$ while Amy's drops to $x - 7$. Subtract $(x + 4) - (x - 7) = 11$, the difference in their chip totals.

11. C Since absolute value must always be greater than or equal to zero, you can eliminate choices (A) and (B). Substitute $y = 4$ into the expression $|1 - y| = |1 - 4| = |-3| = 3$.

12. K FOIL: multiply the First terms $3a \times a = 3a^2$, the Outer terms $3a \times - b^2 = -3ab^2$, the Inner terms $2b \times a = 2ab$, and the Last terms $2b \times -b^2 = -2b^3$. Add these terms to get $3a^2 - 3ab^2 + 2ab - 2b^3$, choice (K).

13. D Simplify the expression: $3 - 2(4 - y) = 3 - 8 + 2y = -5 + 2y$, which is the same as choice (D). Be careful when you multiply two negative values, such as $(-2) \times (-y)$: you should get a positive value.

14. G When raising a number with an exponent to another power, you multiply the exponents; therefore, $(y^3)^8 = y^{3\times8} = y^{24}$.

15. A Sketch out a little calendar until you see a pattern: Day 1 is Monday, 2 is Tuesday, 3 Wednesday, 4 Thursday, 5 Friday, 6 Saturday, 7 Sunday, 8 Monday, and so on. Notice that Sundays are always multiples of 7. Pick a multiple of 7 close to 260, such as 259. That means Day 259 is a Sunday, so Day 260 is a Monday.

16. H Draw yourself a figure to see the relationship between the two shapes. Since the formula for area of a square is $A = s^2$ (where s is the side length of the square), you can find that a square with area 64 has side length 8, which would also be the diameter of the circle inscribed in this square, meaning the circle's radius would be 4. The formula for the area of a circle is $A = \pi r^2$, so $A = \pi(4)^2 = 16\pi$.

17. A Factor $x^2 - 5x - 14 = 0$ to $(x - 7)(x + 2) = 0$; therefore, the solutions (the values of x that make this true) are 7 and -2. Their product: $7 \times -2 = -14$. Also, note than in the standard formula $ax^2 + bx + c$, the product of the solutions will always be c/a.

18. K Factor $x^{12} - 9$ to $(x^6 - 3)(x^6 + 3)$; eliminate choices (F) and (G). Factor $(x^6 - 3)$ to $(x^3 - \sqrt{3})(x^3 + \sqrt{3})$; eliminate choices (H) and (J).

19. C Plug $x = \frac{1}{6}$ into the expression: $\frac{2x+4}{3x} = \frac{2\times\frac{1}{6}+4}{3\times\frac{1}{6}} = \frac{\frac{2}{6}+\frac{24}{6}}{\frac{3}{6}} = \frac{\frac{26}{6}}{\frac{3}{6}} = \frac{26}{3}$.

20. H Use the formula Distance = Rate $\times$ Time. Substitute the values from the problem: $60 = 90 \times t$. Therefore, $t = \frac{60}{90} = \frac{2}{3}$ hours. To convert from hours into minutes, multiply 60 minutes by $\frac{2}{3}$ hours: $60 \times \frac{2}{3} = 40$ minutes.

21. C Begin by drawing vertical lines from the top vertices straight down to the base: these segments are the height of the trapezoid, and your figure should now look like a rectangle and two right triangles. Since the bottom base of the trapezoid is 11" and the top base is 5", the difference is 6".

Assume the two triangles you've created are the same size, which means the base of each is 3" (and the base of your rectangle is 5"). Use the Pythagorean theorem ($a^2 + b^2 = c^2$) to find the height (which we'll call h) of one of the triangles: $h^2 + 3^2 = (3\sqrt{2})^2$, so $h^2 + 9 = 18$, $h^2 = 9$, and $h = 3$. This is also the height of the trapezoid, so plug these values (height and two bases) into the formula in the question: $A = \frac{1}{2}h(b_1 + b_2) = 3(8) = 24$. If you hadn't been given the formula for the area of a trapezoid, or if you just find the formula too confusing, notice that the vertical heights split this figure into three familiar shapes: two triangles and a rectangle. You can find the area of each of these smaller pieces and add them together.

22. F By definition, the roots of a quadratic equation are the values for the variable that cause the equation to equal zero. Starting with the first answer choice, set each factor equal to zero and solve for x: $3x + 2 = 0$ yields $x = -\frac{2}{3}$, and $4x - 1 = 0$ yields $x = \frac{1}{4}$. None of the other answer choices yields both roots given in the problem.

23. C Draw the line segments $\overline{AC}$ and $\overline{BD}$; these are the diagonals. By definition, the diagonals of a rhombus bisect each other; therefore, the two halves of $\overline{AC}$ are 3 each and the two halves of $\overline{BD}$ are 4 each. The diagonals of a rhombus also (by definition) are perpendicular; this means that each of the four triangles inside this rhombus are right triangles. Use the Pythagorean theorem to find the length of the side of the rhombus: $3^2 + 4^2 = s^2$, so $9 + 16 = s^2$, $25 = s^2$, and $5 = s$. Note that these sides create a 3:4:5 Pythagorean triple.

24. G The formula for the area of a rectangle is $A = lw$. Fill in what you know: $80 = l(l - 2) = l^2 - 2l$. Solve for the quadratic to find solutions $l = 10$ and $l = -8$. You can't have a negative side, so the length of the rectangle must be 10. Since this is a tough algebraic problem, you can also work backwards from the answer choices. Try choice (H) first: if the length is 16, then the width (2 shorter) is 14. Area of a rectangle formula is $A = lw$, so $A = 16 \times 14 = 224$. That's too big, so eliminate choices (H), (J), and (K). Try (G) next: if the length is 10, the width is 8, then the area is $10 \times 8 = 80$.

25. E Don't be intimidated by the Cartesian plane: it's the same (x,y) coordinate plane you're used to. Slope is defined as $\frac{rise}{run}$, so use the two points given in the slope formula: $\frac{y_2 - y_1}{x_2 - x_1} = \frac{10-(-5)}{5-1} = \frac{10+5}{4} = \frac{15}{4}$.

26. G The equation of a circle is $(x - 4)^2 + (y - k)^2 = r^2$, where (h,k) is the center of the circle and r is the radius. The first part of the equation tells you that the x-value of the center is -5, since $(x + 5)^2 = (x - [-5])^2$, so $h = -5$. The second part more clearly matches the formula, so it's easier to see that the y-value of the center is 5. Therefore, the center of the circle is $(-5,5)$.

27. D The open circles at $x = 0$ and $x = 4$ mean that $x \neq 0$ and $x \neq 4$; therefore, eliminate choices (A), (B), and (E). The solid line between $x = 0$ and $x = 4$ means that x can be any value between 0 and 4, so eliminate (C). Make sure you read the question carefully. If you chose (C), you may have mistaken it for the range.

28. F The *point exactly halfway between* is another way to describe the midpoint, so plug the two points into the midpoint formula: $\left(\frac{x_1 + x_2}{2}, \frac{y_1 + y_2}{2}\right)$. This gives you $\left(\frac{-1+3}{2}, \frac{-5+3}{2}\right)$, which simplifies to $\left(\frac{2}{2}, \frac{-2}{2}\right)$, or (1,–1).

29. C To find the *average rate of change*, begin by finding the total change: the liquid begins at 0° and eventually reaches 80°, so the total change is the difference, 80°. The question asks for the rate of change *during the times in which Sanjay is* *<u>applying</u>* heat to the container. Sanjay applies heat from minutes 0 to 5, $7\frac{1}{2}$ to 10, and 15 to $17\frac{1}{2}$. Find the difference in each of these pairs of numbers to see that Sanjay applied heat for 5 minutes, then 2.5 minutes, then another 2.5 minutes, or 10 minutes total. Therefore, the average rate of change in degrees per minute is $\frac{80°}{10\text{ min}} = 8$ degrees/min.

30. H When you divide exponentials with the same base, you subtract the exponents, so $\frac{a^x}{a^y} = a^{x-y}$; therefore, $a^{x-y} = a^5$ and $x - y = 5$.

31. E The slope of a line in standard form ($Ax + By = C$) is $-\frac{A}{B}$; therefore, the slope of $-5x + 3y = 8$ is $-\left(\frac{-5}{3}\right) = \frac{5}{3}$. Or, if you prefer, rearrange the equation into slope-intercept form ($y = mx + b$). $8 - 3y = 5x$ becomes $3y = 5x + 8$, or $y = \frac{5}{3}x + \frac{8}{3}$. In slope-intercept form, m is the slope; in this case, $\frac{5}{3}$.

32. J The least common denominator (LCD) must be a multiple of the denominator of each of the three given fractions. Take the factors of each denominator (3, 5, 7, 11) to the highest powers they appear: 3^2 (first fraction), 5^2 (second fraction), 7 (second fraction), and 11^3 (third fraction). This results in $3^2 \cdot 5^2 \cdot 7 \cdot 11^3$, choice (J). Choice (K) is the product of all three denominators and is wrong because (J) is smaller and still a multiple of all three denominators; in other words, both are common denominators but (J) is the "least."

33. C To multiply fractions, you multiply all the numbers on top of the fractions and all the numbers on the bottom of the fractions: $\frac{1}{4} \times \frac{2}{5} \times \frac{3}{6} \times \frac{4}{7} \times \frac{5}{8} \times \frac{6}{9} \times \frac{7}{10} = \frac{1 \times 2 \times 3 \times 4 \times 5 \times 6 \times 7}{4 \times 5 \times 6 \times 7 \times 8 \times 9 \times 10}$. Now, before you pull out the calculator, you can cancel out numbers that appear on both the top and bottom (4, 5, 6, and 7) because a number divided by itself (such as $\frac{4}{4}$) is 1, which doesn't affect the final product. After canceling, you get $\frac{1 \times 2 \times 3}{8 \times 9 \times 10} = \frac{6}{720}$, which reduces to $\frac{1}{120}$.

34. K The figure provided is a right triangle, so use the Pythagorean theorem ($a^2 + b^2 = c^2$) to find the distance asked for. $110^2 + 200^2 = c^2$, so $12{,}100 + 40{,}000 = c^2$, $52{,}100 = c^2$, and $\sqrt{52{,}100} = c$.

35. E The key phrase in this question is *at most.* It's possible that the second pentagon is the same size and is laid directly over the original pentagon. Because all points of one pentagon are the same as the other, choose (E).

36. K When assigning employees to duties, there are 10 available to reserve a venue (the first duty). That leaves 9 remaining to arrange catering (because no one can be assigned more than one duty) and then 8 to plan activities. Then, multiply $10 \times 9 \times 8$ to find how many different ways these duties can be assigned. Note the format of the answer choices—don't do more work than you have to.

37. E The easiest way to work this problem is to sketch it out. Draw $\overline{PQ}$, then draw the line perpendicular to $\overline{PQ}$ at *Q*; *R* is somewhere on this line. All of the answer choices have *x*-values greater than 1 and you can see the line rising to the right of *Q* (1,4) in your sketch. This means that the *y*-value of *R* must be greater than 4, which leaves only choice (E). Alternatively, you could find the slope of $\overline{PQ}$: the slope formula is $\frac{y_2 - y_1}{x_2 - x_1}$, so $\frac{2-4}{6-1} = \frac{-2}{5}$. Since $\angle PQR$ is a right angle, $\overline{PQ} \perp \overline{QR}$. In the coordinate plane, the slopes of perpendicular lines are negative reciprocals, which makes the slope of $\overline{QR}$ $\frac{5}{2}$. Then use the points given in each answer choice to see which gives you the correct slope. It's (E): $\frac{9-4}{3-1} = \frac{5}{2}$.

38. J Solve the given equation for *y*. Start with $y = 0.25(100 - y)$. You can either distribute the 0.25 or divide both sides by the 0.25. In this case, it is easier to divide by 0.25. After doing this your equation becomes: $4y = 100 - y$. Add *y* to both sides to get $5y = 100$. Divide both sides by 5 to get $y = 20$. If you chose to begin the problem by distributing the 0.25, you should have gotten the same answer.

39. B Since $4\cos^2 x = 1$, $\cos^2 x = 0.25$ and $\cos x = 0.5$. You want to know *x*, the degree measure whose cosine is 0.5. A scientific/graphing calculator can help you calculate that: the $\cos^{-1}$ key will tell you the degree measure that yields the cosine you give it. $\cos^{-1}(0.5) = 60°$, so choice (B) is correct. If you prefer, you can try each of the answers in your scientific/graphing calculator. When you plug in (B), you can find that $\cos 60° = 0.5$, so $\cos^2 60° = 0.25$, and $4\cos^2 60° = 1$. Make sure your calculator is in degree mode!

40. H Sketch the rug over the floor to help you visualize the situation. The area of the exposed floor is the difference between the area of the entire floor and the area of the rug. First, find the area of the entire floor: area of a rectangle formula is $A = lw$, so $A = 16 \times 18 = 288$. Area of a circle formula is $A = \pi r^2$, where *r* is the radius. The diameter is 12, so $r = 6$. Therefore, $A = \pi \times 6^2 = \pi \times 36$, which is approximately 113. The difference: $288 - 113 = 175$. If you got a negative number when you did the calculation, you may have used the diameter of the circle in the Area formula rather than the radius.

41. C The equation of the given line is in slope-intercept form: $y = mx + b$, where m is the slope and b is the y-intercept. That tells you the slope of this line is –2. Since the slopes of perpendicular lines are negative reciprocals, the slope of the line in the credited answer choice must be $\frac{1}{2}$: eliminate choices (A), (B), and (E). The question says that the line you're looking for passes through the point (0,–3): that makes the y-intercept (by definition) –3, so eliminate (D).

42. F Draw a vertical line from the point $\left(2\sqrt{3},2\right)$ straight down to the x-axis; this creates a right triangle with base $2\sqrt{3}$ and height 2. Use the Pythagorean theorem ($a^2 + b^2 = c^2$) to find the hypotenuse: $(2\sqrt{3})^2 + 2^2 = c^2$, so $4 \times 3 + 4 = c^2$, $12 + 4 = c^2$, $16 = c^2$, so $4 = c$. (A shortcut is to recognize that this is a 30°-60°-90° triangle. Such a triangle has a ratio of side lengths $1{:}\sqrt{3}{:}2$, which means this triangle's sides are 2, $2\sqrt{3}$, and 4.) Since sine is the ratio of the opposite side to the hypotenuse, $\sin\theta = \frac{2}{4} = \frac{1}{2}$.

43. B Substitute $a = 5$ and $b = -\frac{1}{4}$ into the answer choices. Before you actually work each out, you can eliminate choices (C) and (D) because the product and quotient of a positive and a negative number will be negative. Now try (A): $5+\left(-\frac{1}{4}\right)=4\frac{3}{4}$. (B): $5-\left(-\frac{1}{4}\right)=5\frac{1}{4}$. (E): $\left|5\times\left(-\frac{1}{4}\right)\right|=\left|-\frac{5}{4}\right|=\frac{5}{4}$. (B) is the greatest.

44. G Solve for x: add 1 to both sides to get $\frac{x}{3}=-\frac{13}{12}+1$, or $\frac{x}{3}=-\frac{13}{12}+\frac{12}{12}$. Simplify to $\frac{x}{3}=-\frac{1}{12}$. Multiply both sides by 3 to get $x=-\frac{1}{4}$. Only choice (G) is true.

45. B Because the statement includes an absolute value, you'll need to solve it twice: once assuming the expression inside is positive, once assuming it's negative. First, the positive assumption: $2z - 3 \geq 7$, so $2z \geq 10$ and $z \geq 5$. Eliminate choices (C), (D), and (E). Now, assume the expression is negative: you'd multiply a negative number by –1 to make it positive, so $-(2z - 3) \geq 7$. Solve by multiplying both sides by –1 (remember to flip the sign): $2z - 3 \leq -7$, so $2z \leq -4$ and $z \leq -2$. Eliminate (A). Alternatively, you could try substituting in values for z. Try $z = 4$: $|2 \times 4 - 3| = |8 - 3| = |5| = 5$. This expression is supposed to be ≥ 7; since it isn't, you can eliminate any answer choices that include $z = 4$, so eliminate (C), (D), and (E). Try $z = -3$: $|2 \times (-3) - 3| = |-6 - 3| = |-9| = 9$. This is ≥ 7, so z could be equal to –3; therefore, eliminate (A).

46. H To simplify this expression, recall the identity $\tan x = \frac{\sin x}{\cos x}$. Now $\frac{\sin^2 x}{\cos x \tan x} = \frac{\sin^2 x}{\cos x\left(\frac{\sin x}{\cos x}\right)}$. Simplify: $\frac{\sin^2 x}{\cos x\left(\frac{\sin x}{\cos x}\right)} = \frac{\sin^2 x}{\sin x} = \sin x$.

47. D Try the values of x given in the answer choices in the expression. Try $x = -4$: $\frac{a(-4)-b(-4)}{4a-4b} = \frac{-4a-(-4b)}{4a-4b} = \frac{-4a+4b}{4a-4b} = \frac{-(4a-4b)}{4a-4b}$. Since $\frac{4a-4b}{4a-4b} = 1$, $\frac{-(4a-4b)}{4a-4b}$ simplifies to -1. Since $-1 < 0$, $x = -4$ is valid: eliminate choices (B), (C), and (E). Now try $x = -\frac{1}{4}$: $\frac{a\left(-\frac{1}{4}\right)-b\left(-\frac{1}{4}\right)}{4a-4b} = \frac{-\frac{1}{4}a-\left(-\frac{1}{4}b\right)}{4a-4b} = \frac{-\frac{1}{4}a+\frac{1}{4}b}{4a-4b} = \frac{-\frac{1}{4}(a-b)}{4(a-b)} = \frac{-\frac{1}{4}}{4} = -\frac{1}{16}$. This is also less than 0, so eliminate (A).

48. J The original volume of the figure is described by the equation $V = \frac{1}{3}\pi r^2 h$. The new cylinder has had its radius halved and its height doubled, so the volume of the new cylinder will be $V = \frac{1}{3}\pi\left(\frac{r}{2}\right)^2(2h) = \frac{1}{3}\pi\left(\frac{r^2}{4}\right)(2h) = \frac{1}{6}\pi r^2 h$. This volume is then one-half of the earlier volume, and the ratio is 1:2 . If you chose (H), be careful—you may have forgotten to square the new radius value.

49. B Al's biking time going up the hill was m minutes, and because he went down the hill twice as fast, his time going down was $\frac{1}{2}m$. His total time going up and down the hill was therefore $m + \frac{1}{2}m$ or $\frac{3}{2}m$. If you pick (D), be careful—you're not done here! The variable m represents the time in minutes, and the question asks for the time in hours; therefore, you need to divide the total value by 60: $\frac{\left(\frac{3}{2}m\right)}{60} = \frac{3}{120}m = \frac{m}{40}$.

50. J Since the wheel's diameter is 10, you can find the circumference ($C = \pi d$) of Pippin's wheel: $C = \pi d = 10\pi$. This means Pippin's wheel travels 10π inches in one rotation. Since her wheel rotated 15 times, multiply $10\pi \times 15 = 150\pi$.

51. D Draw a horizontal line, which is also the radius of the circle, from the center of the circle to the right side of the square: this creates a 45°-45°-90° triangle. Recall that the ratio of sides in this type of triangle is $s{:}s{:}s\sqrt{2}$. To find the length of the sides, and hence the radius, divide the hypotenuse (x) by $\sqrt{2}$, giving $\frac{x}{\sqrt{2}}$, which, after multiplying by $\frac{\sqrt{2}}{\sqrt{2}}$ to rationalize the denominator, becomes $\frac{x\sqrt{2}}{2}$, answer choice (D). You just found the radius, so (E) is wrong.

52. K No restrictions are needed because $f_{(x,y)} = f_{(y,x)}$ in all cases. Follow the same rules as the original function, just switch x and y. Because $-2yx = -2xy$, this is the same result that $f_{(x,y)}$ produced in the question and $f_{(y,x)} = -2yx + x + y - 4$. Therefore, all values of x and y will result in $f_{(x,y)} = f_{(y,x)}$, so choice (K) is correct. If you don't see this relationship immediately, you can use real numbers to test each of the answer choices. The question has already told you that $f_{(2,3)} = -11$, so see if $f_{(3,2)} = -11$ also. According to the original definition, $f_{(3,2)} = -2 \times 3 \times 2 + 2 + 3 - 4 = -12 + 1 = -11$. This means that $x = 2$ and $y = 3$ satisfy the goal $f_{(x,y)} = f_{(y,x)}$; therefore, eliminate (G), (H), and (J). Now you need to find out whether both variables must be positive, so try negative values: $x = -2$ and $y = -3$. $f_{(-2,-3)} = -2 \times -2 \times -3 + (-3) + (-2) - 4 = -12 - 3 - 2 - 4 = -21$ and $f_{(-3,-2)} = -2 \times -3 \times -2 + (-2) + (-3) - 4 = -12 - 2 - 3 - 4 = -21$. Since both are equal to -21, x and y don't have to be positive, so eliminate (F).

53. C *Each of the smaller pipes can handle exactly half as much water as the large pipe* means that the area of the cross-section of the small pipe is one-half the area of the cross-section of the large pipe. So start by finding the area of the circular cross-section of the large pipe: $A = \pi r^2$, so $A = \pi r^4 = 16\pi$. Therefore, the area of the cross-section of the smaller pipe is one-half that, or 8π. So for the smaller pipe's circular area $8\pi = \pi r^2$, $8 = r^2$, $r = \sqrt{8} = \sqrt{4} \times \sqrt{2} = 2\sqrt{2}$.

54. H The height (which we'll call h) divides this figure into two right triangles, each with base length of 3 feet. Tangent is the ratio of the opposite side to the adjacent side, so $\tan 40° = \frac{3}{h}$. Solve for h by multiplying both sides by h: $h(\tan 40°) = 3$, so $h = \frac{3}{\tan 40°}$.

55. C Sketch the girls' paths out on the coordinate plane. They start at school (0,0), then Susan walks to (–8,2) and Cindy walks to (3,–1). Use the distance formula $\left(d = \sqrt{(x_1 - x_2)^2 + (y_1 - y_2)^2}\right)$ to find how far apart their homes are: $d = \sqrt{(-8-3)^2 + (2-[-1])^2} = \sqrt{(-11)^2 + 3^2} = \sqrt{121+9} = \sqrt{130} \approx 11.4$.

56. G If a is a positive integer and b is a negative integer, the only answer choice that will never yield a negative exponent (and therefore a fraction) is G. If you're unsure, try substituting values for a and b. Let's say $a = 2$ and $b = -3$. Choice (F) becomes $3^{2-3} = 3^{-1} = \frac{1}{3}$; that's not an integer, so you can eliminate (F). Likewise, for (H), $3^{2(-3)} = 3^{-6} = \frac{1}{3^6} = \frac{1}{729}$, (J), $3^{-2} = \frac{1}{3^2} = \frac{1}{9}$, and (K), $3^{-\frac{2}{3}} = \frac{1}{3^{\frac{2}{3}}} = \frac{1}{\sqrt[3]{3^2}} = \frac{1}{\sqrt[3]{9}}$. Only (G) gives you an integer: $3^{2-(-3)} = 3^{2+3} = 3^5 = 243$.

57. A The question tells you that $0 < \frac{y}{x}$, which means $\frac{y}{x} \neq 0$, so eliminate choices (D) and (E). The only way $\frac{y}{x}$ could be larger than y itself is if $x < 1$ and $y \geq 1$. In other words, y could be 1 in this situation, and since we are told that $\frac{y}{x} > y$, $\frac{y}{x}$ must be greater than 1. This is a tough problem, and if you're not sure how to come up with these relationships, try to find numbers that make the initial relationship true and try them out on the number line. If $x = 0.5$ and $y = 1$, then $\frac{y}{x} = 2$, for example, so you can eliminate choice (C) (and [D] and [E], which you've already eliminated). You'll find that you can't get a number less than 1 for $\frac{y}{x}$.

58. F Sketch out the rectangular 100-ft by 150-ft field described in the question. The 10-ft border within the field creates a new, smaller rectangle, 80 feet by 130 feet. The largest circle that can fit in this rectangle has a diameter of 80 feet, and therefore a radius of 40 feet. If you picked (G), be careful—you may have forgotten to subtract 10 feet on both sides of the track.

59. D Imagine cutting an orange: the first slice (one plane) cuts it into two pieces. If you hold those two pieces together and make another slice (the second plane), you cut both of those pieces, thereby creating 4 sections. Eliminate choices (A) and (C). Now, if you repeat this orange-slicing experiment, but your second slice is parallel to the first slice, it cuts a circular slice off only one piece, thereby creating 3 sections, so eliminate (B). The only way to keep the orange in two pieces after the first slice is for the second slice to repeat the first exactly. Since the question said the sphere was to be cut by two *different* planes, this cannot happen; therefore, it's impossible to get only 2 pieces, so eliminate (E).

60. K "Positive difference" means that when you subtract $a - b$ you can get +5 or −5. (That's also what the absolute value indicates.) So solve for a in both cases: $a - b = 5$, so $a = b + 5$; and $a - b = -5$, so $a = b - 5$. Now subtract these two values: $(b + 5) - (b - 5) = b + 5 - b + 5 = 10$, choice (K). Alternatively, you could substitute a number for b: let's say $b = 2$, so $|a - 2| = 5$. Then solve: $a - 2 = 5$, so $a = 7$; and $a - 2 = -5$, so $a = -3$. The positive difference is $7 - (-3) = 7 + 3 = 10$.

READING TEST

1. C When the narrator first sees her gift, her first response is confusion, followed by devastation that she won't be able to show her gift off to the other girls at school. Eliminate choice (A). She then recognizes that her father put a lot of effort into her gift and tries to be grateful. Eliminate choice (D). She then returns to being confused as to why they made her this house instead of buying her the real Barbie Dream House. Eliminate choice (B). That leaves choice (C), the correct answer. Disappointed and upset as the narrator is, the passage does not state that she hates the house.

2. F The narrator of the story explains that only when she and her sister could smell coffee were they allowed to go downstairs to start Christmas. Therefore, choice (F) is the best answer. Choice (G) incorrectly refers to breakfast, which is not mentioned in the passage. Choice (H) incorrectly refers to the narrator's father's preparation of a gift instead of general morning readiness. Choice (J) is incorrect because the passage explicitly states that the narrator was expected to wait in the kitchen for her parents; she just burst in ahead of them one year because she was too excited to wait.

3. B The narrator talks about her dream of owning the Dream House in the second paragraph, where she says "I knew that if I could only have a Dream House of my own, my life would be complete." Therefore, choice (B) is the best answer, as it is a good paraphrase of that statement. Choice (A) incorrectly refers to the other girl who owns the house and is not meant to be taken literally. Choice (C) confuses the actual result, based on her parents' hard work, with the narrator's dream, based on buying a particular toy. Choice (D) refers to the narrator's eventual comment that she will pass her gift on to her children someday, but that refers not to the Dream House but to her father's actual gift.

4. G The first paragraph describes the family's tradition of waiting until the parents have had a chance to wake up and make coffee before beginning to open the presents. Choice (G) is the best paraphrase of that summary and is the best answer. Choice (F) might be true but it is not mentioned in the passage and is not the best summary of the entire paragraph. Choice (H) states the opposite of what the passage says. Choice (J) is true, but is not the main point of the paragraph.

5. A When the narrator first sees her handmade doll house, she is confused and upset as she compares her house to her idealized Barbie Dream House. Choice (A) is the best paraphrase of her reaction. Choice (B) is incorrect because although the narrator does eventually try to be grateful, that is not her first response and she is not immediately successful in her attempt. Choice (C) goes against the passage—she compares the old-fashioned style of her house with the modern Barbie house and finds her house lacking. Choice (D) is incorrect because that was her goal before she saw her house, when she believed she would receive the official Barbie Dream House.

6. H The narrator's father is described in a few different places in the passage. First, he is overheard reassuring Mel, the mother, regarding Christmas. Then, when he is preparing to present his daughter with her gift, he is described as *smiling anxiously*. Finally, the narrator eventually realizes that her father had "spent countless hours working on the house." Therefore, choice (H) is the best characterization of the father in the story.

7. A In lines 25–30, the narrator overhears her parents discussing Christmas, wondering what they will do. This implies that there is some kind of problem. Her father then proceeds to make a homemade version of the Dream House that his daughter wants, implying that for some reason, he cannot give her the gift she wants but is willing to work very hard to give her something similar. Therefore, choice (A) is the best answer, because it explains what problem might cause him to act in such a manner. Choice (B) is incorrect because it refers to an early comment regarding a previous Christmas, not the one being described. Choice (C) is incorrect because there is no evidence

that the father made the dollhouse because he had always wanted to do so. Choice (D) is incorrect because the fact that the father put so much time and effort into making the dollhouse implies that they do in fact want their daughter to be happy.

8. J At the end of the passage, the narrator comments that she still has the dollhouse and that she hopes to someday give it to her own children along with the story of how she got it. Therefore, choice (J) is the best answer, since it refers only to her hopes of passing on the story. Choice (F) incorrectly refers to the narrator's initial hopes of impressing other children with an official Barbie Dream House. Choice (G) focuses on the possible value of the house, which is not discussed in the passage. Choice (H) is incorrect because the narrator did not in fact appreciate the gift initially.

9. D The narrator concludes, at the time of the gifting, that although she does not like her dollhouse as much as she would have liked a Barbie Dream House, it must have taken her father a lot of time and effort to build. Therefore, choice (D) is the best answer. Choice (A) is incorrect because she refers to the dollhouse as a crude approximation of what she wanted. Choice (B) is incorrect because the absence of an elevator is not mentioned in the passage. Choice (C) is incorrect because there is no evidence that her eventual decision to pass the house on to her children was anticipated by her or her parents at the time when it was given to her.

10. J The last paragraph is told as if the narrator is looking back on her childhood and having trouble remembering the events that followed the previous part of the passage. She reflects that she now more fully understands her parents' actions and wishes she could go back in time and explain things to her younger self. Therefore, the best answer is choice (J). Choice (F) might be true, but the focus of the last paragraph is on the narrator as an adult, not as a child. Choice (G) is incorrect because the passage does not discuss the narrator's sister's gift. Choice (H) is too negative—the narrator is looking back on the events with greater wisdom and understanding, not bitterness.

11. D This passage describes the formation and activities of the CCC. No one was "forced" to work in the CCC, so you can eliminate choice (A). The CCC did employee many veterans, but nothing in the passage supports the claim that veterans had suitable employment "only after" the creation of the CCC.

12. G Choice (F) gives a too literal interpretation of the quotation used in the middle of this paragraph. Choice (H) is incorrect because the bonuses were never paid. For choice (J), the paragraph says that the age restriction was "waived," but at no point does it say whether these veterans were over the age limit. Only choice (G) gives a reasonable summation of the content of the paragraph.

13. D The passage states that Roosevelt "also cared about the fate of trees, having practiced the art of silviculture on his Hyde Park estate with such enthusiasm that on various official forms he was fond of listing his occupation as 'tree farmer.'" Choice (A) makes an assumption that is not supported in the passage; there is nothing to suggest that his interest in silviculture predated his political life. Choices (B) and (C) are not supported in the passage. Only choice (D) is supported by the sentence cited above.

14. G Read this question carefully. The lines you need are 61–63: "For the National Park Service, they built roads, campgrounds, bridges, and recreation and administration facilities." This clearly supports choice (G). The other activities in the answer choices are mentioned in the passage, but not as things the CCC did *for the National Park Service.*

15. A Starting on line 72, the passage reads, "the program taught more than a hundred thousand to read and write, passed out twenty-five thousand eighth-grade diplomas and five-thousand high-school diplomas." This line most clearly supports choice (A). Choices (B), (C), and (D) contain deceptive language from elsewhere in the passage, but they do not describe the CCC.

16. G Lines 24–25 describe the terms of payment in the CCC, so eliminate choice (F). Line 58 describes the "4.1 million man-hours" spent fighting forest fires; it does NOT say that the CCC employed 4.1 million men, so eliminate choice (H). The states referred to in choice (J) are described in the passage as the sites of "flood control projects," not firefighting projects. Only choice (G) has support in the passage.

17. C Lines 60–61 describe the "first major reforestation campaign in the country's history." Although the specific years during which this reforestation campaign took place are unclear, the campaign must have taken place after the establishment of the CCC in 1933. It can therefore be inferred, since this was the "first," that the nation had not undergone a major reforestation campaign before, as choice (C) suggests.

18. F Lines 11–16 state the following: "When he went to Congress for authorization of the program, he called the new agency the Civilian Corps Reforestation Youth Rehabilitation Movement, but before sinking under the weight of an acronym like CCRYRM, it was soon changed to the Civilian Conservation Corps (known forever after as the CCC)." These lines describe the change, and only (F) is supported by the time of these events. The only other answer that might work chronologically would be (G), but nothing in the passage supports the claim that Congress complained about the length of the name.

19. C Lines 29–30 state that the "men had to be US citizens between the ages of seventeen and twenty-seven (later twenty-four)." Since the question asks about enrollees when the CCC was founded, you can disregard the "later" age; choice (C) gives the correct age range.

20. G Lines 21–24 state that "the Departments of Agriculture and Interior... would design and supervise projects in regional and national forests, national parks, and other public lands." These lines give direct support to answer (G), and show that the others are incorrect or inadequate responses to the question.

21. C This passage deals with the importance of the totem pole and the role the totem pole plays in Native American culture. Even with this very general overview of the passage, the only answer that fits is (C). The others are too specific or suggest incorrectly that the tone of the passage is negative.

22. G The question in choice (F) is answered in lines 2–3. The question in choice (H) is given in line 65. The question in choice (J) is answered in lines 8–9. Only the question posed in choice (G) goes unanswered in the passage. The discussion in the fourth paragraph is distracting, but notice this paragraph does not claim that the pole in Pioneer Square is the largest.

23. C Note the opening sentence of the fifth paragraph on line 39: "Poles serve the important purpose of recording the lore of a clan, much as a book would." The other choices describe some minor functions of totem poles, but only the function described in choice (C) is described as "important."

24. G This paragraph describes the meanings of some of the symbols used on totem poles. Choice (F) would be fine if it did not contain the word "every." Clearly, a short paragraph cannot describe *every* possible symbol. There are no regional comparisons, so you can eliminate choice (H). Choice (J) is too limited. Think in terms of the larger point of this paragraph; it describes figures other than the Raven. Only (G) adequately describes the main idea of the paragraph.

25. D Choice (A) is addressed in lines 40–41. Choice (B) is addressed just after this in lines 42–44. Choice (C) is addressed in lines 64–66. Choice (D) may seem like it is addressed in the passage, but read this part of the passage carefully. There is no reference to the importance of this pole in Native American culture; after all, the group that took it, according to line 33, were "Seattle businessmen," not the Tlingit.

26. J Choice (F) is addressed in lines 13–15. Choice (G) is addressed in line 12. Choice (H) is addressed in line 17. Choice (J) is not addressed in the passage; the "family crest" is mentioned in line 16, but there is no evidence in the passage that the poles were constructed exclusively by clans who had family crests.

27. B As lines 39–41 indicate, one of the main functions of the poles is to identify the lore of a clan. The points mentioned in choices (A), (C), and (D) are mentioned, but none could be described as a "main point." Only choice (B) is general enough to be described as a "main point."

28. J When the Tlingit are introduced in line 31, they are described as coming from "the southeastern coast of Alaska." Only choice (J) could work. Don't be distracted by the other places mentioned in this paragraph; those places may have some significance for the Tlingit, but could not be described as the "home of the Tlingit."

29. A This paragraph is used to conclude some of the ideas in the preceding paragraphs and to suggest the broader importance of totem poles beyond their physical beauty. Choices (B), (C), and (D) all use words from the passage, but they use those words in misleading ways. Only choice (A) can be supported by evidence from the passage.

30. H All we know about the employers is that they "complained that their Indian workers were unreliable when a pole was being carved or a potlatch planned" (lines 27–28). Because this is the only reference the author gives to these employers, we can only infer that the employers were "irritated," as choice (H) suggests.

31. C Lines 14–16 state, "...in the present climate of fiscal austerity, there is no telling when humans will next get a good look at the earth's nearest planetary neighbor." Choice (A) can be eliminated because the author is clearly not cheerful and optimistic. Choice (B) can be eliminated because the author's tone does not suggest sarcasm or condescension. Choice (D) can be eliminated because of the word *withdrawn*. Only choice (C) is supported by the lines quoted above: he is doubtful ("there is no telling") and pragmatic ("in the present climate of fiscal austerity.")

32. H Lines 28–33 discuss the state of scientific knowledge before the arrival of *Pioneer Venus*. The paragraph discusses in detail the differences in surface temperatures and atmospheric pressures. Choice (G) is too strong: the two planets are not "twins," but the passage does not say that they are anything like "polar opposites." The best choice is (H), because the paragraph details the objections to the term *twins*.

33. D This question asks about the same portion of the passage as question 32. Lines 28–33 detail some of the ways in which the "twin" characterization of Earth and Venus was reconsidered. The main evidence in this paragraph relates to surface temperature and atmosphere.

34. G The paragraph in question concerns the *Magellan* and *Pioneer Venus* missions. Each mission studied different elements of Venus's physical composition, and the information from each can be used in tandem with the other. The missions are contrasted, but neither is cast in a negative light, so you can eliminate choices (F) and (H), and choice (J) is too narrow in that it does not include the findings of the *Magellan*. Only choice (G) adequately summarizes the paragraph.

35. C Lines 34–35 state, "Even aside from the heat and the pressure, the air of Venus would be utterly unbreathable to humans." It then goes on to discuss the atmospheric conditions in more detail. Choice (C) is the only one of the answer choices that addresses these issues. Choices (B) and (D) describe the physical properties of the planet, but they do not give any indication why human survival would not be possible.

36. J Choice (J) is supported in lines 31–32, which say that Venus's "surface temperature of 450 degrees Celsius is hotter than the melting point of lead." Choice (H) is misleading; these physical properties describe the Earth. Choice (F) can be eliminated because "lead" is introduced as a point of comparison, not as one of the constitutive elements of Venus's surface. Choice (G) can be eliminated because it does not contain any mention of Venus.

37. C The full sentence in lines 56–57 reads as follows: "Unlike the Earth, Venus harbors little if any molecular oxygen in its lower atmosphere." In other words, Venus contains or holds or has little if any molecular oxygen in its lower atmosphere.

38. H The word *primordial* appears in line 65. The lines that follow state that Venus is "more primordial" than Earth because it "has held on to a far greater fraction of its earliest atmosphere." Only choice (H) contains the appropriate reference to these early formations.

39. A The full sentence starting on line 57 establishes a clear link between the activity of these plants (i.e., living things) and the composition of the earth's atmosphere. The only answer that even mentions the earth is (A), and this choice provides a reasonable paraphrase of the passage.

40. J Choice (J) is the only answer that accurately paraphrases lines 20–22.

SCIENCE TEST

1. C Looking at Table 1 and examining the trials with coin samples II and IV shows that electric current is held constant at 2000 mA. The current does not change, eliminating choices (A) and (B). The variable that does change is the identity of precious metal solution. For coin sample II exposed to silver nitrate, 4.0 mg of precious metal plates out. For coin sample IV exposed to copper sulfate, only 2.4 mg of precious metal plates out. Therefore, choice (D) is eliminated and choice (C) is correct.

2. F The precious metal solutions react with zinc to form a coating of pure precious metal on the coin samples. If the available surface area exposed to the solutions decreased, the amount of precious metal coating is expected to decrease. There is no specific evidence in the passage to support the plating amount remaining constant or increasing.

3. A Table 2 shows that increasing the exposure time of a zinc coin to silver nitrate results in higher concentrations of zinc nitrate in the surrounding solution. Therefore, choices (C) and (D) are eliminated. The passage states that *silver nitrate, formed when silver dissolves in nitric acid, reacts with zinc to form solid silver and zinc nitrate.* Therefore, increasing the amount of silver nitrate available to react with zinc is expected to result in higher concentrations of zinc nitrate. This eliminates choice (B) and makes choice (A) the best answer.

4. H The question describes using the same sized sample of zinc and same exposure time as Experiment 1. Table 1 shows that when electric current is increased from 1000 to 2000 mA for zinc coins exposed to copper sulfate for 30 minutes, the plated copper increases from 1.2 to 2.4 mg. 1580 mA is between 1000 and 2000 mA, so the amount of plated copper should fall between 1.2 and 2.4 mg.

5. D In the description of Experiment 1, all coin samples were stated to have a radius of 1 cm. Table 1 shows that the change in mass from precious metal plating, electric current applied, and identity of precious metal solution used were not constant for samples I–IV.

6. G The passage states that *silver nitrate, formed when silver dissolves in nitric acid, reacts with zinc to form solid silver and zinc nitrate.* Therefore, when zinc is plated with solid silver, zinc nitrate is also formed as a product. Choices (F), (H), and (J) are not involved in this reaction.

7. B Melting point is the temperature when a substance changes from a solid to a liquid. Any compound with a melting point above 215 K will still be a solid at that temperature. For alkanes, ac-

cording to Table 2, only octane will still be a solid at 215 K. Octane must be in the answer, and on this basis alone, choices (A), (C), and (D) can all be eliminated, leaving only choice (B). The remaining data in choice (B) are supported in Table 2 as well.

8. F According to Table 3, the 8-carbon alcohol has the highest value for viscosity. Referring to Table 1 for the prefix and suffix of the compound's name, the structure is called octanol.

9. D Reading across any single row of Table 3 demonstrates that for a fixed number of carbons in the molecule, the alcohol has the highest viscosity. This eliminates choices (A) and (B). Further, for any given row, the alkane has the lowest viscosity, eliminating choice (C).

10. G Reading down any single column in Table 2 demonstrates that as the number of carbons in the molecule increases, the melting point increases. Therefore, choices (F) and (J) are eliminated. Reading down any single column in Table 3 demonstrates that as the number of carbons in the molecule increases, the viscosity increases as well, eliminating choice (H) and making (G) the correct answer.

11. C Compare the melting points of the alkanes and alcohols in Table 2. For any given number of carbons in the molecule, the melting points between these two types of compounds differ by varying but similar amounts between 40 and 50 K. Of the possible answer choices, choice (C) is the best approximation of the average of these differences.

12. G When testing the effects of different variables, all variables must be held constant except those being tested. To determine the effects of drag force or air resistance, therefore, all variables except drag force and air resistance must be held constant. Altering the apparatus to use a spring makes this into a completely different experiment, so choices (F) and (H) are eliminated. To negate the effects of air resistance, using a vacuum with no air pressure would be best, making choice (G) the best answer.

13. A In experiments, more precision is nearly always better. A timer that reads to the nearest second can give only whole number results. Therefore, it would read either "1" or "2" for each trial. This would not greatly alter the results for the tin cube (Trials 1 and 5 would be 2 sec, and Trials 2–4 would be 1 sec for an average of 1.4 sec). However, all of the trials for the lead cube would round down to 1 sec for an average of 1 sec. This is significantly different from the 1.46 sec obtained with the more precise timer, eliminating choices (C) and (D). Choice (B) is eliminated because the period of both pendulums is greater than 1 sec, meaning they would travel a shorter distance in 1 second than they would in the time it takes them to complete a cycle.

14. H Choices (F) and (G) are true statements, but they do not explain why forces other than gravity must be acting on the pendulums. The passage states that for a *simple gravity pendulum, gravity is the only force acting on the mass causing an acceleration of 9.8 m/sec^2*. The times obtained in Experiments 1 and 2 resulted in acceleration calculations less than this, indicating some other force was slowing the pendulum down (air resistance and friction). This eliminates choice (J) and makes choice (H) the best answer.

15. D Comparing the results of Experiments 1 and 2 presented in Tables 1 and 2, doubling the length of the thread from 0.5 m to 1.0 m increases the observed period by about .5 sec. Since the average period observed for the tin cube in Experiment 2 (pendulum length of 1.0 m) was 2.09 sec, doubling the length of the thread once again would be expected to result in a similar increase in average period observed.

16. G The text below Table 2 states that the average period for the lead cube in Experiment 2 was 2.06 sec. An additional trial of the same experiment would be expected to give a result closest to this value.

17. D For both Experiments 1 and 2, comparisons between the lead and tin pendulums held length and starting angle constant, eliminating choices (A), (B), and (C). The mass and density of the lead and tin cubes were different. The main difference noted in the text of the passage is that between the masses of the two objects, so choice (D) provides the best-supported option.

18. F In the description of the Coevolution Hypothesis, the passage states that *RNA sequences developed enzyme-like abilities including the ability to self-replicate.* Development of capsids was mentioned in the Regressive Evolution Hypothesis, but not in Coevolution, eliminating choice (G). DNA was not mentioned in the Coevolution Hypothesis, eliminating choice (H). Cell membrane transit was mentioned only in the Cellular Origin Hypothesis, eliminating choice (J).

19. D The first paragraph states that biologists agree that viruses originated from nucleic acid. Choice (A) is eliminated because the Coevolution Hypothesis does not provide an explanation for viruses evolving from bacteria. Choice (B) is eliminated because according to the passage, viruses cannot replicate unless they first infect a cell. Choice (C) is eliminated because only the Regressive Evolution Hypothesis mentions anything about viruses having membranes or envelopes.

20. J The Coevolution Hypothesis specifically mentions that the first virus particles were RNA nucleotides with enzyme-like activity that incorporated into protein structures. Therefore, choices (F), (G), and (H) are all eliminated. DNA is not mentioned as a component of the earliest virus particles in this hypothesis.

21. B The Cellular Origin Hypothesis states that viruses originated from cellular-organism ancestors. They could have come from prokaryotic or eukaryotic organisms, and the type of ancestor cell does not necessarily determine what type of cell they will evolve to infect. Therefore, choices (C) and (D) are eliminated because this cannot necessarily be determined from the information given. Given that both T4 and PP7 infect bacteria, they likely contain genetic material similar to the bacteria they infect. However, given that one is a DNA virus and one is an RNA virus, if they are related at all it is likely through a very distant ancestor virus that escaped a cellular organism long ago. This eliminates choice (A) and makes choice (B) the best answer.

22. H Since the Regressive Evolution Hypothesis suggests that viruses originated from obligate intracellular parasites, one would expect that they would share features of these ancestors. The hypothesis

specifically states that intracellular parasites evolved into viruses, eliminating choices (F) and (G). Between the remaining choices, finding a parasite with DNA similar to a known virus could suggest that this organism and the known virus evolved from a common ancestor, making choice (H) the best answer.

23. B The passage states that viruses cannot replicate unless they first infect a cell. Therefore, the first viruses were unlikely to originate before cells, making choice (B) the best answer. There is nothing in the passage to support that viral capsids are similar to bacterial cell walls, and the word "capsid" does not even appear in the first hypothesis, eliminating choice (A). Choice (C) is eliminated because the differences in RNA and DNA viruses are not elaborated in the passage. Moreover, given that RNA viruses are mentioned in the Coevolution Hypothesis and DNA viruses are mentioned in the hypotheses that relate to more complex cellular organisms, it seems unlikely that RNA viruses would be considered more advanced than DNA viruses. Choice (D) is eliminated because the Coevolution Hypothesis specifically states that the first viruses contained RNA.

24. F The incorporation of RNA sequences into protein structures versus cell structures is specifically mentioned in the Coevolution Hypothesis. Choices (G) and (J) relate to the Regressive Evolution Hypothesis and choice (H) relates to the Cellular Origin Hypothesis.

25. C Table 1 shows that as organic cover percentage increases, erosion from topsoil deflation decreases, eliminating choices (A) and (B). Choices (C) and (D) both state that increased rainfall will reduce erosion as shown in Table 3. The choice comes down to the type of topsoil. Tables 1 and 3 consistently show that soil Y resists erosion more than X, eliminating choice (D).

26. G Soil X contains 5% clay and soil Y contains 40% clay. A soil with 10% clay should have topsoil deflation between the values for X and Y with 0% organic cover in Table 1, eliminating choices (F) and (J). Since 10% clay is most similar to the 5% clay found in soil X, the topsoil deflation value is expected to be closer to 105,000 kg/ha than to 65,000 kg/ha, eliminating choice (H) and making choice (G) the best answer.

27. D Only Experiment 2 involved a variation in water content, eliminating choices (A) and (B). Between choices (C) and (D), only choice (D) provides a clear manner of comparing soils with different water contents.

28. H Experiment 1 investigates wind erosion of different types of topsoil with varying amounts of organic cover. If the fans did not adequately simulate the effects of real wind, it would be difficult to apply the findings to any practical situation, making choice (H) the best answer. Choice (F) is not an assumption but a variable being tested by the experiment. Choice (G) is the opposite of an assumption made in the experiment, that compost and straw do adequately simulate vegetation and organic cover. Choice (J) is not addressed in Experiment 1 because water content is not varied.

29. C Table 3 demonstrates that regardless of the water content, soil X with the smaller clay percentage is more prone to topsoil deflation, making choice (C) the correct answer. Table 3 shows that

erosion is related to water content for both soils, eliminating choice (A). Further, erosion takes place in the presence of water content, eliminating choice (B). Finally, Table 3 demonstrates that increased water content tends to decrease topsoil deflation, eliminating choice (D).

30. F Soil X contains 5% clay and soil Y contains 40% clay. A soil with 10% clay should have water content and topsoil deflation in Tables 2 and 3 that are between the values for soils X and Y after 8 hours of sprinkling. Choices (H) and (J) have water contents that are too low, and choice (G) has an erosion value that is too low. Therefore, only choice (F) can be correct.

31. C According to Figure 1, bathypelagic, mesopelagic, and epipelagic zones are all within mutually exclusive depth ranges. In other words, none of them overlap, so answer choices (A), (B), and (D) are all eliminated and only choice (C) is possible. Depths between 100 and 200 m can be categorized in either the epipelagic or thermocline zone according to Figure 1.

32. J According to Figure 1, when total pressure is 1,200 kPa the ocean zone can be classified as epipelagic, continental shelf, or thermocline. Therefore, choice (J) is the best answer. Choices (F) and (G) are at higher pressures, and choice (H) is at a lower pressure.

33. C The points on Figure 2 where the two oceans would be indistinguishable for any temperature and depth combination would be where the two lines intersect. The tropical and temperate lines on Figure 2 intersect at two points, at depths of approximately 125 m and 625 m. This makes choice (C) the best answer. All other answer choices give depths where the two lines would yield different values of temperature and would thus be distinguishable from one another.

34. G The general trend for both regions in Table 1 is a decrease in ocean temperature with an increase in depth. This eliminates choices (F) and (H). However, Region 2 had a temperature of 8° C at a depth of both 39.7 and 49.6 m whereas Region 1 showed a decrease in temperature for every increased depth. Therefore, only Region 1 showed a consistent decrease in ocean temperature with increasing depth.

35. B Both Figure 1 and Table 1 demonstrate that as depth increases, total pressure increases. If the pressure at 79.5 m is 900 kPa, it would be expected to *increase* beyond 900 kPa at greater depth. Only choice (B) is possible. Note that choice (D) is eliminated because it is impossible to increase from 900 to 101 kPa.

36. J Looking at Figure 1, since 800 mg of sulfamethoxazole results in greater bacterial elimination than 400 mg over time, choices (F) and (G) are both eliminated. Table 1 provides insight to the mechanism of action of sulfamethoxazole, so choice (H) is also eliminated. According to Figure 1, combining sulfamethoxazole (SMX) with either doxycycline or azithromycin increases overall elimination of a common skin infection bacterium, making choice (J) the best answer.

37. A According to Figure 1, it takes 120 minutes for an 800 mg dose of sulfamethoxazole to achieve 80% bacterial elimination and hence 20% original bacterial survival. At the same time, the 400 mg dose only achieves between 40–50% elimination. A 600 mg dose would be expected to give results between these two values at the 120 minute mark. Therefore, only choice A is possible because the time required to reach 20% survival would be greater than 120 minutes for a 600 mg dose.

38. F According to the passage and the data in Figure 1, penicillin is not very effective against the bacterium studied, but it does eliminate some bacteria, eliminating choices (H) and (J). In the experiment in the passage, less than 10% of the bacteria are eliminated by penicillin after 120 minutes (2 hours), meaning most survived. Therefore, choice (F) is better than choice (G).

39. D Figure 1 shows greater bacterial elimination by doxycycline and azithromycin when compounded with sulfamethoxazole (SMX). This eliminates choices (A) and (B). Choice (C) is a true statement. However, even though sulfamethoxazole 800 mg is more effective than SMX/azithromycin according to the figure, this does not answer the question of whether or not azithromycin is more effective when *combined with* sulfamethoxazole. Therefore, choice (D) is the best answer.

40. H The passage describes the goal of antibiotics as eliminating bacteria, so choices (F) and (G) are incorrect. From the data in Figure 1, it can be inferred that antibiotics that eliminate a large amount of bacteria in a short amount of time are most effective. This eliminates choice (J) and makes choice (H) the best answer.

WRITING TEST

To grade your essay, see the Essay Checklist on the following page. The following is an example of a top-scoring essay for the prompt given in this test. Note that it's not perfect, but it still follows an organized outline and has a strong introductory paragraph, a concluding paragraph, and transitions throughout.

The traditional academic calendar of school in the fall, winter, and spring, with summers off, was developed to accommodate the needs of an agrarian society. Simply put, children were needed to work in the fields during the summer. There is an argument that spring break existed to allow for help with planting, and fall break to help with the harvests. Although the shape of our nation has changed dramatically since the academic calendar was created, there are still powerful reasons for keeping it in place: School has become much more stressful, and students need the break during summer; colleges have become much more expensive, and students need the chance to earn money in the summer; childhood is something special, and the things which make it special should not be casually stripped from the young simply because we're no longer a nation of farmers.

Contrary to high school in years past, high school is no longer a gentle nine-month trek through classes. High school today is a very difficult academic exercise designed to prepare students for college, not just for getting a job when they graduate. Consequently, the classes have become harder, and the amount of homework and other preparation has increased. Every student has heard his or her parents comment that they never worked so hard when they were in school. The fact is, this is the truth. Students today have to take AP classes (which are really college-level classes in high school) if they are serious about getting into a top college. These classes run all year and end with a very difficult exam in May. The amount of work being demanded from students is so high that during the year many students need help coping with the stress. If summer vacation did not exist and students had to go at this pace all the time, it would be disasterous.

Furthermore, summer is also for more than just recovering from the school year. Most students today have jobs in the summer, which are critically important to their ability to pay for college. Because college has become more expensive, and because financial aid is so hard to get, many high school students work during the summers. The money they earn is usually for their college savings, although some of them even give this money to their families to help support them. If this flow of money were cut off, perhaps some students would not be able to afford college, or their families would suffer.

Also, we should be cautious about altering the academic calendar in high school because summer vacation is one of those things that make being a child special. Every parent has fond memories of their summers playing, and tells those stories to his or her children. Teachers talk about this in classes as well. The truth is, there is a difference between children and adults, and we should not act rashly to take away those things which mark that difference. We should be cautious when considering decisions that will make childhood less like childhood and more like the "real world" inhabited by adults. Although it is hard to explain in a concrete way exactly how this is a damaging thing to do, that difficulty makes it no less damaging. The simple pleasures mean a lot and should be protected, not eliminated in the name of efficiency.

For a wide variety of reasons, from the very concrete to the somewhat abstract, it would be a bad idea to force students to go to school year-round. Although there may be problems like overcrowding, which cause administrators to consider abolishing the academic calendar and going to a year-round calendar, the proper solution is not changing the calendar, the proper solution is spending more money on education. Because students need a break from the rigors of the classroom, a chance to earn much needed money, and a childhood full of memories to pass on to their own kids, the academic calendar should remain the way it is.

Essay Checklist

1. The Introduction
   Did you
   - o start with a topic sentence that paraphrases or restates the prompt?
   - o clearly state your position on the issue?

2. Body Paragraph 1
   Did you
   - o start with a transition/topic sentence that discusses the opposing side of the argument?
   - o give an example of a reason that one might agree with the opposing side of the argument?
   - o clearly state that the opposing side of the argument is wrong or flawed?
   - o show what is wrong with the opposing side's example or position?

3. Body Paragraphs 2 and 3
   Did you
   - o start with a transition/topic sentence that discusses your position on the prompt?
   - o give one example or reason to support your position?
   - o show the grader how your example supports your position?
   - o end the paragraph by restating your thesis?

4. Conclusion
   Did you
   - o restate your position on the issue?
   - o end with a flourish?

5. Overall
   Did you
   - o write neatly?
   - o avoid multiple spelling and grammar mistakes?
   - o try to vary your sentence structure?
   - o use a few impressive-sounding words?

SCORING YOUR PRACTICE EXAM

Step A

Count the number of correct answers for each section and record the number in the space provided for your raw score on the Score Conversion Worksheet below.

Step B

Using the Score Conversion Chart on the next page, convert your raw scores on each section to scaled scores. Then compute your composite ACT score by averaging the four subject scores. Add them up and divide by four. Don't worry about the essay score; it is not included in your composite score.

Score Conversion Worksheet		
Section	Raw Score	Scaled Score
1	_____/75	_____
2	_____/60	_____
3	_____/40	_____
4	_____/40	_____

SCORE CONVERSION CHART

Scaled Score	Raw Scores			
	Test 1 Engish	Test 2 Math	Test 3 Reading	Test 4 Science
36	75	60	40	40
35	73–74	59	39	39
34	72	58	38	--
33	71	57	37	38
32	70	54–56	36	37
31	69	52–53	35	36
30	68	50–51	34	--
29	66–67	48–49	33	35
28	65	46–47	32	33–34
27	63–64	44–45	30–31	32
26	61–62	42–43	29	31
25	59–60	40–41	28	29–30
24	57–58	37–39	26–27	28
23	55–56	35–36	25	26–27
22	52–54	33–34	24	24–25
21	49–51	31–32	23	23
20	46–48	29–30	21–22	21–22
19	44–45	26–28	20	19–20
18	41–43	23–25	19	17–18
17	39–40	20–22	18	14–16
16	36–38	17–19	16–17	13
15	33–35	14–16	15	11–12
14	31–32	12–13	14	09–10
13	29–30	10–11	12–13	08
12	27–28	08–09	10–11	06–07
11	25–26	06–07	09	05
10	23–24	05	07–08	--
09	22	04	06	04
08	18–21	--	--	03
07	15–17	03	05	02
06	12–14	02	04	--
05	09–11	--	03	--
04	07	--	--	01
03	05–06	01	02	--
02	03–04	--	01	--
01	00–02	00	00	00

About the Authors

Geoff Martz attended Dartmouth College and Columbia University before joining The Princeton Review in 1985 as a teacher and writer. His first book for The Princeton Review was *Cracking the GMAT*, published in 1989. He is also the author or coauthor of *Cracking the GED* and *Paying for College Without Going Broke.*

Kim Magloire is a graduate of Princeton University with a master's degree from Columbia University where she is currently completing her doctorate in Epidemiology. She joined The Princeton Review in 1984 as an SAT teacher and has since taught SAT, MCAT, GMAT, LSAT, GRE, and science SAT Subject tests.

Ted Silver is a graduate of Yale University, the Yale University School of Medicine, and the law school at the University of Connecticut. He has been intensely involved in the fields of education and testing since 1976 and has written several books and computer tutorials pertaining to those fields. He became affiliated with The Princeton Review in 1988 as the chief architect of The Princeton Review's MCAT course. Dr. Silver's full-time profession is as Associate Professor of Law at Touro College Jacob D. Fuchsberg Law Center.

NOTES

NOTES

NOTES

NOTES

Ace the APs

Cracking the AP Biology Exam, 2010 Edition
978-0-375-42914-9 • $18.99/C$23.99

Cracking the AP Calculus AB & BC Exams, 2010 Edition
978-0-375-42915-6 • $19.99/C $24.99

Cracking the AP Chemistry Exam, 2010 Edition
978-0-375-42916-3 • $18.00/C $22.00

Cracking the AP Computer Science A & AB Exams, 2006–2007 Edition
978-0-375-76528-5 • $19.00/C$27.00

Cracking the AP Economics Macro & Micro Exams, 2010 Edition
978-0-375-42917-0 • $18.00/C $22.00

Cracking the AP English Language & Composition Exam, 2010 Edition
978-0-375-42918-7 • $18.00 /C$22.00

Cracking the AP English Literature & Composition Exam, 2010 Edition
978-0-375-42943-9 • 18.00/C$22.00

Cracking the AP Environmental Science Exam, 2010 Edition
978-0-375-42944-6 • $18.00/C $22.00

Cracking the AP European History Exam, 2010 Edition
978-0-375-42945-3 • $18.99/C $23.99

Cracking the AP U.S. Government & Politics Exam, 2010 Edition
978-0-375-42951-4 • $18.99/C $23.99

Cracking the AP Human Geography Exam, 2010 Edition
978-0-375-42919-4 • $18.00/C $22.00

Cracking the AP Physics B Exam, 2010 Edition
978-0-375-42946-0 • $18.00/C $22.00

Cracking the AP Physics C Exam, 2010 Edition
978-0-375-42947-7 • $18.00/C $22.00

Cracking the AP Psychology Exam, 2010 Edition
978-0-375-42948-4 • $18.00/C $22.00

Cracking the AP Spanish Exam with Audio CD, 2010 Edition
978-0-375-42949-1 • $24.99/C $29.99

Cracking the AP Statistics Exam, 2010 Edition
978-0-375-42950-7 • $19.99/C $24.99

Cracking the AP U.S. History Exam, 2010 Edition
978-0-375-42952-1 • $18.99/C $23.99

Cracking the AP World History Exam, 2010 Edition
978-0-375-42953-8 • $18.00/C $22.00

Score High on the SAT Subject Tests

Cracking the SAT Biology E/M Subject Test, 2009–2010 Edition
978-0-375-42905-7 • $19.00/C$22.00

Cracking the SAT Chemistry Subject Test, 2009–2010 Edition
978-0-375-42906-4 • $19.00/C$22.00

Cracking the SAT French Subject Test, 2009–2010 Edition
978-0-375-42907-1 • $19.00/C$22.00

Cracking the SAT U.S. & World History Subject Tests, 2009–2010 Edition
978-0-375-42908-8 • $19.00/C$22.00

Cracking the SAT Literature Subject Test, 2009–2010 Edition
978-0-375-42909-5 • $19.00/C$22.00

Cracking the SAT Math 1 & 2 Subject Tests, 2009–2010 Edition
978-0-375-42910-1 • $19.00/C$22.00

Cracking the SAT Physics Subject Test, 2009–2010 Edition
978-0-375-42911-8 • $19.00/C$22.00

Cracking the SAT Spanish Subject Test, 2009–2010 Edition
978-0-375-42912-5 • $19.00/C$22.00